THE GREAT LIE

RELIGION AND CONTEMPORARY CULTURE SERIES

———————————————————

Edited by Peter Augustine Lawler

Stuck with Virtue:
The American Individual and Our Biotechnological Future
Peter Augustine Lawler

Till We Have Built Jerusalem:
Architecture, Urbanism, and the Sacred
Philip Bess

The Future of Conservatism:
Conflict and Consensus in the Post-Reagan Era
Charles W. Dunn, ed.

A Consumer's Guide to the Apocalypse:
Why There Is No Cultural War in America
and Why We Will Perish Nonetheless
Eduardo Velásquez

The Skies of Babylon:
Diversity, Nihilism, and the American University
Barry Bercier

Christians as Political Animals:
Taking the Measure of Modernity and Modern Democracy
Marc D. Guerra

THE GREAT LIE

CLASSIC AND RECENT APPRAISALS
OF IDEOLOGY AND TOTALITARIANISM

EDITED BY
F. FLAGG TAYLOR IV

WILMINGTON, DELAWARE

ISBN: 9781935191360
Library of Congress Cataloging-in-Publication Data

The great lie: classic and recent appraisals of ideology and totalitarianism / edited by F. Flagg Taylor, IV.
    p. cm.
    Includes bibliographical references and index.
    ISBN 978-1-935191-36-0
    1. Totalitarianism. I. Taylor, F. Flagg.

JC480.G72 2011
320.53—dc23   2011021518

Published in the United States by:

ISI Books
Intercollegiate Studies Institute
3901 Centerville Road
Wilmington, Delaware 19807-1938
www.isibooks.org

CONTENTS

Contents

III. Origins

IV. Seduction

Contents

V. Dissent

VI. Lessons

A living lie—and that is the tragedy of human life—is superior, as force, to a dead truth.

—Waldemar Gurian

The ideal subject of totalitarian rule is not the convinced Nazi or the convinced Communist, but people for whom the distinction between fact and fiction (i.e., the reality of experience) and the distinction between true and false (i.e., the standards of thought) no longer exist.

—Hannah Arendt

There is always this fallacious belief: "It would not be the same here; here such things are impossible." Alas, all the evil of the twentieth century is possible everywhere on earth.

—Aleksandr Solzhenitsyn

The totalitarian state attempts to turn all its subjects into accomplices in its great lie.

—Václav Benda

INTRODUCTION

The purpose of this volume is simple: to bring together in one book the most incisive and profound reflections on the phenomenon that dominated the twentieth century: totalitarianism or ideocratic tyranny.

I

THE HISTORY AND STATUS OF THE DEBATE AROUND TOTALITARIANISM

There is no shortage of books examining Soviet Communism and Nazi Germany. These two regimes unleashed unprecedented violence on neighboring populations and their own citizens, while subjecting these same peoples to utopian, inhuman schemes of social engineering. Such monstrous crimes and projects continue to fascinate scholars and students of history alike. Scholars steadily churn out volumes on the Third Reich, while the opening of the Soviet archives after 1991 continues to offer a wealth of new material. Yet much of this material does not touch on the all important questions relating to these regimes. What ideas do they share? Why did ideocratic regimes come into being only in the twentieth century? Does the term totalitarian capture something central here? Are Nazism and Communism best understood as political religions? These are difficult questions, involving historical, political and philosophic themes. As Michael Burleigh pointed out in his book, *The Third Reich: A New History*, "The literature on which Nazism is studied as a political religion or as a form of totalitarianism is dwarfed by the industrial scale of literature on Nazi Germany as a whole."* The bulk of Soviet scholarship has not caught up with that of Nazi Germany, and therefore the disproportion of which Burleigh speaks is not as true of the Soviet field, but it exists nonetheless. In a sense, this disproportion ought to be surprising. Treating these two regimes (or others like Mussolini's Italy or Mao's China) as similar phenomena—whether from the angle of totalitarianism or political religion or both—has a long and venerable tradition dating back to the 1920s and 1930s with such giants of the twentieth century as Eric Voegelin, Hannah Arendt, and Raymond Aron. What accounts then for the partial eclipse of this approach?

The Problem of Comparison

First, the Soviet Union was wildly successful in imposing its own ideological vision of the political landscape on the West. While Nazism became the incarnation of the Right, Communism the Left, despite the fact that both movements had socialist roots.† During the 1930s, Communism became the vanguard of anti-fascism, and the creation of the Popular Front meant that there were "no enemies to the left." Thus a variety of

---

* Michael Burleigh, *The Third Reich: A New History* (New York: Hill and Wang, 2000), 21.

† As Friedrich Hayek put it in his classic *The Road to Serfdom*, "The conflict between the Fascist or National Socialist parties must, indeed, very largely be regarded as the kind of conflict which is bound to arise between rival socialist factions. There was no difference between them about the question of its being the will of the state which should assign to each person his proper place in society." See *The Road to Serfdom: Texts and Documents*, ed. Bruce Caldwell (Chicago: The University of Chicago Press, 2007), 145. Included in this edition is a memorandum Hayek wrote to Lord Beveridge on this topic in the spring of 1933—see appendix 1, "Nazi-Socialism." For more on the common matrix, see Domenico Settembrini, "Mussolini and the Legacy of Revolutionary Socialism," in *International Fascism: New Thoughts and New Approaches*, George Mosse ed. (London: Sage Publications, 1979), 91–123; Richard Pipes, chapter 5 of *Russia Under the Bolshevik Regime* (New York: Knopf, 1994), 240–81; and François Furet, chapter 6 of *The Passing of an Illusion* (Chicago: University of Chicago Press, 1999), 156–208.

left-wing movements could find common ground in their opposition to fascism. As Francois Furet has argued, the goal of the workers' revolution could now be affirmed and emphasized, not as a distant prospect, but rather as the "natural outcome of the anti-Fascist battle."[*]

The subsequent alliance of the Western powers with the Soviet Union after the Nazi's eastern offensive further weakened Western awareness of Soviet reality. Stalin was now on the side of the victors, and the Soviets were among the judges at Nuremberg. And unlike central Europeans, Westerners were never subjected to the brutality of the Red Army. Nazism was defeated during the "the prime of its iniquity," while Communism, "at the peak of *its* iniquity, was rewarded with an epic victory."[†] This is surely one of the most extraordinary stories of the twentieth century. Enveloping their own citizens in an ideological fiction or what Aleksandr Solzhenitsyn simply called the Lie is one thing. The Soviets' success in getting Western elites to perpetuate the Lie is quite another.

This notion of the Lie is distinct from ordinary political falsehoods or the Machiavellian manipulations of political leaders. It is derived from the function of ideology as the principle of legitimacy in totalitarian regimes. In this context the Lie is comprehensive and utterly destructive. Ideology creates reality by ceaselessly demanding that everyone embrace the lies of the regime: there is no truth other than that proclaimed by the regime. Leszek Kolakowski locates the distinctiveness of totalitarian regimes in precisely this: "This is the great cognitive triumph of totalitarianism: it can no longer be accused of lying, because it has succeeded in abrogating the very idea of truth."[‡] Again, the perpetuation of the Lie in the West was critical to the longevity of the Communist project. As Furet notes, "The capacity to mythologize its own history is one of the most extraordinary performances of the Soviet regime. But that capacity would have been less effective if it had not encountered a credulous tendency that is part and parcel of the culture of European revolutionary democracy."[§]

---

[*] Furet, *The Passing of an Illusion*, 222.

[†] Martin Malia, "The Uses of Atrocity," forward to *The Black Book of Communism* (Cambridge: Harvard University Press, 1999), xii.

[‡] Leszek Kolakowski, "Totalitarianism and the Virtue of the Lie," *My Correct Views on Everything*, ed. Zbigniew Janowski (South Bend, IN: St. Augustine's Press, 2005), 70.

[§] Furet, 144.

This brings us to another reason for the suspicion of this old approach. Comparison may suggest, directly or indirectly, a moral equivalence between Communism and Nazism. This has not been a popular notion given the success of the Soviet vision, while many found the comparison repugnant due to the supposedly benign or humanitarian intentions of Communism as opposed to the genocidal intentions of the Nazis. It is also true that Nazi crimes have been well known due to the Allied victory and the discovery of the death camps by Allied forces. The Gulag was known by the 1930s but Westerners had to rely on the testimony of survivors. Knowledge was uncertain and spotty. Only with the publication of Aleksandr Solzhenitsyn's monumental *The Gulag Archipelago* was much of Western elite opinion forced to undergo a dramatic change. As Alain Besançon has put it, that book "acted as a battering ram that came crashing into the back door of the lie."* The publication of the works of Western academics such as Robert Conquest also shed light on the criminal aspects of the Soviet regime.† The last decade has seen the publication of important volumes such as *The Black Book of Communism*, Alexander Yakovlev's *A Century of Violence in Soviet Russia*, Anne Applebaum's *The Gulag: A History*, and Paul Hollander's *From the Gulag to the Killing Fields*.‡

The Black Book was quite a lightning rod upon its publication in France.§ The main editor of the volume, Stephane Courtois, raises the issue of the scholarly neglect of the crimes of Communism in contrast to the attention paid to the crimes of the Nazis. "While names such as Himmler and Eichmann are recognized around the world as bywords for

---

* Alain Besançon, *A Century of Horrors: Communism, Nazism, and the Uniqueness of the Shoah*, Ralph C. Hancock and Nathaniel Hancock trans. (Wilmington, DE: ISI Books, 2007), xxi.

† See in particular *The Great Terror* (New York: The Macmillan Company, 1968) and *The Harvest of Sorrow* (New York: Oxford University Press, 1986).

‡ *A Century of Violence in Soviet Russia* (New Haven: Yale University Press, 2002); *The Gulag: A History* (New York: Doubleday, 2003); *From the Gulag to the Killing Fields* (Wilmington, DE: ISI Books, 2006).

§ For a summary of the controversies surrounding *The Black Book* by one of its contributors, see Andrej Paczkowski, "The Storm over *The Black Book*," *The Wilson Quarterly* (Spring 2001), 28–34. See also Jean-Francois Revel's *Last Exit to Utopia: The Survival of Socialism in a Post-Soviet Era* (New York: Encounter Books, 2009), esp. chapters 5–6.

twentieth-century barbarism, the names of Feliks Dzerzhinsky, Genrikh Yagoda, and Nikolai Ezhov languish in obscurity. As for Lenin, Mao, Ho Chi Minh, and even Stalin, they have always enjoyed a surprising reverence. A French government agency, the National Lottery, was crazy enough to use Stalin and Mao in one of its advertising campaigns. Would anyone even dare to come up with the idea of featuring Hitler and Goebbels in commercials?"* This disinclination to confront the criminal nature of Communism is related to the reluctance to approach Communism and Nazism as two species of the same genus.

Another related obstacle to the common approach has been the proliferation of alternatives generated by the scholarly community from various disciplines. Let us look at the approaches to Nazi Germany first.[†] German historians such as Karl D. Bracher were sympathetic to the totalitarian approach but other alternatives soon emerged. Many thought Nazi Germany was best understood as a species of interwar European fascism. Marxists historians who took this path saw a deep connection between fascism and capitalism—an approach that was a great boon to Soviet propaganda. Ernst Nolte sought to reveal the connections between Italian Fascism, the Action Française, and National Socialism, and thus spoke of an epoch of fascism. Another group of scholars linked the development of Nazi Germany to modernization theory. Also known as structural functionalism, such scholars argued that fascism gained traction when elites, during their society's passage to industrial society, felt threatened by communism or more general egalitarian tendencies. Finally, some historians argued that National Socialism was more or less the inevitable product of a German *Sonderweg* (special path)—and thus not a part of more general phenomenon at all, whether it be fascism or a modernization process.

---

* Courtois, *The Black Book of Communism*, 17.

† Here I am indebted to Michael Burleigh and Wolfgang Wippermann, "How Modern, German, and Totalitarian was the Third Reich? Some Major Historiographical Controversies," in *The Racial State in Germany 1933–1945* (Cambridge: Cambridge University Press, 1991), 2–77; and Ian Kershaw, "The Essence of Nazism: form of fascism, brand of totalitarianism, or unique phenomenon?" in *The Nazi Dictatorship: Problems and Perspectives of Interpretation*, 4th ed. (London: Arnold, 2000), 20–46.

Now let us look at how scholars have analyzed the Soviet Union.[*] The totalitarian approach gained prominence in 1951 when Stalin was still in power with the publication of Hannah Arendt's *The Origins of Totalitarianism*. Five years later two political scientists, Carl Friedrich and Zbigniew Brzezinski, developed a model that characterized totalitarian rule by six features: an official ideology, a mass party with a leader, institutional terror, an information monopoly, a weapons monopoly, and a centralized and planned economy. This model was thus applied to Hitler's Germany and to the Soviet Union under Stalin. Arendt argued that Stalin transformed a "Russian one-party dictatorship into a totalitarian regime"—and thus that the Soviet Union was not totalitarian under Lenin.[†] The model's applicability to the Soviet Union was soon questioned with Stalin's death, Khrushchev's secret speech in 1956, and a mellowing of the regime. Thus the totalitarian model only seemed to apply to a discrete period in Soviet history.

------

[*] Here I am indebted to Martin Malia, "From Under the Rubble, What?" *Problems of Communism* (Jan.-April 1992), 89–106 and in this volume; and Pierre Hassner, "Communist Totalitarianism: The Transatlantic Vagaries of a Concept," in *Violence and Peace: From the Atomic Bomb to Ethnic Cleansing* (Budapest: Central European University Press, 1997), 139–154 and in this volume.

[†] Hannah Arendt, *The Origins of Totalitarianism* (New York: Harcourt, Brace and World, 1951), 379. Arendt's contention cohered somewhat with a view that would soon become prominent among apologists for the Soviet regime in the West (and was therefore useful to Soviet propagandists after Khrushchev's "secret speech")—the myth of the good Lenin/bad Stalin. Robert Conquest has noted that this view has not been abandoned: "It is still maintained that he [Stalin] perverted Bolshevism—not merely that Stalin was worse than Lenin (not in itself much of a humanitarian criterion) but even that Lenin and Leninism are to some extent admirable." See *The Great Terror: A Reassessment*, 40th anniversary edition (New York: Oxford University Press, 2008), xxi. Robert Gellately confirms this is his *Lenin, Stalin, and Hitler: The Age of Social Catastrophe* (New York: Knopf, 2007), 579. He notes quite a few of his colleagues were "disconcerted" by his inclusion of Lenin and "castigated" him for not giving Lenin his due for his good intentions. The good Lenin/bad Stalin myth has been challenged most effectively in my view by Kolakowski who notes: "There is absolutely nothing in the worst years of Stalinism that cannot be justified on Leninist principles, if only it can be shown that Soviet power was increased thereby." See *Main Currents of Marxism* (New York: Norton, 2005), 769 (originally published in English by Oxford University Press in 1978).

Introduction

In the 1960s the totalitarian model came under attack for, among other reasons, being unable to account for change. The change within the Soviet regime coincided with a revolution in the study of politics. As Martin Malia noted, academic Sovietology "came of age entirely in the behavioral era, and within the institutional confines of the third, new domain of learning, the social sciences."* So just as social science began to acquire the prestige it needed to compete with the natural sciences, the Soviet Union seemed to be abandoning those features which had connected it to the early postwar totalitarian model. Social science demanded its practitioners operate in a "value-free" mode, setting aside any moral judgments in favor of objective, impartial analysis. As social scientists developed methodologies to study the Soviet system, they cast off "totalitarianism" in favor of new models such as "modernization" and "institutional pluralism."† Now, rather than trying to come to terms with something fundamentally new in human affairs, social scientists proceeded to see the Soviet system in terms of a society that had the same features everywhere.‡ In one theory Communism was seen as a kind of forced modernization; this type of autocratic economic development had unfortunate side affects, but the

---

* Malia, 75 (in this volume).

† Michael Geyer notes, "If you learned your Sovietology in the 1960s, you were almost as likely to develop an interest in modernization theory as in totalitarianism, given that Barrington Moore held more sway over first-generation totalitarian theorists than either Friedrich or Brzezinski." See Geyer in Michael Geyer and Sheila Fitzpatrick eds., *Beyond Totalitarianism: Stalinism and Nazism Compared* (Cambridge: Cambridge University Press, 2009), 7.

‡ Hannah Arendt was an early critic of the efforts of social scientists to take the measure of Nazi Germany and the Soviet Union. See three essays in particular: "Social Science Techniques and the Study of Concentration Camps," "On the Nature of Totalitarianism: An Essay in Understanding," and "Religion and Politics." All can be found in *Essays in Understanding, 1930–1954*, ed. Jerome Kohn (New York: Harcourt Brace, 1994). For a particularly illuminating exploration of Arendt's critique and the replies of her interlocutors, see Peter Baehr, *Hannah Arendt, Totalitarianism, and the Social Sciences* (Stanford: Stanford University Press, 2010). As Baehr shows, not all social scientists fell victim to the temptations I mention above. And further, some of Arendt's critics (David Riesman in particular) were successful in pointing out that Arendt's own model was susceptible to some of the same pitfalls she had found in the work of other analysts.

Soviet Union was nonetheless converging with Western industrial societies. Perhaps the regime was evolving toward a more benign authoritarianism. This made Communism, as Malia puts it, both "reformable and intrinsically different from fascism."[*]

During the 1970s in the United States the concept of totalitarianism came under increasing criticism. With the growing fragmentation of the Communist world and the Soviet Union's movement away from the Stalin era, perhaps the term was no longer applicable to *any* existing regime. Some scholars also suggested that those who persisted in their use of term were trying to fan the flames of the Cold War.[†] But then something curious happened. The publication of Solzhenitsyn's *Gulag* brought the question of ideology back to center stage, at least in France. At the same time, the ugliness of a "liberated" Vietnam, the horrific rule of Pol Pot in Cambodia, and the suffocating atmosphere of a normalized Czechoslovakia "made nonsense of the reassuring chatter of scientific Sovietology by showing that if totalitarianism was dead, it had left behind some rather strange offspring."[‡] So it was that "by a curious reversal, American professors came to hate the concept of totalitarianism after having studied it and written about it, whereas French intellectuals, at just about the same time, were beginning to study it after having ignored it."[§] So in the case of both Germany and the Soviet Union the proliferation of approaches never completely discredited the understanding of these regimes as totalitarian.

The Fortunes of Totalitarianism

The twisted history of the term totalitarianism has been recounted many times.[¶] Here I will highlight some of the important moments in this his-

---

[*] Malia, 79 (in this volume).

[†] Herbert J. Spiro and Benjamin R. Barber, "Counter-Ideological Uses of 'Totalitarianism,'" *Politics and Society* Vol. 1, No. 1 (November 1970), 3–21.

[‡] Hassner, 54 (in this volume).

[§] Furet, 496.

[¶] See, for example: Carl Friedrich, Michael Curtis, and Benjamin R. Barber, *Totalitarianism in Perspective: Three Views* (New York: Praeger, 1969); Maurice Cranston, "Should we Cease to Speak of Totalitarianism," *Survey* Vol. 23 (Summer 1978),

tory while addressing some of the criticisms leveled against this approach. Two common criticisms are the related claims that the term "totalitarianism" is a relic of the Cold War (and was used for primarily political purposes) and that it is used widely and indiscriminately. The first claim is historically false. The term "totalitarianism" in noun or adjectival form was coined by an early opponent of Italian Fascism, Giovanni Amendola in 1923. It was then picked up by Mussolini himself in 1925. Anti-Nazi intellectuals such as Franz Borkenau, Franz Neumann, and Sigmund Neumann used the term, as did Joseph Goebbels, Leon Trotsky, and Otto Bauer. Various forms of the term have thus been used by opponents and proponents of the concept from all across the political spectrum.* During this period the word emphasized the "magnification, intensification, and vitalization of political power."† Permanent mobilization of the masses by a self-conscious, dedicated movement would overcome the divisions that seemed to pervade post-war societies.

62–69; Raymond Aron, "Is There a Nazi Mystery," *Encounter* (June 1980), pp. 29-41; Walter Laqueur, "Is There Now, or Has There Ever Been, Such a Thing as Totalitarianism," *Commentary* (October 1985), 29–35; Martin Malia, *"From Under the Rubble, What?"*, in this volume and *The Soviet Tragedy: A History of Socialism in Russia*, 1917–1991 (New York: The Free Press, 1994), 6–17; Abbott Gleason, *Totalitarianism: The Inner History of the Cold War* (New York: Oxford University Press, 1995); Pierre Hassner, "Communist Totalitarianism: The Transatlantic Vagaries of a Concept", in this volume; François Furet, *The Passing of an Illusion*, 156–66; Ian Kershaw, "The Essence of Nazism: form of fascism, brand of totalitarianism, or unique phenomenon?"; Michael Burleigh, *The Third Reich: A New History*, 14–23; Hans Maier, "Concepts for the Comparison of Dictatorships: 'Totalitarianism' and 'Political Religions'," in *Totalitarianism and Political Religions*, Vol. I, Hans Maier ed. (London: Routledge, 2004), 119, 215; Maier, "The Interpretation of Totalitarian Rule 1919–89," in *Totalitarianism and Political Religions*, Vol. III, Hans Maier ed. (London: Routledge, 2007), 3–21; Peter Grieder, "In Defence of Totalitarianism Theory as a Tool of Historical Scholarship," *Totalitarian Movements and Political Religions*, Vol. 8, Nos. 3–4 (September-December 2007), 563–89; and Michael Geyer and Sheila Fitzpatrick eds., *Beyond Totalitarianism: Stalinism and Nazism Compared* (Cambridge: Cambridge University Press, 2009).

* Grieder, "In Defence of Totalitarianism Theory as a Tool of Historical Scholarship," 566.

† Maier, "The Interpretation of Totalitarian Rule 1919–1989," 4.

In the 1930s prominent European intellectuals increasingly used the term to compare Fascist Italy, Nazi Germany, and the Soviet Union. The first academic symposium on totalitarianism was held in November 1939. The term gained more traction in scholarly circles and found its way into more popular usage in the 1950s with the publication of the two aforementioned works by Friedrich and Arendt. As noted above, usage has waxed and waned since coming under criticism. But the present accusation that the term is merely a political tool cannot hold. As Greider and Burleigh have both noted, one only need look at a list of commentators who have found it useful: Karl-Detriech Bracher, Robert Conquest, Norman Davies, Timothy Garton Ash, Emilio Gentile, Ulrich Herbert, Michael Ignatieff, Barrington Moore Jr., Jeremy Noakes, Fritz Stern, Leonard Schapiro, Richard Crampton, and Niall Ferguson. Even Ian Kershaw, who questions the overall utility of the concept, notes, "The underlying assumption that both regimes [Nazi Germany and the Soviet Union under Stalin] made total claims upon society, based upon a monopolistic set of ideological imperatives and resulting in unprecedented levels of repression and attempted indoctrination, manipulation and mobilisation—giving these regimes a dynamic missing from more conventional authoritarian regimes—again seems largely incontestable."[*]

As to the charge that the term is used indiscriminately, this certainly does not invalidate the concept itself. One could make a similar charge about terms such as "democracy" and "fascism." It is true, as Barber and other critics have noted, that those who employ the term often have serious disagreements with one another. Barber, for example, notes that there is a significant division between the "phenomenologists" and the "essentialists."[†] The former are intent upon isolating objective attributes while minimizing questions about the ends of rule, and the latter focus on ideological content and goals. We will come back to this issue of the different understandings.

The third important claim made by the opponents of the concept is that totalitarianism points to similarities between regimes at the expense

---

[*] Kershaw, "'Working Towards the Fuehrer': Reflections on the Nature of the Hitler Dictatorship," in *Hitler, the Germans, and the Final Solution* (New Haven: Yale University Press, 2008), 29–30.

[†] Barber, "Conceptual Foundations of Totalitarianism," in *Totalitarianism in Perspective: Three Views*, 3–52.

of real differences. Two responses immediately come to mind. This certainly is not true of the more well-known and distinguished commentators such as Waldemar Gurian, Raymond Aron, and Alain Besançon. Nobody can read the works of these three thinkers and claim they are not extremely sensitive to the differences between Nazi Germany and the Soviet Union. Indeed, they use the concept for the purpose of identifying similarities *and* differences. These analysts would not be so concerned with the phenomenon of totalitarianism were it not the case that such regimes could reveal themselves in different guises and adapt themselves to different circumstances. All of them were struck, for example, by the different manner in which the Nazis and Bolsheviks came to power.

It also is true that the totalitarians themselves recognized their affinities. Hitler "instructed the Nazi Party to welcome disenchanted Communists while barring Social Democrats: for hatred was easily redirected from one object to another. So it happened that in the early 1920s, the largest number of adherents of the Italian Fascist Party were ex-communists."[*] One might add that it was not only the transferability of hate, but a certain habit of mind that made such changes in allegiance possible. Mussolini and Hitler were each impressed by their respective commonalities with the Bolsheviks, and the Bolsheviks watched as both copied their political techniques. As Bukharin observed at the Twelfth Party Congress, "It is characteristic of Fascist methods of combat that they, more than any other party, have adopted and applied in practice the experiences of the Russian Revolution. If one regards them from the formal point of view . . . then one discovers in them a complete application of Bolshevik tactics."[†]

Those scholars who recommend avoiding the term "totalitarianism" to preserve differences often highlight trivial distinctions or, more problematically, make distinctions that reveal profound misunderstandings of the phenomena in question—ideology most importantly. Kershaw, for example, characterizes Stalin as a paradigmatic committee man while Hilter was just the opposite. Stalin was quite interventionist in his style of rule, while Hitler took a much more distant approach. Kershaw accuses those who utilize "totalitarianism" of remaining wedded to a superficial level of analysis, but this seems much more true of some of his own efforts to assert differences.

---

[*] Pipes, 264.

[†] Quoted in Pipes, 253.

Now let us examine of some examples of a deeper misunderstanding. Kershaw characterizes the Nazi goal "of national redemption through racial purification and racial empire" as a "chimeric, utopian vision" and argues that "barbarism and destructiveness" were "inherent" in the attempt to realize it. True enough. But here is his contrasting picture of Communist rule under Stalin:

> Stalin's rule, for all its dynamic radicalism in the brutal collec-tivisation programme . . . was not incompatible with a rational ordering of priorities and attainment of limited and comprehen-sible goals, even if the methods were barbarous in the extreme and the accompanying inhumanity on a scale defying belief. Whether the methods were the most appropriate to attain the goals in view might still be debated, but the attempt to force industrialization at breakneck speed on a highly backward economy and to intro-duce 'socialism in one country' cannot be seen as irrational or limitless aims.[*]

So we might still debate whether the terror famine was an appropriate means to attain socialism? What, for that matter, of the entire gulag system? Further, what gives Kershaw confidence that the establishment of socialism is not a limitless aim? How does one know when full socialism, or communism, is attained? Drawing a similar contrast between Nazism and Soviet Communism in his review of *The Third Reich: A New History*, Omer Bartov argues that Michael Burleigh fails to make the distinction between "a regime whose ideology was genocidal, and a regime whose ideological promise of a better life to 'the masses' ended in mass violence."[†] Elsewhere Bartov contrasts Nazism's apocalyptic longings with Communism, which offered "an optimistic world view whose goal was construction (albeit on the debris of the old world)." Both Kershaw and Bartov reveal a profound blindness to the hubristic ambition of the Communists to reengineer human nature—to end what Marx called alienation—and

---

[*] Kershaw, "'Working Towards the Fuehrer': Reflections on the Nature of the Hitler Dictatorship," 34–35.

[†] Omer Bartov, "Hitler's Willing Believers," *The New Republic* (November 20, 2000), 32.

build a wholly new social order.* Kershaw seems to think the deaths of the 1930s during the terror famine and the purges resulted from poor methods—thus having nothing intrinsically to do with the ideological goals of Communism. Similarly, Bartov notes the ideological promise of a better life merely "ended" in mass violence, backing away from any causal connection between the ideological project and the bloody results. But why take the Nazis at their word, but not the Communists? There is a serious imbalance here that underlies the effort to maintain distinctions. Much better to acknowledge the striking ideological aims of both regimes, in each case emblematic of an extreme political voluntarism redolent of the Jacobins, but unprecedented in ambition.

The great Russian novelist Vasily Grossman recognized the horrifying kinship. In his masterpiece *Life and Fate*, a Nazi Commandant Liss interviews an old Bolshevik called Mostovskoy. Liss presses his interlocutor, "When we look one another in the face, we're neither of us just looking at a face we hate—no, we're gazing into a mirror. That's the tragedy of our age. Do you really not recognize yourselves in us—yourselves, the strength of your will? Isn't it true that for you too the world *is* your will? Is there anything that can make *you* waver?"† Neither the Communists nor the Nazis recognized limits—the building of socialism required liquidating kulaks and the building of Nazi Europe required liquidating Jews. Of course we ought to investigate the particulars of each of these inhuman projects and draw contrasts where appropriate, but we should not turn away from the kinship. At Furet puts it, "The totalitarian ideologies of the twentieth century were distinguished from all other ideologies by the uncannily narrow constraints they exercised upon the actions of those

---

* See Peter Fritzsche and Jochen Hellbeck, "The New Man in Stalinist Russia and Nazi Germany," *Beyond Totalitarianism*, 302–41; Orlando Figes, *A People's Tragedy: The Russian Revolution 1891–1924* (New York: Penguin, 1996), 732–51; Stephen Kotkin, *Magnetic Mountain: Stalinism as Civilization* (Berkeley: University of California Press, 1995), 198–237; Michael Burleigh and Wolfgang Wippermann, *The Racial State in Germany 1933–1945*, 201–303; Michael Burleigh, *The Third Reich: A New History*, 219–77.

† Vasily Grossman, *Life and Fate* (New York: New York Review Books Classics, 2006), 395.

who professed or followed them, from party leaders to rank and file, from rank and file to the people at large."*

There are two other important criticisms leveled against the concept of "totalitarianism." They are related in that both find that totalitarian analysts take a "top-down" perspective that distorts their view of things. By focusing on the apparatus of rule, such a perspective assumes a strict separation of state and society that is false to the reality of these regimes. It is true that a totalitarian model like Arendt's or Friedrich's concentrates on the nature and methods of the state.† But those writers taking a more capacious, philosophic approach focus on the interpenetration of state and society. In fact, the logic of ideology goes further. As Cranston argues, "The most totalitarian regime is the one where the penetration of the regime into the soul of the individual is complete."‡ That is, the people must be made to want what they are allowed to have or to behave as if they want what they have. This is what makes totalitarian domination truly distinctive. Those thinkers who do not focus on this aspiration must explain how the regime elicits ideological conformity. Here the regime seduces its citizens through constant, ever-present participatory schemes—clubs, festivals, rituals—strategies highlighted by those thinkers who understand Nazism and Communism as political or totalitarian religions. So while there is something to this criticism that merely focusing on the apparatus of rule provides a somewhat shallow basis for comparison, this is a mistake that the most insightful analysts of totalitarian domination avoid.

Similarly, critics of totalitarianism often argue that the model is static and cannot account for change.§ Thus, while the Soviet Union was totalitarian under Stalin, it seemed to evolve into something else after his death. These critics thus seem to focus on terror and repression as the most significant criterion. They make a similar mistake as those whom they criticize by focusing on the state and its instruments. As Hans Maier has put it:

---

* Furet, 190.

† See, for example, David Riesman's critique of Arendt as explored in Baehr, *Hannah Arendt, Totalitarianism, and the Social Sciences*, ch. 2.

‡ Cranston, "Should we Cease to Speak of Totalitarianism?" 69.

§ Michael Curtis, "Retreat from Totalitarianism," in *Totalitarianism in Perspective: Three Views*, 53–121.

Introduction

It would be false to believe that political power was attained in the totalitarian systems solely through threat and terror, or that such systems solely spread fear and trembling and compelled blind obedience. Both totalitarian power and its centre of power, the party, live not merely according to their power to translate its goals into fact, according to the right of the stronger. They live just as much—if not even more—from their claim to know the right, the true. The party is consecrated with knowledge of the purposes of history; it knows where history will lead . . . It is this fortification with an infallible ideology—or at least one that seems infallible—that grants totalitarian movements their power to establish themselves. Not only hands and feet are taken prisoner, but thought is as well.[*]

Once one realizes the fundamental place of ideology as it seduces and integrates the masses, one can understand how the use of terror might wax and wane at different periods, and that different regimes might utilize different means "in their relentless quest for panoptic supervision."[†] Thus, as has been pointed out by many scholars, the Gestapo in Nazi Germany was much smaller as a proportion of the general population than the Stasi in the Communist German Democratic Republic.[‡] The former, therefore, relied very heavily on spying and collaboration by ordinary citizens (as did the Stasi, to be sure).[§] Bartov seems to think this difference undercuts a key totalitarian feature—the suppression of the rule of law and police terror—so that the difference with the Soviet Union is more profound than the similarity. He argues, "But for much of the regime's twelve year existence, as long as one was not a Jew, or a Gypsy, or a Communist, or a handicapped person, or a member of the resistance (and the vast major-

---

[*] Maier, "The Interpretation of Totalitarian Rule 1919-89," 11–12.

[†] Grieder, "In Defence of Totalitarianism Theory as a Tool of Historical Scholarship," 578.

[‡] Ibid.

[§] See Gary Bruce, *The Firm: The Inside Story of the Stasi* (Oxford: Oxford University Press), 12–14 and Robert Gellately, "Denunciations in Twentieth Century Germany: Aspects of Self-Policing in the Third Reich and the German Democratic Republic," *Journal of Modern History* 68, no. 4 (December 1996), 931–67.

ity of the population belonged to none of these categories), one was quite safe."* Apart from the fact the universal espionage is a crucial feature of the Communist experience (identified by Solzhenitsyn, Orwell, and many others), in Nazi Germany, even if one belonged to none of those categories, one still had to live in an ideological universe of lies.† That is, one had to contribute to the right funds, attend the right rallies, mouth the right platitudes. Once the distinction between an ordinary crime and a political crime is erased, there are dire consequences for even voicing unguarded, heterodox opinions—or even not expressing enough optimism. And all of this is quite true to the Communist experience as well.‡

II

THE PRESENT VOLUME: THE CONTINUING RELEVANCE OF ANTI-TOTALITARIAN THOUGHT

Where do we go from here?

Paradoxically, the collapse of Communism in Russia and East Europe reignited interest in totalitarianism in some quarters. This is partly connected to the fact that the material conditions for comparison have improved with the opening of the Soviet archives and the growth in Soviet historiography. For historians at least, argues Geyer, "Comparison is now a matter of doing it—and doing it intelligently and productively."§ But as Geyer notes later in this essay, good work here is not only a matter of digging into the archives and making use of new material. Far too many historians, he says, remain in a "posttheoretical and posttotalitarian mode."¶ Empirically focused efforts can fall into parochialism. "For if the totalitarian presumption of sameness is gone, the phenomenon of twentieth century

---

* Bartov, "Hitler's Willing Believers," 32.

† Solzhenitsyn, "Our Muzzled Freedom," (in this volume).

‡ Burleigh, *The Third Reich: A New History*, 158–77.

§ Geyer, *Beyond Totalitarianism*, 2.

¶ Ibid., 8.

tyrannical rule is as urgent as ever—but, unfortunately, in knowing more about each regime, it turns out that we know altogether less about the nature of their rule."* All the more reason then to return to the greatest analysts of the phenomenon.

Social scientists have criticized "totalitarianism" for being merely a term of description, and not a "theory." That is, they want a term that is predictive, or one that can explain the coming into being of the phenomenon itself. But such a theoretical point of view increasingly removes one from how those who experienced these regimes know them. The more one searches for an abstract model on which to base such an account, the further away one moves from the phenomenon itself. So perhaps the answer lies not in the archives—in more empirically minded studies—nor in a better, more scientific, model. It is not that archival work is unimportant in itself—witness, for example, the impressive Annals of Communism series put out by Yale University Press. Yet a certain archival fetishness can lead to the downplaying of the utility of eyewitness accounts and the philosophical and moral insights of those engaged with the phenomenon at the deepest of levels. We will always require the contributions of a Solzhenitsyn or a Grossman, no matter what is turned up in the archives.

One alternative that has received more attention of late is pursuing Nazism, Communism, and fascism as political religions.† Though surely not as prominent as the idea of totalitarianism, the concept of political religion has a distinguished history whose early proponents included Eric Voegelin, Raymond Aron, and Waldemar Gurian.‡ As Burleigh has

---

* Ibid., 19.

† Emilio Gentile, "Fascism as Political Religion," *Journal of Contemporary History*, vol. 25, no. 2/3 (May-June 1990), 229–51; "The Sacralization of Politics," *Totalitarian Movements and Political Religions* vol. 1, no. 1 (Summer 2000), 18–55; *Politics as Religion*, George Staunton trans. (Princeton: Princeton University Press, 2006). Philippe Burrin, "Political Religion: The Relevance of a Concept," *History and Memory*, vol. 9 (Spring-Summer 1997), 321–49. Michael Burleigh, "National Socialism as a Political Religion," *Totalitarian Movements and Political Religions* vol. 1, no. 2 (Autumn 2000), 1–26, and in this volume. Hans Maier, "Political Religion: A Concept and its Limitations," *Totalitarian Movements and Political Religions* vol. 8, no. 1 (Spring 2007), 15.

‡ Eric Voegelin, *Modernity without Restraint, The Collected Works of Eric Voegelin, vol. 5*, Manfred Henningsen ed. (Columbia: University of Missouri Press, 2000). This

argued, such "disparate figures were heroically searching for explanations which rose above the horizons imposed, and often slavishly followed, by the devotees of such counter-ideologies as Marxism, which they sometimes felt were part of the problem rather than the solution; that is in the sense of narrowing down the fullest meanings of what it is to be human."* Contemporary scholars have focused their efforts here to further their understanding of the commonalities of these tyrannical regimes. Hans Meier has argued that totalitarianism "is to a great extent formal and in need of extension and development," and political religion makes these regimes "more comprehensible with the help of religious-psychological and sociological categories."† The three great political religions offer their followers redemption, the overcoming of evil in this world through revolutionary action. Leaders like Hitler claim to be agents of divine providence who move their societies from fractiousness to harmony and wholeness. Nazism and Communism also imbue their ideological claims with references to science to buttress these quasi-religious sentiments. This gives each movement the legitimacy and resoluteness to pursue their revolutionary, transformative aims without wavering.

Political religion points us away from the formalistic, social scientific model of totalitarianism toward a broader conception of the political. As Philippe Burrin argues, "The specific nature of political religions lies in the fact that they utterly deny the legitimacy of the liberal idea of separate spheres in social life and that they replace the liberal distrust of politics with an absolutization of the latter. Their goal is not to return to a state religion, much less to a theocracy or Caesar-Papism, but to realize the historically new will to encompass the entire life of society in the political."‡ This is where the earliest and best analysts of the totalitarian phenomenon rooted their efforts, in a broad humanistic tradition that includes the insights from literature and philosophy. As Hassner argues:

---

volume contains *The Political Religions*, first published in Austria in 1938. Raymond Aron, "The Future of Secular Religions," in this volume, first published in 1944. Waldemar Gurian, "Totalitarian Religions," in this volume, first published in 1952.

* Michael Burleigh, "National Socialism as a Political Religion," 196–97 (in this volume).

† Hans Maier, "Political Religion: A Concept and its Limitations," 15.

‡ Philippe Burrin, "Political Religion: The Relevance of a Concept," 328.

It is the great literary works (Orwell, Solzhenitsyn, Zinoviev, Grossman) and philosophical interrogations which, periodically, force us to recognize that something escapes the conceptual frameworks and the empirical research of the social sciences applied to Sovietology, and that this 'something' has something to do with totalitarianism. Should it not be sought in the direction of Arendt's 'supersence,' Besancon's 'surreality,' Orwell's 'doublethink' and 'newspeak,' Jaspers' institutionalized lie,' Kostas Papaioannou's 'cold ideology,' or Leszek Kolakowski's 'great lie'? . . . If so, the mistake of the theory of totalitarianism would have to be located in the transition from Arendt to Friedrich and Brzezinski, in the attempt to translate what can be caught only by a global view, intimately linked to a political philosophy into a set of empirical criteria.*

Enduring Themes

The first inspiration for this book came after I began teaching a class called "Dissident Political Thought" that focused on the great anti-communist dissidents—Solzhenitsyn, Czeslaw Milosz, and Václav Havel. I thought of a volume that would bring the writings of these and other dissidents together in one place. As I taught this course I discovered these thinkers addressed questions of enduring political and philosophical interest—that is to say, they were much more than merely "anti-communist thinkers." They addressed themselves to questions political philosophers had been addressing for centuries such as the nature of tyranny, while speaking directly to the political dilemmas of their own time. What enabled human beings to carry out such horrific crimes against their fellows? What does the endurance of Communist regimes reveal about human liberty? Why did human beings suffer rule by ideological lies for so long, and what kept them open to the truth? Finally, and most disconcertingly, what is the relationship between the totalitarian enterprise and the foundational principles of democratic modernity? And they all had something important to

---

* Pierre Hassner, "Communist Totalitarianism: The Transatlantic Vagaries of a Concept," 67 (in this volume).

say about the utter strangeness, the novelty of totalitarian tyranny—even if all of them did not use that term.

It was not just the great anti-communist dissidents who addressed these questions. Some of the best minds of the century past harnessed their gifts in search of answers: Aron, Voegelin, Gurian, Arendt, Leo Strauss, Aurel Kolnai, and Leszek Kolakowski all weighed in on the origins and nature of tyranny in the short and bloody twentieth century. By putting these thinkers together with the great dissidents and adding some penetrating analyses from more contemporary thinkers like Pierre Manent, Claude Lefort, and Alain Besançon, I realized such a volume would present quite an intellectual feast.

The thinkers in this volume all share the sense that tyranny is a problem coeval with political life, and that the totalitarian tyrannies of the twentieth century are in some sense unprecedented. They are not all in agreement about the precise nature of the phenomenon, its origins, or its relation to tyranny simply. They approach the phenomenon from a variety of angles, giving readers access to the fullest and deepest account available. I trust readers will welcome having the writings of such giants as Solzhenitsyn, Havel, Milosz, and Aron in one volume. There is also a measure of intellectual justice at stake in helping lesser known thinkers such as Gurian, Kolnai, Kolakowski, Jan Patočka, and Václav Benda receive the wide audience they deserve.

A Landscape of Modern Tyranny

Here I would like to adumbrate a few of the themes raised by the authors in the volume—themes that illustrate powerfully why these concepts and arguments are not of merely historical interest. I have already alluded to the fact that these thinkers address enduring philosophical and political themes. These writings are also important in thinking through the present and future political landscape. They can help us do what the great political thinkers of the past have always done, lay out the political alternatives, both good and bad, before us. Aristotle and Montesquieu most famously articulated comprehensive regime typologies that described various options and set forth judgments about the merits of each. None of the essays in this volume aims at such a comprehensive goal, but a number of them address the critical question of the distinction between ideocratic or totalitarian regimes and ordinary tyranny—thus, they aid us in articulating a landscape of political evil. Rather than positing a simplistic alternative—"totalitarianism or democracy," as some critics have claimed—thinking through the problem of totalitarian tyranny can enhance the comprehensiveness and the subtlety of our grasp of tyrannical regimes in general.* As Gurian puts it, "It is of crucial importance for the understanding of the totalitarian systems of our time not to identify them with non-democratic or even with non-liberal regimes . . . The assumption that the totalitarian state is the alternative of modern democracy is erroneous."† Contemporary scholars such as Daniel Chirot have also utilized this distinction—Chirot contrasts the "tyranny of corruption" with the "tyranny of ideological certitude" and fleshes out examples of each type as well as those regimes which blend the two.‡

To what extent do we see the totalitarian phenomenon today? North Korea is the clearest example, while Cuba certainly exhibits many key features. This paucity, however, may not adequately express the urgency of the topic. One of the most interesting debates in elite opinion and scholarly circles is the extent to which radical Islam or Islamist movements are kindred phenomena with the totalitarian movements of the twentieth century—obviously a question of great importance.§ Many of the writers

---

* Mark Lilla, "The New Age of Tyranny," *The New York Review* (October 24, 2002), 28–29.

† Waldemar Gurian, "The Totalitarian State," *Proceedings of The American Catholic Philosophical Association*, vol. XV (December 28–29, 1939), 53. Gurian goes on to distinguish totalitarian regimes from "authoritarian absolutistic" and "aristocratic liberal" regimes. See also his discussion of the difference between totalitarian and authoritarian regimes in "Totalitarian Religions," in this volume.

‡ Daniel Chirot, *Modern Tyrants: The Power and Prevalence of Evil in Our Age* (New York: The Free Press, 1994), 167–73.

§ Jeffrey Herf, "What Old and What is New in the Terrorism of Islamic Fundamentalism," *Partisan Review* (Winter 2002), 25–31; Paul Berman, *Terror and Liberalism* (New York: Norton, 2004); Ladan Boroumand and Roya Boroumand, "Terror, Islam, and Democracy," in *Islam and Democracy in the Middle East*, Larry Diamond, Marc F. Plattner, and Daniel Brumberg eds. (Baltimore: Johns Hopkins University Press, 2003), 282–98; Barry Cooper, *New Political Religions, or an Analysis of Modern Ter-*

currently addressing this issue are indebted to a number of thinkers in this volume such as Voegelin and Aron. There is no space to wade into the specifics of this debate here, but whatever one's opinion on the matter, the thinkers included in this volume certainly have much to contribute.

Totalitarianism, Unity, and Mastery

These anti-totalitarian thinkers encourage us to reflect on a problem that seems to emerge with the birth of liberal politics and the separation of the state and civil society. On the one hand, the separation of these spheres is meant to secure the promise of freedom for individuals whose natural rights exist prior to the institution of government. The separation is intended to create the conditions for human flourishing where rights are exercised, interests are pursued, and associations and corporations are created, resulting in a dynamic, semi-autonomous society. On the other hand, thinkers as different as Rousseau, Marx, and Tocqueville have also understood this separation to carry a danger—liberal politics seems to separate people from one another. Human beings, in this optic, are first and foremost individuals without any social bonds that obligate them to one another. Tocqueville famously describes the looming danger of "individualism," the steady retreat by citizens into an ever narrower circle of people and interests.

Totalitarianism can be seen as a rebellion against this separation, as a project to reintegrate people into a social whole where they find community, duty, and higher purpose. To the extent that liberal democracy fails to provide these goods, the totalitarian temptation will not disappear. To be sure, the totalitarian "cure" is infinitely worse than the liberal "disease." It is well worth examining just how totalitarianism has affected human

---

rorism (Columbia: University of Missouri Press, 2005); Bassam Tibi, "The Totalitarianism of Jihadist Islamism and its Challenge to Europe and to Islam," *Totalitarian Movements and Political Religions*, vol. 8, no. 1 (March 2007), 35–54; Hendrik Hansen and Peter Kainz, "Radical Islamism and Totalitarian Ideology: A Comparison of Sayyid Qutb's Islamism with Marxism and National Socialism," *Totalitarian Movements and Political Religions*, vol. 8, no. 1 (March 2007), 55–76; Laurent Murawiec, *The Mind of Jihad* (Cambridge: Cambridge University Press, 2008).

relations. Kolakowski has described totalitarianism as striving for perfect integration through perfect fragmentation. That is, the perfect unity of the state requires the utter destruction of all autonomous social bonds, rendering each individual more isolated and powerless than any inhabitant of any regime in human history. The Polish poet Alexander Wat calls this "socialization through desocialization," or "the law of third." He writes, "Wherever two of you gather, I shall be there with you, 'I' meaning the party, Stalin, an agent. It is through the police that a brother is a brother to his brother, and a friend a friend to his friend. *The law of the greatest possible disjunction of the social bonds between people.*"*

Nonetheless, totalitarianism holds out the prospect of constructing society from above through an exact science. As Claude Lefort argues, "What is being created is the model of a society without divisions, which seems to have mastery of its own organization . . ."† Pierre Manent has pointed out that this impulse of totalitarianism is connected in some way to the "modern artificialism" of Thomas Hobbes—human beings are both "matter" and "artificer."‡ Totalitarian power in its most radical phase seeks to overcome all divisions internal to civil society. The core of this project seems to be the complete homogenization of the human world. All aspects of life are equally subject to the same social power and subsumed under the task of "building socialism."

Citizens of liberal democracies therefore have to be aware of these longings for unity and the seductions of social self-mastery. Though most totalitarian regimes have become part of history, the totalitarian temptation is not dead. As Furet puts it, "The end of the Soviet world in no way alters the democratic call for another society, and for that reason we have every reason to believe that the massive failure of Communism will con-

---

* Alexander Wat, *My Century: The Odyssey of a Polish Intellectual*, Richard Lourie ed. and trans. (Berkeley: University of California Press, 1988), 243, emphasis added. This is a little known gem of a book. It is actually a transcription of an extended interview of Wat by Czeslaw Milosz.

† Claude Lefort, "The Logic of Totalitarianism," in *The Political Forms of Modern Society* (Cambridge: The MIT Press, 1986), 284.

‡ See Pierre Manent, "Totalitarianism and the Problem of Political Representation," in *Modern Liberty and its Discontents*, Daniel J. Mahoney and Paul Seaton eds. and trans. (Lanham, MD: Rowman and Littlefield, 1998).

tinue to enjoy attenuating circumstances in world opinion, and perhaps even renewed admiration."[*]

Modern Democracy and Totalitarianism: A Common Matrix?

Whatever the prevalence or scarcity of the phenomenon of ideocratic or totalitarian tyranny today, there are strong arguments to be made that we have yet to see the last of the phenomenon. As Jean-Francois Revel has put it, "As long as we have not really understood the genesis of this phenomenon, who can say we are safe and immunized against new outbreaks of madness?"[†] Revel's is a crucial question, and one that many thinkers have shied away from. Perhaps we were too confident that 1989–91 put ideocratic tyranny to rest, too tempted by the idea of an end to history. But we must confront the philosophic conditions for the emergence of these regimes and reflect on the present status of those conditions. That is the first step in our immunization against new outbreaks of madness. Many of the thinkers in this volume certainly aid us in this task.

Gurian characterizes totalitarian movements and regimes as the "product of fatigue." They are "a reaction against the skepticism, relativism, and historicism characteristic of the modern democracy of our days."[‡] Philosophic currents prevalent in the early part of the twentieth century continue to pervade our time. Leo Strauss, in his attempt to lay bare the nihilism requisite for the emergence of Hitler and National Socialism, argues that "nihilism is the rejection of the principles of civilization as such." Strauss attempts to elucidate the cultural conditions for the emergence of these tyrannies, arguing:

> By civilization, we understand the conscious culture of humanity, i.e. of that which makes a human being a human being, i.e. the

---

[*] Furet, 502.

[†] Revel, "But We Follow the Worse . . ." *The National Interest* (Winter 1989/90), 99. See also Revel's *Last Exit to Utopia: The Survival of Socialism in a Post-Soviet Era* (New York: Encounter Books, 2009).

[‡] Waldemar Gurian, "The Totalitarian State," 57.

conscious culture of reason. Human reason is active, above all, in two ways: as regulating human conduct, and as attempting to understand whatever can be understood by man; as practical reason and theoretical reason. The pillars of civilization are therefore morals and science, and both united. For science without morals degenerates into cynicism, and thus destroys the basis of the scientific effort itself, and morals without science degenerates into superstition and thus is apt to become fanatic cruelty.[*]

What we have witnessed in the twentieth century, according to Strauss, is the increasing separation between these two pillars of civilization. Pierre Manent picks up on Strauss's argument and points to the radicalization of this separation evident in the Weberian distinction between facts and values. The realm of facts, of course, belongs to science, while values are what guide our moral life. The separation is problematic, as Strauss points out, when one of these realms is not allowed to illuminate the other. Science or theoretical reason has grown immensely powerful in learning new, efficient ways to conquer and manipulate nature, but it has little to say about lived experience. As Manent argues, "Through separating facts from values we are able to divert the mighty flow of reality into the bottles of science. But there is no reciprocity: science is never allowed to come back to illuminate reality and life. Democracy is predicated on the basic intelligibility of the common man, which in turn is predicated on the inherent intelligibility of life, at least of the current occurrences of life. As a result, democracy is the regime that has the least tolerance for nihilism."[†]

Totalitarianism presents itself as a solution to this separation, a political remedy whereby science and life can become fused once again. The Communist fusion occurs through a despotic science while the Nazi fusion occurs through the despotism of life. The writings of the dissidents indicate that this attempted fusion actually radicalizes the separation—the fusion as experienced by human beings becomes increasingly unbearable. Milosz refers to this experience as the "menace of total rationalism." The total rationalism to which he refers is "Diamat," or dialectical materialism, which purports to explain everything—one's actions and

---

[*] Strauss, "German Nihilism," 230–31 (in this volume).

[†] Manent, "The Return of Political Philosophy," 579 (in this volume).

views can be explained through one's economic class and the movement of history. The "science" of Marxist-Leninism provides a comprehensive account of the human world, but it leaves out the common intelligence of individual human beings and their connection to an intelligible world. Milosz emphasizes that this total rationalism is menacing because the individual is, so to speak, remaindered. The experience of wonder and mystery is thought to be irrational because of the despotism of Marxist "science"—it is apparently the only rational game in town. As Milosz puts it, "The resistance against the new set of values is, however, emotional. It survives, but it is beaten whenever it has to explain itself in rational terms. A man's subconscious or not-quite-conscious life is richer than his vocabulary. His opposition to this new philosophy of life is much like a toothache. Not only can he not express the pain in words, but he cannot even tell you which tooth is aching."* This is perhaps the most destructive element of the totalitarian experiment. It saps people's confidence in their own capacities as rational and moral beings—as beings fit to confront questions of justice and human dignity. This is what Havel calls the crisis of human identity that is so evident in totalitarian regimes. Such regimes depend for their perpetuation on the demoralization of their citizens.†

Civilization in Crisis?

This brings us to another prominent theme in the volume that belies the criticism that totalitarianism allows for a simplistic division between the evil, totalitarian East and the good, liberal West. Solzhenitsyn, Havel, and Patočka all suggest that a broad civilizational crisis infects the whole world, both East and West. As Solzhenitsyn puts in his famous Harvard Address, "The split in the world is less terrifying than the similarity of the disease afflicting its main sections."‡ He roots the crisis of the West in what he variously terms rationalistic humanism or anthropocentric humanism.

---

* Milosz, "Man, This Enemy," 441 (in this volume).

† Havel, "The Power of the Powerless," (in this volume).

‡ Aleksandr Solzhenitsyn, *The Solzhenitsyn Reader: New and Essential Writings 1947–2005*, Edward E. Ericson, Jr. and Daniel J. Mahoney eds. (Wilmington, DE: ISI Books, 2006), 575.

Introduction

There are a number of key elements that comprise this: (1) the denial of intrinsic evil in human beings; (2) the denial of any higher task than the attainment of happiness on earth (happiness understood as physical, material well-being); and (3) the claim that material progress automatically entails moral progress, and more specifically, that material progress will soften human beings, make them gentler—the replacement of a world dominated by conflict and war with a world dominated by cooperation and commerce. All these elements depend on a common premise: the strict separation of politics from morality. Technological civilization has brought us many material comforts, but it has come at the result of a weakened, yet anxious spirit prevalent in both East and West.[*]

Havel has a complementary account of the human personality under the dominance of technological civilization that is indebted to Patočka. According to Havel, totalitarian systems are: "a convex mirror of all modern civilization" or "the avant-garde of a global crisis of this civilization." Havel argues that human beings are the only beings aware of an order of Being. This awareness, the natural condition of humanity, is painful since it is a condition of separation. Yet this experience, this longing, Havel also calls the "miracle of the subject," because human beings know that there is something in need of recovery. So we strive for meaning, to recover and rejoin what he calls the integrity of Being, though we know we can never get there fully. Our pre-reflective experience of ourselves as responsible to and for others is the ground of our freedom. According to Havel, modern, technological civilization has enabled us to turn away from our longing for meaning and responsibility by succumbing to mere "existence-in-the-world." We envelope ourselves in everyday desires, in consumption, and invest our efforts in ever more efficient strategies to fulfill these desires.

This retreat is one of the two ways that human beings turn away from transcendence. Havel argues that another temptation is a "reified morality" or "fanaticism." Our pre-reflective orientation towards Being has to be reflected upon and developed. The path of responsibility and transcendence is arduous and must be constantly nurtured. Human beings may be tempted to

---

* See Daniel J. Mahoney, *Aleksandr Solzhenitsyn: The Ascent from Ideology* (Lanham, MD: Rowman and Littlefield, 2001); James F. Pontuso, *Assault on Ideology: Aleksandr Solzhenitsyn's Political Thought*, 2nd Edition (Lanham, MD: Lexington Books, 2004).

solve this problem of longing once and for all, but the attempt to grab Being and hold it place will result in fanaticism—the mind will debase itself before the logicality and unreality of an ideological project. Service to such a project becomes self-alienating, because there is no place for common sense or reason, for thinking together. When we try to eliminate reality when it comes into conflict with our project, violence, terror, repression, and the destruction of history and memory result. This is the totalitarian temptation.[*]

Another thinker from the volume who provides an argument for the continuing relevance of anti-totalitarian thought is Chantal Delsol. In *The Unlearned Lessons of the Twentieth Century: An Essay on Late Modernity*, Delsol delivers a disquieting thesis: "The foundations of contemporary thought remain those of the same revolutionary modernity that gave rise to totalitarianism."[†] Her book is an extended meditation on the meaning and legacy of the totalitarian nightmare and the consequences of the failure to confront that legacy.[‡] She argues that the idea of an autonomous or sovereign subject, free from any external truths or limits, is the precondition for the totalitarian project to transform human nature. Though we inhabitants of the twenty-first century think we have turned a corner and left those nightmares behind, we stand in the same dark hallway. Whereas totalitarian regimes—through their "demiurgic will to change human nature"—created "antiworlds," we in the West strive to create "nonworlds" through our efforts to undermine common values. "What makes the analogy work," she suggests, "is a mixture of relativism and dogmatism. Truths are at once changing and rendered absolute: a paradoxical superimposition of the cynic and self-appointed righter of wrongs—someone who engages in constant derision, devaluing everything, but at the same time decrees what is good and what is true with inspired self-assurance."[§]

---

[*] See Aviezer Tucker, *The Philosophy and Politics of Czech Dissidence from Patočka to Hável* (Pittsburgh: University of Pittsburgh Press, 2000); James F. Pontuso, *Václav Havel: Civic Responsibility in the Postmodern Age* (Lanham, MD: Rowman and Littlefield, 2004).

[†] Chantal Delsol, *The Unlearned Lessons of the Twentieth Century: An Essay on Late Modernity*, Robin Dick trans. (Wilmington, DE: ISI Books, 2006), 177.

[‡] For an account and investigation of this failure, see Jeffrey Isaac, "The Strange Silence of Political Theory," *Political Theory*, vol. 23, no. 4 (November 1995), 636–52.

[§] Delsol, *The Unlearned Lessons of the Twentieth Century: An Essay on Late Modernity*, 87.

We think we have been liberated from these temptations because the ideological contents of Nazism and Communism have been rejected, but Delsol argues that real liberation will only come through a rejection of their form, or their mode of thought. She points to the many Central European intellectuals who aimed to convince people of the need for precisely this. "The authentic subject is neither a fanatic nor a nihilist, but a witness."* The dignity of the human person will not be restored through cool detachment, but through the recognition of truths outside of oneself. These external referents guide the "authentic subject" as he strives to think and act in accord with them. However, because he is not the author of these truths, he must confront his finitude and insufficiency during his pursuit.

Organization

This volume is not meant to be representative in the sense of bringing together all perspectives on the phenomenon of totalitarianism. I have sought rather to bring together the thinkers who in my judgment have offered the most incisive and profound analyses of totalitarianism—from dissidents such as Havel, Michnik, and Benda, to intellectual giants such as Aron, Strauss, and Voegelin, to neglected but important thinkers such as Gurian and Kolnai, and to contemporary thinkers such as Manent, Todorov, and Lefort. Not that they all agree with one another on every aspect of these matters, far from it—Arendt, Voegelin, and Aron, for example, all have significant disagreements. Most of them do share the conviction that ideology is not just one aspect of totalitarian tyranny among many, but the defining feature.† It is this insight that is largely rejected by a social scientific approach or historians working in a "posttheoretical" mode.

The volume is divided thematically into six parts. Part I provides readers with an introduction to the debate around the concept of totalitarianism. It aims to address two issues: first, how might we distinguish totalitar-

---

* Ibid., 106.

† Besançon is perhaps the most insightful on this point. See "On the Difficulty of Defining the Soviet Regime," in this volume and "Language and Power in Soviet Society (Parts I & II): A Conversation Between Alain Besançon and George Urban," *Encounter* (May, June 1987), 3–13, 12–22.

ian tyranny from ordinary tyranny; and second, when and why was this category first introduced, and why has it often met with resistance? So this section includes classic essays by Carl Friedrich and Havel that address this first question and essays by Malia and Hassner that address the second. Part II is devoted to the elucidation of the nature of totalitarianism. What are its essential features? What is its internal logic or "genetic" code that makes such regimes in different times and places behave so similarly? Part III examines the origins of the phenomenon, not so much in a historical sense, but in a philosophic sense. If totalitarianism is not merely a particularly vicious form of tyranny, but indeed a novel, distinctly modern enterprise, what are the philosophic conditions necessary for its emergence? Part IV addresses the question of why and how these regimes attracted so many people into their ideological fold. The classic treatment of this problem is the first chapter of Milosz's *The Captive Mind*, and is included here. Part V treats the opposite problem: what are the possibilities for dissent in totalitarian regimes, how did dissent reveal itself, and what does this tell us about the nature and novelty of totalitarianism and the ultimate limits of its aspirations? Here we focus on Czech authors, who were quite self-conscious about the meaning of their engagement and confrontation with totalitarian power.[*] I should note that it is purely accidental that the Seduction section is dominated by Polish authors while the Dissent section by Czechs. I thought it fortuitous that during my search for possible works to include, I found authors and essays engaged in conversation. The volume as whole is enhanced by the dialogue between Wierzbicki and Michnik and the conversation initiated by Benda and continued by Havel, Kantůrková, and Palouš.

The final part of the volume includes efforts by seminal figures like Solzhenitsyn and contemporary thinkers like Pierre Manent to reflect on the meaning of the totalitarian experience as a whole and its bearing on the future.

These categories are of course not air tight, and some essays might well fit into more than one of them. This is especially true of the Nature and Origins section. My organization is meant to be a useful if imperfect framework to begin to study these thinkers and themes.

---

[*] For an excellent collection of Czechoslovak dissident writing, see *Good-Bye, Samizdat: Twenty Years of Czechoslovak Underground Writing*, ed. Marketa Goetz-Stankiewicz (Evanston, IL: Northwestern University Press, 1992).

Introduction

Many of the thinkers in this volume are long dead. The greatest witnesses to the twentieth century are passing before our eyes, and those who are now entering their college-age years were born during the collapse of Communism in Russia and Eastern Europe. We who must navigate the political challenges and temptations of this century are fortunate to have the wisdom of those who sought to comprehend of the horrors of the twentieth century. But we must ensure that this inheritance endures as a living wisdom. "A living lie—and that is the tragedy of human life—is superior, as force, to a dead truth. It is not possible to accept liberty as something self-evident or absolutely protected by political mechanisms. It is necessary to fight for it, disregarding the risks and dangers."* May the anti-totalitarians of the future profit from the wisdom collected here. It is to them, whoever and wherever they are, that this volume is dedicated.

---

* Waldemar Gurian, "Trends in Modern Politics," *The Review of Politics* (July 1940), 336.

Note on the Text

Most of the essays published here appear as they did in the place of their original publication. Besançon's "On the Difficulty Defining the Soviet Regime," appears here in English for the first time. In all other cases the essays not originally written in English were previously translated. Martin Malia's, "From Under the Rubble, What?," Solzhenitsyn's "The Smatterers," and Havel's "The Power of the Powerless" appear here in abridged form.

The endnotes in the back of the volume are the notes provided by the authors themselves, the translators, or the original editors. The footnotes are mine. As unobtrusively as possible, I have sought to supply information about names or events not likely to be known by the student or casual reader. These notes are in no way meant to be comprehensive, but only to provide a quick reference so as not to be too distracting from the argument of the author.

In a number of cases, where the provenance of an essay is of historical interest, I have provided information on this score in a footnote. Information about the previous publication of the essays can also be found in the Sources and Permissions. The years given in the table of contents are the years of the original publication of the essays, or, in a few cases, the years of composition.

I
CONCEPTS

1

Totalitarian Religions
(1952)

WALDEMAR GURIAN

We observe today an astonishing spectacle. Just as during the worst period of the French Revolution, Christianity, and particularly the Catholic Church, is under systematic attack in wide parts of the world, in the Soviet Union, in its European satellites, and in Red China. These countries are under control of groups which profess an atheistic doctrine. The official doctrine of the Soviet world expresses the belief that religion will disappear; it permits the application of tactics which strangulate Church life slowly, but successfully. Leading members of the hierarchy have been arrested and sentenced; schools and monasteries have been closed down; religious orders disbanded; missionary work of centuries has been destroyed. All this is accomplished by systematic and carefully planned campaigns. Every means of deception is used. In profoundly Catholic countries like Poland, caution prevails; in others brutal terror is applied. And all measures against Church life are presented, despite the clear atheism of the official doctrine, as measures against reactionaries and political counter-revolutionaries; churchmen are accused of being American agents and allies of Imperialism and Capitalism.[*]

But it is not only the Communists who have persecuted the Church in our time; the anti-Communist Nazi regime tried also to destroy the

---

[*] For a detailed chronicle of the spectacle here described by Gurian, see Michael Burleigh's *Sacred Causes: The Clash of Religion and Politics, from the Great War to the War on Terror.*

Church, though this attack was made in the name of another doctrine, a racial philosophy. What both systems, Communism and Nazism, have in common is their totalitarian character. This common totalitarianism of course does not mean that they must always be friendly to each other; on the contrary, both fought against each other, accusing each other of being barbaric, inhuman, sadistic.

In this article I will not try to present the history of the antireligious policies of the two totalitarian systems of our time. I will try to show the basis of these policies, the spirit which makes them develop an absolute hostility against Christ and His Church.

The totalitarian movements which have arisen since World War I are fundamentally religious movements. They aim not at changes of political and social institutions, but at the reshaping of the nature of man and society. They claim to have the true and obligatory knowledge about life and its aims. They emphasize that they are based on doctrines which describe and determine totally and completely the existence and activities of men and society. It does not matter if these doctrines are presented as the exclusively correct expression of a scientific knowledge of society and the laws according to which history develops—as the Marxist Bolshevik variety of totalitarianism does—or if they pretend to justify the domination of the master race and express the myth destined to prevail in the twentieth century as the National Socialist variety asserts. The pretense of having the true doctrine gives to the totalitarian movements their basic character. They are intolerant. They aim at the extirpation of all other doctrines and philosophies. They cannot tolerate any limitation of their claims and their power. Totalitarian movements cannot conceive of realms of life outside and beyond their control; they cannot accept the fact that there are other doctrines or institutions with the right to remain independent, having a dignity and a validity of their own. That they do accept for a time, as long as power considerations demand it, the existence of other groups and other doctrines does not mean that they abandon their aim of absolute domination, of making all other doctrines disappear.

It is a fatal misunderstanding of totalitarian movements to confuse and identify them with authoritarian political regimes. True, authoritarian regimes do not know and accept real democratic institutions and processes, for example, periodical elections based upon universal suffrage which determine the composition of government; they reject constitutional limitations which do not depend upon decisions of the ruler. But they accept (or at least do not reject) an objective traditional social order which is independent of the ruler and the ruling group. Authoritarian regimes do not claim to bring a new faith, an all-embracing doctrine determining the whole of life; though they are nondemocratic, opposed to representative government based on universal suffrage, rejecting parties and the political influence of public opinion which expresses itself in free, not controlled, discussions.

The authoritarian regimes which in their traditional monarchic form became outmoded after the French Revolution, reappear today as reactions against the dissolution of unifying forces and institutions among nations. Nations in our time are often threatened by anarchy, by the deadly strife of parties which put their particular interests above the common good; for the parties have developed into instruments of the egoistic interests of their members or leaders who have forgotten their obligation towards the community as a whole. Authoritarian regimes of today may try, as the absolute monarchies of the Enlightenment did, to control all institutions—including the Church—claiming that the governments know best what the welfare of the community requires. They are surely antidemocratic, rejecting the participation of the people by national suffrage in government; they believe in a system of government exercised from above by a wise man or by a ruling elite. But they are not based upon the belief that the political regime must regulate the whole of life, that everything, including science and cultural activities, is subordinate to the movement which shapes the public power, that the doctrine of this movement is the key to the understanding of history and nature of society as well as of the destiny of man. The authoritarian regimes do not deny the existence of an objective order which is beyond the reach of political power, and they do not claim that political power determines what is the objective order and the truth. The authoritarian regimes express political views not shared by those who accept democracy and who believe that policies ought to be influenced by public opinion and its discussions. But they are not based upon political religions; their political power, unlike totalitarian power, does not determine the whole life of men and society.

Today, of course, it is not always easy to distinguish between totalitarian and authoritarian regimes. The Fascist regime in Mussolini's Italy rose with totalitarian pretenses; Mussolini himself wrote an article about

5

the Fascist doctrine. But I agree fully with Hannah Arendt, who in her study *The Origins of Totalitarianism* (New York: Harcourt, Brace & Co., 1951) cited Nazism and Bolshevism as the prototypes of totalitarianism. For Mussolini employed claims about a particular Fascist doctrine for propaganda purposes in order to justify his superiority over the liberal-parliamentary regime of the past. The Fascist doctrine did not prevent him—despite all clashes and conflicts from coming to terms with the Church. He accepted—true, for pragmatic reasons—the Catholic tradition prevailing in Italy. His rule had an authoritarian character despite totalitarian trimmings; he emphasized—as authoritarians are inclined to do—the power of the state, and therefore the right of the state to control all life and all institutions, including the Church. The Fascist attitude towards the Church brought about a renewal of the traditional conflicts between the Church and a strong State which would try to put the Church under its control, denying her independence in public life. Fascism tried, for example, to control Catholic Action; this attempt caused Pius XI to write the encyclical *Non Abbiamo Bisogno.** But despite all rhetorical boasts against which the Church took a stand Italian Fascism did not try seriously to replace the faith of the Church by a new religion, a political religion making the totalitarian movement the single force dominating all realms of life and giving true meaning to society and men.

What has been said about Italian Fascism must be said too about Franco's Spain. Franco's regime is authoritarian, but not totalitarian. It uses fewer totalitarian trimmings than Mussolini did—for it appeals more directly and intensely to Spanish traditions. It opposes liberalism and modern democracy in the name of those traditions, and it tries to emphasize the power of the state, but it does not assert the mission of a movement destined to bring a new faith and to shape the whole of life correspondingly.

The difficulty in making clear the distinction between authoritarian and totalitarian regimes is increased by the tendencies of totalitarian movements to utilize both traditional ideas and conservative-minded groups

---

* *Non Abbiamo Bisogno* ("We Do Not Need"), promulgated on June 29, 1931, was a defense of Catholic Action and other Catholic youth organizations dedicated to religious education and faith cultivation that had come under attack from the Fascist regime of Mussolini.

6

to bring themselves and their policies into power. A particularly striking example of this tendency was provided by Hitler and his National-Socialism. One of his most efficient propaganda slogans was the claim that he alone was able to crush Communism—as whose allies liberals and democrats were denounced—and that, therefore, he would preserve and rescue traditional values and religion. He was anti-Communist; so his propaganda tried to spread the wrong impression that his movement was pro-Christian. It was overlooked by his conservative admirers that one can fight one error not only in the name of truth, but in the name of other errors. Not only did the party program mention "positive Christianity," but the first proclamation of Hitler after his appointment as chancellor mentioned protection of religion. Likewise, the Bolsheviks, who began as the fiercest opponents and destroyers of all traditional institutions and beliefs and as indefatigable workers for an international atheistic classless society, have learned to press traditional forces into their service. Stalin's Soviet Union proclaims today that its policies realize Russian national aspirations; and the state Church of the Tsarist past is again utilized as an instrument of the government and its propaganda. Therefore, the strong state whose rulers are not dependent upon elections, parties, and a free public opinion, appears as characteristic of totalitarian regimes; their claim to have an all-embracing doctrine seems to be only an instrument for the erection of a political system where the state concentrates in its hands the maximum of power.

But I think this attempt to interpret totalitarianism only as a particularly ruthless form of authoritarianism and to explain away the importance of the totalitarian doctrine prevents real understanding of the political religions of the twentieth century. These political religions, the various kinds of totalitarianism, aim not only at the establishment of a strong state, but at the complete transformation and control of men and society. The totalitarian state which intervenes in all realms of life is not the end but merely an instrument of the totalitarian movement. The decisive feature of this movement is the acceptance of a doctrine which justifies absolute domination by those who have accepted it—the leaders and members of the totalitarian party. This doctrine does not exclude practical adaptations. The masses are not told the consequences of the doctrine; they must be seduced and tamed by giving the impression (especially before power is achieved) that their needs and demands will be satisfied.

The Bolsheviks said in 1917 that they were for peace—the masses, the Russian soldiers and peasants did not understand that they were really only for the ending of the imperialist wars, for the transformation of these wars into revolutionary wars. They told the peasants that all landed estates would be turned over to them. The peasants did not realize that all land, including their own, would be finally put under the control of the state. The Nazis told the middle-class businessmen that they would abolish department stores, and end an economic order dominated by the easy gains of interest-takers. The nature of the totalitarian doctrines was but slowly realized. Hitler introduced even the measures against the Jews only step by step. He began with the Concordat* in order to deceive the Catholics about his Church policies. The final status promised by the totalitarian doctrine can even become a myth whose realization is beyond human control. Stalin has extended the transitional period during which a strong political power would be necessary; therefore, he has delayed the withering away of the state as an instrument of coercion to the uncontrollable and unpredictable far-distant future.

What matters is not the content of totalitarian doctrine; its function of establishing total domination by the totalitarian leaders and elites is decisive—to use an expression of Hannah Arendt. Totalitarian doctrine justifies a continuous drive for more and more power as well as the dynamism and expansionism without end characteristic of totalitarian regimes; totalitarian doctrine makes totalitarian rulers deal with men and human groups as pure material; for what matters are not human beings and their reality, but the constant proof presented again and again that the doctrine is right, for it determines reality by power exercised in its name;

---

* The Concordat was an agreement signed between the Nazi government and the Vatican in July 1933. In exchange for the Vatican's pledge not to involve itself in German politics by promoting a political party (e.g., the Catholic Centre Party), the Nazi government legally authorized Church activities such as youth organizations, rallies, etc. The Nazis wasted no time in breaking their pledge and quickly began to undermine the autonomy of these Catholic lay organizations in myriad ways. It is worth pointing out that Gurian knew whereof he spoke. Gurian, after leaving Germany for Switzerland in 1933, published "German Letters" with another exiled journalist. These letters provide a detailed picture of Nazi policies and the resulting conditions. In 1936 Gurian also published *Hitler and the Christians*.

this power that has no limits it is expanded and demonstrated again and again—becomes an end in itself, for it is proved to be meaningful because it corresponds to the doctrine and therefore justifies the actions of those who realize and interpret it.

Men and groups are not only to obey and to avoid any public opposition as in authoritarian regimes—but they are forced to be active and enthusiastic supporters. They are forced in such a way that they do not appear to be forced. They are liquidated, thrown away as if they were unnecessary and useless parts of a machine—according to the whims of the rulers, who show by this behavior their limitless, all-embracing power. The totalitarian masters shape the world according to their doctrine; any reality not corresponding to the doctrine is wrong, and its existence is rejected if the doctrine demands it. Hannah Arendt illustrates this attitude by mentioning a story which denies that there are other subways besides those of Moscow, for to admit of other subways would be to oppose Soviet propaganda whose claims the inhabitants of the Soviet Union must accept as reality. The policy of the iron curtain is a consequence of the totalitarian attempt to make the totalitarian world appear as the real world. The authoritarian regime establishes a form of political rule; the totalitarian regime tries to create an artificial world and impose it as reality. This world has to correspond to the demands of the totalitarian doctrine as interpreted by the rulers so that their power is constantly maintained and demonstrated by expansions. A vicious circle characterizes totalitarian rule: the doctrine justifies the absolute domination by such a group as the party—the instrument for the realization of Socialism and Communism or the racial elite—and the doctrine is proved to be true by the successful absolute domination consisting not only in the establishment of the totalitarian state, but in the imposition of an artificial world. God's order is replaced by a man-made order, the artificial order required by the doctrine and created by the power exercised in its name.

Therefore, the conflict between the Church and the totalitarian regimes goes much deeper than the conflicts between the Church and the authoritarian regimes. The latter are conflicts caused by attempts of the secular power to put the spiritual power with its public functions under its control, to determine, for example, appointments of bishops, to control all educational activities of the Church, to restrict the formation of Catholic associations, to supervise or to forbid religious orders, to make the publication of papal and episcopal pronouncements dependent upon permission by state authorities (the so-called *placet*). The totalitarian regimes take over all methods of the authoritarian state to control and restrict Church activities; they do not admit, of course, any obligation to regard the Church as modern liberal-democratic regimes do as an association of citizens in whose internal life the government does not interfere. For all associations ought to be under control of the totalitarian movement; their "coordination" (*Gleichschaltung*) is carried out as one of the most important policies of the totalitarian regime, and only on account of power politics and propagandist considerations is the Church provisionally exempted from this coordination—Hitler concluded a Concordat not actually to comply with its terms, but to avoid an immediate open conflict with Catholics and to confuse them. The land and other property of the Catholic Church in Poland are not confiscated in order to keep the Catholic believers quiet.

The totalitarian regimes also apply methods and legislative measures which have been used by authoritarian regimes which tried to put the Church under political control, regarding it as an intolerably dangerous competitor of the secular civil authority and threatening loyal behavior towards the government or the nation. But this legislation and these measures are not specific in the totalitarian Church policies. The application of these means by totalitarian regimes has as its aim not the restriction and the control of the public activities of the Church but the complete destruction of religion and the Church. The faith of the Church will be replaced by the myth of the twentieth century, the racialist religion of the leaders of the Nazi movement. True, Rosenberg,* the authoritative teacher of the Nazi doctrine, maintained that the racial People's Church of the future would tolerate Catholic and Protestant chapels, "positive Christianity," but racialism would determine what could be accepted as "positive" and what must be rejected as "negative Christianity." The Bolshevik anti-religious religion does not use, as the Nazis did, a misleading pseudo-religious terminology even though asserting that its atheism will necessarily triumph and can afford to accept freedom of religion and conscience. The Communists claim that the realization of Socialism and Communism will destroy the social roots of religious beliefs, which are "opiates" used either by exploit-

---

* Alfred Rosenberg, an early member of the Nazi party, wrote key Nazi treatises on foreign policy and the nature of German racial purity.

ing groups to fool the masses or by the masses themselves as means of self-deception in order to escape from intolerable realities. If men become masters of society through and in Socialism and Communism, the Bolsheviks as followers of Marxism pretend there will be no need for a God Who has created men and the world—all religious mysteries will evaporate when faced by the reality of the perfect, man-made world of the classless society. The totalitarian movements are hostile to the Church not only on account of their policies towards the Church but on account of their basic belief, of the consciously formulated doctrine which, allegedly, is alone able to explain history and to give the right aim to all human activities.

The totalitarian doctrines are not only political ones, they claim to provide the key to the whole universe, to all realms of human life; they deny to the Church any independence in public activities. They are bitterly opposed to her doctrine, to her influence on the souls of men. This doctrine and this influence must be replaced by the totalitarian ones. Here appears the similarity between the totalitarian movements of the twentieth century and the antireligious ideologies of the French Revolution in the eighteenth century. These ideologies went beyond the original aim of the new French regime to control the Church; they tried to replace its doctrines by new ones corresponding to reason and the true nature of men. Modern totalitarianism is distinct from its predecessor by creating its doctrines as explanations of the historical processes—they can be realized only in their culmination, not at once, immediately, by proclamations, pressure and legislative actions. Marx made satirical remarks about the behavior of Bakunin* who, during one of his putsches, issued a decree abolishing belief in God; the Soviet regime has always pretended to respect religious feelings, but this of course has not prevented all kinds of persecution of religious groups, whereas atheistic propaganda is favored and supported. Hitler carefully avoided publicizing his hostility to Christianity— the Nazis fought allegedly only against so-called "political" Catholicism and against ministerial intervention in affairs of state. Another distinction is the abandonment of the attempts made, for example, by Robespierre with his introduction of the cult of the Supreme Being to create special new moral-religious cults; some Nazi fanatics did attempt such a creation but the Germanic religion did not work. The modern totalitarian cult is

---

* Michael Bakunin was a nineteenth-century Russian theorist of anarchism.

exercised by demonstrations of power and domination by the totalitarian regime and its leaders. Party congresses, May Day processions, incessant adulatory praise of the leaders, constant announcement that a new era has started and that all representatives of old epochs are doomed—these are the cult and the liturgy of the totalitarian movements. The totalitarian movements have their devils, too—not only external enemies but internal traitors, who are constantly unmasked and defeated, purged and liquidated.

Just because the totalitarian movements believe that their doctrine will be victorious and that all reality will be shaped in their image, they are able to apply deceptive tactics. The masses, which are kept in constant motion, must be educated and prepared to understand the goal grasped at the beginning only by the leaders. When the enemy is too strong, complicated maneuvers are necessary. As Lenin put it, it is necessary to retreat one step in order to be able to advance again. The Bolsheviks abandoned their attempts to destroy the prestige of the Orthodox Church or to split it by supporting the faction known as the so-called Living Church which accused the old Church leadership of being reactionary; they realized soon that this policy would not work; but they have continued to expect the disappearance of all religion as a result of their policies—even today when they use the Orthodox Church both as an instrument for their propaganda, and as a means to refute the accusation that antireligious policies prevail in the Soviet Union. A final objective here is also to weaken the Catholic Church; the Catholics of the Greek rite, the so-called Uniates, recognizing the authority of Rome, have been put under the authority of the Patriarch of Moscow. Groups of priests cooperating with Communism are established and favored in order to confuse and split the believers.

The Nazi policies towards the Church at the beginning were more disguised than those of the Bolsheviks. They tried to mislead Christian believers by their opposition to atheistic Communism and by concluding a concordat with Rome. They emphasized always that they were fighting only against political Catholicism and the representatives of religion who—by becoming too power-hungry or even allegedly indulging in vices—were in reality betrayers of the faith. In the name of national unity and the necessity of keeping religion pure the Church was eliminated step by step from the exercise of influence on public life. Catholic schools were abolished, Catholic publications had to stop because of a paper shortage which Nazi publications did not experience. Religious orders no longer had a chance to exist; there was no longer any opportunity to recruit seminarians. But all this was done step by step, cautiously. It is characteristic that Goebbels* prevented the arrest of Bishop Count Galen (who publicly criticized such Nazi policies as the liquidation of insane and feeble-minded people) in accordance with the principle: "We do not want martyrs." Churchmen were arrested, allegedly, only because they were criminals and enemies of the national unity, the community of the German people.

Peculiar to totalitarian movements is their attempt to change the center of life. The transcendent world is either absolutely denied as in the Bolshevik belief in the inevitable coming of the atheistic classless society, or it is made into an instrument of purely immanent political and social forces as in the Nazi order. Pope Pius XI's encyclical of 1937 "With Utmost Anxiety," (*Mit brennender Sorge*) gives a classical analysis of this misuse of religious words and concepts for purely secular meaning. The Pope rejects the Nazi talk about God, which makes God a symbol of the power of a race. He rejects the use of sacred words for the purpose of praising the policy and public acts of the Nazi totalitarian movement. He reveals the misuse of the word justice when it is made to express racial feelings, as in the sentence: "Just is what Nordic-Aryan men regard as just."

The fact that a political movement informed and guided by the allegedly just and at the same time true doctrine *is* put at the center of life makes this doctrine the aim of life. If religion is not openly rejected— and explained away in Marxian fashion as the product of an imperfect society—it is deprived of all dignity and independence by being made a tool of political and social power politics, a collection of myths which strengthen the will to live and die for the totalitarian movement. The politico-social religions compel the swallowing-up of true religion and universal human ethics by arbitrary pseudoscientific and pseudomythical doctrines. These doctrines claim to correspond to and to be reality—because they are backed by groups which, having achieved political power, can make the system of domination established by them appear to be the reality.

The conflict between the Church and totalitarianism is, therefore, not only a conflict of power and influence, but a conflict over the nature of men and society. Totalitarianism will reduce men not merely to cogs in its

---

* Joseph Goebbels was the Nazi minister of propaganda.

power machinery but to creatures utilizing all their capacities to celebrate their own enslavement. What is just, what is good, what is beautiful, what is free, is defined by the totalitarian rulers, for they must always be right and competent in all fields according to the doctrine, the obligatory philosophy, pseudotheology and mythology of history. This must be constantly confirmed by demonstrations of public enthusiasm and by display of unceasing efforts to prove that the totalitarian fiat has no limitations.

The Church thus must appear to the totalitarians as an intolerable challenge. Even if they succeed in depriving it of any independent role in public life, the fact remains that the Church is not based upon the totalitarian faith, the totalitarian doctrine. And the Christian faith is not compatible with an image of man which can regard as the meaning of his life only participation in worldly society based either on economic achievements or on the master race. The Catholic faith does not accept belief in the power of man to create by his own forces a world in which he is absolute master and which is absolutely perfect and self-sufficient. The Catholic faith does not permit an absolute domination over men, one which regards them simply as material for the achievement and demonstration of power and as instruments of an earthly development looked upon as necessary by the totalitarian doctrine.

The totalitarian movements, the pseudoreligious movements and exponents of antireligious politico-social religions, have arisen in the twentieth century as products of a religious and spiritual crisis. In the modern secularized world, religion—if not deemed superfluous or unimportant—has continued to be widely accepted only as a traditional force linked with familiar social orders. As these orders experienced a crisis the basic secularistic belief became manifest. What matters is economic productivity and right organization; what matters is political power to form and establish a new society. The totalitarian political religions are expressions of secularist thought in a world where the inherited traditional stability and continuity are threatened or have disappeared. They try to establish again a secure world without uncertainties and internal crises by accepting an interpretation of history and society which claims to be absolute truth, which explains all the failures of the past and present and which announces a happy future. This future will come after a merciless fight to the finish. This belief in the future golden age is connected with a belief in the particular mission of a group, the party which formulates and applies the right

14

revolutionary consciousness of the masses or the racial elite which ends misrule by evil and inferior elements. The present is sacrificed to the future and the individual is regarded as material in and for the necessary and, therefore, just development. World and history are explained by natural laws which are known to those who master the doctrine.

Secularism in its totalitarian form becomes a secular religion, putting a human doctrine in the place of Revelation, a visible worldly society in the place of union with God as the aim of life. Not utilitarian calculations but demonstrations of faith in the unlimited power of the doctrine and its representatives really matter. Utilitarian calculations would limit the policies of expansion and the urge to absolute domination. This totalitarian, immanentist faith cannot be met by an optimistic secularism which is not aware of the fundamental crisis of our time or by an apparently religious attitude for which religion is, despite theoretical denials, indissolubly bound to a particular social order. The pseudocertainty of totalitarianism which establishes by terror and a refined system of pressure a closed pseudoreal world can be opposed only by the true certainty based upon belief in true revelation and by the realization that man is infinitely more than an instrument for life and society in this world, that there are rights and duties of the human person which cannot be sacrificed to a doctrine about political and social development. The conflict between the Church and totalitarianism is, therefore, much more than a conflict between Church and state, for totalitarianism tries to establish a reality in which all human forces and beliefs serve only this world, an earthly society, which is self-sufficient and has no other end than itself. The world leading to God, totalitarianism replaces by a self-sufficient world which, through the effort and struggles of men, makes God appear merely as a superstitious creation of men before they were able to master their life and society or simply as a mythical symbol of the power exercised by their social or racial elites.

2

The Unique Character of a
Totalitarian Society
(1954)

Carl J. Friedrich

It is the contention of this paper that (a) Fascist and Communist totalitarian society are basically alike, that is to say are more nearly alike to each other than to any other systems of government and society, and (b) totalitarian society is historically unique and sui generis. These two theses are closely linked and must be examined together. At the outset, it should be stated that these contentions do not presuppose that our understanding of totalitarian society is complete or even adequate; these theses are based upon what we at present know reasonably surely about them. Nor do the two theses presuppose that totalitarian societies are fixed and static entities—on the contrary, it is being assumed that they have undergone and continue to undergo a steady evolution; presumably involving both growth and deterioration.[1] The debate about these causes or origins of totalitarianism, and more especially of Fascism, has run all the way from a primitive bad-man theory to the "moral crisis of our time" kind of argument. A detailed inspection of the available evidence would seem to suggest that virtually every one of the factors which has been stressed as offering by itself an explanation of the origin of totalitarianism has played its role. For example, in the German case, Hitler's moral and personal defects, weaknesses in the German constitutional tradition, certain traits involved in the German "national character," the Versailles Treaty and its aftermath, the economic crisis and the "contradictions" of an aging capitalism, the "threat" of Communism, the decline of Christianity and other spiritual moorings, and so forth have all played a role in the total configuration of factors contributing to the overall result. As in the case of other broad developments in history, only a multiple-factor analysis will do. In keeping with his general philosophical methodological position, the author is presupposing that *ta politika* are decisive for the patterning of any society.[2]

The argument of historical uniqueness of any configuration does not mean that it is "wholly" unique; for nothing is. All historical phenomena belong to broad classes of analytical objects. When we say that the Greek polis was historically unique, we do not mean that there were never any cities, or city-states, but we do mean that the Greek and more particularly the Athenian polis had so many and such striking traits peculiar to it that it deserves to be considered "historically unique." History is primarily concerned with individualities, whether these be persons, things, or events, and a sufficiently variegated pattern of distinctive elements therefore constitutes historical uniqueness.[3] In passing, one should perhaps safeguard oneself against the objection that everything historically considered is "historically unique." This objection, while often made, is not actually correct. A great many events (as well as persons and things) are so nearly alike that they lack that distinctive quality which constitutes historical uniqueness; but it is true that when taken in sufficiently large "classes" and broad enough perspective, their uniqueness often appears. Thus the monarchy in this or that German territory in the eighteenth century is not in any sense historically unique, but the monarchical paternalism of all these and a number of related societies in the seventeenth and eighteenth centuries does indeed constitute what we may call a "historically unique" configuration.

Why do we say that Fascist and Communist totalitarian society and government are *basically alike*? In the first instance, the qualifying adverb "basically" is intended to indicate that they are *not wholly alike*. Popular and journalistic interpretation has oscillated between these two extremes of proclaiming the two societies as wholly alike or as not at all basically alike. The latter was the prevailing mood during the popular front days in Europe, and in "liberal" circles in the United States; it was even more popular during the Second World War, and more especially among Allied propagandists. It is, of course, the insistently promoted official Soviet and Hitler party line. The proposition that they are wholly alike is presently favored in the United States and western Europe, and hence it may seem unnecessary to labor the point. But there is, in the first place, a lingering doubt remaining from former days, and there is secondly and perhaps more importantly the problem of the range of alikeness, or to put it another way, the question of what makes them "basically" alike. For it is obvious that they are not alike in "intention." The sharply divergent content of their ideologies proves it. So do the historical facts which show the Fascist movements to arise in reaction to the Communist challenge and to offer themselves to a frightened bourgeoisie as saviors from the Communist threat.* These facts are so familiar that they do not require documentation. The well-known frauds involved in the argument are part of the pattern of psychic antagonism and combative projection.

It is equally obvious that more of the preceding liberal and constitutional society survives in the Fascist than in the Communist society; but this is in part due to the fact that no liberal, constitutional society preceded Soviet Communism. It is conceivable that at least for a considerable initial period, the situation in this respect would be sharply different in, say, Great Britain or the United States. This tendency of isolated fragments of the preceding state of society to survive has been a most potent source of misinterpretation of the Fascist totalitarian society. In the twenties, Italian totalitarianism was very commonly misinterpreted as being "merely" this and that, with the "trains on time" and "the beggars off the street" thrown in for symbolic measure.[4] In the thirties, various authors, some Marxist, others of Marxist antecedents, still others just befuddled, undertook to interpret German totalitarianism as either "the end phase of capitalism"[5] or of "militarist imperialism" (in the manner of Veblen†).[6] It is not generally appreciated, even by scholars, how profound a shock to Marxist orthodoxy the rise of German Fascism turned out to be. Men of the dogmatic acumen of Hilferding‡ were so struck by it

---

* Friederich Hayek was an early and notable critic of this view. See in particular *The Road to Serfdom*, especially chapter 12, "The Socialist Roots of Naziism." The germ of this book was, in part, a memorandum Hayek wrote in the spring of 1933 to Lord Beveridge, the chair of the London School of Economics, on this same topic. Titled "Nazi-Socialism," it can be found as an appendix in *The Road to Serfdom: Texts and Documents*, edited by Bruce Caldwell (Chicago: The University of Chicago Press, 2007).

† Thorstein Veblen, the American sociologist and economist. His best-known work is *The Theory of the Leisure Class* (1899).

‡ Rudolf Hilferding was a prominent German economist who first gained attention in

that they felt a complete reassessment of Marxist doctrine was called for.[7] For there was no trace in Marx and Engels of this eventuality emerging. To be sure, Marx was not unaware (how could he be?) that a frightened bourgeoisie might rally behind a rider on horseback, such as Napoleon III, but this kind of amiable *opera bouffe* of mid-nineteenth-century politics is a far cry indeed from the totalitarian society of our time. All one has to do is to look at the intellectual life of France in that period to sense the difference. It was a natural escape for such Marxist and Veblenian interpreters to try and depict the totalitarian society Hitler and Himmler were building as nothing but a capitalist one, totally at variance with the socialist society which was being formed in the Soviet Union. Blinded by the dichotomy of capitalism and socialism of the Marxian heritage, and afflicted by its preoccupation with the economic as contrasted with the governmental and political aspects of society, they did not see that the "planned," that is to say the thoroughly coordinated and governmentally controlled, economy of the Nazi state was different from that of the Soviet state only by the degree of thoroughness with which the coordination and subordination of the "managerial" as well as "labor" elements had been carried forward; this process was advancing apace and given another ten to twenty years would probably have become as nearly complete as in the Soviet Union.[8] Characteristically, however (to mention only one common feature), strikes are completely barred, as criminal sabotage of the "workers' state" in both totalitarian societies. Having said this much, one has at the same time indicated once more some significant divergences between the two totalitarian societies as well: they do not advance toward the totality of their economic controls either by the same stages, or at the same tempo. (It might, as an amusing variant of this line of reasoning, be recalled that Sidney and Beatrice Webb* in *The Truth about Soviet Russia* (1942) argued that Stalin was no dictator at all, but had brought not

---

1904 when he provided an influential defense of Marxist economics against a prominent critic, Eugen von Böhm-Bawerk. Hilferding's 1910 work *Finance Capital* has been called the most important work in Marxian economics in the twentieth century. He was a leader in the German Social Democrat Party prior to World War I.

* Sidney and Beatrice Webb were socialist economists and early members of the Fabian Society. They authored *Soviet Communism: A New Civilization?* (1935) among other books.

only political but economic democracy to Russia, whereas the real dictator appeared to them to be the American president, Franklin D. Roosevelt.)

Other attempts at differentiating sharply between the Soviet Communist and the Fascist regimes turn upon such items as the content of their divergent ideologies, the national characters of the peoples within which they arise, the stage of respective economic development, and the like. It would be tedious to refute these various lines of reasoning, especially as their positions will by implication be denied through a more positive analysis of the basic features which, according to general agreement, they have in common. These same features do at the same time constitute the ground for asserting that these totalitarian societies are historically unique.

The factors or aspects which basically are shared by all totalitarian societies of our time are five, or can be grouped around five closely linked clusters of characteristic features. These societies all possess:

1. An official ideology, consisting of an official body of doctrine covering all vital aspects of man's existence, to which everyone living in that society is supposed to adhere at least passively; this ideology is characteristically focused in terms of chiliastic claims as to the "perfect" final society of mankind.[9]

2. A single mass party consisting of a relatively small percentage of the total population (up to 10 percent) of men and women passionately and unquestioningly dedicated to the ideology and prepared to assist in every way in promoting its general acceptance, such party being organized in strictly hierarchical, oligarchical manner, usually under a single leader and typically either superior to or completely commingled with the bureaucratic governmental organization.

3. A technologically conditioned near-complete monopoly of control (in the hands of the party and its subservient cadres, such as the bureaucracy and the armed forces) of all means of effective armed combat.

4. A similarly technologically conditioned near-complete monopoly of control (in the same hands) of all means of effective mass communication, such as the press, radio, motion pictures, and so on.

5. A system of terroristic police control, depending for its effectiveness upon points 3 and 4 and characteristically directed not only against demonstrable "enemies" of the regime, but against arbitrarily selected classes of the population; such arbitrary selection turning upon exigencies of the regime's survival, as well as ideological "implications," and systematically exploiting scientific psychology.

The suggestion that to these five clusters of basic traits there should be added that of the secret police gaining ascendancy over the army, seems unacceptable, because both of these factors are controversial, whereas the five which have been delineated are quite generally admitted to be factually established features of these regimes. In the nature of the case, it is very difficult to determine whether, when, and to what extent the secret police gained ascendancy over the army; another difficulty arises from the fact that insofar as the police is a branch of the civilian government, it is in the ascendancy in constitutional states as well.

The argument that total subversion is another distinctive feature of totalitarian systems has merit, but it is arguable whether this aspect of totalitarianism constitutes a sufficiently separate item. It would seem to me that it is comprehended under the first of the five characteristics, where we state that the official ideology is one "to which everyone living in that society is supposed to adhere." The five main clusters of traits, for the sake of clarity, ought not to be unnecessarily expanded.

Within this broad similarity, there are many significant variations, both in time and in place, as already mentioned. For instance, the party appears to play less of a role in the Soviet Union today than earlier;[10] the ideology of the Soviet Union is more rigid, because of its Marxist bible, than that of Italian or German Fascism, where ideology was formulated by the leader of the party;[11] and—to give a third illustration at random—Hitler's extermination of the Jews was ideologically motivated and contrary to the apparent immediate needs of the regime, whereas Stalin's recent Jewish purges appear to be taking place in response to exigencies of the international situation, rather than to ideology, hence the vigorous denial of anti-Semitism.[12]

It is submitted that every one of these factors to a large extent, and all of them in combination, are certainly lacking from all historically known despotic, let alone authoritarian, societies of the past. It might be mentioned in passing that many authoritarian societies of the past should in point of fact be sharply differentiated from autocratic societies. The medieval and early modern distinction of monarchy and tyranny was in many ways sounder than our common differentiation of "democratic" and "autocratic."[13] Neither the oriental despotisms of the more remote past nor the absolute monarchies of modern Europe, neither the tyrannies of the ancient Greek polis nor the imperial establishment of Rome, nor yet the tyrannies of the city-states of the Italian Renaissance exhibit any one of these factors to any marked extent. Attempts, such as Thornton Wilder's *The Ides of March* (in which he tries to show Caesar to have been a totalitarian dictator in the making) or more learned efforts along similar lines,[14] collapse when subjected to a more detailed scrutiny in terms of these five factors. To be sure, there have often been made efforts to organize some kind of secret police, but they are not even horse-and-buggy affairs compared to the enterprises of a Himmler* or a Beria.† Similarly, there have been in the past both military and propagandistic concentrations of power and control, but as in the previous case, the limits of technology prevented any thorough-going development along totalitarian lines. Rather than elaborate this point, which is obvious enough, once one has faced up to it, it seems more urgent to stress the common reason for the uniqueness of factors 3, 4, and 5, and thus to turn back to the other side of the general thesis.

This common cause appears to be our advanced technology. Without the inventions of the last few generations, none of these features could have been created, no matter how glad Peter or Frederick the Great might have been to do so. This technological aspect of totalitarianism is, of course, particularly striking in the matter of arms and communications. The constitution of the United States guarantees to every citizen the "right to bear arms." In the days of the Minutemen this was a very important right, and the freedom of the citizen was indeed symbolized by the gun over the hearth, as it is in Switzerland to this day. But who can "bear" such arms as a tank, a bomber, or a flame-thrower, let alone an atom bomb? The citizen as an individual, and indeed in larger groups, is simply defenseless against the overwhelming technological superiority of those who can centralize in their hands the means wherewith to wield these modern arms and thereby physically to coerce. Similar observations readily apply concerning the press, the radio, and so forth. "Freedom" does not have the same intrinsic value, resting upon individual effort and exertion, which it had a hundred and fifty years ago. The trend of technological advance carries with it,

---

* Heinrich Himmler was the leader of the Nazi SS. This group, which began as a bodyguard service for senior Nazi leaders, would become a massive internal security force with responsibility for enforcing racial purity. Hitler entrusted Himmler with the implementation of the "Final Solution"—the destruction of eastern European Jewry.

† Lavrenty Beria was head of the NKVD, the Soviet secret police, from 1938 to 1953.

with relatively few exceptions, the trend toward greater and greater size of organization. Thus, totalitarian societies appear in this respect to be merely exaggerations, but nonetheless logical exaggerations, of inherent implications of the technological state in which we find ourselves.[15]

The situation is rather different with respect to the first two distinctive features of totalitarian societies. Neither ideology nor party have any significant relation to the state of technology.[16] But they do have a vital relation to another common feature of all contemporary societies, namely, the increasing amount of general literacy.[17] To this literacy must be added (in Russia, Italy, Germany, and other countries where totalitarian societies have arisen within the context of the Christian tradition) the fact that Christianity has tended to establish a broad predilection for convictional certainty.[18] But probably more important than either is the "democratic" antecedents of these totalitarian societies. Marx and Engels saw themselves as constituting the vanguard of the democratic movement of their day, and Stalin talked of the Soviet totalitarian society as the "perfect democracy" with evident conviction.[19] However, not only Marx and Engels, but Mussolini and Hitler organized parties with a program intended for mass appeal, designed to win as many adherents as possible.[20] It would never have occurred to the absolute monarchs of seventeenth- and eighteenth-century Europe to stoop so low, nor would the Roman Emperors have considered such an undertaking as politically significant. They appealed to the masses against senatorial privilege from time to time, but an organized and ideologically homogeneous party was "inconceivable." There was, to be sure, a party of the Medicis* in Florence,[21] but this was in the days of flourishing factions contesting for power with each other—in other words, during a period resembling in some limited ways the democratic condition. But the carefully organized single mass party, complete with program and ideology, is a distinct peculiarity of the totalitarian societies of our time. The tie to its Christian and democratic antecedents may gradually weaken—there are signs that both the ideology and the party in Soviet totalitarian society are declining in importance[22]—but there is some room for doubt as to whether a totalitarian society could survive their destruction.

---

* The Medici family was extremely influential in Florentine politics and Italian politics more broadly from the fourteenth to the eighteenth century.

The foregoing may lend itself to the misinterpretation that democracy, Christianity, or technology had, in the author's view, "caused" totalitarianism. No proposition of the kind is intended. All that is meant is that it could only have arisen in the kind of context created by Christianity, democracy, and modern technology. But it seems basically unsound to pick out of past intellectual history some one or several exponents or supposed exponents of some aspect of totalitarian views—for instance, of an authoritarian society, be it Plato or Thomas Aquinas, Hobbes or Rousseau, Hegel or Carlyle—and hold him "responsible" for the totalitarian movements or societies by claiming that he was a totalitarian. None of those mentioned were, because none of them could be: the historically unique features of the totalitarian society were unknown to them.[23] Usually, it is quite easy to show that the particular thinker would, on his own terms, have turned with disgust and indignation upon these latter-day totalitarians, for a variety of reasons inherent in his system. The peculiar moral obtuseness of contemporary totalitarian societies which has been stressed as *the* distinguishing feature of these societies (we think, wrongly),[24] manifesting itself in violence on an unprecedented scale, is demonstrably entirely alien to the thinkers we have named. They are all ardent rationalists, if not moralists, whereas the totalitarians of today are indifferent to such considerations because theirs is essentially an engineering approach to society. They solve problems in a manner which they believe to be "scientific," while at the same time denying the importance of freedom and more especially freedom of inquiry, of teaching and learning, the essential conditions of scientific truth.

Closely related to these issues of novelty and conceptual distinctiveness is the as yet unresolved problem of succession in totalitarian regimes. This issue has recently been highlighted by the death of Stalin. Most of the comments revealed as in a flash the hopeless noncomprehension of the totalitarian reality, as men gravely disputed about the successor to Stalin as if he had been occupying a legally or traditionally defined office, such as the King of France, or even the Tsars of Russia. In fact, the problem of succession in government has to date not been solved in any totalitarian society. This is a most important shortcoming, in view of the millennial importance of succession. Constitutional democracy and hereditary monarchy, oriental despotism with its deification of the ruler as well as its ancient tribal antecedents—they all revolve around this issue of succession. Tyranny has perennially been weak on this score, as Aristotle noted, and as the history of the two Napoleons suggests. Maybe totalitarian societies will discover a means to cope with the problem. The vast array of documentary evidence we now have about Fascism does not contain any really viable scheme for succession. The obstacles to evolving one are formidable. The building up of concentrated veneration for the one "father of the people" or "leader," which approximates and at times exceeds what the deifiers of kings used to do, obviously must create a vacuum the moment this unique person has gone "the way of all flesh." How the then-controller of the machinery of communication can be brought to shift, and shift dramatically, to a new man who only yesterday was his equal and maybe competitor seems perplexing. Equally puzzling appears the question of what will be done by him who controls the terror apparatus.[25]

The sharp delineation of what distinguishes the past from the present in thought as well as action should not be mistaken, of course, for a denial of significant links. One does not have to mistake Hobbes for a totalitarian in order to recognize the connection between his failure to understand the vital role of religion and of intermediary groups in a well-ordered commonwealth and the totalitarians' comparable blindness in these matters. The road of Western thought runs from Luther to Lincoln, as it does from Luther to Hitler; the seamless web of history is woven of many intertwined strands, and totalitarianism, for all its uniqueness, does not spring from the head of any ideologue or demagogue without antecedents. But these antecedents did not "cause" the phenomenon, and there was nothing inevitable about Hitler or Stalin. The totalitarian societies are basically alike, and they are historically unique; but why they are what they are we do not know.[26] Like everything genuinely novel in history, whether good or bad, whether beautiful or ugly, totalitarianism remains wrapped in the womb of creation. Hence only the genuinely creative answer will do effective service in supplanting and superseding it. The future, if there is one, will be a future beyond Communism and Fascism; not some neo-ism of recent or more ancient prescription.

25

3

The Power of the Powerless[*]
(1978)

VÁCLAV HAVEL

To the memory of Jan Patočka

II

Our system is most frequently characterized as a dictatorship or, more precisely, as the dictatorship of a political bureaucracy over a society which has undergone economic and social leveling. I am afraid that the term "dictatorship," regardless of how intelligible it may otherwise be, tends to obscure rather than clarify the real nature of power in this system. We usually associate the term with the notion of a small group of people who take over the government of a given country by force; their power is wielded openly, using the direct instruments of power at their disposal, and they are easily distinguished socially from the majority over whom they rule. One of the essential aspects of this traditional or classical notion of dictatorship

---

[*] This essay, written in October 1978, was intended to be part of a joint venture between Polish and Czechoslovak authors on the subject of freedom and power. Havel's essay was circulated in samizdat in Poland and in his own country to get the conversation started. The Czechoslovak authors completed their essays, but in March of 1979 a number of them were arrested, including Havel. The decision was made to go ahead with publication in the absence of the Polish contributions. Havel's essay and its companions (in a volume called *On Freedom and Power*) had quite an impact in Czechoslovakia and Poland.

26

is the assumption that it is temporary, ephemeral, lacking historical roots. Its existence seems to be bound up with the lives of those who established it It is usually local in extent and significance, and regardless of the ideology it utilizes to grant itself legitimacy, its power derives ultimately from the numbers and the armed might of its soldiers and police. The principal threat to its existence is felt to be the possibility that someone better equipped in this sense might appear and overthrow it.

Even this very superficial overview should make it clear that the system in which we live has very little in common with a classical dictatorship. In the first place, our system is not limited in a local, geographical sense; rather, it holds sway over a huge power bloc controlled by one of the two superpowers. And although it quite naturally exhibits a number of local and historical variations, the range of these variations is fundamentally circumscribed by a single, unifying framework throughout the power bloc. Not only is the dictatorship everywhere based on the same principles and structured in the same way (that is, in the way evolved by the ruling superpower), but each country has been completely penetrated by a network of manipulatory instruments controlled by the superpower center and totally subordinated to its interests. In the stalemated world of nuclear parity, of course, that circumstance endows the system with an unprecedented degree of external stability compared with classical dictatorships. Many local crises which, in an isolated state, would lead to a change in the system, can be resolved through direct intervention by the armed forces of the rest of the bloc.*

In the second place, if a feature of classical dictatorships is their lack of historical roots (frequently they appear to be no more than historical freaks, the fortuitous consequence of fortuitous social processes or of human and mob tendencies), the same cannot be said so facilely about our system. For even though our dictatorship has long since alienated itself completely from the social movements that give birth to it, the authenticity of these movements (and I am thinking of the proletarian and socialist movements of the nineteenth century) gives it undeniable historicity. These origins provided a solid foundation of sorts on which it could build until it became the utterly new social and political reality it is today, which has become so inextricably a part of the structure of the modern world. A feature of those

---

* Havel is of course alluding to the Soviet interventions in Hungary in 1956 and in Czechoslovakia in 1968.

27

historical origins was the "correct" understanding of social conflicts in the period from which those original movements emerged. The fact that at the very core of this "correct" understanding there was a genetic disposition toward the monstrous alienation characteristic of its subsequent development is not essential here. And in any case, this element also grew organically from the climate of that time and therefore can be said to have its origin there as well.

One legacy of that original "correct" understanding is a third, peculiarity that makes our systems different from other modern dictatorships: it commands an incomparably more precise, logically structured, generally comprehensible and, in essence, extremely flexible ideology that, in its elaborateness and completeness, is almost a secularized religion. It offers a ready answer to any question whatsoever; it can scarcely be accepted only in part, and accepting it has profound implications for human life. In an era when metaphysical and existential certainties are in a state of crisis, when people are being uprooted and alienated and are losing their sense of what this world means, this ideology inevitably has a certain hypnotic charm. To wandering humankind it offers an immediately available home: all one has to do is accept it, and suddenly everything becomes clear once more. Life takes on new meaning, and all mysteries, unanswered questions, anxiety, and loneliness vanish. Of course, one pays dearly for this low-rent home: the price is abdication of one's own reason, conscience, and responsibility, for an essential aspect of this ideology is the consignment of reason and conscience to a higher authority. The principle involved here is that the center of power is identical with the center of truth. (In our case, the connection with Byzantine theocracy is direct: the highest secular authority is identical with the highest spiritual authority.) It is true of course that, all this aside, ideology no longer has any great influence on people, at least within our bloc (with the possible exception of Russia, where the serf mentality, with its blind, fatalistic respect for rulers and its automatic acceptance of all their claims, is still dominant and combined with a superpower patriotism which traditionally places the interests of empire higher than the interests of humanity). But this is not important, because ideology plays its role in our system very well (an issue to which I will return) precisely because it is what it is.

Fourth, the technique of exercising power in traditional dictatorships contains a necessary element of improvisation. The mechanisms for wielding power are for the most part not established firmly, and there is considerable room for accident and for the arbitrary and unregulated application of power. Socially, psychologically, and physically, conditions still exist for the expression of some form of opposition. In short, there are many seams on the surface which can split apart before the entire power structure has managed to stabilize. Our system, on the other hand, has been developing in the Soviet Union for over sixty years, and for approximately thirty years in eastern Europe; moreover, several of its long-established structural features are derived from Czarist absolutism. In terms of the physical aspects of power, this has led to the creation of such intricate and well-developed mechanisms for the direct and indirect manipulation of the entire population that, as a physical power base, it represents something radically new. At the same time, let us not forget that the system is made significantly more effective by state ownership and central direction of all the means of production. This gives the power structure an unprecedented and uncontrollable capacity to invest in itself (in the areas of the bureaucracy, and the police, for example) and makes it easier for that structure, as the sole employer, to manipulate the day-to-day existence of all citizens.

Finally, if an atmosphere of revolutionary excitement, heroism, dedication, and boisterous violence on all sides characterizes classical dictatorships, then the last traces of such an atmosphere have vanished from the Soviet bloc. For some time now this bloc has ceased to be a kind of enclave, isolated from the rest of the developed world and immune to processes occurring in it. To the contrary, the Soviet bloc is an integral part of that larger world, and it shares and shapes the world's destiny. This means in concrete terms that the hierarchy of values existing in the developed countries of the West has, in essence, appeared in our society (the long period of coexistence with the West has only hastened this process). In other words, what we have here is simply another form of the consumer and industrial society, with all its concomitant social, intellectual, and psychological consequences.* It is impossible to understand the nature of power in our system properly without taking this into account.

The profound difference between our system—in terms of the nature of power—and what we traditionally understand by dictatorship, a differ-

---

* This thought is more fully developed in *Politics and Conscience* and in *Letters to Olga* (especially letters 141 and 142—both in this volume).

ence I hope is clear even from this quite superficial comparison, has caused me to search for some term appropriate for our system, purely for the purposes of this essay. If I refer to it henceforth as a "post-totalitarian" system, I am fully aware that this is perhaps not the most precise term, but I am unable to think of a better one. I do not wish to imply by the prefix "post-" that the system is no longer totalitarian; on the contrary, I mean that it is totalitarian in a way fundamentally different from classical dictatorships, different from totalitarianism as we usually understand it.

4

On the Difficulty of Defining the Soviet Regime[1]
(1976)

ALAIN BESANÇON

The Soviet regime eludes with remarkable ease both Aristotle's and Montesquieu's classifications of regimes. Let's start with Aristotle's *Politics*. The Soviet regime claims the combined advantages of all three forms of "correct" governments, those which have as their goal or purpose the common good. Socialism, and even more completely Communism, is the common good. To be sure, instead of being actual or real as is Aristotle's common good it exists potentially—*in potentia*—but this comprehensive good is the true significance and final goal of the dictatorship of the proletariat or of so-called "people's democracy." The regime thus presents itself as a *republic* since it is "the multitude which administers the state in view of the common good."[2] In this connection one can take into account article 126 of the 1936 Constitution:

> The most active and self-conscious members of the working class, as well as of other strata of workers, join together in the (Bolshevik) Communist Party of the USSR. The Party is the avant-garde of workers in their struggle to strengthen and develop the socialist regime, it is the guiding center of all worker organizations, those in society as well as in the state.

Thus one can also say that the regime is equally *aristocratic,* in the sense that it is the best who govern. Finally, for decades it was the best of the best who governed for the good of the city: Lenin's regime and Stalin's

31

(and even, after all, Khrushchev's and Brezhnev's) could claim to be a perfect form of *monarchy.*

This, however, was not the view of the opponents of the Soviet regime. They applied to it the labels of the three forms of bad or "perverse" governments. The day after the Revolution the adherents of the previous autocratic order believed that the new order was a *democracy,* that is, rule exercised by the poor for their own exclusive interest. A more attentive observation revealed soon enough the absolute power of an *oligarchy,* that of the Communist Party. And finally it became evident that Lenin, and even more so Stalin, governed the political community in a despotic manner and, consequently, that the regime corresponded to the definition of *tyranny.*

AN ELUSIVE PERVERSION

But there was a troubling fact: further observation and examination showed that even these new definitions fit the regime as poorly as the original ones. Even if one denied the Soviet regime the right of appearing among the "correct" forms of government it nonetheless did not correspond to the perverse forms. All in all, the classificatory scheme did not fit the facts. What characterizes perverse forms is that they only aim at the personal interest of the rulers: in democracy, the poor; in oligarchy, the wealthy; in monarchy, the monarch. However, in Communist reality the notion of someone's individual or particular good is as elusive as that of the common good. All reference to transcendent Justice being put aside, it becomes equally impossible to recognize injustice, and even less so to be able to profit from injustice as one was able to do in the classical perversions of good constitutions.

The Soviet regime established itself by claiming to base itself upon the "democratic" aspirations of the Russian people. And in fact in the first years there was a violent government of the poor over the rich with the confiscation of the latter's goods. But the state reserved for itself the fundamental ownership of almost everything and increasingly it also reserved the usufruct. One only had to wait a dozen years for the principal beneficiaries of the original expropriation and redistribution, the peasants, to be expropriated in their turn. And they never governed; strictly speaking, in Russia there never was a *democracy* in the pejorative sense that Aristotle gave to the term. Certainly there remained no trace of any such thing after collectivization. Was it therefore an *oligarchy?* Marxists in opposition adopted this view. In 1904 Rosa Luxemburg[*] feared the Bolshevik understanding of power:

> Nothing could more surely subjugate a workers' movement that is so young to an intellectual elite hungry for power than this democratic armor in which one encases it, in order to make it an autocracy managed by a committee.[3]

The same year Trotsky foresaw that the Leninist formula would lead from oligarchy to tyranny:

> These methods will lead to the result that the Party organization "will replace" the Party itself, that the Central Committee will replace the organization, and finally that a "dictator" will replace the Central Committee itself.[4]

The Party monopolized power. In order to implement its economic projects it had almost overt recourse to exploitation. For workers there were neither unions nor social protection, and their salaries were the lowest in Europe. For peasants there was the restoration of forced labor. Moreover, the Party reserved for itself the most advantageous posts, the best and most "fast track" careers. And lastly, it granted itself material privileges (even if of an elementary sort): better food, better clothes, special stores, special vacation spots, trips forbidden to others, etc. One can understand why the former Yugoslav Communist Milovan Djilas came up with the notion of a *new class.* The Communist bureaucracy had replaced the bourgeoisie as the new exploiting class. Trotsky, who held firm to Marxist orthodoxy, rejected the phrase "class exploitation" and only conceded a widespread "social parasitism" (which is not contrary to Aristotle's definition of oligarchy). However, even taking into account the exploitation and privileges it remains grossly inadequate to say that the Party and

---

* Rosa Luxemburg (1870–1919), born in Russian Poland, was an influential Marxist political economist who participated in Socialist International congresses and taught at the German Social Democratic Party's school in Berlin.

those associated with it governed in their own particular interest. This, however, is necessary for a regime to be properly called oligarchic.

Aristotle had in mind the division and distribution of wealth in an oligarchy. Nowhere have the Communists confiscated property and wealth simply for themselves. The state grants them a level of comfort we would call "middle class," but nothing more. When they steal and enrich themselves they become subject to the law. One could object that the true satisfactions found in these regimes are found in exercising power, not those of wealth. True enough, but it then becomes necessary that this power should be peacefully exercised, that is, that it constitute a *jus* or right that is securely possessed and peacefully transmitted as personal or familial property. This is not the case at all. The only study we have that is based upon archival materials, *Smolensk under the Soviet Rule,*[5] on the contrary shows members of the bureaucracy harassed by an ever-present threatening force. It leaves no one in peace. To enter into a career in the Party is to agree to live dangerously. Of course nepotism exists. It is easier for someone who can appeal to a "good social origin" to pursue higher education and there is none better than being the child of a Party member. That is a lot, but it is not enough to guarantee the hereditary character of conditions, as in a social order composed of estates or ranks. At most it is a corrective to social mobility, like other sorts that exist in societies that have social and economic classes. Since political life is entirely concentrated in the Party, political change can only occur by a change in the Party. From this necessity came the periodic purges, of which Stalin's were only the most energetic. Can one therefore call a regime "oligarchic" in which the oligarchy daily runs such risks, in which the oligarchy as a whole sometimes—as in 1937—seems on the edge of being exterminated?

One is therefore tempted to call it a *tyranny.* As he grew old Stalin conducted himself in the ways described by the classical authors. He rejoined the Russian type of the terrible tsar, of the Great Sinner; he thus exceeded the contours of the regime which did not recognize itself in him. Once it was free of Stalin the Party took precautions so that the unity of direction would not deviate into tyranny, into a form of government in which the leader governs for his own interest. The ideal norm in this view is Lenin, not Stalin. It was to Lenin that Stalin himself referred, as did Khrushchev and Brezhnev. (According to a number of the Bolsheviks,

Stalin did so wrongly.) But Lenin himself governed by secret police and bureaucracy. He wrote to the minister of justice:

> The fundamental idea is clear. . . . To put forth clearly, first on the political plane (and not in a narrow juridical sense), the principle motivating and justifying terror, its necessity, its limits. . . . It is only the conception of revolutionary justice and, more broadly, revolutionary consciousness that will determine the extent of its practical application.[6]

The principle of justice, which is the equal and proportional sharing among persons, is repudiated by Lenin because "the other" is not considered by him as a legitimate or respectable party in a legal process but as an adversary whom the revolutionary terrorizes and eliminates at will. This is an adequate definition of tyranny. And yet one hesitates. The tyrant, as we have seen, governs in his own interest, which presupposes a certain self-awareness as a tyrant. Lenin himself never had this awareness. He governed in the name of his idea of the common good—socialism—and in the name of the historical carriers of the common good—the proletariat, the Party, the Central Committee. The idea that he was a dictator never occurred to him. His methods of governing were dictatorial and were avowed as such, but they were not tyrannical because ideology did not allow him to recognize, nor even imagine, a particular interest. The Aristotelian tyrant is self-interested; the secretary-general is not.

A BAD DREAM

Aristotle's classification is formal, even though it implicitly presupposes the Greek city-state. Montesquieu attempted, in an empirical manner, to connect political regimes with the types of society in conformity with them. His initial classification is dualistic. He contrasts the *republican* regime (whether democratic or aristocratic) to the *monarchical* regime, on one hand, and to the *despotic* regime, on the other. The first are regimes of liberty, moderate regimes in which each one feels himself to be secure, while the latter is an arbitrary regime whose sole "principle" or psychological wellspring is fear.

Here, too, the Soviet regime appears to be a combination. It claims to be based upon republican *virtue,* and the Communist "new man" is educated in this spirit. The members of the Party who enjoy distinction of rank are in principle held to *honor* as in monarchies according to Montesquieu. Witnesses, however, oblige us to accept the reality of apprehension and *fear,* as in despotisms. Montesquieu grasped despotism through the reports of Chardin, Bernier, and the documentation he had been able to gather on the Persia, India, and China of his time.

> The absolute sovereign is alone, all powerful, although he eventually delegates his powers to a grand vizier; but whatever may be the modes of relationship between the despot and his entourage, there are no social classes in a sort of balance or equilibrium and no equivalent of ancient virtue, nor of honor as found in Europe. Fear reigns over millions of men spread through the immeasurable extent of the state, a state that cannot preserve itself except on the condition that one man can do anything.[7]

This approximates well enough to the USSR. Nonetheless, one should be cautious. Montesquieu's own description corresponds to reality as much as Custine's* corresponded to the Russian reality of 1839. With both there was exaggeration. The Westerner projected his fears outside the West and placed images of his nightmares in the endless steppes and exotic locales of Asia or Russia.

Asiatic despotism, from Montesquieu to Wittfogel,[†] is the terrible fantasy of a European who fears the loss of his liberties, the destruction of civil society. It is an imaginary construct. The Soviet regime, however, does not allow itself to be placed among the regimes of the Asiatic empires. In these empires the social *bodies* had not been destroyed for the good reason that they had not yet emerged. Civil society had not yet arrived at the delicate differentiation which is the privilege of the West. If they were to emerge, these empires would improve. In the USSR, on the

---

* Astolphe de Custine, author of *La Russie en 1839.* Available in English as *Letters from Russia*, ed. with intro. Anka Muhlstein (New York: Review Books, 2002).
† Karl Wittfogel, author of *Oriental Despotism: A Comparative Study of Total Power* (New Haven: Yale University Press, 1957).

contrary, the atomization of civil society is the object of a *deliberate* political project, one constitutive of the regime, which reversed the centuries'-old evolution of the old tsarist "despotism."

Therefore in contrast to the USSR these classical despotisms would merit the title of "moderate." They leave the 'little people' undisturbed in their occupations, their work, their pleasures; they leave room for the shopkeeper, the artisan, and the merchant; they were the guardians of mores, legal customs, and established religions. In their own self-understanding, they constituted a political and economic order reflective of the cosmic and spiritual order. The sovereign was their guarantor and symbol. The first act of the newly installed Chinese emperor, for example, was to provide the *la,* to determine the scales. It could happen, of course, that the sovereign degenerated and became corrupt, that he disturbed the established order, that he conducted himself as a tyrant. Instead of magnifying the harmony of the social order, his numerous palaces, wives, eunuchs, and horses could betray a blameworthy, even disgraceful, pursuit of glory and of his own pleasure. Given the simplicity of civil society and the little resistance it could offer him, the Asiatic despot multiplied absurd and socially damaging actions:

> When the savages of Louisiana want to have fruit, they cut down the tree and harvest the fruit. Behold despotic government.[8]

This, however, is not the Soviet government. It does not recognize any legitimate stability in the established order. On the contrary, in order to overturn it it imposes previously unheard-of burdens and constraints upon the populations, it seeks to transform mores and weaken religions. Its actions are not "absurd" as would be that of a crazy sultan but are planned and aimed at a goal which is never simply individually self-interested.

So where have we arrived? Perhaps the following formulation summarizes what we have seen. The reason the Soviet regime does not fit into either Aristotle's or Montesquieu's classification of good, or bad, governments is that its principle is neither the common good nor the particular good. It aims at a pseudocommon good and only attains a pseudoindividual good.

The beast is new. Montesquieu seeing these facts today would retain and expand his dualistic scheme. On one hand, we have the historically known regimes, on the other, the Soviet regime. Better informed, he would recognize that his anxious imagination had anticipated reality. But what name to give to it?

THE PRIMACY OF IDEOLOGY

Raymond Aron, who continued Montesquieu's investigations, proposed the term "totalitarianism."

> To the ordinary features of despotic bureaucracies is added the revolutionary party's will to change ["man and society at a stroke"] and an ideology of rationalist inspiration which constitutes by itself a critique of reality. Finally, modern industrial society gave the Soviet regime means of action which no despotism in the past had at its disposal, the monopoly of means of propaganda and new techniques of psychological influence. Asiatic despotism did not entail the creation of a new man and the expectation of the end of prehistory.[9]

One could not put it more clearly. In what does the totalitarian phenomenon consist then? Aron lists the following five elements:

1. The monopoly of political activity given to—arrogated by— a single party.
2. A Party which is animated by an ideology that becomes the official truth of the state because it confers upon it an absolute authority.
3. In order to promulgate this truth, the state reserves to itself and exercises a monopoly of means of coercion and of propaganda.
4. Most economic and professional activities are subject to the state and become in some way or other part of the state itself.
5. Everything henceforth becomes a state activity and all activity being subject to ideology, a mistake made in economic or professional activity is simultaneously an ideological fault.[10]

It was nearly twenty years ago that this analysis was given.* The wonder is not that it has not grown dated vis-à-vis reality but that reality, despite the hopes of the author, has not outgrown it. This definition is not sociological in any ordinary sense. It is not industrial society, not the single party, nor a combination of the two that entails totalitarianism. There must be another factor:

> The principal cause seems to me to be the revolutionary party itself. Regimes did not become totalitarian by some sort of gradual development but from an original intention, from the will of fundamentally transforming the existing order in function of an ideology. Despotism and ideology are interconnected and the fact is that "the pathological forms of despotism are inconceivable outside of an ideological frenzy."[11]

On two points, however, I would like to develop and render more precise the Aronian analysis. Is the word "totalitarianism" well chosen? It signifies an absorption by the state of the particular activities which normally take place in civil society. "Totalitarianism" is therefore well suited to designate points 4 and 5 of the list, as well as point 1. But the concept does not at all grasp point 2, that is, ideology taken as the absolute truth and imposed as such.

Now, it would appear—and Raymond Aron would be the first to acknowledge this—that "totalitarianism," taken in its obvious and limited sense, comes second after ideology. *Ideology is not a means of totalitarianism,* on the contrary, totalitarianism is the political consequence, the incarnation in social life, of the ideology; it is chronologically and logically first. It is therefore misleading to characterize a phenomenon by its effects rather than by its causes and principles. The effects can occur, locally and temporarily, in other regimes. In this way, for example, people have spoken equivocally about the "totalitarianism" of the Late Roman empire, of the Incan empire, of Sparta. In saying this, I do not wish to deny that at any specific moment, for any particular group, the imperial cult at Constantinople, the division of property in Peru, the control of private life in Sparta, were perhaps subjectively equivalent to what a citizen

---

* At the time of Bescançon's writing.

in Moscow experiences today, as she is obliged in the morning to demonstrate her enthusiasm on the Red Square, in the afternoon to wait in line for vegetables at the grocery store, and in the evening to hold her tongue in a crowded communal apartment.

But in this perspective totalitarianism loses its novelty. It remains in the lineage of Montesquieuan despotism, not one that he observed but one that he could at least imagine by extrapolating from developments he saw. Thus, for Kostas Papaïoannou all the elements that make up the Soviet regime existed separately in previous historical experience. What is original is "the extraordinary *rapidity* with which all of these traditional, even archaic, elements of power were able to come to life again, amalgamated and perfected, this occurring after a century of 'progress' and the triumph of a double revolution that had *promised* socialism in the cities and *actually established* widespread exploitation of the peasants in the countryside." [12]

On the other hand, according to him it is the *intensity* with which henceforth all these elements exist, the *absolute concentration and centralization* of total power. In this way there is among despotisms—at least among a certain core of previous despotisms and the Soviet regime, a difference of degree—one that is as extensive as one would like to acknowledge, but still only of degree, not kind.

This, however, is not true in the final analysis. It misses the absolute originality of this regime vis-à-vis all known regimes, an originality such that it could not have been imagined beforehand nor understood as long as it had not yet seen the light of day. This is owing to the role played in it by *ideology.* Ideology is the principle and the end of the regime, and totalitarianism is connected to it as its means. Ideology alone—and Aron underscores this point—gives to despotism its new face and obliges it to mobilize in an unprecedented manner all the immense social resources generated by industrial society. The word *ideocracy* (which Aron cites) or *logocracy* (proposed by the Polish writer Czeslaw Milosz), rather than "totalitarianism," is therefore more fitting. We will simply call it, following Solzhenitsyn—and Aron himself in a digression in his book—*the ideological regime.* [13]

On the Difficulty of Defining the Soviet Regime

BOLSHEVISM AND NAZISM

Historically there have been two variants of totalitarianism, the Hitlerian and the Soviet. After having laid out their similarities, Raymond Aron contrasts them in terms of their fundamental objective. According to him the first was nefarious from the beginning, the second noble at its beginning:

> The difference is essential because of the idea that animated the one and the other enterprise; in one case it ended in work camps, in the other, in the gas chambers. In one case [the Communist], at work is the will to construct a new regime and perhaps another [sort of] human being by any means; in the other case [National Socialism], a properly demonic will to destroy a pseudo-race.[14]

I am not sure that by proceeding in this way one does justice to the two regimes and that one in fact misses their true meaning. The will to destroy a pseudorace is neither more noble nor more nefarious than the will to destroy a pseudoclass, granting that here "pseudo-" means as much as "race" or "class." Objective justice is not concerned with the motives that derive from these two ideological systems and which do not recognize objective forms of justice in any event, since both justify themselves internally and deny universal criteria outside of themselves. What matters to objective justice, however, is the act that is done, the crime defined by universal criteria of right. It is impossible to decide if the woman or the man who dies in a camp suffers a greater injustice because the camp is a work camp or an extermination camp. Or if it is more unjust to be killed as a kulak or as a Jew. One can argue that the crime committed in the name of a high ideal (or which at least seems elevated) is greater than a crime which admits that it is a crime—but in Hitler's eyes the extermination of the Jews was a humanitarian aim! In fact, this was the sole point where Nazism believed that it transcended national egoism and merited mankind's gratitude. Following the traditional adage *corruptio optimi, pessima* (the corruption of the best is the worst), one could argue that the more the ideal is elevated and the cause sublime, the worse is its betrayal. The self-imposed limitation of the Nazi ambition perhaps guaranteed a lesser destruction than Soviet universalism. One can also argue the contrary.

41

Contrasting in this way the two regimes by their objectives leads to understanding their histories in two different ways. Considered in its traditional goals, its Ceasarism, its nationalistic character, Hitlerism is understandable enough. Add the racialist premise and it still is, that is, in its project of remaking the racial map of Europe. I therefore cannot follow Aron when he writes:

> At this moment arose a terror even more unforeseeable than that which could strike Soviet citizens, whose purpose, above all, was different. The objective of Soviet terror is to create a society entirely conformed to an ideal, while in Hitler's case the objective is purely and simply extermination.[15]

In Hitler's case it was also a matter of constructing a society conformed to an ideal. The ideal does not appear to us more monstrous than the other only because there no longer are Nazis. Moreover, the Hitlerian terror was more predictable than the Communist terror because the categories to be exterminated had extra-ideological conceptual contours. Jews and Slavs existed before Nazism and continued to exist after it, even if their definition did not correspond to what was laid down in the racial laws. One cannot say the same of the concepts inventoried in article 58 of the Penal Code of 1927, whose first paragraph defined as counter-revolutionary any action—and in terms of paragraph 6, any inaction—that contributed to the weakening of Communist power. It remains true that between the Hitlerian project and the history of Nazi Germany there is a fundamental coherence, because of which Aron judges the enterprise to be radically evil. In the Soviet case, however, Aron believes there was a contradiction between the project and the history. Aron writes:

> Historically the Soviet regime emerged from a revolutionary will inspired by a humanitarian ideal. The goal was to create the most humane regime that history had ever known, the first regime in which all men would fulfill their humanity, in which classes would have disappeared, and in which society's homogeneity would permit the mutual recognition of all citizens. But this movement aimed at an absolute goal did not hesitate before any means because according to the doctrine only the will could

create this absolutely good society and because the proletariat was engaged in a war to the death with capitalism. From this combination of a sublime goal and pitiless means came all the different phases of the Soviet regime.[16]

From the perspective of its goal, therefore, Soviet history was a repeated accident. Civil war, collectivization, and the terror that accompanies them are not desired or willed. They can even be rationally understood: they rise up against the resistance that reality presents to the revolutionary endeavor. Stalin's Great Purge, however, is "perfectly irrational," "unreasonable." Only one explanation, even more of an accident, is plausible:

> In order to move from possible to actual, from an understandable purpose (purification) to the excesses of the Great Purge, there had to be something unique, an individual, Stalin himself.

Such a description is certainly faithful to the unfolding of events. A certain number of Communists, at all stages, have felt the disjunction between the intention and the result as a disjunction between justice and injustice. They said so and often paid for it with their lives. And the great purges are incomprehensible if one does not take into account the political personality of Stalin, his decision to forge a new party, one more devoted to him than the existing party—which was Stalinist, but more in terms of shared views than of being created by him.

Nonetheless the "accidental" theory of Soviet history looks both too far and too short and misses the mark. "Too short" because the perception of this history as a failed attempt to establish justice arises from naïveté from the ideological perspective. The naiveté consists in judging the value of the action, not by criteria intrinsic to the doctrine but by universal criteria that the ideology does not acknowledge. Such claims of potential justice and actual injustice arise from a nonideological viewpoint, insofar as ideology denies the autonomy of morality vis-à-vis itself. The view also looks "too far" because the exercise of power for power's sake and the introduction of a personal factor in its exercise emerges from another imperfection in ideological adherence, which I call *cynicism*.[17] The Aronian interpretation encompasses on both sides a correctly defined phenomenon, the ideological regime, but only comprehends it on the margins, in its excesses and its defects.

The ideological project is not humanitarian, precisely because it is ideological. In the city it is attempting to construct, a part of humanity finds itself ontologically excluded. The exclusion does not allow for any debate over the just and the unjust because by its essence the excluded part cannot take part in the proceedings. As for the other part of humanity, the "elected" part, it too is in no way subjected to the eternal rules of justice and injustice but by conformity to the norms of thought and action defined by Soviet ideology. Nazism avowed the particular character of its aims (except for the extermination of the Jews, to which it attributed a universal value). It therefore openly proposed to establish on a world-wide scale an oligarchy or tyranny, and within the German people itself an aristocracy or a monarchy. In contrast, Soviet ideology appropriated the authentically universal and humanitarian ideals of religion and morality. There is therefore some overlap between the humanitarian or universalistic project and the ideological one. The second claims to realize the first, but from the beginning only partially—which falsifies and even annuls the claim.

It is wrong therefore to ascribe justice—especially the sublimity of absolute Justice—to an enterprise which arrogates to itself the right, or more exactly (since it denies objective right) the opportunity to lie and to kill. Even when the ideological regime enacts a just reform—a division of land, for example—it cannot be qualified as just because it is not performed in the name of justice but of ideology. That is why the consistent Bolshevik feels as little scruple when he repossesses land as he felt meritorious when he distributed it originally. The difference between the Nazi enterprise and the Bolshevik project is not that between evil and good (or inhuman versus humane), but the univocal in contrast to the equivocal such that the latter's superiority is not moral but functional. Each believes that justice "envelops" them and thus justifies what he is doing, while in truth it is the project or enterprise which gobbles up and perverts justice.

THE DIALECTIC OF TWO REALITIES

The regime, writes Raymond Aron, becomes totalitarian from its original intention: the will to fundamentally transform the existing order in function of an ideology. The regime therefore has recourse to three kinds of terror. The first can be called "normal." It is that which is practiced by one faction against enemy factions. It is as old as the history of revolutions. The new power has many enemies and in order to survive has to crush them. The second sort, that of collectivization (and, one can add, of five year plans) is rationally explainable, despite the absurdity of the projects of which this terror is the logical consequence. The third sort, the use of terror against the Party itself, is mysterious according to Aron:

> No one was entirely duped, but few had the courage to say in English, Nonsense!, or in French, Mensonge! Mensonge! Mensonge! Even more astonishing still, the world of macabre fictions was not simply, or only, base or odious. In a certain way it attracted attention or fascinated, because everything in it had its meaning, nothing happened by chance. Profound historical forces combined with the concept of classes and the machinations of particular individuals. Hegel's dialectic results in a delirium of purgation.[18]

This clinically dispassionate description of the fascination that the spectacle exercises on the observer who does not share the ideology seems quite accurate and admirable to me. However, there is an opportunity to break the spell and to penetrate the *mysterium magnum* which is the terror whose effects grow as its causes disappear. To do so, though, one needs to take into consideration a fourth sort of terror which commands the other three. This is the heart of the matter. In addition to the effort to absorb reality, which very well explains the first sort of terror, but less well the second sort and poorly the third, ideology imposes the fiction of another already existing reality, its own. The regime is not terroristic only because it brings the ideology from potency to act, but also and especially because it claims that the ideals of the ideology already actually exist.

The pre-ideological revolutionary project respected and preserved the unicity, the integrity, of reality—even though it violated it—as well as the continuity of time—even though it hastened its advent. Peter the Great represents very well what we could call this "simple revolutionary power." In order to transform Russia, he instituted terror. But at the same time he was transforming it, he did not claim that Russia was already transformed! Thus, even while being vigilant about his propaganda, he did not falsify information and he did not establish the reign of the Lie. To the contrary, he demystified the Russian situation in order for it to be better known, and he reduced it to a common measure in order better to transform it. He broke the Church, he opened borders. As for severed heads, he displayed them at the gates of cities.

The old apocalyptic accounts distinguished the present world from the world to come as two distinctly separated *aeons*. Ancient Gnosticism, however, unveiled behind this world another world which was immanent to it, already there and which was only separated from the first by a still-darkened consciousness. By right, in principle the two *aeons* only formed one. Peter the Great worked for "the world to come." Therefore the Old Believers applied to him the apocalyptic formulas, calling him the Antichrist; the official bishops called him Constantine. The ideological regime devotes the essential thrust of its terroristic efforts to make men who are its subjects, and its agents, to believe in this ideological world, to believe that the essence of the social cosmos is *already transfigured*. With socialism mankind has actually entered into its definitive state. It is only secondarily that "normal" or "rationally explainable" terror is required to make him enter into it. But the specific terror of ideology goes well beyond even this. It must plug all the fissures that show up in the partition separating "real reality" from ideological "reality." Its first act is to close all borders and to control all information. The part of reality that finds itself under the control of the regime must be treated as nonreality (and the pseudoreality of ideology, as reality). The second step is the reeducation of the masses. This reeducation must be pushed to the point where the senses cease to fulfill their office, that of providing information about the world; now white can be called black and vice versa without contradiction. In the presence of the Lie, the tongue becomes paralyzed and cannot even exclaim: Lie! Lie! Lie!

Nor is this terror merely extensive; this would only generalize and push to their limits modes of oppression that mankind has already experienced, albeit in interrupted and fragmented ways. It is of a new kind. It is more deep-reaching and painful, in that the unity of the world is broken and the powerless individual who is wrenched from the real world is supposed to live in an nonexistent world. Without being able to extricate himself from real historical time, he is supposed to live in the imaginary eschatological time. In this way he finds himself within a falsehood even more intolerable than oppression itself. What is more, this massive terror and this intense, excruciating pain have to be publicly denied. The terror of the first years of the regime resembled "normal" terror enough that it could be acknowledged. In fact, it was celebrated. Lenin extolled the Cheka. Of all the heads of the police that history names, only Dzerżhińsky* has a statue erected to him in Moscow. But when that terror had done its work and the regime no longer had actual enemies of flesh and blood it was reality itself which became the enemy, because by its very existence it compromised the ideological pseudocreation. There had to be another, infinitely more horrible, terror. But because terror was intrinsically incompatible with the proclaimed ideological reality, it had to become the great secret of the regime. As soon as it would become known, it would have ruined the regime.

Thus at the heart of the new regime there grew a repressive system of denial upon which it rested. At the height of Stalinism the radiant Soviet creation was reduced to a thin film which displayed a harmonious, continuous surface to the outside world but which, once breached by accident, immediately opened to the Gulag, as several Western Communists found out. As thin as this film was, it was not to be broken. Because of its ubiquity, the terror knew how to maintain invisibility. At this culminating stage, however, it was no longer humanly controllable. The task of the secret police became strictly speaking metaphysical. It was on the shoulders of Yezhov, of Beria, on the *organs*† that the new reality rested, as well as belief in it. The mundane goals assignable in the realm of *phusis*—constructing factories, reconstituting the Party—became secondary in comparison to the grandiose work of substituting a new *metaphusis*. If in order to attain the first sort of goals it was not necessary, for example, to ruin agriculture, the total submission of the peasants (and thus the liquidation of its elites) belonged to the second order and its necessities. The Great Purge was not necessary in order to preserve the Party's political monopoly. But to preserve ideological purity, it was, perhaps, not excessive.

The problem of the ideological regime is to control this dialectic of two realities. Drawing its substance from "real reality," the fictive reality cannot destroy it completely without perishing in turn. There is an equilibrium to maintain between the parasite and the host. The Soviet regime today avoids

---

* Feliks Dzerżhińsky was born in the Wilno province of the Russian Empire to Polish Catholic parents. He was a central figure in the creation and expansion of the Cheka (the Soviet secret police).

† Besançon refers here to the secret police.

a return to Stalinism because under Stalin the equilibrium came close to being destroyed. If it was not broken during the first months of the German invasion in World War II, it was because the Soviet government jumped very quickly to the other side of the equilibrium: it accepted a temporary eclipse of ideology. During the "Great Patriotic War," it tolerated a massive infusion of "real reality," so much so that it was taken by its allies, even by its subjects, as a traditional regime not too far removed in appearance from what Solzhenitsyn says is his preference.* The Party retained power but it united the best citizens to its actions. The Church lived under a de facto concordat. The Lie was covered by nationalism, which was much more effective as a motivator. Solzhenitsyn does not have a bad memory of this period when he entered into adulthood. He sees in it a sort of promise. Nonetheless, as everyone knows, as easily as it had restrained itself Soviet reality came back as soon as the danger was passed. Solzhenitsyn had direct experience of this. Hidden from view, the *organs* had remained intact. The metaphysical project of construction, suspended for a moment, was vigorously reprised the day after the war was over and came up just short of bleeding the country to death. Since Stalin's death the regime has found a better equilibrium than at any time in its history. It remains intact, however, in its essence.

"Be quiet, Sancho!"

But what is this essence? Where can one look for its principle, its wellspring, its vital essence? As we have seen, the Soviet regime is entirely dependent upon ideology, and ideology in its turn depends upon a fictive "reality" to which it constantly tries to give reality and consistency—this is why the regime is harsh and oppressive—but which nonetheless refuses to exist, thereby denying the regime itself any consistency, depriving it of reality. If one looks at it in what I have called *phusis,* there is nothing so imposing as this regime, nothing so impressive as the *organs*. But since the ideological regime so to speak has nothing in common with *phusis* it

---

* See Solzhenitsyn's 1973 *Letter to the Soviet Leaders.* Here he calls on the leaders to jettison their failed ideology and establish a nonideological, authoritarian regime as a first step back to reality. Published in English as *Letter to the Soviet Leaders*, trans. Hilary Sternberg (New York: Harper and Row, 1974).

appears quite impotent in its omnipotence and it governs *phusis* no more than does the weasel tethered to the rabbit. If one considers the fictive reality, one has to believe in it in order to believe in the regime. And in order to believe in it "real reality" has to be denied.

At this point of accumulating paradoxes where reasoning apparently fails, I will turn to a famous story. When it is the wise who are perplexed, it is the crazy man who can explain the nature of the Soviet regime. I open *Don Quixote,* part two, chapter 19:

> They discovered a great windmill erected in the midst of a river; Don Quixote had barely glimpsed it when he cried in a loud voice: "Look, dear Sancho, behold the town, the chateau or the fortress, in which there must be some captive knight, some infant queen, some stolen princess to whose aid I am here come."
>
> "What imaginary town, fortress, or chateau are you talking about, my lord?" replied Sancho. "Don't you see that it is a windmill, built on a river, a mill to grind wheat?"
>
> "Be quiet, Sancho!" cried Don Quixote, "even though that appears to be a windmill, it is nothing of the sort. Haven't I told you that spells transform objects and cause them to depart from their natural state? I do not want to say that they are really transformed from one thing into another, but that they cause them to appear to be other things."

The windmill is Russia. The chateau where the infant is imprisoned is the Russia imagined by the revolutionary. The revolutionary power is the power of Don Quixote. But is the latter a power over a windmill or over a chateau? The ideology makes one see a chateau behind the appearances of a windmill, and by a truly mad inversion it is reality which seems to be the product of a spell. There is no apocalyptic transformation of an imaginary reality by "real reality," of the chateau by the windmill. The windmill therefore will be governed as a chateau and not as a windmill. According to the point of view that one adopts, this government will appear alternatively powerful and impotent. Everything in the windmill that recalls the windmill is eliminated; the millstones and the wheels are broken and the miller reeducated. The miller therefore believes he lives under a perfect despotism, one he cannot avow: Be quiet, Sancho! And yet the windmill remains a windmill, the chateau refuses to appear. Since one has to live, the miller shares with the governor the bread the miller makes as best he can in the corner left to him. Then, the miller in the ruined windmill (but more a windmill than ever before) asks himself if he, the miller, is not the master, after all he is a miller and not a captive child. In any event he suffers power as an inconvenient guest or a bad dream. In this sense he lives under an anarchy: *tyrannical anarchy* might be the most suitable definition of a regime that defines itself as a wholly organic "rule," one without conflict.

The story allows us to understand why the Soviet regime eludes Aristotle, Montesquieu, and Aron. Like an illusionist's trick, it cannot be "located." It aims to combine the three good governments. But driven from this place, it does not find rest in any of the three bad ones. It corresponds to Montesquieu's despotism, on the condition that we acknowledge that Montesquieu did not actually see the despotism he wrote about, rather it was one he imagined. But then one sees that this despotism is without a despot. The Marxist is as disoriented as anyone. He seeks the social basis of the ideological superstructure at the very moment when power applies itself to transform society into an epiphenomenon of his doctrine. The regime acts like an absolute idealist. It subjects ontology to logic. But in imitation of Don Quixote it transfers the spell of its thought to things and believes itself to be a materialist.

Does totalitarianism derive from the revolutionary project? Yes. But beside the project the ideological was already there. The transformation of reality according to the model of a reality declared to be immanent but which is in truth fictive and illusory "freezes" the former while obliging it to mimic itself. But it is not by ceasing to grind wheat that the windmill becomes a chateau. The windmill simply comes to a halt. The regime thus harbors both revolution and conservation. Utopia, because it is held to be actualized, gums up reality and sterilizes the imagination. Ultimately, destruction (which Bakhunin* identified with creation) is not decreed by some Promethean ambition but by the leaden fantasy of some subordinate functionary. In order to surgically operate on the societal clubfoot, that is, recalcitrant reality, all of art's resources are summoned. Here comes Charles Bovary with his sharpened instruments.

Translated by Paul Seaton & Daniel J. Mahoney

---

* See note on page 11.

5

Communist Totalitarianism:
The Transatlantic Vagaries of a Concept
(1984)

PIERRE HASSNER

> Where I feel that people like us understand the situation better
> than so-called experts is not in any power to foretell specific events,
> but in the power to grasp what kind of world we are living in.
> —George Orwell, *Wartime Diary*, June 8, 1940

To write about totalitarianism is to write about oneself. For this writer
the question of how to think about totalitarianism lies at the crossroads
of two personal itineraries: the first one is geographic—between eastern
Europe and the West and, within the latter, between the cultural atmo-
spheres of France and the United States; the second one is conceptual—
between the study of political philosophy, ideologies, and contemporary
international relations.

It is perhaps because of personal circumstances that these historical
questions—Is it true that there is something fundamental in common
between the Nazi and the Communist regimes that sets them apart from
constitutional or pluralist systems? Is this bond central and permanent, or
partial and transient? Why do some people ignore it and others become so
obsessed by it that they are unable to see anything else?—merge, for me,
with the theoretical ones: Can one understand what is completely alien?
Must the nonideologue become an ideologue, just as, for Plato, the judge
must be able to turn himself into a criminal? Faced with the reality of
totalitarianism, is there no choice but to trivialize it by denying its originality and hiding it behind the diversity of its origins, its incarnations, its

51

phases or its consequences, or to absolutize it by imitating its methods and substituting, once more, the logic of an abstract idea for the complexity of reality? Is Manichaeism forced upon us by the very nature of totalitarianism? And if the only way to understand totalitarianism is to be antitotalitarian, can one be antitotalitarian without recreating an anti-ideological ideology, an antitotalitarian totalitarianism?

These problems were faced by Arthur Koestler and George Orwell, by Albert Camus and Ignazio Silone,* by Raymond Aron and Richard Löwenthal,[†] and have inspired their moral and intellectual stance since the 1930s. But the dominant impression left by thirty-five years of ardent curiosity is one of constant surprise and irritation at the way in which the problem of totalitarianism has been disappearing and reappearing according to the vagaries of ideological and political, individual, and collective fashions and whims.

In France, or even in Europe, the postwar debate over concentration camps and the Stalinist trials (which were central to the Kravchenko[‡] and Rousset[§] affairs, and to the polemics among Sartre, Camus and Merleau-Ponty[¶]) did not lead to a deeper theoretical analysis, except through the

---

* Ignazio Silone was an Italian novelist who gained international recognition after the publication of his acclaimed first novel, *Fontamara*, in 1930. He had been a founding member of the Italian Communist Party, but was then expelled in 1931. He became a prominent figure in anti-Communist circles, like his countryman Nicola Chiaramonte.

† Richard Löwenthal was a member of the German Communist Party in the 1920s and then a key member of the anti-Nazi group New Beginnings in the 1930s. He would go on to become a prominent analyst of Soviet and Eastern Communism during the Cold War.

‡ Victor Kravchenko, Soviet defector and author of the memoir *I Chose Freedom*, found asylum in the United States in 1944. After his memoir was published in France, Kravchenko was attacked in a French Communist newspaper which he subsequently sued for libel. The resulting "trial of the century" drew hundreds of witnesses and brought him international attention.

§ David Rousset, Nazi concentration camp inmate, published *The Concentration Camp Universe* in 1947 and won international acclaim. He subsequently attacked the Soviet Union and its Gulag system and was then repeatedly denounced by French Communist intellectuals as a tool of American anti-Soviet propaganda.

¶ Maurice Merleau-Ponty was an extraordinarily influential philosopher in postwar France. In his *Humanism and Terror* (1947), a response to Arthur Koestler's *Darkness at Noon*, he offered a defense of the Communist enterprise.

great novels of Koestler and, above all, Orwell. It was in the United States, often through the works of German émigrés who had known Nazism and had started to formulate the concept of totalitarianism as far back as the 1920s, that the latter, after being temporarily shelved because of the alliance with the Soviet Union, re-emerged triumphantly in the early 1950s—a triumph soon extended to the Federal Republic of Germany and, to a lesser extent, to Great Britain. In France, those who had forestalled the wave of U.S. books became the only ones to take it into account. A solitary review of Hannah Arendt's *Origins of Totalitarianism* (New York, 1951) by Raymond Aron, in 1954, did not succeed in breaking the wall of silence, and the book was not translated until the 1970s. Hence the surprise of opposite but quasi-unanimous attitudes in the United States and in France.

After 1956 the atmosphere changed on both sides of the Atlantic. In France, through a process witnessed again today in their attitude towards China, intellectuals began to turn away from totalitarianism as soon as it became a little less bloody and attempted a certain reconciliation with society and reality. Meanwhile, in the United States, the death of Stalin, the decline of terror, and the events in Poland and Hungary led to a questioning (anticipated by Aron in his 1954 article) of the classical and maximalist model of authoritarianism (Arendt's and that of Carl-Joachim Friedrich and Zbigniew Brzezinski[1]). This questioning was shared, with various nuances and delays, by these authors themselves. But the decline in the fascination with totalitarianism led most U.S. Sovietologists to reinterpret the Soviet Union by denying its uniqueness. In the United States as well as the FRG, the decade from 1956 to 1966 is full of polemics around the notion of totalitarianism—now charged with underestimating the complexity of the regimes to which it is applied and their capacity for change, as well as the differences between them and their features in common with other dictatorships. By the end of the 1960s, the debate seemed to be over: the opponents of totalitarianism, found guilty of Cold-War bias, won by a knockout in the United States, and on points in the FRG and in Great Britain. In the 1970s, while the debate lingered in these two countries, it was replaced in the United States by a quasi-unanimity in favor of broader notions, which were either classical (authoritarianism), novel ("movement" or "mobilization" regimes) or Westernized ("institutional pluralism," or bureaucratic and corporate models). Hence a new malaise: for what the social sciences seemed to have done was, in effect, to provide totalitarian power with a set of new clothes about as useful as those of the naked emperor.

Fortunately or unfortunately, however, the cunning of reason, that old friend of totalitarianism, did not stay idle. From Mao's little red book to the normalization of Czechoslovakia, from the new forms of psychiatric repression in the Soviet Union to the grim Stalinism of liberated Vietnam and the demonstration by Cambodia's Pol Pot that the most monstrous monster can give birth to even more monstrous caricatures, it made nonsense of the reassuring chatter of scientific Sovietology by showing that if totalitarianism was dead, it had left behind some rather strange offspring. Above all it gave totalitarianism a spectacular comeback through the acclaim of a most unexpected public—the Parisian intellectual scene.

At long last came *The Gulag*, a divine surprise for the sad and ageing cohort of Eastern émigrés and their few scattered friends. The door to criticism that had been set ajar by the brutalities of Khrushchev and Mao was now blown wide open by the revelations of Solzhenitsyn, whose impact in France was greater than in any other country. The period of indifference and embarrassment which had replaced, between 1956 and the early 1970s, the positive fascination with the Soviet Union, was now succeeded by a negative fascination with the Gulag. There was a convergence of three trends: specialists like Alain Besançon who furthered Arendt's ideas of the totalitarian "supersense,"[2] or Eric Voegelin's on its gnostic origins;[3] former Maoists or members of the New Left who substituted totalitarianism for imperialism as an incarnation of evil, the dissidents for the colonized people as a suffering incarnation of good, and looked to moral resistance against power and the state rather than to social and political revolution for a substitute to politics; and, finally, a political group, the antitotalitarian Left or the "second" Left, who found in solidarity with the antitotalitarian revolution of eastern Europe the occasion for challenging, from within the Left, some of the latter's traditional dogma. Antitotalitarianism meant the rediscovery of pluralism, of the rule of law, of an analysis in terms of state and society rather than of class and party, of an interest in Europe rather than in the Third World.

One could welcome this evolution and yet express certain doubts. First, the antitotalitarian mood retains the characteristics of French intellectual fashion—the combination of abstraction and romanticism, the reluctance to recognize ambiguity, contradiction and change. Second, even specialists such as Besançon, Claude Lefort and Cornelius Castoriadis describe the two worlds of party and society, ideology and reality, or the military and civilian sector, in terms of an opposition between abstract and coherent models, never in terms of transformation and interpenetration.

The reader is then in danger of falling into a state of acute schizophrenia. When he reads that one of the brightest young stars of U.S. Sovietology, George Breslauer, seems, among *Five Images of the Soviet Future*,[4] to favour "welfare-state authoritarianism," he reacts by thinking of the constant primacy, in the Soviet Union, of power and the warfare state, of the decay of civilian infrastructure and of the progress of totalitarian psychiatry; in short, he reaches for his Besançon or his Castoriadis. But when he sees that, according to Besançon, the concept of economy cannot be applied to the Soviet Union because the Soviet system does not know economic constraints and can apply the criterion of power without ever having to care about the consumer, he is reminded of the sums poured into agriculture and of the Kremlin's concerns about consumer dissatisfaction, and he returns to the specialists of the Soviet economy.

Of course, Breslauer can argue that neototalitarian phenomena fall under the concept of authoritarianism and that the term welfare should not be understood according to the Western model. After all, Zinoviev and Besançon themselves describe a certain type of socialist welfare, based on laziness and corruption. On the other hand, Besançon can argue that the Soviet rulers, even when they abandon their ideological jargon to speak the everyday language of the consumer's preoccupations, are disguising their real priorities, which are built into their budgetary choices.[5] Conversely, when these choices are modified in the direction of consumption, Besançon will argue that this is in order to achieve the goals of the regime, which by definition can only be the pursuit of power in the service of the Bolshevik Revolution.

One is thus faced, in the first case, with the methodological problem of using concepts so broad that they become meaningless and, in the second, with the philosophical problem of whether one should judge a regime (as do both the defenders of the Soviet Union in the name of socialism and its radical critics in the name of totalitarianism) according to the goals set by its ideology or according to the daily experiences of its citizens. In both cases, one is confronted with the epistemological problem of theories which, like the ideologies themselves, do not explain anything because they can always explain everything.

If, however, one tries to get outside the conceptual framework of the two approaches so as to find a way of choosing between them, one has to acknowledge that Besançon's discourse—in spite or because of its internal logic—cannot be used to study the mechanisms and evolution of the Soviet economy, but that he is quite right when he states that those who live within, or in direct contact with, Soviet reality do not recognize their own experience when they read the learned studies of Western specialists. One may even generalize this observation. On the one hand, the evolution of Sovietology away from the notion of totalitarianism reflects, often naïvely and excessively, a very real evolution of its subject matter which French antitotalitarian intellectuals are wrong to dismiss with such contempt. On the other hand, it is not by chance that Solzhenitsyn and Zinoviev have had such influence in France; their respective visions (which incidentally are profoundly contradictory to each other) fit better with Besançon and Lefort than with Breslauer or even Severyn Bialer.[6] Many eastern European dissidents, whose very existence refutes the triumph of totalitarianism, reproduce its classical descriptions or recognize their own experiences when they read *1984*. Somewhere there exists a hard core, a permanent kernel of truth which is the classic view of totalitarianism. The question then is whether it can be reconciled with the empirical studies produced by social scientists, particularly in the United States.

FROM POLITICS TO POLITICAL SCIENCE

The guiding theme in this essay is the double contrast between American and French students of the Soviet Union, and between the 1950s and the 1970s. In the United States, Alex Inkeles and Raymond Bauer[7]—authors of the 1950s studies which gave the totalitarian model its empirical support—had announced from the outset, as Raymond Aron did in France, that the concept of totalitarianism would have to be linked to that of the industrial society. In 1953, Karl Deutsch[8] had already announced that the limits of centralization, mobilization, and control in any organization were bound to produce cracks in the totalitarian monolith. Conversely, at every wave of attack against the totalitarian model, some brave and isolated soldiers heroically took risks to cover its retreat (Peter Wiles in 1961, Paul Hollander in 1967 and William Odom in 1976)[9] and prepare for a counteroffensive which may well be in the making. But dominant trends do exist, and they are best explained by the interaction of the evolution of the Soviet Union and eastern Europe, East-West relations, and the social sciences.

The concept of totalitarianism has never been, as many have claimed, a mere instrument of the Cold War, but neither has it been depoliticized and turned into an operational, let alone a value-free, concept of political science. It was indeed born from a political struggle, but at the same time all the basic features which dominated the postwar discussion had been present since the 1920s (with Don Sturzo[*] calling Fascism a right-wing Bolshevism and Bolshevism a left-wing Fascism[10]) and the 1930s, from Elie Halévy's "organization of enthusiasm"[11] to Waldemar Gurian's and Voegelin's political and secularized religions,[12] from Emil Lederer's[†] "state of the masses" to Sigmund Neumann's[‡] "permanent revolution." In a sense, what Hannah Arendt did was only to tie these elements together in a creative synthesis (of which Friedrich's and Brzezinski's "totalitarian syndrome" represented the academic counterpart) by uncovering their common logic. It is clear, however, that the triumph of the notion of totalitarianism in the 1950s, particularly in the United States and in Germany, is due to the East-West struggle; antitotalitarianism had become, so to speak, the Cold-War cry of the West. But conversely, if nearly fifteen years separate the American Philosophical Society symposium of 1939 on "the totalitarian state from the points of view of history, political science, economics and sociology" from the American Academy of Arts and Sciences symposium on "totalitarianism" in 1953, it was because political reasons—the same ones that had made the Left so reluctant to hear out Koestler and Orwell, namely the alliance with the Soviet Union—had

---

* Don Luigi Sturzo, a Catholic priest, was a leader of the Partito Popolare Italiano (PPI, founded in 1919), a central player in Italian politics during the early 1920s. Sturzo was exiled to England in 1924 and was an important and prolific intellectual critic of Fascism.

† Emil Lederer, author of *The State of the Masses* (1939), was a German sociologist and economist.

‡ Sigmund Neumann, author of *Permanent Revolution: The Total State in a World at War* (1942).

made it undesirable in the meantime to stress the basic kinship between Stalinism and Hitlerism—all the more so since the former was raising hopes of improvement analogous to those connected with de-Stalinization a few years later. At any rate, the rude postwar awakening, brought in particular by the fate of the people's democracies and the trials of the late 1940s and the early 1950s, led the theorists of totalitarianism (particularly Arendt, Friedrich and Brzezinski) to stress, in their definitions, its most extreme forms—namely, those which were rapidly to be seen in the Soviet Union and later in China as linked to the person of the tyrant: the mass terror driven by ideology but increasingly taking on a life of its own, the permanent purges, etc. The theories of the 1950s oscillated between structure and process, between the idea of a new type of regime complete with a set of criteria and operating rules, and that of a mad and constantly paroxysmal system, initially aiming at transforming reality in the name of ideology but ending up with no other aim than itself. These two ideas could be reconciled in the name of the absorption of society by the state and of the state by the party movement, but at the price of difficulties which were pointed out, at the time, by Aron and others.

These difficulties were brought to the fore by Stalin's death. The theorists of totalitarianism were unprepared for the emergence of collective leadership, the relative decline of terror, the replacement of the permanent purge by the oligarchy's concern for security, the reduction in the role of the secret police, and the increase of the party's role. Hannah Arendt, whose conception was centered on the 1932–52 period of the concentration camps, the purges and the trials, did not have to change her interpretation in order to declare that it did not apply to Stalin's successors any more than to his predecessor or to Mao. In 1966 she disavowed the ideological use of the term against all the Communist Party states. Brzezinski, on the contrary, started as early as 1956 the process of revision or of what Michael Curtis was to call "the retreat from totalitarianism."[13] In Brzezinski's article, "Totalitarianism and rationality,"[14] manipulation aimed at total social revolution appeared as a more modern, rational, and efficient substitute for terror. For a whole period, until the early 1960s, a series of formulas stressing the process—such as Löwenthal's "permanent revolution from above"—or the system—like Allen Kassof's "administered society" or "totalitarianism without terror"—developed this idea of a totalitarianism modified by the "rationalization of party control." This period, of course, corresponded to Khrushchev's reign, with its renewal of ideological and utopian dynamism and its attempt to take the needs of society into account while reducing the role of terror and the secret police.

This phase in the odyssey of the concept of totalitarianism was called into question by the combination of a new phase in the evolution of Communist countries and the desire of the Sovietologists to break out of their ghetto in order to jump on the bandwagon of modernization and comparative studies.

In the first dimension, it soon became clear that the Khrushchevian dynamic was stalled. As Löwenthal put it at the time of Nikita Sergeyevich's fall, it was no longer only terror but the revolution itself that was withering away;[15] the Party, however, was clinging to power as tenaciously as ever but limited its ambition to keeping the social aspirations to differentiation in check rather than attempting to eradicate them. The function of ideology was the legitimation of power rather than the inspiration of a dynamic attempt at transforming society. Brzezinski had foreseen the hypothesis of a totalitarian power which would keep its institutional position while having lost its revolutionary dynamism. But then, should one still speak of totalitarianism, or rather of a transformation into a one-party authoritarian regime? Löwenthal pointed out that the label was less important than the need to recognize the exhaustion of the permanent revolution from above, but, like Peter Ludz, Juan Linz and most American authors, he preferred to call the postrevolutionary or postmobilization phase post-totalitarian authoritarianism.

Others in the same period were drawing even more radical conclusions from the same evolution. Looking back at the earlier phase in the light of the new one, they were challenging the concept of totalitarianism even for the period of revolutionary mobilization, or at least they were subordinating it to more general concepts which were just coming to the fore in the social sciences. For Löwenthal and Ludz themselves, the dynamics of totalitarianism conflicted with the rival dynamics of economic development and with the growing complexity of industrial society. At the very least, one had to combine the totalitarian model with the development and industrial-society models. But then, it became very tempting to give priority to the last two, which, compared to the totalitarian, had the advantage of opening the door to the world of the social sciences.

This door was pushed by three trends that can be traced to three authors: Robert C. Tucker and mobilization, Alfred Meyer and organization, and Gordon Skilling and interest groups. For Tucker the notion of totalitarianism is either too broad or too narrow. On the one hand, he stresses the personal role of the dictator[16] in the acute phase—that upon which Hannah Arendt had insisted, and which Tucker calls today the phase of "nightmare regimes."[17] On the other hand, he would like to include totalitarian party movements in a broader comparative framework that would include the nationalist party movements of the Third World. He thus makes a decisive contribution to the launching of the notion of mobilization regimes, which led to the Chalmers Johnson symposium and was criticized, convincingly, by Peter Wiles and Jeremy Azrael.[18]

Alfred Meyer,[19] who tended to underplay the specific role of ideology and politics, was profoundly influenced by theories of convergence and by the analogies between the Soviet Union and a huge corporation; he insisted upon the old Burnhamian idea of the managerial revolution, without drawing clear distinctions between its bureaucratic and its technocratic versions. Here, too, the criticisms of Hollander and Azrael seem close to the mark.

Last, Skilling[20] criticizes the totalitarian model mostly for hiding the complexity of Communist societies and the emerging opposition of interests within them. He does not neglect the precautions that distinguish him from Jerry Hough[21] and acknowledges that Soviet-type regimes cannot be called pluralistic. The fact remains that the theoretical tendency of his work (curiously at odds with his exhaustive and empathetic knowledge of Czechoslovakian society) goes in the direction of de-exceptionalizing Communist regimes and makes him vulnerable to the criticisms of Francis Castles[22] and William Odom,[23] who try to rehabilitate the totalitarian model by distinguishing between the articulation of interests and formation of groups without, however, going as far as the Franco-Czechoslovakian scholar Thomas Lowit, for whom all apparent social diversity is reduced to the hidden unity of a polymorphic party.

Matters are less complicated with the other advocates of the pluralistic model. There the double desire both to de-exceptionalize the Soviet Union in order to be admitted by the social sciences and to save détente is expressed with an almost naive candor. Thus, Susan G. Solomon declares:

The building of real conceptual bridges between comparative politics and Soviet studies would have accomplished two objectives. First, it would have demonstrated more forcefully than any argument that the Soviet Union was not an outsider in the family of nations, a pariah. And, in destigmatizing the Soviet system, it would have moved specialists on Soviet politics more squarely into the mainstream of the discipline of political science.[24]

The result, however, is only partly satisfactory:

> Works on pluralism and on interest groups by specialists of comparative politics now routinely contain references to research conducted by Sovietologists. On the other hand, the goal of eliminating or even reducing the credibility of totalitarianism (either in pure or in modified form) has not been notably furthered.

And Jerry Hough, the most radical advocate of the pluralist model, defends it against the new fashion—corporatism—in the name of its greater effectiveness with the public in the still-to-be-won battle against the common enemy, the totalitarian model:

> Whatever evolution in the views of the Soviet Union has occurred within political science, the old dogmatic views continue to have a deep hold in large and influential portions of the American population. Fifteen years of work on the input side of Soviet politics have made far too little impact on old images of an all-powerful state, directing society and pursuing foreign policy on the basis of a long-established master plan. It seems to me that we should keep in mind the general audience as well as the specialists as we decide what is important to study and to understand.[25]

FROM POLITICAL SCIENCE TO POLITICAL PHILOSOPHY

What had happened, then, to justify this plaintive tone, this confession of failure, coupled with a pressing appeal to a greater political consciousness? Again, the three dimensions that we have distinguished come into play.

First, the social sciences—whose triumphant takeoff had so impressed the Sovietologists—have lost much of their prestige. In particular, theories of modernization and political development have been increasingly questioned.[26] Over the years, the notion of political development has become more and more discredited and its application to the evolution of eastern Europe has looked more and more like black humor. In 1982 Gordon Skilling and Archie Brown, two strong supporters of the comparative model and of limited pluralism, pronounced its death in *Studies in Comparative Communism.*

The notion of pluralism, applied to Communist states, is in only slightly better shape. Already in 1979, in the same *Studies in Comparative Communism*, its critics had renewed their attacks. Moreover, as Susan Solomon points out, the Sovietologists had seized upon that notion at the very time when students of Western societies were beginning to abandon it. Without going so far as to apply the concept of totalitarianism to Western "repressive tolerance," like the Marcusian New Left in the United States in the late 1960s and in Germany today, the Sovietologists point to the sway of large organizations, to their collusion, and to their solidarity towards the outside world. They thus rediscover one of the dimensions of Fascism—corporatism. Hence the fashion of neocorporatism—which the Sovietologists are tempted to embrace, but with a certain prudence. As Hough warns, they do not want to risk falling back into the totalitarian model, all the more so because they feel it risks being revived by the New Cold War.

Clearly, this second factor—the state of East-West relations—is the most conspicuous, even more so than in earlier periods. If the notion of totalitarianism is revived by some and rejected by others, the reason lies less in the evolution of the social sciences or the Soviet Union than in the fact that the latter is again appearing as an enemy and that the term totalitarianism is the most convenient way to brand it as such. This does not detract from the genuine progress in the debate about the validity of the concept. Similarly, one need not share Jeane Kirkpatrick's conclusions[27] when she uses a revived distinction between authoritarian and totalitarian regimes to argue that right-wing dictatorships should be supported against Communist ones, to recognize that she raises a genuine problem, illustrated recently in the cases of Argentina and Poland: the respective reversibility or irreversibility of the two types of regime. But Kirkpatrick's distinction remains a political argument in favor of a political attitude—the priority of opposition to Communism.

As during détente what has changed is less the Communist regimes themselves than Western attitudes towards them. Or rather, what has changed is less the nature of the Soviet Union than its external role and power. The Soviet accession to strategic parity, coupled with the more interventionist quality of its military policy between 1975 and 1980, and the late and partly retrospective discovery of the Gulag by the French intelligentsia—these are what motivates the new fear and hostility towards Moscow.

This reaction relies partly on a non sequitur. It is not inherently obvious that the military danger of a regime or the urgency or necessity of negotiating with it are tied to its internal nature. A country can be totalitarian yet turn its dynamism towards internal oppression rather than external expansion: this was the case for Stalin during the Great Purge, for Mao during the Cultural Revolution. It is by necessity the case for some small countries, often the most totalitarian ones such as Albania and, to some extent, Pol Pot's Cambodia. Conversely, a classical power can be expansionist or imperialist. One can find reasons to negotiate as well as common—albeit provisional—interests with the most totalitarian state. The fact remains, however, that long-range agreements, such as those the West hoped to achieve during détente, are made impossible by the very nature of a totalitarian regime, by its fundamentally conflictual view of the world and by the character of its own citizens. It is also true that, even in the short run, Western democracies seem to have a subjective or exaggerated view of their allies or adversaries. What had happened during the alliance against Hitler was repeated in part during détente. Similarly, in an attenuated form, the failure of East-West cooperation has produced a renewed consciousness of the alien or evil character of the Soviet Union. Since it has not become friendly or democratic, this must mean that it has not ceased being totalitarian. Conversely, the defenders of détente feel obliged to prove that they were not mistaken in claiming that Moscow had changed.

The main reason for wondering whether, by abandoning the notion of totalitarianism, the specialists have not thrown the baby out with the bath water, is what might be called the non-withering-away of dictatorship in Communist states. It is de-Stalinization that has discredited the theory of totalitarianism. Conversely, the theories that replaced it relied on a vision and on concepts directed towards liberalization and democratization, or at least rationalization and compromise between the party and society. The crisis of Communist countries, the domestic immobility of the Soviet Union, at least under Brezhnev, the failure of the Prague Spring, the rise of Solidarity and its repression, lead one to wonder whether one should not speak of a totalitarian residue which would block potential evolutions that are comparable to those of right-wing authoritarian regimes.

It is clear, on the one hand, that the Arendt-Friedrich-Brzezinski model is untenable for the present phase, and that its advocates have had to sacrifice its attributes one after the other—first terror, then revolution. But on the other hand, it is clear that this theoretical striptease is never completed and that the advocates of modernization, technocracy, and pluralism are forced to operate an analogous retreat in the opposite direction.

Can one say, with Michael Walzer,[28] that every existing totalitarianism is a failed one, but in addition that all post-totalitarian liberalizations and democratizations have equally failed? Should one conclude from that double failure a cyclical, ever undecided struggle between system and society? Perhaps, but to defend such a statement with any confidence one would need both an empirical inquiry about the various forms of this struggle and a philosophical and moral gamble on its ultimate significance. Moreover, perhaps both this inquiry and this gamble should deal less with the system than with the societies.

Where the study of totalitarianism went wrong is not in what it said about the system but in its insufficient attention to the opposite pole, to the civil society and national cultures which it destroys but which re-emerge, which it transforms but which keep resisting. Or are this renaissance, and resistance, only an illusion? Could it be that they are only the mirror image of a transformed totalitarian power whose ultimate triumph would consist precisely in society producing its own "totalitarianism from below"? That is the question. Everyone seems to agree with A. Smolar[29] that the dynamics of the "revolution from above" have withered away but that the institutions of the totalitarian system persist. Should one then conclude that the latter, faced with a nascent or renascent civil society, is on the defensive, as seems to be the case in China today according to Jean-Luc Domenach, or, on the contrary, that it no longer needs to be dynamic and to impose revolution from above precisely because it has succeeded in destroying or digesting civil society? We would be dealing (everywhere, according to Besançon, except in Poland) with another society, one where

Communism is a reality, or even with a new type of man, Zinoviev's *Homo sovieticus* or *Homocus*.[30] For Jacques Rupnik, the answers coming from central Europe are profoundly different (whether in the name of civil society as in Poland, or of the market economy as in Hungary, or of European culture as in Czechoslovakia) from those provided by Zinoviev. It seems fair to agree with Rupnik's conclusion that while the system is always the same, how one lives it, adapts to it, or resists it differs according to cultures and historical experiences.

Can one go beyond and try to indicate some features which would be common to the present phase of Communist regimes?

It seems reasonable to accept the notion of post-totalitarian authoritarianism, provided one gives it a meaning that is not too different from that of postrevolutionary totalitarianism. In other words it is true that totalitarian power, as it loses part of its dynamism and ability to control an increasingly complex and resistant society, tends to restrain its ambitions to make them more compatible with its means, and thereby to come closer to an authoritarian power, this certainly seems to be a more plausible view of eastern Europe's evolution, and probably of the Soviet Union's, than Zinoviev's vision. But it is no less true that it does not become an authoritarian power like any other. Post-totalitarian authoritarian regimes are, in a way, a decadent phase of totalitarianism itself; at any rate they are profoundly shaped by their origins.

It seems difficult to deny that we are witnessing, in Milovan Djilas's words, a "disintegration of Leninist totalitarianism."[31] But, as Djilas himself pointed out, this disintegration pertains less to the organizational and ideological framework of totalitarianism than to its content. Totalitarianism seems always present in the background, functioning as a negative point of comparison which makes the current situation look more acceptable, as a threat that may be more and more unreal but projects its shadow upon real life.

Mass terror has declined considerably but enough is left to make its return not entirely unthinkable. What has replaced the threat of labor camps is the threat of being excluded from the social and economic system. What Inkeles called "the institutionalization of anxiety" remains present even though it conflicts with the gerontocracy's aspiration to security.

A certain diffusion of power does take place, but not in the guise of a balance of interest groups. Rather, there can be on the one hand, a renewal of elites and an interpenetration within the ruling class (KGB-ization, militarization, technicalization), through co-optation within the party apparatus; and there can be, on the other hand, an increased tolerance towards the second economy and even towards a certain anomie that would be its social equivalent, even though, beyond certain limits, the party tries to reassert its control. The conflict, as William Odom points out,[32] is less between institutions and groups than between center and periphery, between the various levels of a hierarchical system. The structure remains the same but there is a decline in central control and a withering away of revitalization mechanisms like terror and purges.

Similar tensions and contradictions are found at the ideological level. There is an increasing search for substitutes to Marxism-Leninism as legitimizing ideologies. These can be traditional (nationalism, including, today, in the GDR, where it once seemed impossible) or modernistic (the scientific-technological revolution). Soviet literature today seems to aim more at privatization than at mobilization and to encourage nationalism and the cults of work, nature, and the past more than devotion to social-ism[33]—although tendencies to a reassertion of the old priorities are also visible. There are more and more open windows on reality. And yet the wooden language of ideology survives, both as a symbol and a code of power and of its legitimacy which cannot totally dispense with the two permanent myths of dark conspiracies and a brilliant future.

Finally, foreign policy. One can accept that world revolution has ceased being an operational goal of Soviet policy, if it ever was one; that the latter is driven more by *Realpolitik* than by an irresistible ideological dynamism; and yet one must maintain that its lack of traditional or democratic legitimacy keeps the regime in a state of permanent insecurity; that, to preserve their power, the rulers must keep their empire and their society under control; that, towards that aim, they must protect them against external influences; and for that, in turn, they need an ideology that entertains hostility towards the outside world, and a power that enables them to control, at least potentially, any threat coming from their environment; and finally, that all these defensive and conservative reasons can push Moscow towards expansion and conflict as unmistakably as a triumphant messianism.

These few vague and banal indications are meant only to point out that while change and complexity are characteristic of the present phase, they are not free of the Stalinist heritage. Now more than ever we lack the instruments which would enable us to identify the role of this heritage within the different existing varieties of imperfect and decadent totalitarianism.

At any rate, it does not seem likely that these instruments will be found in the social sciences. It is the great literary works (Orwell, Solzhenitsyn, Zinoviev, Grossman*) and philosophical interrogations which, periodically, force us to recognize that something escapes the conceptual frameworks and the empirical research of the social sciences applied to Sovietology, and that this "something" has something to do with totalitarianism. Should it not be sought in the direction of Arendt's "supersense," Besançon's "surreality," Orwell's "doublethink" and "newspeak," Jaspers's "institutionalized lie," Kostas Papaïoannou's "cold ideology"[34] or Leszek Kolakowski's "great lie"[35]—in other words, in this articulation between language and power analyzed by the eastern European authors quoted by Rupnik?

If so, the mistake of the theory of totalitarianism would have to be located in the transition from Arendt to Friedrich and Brzezinski, in the attempt to translate what can be caught only by a global view, intimately linked to a political philosophy, into a set of empirical criteria.

As Lefort pointed out,[36] it is perhaps only through the experience of democracy and human rights, through the relations between language and society, or between philosophy and politics, that the political scientist can understand the different forms of authoritarianism and grasp the meaning of totalitarianism.

In the end, if one wants to speak of totalitarianism, one can avoid neither a political-philosophical commitment nor a historical gamble.

Of course, abstract antitotalitarian rhetoric is no substitute for the empirical study of totalitarian regimes, and a prevalently political or ideological approach like the French one has much to learn in this respect, from American social scientists. But in the last analysis, the concept of totalitarianism does not belong to political science.

This does not mean, however, that the concept of totalitarianism is not important for political science. On the contrary, political science as a discipline is in the same situation as the theory of totalitarianism: the

---

* Vasily Grossman's two historical novels *Life and Fate* and *Everything Flows* both explore the nature of totalitarianism.

only way either can progress is by acknowledging its limitations. As Pascal would have said, nothing is more in agreement with political science than this disavowal of political science.

6

From Under the Rubble, What?
(1992)

Martin Malia

We have met the enemy and he is us.
——Pogo

The appropriation of Aleksandr Solzhenitsyn's famous title for the present essay refers to two fields of rubble.* The first is that which extends, in the empirical world, over the former Soviet Union's eleven time zones, from Brest-Litovsk to the Bering Straits. The second is that which extends, in the conceptual world, over the four time zones of the continental United States, and through all the universities and think-tanks from Massachusetts Bay to the Pacific Rim. And this conceptual world embraces four social science disciplines: economics, political science, sociology, and their common ancestor, history.

After seventy-four years of Sovietism, and forty-five years of institutionalized Sovietology, the time has come to say openly: Comrades, there is a crisis in our party—both the one we study, and the one to which by professional vocation we all belong. Clearly, something quite unantici-

---

* *From Under the Rubble* (Little, Brown and Co., 1975) by Solzhenitsyn and others sought to restore an older tradition of Russian thought amidst the toxic legacy of an exhausted, empty socialist intelligentsia. It was meant to be a companion volume to another collection of essays published in 1909. That volume, *Landmarks*, had similarly repudiated the revolutionary ethos of the Russian intelligentsia of the nineteenth century.

pated by the Kremlin went wrong with Sovietism, and just as clearly as well, all of us failed to anticipate it.

But perhaps anticipation in history is precluded, for everyone, by the unfathomable ways of what Hegel called the "Cunning of Reason" in human affairs. Perhaps the most we can ever hope for is to devise analytic or conceptual schemes that will make full sense of events only after they have occurred. On this score, how does our Sovietological science measure up? And how well are our post-Soviet colleagues, both in Russia and in eastern Europe, doing in their own efforts to comprehend the Communist catastrophe? For to them, this matter is no academic exercise, since they must urgently cope with the crushing problems that Communism has left in its wake.

Yet, in order to evaluate matters in the conceptual world of Sovietology and in the four social science disciplines, it is first necessary to survey the problems left behind in the empirical world by the recent collapse of Communism. And before we can survey these problems adequately, it is necessary to dispel some of the false perceptions that have surrounded them since August 1991. The present essay, therefore, will begin with a discussion of these recent perceptions, will then proceed to post-Soviet problems, and, finally, will turn to those grander and more systematic perceptions that constitute Sovietology.

THE RUSSIAN REVOLUTION OF 1991

During the four months between the August events of 1991 and the end of the Soviet Union in December, Western public opinion, as well as governmental opinion, was clearly suffering from cognitive lag in registering events in Moscow. And this opinion was struggling with an even more acute case of cognitive dissonance in attempting to organize these events into a mode of discourse appropriate to post-*perestroyka* conditions.

What we heard in our academic colloquia and read on our op-ed and editorial pages is that a "failed coup," which was carried out by an adventitious group of individuals tautologically known as "coup-plotters," took place in Moscow last August. Their evil designs were fortunately thwarted, however, and "President" Mikhail Gorbachev, with the heroic help of Boris Yeltsin, was restored to his rightful place. Thus, the "reform process" begun by *perestroyka* was put back on track, although under more difficult circumstances than before, because of the untoward interruption by the coup of the Soviet Union's "transition to democracy." True, the media also spoke prominently of the "collapse of Communism," yet usually managed to combine this with a focus on Gorbachev that conveyed a message of continuity.

Moreover, we were often told that the post-coup situation in the Soviet Union had brought with it new dangers that apparently had not been so threatening during *perestroyka*, dangers of a chauvinistic authoritarianism, quite possibly promoted by "tsar" Boris, as some called Yeltsin. Such sentiments were not confined to Western liberal opinion; they could also be heard in Moscow, although less in liberal quarters than in former Communist ones. A frequent conclusion of this line of reasoning was that Gorbachev, not Yeltsin and those in Russia who presumed to call themselves "democrats," represented both state legitimacy and the real potential for democracy in Russia.

This perspective, predominant in America in the months after the August events, represents an inversion of reality as it is perceived among Russian democrats. And not just as it is perceived, but an inversion of reality *tout court*. For the August "coup" was no coup at all, but an act of the Soviet government. This "coup" was led by the vice president, the prime minister, the head of the KGB, the ministers of defense and interior, the chief of staff of Gorbachev's personal cabinet, and the president of the Supreme Soviet, among others. Together, they represented the whole Communist establishment—the party, the military-industrial complex, the army command, and the secret police. Gorbachev, moreover, had appointed them all.

As their actions before August demonstrate, these "plotters" no doubt expected to implement their program of repression openly and constitutionally. They rather clearly supposed that faced with the growing anarchy in the country, and the rising strength of the Yeltsinian democrats, their President would ultimately agree to declare a state of emergency, a measure that had, in fact, been under active consideration since Gorbachev had appointed Boris Pugo to be his interior minister and Valentin Pavlov to be his prime minister in December 1990.

Indeed, these "coup-plotters" had already acted with armed force in the Baltic republics in January, and politically in the Russian parliament in March, when they attempted to impeach Yeltsin, only to be thwarted by several hundred thousand democrats demonstrating in the streets of Moscow. And their final effort was Pavlov's public attempt, in June, to usurp Gorbachev's decree powers. If the President during all these months did not know or understand what was going on, then he was incompetent, which is almost as bad as active complicity. The Russian word for such conduct in responsible positions is *khalatnost,* or criminal negligence.

When leading government officials sought to pressure Gorbachev into decreeing a state of emergency and, to their surprise, he refused, they clumsily declared him deposed, thus leaving his vice president, Gennady Yanayev, "legally" able to issue the required decree. In the West, this type of attempted palace revolution is called a "coup." It was to have been followed by what in Moscow is known as the "putsch," that is, a military operation to put down the democrats.

The plotters' effort failed grotesquely. Yeltsin and the democrats then turned the situation into a genuine revolution. They suspended—and later dissolved—the Communist Party. This was tantamount to dismantling the Soviet system itself, together with all its works and pomps—the Union, the Congress of People's Deputies, the five-year plan, the police, the politicized army command, and the administrative apparatus of the military-industrial complex.[1]

This is the basic, indeed self-evident, outline of Russian history in August and September. One can even read about it in the *New York Times.* Yet almost no one publicly uses the self-evident name, "revolution," to designate what is so obviously one of the most revolutionary events of twentieth-century history. For what occurred in August was the end of Communism, not just in its eastern European periphery, but in its heartland and place of origin, the Soviet Union. What more does it take to qualify as a revolution? It is this mysterious refusal to face reality that must first be explained before we can talk realistically about the staggering problems of post-Sovietism.

On closer examination, the mystery really is not so mysterious after all. What is really involved in this matter may be shown by adapting a distinction made in the historiography of the French Revolution, in which the debate was once between proponents of *la thèse du complot* and *la thèse des circonstances. La thèse du complot* held that the revolution was the work of a minority of conspirators, and hence was both avoidable and illegitimate, while *la thèse des circonstances* asserted that the revolution proceeded from objective conditions and hence was both necessary and legitimate. In the present Soviet case, what might be called *la thèse du coup* (*complot*) minimizes the importance of the August events, and thus implies that the passage from *perestroyka* to the new democracy in Russia was an evolutionary one, with a continuity of legitimacy from Sovietism to a liberal order. As such, this passage realized the reform potential of Communism, and by the same token demonstrated that the Soviet system had not in fact been totalitarian. *La thèse de la revolution* (*circonstances*), on the other hand, asserts that there was a fundamental rupture, a radical break between Communism of whatever stripe and Russia's present attempt to build a market economy and democracy. In this perspective, legitimacy stems from entirely different, indeed anti-Communist, roots, and thus demonstrates that the Soviet system was totalitarian, incapable of reform without abandoning its fundamental structures.

But frank recognition of a sharp break with the comfortable illusions of *perestroyka* is unsettling to too many Western political, as well as Sovietological, interests to be readily accepted—hence the urge to believe in continuity. Hence also, a part of the post-August concern about the authoritarian and chauvinistic dangers inherent in the new democratic polity. Although some of this concern was inspired by eastern Europe's turbulent past, much of it constituted an effort of dubious intellectual authenticity to invert reality so as to make a democrat out of the Communist Gorbachev and an autocrat out of the anti-Communist Yeltsin. As Louis Jouvet said in *Drôle de Drame*, "bizarre, bizarre."

Droll though our misperception of post-Communist reality may be, that reality itself, if not yet tragic, is clearly calamitous. For Communism left in its wake, as a poisoned legacy to the democratic August Revolution, nothing but rubble—in the most literal sense of that word. We are all aware that Russia and the other republics of the former Soviet Union face numerous, if not quite innumerable, problems: constitutional, economic, ethnic, nuclear, ecological, and even the most basic of problems—lack of food and shelter.

Yet, once again, our understanding fails us; too often we treat these problems as discrete and separate, as if they could be taken up and solved one at a time. To cite only one example, the U.S. Secretary of Agriculture together with the National Security Council's resident Soviet specialist, economist Ed Hewett, were dispatched to Moscow in mid-1991 to help the Soviets fix "their food distribution system," as if that system could somehow be treated apart from the kolkhoz network and its agrarian *nomenklatura*, three or four ministries, and the inveterate distrust of all state authority on the part of what remains of the Russian peasantry—all of which Dr. Hewett, of course, knew quite well. Or we find the International Monetary Fund, some professors from Harvard's Kennedy School of Government, and Monsieur Jacques Attali of the European Bank for Reconstruction and Development giving the ex-Soviets advice on how to brake inflation and absorb the "monetary overhang," as if all we are talking about are essentially technical measures to be applied to yet another sick, Third-World economy.

To be sure, all of these discrete problems are quite real; and all of them will require technical solutions of the sort just mentioned. Nevertheless, none of them will work unless it is first realized that the post-Soviet crisis is a total crisis, embracing every aspect of life at once. For all basic institutions in the former Soviet Union collapsed together and at once; and thus all of them must be rebuilt together and, if not at once, then in rapid succession.

This is the meaning of an oft-quoted witticism, so universally applicable to Sovietism that it has been variously attributed to Lech Walesa and to the Russian humorist Mikhail Zhvanetsky: It is easy to make fish soup out of an aquarium, but no one has yet found a way to make an aquarium out of fish soup. Such a situation, and such a conundrum, is without precedent in world history. And it will no doubt take a generation and a decade or two to improvise, while still in the soup, Russia's return to a "normal society."

SOVIETOLOGY AND SOCIAL SCIENCE

The great first step taken by the August Revolution in the Soviet Union was to put an end to the Communist ideocratic partocracy. Western Sovietology must now take an answering step by coming to terms intellectually with post-partocratic reality. And this will have to be a rather big step indeed; for long ago mainstream Sovietology threw away the key to understanding Sovietism by discarding the "totalitarian model" in favor of such concepts as "modernization," "institutional pluralism," and "developmental authoritarianism." So, the way out of our Western conceptual soup might well be one that leads us back to a state of pre–social science innocence.

The present inability of our Sovietological "models" to explain the way Sovietism ended concerns not only Sovietology but the four social science disciplines as they have developed in the West since World War II. Until that time, our academic institutions had only two basic faculties—Letters and Sciences. It is only after the war that a third great area of learning was staked out and institutionalized in a separate faculty as the Social Sciences. At the same time, the spirit in which the study of man and society was conducted changed. What the French used to call *les sciences humaines* and the Germans the *Geisteswissenschaften* had been largely informed by the spirit of the humanities, and they were considered to be distinct from the exact or natural sciences. But what the Americans now labeled the social sciences had the ambition of becoming as similar to the natural sciences as possible. Until this "behavioral revolution," the fledgling social disciplines were lodged in the traditional faculties or, in Europe, outside the established university, as in the London School of Economics or France's *Institut d'Etudes Politiques*. Now all the social disciplines were gathered together under one great positivistic roof of their own.

Sovietology came of age entirely in the behavioral era, and within the institutional confines of the third, new domain of learning, the social sciences. And Sovietology developed as the application of general social scientific methodologies to the Communist world. It was considered as a form of "area studies" alongside Latin American area studies and those dealing with other regions of the world. This occurred first in American universities, and was subsequently copied in western Europe; the results are now being imported into the post-Communist countries. We have a professional obligation to inform their scholars of what it is they are getting.

The idea of an empirical, inductive science of society is as old as Aristotle's *Politics*; and in a very basic way this work has never been superseded, because certain aspects of the knowledge we have of ourselves are not cumulative. But it was only after the Scientific Revolution of the seventeenth century that social science in the modern and putatively cumulative sense became possible, because for the first time, mankind developed a form of knowledge that was wholly empirical and yet conceptualized in universal, and often mathematical, laws. And, as such, this new knowledge was regarded as incontrovertible, not to say infallible. It was a kind of knowledge that had hitherto been attributable only to God. In the eighteenth-century Enlightenment, the first systematic effort was made to transfer this model of knowledge to human affairs so as to create a science of man and society. The great prototype of this was the *Encyclopédie* of D'Alembert and Diderot. Its nineteenth-century culmination was the positivism of Auguste Comte, who indeed first gave us the word "sociology" to designate the ultimate science.

In the sphere of practical, empirical application of this aspiration, the first new discipline to emerge was "political economy" in the half century following Adam Smith's *Wealth of Nations* in 1776. By the turn of the century, it had acquired organized academic status. The second discipline to emerge in an institutional fashion was what we now call political science, which gained a separate identity beginning in the 1880s. Sociology was the last to appear, emerging as a discipline in the 1920s and 1930s out of an amalgam of the work of Max Weber and Emile Durkheim (as in the structural functionalism of Talcott Parsons); and after the late 1930s, a great deal of Marx was blended in, while a dash of de Tocqueville was added after World War II. Then, in the wake of that conflict, these social sciences permeated the great parent discipline, history, which was in fact older than Aristotle.

During the forty-odd years after World War II, all four disciplines in this new world of social science lived through the same great "paradigm shift" in Communist studies: from the "totalitarian model" to "modernization theory." The former sought to explain Communist systems essentially from above, as the product of ideology and political will. In this perspective, Sovietism was akin to Nazism and Fascism, and hence radically different from the Western democracies. The second model, which emerged in the 1960s, sought to explain the Soviet system essentially from below, as the product of universal social and economic forces, and hence different only in degree, not in kind, from other "modern" or "modernizing" societies. But how did this overarching paradigm shift unfold in each of the four social sciences?*

---

* Malia tracks the study of the Soviet Union in the disciplines of economics, sociology, political science, and history. In this abridged version of Malia's essay, I have retained only his thoughts on the latter two disciplines.

POLITICAL SCIENCE

In political science studies of Communism, the great issue turned around the "totalitarian model" and its critics. And this struggle touched just as directly the other "soft" social sciences as well—sociology and history. The basic facts are so well known as to make superfluous anything but the briefest recapitulation. The totalitarian model was launched in 1951, while Stalin was still in power, by Hannah Arendt in her *Origins of Totalitarianism*. Her thesis was that the mid-twentieth century experienced a qualitatively new and unique form of despotism, founded on the mass, demotic mobilization of society by ideological political power; and that the supreme expressions of this were Nazism and Communism. In 1956, Carl Friedrich and Zbigniew Brzezinski turned Arendt's thesis into a model, according to which totalitarianism is characterized by an official ideology, a mass party with a leader, institutional terror, a monopoly on information, a monopoly of high-technology weaponry, and a centrally controlled economy.[2]

Beginning in the 1960s, the totalitarian model came increasingly under attack. There were many reasons for this, but here it is possible to mention only the most important. First, times were in fact changing in the Soviet Union, and the system was becoming more mellow. Second, times were changing in the West as well, and the Left, after a long eclipse, was making a comeback. The conjunction of these two factors diminished concern about the Soviet menace, and so the totalitarian model came to be denounced as the academic rationale for the Cold War. Moreover, with the "balance of terror" between the two superpowers producing a stalemate, it seemed clear that the Soviet Union would be a permanent factor in world affairs, and that the time had therefore come to settle down and analyze it soberly, without the emotion of the late Stalin years. And this meant processing Soviet data through the "value-free" categories of the new social sciences. Thus, academic investigation of the USSR, which had begun as a form of mere "area studies," was constantly upgraded by its practitioners through the assimilation of ever more sophisticated social science models. The result was that the Soviet Union's historical specificity as a Communist Party–state was increasingly blurred under a vocabulary that spoke in universal political and social terms. And this process was furthered by a good dose of ignorant innocence in the West about actual Soviet conditions.

By the 1970s, this "revisionist" perspective had produced a vast literature that sought to ground the Soviet regime in the dynamics of Soviet society, and which subordinated politics and ideology to social and economic factors in explaining the system's operation. This revisionism produced no single dominant model; rather, new models came on the scene as thick and perishable as autumn leaves, from the leadership conflicts approach (Kremlinology), to Sovietism as neotraditionalism (in Weber's sense of the traditional), to corporatism, to the view of Brezhnevism as welfare-state authoritarianism. But there were three approaches, characterized by three key words—development, authoritarianism, pluralism—that proved more durable than all the rest.

The first of these was in fact the political equivalent of the GNP model. Its classic statement was given by Richard Löwenthal in "Development vs. Utopia in Communist Policy" published in 1970.[3] Löwenthal began with the totalitarian model, which he combined with the newer perspective of modernization theory, which in turn drew both on Max Weber and on structural functionalism as applied to backward or traditional societies. Thus, for him, Communism was a particular form of modernization, or "a special type of politically forced development" founded on Marxist-Leninist ideology. Yet, totalitarian policies inevitably led to unintended consequences. Thus, under Khrushchev, Sovietism's "last utopian," the ideological goal of "building socialism" gave way to the mundane pursuit of economic development as an end in itself. One conclusion drawn by others from this mode of argument was that Soviet development, as measured by an allegedly expanding GNP, could serve as a model for more backward Third World countries, from Cuba, to India, to Vietnam—an opinion with which the rulers of those countries concurred. Another conclusion was that since economic development was the royal road to modernity everywhere, the Soviet Union itself was well on its way to "converging" with the fully developed First World. And so Sovietism was fitted into a universal pattern of progress.

The second of the political science insights need not be associated with any one name or book, because it was diffused throughout the field: this was the contention that although Sovietism may have been totalitarian under Stalin, it had mellowed into ordinary "authoritarianism" under his successors. Thus, Communism was at the same time reformable and intrinsically different from Fascism. Again, there is factual basis for a distinction between Stalinism and the more decayed regime of his successors, as everyone who lived under Sovietism knew well. But this is not the same as holding that the quantitative decline in terror equaled a qualitative transformation of the system; or that reform Communism could eventuate in genuine democracy without a radical break.

And the reform Communism of *perestroyka* did, in fact, end last August in a rupture. There was no evolutionary "transition to democracy" of the sort that Juan Linz and others have so effectively analyzed in Latin America and Spain. Indeed, the intrinsic irreformability of Communism is the point of Jeane Kirkpatrick's famous—and for some, infamous—distinction of the late 1970's between totalitarian and authoritarian regimes. Her contention was not that totalitarian regimes could never change at all—this is a caricature of her position—but that they could not transform themselves into democracies, whereas merely authoritarian regimes could, as in fact occurred in Spain.

The final conceptual innovation of post-Stalin political science was that if Sovietism was to be understood as "developmental authoritarianism," then its political mode of operation must be "institutional pluralism," a derivative of "interest group" theory. The most notable proponent of this approach was Jerry Hough. Its effect was to present the Soviet Union as just another multipolar polity, in much the same way that the GNP model made Sovietism out to be simply another species of a universal, modern economy. This view received its culminating expression in Hough's *How the Soviet Union Is Governed*, published in 1979, which symbolically annulled the *summa* of the totalitarian approach, Merle Fainsod's *How Russia Is Ruled*, which was first published in 1953. And so with the political system, as with the economy, we were promised a pot of convergence at the end of the Soviet rainbow. But, again, in historical fact things did not work out this way. A true pluralism of institutions—from the factories, to the Academy of Sciences, to the local soviets—did not emerge until the superinstitution of the Party-state, or the "center" as it came to be called, was abolished.

HISTORY

And what, finally, of the mother discipline of the social sciences—history? Well, history offers us more of the same, for the oldest social discipline had been thoroughly modernized in the behavioral era by the new social sciences. Yet, historical writing was still ordered in a temporal sequence, as research advanced after World War II from 1917 to the Stalin era; at the same time, this progression fused with the familiar methodological progression from the totalitarian to the revisionist perspective. So history came to sum up the whole "normalization" of Sovietism in Western scholarship.

In the years after World War II, the Western approach to Soviet history was overwhelmingly political and ideological. The paradigmatic work of the day was Leonard Schapiro's *The Origins of the Communist Autocracy*, published in 1955, which portrayed a Soviet regime already under Lenin as aiming at the elimination of all rival loci of power and the total concentration of this power in the hands of the party, themes later extended in time by his *History of the Communist Party of the Soviet Union* in 1959. And this view of the Soviet Union as a totalitarian monolith paralleled that of its classical formulation in Fainsod's *How Russia Is Ruled*.

But even Schapiro's great adversary, E. H. Carr, who was favorably inclined to the Soviet experiment, gave an essentially political explanation of Bolshevism. Nor did he make any bones about its being a tough autocracy, on the grounds that toughness was necessary to socialism's survival.[4] And Carr's ally in Sovietophilia, the Trotskyite Isaac Deutscher, also gave a political interpretation of his subject, though placing a significantly greater emphasis on ideology than did Carr.[5] It should by pointed out that both these authors had their greatest impact at the height of the cold war, when the totalitarian model supposedly ruled the field.

The revolution in Soviet historical studies came in 1964 in an article in the *Slavic Review* by Leopold Haimson, an article whose mention ever since has invariably, and justifiably, been preceded by the adjective "seminal." At the time it appeared, the prevailing view of 1917 was that the Revolution was a cataclysm produced by the impact of World War I on the fragile political and economic structures of Imperial Russia, which until then, had been evolving toward a Western-style constitutional order.

Haimson, however, argued that the Revolution had to be understood as the product of a dual "polarization" in Russian life—the one between the state and society, and the other between the workers and the bourgeoisie. He argued further that this process had already reached a decisive phase by the summer of 1914. By implication, therefore, October was no "accident" due to war but the logical working out of Russia's social processes, or of what the Russians call *zakonomernost* and what German Hegelo-Marxists call *Gesetzmässigkeit.*[6]

In the same way that the classic Russian novel (in Dostoyevsky's famous phrase) emerged from Gogol's *The Overcoat*, so subsequent American social history writing on Sovietism emerged from Haimson's hardly less seminal endeavor. This tradition of social history may be characterized, in its basic thrust if not necessarily in its empirical elaborations, as neo-Menshevik. Or, more precisely, it is in the intellectual lineage of Left, or internationalist, Menshevism as represented by Julius Martov,* who indeed was the originator of the polarization thesis. In the neo-Menshevik view, Bolshevism, for all its excesses, was a genuine workers' movement, and therefore the Soviet state was authentically socialist, though deformed by the later excesses of Stalinism. Sovietism, in consequence, possessed the capacity for self-reform, so as to yield what the Czechs and Slovaks in 1968 called "socialism with a human face." Given this usually unstated yet constantly lurking postulate, most Western historiography about Soviet Russia, through all its empirical permutations, has in fact lent support to the idea of Communism's eventual transformation into some kind of social democracy.

This enterprise of the historical rehabilitation of Sovietism unfolded in four basic phases. The first was characterized by a wave of studies on 1917 designed to show that October was not a coup d'état, as the totalitarian school held, but a genuine workers' revolution, and that the Bolshevik party was no monolith commanded from above, but an open, "demo-

---

* Julius Martov, along with such figures as Lenin, Trotsky, and Plekhanov, was a member of the Social Democratic Labour Party. At the second Congress of the Party in 1903, a dispute between Martov and Lenin split the Party into two factions: the followers of Martov became the Mensheviks and those of Lenin the Bolsheviks. Along with Kautsky and Rosa Luxemburg, Martov was one of the great Marxist critics of the Bolshevik Revolution in its immediate aftermath.

cratic" entity driven by radical impulses from below.[7] Although there is much in this view that is true with respect to 1917 itself, and with respect to workers only, it totally neglects the rest of society, the extraordinary political conditions created by the war, and the long-term ideocratic purposes of the party, which were quite incompatible with any democratic sharing of, or alternation in, power with other groups. Yet, these factors were largely ignored, and research concentrated on establishing the proletarian legitimacy of October, since this was necessary to give legitimacy to Soviet history as a whole.

The second phase of the neo-Menshevik enterprise was characterized by the argument that the true harvest of October was not War Communism, but the NEP* of Lenin's last two years as this was developed by Nikolai Bukharin until 1929. And, indeed, an economic policy along the lines of the NEP had been the Menshevik program to save the socialist fruits of the Revolution in the 1920s. The argument went that if only the NEP had not been brutally interrupted by Stalin, Russia would have "grown into" socialism, conceived of as a semi-market, quasi-mixed economy. Again, there is minimal empirical plausibility to this characterization of the 1920s, but this is achieved only at the cost of ignoring, not only the persisting hegemony of the party over the economy, but the Communists' ambition to socialize, in more or less short order, all aspects of life. Nevertheless, the mode for some twenty years has been to idealize the NEP—economic, political, and cultural—as the golden age of Sovietism, with the implication that some future reform was destined to return successfully to this source.[8]

The third phase of social-history revisionism of the totalitarian model went beyond neo-Menshevism to what can only be called a soft Stalinism. This approach argued that the first five-year plan took its impetus from below in the form of a "cultural revolution" of working-class and party activists. It resulted in a great upward social mobility, or *vydvizheniye*, of these worker-activists into managerial and party posts, a development that eventually furnished the cadres of the "Brezhnev generation." Such a process of upward mobility would obviously be recognized by any Westerner as democratic social promotion. And, in fact, this *vydvizheniye* did

---

* Lenin's New Economic Policy was a partial retreat from the full collectivism initially enforced during the civil war.

occur on a massive scale. But this is hardly all that occurred in Stalin's revolution, which, moreover, clearly came from above. Almost completely neglected in this perspective are collectivization and the purges; indeed, the latter are minimized with the remark that their victims were in the "low hundreds of thousands." This partial rehabilitation of the Stalinist record is most prominently associated with the name of Sheila Fitzpatrick, and it obviously corresponds to the positive evaluation of mature Soviet-ism given in political science by Jerry Hough.[9]

But matters did not stop with this, and there occurred a fourth phase of revisionism that did not hesitate to rehabilitate the rest of Stalin's record. His collectivization has been portrayed as being, in significant measure, the product of worker enthusiasm for the building of socialism. And his purges have been presented as the result of a struggle by the "cen-ter" to bring the quasi-anarchic "periphery" under control, a process in which Stalin allegedly played a moderating role. It has also been argued that the number of victims is not a subject for proper scientific investiga-tion since contemporary, that is, official, sources are silent on the matter.[10] Proper social science method could hardly obfuscate Soviet reality more thoroughly.

With this oblique sanitization of high Stalinism, the process of revi-sionism reaches a kind of culmination: each phase of Soviet development from October through the final building of socialism in the 1930s has been given a purposeful cast; the overall process, if not every detail, adds up to achievement and success. To be sure, those who hold to Bukharin's NEP vehemently reject the efforts of the defenders of cultural revolution as excessive, and as aberrant to the truth as Stalinism itself was to true Leninism. Nonetheless, both are working in the same social reductionist mode, and the result in both cases is to judge the Soviet experiment to be, on the whole, reformable. Both are linked, moreover, by the fact that the twenty-five years of Stalinism are too central a piece of Soviet history to be written off as an "aberration" lacking a proper "social base." Thus, that bolder revisionism oriented to the 1930's really develops logically out of the more cautious neo-Menshevism, and brings out more clearly the fail-ings of the whole revisionist enterprise. And these failings are that neither Leninism nor Stalinism can plausibly be derived from any class or social base. The Soviet regime determines, and is not determined by, the social process.

And so, by the mid-1980s and the onset of *perestroyka*, revisionist historical writing had spelled out period by period, and in concrete terms, the basically positive evaluation of Sovietism given in different ways by economics, political science, and sociology. And the implied conclusion of this whole interdisciplinary joint venture was that a mature Communism, since it had grown into an advanced industrial urbanized superpower, was ready for a liberalizing "reform" that would make of Russia a wholly "modern" society. So, Gorbachev's *perestroyka* was received by most Sovietologists with enthusiasm, and was happily processed through a panoply of predictive models for portents of success. But as has already been noted, *perestroyka* did not rejuvenate Communism; it killed it. So perhaps we should look to the East for insights and intuitions, if not for outright models, to help us restructure our ailing discipline.

THE EASTERN PERSPECTIVE

In the East, we observe the exact opposite of the Western development, Until well into *perestroyka*, the official Eastern evaluation of Sovietism was the Marxist-Leninist assertion that the system represented "really existing," or "developed," socialism. But in the 1970s, as the system began to decay in eastern Europe, dissident thinkers took up the term totalitarianism. To be sure, these thinkers also adopted some Western social science perspectives; but they almost always subordinated these concepts to the overarching totalitarian concept. By 1988, with *glasnost*, this term came out in the open in the Soviet Union; by 1990, even Gorbachev himself was using it; and by 1991, Yeltsin's government made anti-Communism and the "exit from totalitarianism" its declared policy. Faced with this overwhelming consensus of Eastern opinion about the nature of the system, Western Sovietology will in time have to adapt.

Under early *perestroyka*, down to 1989, Western neo-Menshevik revisionism was an acceptable Sovietological position in both East and West. Indeed, Gorbachev's policy represented a kind of neo-NEP; selections from Bukharin were republished, and Stephen Cohen's work on Bukharin* was

---

* *Bukharin and the Bolshevik Revolution* (Oxford: Oxford University Press, 1980) was first published in English in 1971.

translated. Even the bolder Western eulogists of the Soviet 1930s could be useful in this context, and the whole spectrum of American revisionists gave lectures at Yury Afanasyev's Archival Historical Institute. But this period has passed. Vaclav Klaus, the Czechoslovakian minister of finance, has taken to declaring that now "the greatest danger in the East is ideological infiltration from the West." So, to continue to do business with the East, and perhaps even to make a contribution to its "exit from totalitarianism," Western Sovietology will have to enter into an intellectual joint venture with post-Soviet democrats, preferably as their junior partners. Indeed, the Institute for East-West Security Studies has already done this for eastern Europe at Štiřin Castle in Bohemia—a similar venture will no doubt soon follow for Russia and other former Soviet republics.

What is the view of totalitarianism that has developed in the former Communist countries over the past fifteen years? First of all, it is not a model in the social scientific sense. Rather, it is a concept, general and flexible, yet also reasonably precise in its essential points. This concept is viewed simply as the reflection of a fact of life, indeed of the basic fact of life since October 1917. Moreover, this concept is not a recapitulation or simple endorsement of Arendt, or Friedrich and Brzezinski, or Fainsod, though it does build on their work. The model of totalitarianism of Friedrich and Brzezinski tended to be static and abstract, and it is this version that seems to have become fixed as the totalitarian model per se. But the approaches of Arendt and Fainsod were quite historical, and thus were closer to the current eastern European one, which is both historical and dynamic, deriving as it does from the changing experience of totalitarianism in its decline and decay. This model is not set forth or systematized in any classic treatise or formal work of social science. Rather, it is to be found in the imaginative, polemical, and scholarly writings of such eastern Europeans as Leszek Kolakowski, Adam Michnik, and Tadeusz Konwicki, in Poland; Václav Havel in Czechoslovakia; János Kis and János Kornai in Hungary; and in the writings of such Russians as Aleksandr Solzhenitsyn, Andrey Sakharov, Abram Tertz (Andrei Siniaysky), and Aleksandr Zinoviev. It also appears in the writings of such Russian social scientists as Andranik Migranyan, Aleksandr Tsipko, and Igor Klyamkin, and of historians such as Sergey Kuleshov or Vyacheslav Shostakovsky.

The main points of this concept need not be codified or hypostatized as a model, but they may be conveniently summarized as follows. First,

Communist totalitarianism is not a variation, even a deformed one, of some universal process of modernization. It is historically sui generis, a qualitatively new departure in human affairs. Outsiders have difficulty comprehending it precisely because of its radically new nature. As Alain Besançon put it in the 1970s, when his works were considered classics among dissident Soviet social scientists, the problem in understanding the Soviet Union is that one must "believe the unbelievable." This world is so radically different from the normal world that Besançon could only use the word "surreal" to characterize it.[11]

Second, the fundamental organizational trait of Sovietism is that everything is subordinated to politics, that this politics consists of the "building of socialism," and that this world-historical task is the monopoly of the self-appointed party. Concretely, this means that the state administration, the economy, culture, and even private life are subject to the direct control of the party. This is achieved through a hierarchical directorate of party cells from the top to the bottom of society, an interlocking network of party *nomenklatura* appointments in all key areas, and a constant flow of agitprop to orchestrate the whole. In short, Soviet society is a total, or totalitarian, society, with everything institutionally controlled by the omnipresent Party-state, its plan, and its police. To be sure, at no time, even during the worst years of Stalin, was such total control ever in fact achieved. Nonetheless, such control has been the system's constant aspiration from the beginning of the party's dictatorship, and such a total order is the ideal type of Communism everywhere. In other words, the system has an essence, a logic, or, if you will, a "genetic code," that is always present and acting, however much its empirical and historical accidents may vary from one time and place to another.[12]

But this essence or logic of Communism is in no way static in its concrete manifestations. The system has a history, a life course, with a beginning, a middle, and as we now know, an end. Although its genetic code is a permanent given, this code reveals its potentialities only by stages over time. And the degree to which the system verges upon total control is a function of the historical stage in which it finds itself at any given moment.

Thus, Western critics of the totalitarian model do not have a point at all when they argue that although Sovietism might have been totalitarian under Stalin, it had evolved into a mere authoritarianism under Brezhnev, because the level of terror and the degree of Party-state control had declined. It is of course true that this diminution occurred, and for people who had to live in communist countries, this change was of very great practical importance. Still, these Western critics had mistaken a quantitative change for a qualitative one.

Although its will and muscle had begun to atrophy, the essence or nature of the system remained the same. All functional institutions, from the factory to the schoolhouse, remained subordinated to the Party-state, and "institutional pluralism" under such circumstances remained circumscribed to immediate, functional matters. By the last years of Brezhnev, we were dealing with "totalitarianism with its teeth kicked out," in Adam Michnik's phrase; we were not dealing with a "normal" society, as eastern European dissidents called their ultimate goal. This, indeed, was the meaning of the sharp rupture of 1989 in eastern Europe, and its only somewhat less sharp sequel of 1991 in the Soviet Union. As *la thèse de la revolution* would have it, only after these breaks was it possible to move from reform Communism, however far-reaching, to a genuine exit from the system.

It is necessary to insist on this point, for what ought to be self-evident about the end of Communism is at times disputed in a kind of posthumous prolongation of the revisionist perspective. One of the consequences of *la thèse du complot* and of the minimization of the break of August 1991, is the belief that *perestroyka* was in fact Russia's transition to democracy. The point is made that Gorbachev introduced *glasnost*, parliament, and elections, and that these reforms depended on the Soviet regime's earlier success in industrializing, urbanizing, and educating the country—a position that derives from the corpus of Moshe Lewin's writings, as these are summed up in his *Gorbachev Phenomenon* of 1988. In short, despite all the acknowledged horrors of communist history, the system produced the resources for transforming itself. Thus, Russia's transition to democracy was an evolutionary, not a revolutionary, process.

Although the pre-August developments adduced in this argument are all quite real, the argument itself ignores the fact that the basic components of the system—the party, the plan, the police, and the Union—were not transformed; they were abolished, and in the short span of three months after August. All the things that made Communism what it was had to be destroyed before Russia could embark on the quest for democracy. To argue that this destruction was in reality an evolution is a bit like arguing that because Louis

XVI had summoned the Estates-General, the events of 1789 represented an evolutionary rather than a revolutionary transition from absolutism.

THE SOCIALIST IDEA

But more was involved in the Russian Revolution of 1991 than a change of institutions, however basic; at the heart of the transformation was a change in the defining ethos of life viz., the abandonment of the Idea of Socialism. To understand the significance of this, Aristotle is really more helpful than all the social science of the behavioral age. In the *Politics*, the economy and the polity are viewed as part of ethics. In other words, ethics gives purpose, the final cause, or what would now be called, in functional terms, the value system of a society, that which lends meaning to each of its institutions, and indeed makes it possible for them to function at all. And this ethical purpose must be transcendent to any one of its particular manifestations.

Thus, the essence of the Communist system and the unity of the Soviet experience are defined by a single and supreme task—the "building of socialism." And it is because Western social science has by and large refused to take this ideological aim seriously that Sovietology has failed so woefully to understand its subject. But what is meant in the present instance by the slippery and protean term, socialism?

Basically, two elements are involved. First, there is an ethical goal—the supreme social good is democratic equality among all human beings. Second, there is an instrumental program—since inequalities of wealth inevitably create inequalities of human conditions, the abolition of private property is the great means for achieving democratic equality. This was indeed how Marx defined the essence of the Communist program in his *Manifesto*. But if private property is abolished, its fruit—profit—and the means for realizing profit—the market—must also be abolished. Thus, the moral goal of human equality requires a program of total state control over the economy. At the same time, this coordinated control is deemed to be more rational, and hence more productive, than the selfish profit motive and the "anarchy of the market." And the combination of democratic morality with productive rationality in the socialist aspiration would, in time, provide an extraordinary ethical warrant for using coercion to achieve such unquestionably noble goals.

And coercion did, indeed, prove necessary when it came to realizing this program. In Marxist theory, the logic of history—expressed both in the modern momentum of social democratization and in the constant growth of productive forces—was supposed to produce the transition from capitalism to socialism. In practice, however, the logic of history did not work out this way. The intervention of a special political instrument, the Leninist party, was required to "build socialism." This ideological-cum-political set of circumstances, and not "development" or modernization, represents the key to understanding the Communist system, and the reason why it became totalitarian.

Toward a New T-Model

The Soviet regime began with the October 1917 seizure of power, an act designed to force the hand of history into producing a socialist revolution. When, in the turmoil of the civil war that inevitably ensued, a socialist order did not appear on its own, history had to be forced once again with the militarized economy of War Communism and the first attempts at "planning." But this effort proved more than a society devastated by war could sustain, and so the first attempt at building socialism had to be given up in 1921 for a temporary retreat into the semi-market, semi-private economy of the NEP. In this alternation between a "socialist offensive" and a partial retreat toward a more normal society we have the basic rhythm of the Soviet experience.

The rhythm, however, was hardly regular, for it culminated in one great climax, which was the actual "building of socialism" under Stalin in the 1930s. When, in the late 1920s, the minimal concessions to normality of the NEP began to threaten the party's monopolistic hold over the country, Stalin proceeded to the full implementation of the original program—abolishing private property and the market in both agriculture and industry, subordinating all economic life to the plan, and subjecting the whole of society and of culture to the Party-state and its police. Indeed, by the 1930s, Soviet socialism had effectively annihilated all autonomous forces in the country and thoroughly atomized society. It is in this Stalinist revolution from above that Communism came the closest it ever would to realizing in practice the ideal type of totalitarianism. This was quite close enough, however, to create maximum discomfort for all who lived under it, or for putting beyond cavil the appropriateness of the embattled "T-word." And Stalin's socialism clearly surpassed both Nazism and Fascism in the totality of its control over society, as well as in its staying power.

To be sure, all of this did represent "development," urbanization, and everything else that modernization theory has claimed for Sovietism. But this "modernization" was wholly driven by the political purposes of Communism. Hence, this modernization was rendered sterile. It was capable of imitating and multiplying, on party command, industrial models taken from the West, but as a command structure, it did not have the capacity to innovate and invent on its own. It was a kind of grandiose robot in the service of "building socialism."

It is because of this sterile, robotic quality that Sovietism, after the initial successes of building the system in the 1930s and winning World War II, stagnated and entered into decline under the leadership of Stalin's successors. After the great Stalinist peak, therefore, the basic rhythm of alternation between hard, militant Communism and soft, reform Communism resumed. It did so now, however, in a descending phase of the life-course of the system. In this phase, successive efforts at liberalization gradually eroded the system while seeming to improve it. At the same time, these efforts generated the illusions about the ability of the Communist system to reform itself that for a time made plausible all the various revisionist critiques of the totalitarian model discussed above.

This pattern was first played out in the late 1950s and early 1960s under Khrushchev. It was also during his reign that Sovietology first turned to revisionism. His de-Stalinization seriously destabilized the system, however, and so he was deposed. Under Brezhnev and Mikhail Suslov, Sovietism returned to a soft or routinized Stalinism, that is, a command-administrative partocracy without mass terror and with a now cold ideology. And this stable and stagnant Sovietism was different enough from its grand and terrifying predecessor to pass in the West for an authoritarian, pluralistic system founded on what has quaintly been called an "asymmetrically advantageous social contract" between party and people. But this stagnant system increasingly made the Soviet superpower noncompetitive internationally, and so still another attempt at liberal, reform Communism became necessary to bring forth new elites, to revive energies, and to stimulate innovation. This was the meaning of Gorbachev's *perestroyka*, *glasnost*, and democratization.

In consequence, the whole twenty-five years' accumulation of revisionist, American Sovietology was offered to him as a homage: he was seen as the Second Coming of Bukharin, the maturation of Soviet modernity, the architect of Communism's transition to democracy. But this time, the effort at reform Communism went beyond the point of no return. *Glasnost* made it possible for people to say openly that the system was a failure and a fraud, while democratization made it possible for them to challenge the party's hegemony. So when the apparatus's inevitable attempt to roll back the reform was made in August 1991, it was defeated ignominiously, and the whole system collapsed in three days.

In this manner, the genetic code born of the October overturn of 1917 at last worked itself out fully, that is, to the extinction of the organism. This would not have been the case had the Soviet adventure been simply about development or modernization. But it was about "building socialism." By this is meant integral, full socialism, in the sense of non-capitalism, or suppression of private property and the market. And this is not at all the same as the halfway-house Scandinavian variety of socialism, which preserves the market and private property yet taxes them maximally to finance a super welfare state.

But integral socialism is ultimately an impossible and self-destructive venture. For the moral goal of democratic equality does not result from the instrumental program of the "statization" of all property; quite the contrary, the result is total state tyranny. Nor do greater economic rationality and material abundance result from the suppression of the market in favor of the command-administrative plan. Again, quite to the contrary, the result, after an initial phase of crash growth, is stagnation, obsolescence, and ultimately widespread penury. In the face of such fatal internal contradictions the system can be held together, in its ascending phase, only so long as the socialist Myth is credible, that is, while its realization still lies in the future. Once socialism has been built, however, the Myth is transformed by the results it has produced into the Lie. This transformation occurred at the peak of socialist development under Stalin in the 1930s, and from that time until his death, institutionalized terror became necessary to preserve the "conquests of socialism." But this regimen undermined the system's performance, and so his successors attenuated it in an alternation of reform and retrenchment that sent the system into its long descending phase. Thus, after Stalin, it was only a question of time before the internal contradictions of the impossible enterprise of "building socialism" worked themselves out in the total discrediting, and hence the brusque abandonment, of the system.

In short, there is no such thing as socialism, and the Soviet Union has built it. When a disastrously noncompetitive performance at last made this paradox apparent, the whole institutionalized fantasy of "really existing socialism" vanished into thin air, the "surreality" of Soviet life suddenly ceased, and Russia became a "normal" country once again. But it was a country now existing amid the rubble of its abortive "development." It is under these catastrophic conditions that it must begin its transition to true "modernity," that it must transform the fish soup of spent socialism back into a pluralistic market aquarium.

A POSITIVE NOTE

And what of the fish soup of American Sovietology? First of all, a serious stock-taking is clearly in order. Now that we know how the dynamics of Sovietism worked out, we will have to go back and do our economic, social, and historical calculations all over again, reevaluating each period of the Soviet performance from October and the NEP to *perestroyka* itself. And a similar stock-taking of the social sciences in general is also in order, for the failure of Sovietology, perhaps the greatest case study of the behavioral age, is also a failure of the social sciences per se.

Nor is this effort at correction just an academic matter; the misjudgments of Sovietology have had major practical consequences. For example, the overestimation of the Soviet economy has obviously affected Western defense policy and hence also our budget and domestic policies. There is even reason to believe that the Soviets took the CIA's estimates so seriously that they concluded they had greater resources to devote to the military than was in fact within the possibilities of their economy. Indeed, this misjudgment could be a contributory reason for their collapse. Another Western input into Soviet policy is, as we now know, that Aleksandr Yakovlev, the theoretician of *perestroyka*, when he was director of the social science think-tank IMEMO, assigned to his researchers the work of John K. Galbraith on post-industrial societies, that of Wassily Leontiev on growth, and that of Daniel Bell on the end of ideology as arguments that a mature Soviet society was ready for "*konvergentsiya*." Still another example is the fate of Löwenthal's thesis that Communism meant, in fact, development: this led West German Social Democrats to court and coddle the East German Communists in the hope of producing gradual reform, but the result was simply to prop up the East German order. The governing West German Christian Democrats largely concurred in the Socialists' illusion, with the result that both were totally unprepared when East Germany collapsed. Along similar lines, in the spring of 1991, a number professors at the Harvard Kennedy School of Government, with the benediction of the *New York Times* editorial page, proposed to give a Marshall Plan of some US$30 billion a year for five years, to be called a "Grand Bargain," to the Soviet government of Valentin Pavlov that was then preparing its August coup to save the system.

Nonetheless, the task of Sovietology's reform should be far easier than that of the Soviet Union itself. We now have full access to Russian society, and we will soon have comparable access to all its vital data. We no longer have to submit to the pretext, or to the fantasy, that special Soviet forms and institutions have a value and a future that we must respect. We are now dealing with something that is "just another society," a country that, if not wholly comparable to the West, is of a kindred genus with other urban industrial societies. A number of our models or conceptual schemes based on the experience of the West or the Third World—development, modernization, transition to democracy, etc—are more or less relevant to present former Soviet circumstances. But they are relevant only on the condition that we recognize that these circumstances are still haunted by their Soviet past, by an experience that is radically and surreally different from our own world. And for this unique experience, a historical and dynamic totalitarian model is the only one that is appropriate. With this perspective as a base and a background, our social science techniques, whether in economics, political science, sociology, or history, can at last bear fruit in a manner proportionate to the effort invested in developing them. They can no doubt also aid our Eastern colleagues in effecting the "return to Europe" to which they have aspired since the onset of *perestroyka*.

Sovietology and Communist studies need not go the way of the Soviet Union and Communism into oblivion. For some decades to come, there will be a vast and valid field of post-Soviet, post-Communist studies, applicable from the Caribbean to the China seas, in lands where a third of the human species has for various periods in time been subjected to the Marxist-Leninist fantasy. And this shared calamitous experience will continue to mold their relations with the rest of the world for as long as it will take them to become integrated, at last, into a genuine modernity.

II
NATURE

7

The Future of Secular Religions[*]
(1944)

Raymond Aron

I

"Men will form a society whose goal will be to take from life all it has to give, but solely for the sake of the happiness and contentment of earthly existence. Man will identify himself with God and be filled with divine and Titanic pride. Sovereign lord of nature through knowledge and his own will, man will constantly experience such great satisfaction that it will replace all hopes of happiness hereafter." Thus spoke the Devil to Ivan Karamazov. This was the very definition of temptation: to place the fulfillment of man's vocation in this life is to be guilty of the worst impiety—that of disregarding everything outside the sphere of earthly existence. Lucien Laberthonnière[**] detected the origin of this impiety in Cartesianism: Descartes, good Catholic though he was, cared more about becoming a "master and possessor of nature" than about meditating on eternal life. Socialism, which aims at what the Devil suggests, carries to its logical conclusion this secularization of human thought and ambition. It sees a humanity reconciled with itself and victorious over inequality and injustice, but this reconciliation is clearly dependent on a previous victory

---

[*] Originally published in London in *La France libre*, a monthly review founded in 1940 and edited by Aron.

[**] Lucien Laberthonnière (1860–1932) was a French Catholic priest and philosopher whose books include *Essais de philosophie religieuse* (1903).

over nature. The resources of the planet need to be sufficiently exploited to allow men to dream of an egalitarian, peaceable, classless society.

In this sense, socialism is essentially against religion. In the grandiose expectations of the young Marx, it was to put an end to "religious alien-ations."* Once man is master of his own actions, Marx theorized, he would find complete fulfillment within the real community and no longer seek substitutes for his disappointed hopes in transcendental images.

And yet, insofar as socialism is an antireligion, it is also a religion. It denies the existence of an afterlife, but it brings back to earth certain hopes that, in the past, were inspired by transcendental beliefs alone. I propose to use the term *secular religions* to designate doctrines that, in the souls of our contemporaries, take the place of the faith that is no more, placing the salvation of mankind in this world, in the more or less distant future, and in the form of a social order yet to be invented.

It will, of course, be asked whether it is permissible to use the expres-sion *secular religion* for a phenomenon that excludes the transcendent, or at least sacred, object to which prayer and love have traditionally been addressed. I do not deny that from a Christian point of view, or indeed that of anyone who defines religion by the essential *intentionality* of the feeling it inspires, secular religions seem to have little claim to be so called: at most they might be said to be substitutes for or caricatures of the real thing. But the use of the term can be justified in a number of ways. A psychologist or sociologist might say: "Being religious is not simply a matter of worshiping a divinity; it can also mean putting all the resources of one's mind, all the obedience of one's will, and all the ardors of one's fanaticism at the service of a cause, or making something the end and object of one's feelings and actions." It is a fact that the secular reli-gions are capable of converting souls to the same kinds of devotion, the same kinds of intransigence, and the same unconditional fervor as ever the traditional religious beliefs did in the days of their most universal and authoritarian influence.

This argument alone would not get us far. We could end up using the term *religion* for any doctrine that arouses strong passions and, by the same token, awakens intolerance and the other violent concomitants of faith. But

---

* See in particular Marx's "On the Jewish Question" which can be found in *The Marx-Engels Reader*, Robert Tucker ed. (New York: W. W. Norton & Company, 1978).

it seems to me that some of the doctrines current today really do deserve to be called secular religions in a more precise sense of the phrase.

Such doctrines set up an ultimate and quasi-sacred goal and define good and evil in relation to this ideal. When a movement like the Deutsche Glaubens Bewegung* proclaims, "Everything that is useful to Hitler and the German community is good; everything that is harmful to them is bad," it is simply giving brutally crude expression to the common foundation of all secular religions and the origin of their ruthless Machiavellianism. The followers of these religions of collective salvation know of nothing—not even the Ten Commandments, not even the rules of the catechism or of any formal ethic—that is superior in dignity or authority to the aims of their own movement. That being so, they relate everything—men and things, thoughts and deeds—to that ultimate end, and utility in terms of that end is the measure of all values, even spiritual ones. Partisans of such religions will without any qualms of conscience make use of any means, however horrible, because nothing can prevent the means from being sanctified by the end. In other words, if the job of religion is to set out the lofty values that give human existence its direction, how can we deny that the political doctrines of our own day are essentially religious in character?

Even in their structure these ideologies reproduce some of the typical features of the old dogmas. They give an overall interpretation of the world (the historical world, at least). They explain the meaning of the catastrophes suffered by wretched humanity and vouchsafe a glimpse of some distant outcome to these tragic ordeals. In the present fraternity of the party they offer a foretaste of what the human community of the future will be like, once it is saved. They demand sacrifices that bring immediate rewards; they rescue the individual from the loneliness of crowds without souls and life without hope.

The Religion of Hyper Rationalism

The reign of socialism, as described in Marx's juvenilia, is the reign of free men who are equals and brothers: this ideal sounds fundamentally

---

* Deutsche Glaubens Bewegung or The German Christians were a Protestant movement which attached itself to the Nazi party and had doctrinal affinities with Nazi ideas of racial purity.

very close to the Christian one. The very idea, co-opted by socialism, of man being liberated over the course of history derives from progressivist philosophy, itself a secularization of the Christian vision of mankind on the march toward the millennium. But where Condorcet* imagined a continuous movement toward more knowledge and higher civilization, Marxism sees a dialectic—in this case, a chain of contrasting social regimes succeeding one another by means of violent transitions, or revolutions. By negating capitalism, man will overcome the separateness and slavery to which he has been condemned by a system based on private property.

Revolution, then, the crucial element in what might be called socialist eschatology, is not merely a social upheaval, the replacement of one regime by another. It has a supra-political value in that it marks the leap from necessity to liberty. Salvation lies beyond this apocalyptic catastrophe, this Promethean act by which humanity will break its chains and enter again, so to speak, into possession of itself. But capitalism is supposed to lead by spontaneous evolution to this event, initiating a new era. Anything that infringes on this teaching, any interpretation of capitalist development that compromises the directness or necessity of this march toward liberating collapse, strikes the dogma itself at its most sensitive point. Thus Eduard Bernstein's[†] reformism aroused passionate debates and was finally condemned by a congress of the Social Democrat Party (which some Socialist worthies themselves compared to the councils that established Catholic dogmas). His reformist views were treated much more like a heresy than a scientific opinion, or at least they constituted a scientific opinion (concerning the intensifying or weakening of class conflicts and the disappearance or survival of small property) that assumed the character of a heresy because they deviated from the object of Socialist orthodoxy, a certain conception of historical evolution itself. Socialism has gone on

---

* Marie-Jean-Antoine-Nicolas de Caritat, marquis de Condorcet (1743–1794) was a French philosopher who promoted the idea progress or the perfectibility of mankind in his *Sketch for a Historical Picture of the Progress of the Human Mind* (1795).

† Eduard Bernstein (1850–1932) is known as the father of "revisionism," a broad grouping whose adherents came to doubt Marxist premises like the inevitability of the collapse of capitalism. He dissented from revolutionary socialists who advocated the violent overthrow of liberal governments, instead promoting a gradualist reform agenda to move governments toward socialism.

producing rival sects that, while appealing to the same prophet and the same sacred book, fiercely excommunicate one another.

It may be objected that these analogies underestimate the scientific character of Marxist socialism. And no one thinks of denying the scientific nature of many of the propositions included in the teachings. Historical materialism, in the brilliantly simplified form it is given in the *Communist Manifesto*, marks a great turning point in the development of sociological theory. Even people who do not accept the economic ideas in *Das Kapital* recognize it as a monument of constructive analysis.

And yet there can scarcely be any doubt that the influence of *Das Kapital* is largely independent of the truth or falseness of the theories it contains. These abstract theories, thoroughly comprehensible only to specialists, have influenced hundreds of thousands of people who are convinced they are accurate solely because they confirmed, with apparently conclusive arguments, the feelings that inspired the socialist masses: moral condemnation of the salaried class; the hope that capitalism, through the crises it regularly engenders, tends naturally toward its own destruction; and so on. Whatever scientific merit we may grant Marxist theories of labor and wages, their greatest effect has been as a demonstration of value judgments, a confirmation of the success the future will accord to people's wills. One might say they have been the intelligence of socialist faith: *Fides quaerens intellectum.**

Almost the same can be said of historical materialism. The notion that societies depend on the means and relations of production has become part of the common consciousness. Even non-Marxists have invariably learned something from it. But if on the one hand it is easy to explain many phenomena in terms of economic data (and even so, we may wonder what exactly is meant by the economic factor—whether it entails the technical instruments or the social relationships of production), on the other, this explanation becomes more and more indirect, uncertain, and even arbitrary as one proceeds from material organization to political regime and then to the intellectual plane. To reduce everything to infrastructure, or to state dogmatically that a certain cause is the ultimate cause, is, scientifically speaking, completely arbitrary. Once we admit that between the different causes there is interaction, by what right and in what sense

---

* *Fides quaerens intellectum.* Faith seeking understanding.

can we say that one cause is the ultimate one? The truth is that the choice of an ultimate cause depends on the observer's intentions. A Marxist is interested primarily in the economic system, which he is determined to change. Because, according to him, this change will bring about a complete upheaval in human existence, it suits him to see it as the final cause in social evolution. The object of even the exaggerations of historical materialism is to encourage the necessary belief that economic revolution will ipso facto bring with it total revolution.

This conviction lies at the heart of Marxism. It is what lends the ideology its conquering momentum and makes its propaganda so powerful. It creates the crucial confusion between what is necessary and what is desirable; between historical evolution, described as inevitable, and values adopted naturally and unconsciously. Marxism claims to be scientific and to reflect the real changes taking place in society, whereas Utopian socialisms merely wish for an imaginary just order that contrasts with the injustice and disorder that actually exist. But might it not really be more scientific to recognize that there is a fundamental difference between facts and desires, instead of setting them in a vast context that suggests that they are the same? True, prophecies about the gradual decline of capitalism and the advent of a collectivist economy do fall within the sphere of scientific criticism. Such predictions, however uncertain, do not essentially go beyond the bounds of legitimate speculation. It was a useful hypothesis to conjure up the image of capitalism sliding toward death as it developed and grew more concentrated. But the implicit assertion that the postcapitalist economy would give birth to a new, egalitarian human order transcends knowledge and derives from an act of faith. I realize that Marxism, taken literally, admits it does not know what society will emerge after the private ownership of the instruments of production is abolished. But would a single Socialist passionately desire the end of capitalism if all Socialists did not believe in their hearts that the exploitation of man by man would vanish with it?

But the question of whether political and intellectual liberalism is compatible with a planned economy—the central theme of current controversies calls at least for some sort of demonstration. In other words, the very idea that gives socialism its ability to expand—the identification of what is desirable with what is necessary—far from being self-evident, is now subject to the harsh test of the totalitarian experiments rather than to mere theoretical analysis. Socialist criticism, no matter how keen it is nor how pertinent it may appear when it denounces the present chaos, has not rediscovered the secret source of its former power: the optimistic vision of a future regime that will be both the heir of the present system and its antithesis.

Where did it come from, the anticipation of a radiant future that was to succeed capitalist exploitation? It came from a boundless confidence in man and in human reason. In the eyes of the young Marx, private property, together with the social organization that went with it, was a legacy from the past, an irrationality that it was man's duty to judge and reform. Private property condemns individuals to separateness: each one is imprisoned inside his own sphere, communicating with others only through the medium of the market for which they all labor, and which, free of any conscious control, tyrannizes over them all and makes them the slaves of their own actions. If this fundamental cause of alienation were removed, man, restored to himself, would emerge straight into freedom. To translate into simple terms what lay behind this belief: humankind, without God or master and ruling itself by reason, is bound to become peaceable and fulfilled.

The same rationalism can be detected in the notion of historical evolution. Although Marxism no longer explicitly contains the "ruse of reason" that uses human passions to achieve its own ends, nonetheless there is a certain significance to the way events unfold. This meaning may emerge from the chaos of individual actions and not be intended by anyone, but ultimately the overall, irreversible movement of capitalism toward catastrophe seems to have a kind of supra-individual rationality. Reason wins out over time, just as, via revolution, it will win out in the organization of collective existence.

This rationalism has subsequently been given a less Hegelian and more positivist expression. The popularity of the natural sciences has to some degree repressed that kind of historical philosophy. But what lies behind it has not changed.

Of all secular religions, socialism has been and remains the most rationalistic. It has set out in intellectual terms the faith it fosters; rather than exploiting blind passion it throws light on legitimate revolt; and it sees salvation as the outcome of an intelligible history and of the considered will of human beings who are equipped with knowledge and masters of nature.

The Conflicts between Secular Religions

Socialism's period of greatest expansion came at the beginning of the twentieth century. It was the only, or almost the only, movement that attracted passions without an object. In a world apparently devoted to wealth, comfort, and the spirit of profit, it embodied, despite its materialist philosophy, a principle of spiritual renewal. It had millions of followers all over the world, an imposing mass that gave an impression of strength. The overall unity it managed to preserve in spite of fierce doctrinal quarrels; the quality of its leaders; the enthusiasm of its rank and file—all denoted a movement of liberation destined to build the future.

At the same time, socialism did not conjure up the sense of impending upheaval but maintained a certain balance between revolutionary ambition and a desire for immediate reforms and between a sense of mission, which separated it from the social milieu, and the inevitable incorporation of the working class into its program. The bourgeois world was not driven by fear to give extremist answers to a threatening extremism. The German Social Democrat Party, the pride and model of the International, found a place, despite its dogmatic orthodoxy, inside the Kaiser's Reich.

The 1914 war dealt the socialist religion a heavy blow, showing that, despite words and appearances, when it came to a choice, country easily came before party. Patriotism swept through the crowds, even those that had recently proclaimed their indifference to their fatherland and their exclusive devotion to the workers' International. But above all, the war and the Russian Revolution brought about a proliferation of secular religions, a division of the socialist "church" into rival parties, and the emergence of virulent antisocial religions that used similar means for completely different ends.

The similarities between the secular religions are as obvious as the differences. Let us work from the outside in, from form to content.

1. If we compare social democracy with National Socialism, the superficial resemblance is clear to any impartial observer. Nazi gatherings used the same methods as Socialist ones, bringing thousands, sometimes tens of thousands, of followers together in vast halls or arenas. The walls are hung with enormous portraits of great men and with simple slogans written in huge letters. Cohorts of uniformed militiamen goose-step to "political" music amid

innumerable flags. (Hitler has never tried to conceal the fact that in matters of mass propaganda, he learned from the Socialists and the Communists.)

When it comes to action, there are obvious differences between the methods used by the humanist, rationalist religion of the Socialists and those employed by the pessimistic, irrationalist religion of the Nazis. All propaganda oscillates between two extremes, one oriented toward education, the other marked by obsession. No one who knows the facts about Germany could be so unfair as to underestimate the moral and social influence of the Social Democrat Party or forget the educational endeavors of the working-class activists and their leaders. Those who experienced it still remember the atmosphere of serious, honest research that characterized the everyday life of the party. The Nazis cared nothing about education—all they thought about was winning over consciences, one might even say unconsciousnesses, spreading their hatreds, and disseminating the slogans that helped create collective obsessions. Both socialism and National Socialism offered their supporters the comfort of a close and fraternal community. But in the case of the Nazis this was a militant, not to say military, order aimed at conquering first the nation and then the world. The church degenerated into a sect, the hope of salvation into a will to power.

2. Nazism, too, has its vision of the world, at least of the historical world. And like all secular religions, it is Manichaean. Out of the confusion of men and things, it identifies two parties, and the struggle between them is supposed to fill the universe; but in the place of the impersonal principles of socialism it puts flesh-and-blood people or groups of people. Socialism was against capitalism (though it recognized its historical necessity and usefulness); Nazism anathematizes plutocrats and Jews. Public enemy number one becomes not a system (for which no one in particular is responsible), but a race, a defenseless minority.

It is easy to explain the Manichaeanism of the secular religions. What need would there be for a savior or a purifier if the world were not doomed to perdition? Moreover, authoritarian parties are born out of and thrive because of the obsessive frenzy they foster. Eager to federate hatreds, convinced that men are linked more by shared hostilities than by shared loves, they are forever showing their supporters new Bastilles to tear down. They have enemies in the plural—Weimar, plutocrats, Communism, Jews—but they have one enemy par excellence that they will never finish slaying. Permanent mobilization, which is what crusades for power tend toward,

105

calls for the constant availability that, with the exception of faith, only preoccupation with a hated adversary can produce.

3. Nazism has a doctrine of salvation as well. It heralds a 1,000-year kingdom called the Third Reich, less distant and less perfect than the reign of socialism but therefore more accessible and, for millions of people, more attractive.

True, the differences are not merely those of degree. They concern first and foremost the replacement of an elite class by an elite race. (The distinction is based on historical vocation: the mission of the proletariat is to bring about the revolution and take over from capitalism; the mission of the Germanic race is to found the Third Reich.) They also concern the nature of the ideal goal. The society dreamed of by the Socialists is open to all men and based on universal law, whereas that of the Nazis is confined to one nation and identified with one race. The dialectic that leads to socialism displays a kind of intrinsic rationality. History as seen by the Hitlerites is dominated by a struggle between the races comparable to that between beasts of prey. The ultimate object has nothing to do with the fulfillment of human destiny; it is more like the victory of one species over another.

No doubt the language and the ideology of the Third Reich have some kind of spiritual resonance. They revive the longing that used to torment the Germans when, deprived in the real world of the unity they aspired to, they had to make up for the mediocrity of their innumerable small states by the grandeur of their dreams. They conjure up a Reich that simultaneously ends their divisions and satisfies the desire for community kindled in them by their political humiliation and their religious fervors. In spite of everything, the chiliastic hope has degenerated into what might be described as a stockbreeder's fantasy.

Primitive though it may seem to us, this religion has met with some resounding successes. It is a fact that Germans all over the world, even when not directly subjected to police or propaganda pressure, have responded en masse to the Führer's call. It is a fact this coarse and simplistic doctrine has found partisans at all levels of German society, and that the intellectuals, even the greatest of them, have flocked in thousands to comment on, defend, and illustrate Hitler's philosophy. It is a fact that Nazi-style socialism, or rather pseudosocialism, has won over millions of people whom orthodox socialism left unmoved.

So why has a national form of socialism, without a doctrine, outdone the Marxist parties? To begin with, rationalism has been more of a hindrance than a help to the socialist religion. By subordinating the realization of a millennial kingdom to a historical dialectic, it tended, willy-nilly, to rule out immediate hopes. In any case, it saddled salvation with terrifying conditions—total upheaval, the reorganization of society under the direction of the proletariat and its representatives—things that millions of men, though outraged by their situation, would not accept and did not even desire. Nazism played on the same hates and loathings that socialism traditionally exploited: it anathematized plutocrats, financiers, and the burden of interest; in short, it carried to its logical conclusion the methods of thought and propaganda, familiar to all revolutionaries, that consist in being *against.*

The divisions between the Marxist parties also did much to favor the purposes of their common enemy. When separated, the Socialists and the Communists lost the advantage of a doctrine that was at once reformist and revolutionary, deterministic and activist. The former ended up relying only on everyday reforms and, in the long term, the notion of a historical dialectic; the latter were concerned solely with direct action and seizing power. The former, taking part in all the institutions of the Weimar Republic, seemed to become bourgeoisified and forgetful of their unique mission; the latter, while seeming to represent revolutionary zeal in its pure form, had to fall in with the decisions of a foreign government and by dint of realistic action were visibly inclined to Machiavellianism—which does not offend the conscience of believers but may repel the undecided.

It might be said that in both its forms socialism was compromised because it was confused with a particular reality—social democracy with the Weimar Republic, Communism with the Republic of the Soviets. Nazism thus gained the privilege of novelty. The Nazi Reich was not only nearer and more accessible than the socialist kingdom: it was also free from the flaws of imperfect incarnation.

In addition to all these reasons we can descry another that is simpler and probably more decisive. As early as 1871, Joseph Ernest Renan[*] noted that the life of the peoples of Europe continually alternated between social and national concerns. In his view, France was then dominated by

---

[*] Joseph Ernest Renan was an influential philosopher and historian of religion in nineteenth-century France.

the social question, Germany by national feeling. He expected these roles eventually to be reversed. Clearly, in our own day, those preoccupations are simultaneous and concurrent. But they occur in a variety of forms. Patriotism—or these days, nationalism—survives ineradicably in the depths of people's souls, but it is often all the stronger for being unexpressed. New enthusiasms are directed toward forthcoming conquests and dreams of the future. Unlike Germany, nations that are permanently unified feel no need to be forever defining themselves. But if in exceptional circumstances, for example in an atmosphere of defeat, nationalism becomes overheated, a social doctrine that is nationalistic by nature is much more persuasive than social doctrines in which the idea of a homeland is merely tangential or incidental. In such circumstances the secular religion, with its hope of earthly salvation, merges with love of nation, the highest loyalty to remain intact in a West riven by doubt. The other secular religions are the victims of their own universalism. Real religions must of course speak to each and every individual, but if nothing is known except this world, and if the audience addressed consists of collectivities, is there any reason why particularism, which after all is easiest, should not win the day?

And so the pros and cons are reversed: the religion of hyper-rationalism is succeeded by the religion of biological impulse. The contrast is seen most clearly in the realm of ideology. The Third Reich accords as much importance as socialism does to administrative and industrial rationalization. But the man leading this religion to victory, the man whom this religion takes as its model, is not a man of reason but a beast of prey, triumphant in the animal struggle for life. "The earthly paradise has become the paradise of beasts."*

—

In the last years of the republic, German "democracy" was reduced to a juxtaposition of competing totalities. The complete control of education, youth, sport, and leisure, so strikingly demonstrated by the Nazi regime, already existed within each of the main parties before 1933. The violence of the quarrels between the great organizations, each armed with its own creed, its own prophet, and its own banners, ultimately made it almost

---

* From George Bernanos, *Lettre aux Anglais* (Rio de Janeiro: Atlantica, 1942), 287.

impossible for the Constitution to function. Above all it gradually made everyone think that such unbearable tension must resolve itself in an abrupt unification: as soon as one or more minorities had the state at their mercy and were ready to misuse their power, there would be no more real democracy. Everything would be reduced to a choice between the tyrannies on offer. Germany exemplified first a plurality of secular religions culminating in the anarchy of war between them all, then the unity of one secular religion completing the conquest and conversion of the whole nation.

But even in the fateful years between 1930 and 1940, these two extreme forms did not cover all the possibilities. Britain, with its good sense and its privileged stability, escaped the secular religions. No political opinion there took on the pervasive fervor of faith. No party adopted the strict internal discipline and the eternal aggressiveness typical of sects. Nothing has so far destroyed or even seriously undermined the self-evidence of the people's moral and religious imperatives, whether personal or universal. Nothing impaired a long-silent patriotism that awoke as fervently as ever when danger dawned.

France, in this respect, was midway between the Weimar Republic and Britain, though closer to the latter, despite appearances. In France, parties and beliefs became virulently dogmatic only in reaction to external conflicts that happened to be both national and religious. The identification of a country with a creed eliminates rivalry between secular beliefs on a national level but exacerbates them on the international plane. The relations of a democratic country with the totalitarian countries becomes the stake in the struggle between parties. And to conceal his purposes, the conqueror encounters little difficulty denouncing any attempt at resistance as ideological warfare. As long as the secular religions are with us, the doors to the temple of Janus will never be closed.

II

The counterrevolutionary religions will collapse in unprecedented catastrophe amid the ruins of a devastated continent. Fascism is ending in a grotesque escapade that discredits it forever. Never before has a Caesar, even a miniature one, outlived himself in a comedy put on against his king and country. It is a harsh lesson. The Italian people, who never fundamentally accepted the imperial myth, will hate their Duce even more vociferously than they acclaimed him on June 12, 1940, in the square in Venice.

The Germans, in contrast, will go on dreaming of their Führer for some time. They will repeat in the depths of their hearts the comment attributed to a young German to whom someone was explaining the inevitability of his country's defeat: "It was a very good idea, though." But nostalgia for the 1,000-year empire will torture the German masses in vain: this time the peace will be based on the Reich's helplessness, not on its acceptance of defeat. After all, it is not a matter of forgetting dreams, but of time. This question has a wider bearing, for the secular religions are symptoms. Will the great upheaval have torn up the roots of the evil?

Are Secular Religions Inevitable?

It is more than half a century since Friedrich Nietzsche uttered the famous phrase on which our present ordeals are a diabolical comment: "God is dead; anything goes."

The spiritual conflicts of our own day attack men's souls more deeply than any of those that have divided Europe since the Renaissance. It is not enough to say that spiritual unity no longer exists: it has become inconceivable. Christian churches have congregations of millions, but the greatest crises of conscience, including the present one, take place outside the sphere of traditional belief. The Christians in Germany have fought for their Führer without their pastors telling them, or even dreaming of telling them, that they were fighting in the unjust cause of conquest by the sword. Moreover, Nietzsche's inversion of values has been morally accepted and put into practice by millions of people. Despite their different origins, secular morality and the catechism have joined together to form spiritual families akin to one another in their very opposition. The young barbarians trained by Hitler belong to another universe. Can we be sure they will ever be eradicated? What miracle could ever restore peace between them and us?

It is true that men can live without believing in an afterlife. For century upon century, the peasants of every civilization have plowed the earth, bent under the yoke of seasons and myths. How many lives, even today, fail to rise above the unconsciously accepted tradition! How many people are fulfilled, without being driven by atheism into a sense of deprivation and failure! But there are also souls to whom the good news has given a hunger that nothing can satisfy except a plenitude comparable to that which was promised. And even if man can manage to live without expecting anything from God, it is doubtful whether he can live without hope. But there are millions of people, imprisoned in dreary jobs, lost in the multitude of cities, who have no other share in a spiritual community but what is offered them by the secular religions. The crowds who acclaim false prophets bear witness to the intensity of the aspirations mounting to an empty heaven. As Bernanos* has said, the tragedy is not that Hitler proclaims or takes himself for a god, but that millions of people are desperate enough to believe him. Any crisis, whether economic or political, that severs the multitudes from their roots will deliver them yet again to the combined temptations of despair and enthusiasm.

At the same time, the secular religions do offer a substitute system of unification. Surprisingly, scientists sometimes discover, as if touched by grace, the virtues of even a watered-down Marxism. Here again it is a matter of an unmet need. When knowledge accumulates ceaselessly but at random, it increases the desire for a system. Charles Maurras† owed his prestige largely to the fact that every morning he added some other example or detail to his doctrine as a whole. Whatever one thinks of Marxist materialism, it is certainly better than the ordinary materialism that served as a philosophy for the physicist before he or she was converted. Even Nazi racism supplies a kind of principle on which to base some sort of philosophy of human existence.

It might be said that these spiritual needs are in a sense created by those who exploit them for their own advantage. But there are times and situations when secular religions seem to fill an abyss into which society might otherwise fall. In short, they introduce a supreme principle of authority when all the others are collapsing.

Today's fashionable formula, according to which the world, in the absence of legitimate powers, is given over to fear and violence, does no

---

* George Bernanos was a French Catholic novelist whose works include *Diary of a Country Priest* (1936).

† Charles Maurras was a French author whose doctrines were the driving force behind Action Française, an influential monarchist and nationalist political movement in the early twentieth century.

more than state a fact. If there is to be social stability, men must agree to obey and recognize that their superiors have the right to command. The reasons for obedience vary according to history and circumstance. Sometimes they are to be found in the depths of the past, in the collective unconscious, inherited from ancient custom; sometimes they are rational and self-evident in terms of a particular technique or function (performed in any given instance by a merely temporary incumbent); sometimes, as in an ideal army, the two kinds of reason coexist and reinforce one another.

Nowadays the traditional legitimacy that sustained monarchies and aristocracies is becoming extinct. In addition, the constitutional forms in which the idea of democratic legitimacy was embodied have lost some of their former prestige. The moral and political ideas that guaranteed them have been undermined by the criticism of counterrevolutionary thinkers and the lessons taught by events. The pessimism of mass psychology has repressed the optimistic notion of a general will. How can we believe that truth or the common good could emerge from free discussion when everywhere we see passions unleashed against one another? Moreover, the mechanisms of democracy have been degraded by the uses to which they have been put, and by the way authoritarian parties have caricatured them. National Socialism gained absolute power by means of repeated elections. Where is the dividing line between plebiscite and election, between votes that are genuine and votes that are rigged?

In France, even before the war, one was struck by the way discipline inside an organization like the Communist Party was much better than that among ordinary citizens or even in the army. Officials at all levels were called *responsables*, reflecting the notion, not confined to the military, that whoever gives orders is the one who assumes responsibility. And the *responsables*, conscious of their position, had no difficulty in winning the trust of the activists. There was none of the ill-humor and continual suspicion that Alain* recommended toward all wielders of power, and that the French readily manifest toward their rulers.

Since 1940 we French have been through the tragic experience of seeing first the disintegration and then the restoration of our state. When France collapsed under the shock of Hitler's war machine, when the armistice left us with a government that was "half-prisoner," whose words and

---

* Émil Chartier (1868–1951), known as Alain, was a French philosopher and pacifist.

decisions might at any moment betray the country and serve the enemy, people clung on all sides to flags, standards, and standard-bearers. One saw the most extreme reactions. Some people, in despair because of their love for their country, became suspicious of everything and everybody and no longer believed in or obeyed anything but their consciences. Others, though often motivated by the same fundamental feelings, obeyed all the more implicitly the orders of their superiors because their authority was so flimsy they feared a social vacuum. Here and there some practically isolated pockets of traditional order survived. For a few months, as Spengler* prophesied, armies were known by the names of their generals, as if the ultimate loyalty, amid the collapse of all other values, was fidelity to one person. This phenomenon is more natural than may appear. The "depersonalization" of the state comes about at the end of a long process of evolution: before a state can be recreated it has to pass once again through the original stage, when power was embodied in one man.

The situation, we have just been examining, where a regime is based on the ascendancy of a secular religion, on the fraternity between followers of the same cult, and on the prestige of one man, seem to be poles apart from one another. Prestige is something mysterious and incommunicable, linked to the very being of a leader and to the distance that exists or is artificially created between that leader and his fellow men. It does not in itself offer a rational or even a pseudorational justification for the doctrine he espouses. The fact is that in our day and age the adventurers brought to power by popular acclamation reinforce their assumed dignity by the myths they claim to fulfill. Though they derive their authority neither from God nor from history, they never rule in their own name, but always by virtue of a "mission."

Men are tired of obeying "officials" and an authority without a face or a name: in reaction to the anonymity of rational organizations, heroes suddenly emerge. Men are weary of submitting to an order that they do not understand and that, in the absence of any moral inspiration, degenerates into force or inevitability. The hope of salvation can transfigure that order by giving it a spiritual significance. The two kinds of aspiration tend to merge: collective beliefs generate prophets, and Caesars invent their

---

* Oswald Spengler was a German philosopher and author of the influential *Decline of the West* (1928).

own religions. Even if all images of an earthly paradise vanished, the primal belief in a man of destiny would remain. When their empire was in decline, the Romans made their emperors into gods.

The Decline of Dogma

As long as men see politics as the vehicle of their fate, they will actively worship the regimes that, dangling before them an illusory future, reflect their desires and console them for their disappointments. As long as troubled masses think themselves betrayed or exploited, men will dream of liberation, and the image of their dream will be the face of their god.

But it seems unlikely that we shall see a repetition of the events that followed World War I. When the current crisis is over, the moral climate will be different from that in which the previous one ended. The messages of President Woodrow Wilson, with his Fourteen Points, created a great illusion; the same cannot be said of the Atlantic Charter. The misuse of propaganda and the excesses of cheap ideology have ended by producing a kind of satiety.

The present phase seems to mark a decline in dogma. At the heart of Marxist dogma, as I have said, was a confusion between socialism and anticapitalism, a belief that socialism would put into practice the values in whose name capitalism was condemned. But what once seemed obvious has become a subject of argument: What human or political regime will succeed capitalism? Assuming that it is bound to have a planned economy, what will be its other characteristics? Socialists probably reject the idea that totalitarianism—with its single party and its abolition of representative institutions and intellectual liberties—is *bound* to accompany state direction of production and trade. But no one denies that the danger exists. Which means that socialism is thrown on the defensive. Victorious religions are not content with repelling attacks; they seek enemies.

Moreover, the Socialist Party is only one of the groups that offer to take on the legacy of capitalism and carry out the task of renewal. Far from uniting the vast majority of the oppressed against the absurd minority of the profiteers, as early predictions anticipated, all these groups merely represent certain masses that are opposed by other masses who may be even more disadvantaged (as in Weimar Germany, for instance).

114

There is not one large country where parliamentary and democratic socialism has managed by peaceful means to bring about a complete overhaul of the economic system. Communism has managed it, but by violent means of which liberal socialists disapprove. Probably, in the Scandinavian countries and in some dominions in the British Empire, a kind of social democracy has been created; these are based on negotiated relations between entrepreneurs and workers and involve some degree of economic control without eliminating or expropriating the capitalists. But in Germany and France, the socialists have neither, in theory, given up the idea of a socialist revolution, nor, in practice, succeeded in working out a viable system in which the working class could at once modify and be incorporated into society as it exists at present.

Their reformism has been compromised by lack of immediate success, their revolutionary zeal called into doubt by the part they have played in the existing order. They no longer offer the attraction of a new and unknown world. Whatever they may say, they are still half in sympathy with the prewar world everyone professes to reject, even though millions of people secretly hanker after it.

No doubt Communism escapes this descent into the prosaic. Throughout Europe it profits from and will go on profiting from the enormous prestige reflected on the Soviet regime and people by the victories of the Russian armies. In France, the Communists have won sympathy in all classes and dispelled some instinctive fears by their heroism in the struggle against Germany. But admiration for the fighters is not the same thing as belief in the message. This belief does exist, vibrant and total, among the officials and the activists of the party, as is shown by their obedience to the numerous and sometimes contradictory orders directed at them and by their loyalty throughout the twists and turns of official dialectics. But in western Europe they are only a minority, and in the absence of any foreign intervention they have little chance of gaining the upper hand, at least during the first phase after the Liberation.

But if socialist dogmas are in decline, the ideologies common to all forms of socialism are extremely popular. The usual arguments against capitalism—the tyranny of trusts, the scandal of poverty in the midst of plenty—remain in the forefront of people's minds. And few intellectuals will defend an economic system based on the search for profit. At the same time, the efficiency of the Communist regime's performance during the war has refuted some classical arguments on the inevitable decadence inherent in a bureaucratic economy. A preference for a planned economy instead of reliance on automatic market mechanisms, the desire for rational state organization of economic life—all these ideas, more or less related to socialism, are now virtually part of the common consciousness. In this sense, socialism can be said to have triumphed: It only remains to be seen which *kind* of socialists will benefit from this victory.

Despite the differences among countries, a unity did nevertheless exist prior to 1914. I am thinking not so much of international unity—no more than a fragile facade, as events would show—as of the unity within every country, for at that time a single party embodied the socialist hope. Now, however, several groups offer to take over the state and direct its economy. This is the essential and inevitable factor. Will these groups agree to conduct their struggle according to democratic rules? Or will they merely be new candidates for despotism, eager, on the pretext of introducing renovation, to assume absolute power? With the decline of dogma coinciding with the popularity of socialist ideas and the reawakening of nationalistic feeling, is not this a situation propitious to the birth of National Socialisms?

Cynicism or Faith in Man?

The future remains to be written. We project on it, in turn, our memories, hopes, and fears. Resignation to a future perceived as inevitable is always a form of defeatism. At present, according to circumstance and mood, we hesitate between two views: either the age of secular religions will continue as an age of fanaticism devoid of doctrine, or we shall emerge from the war of the nations and myths and rebuild a human order.

Both prospects are logical developments from the present situation. The secular religions have discredited universal ethics, whether Christian or secular. What are justice and truth but "metaphysical prostitutes"? What is the use of teaching us that we should respect other people's property unless the lesson begins by defining legitimate possession? Are not rules that apply to everyone, at all times and in all circumstances, necessarily meaningless, unable to deal with any bone of contention? What answer could they give to men's urgent and passionate questions about the most humane and efficient modes of production and trade? In this context, feeling attaches not to universal imperatives—which either signify nothing, or else by concealing it justify the established disorder—but to the goals put forward by the secular religions.

But by fighting and imitating one another as they do, the secular religions have helped to discredit themselves. Have not the irreconcilable ideologies revealed the partial similarity of the methods of their groups, which oppose one another all the more fiercely because each one, if successful, would arrogate all rights to itself and deny them to its unsuccessful rivals? Whichever team wins the state will do as it pleases. The only question is who *will* abuse state power.

Pursuing this line of thought, we can distinguish the main lines of what might be called the cynical view. Half a century ago, in a book that was scorned in France but widely appreciated abroad, Gustave Le Bon declared that we were entering the age of the crowd. "It is no longer in the councils of princes," he wrote, "but in the souls of the crowds that the fates of nations are prepared. . . . For a moment, the blind force of numbers becomes the only philosophy of history."* We know now that the age of the crowd really conceals the age of the elites. It is true that without the passive or passionate support of the masses no regime is possible in our own century. But it is also true that the masses are manipulated rather than autonomous. They are maneuvered into worshiping someone they know nothing about. And modern life, complicated as it is, constantly presupposes a mechanism of authority that all must obey, even when they are allowed the illusion of choice. We know now that the industrial age does not produce an egalitarian society, but rather the reign of the engineers, and first among these is he who engineers souls.

As a result, the very image of historical evolution is transformed. In the nineteenth century, most minds were dominated by the idea of a single irreversible movement. In a climate of rationalist optimism, this was an idea of progress. No one doubted that knowledge accumulated and with it grew man's power over nature. But however often economists assert that the standard of living of a worker in the United States today is more or less the same as that of Louis XIV, the nature of man and the organization of societies have not necessarily been fundamentally changed by technical advances. Indeed, this is the essential point. Psychoanalysts find evidence

---

* See Gustave Le Bon's *The Crowd: A Study of the Popular Mind* (1896).

of the same psychological mechanisms in the souls of our ancestors, how-ever distant, as in those of our contemporaries. The reactions of a citizen of a modern democracy are just as shallow as those of a citizen of Athens. Minorities always rule and keep benefits and privileges for themselves, even if their members and methods of governance change. Some people are angry at the thought that politics goes on existing amid the same old confused words in an age when scientists can calculate an eclipse to the seventh decimal point. But the same scientist, with his dazzling but vain triumphs, does not, outside his science, think or act any differently from his lab assistant. Politics lives on myths because the men it manipulates have not emerged from the age of myths.

But even if man remains the same turbulent, passionate, envious being described by Machiavelli, La Rochefoucauld, Pareto,* and Freud, and even if the egoism of the elites and the blindness of the masses sur-vive all revolutions, history is not heading toward a fixed end. Either it just goes on, irregular and unpredictable, as chance concerning things, men, and encounters will have it, or it is shaped according to an irrational mechanism: there are but a few types of organization, all imperfect and all attacked by an inner principle of corruption. Authoritarian elites wear out, either because they shed too much blood in combat or because they wallow in self-indulgence. Cunning elites ultimately succumb through lack of energy and resolution. So contrasting types naturally succeed one another, and the more or less regular repetition of such sequences amounts to a roughly cyclical pattern. Throughout the centuries mankind has hesi-tated between two images of its own history: the inexorable sterility of alternation, or progression toward a more or less determined end. Unable to believe that scientific progress will expand into the progress of human-ity itself, people resign themselves to a history that repeats itself.

To look at a different approach, science itself suggests a "realistic" pol-icy. Do not psychology, biology, and sociology all treat men and societies as a kind of matter, with a life and evolution from which causal laws may be deduced? The geneticist proposes crossbreeding, the sociologist talks of creating artificial elites, the psychologist of deliberately exploiting mass passions. They all treat man no longer as a subject but as an object. The philosophy of progress did the opposite. A little while ago we hoped for

---

* Vilfredo Pareto (1848–1923), an Italian sociologist and economist.

a humanity grown knowledgeable or at least reasonable. Now we either hope for or dread a humanity subjected to applications of the knowledge of our species acquired by a few individuals.

None of these ideas forces us to be cynical, but all of them taken together encourage us to be so. If in the long run all regimes are equal, the main thing is to be on the right side of the barricade—in other words, a member of the party in power. If ideologies can be regarded merely as instruments for winning souls, the political culture of the elites is more or less tantamount to the art of juggling with words. Such cynicism, which is more widespread than is generally thought, fosters both skepticism and fanaticism. Religions devoid of doctrine are the ones most impatient of orthodoxy and most inflexibly opposed to dissidents, because of the simple fact that they feel more vulnerable than the rest. Their leaders are all the more eager to foster fanaticism because they know they are incapable of defining exactly what the mission is on which their claim to legitimacy is based. Fanaticism and skepticism, although diametrically opposed, fight for possession of the same souls. The masses, like individuals, oscillate between two extremes, sometimes weary of everything and wallowing in passivity, sometimes caught up in a dream of grandeur. National Socialism, as it nears its end, seems to encompass three attitudes: that of the masses, shattered by their misfortune and the painful memory of a once-imminent victory; that of the young Nazis, who, having never known any other universe, are still the same barbarians Hitler dreamed of fifteen years ago; and that of the Party leaders, ready to go on desperately playing to the bitter end a game in which they have nothing to lose, because if they fail there will nothing left.

But another outcome is equally feasible. It, too, begins by discrediting the secular religions because of both their conflicts and similarities. But in this case the decline of dogma, instead of leading to nihilism, would tend to revive what the primacy of politics, common to all the competing ideologies, was ultimately stifling: a sense of universal values.

Such a suggestion may seem paradoxical: Have not the demands of clandestine warfare inevitably made human life cheap and spread contempt for the law (which was that of the oppressor)? This is probably true, but at the same time one observes a completely different reaction: people long for security, national independence, and all those liberties—freedom to think and speak and spend one's money as one pleases—of which a whole continent was deprived by the enemy and his accomplices. It may be that these aspirations include a hankering, impossible to satisfy, after a return to prewar ease. It certainly includes a nostalgia for things only really appreciated after they were lost: liberty is a "metaphysical prostitute," and theorists will tell us that the formal freedoms of bourgeois democracy—the right to vote, the right of free speech, the right of assembly—are nothing in comparison with the concrete freedom that only a collectivist society can supply. At any rate, there are liberties, whether formal or concrete, that peoples emerging from servitude will soon be demanding, unconditionally and without reservations. They will not tolerate a Gestapo of whatever stripe, nor the abolition of basic individual rights, on no matter what pretext. Or rather, they may endure these things if some tyrannical power establishes itself by surprise and maintains itself by violence; they will not resign themselves to them.

People will try to create a new doctrine on the basis of such feelings as patriotism and desire for freedom and individual rights. This new doctrine may arise, not from a new dogmatism, but from a search for institutions that, while meeting the necessities of the twentieth century, can safeguard the legacy of the nineteenth. The reawakening of rationalism and fundamental liberalism in the occupied countries, for example, demonstrate a persistent vitality in this new era.

There can be no doubt that the revolutions of the twentieth century have prolonged and "normalized" the use of despotic methods. This does not mean these methods are an unavoidable feature of our present epoch, but it does mean that the desire to reconstruct society quickly, via a discretionary authority and in accordance with the preferences of a particular group, inevitably leads to a total state. Before we resign ourselves to an inescapable transition to tyranny, we need to be convinced that there is no progressive solution to the problems of our age.

The search for proof would begin from the fact that also encourages skepticism: that there are similarities between regimes that are verbal enemies. For from that beginning we might be able to identify the things that must be done if we are to avoid a revolution leading to tyranny: these things are the special tasks facing the twentieth century. It is now clear that the quarrels of the nineteenth century led, on the social plane, to a generalizing of the advances made by the revolutions of the eighteenth (equality before the law, abolition of castes and hereditary privileges), and, on the political plane, to a wider spread of parliamentary institutions and individual liberties. Today all regimes, of whatever kind, have to guarantee a minimum of economic security (and, in the first place, security of employment) to every citizen, which means that the state accepts responsibility for some degree of control, direct or indirect, of the economy as a whole. Totalitarian regimes boast of performing this task en bloc. The team that is in power controls all aspects of life and directs the national resources toward whatever end it chooses, perhaps a war of conquest, perhaps an improvement in the standard of living. So in our day and age any revolution will be, and will long remain, totalitarian, for if we transfer to the state responsibility for decisions that used to be made unconsciously by each individual and by all (for example, decisions about the division of labor among different sectors), we condemn the state to act independently of the many competing groups, and thus to become the property of the group in power. Government that wants to preserve pluralism and liberties must take on such responsibilities as their citizens will not forgive them for refusing and, at the same time, leave room for the play of automatic market mechanisms conducive to the general interest within the operative limits.

No doubt, in the twentieth century, belief in parliamentary constitutions, economic liberalism, and national sovereignty is no longer what it was in the nineteenth. Having been at least partly put into practice, these ideas have lost the charm of novelty. But it would be absurd to underestimate the reawakening of nationalism and a kind of humane liberalism on the ravaged continent of Europe. And some parliamentary institutions and certain forms of free initiative may well find a new justification, even in the eyes of the masses, as the best means of fulfilling the burning desire for personal autonomy.

I firmly believe that an intermediate kind of government, free from the rival dogmatisms, is economically and socially viable. A cloud of the gravest uncertainty hangs over the political future. For in order to produce the infinitely complex mechanisms necessary for such a government, what is needed is nothing less than the prestige of a recognized elite and the collaboration of the masses, mediated by their "ringleaders." Such a collaboration is very likely to develop in Britain. But the prospects are less favorable on the continent of Europe, where popular demands will be sharpened by the sufferings of the occupation, and where the reactionary blindness of the former ruling classes has not always been enlightened by tragic experience.

It would be foolish to accuse the secular religions of organizing intolerance and spreading war. After all, the religions preaching salvation, when they ruled unchallenged over men's souls, were no less intolerant. Acting brutally in the name of purity, they persecuted heretics unmercifully and did not shrink from victories won by fire or sword. Even if temporal motives mingled with the passions of the crusaders, it is true that the Albigensians,* among others, experienced cruelty at the hands of those who claimed to believe in the God of love.

I would stress two main arguments against the secular religions. The first is that they are religions of collective salvation. They do not offer individuals the same consolations or hopes, nor do they impose on them the same disciplines, as the personal religions. Moreover, insofar as they are put into practice, they are doomed either to disappear or to prolong themselves through worship of the collectivity or of its leaders. Bernanos saw clearly when he denounced the totalitarian state as the pagan state resurrected.

The second objection is that these substitute religions are undermined from the outset by a secret unbelief. The earthly reality they offer the faithful as an objective ideal gives them no lasting intellectual satisfaction and fills their souls only by the grace of uncertainty and struggle. That is why the enthusiasm they arouse degenerates so readily into blind transports or conscious cynicism. It is not easy for representatives of *Homo sapiens* to believe that Mussolini is always right or that Hitler's words define good and evil.

But whatever the ravages wrought by the secular religions, they alone seem nowadays to possess the secret of arousing the passions that can move mountains and of producing leaders who can send their supporters to death with a word. Nothing great in history is ever achieved unless the masses have faith in ideas and in men. But can we prevent that faith from degenerating into barbaric fury? Will we give that faith monuments to build that bear witness to something other than the sacrifice of millions of

---

* The Albigensians were a neo-Manichean sect prominent in southern France in the twelfth and thirteenth centuries. They were severely repressed by the Catholic Church.

slaves? This faith, born out of an aspiration to greatness, out of a desire for devotion to a more than human task, will we teach it to first respect the virtues of mere humanity?

At the end of June 1940, at the Olympia Hall in London, the first order of the day read out to the Free French volunteers ended with the famous words of Tacitus: "One need not hope in order to try, nor succeed in order to persevere." I saw in that phrase, and I see still, the watchword of revolt, always vanquished yet always victorious—the revolt of conscience.

—London, July 1944

8

Ideology and Terror:
A Novel Form of Government
(1953)

Hannah Arendt

I

The following considerations have grown out of a study of the origins, the elements and the functioning of that novel form of government and domination which we have come to call totalitarian. Wherever it rose to power, it developed entirely new political institutions and destroyed all social, legal, and political traditions of the country. No matter what the specifically national tradition or the particular spiritual source of its ideology, totalitarian government always transformed classes into masses, supplanted the party system, not by one-party dictatorships, but by a mass movement, shifted the center of power from the army to the police, and established a foreign policy openly directed toward world domination. Present totalitarian governments have developed from one-party systems; whenever these became truly totalitarian, they started to operate according to a system of values so radically different from all others, that none of our traditional legal, moral, or common- sense utilitarian categories could any longer help us to come to terms with, or judge, or predict its course of action.

If it is true that the elements of totalitarianism can be found by retracing the history and analyzing the political implications of what we usually call the crisis of our century, then the conclusion is unavoidable that this crisis is no mere threat from the outside, no mere result of some aggressive foreign policy of either Germany or Russia, and that it will no more disappear with the fall of Soviet Russia than it disappeared with the fall of Nazi Germany. It may even be that the true predicaments of our time will assume their authentic form—though not necessarily the cruelest—only when totalitarianism has become a thing of the past.

It is in the line of such reflections to raise the question whether totalitarian government, born of this crisis and at the same time its clearest and only unequivocal symptom, is merely a make-shift arrangement, which borrows its methods of intimidation, its means of organization, and its instruments of violence from the well-known political arsenal of tyranny, despotism, and dictatorships, and owes its existence only to the deplorable, but perhaps accidental failure of the traditional political forces—liberal or conservative, national or socialist, republican or monarchist, authoritarian or democratic. Or whether, on the contrary, there is such a thing as the *nature* of totalitarian government, whether it has its own essence and can be compared with and defined like other forms of government such as Western thought has known and recognized since the times of ancient philosophy.

Questions of this sort have been out of fashion for a long time and for reasons which may have more than a little to do with those modern developments which eventually brought about a crisis of Western politics no less than of Western political thought. More specifically, such questions have been thought superfluous, if not meaningless, ever since the social sciences established their rule over the whole field of politics and history. Interesting in this development, which easily can be traced back to Marx, was that sociology from its beginnings showed a marked tendency to explain political institutions and historical developments in terms of psychological types; all the well-known clichés of the lower middle classes, the bureaucracy, the intelligentsia have already that particular tinge of typification which shows itself openly in categories such as "the authoritarian personality." More recently, with the growing disappointment in the strictly Marxist explanation of history, psychology itself with its new Freudian concepts of superego, father-image, and oedipus complex, has invaded the social sciences and continues to provide them with their chief tools of "evaluation" to such an extent that it has become difficult to tell the two sciences from each other.

This new-fangled mixture of sociology and psychology is no accident. Both sciences have their origin in a liberalism that viewed politics (and more or less all human affairs) under the dual category of society and individual. Men became mere parts of a society that conditioned or determined the individuals, as the whole determines its parts. In this sense, sociology and psychology have always been two sides of the same medal, the one dealing with the functioning of the whole (society), the other with the functioning of the parts (individuals). The trouble came when psychology, notwithstanding its respect for society, discovered that even these individuals, whose whole interior life was supposed to be conditioned by, or to react against, social circumstances, possess a "soul." But we have souls only as long as we are more than mere members of society where this psychological side of our being has always created disturbances. Manners and conventions, all public morals and mores help us to control our souls so that we can function on a merely social level. Individual psychology, since it looked on man as though he were nothing but an individual part of society, has developed into a science which deals mostly with abnormal behavior patterns: all "psychological" attitudes become abnormal when they occur in society because they have been stripped of the privacy in which alone a man's soul can function "normally." Individual psychology became fashionable wherever customs and conventions, the whole texture of morality which is the lifeblood of society, lost their authority. The modern individual is the surviving member of a society which no longer exists; it is a part that lost its place in the whole. In this situation, the psychological sciences have become increasingly social-minded and direct their greatest efforts toward the re-adjustment of isolated individuals. The trouble is that society as a whole, that is, as something which is greater than the sum total of its parts, no longer exists. The best demonstration of this is that the social sciences can conceive of society now only in terms of individual behavior patterns, which they indiscriminately apply to collective bodies where such behavior never occurs.

The great merit of this confusion is that it somehow has awakened us to the fact that political bodies, to quote a long-forgotten remark of Plato, do not spring from oak and rock (Republic 8.544d). Yet, they do not spring from within our particular and individual selves either. The old Roman distinction between *res publica* and *res privata* is still valid. Political forms of organization concern matters which are of equal concern to each of us because they occur *between us.* Our question whether there is such a thing as the nature of totalitarian domination means actually whether the entirely new and unprecedented forms of totalitarian organization and course of action rest on one of the few basic experiences which men can make whenever they live together, and are concerned with public affairs. If there is a basic experience which finds its political expression in totalitarian domination, then, in view of the novelty of the totalitarian form of government, this must be an experience which, for whatever reason, has never before served *as* the foundation of a body politic and whose general mood—although it may be familiar in every other respect—never before has pervaded, and directed the handling of, public affairs.

If we consider this in terms of the history of ideas, it seems extremely unlikely. For the forms of government under which men live have been very few; they were discovered early, classified by the Greeks, and have proved extraordinarily long-lived. If we apply these findings, whose fundamental idea, despite many variations, did not change in the two and a half thousand years that separate Plato from Kant, we are tempted at once to interpret totalitarianism as some modern form of tyranny, that is a lawless government where power *is* wielded by one man. Arbitrary power, unrestricted by law, yielded in the interest of the ruler and hostile to the interests of the governed, on one hand, fear as the principle of action, namely fear of the people by the ruler and fear of the ruler by the people, on the other—these have been the hallmarks of tyranny throughout our tradition.

Instead of saying that totalitarian government is unprecedented, we could also say that it has exploded the very alternative on which all definitions of the essence of governments have been based in political philosophy, that is, the alternative between lawful and lawless government, between arbitrary and legitimate power. That lawful government and legitimate power, on one side, lawlessness and arbitrary power on the other, belonged together and were inseparable has never been questioned. Yet, totalitarian rule confronts us with a totally different kind of government. It defies, it is true, all positive laws, even to the extreme of defying those which it has itself established (as in the case of the Soviet Constitution of 1936, to quote only the most outstanding example) or which it did not care to abolish (as in the case of the Weimar Constitution which the Nazi government never revoked). But it operates neither without guidance of law nor is it arbitrary, for it claims to obey strictly and unequivocally those laws of Nature or of History from which all positive laws always have been supposed to spring.

127

It is the monstrous, yet seemingly unanswerable claim of totalitarian rule that, far from being "lawless," it goes to the sources of authority from which positive laws received their ultimate legitimation, that far from being arbitrary it is more obedient to these suprahuman forces than any government ever was before, and that far from wielding its power in the interest of one man, it is quite prepared to sacrifice everybody's vital immediate interests to the execution of what it assumes to be the law of History or the law of Nature. Its defiance of positive laws claims to be a higher form of legitimacy which, since it is inspired by the sources themselves, can do away with petty legality. Totalitarian lawfulness pretends to have found a way to establish the rule of justice on earth—something which the legality of positive law admittedly could never attain. The discrepancy between legality and justice could never be bridged because the standards of right and wrong into which positive law translates its own source of authority—"natural law" governing the whole universe, or divine law revealed in human history or customs and traditions expressing the law common to the sentiments of all men—are necessarily general and must be valid for a countless and unpredictable number of cases, so that each concrete individual case with its unrepeatable set of circumstances somehow escapes it.

Totalitarian lawfulness, defying legality and pretending to establish the direct reign of justice on earth, executes the law of History or of Nature without translating it into standards of right and wrong for individual behavior. It applies the law directly to mankind without bothering with the behavior of men. The law of Nature or the law of History, if properly executed, is expected to produce mankind as its end product; and this expectation lies behind the claim to global rule of all totalitarian governments. Totalitarian policy claims to transform the human species into an active unfailing carrier of a law to which human beings otherwise would only passively and reluctantly be subjected. If it is true that the link between totalitarian countries and the civilized world was broken through the monstrous crimes of totalitarian regimes, it is also true that this criminality was not due to simple aggressiveness, ruthlessness, warfare and treachery, but to a conscious break of that *consensus iuris* which, according to Cicero, constitutes a "people," and which, as international law, in modern times has constituted the civilized world insofar as it remains the foundation-stone of international relations even under the conditions of war. Both moral judgment and legal punishment presuppose this basic consent; the criminal can be judged justly only because he takes part in the *consensus iuris,* and even the revealed law of God can function among men only when they listen and consent to it.

At this point the fundamental difference between the totalitarian and all other concepts of law comes to light. Totalitarian policy does not replace one set of laws with another, does not establish its own *consensus iuris,* does not create, by one revolution, a new form of legality. Its defiance of all, even its own positive laws, implies that it believes it can do without any *consensus iuris* whatever, and still not resign itself to the tyrannical state of lawlessness, arbitrariness, and fear. It can do without the *consensus iuris* because it promises to release the fulfillment of law from all action and will of man; and it promises justice on earth because it claims to make mankind itself the embodiment of the law.

This identification of man and law, which seems to cancel the discrepancy between legality and justice that has plagued legal thought since ancient times, has nothing in common with the *lumen naturale* or the voice of conscience, by which Nature or Divinity as the sources of authority for the *ius naturale* or the historically revealed commands of God, are supposed to announce their authority in man himself. This never made man a walking embodiment of the law, but on the contrary remained distinct from him as the authority which demanded consent and obedience. Nature or Divinity as the source of authority for positive laws are thought of as permanent and eternal; positive laws were changing and changeable according to circumstances, but they possessed a relative permanence as compared with the much more rapidly changing actions of men; and they derived this permanence from the eternal presence of their source of authority. Positive laws, therefore, are primarily designed to function as stabilizing factors for the ever changing movements of men.

In the interpretation of totalitarianism, all laws have become *laws of movement.* When the Nazis talked about the law of Nature or when the Bolsheviks talk about the law of History, neither Nature nor History is any longer the stabilizing source of authority for the actions of mortal men; they are movements in themselves. Underlying the Nazis' belief in race laws as the expression of the law of Nature in man, is Darwin's idea of man as the product of a natural development which does not necessarily stop with the present species of human beings, just as under the Bolsheviks' belief in class struggle *as* the expression of the law of History lies Marx's notion of society as the product of a gigantic historical movement which races according to its own law of motion to the end of historical times when it will abolish itself.

The difference between Marx's historical and Darwin's naturalistic approaches has frequently been pointed out, usually and rightly in favor of Marx. This has led us to forget the great and positive interest Marx took in Darwin's theories; Engels could not think of a greater compliment to Marx's scholarly achievements than to call him the "Darwin of history." If one considers, not the actual achievement, but the basic philosophies of both men, it turns out that ultimately the movement of History and the movement of Nature are one and the same. Darwin's introduction of the concept of development into nature, his insistence that, at least in the field of biology, natural movement is not circular but unilinear, moving in an infinitely progressing direction, means in fact that nature is, as it were, being swept into history, that natural life is considered to be historical. The "natural" law of the survival of the fittest is just as much a historical law and could be used as such by racism as Marx's law of the survival of the most progressive class. Marx's class struggle, on the other hand, as the driving force of history is only the outward expression of the development of productive forces which in turn have their origin in the labor *force* of men. Labor, according to Marx, is not a historical but a natural-biological "force," namely man's "metabolism with nature" by which he conserves his individual life and reproduces the species. Engels saw the affinity between the basic convictions of the two men very clearly because he understood the decisive role which the concept of development played in both theories. The tremendous intellectual change which took place in the middle of the last century consisted in the refusal to view or accept anything "as it is" and in the consistent interpretation of everything as being only a stage of some further development. Whether the driving force of this development was called nature or history is relatively secondary.

In these theories, the term "law" itself changed its meaning: from expressing the framework of stability within which human actions and motions can take place, it became the expression of the motion itself.

130

II

By lawful government we understand a body politic in which positive laws are needed to translate and realize the immutable *ius naturale* or the eternal commandments of God into standards of right and wrong. Only in these standards, in the body of positive laws of each country, do the *ius naturale* or the Commandments of God achieve their political reality. In the body politic of totalitarian government, this place of positive laws is taken by total terror, which is designed to translate into reality the law of movement of History or Nature. Just as positive laws, though they define transgressions, are independent of them—the absence of crimes in any society does not render laws superfluous but, on the contrary, signifies their most perfect rule—so terror in totalitarian government has ceased to be a mere means for the suppression of opposition, though it is also used for such purposes. Terror becomes total when it becomes independent of all opposition; it rules supreme when nobody any longer stands in its way. If lawfulness is the essence of nontyrannical government and lawlessness is the essence of tyranny, then terror is the essence of totalitarian domination.

Terror is the realization of the law of movement; its chief aim is to make it possible for the force of Nature or of History to race freely through mankind, unhindered by any spontaneous human action. As such, terror seeks to "stabilize" men in order to liberate the forces of Nature or History. It is this movement which singles out the foes of mankind against whom terror is let loose, and no free action of either opposition or sympathy can be permitted to interfere with the elimination of the "objective enemy" of History or Nature, of the class or the race. Guilt and innocence become senseless notions; "guilty" is he who stands in the way of the natural or historical process which has passed judgment over "inferior races," over individuals "unfit to live," over "dying classes and decadent peoples." Terror executes these judgments, and before its court, all concerned are subjectively innocent: the murdered because they did nothing against the system, and the murderers because they do not really murder but execute a death sentence pronounced by some higher tribunal. The rulers themselves do not claim to be just or wise, but only to execute historical or natural laws; they do not apply laws, but execute a movement in accordance with its inherent law. Terror is lawfulness, if law is the law of the movement of some suprahuman force, Nature or History.

Terror as the execution of a law of movement whose ultimate goal is not the welfare of men or the interest of one man but the fabrication of mankind, eliminates individuals for the sake of the species, sacrifices the "parts" for the sake of the "whole." The suprahuman force of Nature or History has its own beginning and its own end, so that it can be hindered only by the new beginning and the individual end which the life of each man actually is.

Positive laws in constitutional government are designed to erect boundaries and establish channels of communication between men whose community is continually endangered by the new men born into it. With each new birth, a new beginning is born into the world, a new world has potentially come into being. The stability of the laws corresponds to the constant motion of all human affairs, a motion which can never end as long as men are born and die. The laws hedge in each new beginning and at the same time assure its freedom of movement, the potentiality of something entirely new and unpredictable; the boundaries of positive laws are for the political existence of man what memory is for his historical existence: they guarantee the pre-existence of a common world, the reality of some continuity which transcends the individual life span of each generation, absorbs all new origins, and is nourished by them.

Total terror is so easily mistaken for a symptom of tyrannical government because totalitarian government in its initial stages must behave like a tyranny and raze the boundaries of man-made law. But total terror leaves no arbitrary lawlessness behind it and does not rage for the sake of some arbitrary will or for the sake of despotic power of one man against all, least of all for the sake of a war of all against all. It substitutes for the boundaries and channels of communication between individual men a band of iron which holds them so tightly together that it is as though their plurality had disappeared into One Man of gigantic dimensions. To abolish the fences of laws between men—as tyranny does—means to take away man's liberties and destroy freedom as a living political reality; for the space between men as it is hedged in by laws, is the living space of freedom. Total terror uses this old instrument of tyranny but destroys at the same time also the lawless, fenceless wilderness of fear and suspicion which tyranny leaves behind. This desert, to be sure, is no longer a living space of freedom, but it still provides some room for the fear-guided movements and suspicion-ridden actions of its inhabitants.

By pressing men against each other, total terror destroys the space between them; compared to the condition within its iron band, even the desert of tyranny, insofar as it is still some kind of space, appears like a guarantee of freedom. Totalitarian government does not just curtail liberties or abolish essential freedoms; nor does it, at least to our limited knowledge, succeed in eradicating the love for freedom from the hearts of man. It destroys the one essential prerequisite of all freedom which is simply the capacity of motion which cannot exist without space.

Total terror, the essence of totalitarian government, exists neither for nor against men. It is supposed to provide the forces of Nature or History with an incomparable instrument to accelerate their movement. This movement, proceeding according to its own law, cannot in the long run be hindered; eventually its force will always prove more powerful than the most powerful forces engendered by the actions and the will of men. But it can be slowed down and is slowed down almost inevitably by the freedom of man, which even totalitarian rulers cannot deny, for this freedom—irrelevant and arbitrary as they may deem it—is identical with the fact that men are being born and that therefore each of them is a new beginning, begins, in a sense, the world anew. From the totalitarian point of view, the fact that men are born and die can be only regarded as an annoying interference with higher forces. Terror, therefore, as the obedient servant of natural or historical movement has to eliminate from the process not only freedom in any specific sense, but the very source of freedom which is given with the fact of the birth of man and resides in his capacity to make a new beginning. In the iron band of terror, which destroys the plurality of men and makes out of many the One who unfailingly will act as though he himself were part of the course of History or Nature, a device has been found not only to liberate the historical and natural forces, but to accelerate them to a speed they never would reach if left to themselves. Practically speaking, this means that terror executes on the spot the death sentences which Nature is supposed to have pronounced on races or individuals who are "unfit to live," or History on "dying classes," without waiting for the slower and less efficient processes of Nature or History themselves.

In this concept, where the essence of government itself has become motion, a very old problem of political thought seems to have found a solution similar to the one already noted for the discrepancy between legality and justice. If the essence of government is defined as lawfulness, and if it is understood that laws are the stabilizing forces in the public affairs of men (as indeed it always has been since Plato invoked Zeus, the God of the boundaries, in his Laws) then the problem of movement of the body politic and the actions of its citizens arises. Lawfulness sets limitations to actions, but does not inspire them; the greatness, but also the perplexity of laws in free societies is that they only tell what one should not, but never what one should do. The necessary movement of a body politic can never be found in its essence if only because this essence—again since Plato—has always been defined with a view to its permanence. Duration seemed one of the surest yardsticks for the goodness of a government. It is still, for Montesquieu, the supreme proof for the badness of tyranny that only tyrannies are liable to be destroyed from within, to decline by themselves, whereas all other governments are destroyed through exterior circumstances. Therefore what the definition of governments always needed was what Montesquieu called a "principle of action" which, different in each form of government, would inspire government and citizens alike in their public activity and serve as a criterion beyond the merely negative yardstick of lawfulness, for judging all action in public affairs. Such guiding principles and criteria of action are, according to Montesquieu, honor in a monarchy, virtue in a republic, and fear in a tyranny.

In a perfect totalitarian government, where all men have become One Man, where all action aims at the acceleration of the movement of Nature or History, where every single act is the execution of a death sentence which Nature or History has already pronounced, that is, under conditions where terror can be completely relied upon to keep the movement in constant motion, no principle of action separate from its essence would be needed at all. Yet as long as totalitarian rule has not conquered the earth and with the iron band of terror made each single man a part of one mankind, terror in its double function as essence of government and principle, not of action, but of motion cannot be fully realized. Just as lawfulness in constitutional government is insufficient to inspire and guide men's actions, so terror in totalitarian government is not sufficient to inspire and guide human behavior.

While under present conditions totalitarian domination still shares with other forms of government the need for a guide for the behavior of its citizens in public affairs, it does not need and could not even use a principle of action strictly speaking, since it will eliminate precisely the capacity of man to act. Under conditions of total terror not even fear can any longer serve as an advisor of how to behave, because terror chooses its victims without reference to individual actions or thoughts, exclusively in accordance with the objective necessity of the natural or historical process. Under totalitarian conditions, fear probably is more widespread than ever before; but fear has lost its practical usefulness when actions guided by it can no longer help to avoid the dangers man fears. The same is true for sympathy or support of the regime; for total terror not only selects its victims according to objective standards; it chooses its executioners with as complete a disregard as possible for the candidate's conviction and sympathies. The consistent elimination of conviction as a motive for action has become a matter of record since the great purges in Soviet Russia and the satellite countries. The aim of totalitarian education has never been to instill convictions but to destroy the capacity to form any. The introduction of purely objective criteria into the selective system of the SS troops was Himmler's great organizational invention; he selected the candidates from photographs according to purely racial criteria. Nature itself decided, not only who was to be eliminated, but also who was to be trained as an executioner.

No guiding principle of behavior, taken itself from the realm of human action, such as virtue, honor, fear, is necessary or can be useful to set into motion a body politic which no longer uses terror as a means of intimidation, but whose essence is terror. In its stead, it has introduced an entirely new principle into public affairs that dispenses with human will to action altogether and appeals to the craving need for some insight into the law of movement according to which the terror functions and upon which, therefore, all private destinies depend.

The inhabitants of a totalitarian country are thrown into and caught in the process of Nature or History for the sake of accelerating its movement; as such, they can only be executioners or victims of its inherent law. The process may decide that those who today eliminate races and individuals or the members of dying classes and decadent peoples are tomorrow those who must be sacrificed. What totalitarian rule needs to guide the behavior of its subjects is a *preparation* to fit each of them equally well for the role of executioner and the role of victim. This two-sided preparation, the substitute for a principle of action, is the ideology.

III

Ideologies—isms which to the satisfaction of their adherents can explain everything and every occurrence by deducing it from a single premise—are a very recent phenomenon and, for many decades, this played a negligible role in political life. Only with the wisdom of hindsight can we discover in them certain elements which have made them so disturbingly useful for totalitarian rule. Not before Hitler and Stalin were the great political potentialities of the ideologies discovered.

Ideologies are known for their scientific character: they combine the scientific approach with results of philosophical relevance and pretend to be scientific philosophy. The word "ideology" seems to imply that an idea can become the subject matter of a science just as animals are the subject matter of zoology, and that the suffix *-logy* in ideology, as in zoology, indicates nothing but the *logoi*, the scientific statements made on it. If this were true; an ideology would indeed be a pseudoscience and a pseudophilosophy, transgressing at the same time the limitations of science and the limitations of philosophy. Deism, for example, would then be the ideology which treats the *idea* of God, with which philosophy is concerned, in the scientific manner of theology for which God is a revealed reality. (A theology which is not based on revelation as a given reality but treats God as an idea would be as mad as a zoology which is no longer sure of the physical, tangible existence of animals.) Yet we know that this is only part of the truth. Deism, though it denies divine revelation, does not simply make "scientific" statements on a God which is only an "idea," but uses the idea of God in order to explain the course of the world. The "ideas" of isms—race in racism, God in deism, etc.—never form the subject matter of the ideologies and the suffix *-logy* never indicates simply a body of "scientific" statements.

An ideology is quite literally what its name indicates: it is the *logic of an idea*. Its subject matter is history to which the "idea" is applied; the result of this application is not a body of statements about something that *is,* but the unfolding of a *process* which is in constant change. The ideology treats the course of events as though it followed the same "law" as the logical exposition of its "idea." Ideologies pretend to know the mysteries of the whole historical process—the secrets of the past, the intricacies of the present, the uncertainties of the future—because of the logic inherent in their respective ideas.

Ideologies are never interested in the miracle of being. They are historical, concerned with becoming and perishing, with the rise and fall of cultures, even if they try to explain history by some "law of nature." The word "race" in racism does not signify any genuine curiosity about the human races as a field for scientific exploration, but is the "idea" by which the movement of history is explained as one consistent process.

The "idea" of an ideology is neither the eternal essence grasped by the eyes of the mind nor the regulator of reason—as it was from Plato to Kant—but has become an instrument of explanation. To an ideology, history does not appear in the *light* of an idea (which would imply that history is seen *sub specie* of some ideal eternity which itself is beyond historical motion) but as something which can be *calculated* by it. What fits the "idea" into this new role is its own "logic," that is a movement which is the consequence of the "idea" itself and needs no outside factor to set it into motion. Racism is the belief that there is a motion inherent in the very "idea" of race, just as deism is the belief that a motion is inherent in the very notion of God.

The movement of history and the logical process of this notion are supposed to correspond to each other, so that whatever happens, happens according to the logic of one "idea." However, the only possible movement in the realm of logic is the process of deduction from a premise. Dialectical logic, with its process from thesis through antithesis to synthesis which in turn becomes the thesis of the next dialectical movement is not different in principle, once an ideology gets hold of it; the first thesis becomes the premise and its advantage for ideological explanation is that this dialectical device can explain away factual contradictions as stages of one identical, consistent movement.

As soon as logic as a *movement* of thought—and not as a necessary control of thinking—is applied to an idea, this idea is transformed into a *premise*. Ideological world explanations performed this operation long before it became so eminently fruitful for totalitarian reasoning. The purely negative coercion of logic, the prohibition of contradictions, became "productive" so that a whole line of thought could be initiated, and forced upon the mind, by drawing conclusions in the manner of mere argumentation. This argumentative process could be interrupted neither by a new idea (which would have been another premise with a different set of consequences) nor by a new experience. Ideologies always assume that one idea is sufficient to explain everything in the development from the premise, and that no experience can teach anything because everything is comprehended in this consistent process of logical deduction. The danger in exchanging the necessary insecurity of philosophical thought for the total explanation of an ideology and its *Weltanschauung,* is not even so much the risk of falling for some usually vulgar, always uncritical assumption as of exchanging the freedom inherent in man's capacity to think for the straightjacket of logic with which man can force himself almost as violently as he is forced by some outside power.

The transformation of an idea into a premise and the use of the logic of deduction as the only demonstration for truth, is certainly only one of the totalitarian elements in ideologies. Another is obviously the claim of all *Weltanschauungen* to offer total explanations of everything, mainly, of course, of past, present, and future. And the emancipation from reality this method always implies, since it pretends to know beforehand everything that experience may still have in store, might, psychologically speaking, be even more important. Yet, we insisted on this peculiar logicality of ideologies because the true totalitarian rulers (Hitler and Stalin, not their forerunners) used it more than any other element when they converted ideologies—racism and the premise of the law of Nature, or dialectical materialism and the premise of the law of History—into foundation stones for the new totalitarian body politic.

The device both totalitarian rulers used to transform their respective ideologies into weapons with which each of their subjects would force himself into step with the terror movement was deceptively simple and inconspicuous: they took them dead seriously, took pride the one in his supreme gift for "ice cold reasoning" (Hitler) and the other in the "mercilessness of his dialectics," and proceeded to drive ideological implications into extremes of logical consistency which, to the onlooker, looked preposterously "primitive" and absurd: a "dying class" consisted of people condemned to death; races that are "unfit to live" were to be exterminated. Whoever agreed that there are such things as "dying classes" and did not draw the consequence of killing their members, or that the right to live had something to do with race and did not draw the consequence of killing "unfit races," was plainly either stupid or a coward. This stringent logicality as a guide to action permeates the whole structure of totalitarian movements and governments. It is exclusively the work of Hitler and Stalin who, although they did not add a single new thought to the ideas and propaganda slogans of their movements, for this reason alone must be considered ideologists of the greatest importance.

What distinguished these new totalitarian ideologists from their predecessors was that it was no longer primarily the "idea" of the ideology—the struggle of classes and the exploitation of the workers or the struggle of races and the care for Germanic peoples—which appealed to them, but the logical process which could be developed from it. According to Stalin, neither the idea nor the oratory but "the irresistible force of logic thoroughly overpowered (Lenin's) audience." The power, which Marx thought was born when the idea seized the masses was discovered to reside, not in the idea itself, but in its logical process which "like a mighty tentacle seizes you on all sides as in a vise and from whose grip you are powerless to tear yourself away; you must either surrender or make up your mind to utter defeat."* Only when the realization of the ideological aims, the classless society or the master race, were at stake, could this force show itself. In the process of realization, the original substance upon which the ideologies based themselves as long as they had to appeal to the masses—the exploitation of the workers or the national aspirations of Germany—is gradually lost, devoured as it were by the process itself: in perfect accordance with "ice cold reasoning" and the "irresistible force of logic," the workers lost under Bolshevik rule even those rights they had been granted under Tsarist oppression and the German people suffered a kind of warfare which did not pay the slightest regard to the minimum requirements for survival of the German nation. It is in the nature of ideological politics—and is not simply a betrayal committed for the sake of self-interest or lust for power—that the real content of the ideology (the working class or the Germanic peoples), which originally had brought about the "idea" (the struggle of classes as the law of History or the struggle of races as the law of Nature), is devoured by the logic with which the "idea" is carried out.

The preparation of victims and executioners which totalitarianism requires in place of Montesquieu's principle of action is not the ideology

---

* Stalin's speech of January 28, 1924; quoted from Lenin, *Selected Works*, vol. I (Moscow, 1947), 33.

itself—racism or dialectical materialism—but its inherent logicality. The most persuasive argument in this respect, an argument of which Hitler, like Stalin, was very fond, is: you can't say A without saying B and C and so on, down to the end of the murderous alphabet. Here, the coercive force of logicality seems to have its source; it springs from our fear of contradicting ourselves. To the extent that the Bolshevik purge succeeds in making its victims confess to crimes they never committed, it relies chiefly on this basic fear and argues as follows: we are all agreed on the premise that History is a struggle of classes and on the role of the Party in its conduct. You know therefore that, historically speaking, the Party is always right (in the words of Trotsky: "We can only be right with and by the Party, for history has provided no other way of being in the right"). At this historical moment, that is in accordance with the law of History, certain crimes are due to be committed which the Party, knowing the law of History, must punish. For these crimes, the Party needs criminals; it may be that the Party, though knowing the crimes, does not quite know the criminals; more important than to be sure about the criminals is to punish the crimes, because without such punishment, History will not be advanced but may even be hindered in its course. You, therefore, either have committed the crimes or have been called by the Party to play the role of the criminal—in either case, you have objectively become an enemy of the Party. If you don't confess, you cease to help History through the Party, and have become a real enemy. The coercive force of the argument is: if you refuse, you contradict yourself and, through this contradiction, render your whole life meaningless; the A which you said dominates your whole life through the consequences of B and C which it logically engenders.

Totalitarian rulers rely on the compulsion with which we can compel ourselves, for the limited mobilization of people which even they still need; this inner compulsion is the tyranny of logicality against which nothing stands but the great capacity of men to start something new. The tyranny of logicality begins with the mind's submission to logic as a never-ending process, on which man relies in order to engender his thoughts. By this submission, he surrenders his inner freedom as he surrenders his freedom of movement when he bows down to an outward tyranny. Freedom as an inner capacity of man is identical with the capacity to begin, just as freedom as a political reality is identical with a space of movement between men. Over the beginning, no logic, no cogent deduction can have any power, because its chain presupposes, in the form of a premise, the beginning. As terror is needed, lest with the birth of each new human being a new beginning arise and raise its voice in the world, so the self-coercive force of logicality is mobilized lest anybody ever start thinking— which as the freest and purest of all human activities is the very opposite of the compulsory process of deduction. Totalitarian government can be safe only to the extent that it can mobilize man's own will power in order to force him into that gigantic movement of History or Nature which supposedly uses mankind as its material and knows neither birth nor death.

The compulsion of total terror on one side, which, with its iron band, presses masses of isolated men together *and supports* them in a world which has become a wilderness for them, and the self-coercive force of logical deduction on the other, which prepares each individual in his lonely isolation against all others, correspond to each other and need each other in order to set the terror-ruled movement into motion and keep it moving. Just as terror, even in its pre-total, merely tyrannical form, ruins all relationships between men, so the self-compulsion of ideological thinking ruins all relationships with reality. The preparation has succeeded when people have lost contact with their fellow men as well as the reality around them; for together with these contacts, men lose the capacity of both experience and thought. The ideal subject of totalitarian rule is not the convinced Nazi or the convinced Communist, but people for whom the distinction between fact and fiction (i.e., the reality of experience) and the distinction between true and false (i.e., the standards of thought) no longer exist.

IV

The question we raised at the start of these considerations and to which we now return is what kind of basic experience in the living-together of men permeates a form of government whose essence is terror and whose principle of action is the logicality of ideological thinking. That such a combination was never used before in the varied forms of political domination is obvious. Still, the basic experience on which it rests must be human and known to men, insofar as even this most "original" of all political bodies has been devised by, and is somehow answering the needs of, men.

It has frequently been observed that terror can rule absolutely only over men who are isolated against each other and that, therefore, one of the primary concerns of all tyrannical government is to bring this isolation about. Isolation may be the beginning of terror; it certainly is its most fertile ground; it always *is* its result. This isolation is, as it were, pretotalitarian; its hallmark is impotence, insofar as power always comes from men acting together, "acting in concert" (Burke); isolated men are powerless by definition.

Isolation and impotence, that is the fundamental inability to act at all, have always been characteristic of tyrannies. Political contacts between men are severed in tyrannical government and the human capacities for action and power are frustrated. But not all contacts between men are broken and not all human capacities destroyed. The whole sphere of private life with the capacities for experience, fabrication, and thought are left intact. We know that the iron band of total terror leaves no space for such private life and that the self-coercion of totalitarian logic destroys man's capacity for experience and thought just as certainly as his capacity for action.

What we call isolation in the political sphere is called loneliness in the sphere of social intercourse. Isolation and loneliness are not the same. I can be isolated—that is, in a situation in which I cannot act, because there is nobody who will act with me—without being lonely; and I can be lonely—that is, in a situation in which I as a person feel myself deserted by all human companionship—without being isolated. Isolation is that impasse into which men are driven when the political sphere of their lives, where they act together in the pursuit of a common concern, is destroyed. Yet isolation, though destructive of power and the capacity for action, not only leaves intact but is required for all so-called productive activities of men. Man, insofar as he is *homo faber*, tends to isolate himself with his work, that is, to leave temporarily the realm of politics. Fabrication (*poiesis,* the making of things), as distinguished from action (*praxis*) on one hand and sheer labor on the other, is always performed in a certain isolation from common concerns, no matter whether the result is a piece of craftsmanship or of art. In isolation, man remains in contact with the world as the human artifice; only when the most elementary forms of human creativity, which is the capacity to add something of one's own to the common world, are destroyed, isolation becomes altogether unbearable. This can happen in a world whose chief values are dictated by labor, that is where all human activities have been transformed into laboring. Under such conditions, only the sheer effort of labor, which is the effort to keep alive, is left, and the relationship with the world as a human artifice is broken. Isolated man, who lost his place in the political realm of action, is deserted by the world of things as well, if he is no longer recognized as *homo faber* but treated as an *animal laborans* whose necessary "metabolism with nature" *is* of concern to no one. Isolation then becomes loneliness. Tyranny based on isolation generally leaves the productive capacities of man intact; a tyranny over "laborers," however, as, for instance, the rule over slaves in antiquity, would automatically be a rule over lonely, not only isolated, men and tends to be totalitarian.

While isolation concerns only the political realm of life, loneliness concerns human life as a whole. Totalitarian government, like all tyrannies, certainly could not exist without destroying the public realm of life, that is, without destroying, by isolating men, their political capacities. But totalitarian domination as a form of government is new in that it is not content with this isolation and destroys private life as well. It bases itself on loneliness, on the experience of not belonging to the world at all, which is among the most radical and desperate experiences of man.

Loneliness, the common ground for terror, the essence of totalitarian government, and for ideology or logicality, the preparation of its executioners and victims, is closely connected with uprootedness and superfluousness which have been the curse of modern masses since the beginning of the Industrial Revolution and have become acute with the rise of imperialism at the end of the last century and the break-down of political institutions and social traditions in our own time. To be uprooted means to have no place in the world, recognized and guaranteed by others; to be superfluous means not to belong to the world at all. Uprootedness can be the preliminary condition for superfluousness, just as isolation can (but must not) be the preliminary condition for loneliness. Taken in itself, without consideration of its recent historical causes and its new role in politics, loneliness is at the same time contrary to the basic requirements of the human condition *and* one of the fundamental experiences of every human life. Even the experience of the materially and sensually given world depends upon my being in contact with other men, upon our *common* sense which regulates and controls all other senses and without which each of us would be enclosed in his own particularity of sense data which in themselves are unreliable and treacherous. Only because we have common sense, that is, only because not one man, but men in the plural, inhabit the earth, can we trust our immediate sensual experience. Yet, we have only to remind ourselves that one day we shall have to leave this common world which will go on as before and for whose continuity we are superfluous in order to realize loneliness, the experience of being abandoned by everything and everybody.

Loneliness is not solitude. Solitude requires being alone, whereas loneliness shows itself most sharply in company with others. Apart from a few stray remarks—usually framed in a paradoxical mood like Cato's statement (reported by Cicero, *De Re Publica*, 1.17): *numquam minus solum esse quam cum solus esset,* "never was he less alone than when he was alone," or never was he less lonely than when he was in solitude—it seems that Epictetus, the emancipated slave philosopher of Greek origin, was the first to distinguish between loneliness and solitude. His discovery, in a way, was accidental, his chief interest being neither solitude nor loneliness, but being alone (*monos*) in the sense of absolute independence. As Epictetus sees it (*Dissertationes,* bk. 3, ch. 13) the lonely man (*eremos*) finds himself surrounded by others with whom he cannot establish contact or to whose hostility he is exposed. The solitary man, on the contrary, is alone and therefore "can be together with himself" since men have the capacity of "talking with themselves." In solitude, in other words, I am "by myself," together with my self, and therefore two-in-one, whereas in loneliness I am actually one, deserted by all others. All thinking, strictly speaking, is done in solitude and is a dialogue between me and myself; but this dialogue of the two-in-one does not lose contact with the world of my fellow men because they are represented in the self with whom I lead the dialogue of thought. The problem of solitude is that this two-in-one needs the others in order to become one again: one unchangeable individual whose identity can never be mistaken for that of any other. For the confirmation of my identity I depend entirely upon other people; and it is the great saving grace of companionship for solitary men that it makes them "whole" again, saves them from the dialogue of thought in which one remains always equivocal, restores the identity which makes them speak with the single voice of one unexchangeable person.

Solitude can become loneliness; this happens when all by myself I am deserted by my own self. Solitary men have always been in danger of loneliness, when they can no longer find the redeeming grace of companionship to save them from duality and equivocality and doubt. Historically, it seems as though this danger became sufficiently great to be noticed by others and recorded by history only in the nineteenth century. It showed itself clearly when philosophers, for whom alone solitude is a way of life and a condition of work, were no longer content with the fact that "philosophy is only for the few" and began to insist that nobody "understands" them. Characteristic in this respect is the anecdote reported from Hegel's deathbed which hardly could have been told of any great philosopher before him: "Nobody has understood me except one; and he also misunderstood." Conversely, there is always the chance that a lonely man finds himself and starts the thinking dialogue of solitude. This seems to have happened to Nietzsche in Sils Maria when he conceived of *Zarathustra*. In two poems ("Sils Maria" and "Aus hohen Bergen") he tells of the empty expectation and the yearning waiting of the lonely until suddenly *"urn Mittag wars, da wurde Eins zu Zwei . . . Nun feiern wir, vereinten Siegs gewiss, / Das Fest der Feste: Freund Zarathustra kam, der Gast der Gäste!"* ("Noon was, when One became Two . . . Certain of united victory we celebrate the feast of feasts; friend Zarathustra came, the guest of guests.")

What makes loneliness so unbearable is the loss of one's own self which can be realized in solitude, but confirmed in its identity only by the trusting and trustworthy company of my equals. In this situation, man loses trust in himself as the partner of his thoughts and that elementary confidence in the world which is necessary to make experiences at all. Self and world, capacity for thought and experience are lost at the same time.

The only capacity of the human mind which needs neither the self nor the other nor the world in order to function safely and which is as independent of experience as it is of thinking is the ability of logical reasoning whose premise is the self-evident. The elementary rules of cogent evidence, the truism that two and two equals four cannot be perverted even under the conditions of absolute loneliness. It is the only reliable "truth" human beings can fall back upon once they have lost the mutual guarantee, the common sense, men need in order to experience and live and know their way in a common world. But this "truth" is empty, or rather no truth at all, because it does not reveal anything. (To define consistency as truth as some modern logicians do means to deny the existence of truth.) Under the conditions of loneliness, therefore, the self-evident is no longer just a

145

means of the intellect and begins to be productive, to develop its own lines of "thought." That thought processes characterized by strict self-evident logicality, from which apparently there is no escape, have some connection with loneliness was once noticed by Luther (whose experiences in the phenomena of solitude and loneliness probably were second to no one's and who once dared to say that "there must be a God because man needs one being whom he can trust") in a little-known remark on the Bible text "it is not good that man should be alone": a lonely man, says Luther, "always deduces one thing from the other and thinks everything to the worst." *("Ein solcher (sc. einsamer) Mensch folgert immer eins aus dem andern und denkt alles zum Argsten."* In: *Erbauliche Schriften,* "Warum die Einsamkeit zu fliehen?") The famous extremism of totalitarian movements, far from having anything to do with true radicalism, consists indeed in this "thinking everything to the worst," in this deducing process which always arrives at the worst possible conclusions.

What prepares men for totalitarian domination in the nontotalitarian world is the fact that loneliness, once a borderline experience usually suffered in certain marginal social conditions like old age, has become an everyday experience of the ever-growing masses of our century. The merciless process into which totalitarianism drives and organizes the masses looks like a suicidal escape from this reality. The "ice cold reasoning" and the "mighty tentacle" of dialectics which "seizes you as in a vise" appear like a last support in a world where nobody is reliable and nothing can be relied upon. It is the inner coercion whose only content is the strict avoidance of contradictions that seems to confirm a man's identity outside all relationships with others. It fits him into the iron band of terror even when he is alone, and totalitarian domination tries never to leave him alone except in the extreme situation of solitary confinement. By destroying all space between men and pressing men against each other, even the productive potentialities of isolation are annihilated; by teaching and glorifying the logical reasoning of loneliness where man knows that he will be utterly lost if ever he lets go of the first premise from which the whole process is being started, even the slim chances that loneliness may be transformed into solitude and logic into thought are obliterated.

If it is true that tyranny bears the germs of its own destruction because it is based upon powerlessness which is the negation of man's political condition, then one is tempted to predict the downfall of totalitarian domination without outside interference, because it rests on the one human experience which is the negation of man's social condition. Yet, even if this analogy were valid—and there are reasons to doubt it—it would operate only after the full realization of totalitarian government, which is possible only after the conquest of the earth.

Apart from such considerations—which as predictions are of little avail and less consolation—there remains the fact that the crisis of our time and its central experience have brought forth an entirely new form of government which, as a potentiality and an ever-present danger, is only too likely to stay with us from now on, just as other forms of government which came about at different historical moments and rested on different fundamental experiences have stayed with mankind regardless of temporary defeats—monarchies and republics, tyrannies, dictatorships, and despotism.

But there remains also the truth that every end in history necessarily contains a new beginning; this beginning is the promise, the only "message" which the end can ever produce. Beginning, before it becomes a historical event, is the supreme capacity of man; politically, it is identical with man's freedom. *Initium ut esset homo creatus* est—"that a beginning be made man was created" said Augustine. *(Civitas Dei, Book* 12, ch. 20) This beginning is guaranteed by each new birth; it is indeed every man.

9

Our Muzzled Freedom
(1975)

ALEKSANDR I. SOLZHENITSYN

But even when all the main things about the Gulag Archipelago are written, read, and understood, will there be anyone even then who grasps what our *freedom* was like? What sort of a country it was that for whole decades dragged that Archipelago about inside itself?

It was my fate to carry inside me a tumor the size of a large man's fist. This tumor swelled and distorted my stomach, hindered my eating and sleeping, and I was always conscious of it (though it did not constitute even one-half of 1 percent of my body, whereas within the country as a whole the Archipelago constituted 8 percent). But the horrifying thing was not that this tumor pressed upon and displaced adjacent organs. What was most terrifying about it was that it exuded poisons and infected the whole body.

And in this same way our whole country was infected by the poisons of the Archipelago. And whether it will ever be able to get rid of them someday, only God knows.

Can we, *dare* we, describe the full loathsomeness of the state in which we lived (not so remote from that of today)? And if we do not show that loathsomeness in its entirety, then we at once have a lie. For this reason I consider that *literature did not exist* in our country in the thirties, forties, and fifties. Because without the *full* truth it is not literature. And today they show this loathsomeness according to the fashion of the moment—by inference, an inserted phrase, an afterthought, or hint—and the result is again a lie.

This is not the task of our book, but let us try to enumerate briefly those traits of *free* life which were determined by the closeness of the Archipelago or which were in the same style.

1. *Constant Fear.* As the reader has already seen, the roster of the waves of recruitment into the Archipelago is not exhausted with 1935, or 1937, or 1949.* The recruitment went on *all the time.* Just as there is no minute when people are not dying or being born, so there was no minute when people were not being arrested. Sometimes this came close to a person, sometimes it was further off; sometimes a person deceived himself into thinking that nothing threatened him, and sometimes he himself became an executioner, and thus the threat to him diminished. But any adult inhabitant of this country, from a collective farmer up to a member of the Politburo, always knew that it would take only one careless word or gesture and he would fly off irrevocably into the abyss.

Just as in the Archipelago beneath every trusty lay the chasm (and death) of general work, so beneath every inhabitant lay the chasm (and death) of the Archipelago. In appearance the country was much bigger than its Archipelago, but all of it and all its inhabitants hung phantomlike above the latter's gaping maw.

Fear was not always the fear of arrest. There were intermediate threats: purges, inspections, the completion of security questionnaires—routine or extraordinary ones—dismissal from work, deprivation of residence permit, expulsion or exile. The security questionnaires were so detailed and so inquisitive that more than half the inhabitants of the country had a bad conscience and were constantly and permanently tormented by the approach of the period when they had to be filled out. Once people had invented a false life story for these questionnaires, they had to try not to get tangled up in it.

The aggregate fear led to a correct consciousness of one's own insignificance and of the lack of any kind of *rights.*

Nadezhda Mandelstam[†] speaks truly when she remarks that our life is so permeated with prison that simple meaningful words like "they took,"

---

* Solzhenitsyn described the nearly constant flow of people into the Gulag system in part 1, chapter 2 of *Gulag*, "The History of Our Sewage Disposal System."

† Nadezhda Mandelstam is the author of the memoir *Hope against Hope* and wife of the famous Russian poet Osip Mandelstam—Osip was arrested in 1934 and died in Stalin's Great Purge.

or "they put inside," or "he is inside," or "they let out," are understood by everyone in our country in only one sense, even without a context.

Peace of mind is something our citizens have never known.

2. *Servitude.* If it had been easy to change your place of residence, to leave a place that had become dangerous for you and thus shake off fear and refresh yourself, people would have behaved more boldly, and they might have taken some risks. But for long decades we were shackled by that same system under which no worker could quit work of his own accord. And the passport regulations also fastened everyone to particular places. And the housing, which could not be sold, nor exchanged, nor rented. And because of this it was an insane piece of daring to protest in the place where you lived or worked.

3. *Secrecy and Mistrust.* These feelings replaced our former open-hearted cordiality and hospitality (which had still not been destroyed in the twenties). These feelings were the natural defense of any family and every person, particularly because no one could ever quit work or leave, and every little detail was kept in sight and within earshot for years. The secretiveness of the Soviet person is by no means superfluous, but is absolutely necessary, even though to a foreigner it may at times seem superhuman. The former Tsarist officer K.U. survived and was never arrested only because when he got married he did not tell his *wife* about his past. His brother, N.U., was arrested—and the wife of the arrested man, taking advantage of the fact that they lived in different cities at the time of his arrest, hid his arrest from her own *father and mother*—so they would not blurt it out. She preferred telling them and everyone else that her husband had abandoned her, and then playing that role a long time! Now these were the secrets of one family which I was told thirty years later. And what urban family did not have such secrets?

4. *Universal Ignorance.* Hiding things from each other, and not trusting each other, we ourselves helped implement that *absolute secrecy,* absolute misinformation, among us which was *the cause of causes* of everything that took place—including both the millions of arrests and the mass approval of them also. Informing one another of nothing, neither shouting nor groaning, and learning nothing from one another, we were completely in the hands of the newspapers and the official orators.

5. *Squealing.* Was developed to a mind-boggling extent. Hundreds of thousands of Security officers in their official offices, in the innocent

rooms of official buildings, and in prearranged apartments, sparing neither paper nor their unoccupied time, tirelessly recruited and summoned stool pigeons to give reports, and this in such enormous numbers as they could never have found necessary for collecting information. One of the purposes of such extensive recruitment was, evidently, to make each subject feel the breath of the stool pigeons on his own skin. So that in every group of people, in every office, in every apartment, either there would be an informer or else the people there would be afraid there was.

I will give my own superficial speculative estimate: out of every four to five city dwellers there would most certainly be one who at least once in his life had received a proposal to become an informer. And it might even have been more widespread than that. Quite recently I carried out my own spot check, both among groups of ex-prisoners and among groups of those who have always been free. I asked which out of the group they had tried to recruit and when and how. And it turned out that out of several people at a table *all* had received such proposals at one time or another!

Nadezhda Mandelstam correctly concludes: beyond the purpose of weakening ties between people, there was another purpose as well. Any person who had let himself be recruited would, out of fear of public exposure, be very much interested in the continuing stability of the regime.

6. *Betrayal as a Form of Existence.* Given this constant fear over a period of many years—for oneself and one's family—a human being became a vassal of fear, subjected to it. And it turned out that the least dangerous form of existence was constant betrayal.

The mildest and at the same time most widespread form of betrayal was not to do anything bad directly, but just not to notice the doomed person next to one, not to help him, to turn away one's face, to shrink back. They had arrested a neighbor, your comrade at work, or even your close friend. You kept silence. You acted as if you had not noticed. (For you could not afford to lose your current job!) And then it was announced at work, at the general meeting, that the person who had disappeared the day before was . . . an inveterate enemy of the people. And you, who had bent your back beside him for twenty years at the same desk, now by your noble silence (or even by your condemning speech!), had to show how hostile you were to his crimes. (You had to make this sacrifice for the sake of your own dear family, for your own dear ones! What right had you not to think *about them?*) But the person arrested had left behind him a wife, a mother, children, and perhaps they at least ought to be helped? No, no, that would be dangerous: after all, these were the wife of an *enemy* and the mother of an enemy, and they were the children of an enemy (and your own children had a long education ahead of them)!

And one who concealed an enemy was also an enemy! And one who abetted an enemy was also an enemy! And one who continued his friendship with an enemy was also an enemy. And the telephone of the accursed *family* fell silent. And in the hustle of a big city people felt as if they were in a desert.

And that was precisely what Stalin needed! And he laughed in his mustaches, the shoeshine boy!

In evaluating 1937 for the Archipelago, we refused it the title of the crowning glory. But here, in talking about *freedom,* we have to grant it this corroded crown of betrayal; one has to admit that this was the particular year that broke the soul of our *freedom* and opened it wide to corruption on a mass scale.

Yet even this was not yet the end of our society! (As we see today, the end never did come—the living thread of Russia survived, hung on until better times came in 1956, and it is now less than ever likely to die.) The resistance was not overt. It did not beautify the epoch of the universal fall, but with its invisible warm veins its heart kept on beating, beating, beating, beating.

Every act of resistance to the government required heroism quite out of proportion to the magnitude of the act. It was safer to keep dynamite during the rule of Alexander II* than it was to shelter the orphan of an *enemy* of the people under Stalin. Nonetheless, how many such children were taken in and saved . . . Let the children themselves tell their stories. And secret assistance to families . . . did occur. And there was someone who took the place of an arrested person's wife who had been in a hopeless line for three days, so that she could go in to get warm and get some sleep. And there was also someone who went off with pounding heart to warn someone else that an ambush was waiting for him at his apartment and that he must not return there. And there was someone who gave a fugitive shelter, even though he himself did not sleep that night.

---

* Czar Alexander II ruled Russia from 1855 to 1881. He set in motion a wave of domestic reforms, including the abolition of serfdom. He was assassinated by revolutionary terrorists.

Nowadays it is quite convenient to declare that *arrest* was a lottery (Ehrenburg[*]). Yes, it was a lottery all right, but some of the numbers were "fixed." They threw out a general dragnet and arrested in accordance with assigned quota figures, yes, but every person who *objected publicly* they grabbed that very minute! And it turned into a *selection on the basis of soul*, not a lottery! Those who were bold fell beneath the ax, were sent off to the Archipelago—and the picture of the monotonously obedient *freedom* remained unruffled. All those who were purer and better could not stay in that society; and without them it kept getting more and more trashy. You would not notice these quiet departures at all. But they were, in fact, the dying of the soul of the people.

7. *Corruption.* In a situation of fear and betrayal over many years people survive unharmed only in a superficial, bodily sense. And inside . . . they become corrupt.

So many millions of people agreed to become stool pigeons. And, after all, if some forty to fifty million people served long sentences in the Archipelago during the course of the thirty-five years up to 1953, including those who died—and this is a modest estimate, being only three or four times the population of Gulag at any one time, and, after all, during the war the death rate there was running *1 percent per day*—then we can assume that at least every third or at least every fifth case was the consequence of somebody's denunciation and that somebody was willing to provide evidence as a witness! All of them, all those murderers with ink, are still among us today. And most often they are prospering. And we still rejoice that they are "our ordinary Soviet people."

8. *The Lie as a Form of Existence.* Whether giving in to fear, or influenced by material self-interest or envy, people can't nonetheless become stupid so swiftly. Their souls may be thoroughly muddied, but they still have a sufficiently clear mind. They cannot believe that all the genius of the world has suddenly concentrated itself in one head with a flattened, low-hanging forehead. They simply cannot believe the stupid and silly images of themselves which they hear over the radio, see in films, and read in the newspapers. Nothing forces them to speak the truth in reply, but

---

[*] Ilya Ehrenburg was a prominent novelist, journalist and memoirist. With Vasily Grossman, he compiled, edited, and wrote portions of *The Complete Black Book of Russian Jewry.*

153

no one allows them to keep silent! They have to talk! And what else but a lie? They have to applaud madly, and no one requires honesty of them.

The permanent lie becomes the only safe form of existence, in the same way as betrayal. Every wag of the tongue can be overheard by someone, every facial expression observed by someone. Therefore every word, if it does not have to be a direct lie, is nonetheless obliged not to contradict the general, common lie. There exists a collection of ready-made phrases, of labels, a selection of ready-made lies. And, not one single speech nor one single essay or article nor one single book—be it scientific, journalistic, critical, or "literary," so-called—can exist without the use of these primary clichés. In the most scientific of texts it is required that someone's false authority or false priority be upheld somewhere, and that someone be cursed for telling the truth; without this lie even an academic work cannot see the light of day. And what can be said about those shrill meetings and trashy lunch-break gatherings where you are compelled to vote against your own opinion, to pretend to be glad over what distresses you?

In prison Tenno* recalled with shame how two weeks before his own arrest he had lectured the sailors on "The Stalinist Constitution—The Most Democratic in the World." And of course not one word of it was sincere.

There is no man who has typed even one page . . . without lying. There is no man who has spoken from a rostrum . . . without lying. There is no man who has spoken into a microphone . . . without lying.

But if only it had all ended there! After all, it went further than that: every conversation with the management, every conversation in the Personnel Section, every conversation of any kind with any other Soviet person called for lies. And if your idiot interlocutor said to you face to face that the Colorado beetles had been dropped on us by the Americans—it was necessary to agree! (And a shake of the head instead of a nod might well cost you resettlement in the Archipelago. Remember the arrest of Chulpenyov, in part I, chapter 7.)

But that was not all: your children were growing up! And if the children were still little, then you had to decide what was the best way to bring them up; whether to start them off on lies instead of the truth (so that it would be *easier* for them to live) and then to lie forevermore in front of them too; or to tell them the truth, with the risk that they might make a slip, that they might

---

* Solzhenitsyn writes about Georgi Tenno in part 5, chapter 6 of *Gulag*, "The Committed Escaper."

let it out, which meant that you had to instill into them from the start that the truth was murderous, that beyond the threshold of the house you had to lie, only lie, just like papa and mama.

The choice was really such that you would rather not have any children.

9. *Cruelty.* And where among all the preceding qualities was there any place left for kindheartedness? How could one possibly preserve one's kindness while pushing away the hands of those who were drowning? Once you have been steeped in blood, you can only become more cruel. And, anyway, cruelty ("class cruelty") was praised and instilled, and you would soon lose track, probably, of just where between bad and good that trait lay. And when you add that kindness was ridiculed, that pity was ridiculed, that mercy was ridiculed—you'd never be able to chain all those who were drunk on blood!

10. *Slave Psychology.* In various parts of our country we find a certain piece of sculpture: a plaster guard with a police dog which is straining forward in order to sink its teeth into someone. In Tashkent there is one right in front of the NKVD school, and in Ryazan it is like a symbol of the city, the one and only monument to be seen if you approach from the direction of Mikhailov.

And we do not even shudder in revulsion. We have become accustomed to these figures setting dogs onto people as if they were the most natural things in the world.

Setting the dogs onto us.

10

The Marxist Roots of Stalinism
(1977)

Leszek Kolakowski

The Questions We Ask and the Questions We Don't

When we ask about the relation between Marxism and the Stalinist ideology and system of power, the main difficulty is in how to formulate the question. This can be done, and in fact has been done, in a number of ways. Some of the resulting questions are unanswerable or pointless; others are rhetorical, since the answers are obvious.

An example of a question that is both unanswerable and pointless: "What would Marx have said had he lived to see his ideas embodied in the Soviet system?" If he had lived, he would inevitably have changed. If by some miracle he were resurrected now, his opinion about which practical interpretation of his philosophy is the best one would be just one opinion among others, and could easily be dismissed by saying that a philosopher is not necessarily infallible in recognizing the implications of his own ideas.

Examples of questions to which the answers are obvious and indisputable: "Was the Stalinist system causally generated by Marxist theory? Do Marx's writings contain any implicit or explicit value judgments that conflict with the value system established in Stalinist societies?" The answer to the first question is obviously "no": there has never been a society entirely begotten by an ideology or entirely explicable by the ideas of those who contributed to its origin. Anyone is Marxist enough to admit that. All societies reflect in their institutions their members' and makers'

156

(mutually conflicting) ideas about how society ought to be, but no society has ever been produced from such ideas alone—from conceptions of it before its existence. To imagine that a society could ever spring up entirely from a utopia (or indeed from a *kakotopia*) would amount to believing that human communities are capable of doing away with their history. This is common sense—a platitude, and a purely negative one at that. Societies have always been molded by what they thought about themselves, but this dependence has never been more than partial.

The answer to the second question is obviously "yes," and is irrelevant to our problem. It is easily established that Marx never wrote anything to the effect that the socialist kingdom of freedom would consist in one-party despotic rule; that he did not reject democratic forms of social life; that he expected socialism to lead to the abolition of economic coercion *in addition to*, and not *as opposed to*, political coercion; and so on. Nevertheless, his theory may logically imply consequences that are incompatible with his ostensible value judgments; or it may be that empirical circumstances prevented its being implemented in any other way. There is nothing odd in the fact that political and social programs, utopias, and prophecies lead to outcomes not only very different from but significantly in conflict with the intentions of their authors; empirical connections previously unnoticed or neglected may make it impossible to implement one part of the utopia without abandoning some other ingredient. This, again, is common sense, and trivial. Most of what we learn in life is about which values are compatible and which mutually exclusive; and most utopians are simply incapable of learning that there *are* incompatible values. More often than not, this incompatibility is empirical, not logical, and this is why their utopias are not necessarily self-contradictory in logical terms, only impracticable, because of the way the world is.

Thus in discussing the relationship between Stalinism and Marxism I dismiss as irrelevant pronouncements like "This would make Marx turn in his grave" or "Marx was against censorship and in favor of free elections," whether or not their truth could be decided with certainty (which is somewhat doubtful in the case of the former).

My own curiosity would be better expressed in another way: Was (the characteristically Stalinist ideology that was designed to justify the Stalinist system of societal organization a legitimate (even if not the only possible) interpretation of Marxist philosophy of history? This is the milder version of my question. The stronger version is: Was every attempt to implement all the basic values of Marxist socialism likely to generate a political organization that would bear the unmistakable marks of Stalinism? I shall argue for an affirmative answer to both questions, while realizing that saying "yes" to the first does not logically entail "yes" to the second: it is logically consistent to maintain that Stalinism was one of several admissible variants of Marxism and to deny that the very content of Marxist philosophy favored this particular version more strongly than any other.

HOW CAN "STALINISM" BE IDENTIFIED?

It makes little difference whether we use the word "Stalinism" to refer to a well-defined period of one-man despotism in the Soviet Union (i.e., roughly from 1930 to 1953) or to any system that clearly manifests similar features. Nevertheless, the question of the degree to which post-Stalinist Soviet and Soviet-style states are essentially extensions of that system is obviously not a terminological one. For a number of reasons, however, the second, less historical and more abstract definition, which stresses the continuity of the system, is more convenient.

"Stalinism" may be characterized as an (almost perfect) totalitarian society based on state ownership of the means of production. I use the word "totalitarian" in its common sense of a political system where social ties have been entirely replaced by state-imposed organization and where, consequently, all groups and all individuals should be guided in their actions only by goals which are goals of the state, and which the state has defined as such. In other words, an ideal totalitarian system would entail the utter destruction of civil society: it would be a system in which the state and its organizational instruments were the only forms of social life, and where all forms of human activity—economic, intellectual, political, and cultural— were allowed and imposed (the distinction between what is allowed and what is imposed tending to disappear) only if they were at the service of state goals (again, as defined by the state). In such a system, every individual (including the rulers themselves) is considered the property of the state.

The concept so defined—and in so defining it I believe I do not differ from most authors who have dealt with the subject—calls for a few explanatory remarks.

First, it is clear that in order to achieve the perfect shape, a totalitarian principle of organization requires state control of the means of production. In other words, a state which leaves significant parts of productive activity and economic initiative in the hands of individuals, and in consequence permits segments of society to be economically independent of the state, cannot attain the ideal form. Therefore totalitarianism has the best chances of fulfilling this ideal within a socialist economy.

Second, it should be stressed that no absolutely perfect totalitarian system has ever existed. However, we do know some societies with a very strong, built-in, and constantly operative tendency to "nationalize" all forms of individual and community life. Both Soviet and Chinese society are, or have been, in certain periods, very close to this ideal; so was Nazi Germany, even if it did not last long enough to develop itself fully, and even though it was satisfied with subordinating economic activity to state goals through coercion, without nationalizing everything. Other Fascist states were (or are) far behind Germany on this path; nor have European socialist states ever achieved the Soviet level of totalitarianism, despite a permanent and undiminished determination to do so.

It is unlikely that the *entelechia** of totalitarianism could ever be realized in an ideal form. There are forms of life—among them familial, emotional, and sexual relationships—which stubbornly resist the pressure of the system; they have been subjected to all sorts of strong state pressure, but apparently never with complete success (at least not in the Soviet state; perhaps more was achieved in China). Similarly with individual and collective memory, which the totalitarian system constantly tries to annihilate by reshaping, rewriting, and falsifying history according to current political needs. Factories and labor are obviously easier to nationalize than feelings; and hopes easier than memories. Resistance to state ownership of the past is an important part of antitotalitarian movements.

Third, the above definition implies that not every despotic system or reign of terror is necessarily totalitarian. Some, even the bloodiest, may have limited goals, and may not need to absorb all forms of human activity within them. The worst forms of colonial rule, in their worst periods, were usually not totalitarian; the goal was to exploit the subjugated countries

---

* *Entelechia*, from Greek, is an Aristotelian term. Kolakowski uses it here to mean something like the complete or perfect end.

economically, and many spheres of life which were neutral from this point of view could be left more or less untouched. Conversely, a totalitarian system does not need to use terror permanently as a means of oppression.

In its perfect form, totalitarianism is an extraordinary form of slavery: slavery without masters. It converts all people into slaves; because of this it bears certain marks of egalitarianism.

I realize that the concept of totalitarianism, applied in this way, has of late increasingly been dismissed as "outdated" or "discredited"; its validity has been questioned. Yet I know of no analysis, either conceptual or historical, that does discredit it, although I am acquainted with many earlier analyses which justify it. Indeed, the prediction that Communism would mean state-ownership of persons appears in Proudhon;* and so many well-known authors have pointed out (whether or not they used the word "totalitarianism" in doing so) that this was what did in fact happen in Soviet society, and gone on to describe it, that it would be pointless pedantry to quote them here.

THE MAIN STAGES OF STALINIST TOTALITARIANISM

The Soviet variety of totalitarianism spent many years ripening before reaching its apogee. The main stages of its growth are well known, and need only to be briefly mentioned.

In the first stage, the basic forms of representative democracy—parliament, elections, political parties, a free press—were done away with.

The second stage (which overlapped with the first) is known by the misleading name of "War Communism." The name suggests that the policies of this period were conceived of as temporary and exceptional measures to cope with the monstrous difficulties imposed by civil war and intervention. In fact, it is clear from the relevant writings of the leaders—in particular Lenin, Trotsky, and Bukharin—that they all envisaged this economic policy (the abolition of free trade, coercive requisitioning of "surplus"—i.e., whatever the local leadership considered to be surplus—from the peasants, universal rationing, forced labor) as a permanent achievement of the new society, and that it was eventually abandoned not

---

* Pierre Proudhon (1809–1865) was a prominent French socialist.

because the war conditions which had made it necessary no longer existed, but as a result of the economic disaster it had caused. Both Trotsky and Bukharin were emphatic in their assurances that forced labor was an organic part of the new society.

Important elements of the totalitarian order that was set up in this period persisted and became permanent components of Soviet society. One such lasting achievement was the destruction of the working class as a political force: the abolition of the soviets as an independent expression of popular initiative and the end of independent trade unions and political parties. Another was the suppression—not yet definitive—of democracy within the party itself: the ban on factional activity. Throughout the NEP era the totalitarian traits of the system were extremely strong, despite the fact that free trade was accepted and that a large section of society—the peasants—enjoyed economic independence from the state. Both politically and culturally, the NEP meant mounting pressure of the party-owned state on all centers of initiative that were not yet, or not entirely, state-owned, although it was only in subsequent stages of development that full success was achieved in this respect.

The third stage was forced collectivization, which amounted to destroying the last social class not yet nationalized and gave the state full control over economic life. Which did not mean, of course, that it enabled the state to engage in real economic planning: it did not.

The fourth stage was to destroy the party itself, through purges; for it was still a potential, though no longer actual, non-nationalized force. Although no effective forces of rebellion survived within it, many of its members, especially the older ones, remained loyal to the traditional party ideology. Thus even if they were perfectly obedient, they were (rightly) suspected of dividing their loyalties between the actual leader and the inherited ideological value system—in other words, of being potentially disloyal to the leader. It had to be made clear to them that ideology was whatever the leader at any given moment said it was. The massacres successfully accomplished this task; they were the work of an ideological Führer, not a madman.

THE MATURE FACE OF STALINISM

Each stage of this process was deliberately decided and organized, although not all were planned in advance. The result was a fully state-owned society that came very close to the ideal of perfect unity, cemented by party and police. It was both perfectly integrated and perfectly fragmented, and for the same reason: integrated in that all forms of collective life were entirely subordinated to, and imposed by, one ruling center, and fragmented in that civil society had been to all intents and purposes destroyed, and each citizen, in all his relations with the state, faced the omnipotent apparatus alone, an isolated and powerless individual. Society was reduced to a thing like a "sack of potatoes," as Marx said of French peasants in the *Eighteenth Brumaire*.

This situation—a unified state organism facing atom-like individuals—defined the all-important features of the Stalinist system. They are well known and have been much-described, but it is worth briefly mentioning a few of the ones most relevant to our topic.

First, the abolition of law. Law persisted, to be sure, as a set of procedural rules governing public life. But as a set of rules which could infringe upon the state's omnipotence in its dealings with individuals it was entirely abolished. In other words, it could contain no rules which might restrict the principle that citizens are the property of the state. In its crucial points totalitarian law had to be vague, so that its application might hinge on the arbitrary and changing decisions of the executive authorities, and so that each citizen could be considered a criminal whenever these authorities chose so to consider him. The notable examples have always been political crimes as defined in penal codes; these are constructed in such a way that it is well-nigh impossible for a citizen not to commit crimes almost daily. Which of these crimes are actually prosecuted and how much terror is used depends on the political decisions of the rulers. In this respect nothing has changed in the post-Stalinist period: the law remains characteristically totalitarian, and neither the transition from mass to selective terror nor the better observance of procedural rules is relevant—as long as they do not limit the effective power of the state over individual lives—to its persistence. People may or may not be jailed for telling political jokes; their children may or may not be forcibly taken away from them if they fail in their legal duty to raise them in the Communist spirit (whatever this means). Totalitarian lawlessness consists not in the actual application of extreme measures always and everywhere but in the fact that the law gives individuals no protection against whatever forms of repression the state wants to use at any given moment The law as a mediator between the state and the people disappears, and is converted into an endlessly malleable instrument of the state. In this respect the Stalinist principle persists unchanged.

Second, one-person autocracy. This seems to have been a natural and "logical" outcome of the perfect-unity principle which was the driving force in the development of the totalitarian state. In order to achieve its full shape, the state required one and only one leader, endowed with limitless power. This was implicit in the very foundations of the Leninist party (in accordance with Trotsky's often quoted prophesy of 1903, soon forgotten by the prophet himself). The whole progress of the Soviet system in the 1920s consisted in a step-by-step narrowing of the forum where conflicting interests, ideas, and political tendencies could be expressed. For a short period they continued to be articulated publicly in society, but their expression was gradually confined, in a narrowing upward movement, first to the party; then to the party apparatus; then to the Central Committee; and finally to the Politburo. But here, too, expressions of social conflict could be prevented, although the sources of conflict had not been eradicated. It was Stalin's well-grounded contention that even here, in this narrowest caucus, conflicting expressions of opinion, if allowed to continue, would convey the pressure of those conflicting interests which still survived within society. This is why the destruction of the civil society could not be fully accomplished so long as different tendencies or factions had room to express themselves, even in the supreme party organ.

The changes which occurred in the Soviet system after Stalin—the transition from personal tyranny to oligarchy—seem most salient here. They resulted from an incurable contradiction inherent in the system: perfect unity of leadership, required by the system and embodied in personal despotism, was incompatible with other leaders' need for a minimum of security. Under Stalin's rule they were demoted to the same precarious status as other people—the status of slaves. All their enormous privileges could not protect them against a sudden fall from grace, imprisonment and death. The oligarchical rule after Stalin was a sort of mutual security pact among the party apparatus. But such a contract, insofar as it is in fact applied, runs counter to the principle of unity. In this sense the decades after Stalin's death may properly be described as an ailing form of Stalinism.

Nevertheless, Soviet society, even in its worst periods, has never been ruled by the police. Stalin governed the country and the party with the aid of the police machine, but he governed as party leader, not as chief of police. The party, which for a quarter of a century was identical with Stalin, never lost its all-embracing sway.

Third, universal spying as the principle of government. People were encouraged—and compelled—to spy upon one another, but this was obviously not how the state defended itself against real dangers; rather, it was a way of pushing the principle of totalitarianism to its extreme. As citizens, people were supposed to live in a perfect unity of goals, desires, and thoughts—all expressed through the mouth of the leader. As individuals, however, they were expected to hate one another and to live in constant mutual hostility. Only thus could the isolation of individuals from one another achieve perfection. In fact, the unattainable ideal of the system seems to have been one where everyone is at the same time an inmate of a concentration camp and a secret police agent.

Fourth, the apparent omnipotence of ideology. This is a point on which, in all discussions of Stalinism, there is more confusion and disagreement than on any other. This is evident if we look at the exchange of views on the subject between Solzhenitsyn and Sakharov. The former says, roughly, that the whole Soviet state, in both its home and its foreign policy, in both economic and political matters, is subjugated to the overwhelming rule of Marxist ideology, and that it is this (false) ideology which is responsible for all the disasters that have struck both the state and the society. The latter replies that the official state ideology is dead and that no one any longer takes it seriously, so it is silly to imagine that it could be a real force in guiding and shaping practical policies.

It seems that both these observations are valid, within certain limits. The point is that the Soviet state has an ideology built into its very foundations, from the very beginning, as the only principle of its legitimacy. Certainly, the ideological banners under which the Bolshevik party seized power in Russia (peace and land for the peasants) had no specifically socialist, let alone Marxist, content. But it could only establish its monopoly rule on the Leninist ideological principle: as a party which by definition was the only legitimate mouthpiece of the working class and of all the "toiling masses," of their interests, goals, and desires (even if these were unknown to the masses themselves), and which owed its ability to "express" the will of the masses to its "correct" Marxist ideology. A party that wields despotic power cannot abandon the ideology which justifies this power and which remains, in the absence of free elections or an inherited royal charisma, the only basis of its legitimacy. In such a system of rule ideology is indispensable, no matter how few or many people believe it, who they are and how seriously they take it; and it remains indispensable even if—as is now the case in European socialist countries—there are virtually no more believers left, either among the rulers or among the ruled. The leaders clearly cannot afford to reveal the real and notorious principles of their policy without risking the utter collapse of the system of power. A state ideology believed by no one must be binding on all if the entire fabric of the state is not to crumble.

This does not mean that the ideological considerations appealed to in order to justify each step in practical policy are real, independent forces before which Stalin or other leaders bowed. But to a certain extent they do limit this policy. The Soviet system, both under and after Stalin, has always pursued the *Realpolitik* of a great empire, and its ideology had to be vague enough to sanctify any given policy: NEP and collectivization, friendship with the Nazis and war with the Nazis, friendship with China and the condemnation of China, support for Israel or support for Israel's foes, Cold War and détente, the tightening of the internal regime and its relaxation, the oriental cult of the satrap and the denunciation of that cult. And still this ideology preserves the Soviet state and holds it together.

It has often been pointed out that the Soviet totalitarian system is not intelligible unless we take into account the historical background of Russia, with its strongly pronounced totalitarian traits. The autonomy of the state and its overwhelming powers over civil society was stressed by Russian historians of the nineteenth century, and this view was endorsed, with some qualifications, by a number of Russian Marxists (such as Plekhanov, in his *History of Russian Social Thought*, and Trotsky in his *History of the Russian Revolution*). After the revolution this background was repeatedly referred to as the genuine source of Russian Communism (Berdyaev[*]). Many authors

---

[*] Nikolai Berdyaev (1874–1948) is regarded as one of the outstanding Russian philosophers of the twentieth century.

(Kucharzewski[*] was one of the first) saw in Soviet Russia a direct extension of the czarist regime; they saw it in, among other things, her expansionist policy and her insatiable hunger for new territories, and also in the "nationalization" of all citizens and the subordination of all forms of human activity to the state's goals. Several historians have published very convincing studies on the subject (most recently R. Pipes[†] and T. Szamuely[‡]), and I do not question their conclusions. But this historical background does not explain the peculiar function of Marxist ideology in the Soviet order. Even if we go so far as to admit (with Amalrik[§]) that the whole meaning of Marxism in Russia ultimately consisted in injecting a shaky ideological empire with flesh and blood that would allow it to survive for a time before definitively falling apart, the question of how Marxism fitted into this task still remains unanswered. How could the Marxist philosophy of history, with its ostensible hopes, aims, and values, supply the totalitarian, imperialist, and chauvinist state with an ideological weapon?

It could and it did; and it did not even need to be essentially distorted, merely interpreted in the appropriate way.

STALINISM AS MARXISM

In discussing this question I am assuming that Marx's thought from 1843 onwards was propelled by that same value-laden idea for which he was continually seeking a better form of expression. Thus I agree with those who emphasize the strong continuity of Marx's intellectual development; I do not believe that there was any significant, much less violent, break in the growth of his main ideas. But I will not argue here in favor of this controversial—although by no means original—view.

In Marx's eyes the original sin of man, his *felix culpa*, responsible both for great human achievements and for human misery, was the division of labor—and its inevitable result, the alienation of labor. The extreme form

---

* Jan Kucharzewski, author of *The Origins of Modern Russia* (1948).

† Richard Pipes, one of the pre-eminent Sovietologists of his generation, and author of many books, including *Russia under the Old Regime* (1974).

‡ Tibor Szamuely, author of *The Russian Tradition* (1974).

§ Andrei Amalrik, author of *Will the Soviet Union Survive Until 1984?* (1969).

of alienated labor is exchange value, which dominates the entire process of production in industrial societies. It is not human needs but the endless accumulation of exchange value in the form of money that is the main driving force behind all human productive efforts. This has transformed human individuals, with their personal qualities and abilities, into commodities which are sold and bought according to the anonymous laws of the market, within a system of hired labor. It has generated the alienated institutional framework of modern political societies; and it has produced an inevitable split between people's personal, selfish, self-centered lives as members of civil society on the one hand and, on the other, the artificial and obscure community which they form as members of a political society. As a result, human consciousness was bound to suffer an ideological distortion: instead of affirming human life and its own function as an "expression" of that life, it built a separate, illusory kingdom of its own, designed to perpetuate this split. With private property, the alienation of labor divided society into hostile classes struggling for the distribution of the surplus product finally, it gave rise to the class in which all society's dehumanization was concentrated, and which was consequently destined both to demystify consciousness and to restore the lost unity of human existence. This revolutionary process starts with smashing the institutional mechanisms which protect existing labor conditions and ends with a society where, with all the basic sources of social conflict removed, the social process is subordinated to the collective will of the individuals associated in it. These latter will then be able to unfold all their individual potentialities not against society but for its enrichment; their labor will have been gradually reduced to the necessary minimum, and free time will be enjoyed in the pursuit of cultural creativity and high-quality entertainment. The full meaning of both history and present struggles is revealed only in the romantic vision of the perfectly united mankind of the future. Such unity implies no more need for the mediating mechanisms which separate individuals from the species as a whole. The revolutionary act that will close the "pre-history" of mankind is both inevitable and directed by free will; the distinction between freedom and necessity will have disappeared in the consciousness of the proletariat as it becomes aware of its own historical destiny through the destruction of the old order.

I suspect it was both Marx's anticipation of man's perfect unity and his myth of the historically privileged proletarian consciousness that led to his theory's being turned into the ideology of the totalitarian movement; not because he conceived of it in such terms, but because its basic values could not be realized in any other way. It was not that Marx's theory lacked a vision of future society; it did not. But even his powerful imagination could not stretch so far as to envisage the transition from "pre-history" to "genuine history" and come up with the proper social technology for converting the former into the latter; this step had to be carried out by practical leaders. And that necessarily implied adding to the inherited body of doctrine and filling in the details.

In his dream of a perfectly unified humanity Marx was not, strictly speaking, a Rousseauist; Rousseau did not believe that the lost spontaneous identity of each individual with the community would ever be restored and the poison of civilization effaced from human memory. But this was precisely what Marx did believe: not because he believed that jettisoning civilization and returning to the primitive happiness of a savage state was possible or desirable, but because he believed that the irresistible progress of technology would ultimately overcome (dialectically) its own destructiveness and offer humanity a new unity—a unity based not on the suppression of needs but on freedom from wants. In this respect he shared the hopes of the St. Simonists.*

Marx's liberated mankind needs none of the machinery with which bourgeois society settles conflicts among individuals or between them and society: law, state, representative democracy, and negative freedom, as conceived and proclaimed in the Declaration of Human Rights. Such machinery is characteristic of societies ruled economically by the market and composed of isolated individuals with their conflicting interests; it is what they must rely on to maintain their stability. The state and its legal skeleton protect bourgeois property by coercion and impose rules on conflicts; their very existence presupposes a society where human activities and desires naturally clash with each other. The liberal concept of freedom implies that my freedom inevitably limits the freedom of my fellow men, and this is indeed the case if the scope of freedom coincides with the scale

---

* St. Simonists were the followers of Claude Henri, comte de Saint-Simon. Saint-Simon argued history was moving inexorably toward socialism and that science properly understood could be a guide for social improvement. Kolakowski elsewhere refers to him as the "founder of modern theoretical socialism."

of ownership. Once the bourgeois order is replaced by a system of communal property, this machinery no longer has any purpose. Individual interests converge with universal ones, and there is no more need to shore up society's unstable equilibrium with regulations that define the limits of individual freedom. And it is not only the "rational" instruments of liberal society that are then done away with: inherited tribal and national ties will also disappear. In this respect the capitalist order paves the way for Communism: under the cosmopolitan power of capital and as a result of the internationalist consciousness of the proletariat, the old, irrational loyalties crumble away. The end of this process is a community where nothing is left except the individual and the human species as a whole, and where individuals will directly identify their own lives, abilities, and activities as social forces: they will have no need of political institutions or traditional national ties to mediate this experience of their identity.

How can this be achieved? Is there a technique for effecting such social transubstantiation? Marx did not answer this question, and from his point of view it seems wrongly put: the point was not to find a technique of social engineering after drawing an arbitrary picture of a desirable society, but to identify and "express" theoretically the social forces which are already at work to bring such a society about. And expressing them meant practically reinforcing their energy and providing them with the self-knowledge necessary for their conscious self-identification.

There were a number of possible practical interpretations of Marx's message, depending on which values one considered fundamental to the doctrine and which formulations one interpreted as basic dues to the whole. There seems nothing wrong with the interpretation which became the Leninist-Stalinist version of Marxism. It went as follows:

Marxism is a ready-made doctrinal body, identical with the class-consciousness of the proletariat in its mature and theoretically elaborated form. Marxism is true both because it has "scientific" value and because it articulates the aspirations of the "most progressive" social class. The distinction between "truth" in the genetic and the ordinary sense of the word has always been obscure in the doctrine; it was taken for granted that the "proletariat," by virtue of its historical mission, has a privileged cognitive position, and therefore that its vision of the social "totality" has to be right. Thus the "progressive" automatically becomes the "true," whether or not this truth could be confirmed by universally accepted scientific procedures.

This is a simplified version of the Marxist concept of class consciousness. Certainly, the party's claim to have a monopoly on truth did not automatically follow from it; the equation also required the specifically Leninist notion of the party. But there was nothing anti-Marxist in this notion. If Marx did not have a theory of the party, he did have a concept of a vanguard group which was supposed to articulate the latent consciousness of the working class, and he saw his own theory as an expression of that consciousness. The idea that a "proper" working class revolutionary consciousness had to be instilled into the spontaneous workers' movement from without was one that Lenin took from Kautsky* and supplemented with an important addition: that since only two basic ideologies can exist in a society torn by class struggle between the bourgeoisie and the proletariat, it follows that an ideology which is not proletarian—i.e., not identical with the ideology of the vanguard party—is necessarily bourgeois. Thus, since the workers are incapable of producing their own class ideology unaided, the ideology they will produce by their own efforts must be a bourgeois one. In other words, the empirical, "spontaneous" consciousness of the workers can only generate what is essentially a bourgeois *Weltanschauung*. Consequently, the Marxist party, while being the only vehicle for truth, is also entirely independent of the empirical (and by definition bourgeois) consciousness of the workers (except that it sometimes has to make tactical concessions in order not to run too far ahead of the proletariat if it is canvassing for its support).

This remains true after the seizure of power. As the sole possessor of truth, the party may completely discard (except in a tactical sense) the (inevitably immature) empirical consciousness of the masses. Indeed it must do so: it cannot do otherwise without betraying its historical mission. It knows both the "laws of historical development" and the proper connections between the "base" and the "superstructure," and is therefore perfectly able to discern which elements of the real, empirical consciousness of the people deserve destruction as surviving remnants from a past historical epoch. Religious ideas clearly fall into this category, but so does everything that makes the minds of the people different in content from the minds of their leaders.

---

* Karl Kautsky (1854–1938) was the central defender of Marxism during the period of the Second International. He was denounced by Lenin for his critique of the Bolshevik Revolution.

Within this conception of the proletarian consciousness, the dictatorship over minds is entirely justified: the party really does know better than society what society's genuine (as opposed to empirical) desires, interests, and thoughts are. And once the spirit of the party is incarnated in one leader (as the highest expression of society's unity), we have the ultimate equation: truth = proletarian consciousness = Marxism = the party's ideology = the party leaders' ideas = the chief's decisions. The theory which endows the proletariat with a sort of cognitive privilege culminates in the statement that Comrade Stalin is never wrong. And there is nothing un-Marxist in this equation.

The concept of the party as the sole possessor of truth was of course strongly reinforced by the expression "the dictatorship of the proletariat," which Marx used casually two or three times without explanation. Kautsky, Martov, and other Social Democrats could argue that what Marx meant by "dictatorship" was the class content of government rather than its form, and that the term was not to be understood in opposition to a democratic state; but Marx did not specifically say anything of the sort in this context. And there was nothing obviously wrong in taking the word "dictatorship" at its face value, to mean precisely what Lenin meant and expressly said: a reign based entirely on violence and not limited by law.

Beside the question of the party's "historical right" to impose its despotism on all domains of life, there was the question of the content of this despotism. This was solved in a way that was basically in keeping with Marx's predictions. Liberated mankind was supposed to abolish the distinction between state and civil society, to eliminate all the mediating devices that had prevented individuals from achieving a perfect identity with the "whole," to destroy the bourgeois freedom that entailed conflicts of private interests, and to demolish the system of hired labor which compelled workers to sell themselves like commodities. Marx did not spell out exactly how this unity was to be achieved, except for one indisputable point: the expropriation of the expropriators—i.e., the elimination of the private ownership of the means of production. One could, and ought, to argue that once this historical act of expropriation has been performed, all remaining social conflicts are merely the expression of a backward (bourgeois) mentality left over from the old society. But the party knows what the content of the correct mentality corresponding to the new relations of productions should be, and it is naturally entitled to suppress all phenomena which are out of keeping with it.

What would, in fact, be the appropriate technique to reach this desirable unity? The economic foundations have been laid. One could argue that Marx did not mean for civil society to be suppressed or replaced by the state, but rather expected the state to wither away, leaving only the "administration of things," with political government becoming superfluous. But if the state is by definition an instrument of the working class on its road to Communism; it cannot by definition use its power against the "toiling masses," only against the relics of capitalist society. And how could the "administration of things," or economic management, not involve the use and distribution of labor, i.e., of all working people? Hired labor—the free market of the labor force—was to be eliminated. This duly happened. But what if Communist enthusiasm alone proves an insufficient incentive for people to work? Clearly, this means that they are imprisoned in bourgeois consciousness, which it is the task of the state to destroy. Consequently, the way to eliminate hired labor is to replace it by coercion. And how is the unity of civil and political society to be implemented if only the political society expresses the "correct" will of the people? Here again, whatever opposes and resists that will is by definition a survival of the capitalist order; so once more the only way toward unity is through the destruction of civil society by the state.

Whoever argues that people should be educated to cooperate freely and without compulsion must answer the question: at what stage and by what means can such education be successful? It is certainly counter to Marx's theory to expect it to be possible in capitalist society, where the working people are weighed down by the overwhelming influence of bourgeois ideology (Did not Marx say that the ideas of the ruling class are ruling ideas? Is it not pure utopia to hope for a moral transformation of society in a capitalist order?). And after the seizure of power, education is the task of the most enlightened vanguard of society; compulsion is used only against the "survivals of capitalism." So there is no need to distinguish between the production of the "new man" of socialism and sheer coercion; in consequence, the distinction between liberation and slavery is inevitably blurred.

The question of freedom (in the "bourgeois" sense) becomes irrelevant in the new society. Did not Engels say that genuine freedom should be defined as the extent to which people were capable of both subjugating their natural environment and consciously regulating social processes? On

172

this definition, the more society is technologically advanced, the freer it is; and the more social life is submitted to a unified directing force, the freer it is. Engels did not mention that this regulation of society would necessarily involve free elections or any other bourgeois contrivances of the sort; and there is no reason to maintain that a society entirely regulated by one center of despotic power is not perfectly free in this sense.

One can find many quotations in Marx and Engels to the effect that throughout human history the "superstructure" has been at the service of the corresponding relations of property in a given society, that the state is nothing but a tool for keeping intact the existing relations of production, and that the law cannot but be a weapon of class power. It is valid to conclude that the same situation continues in the new society, at least as long as Communism in its absolute form has not entirely dominated the earth. In other words, the law is an instrument of the political power of the "proletariat," and since it is just a technique for wielding power (its main task being, more often than not, to cover up violence and deceive the people), it makes no difference whether the victorious class rules with the help of the law or without it. What matters is the class content of power, not its "form." Moreover, it also seems valid to conclude that the new "superstructure" must serve the new "base"; this means, among other things, that cultural life as a whole must be entirely subordinated to political "tasks" as defined by the "ruling class," speaking through the mouth of its most conscious element. It is therefore arguable that universal servility as the guiding principle of cultural life in the Stalinist system was a proper deduction from the "base-superstructure" theory. The same applies to the sciences: again, did not Engels say that the sciences should not be left to themselves, without theoretical philosophical guidance, lest they fall into all sorts of empiricist absurdities? And indeed this was how many Soviet philosophers and party leaders from the start justified the control of all the sciences (in their content as well as their scope of interest) by philosophy—i.e., by party ideology. In the 1920s Karl Korsch had already pointed out the obvious connection between philosophy's claim to supremacy and the Soviet system of ideological tyranny over the sciences.

Many critical Marxists considered this to be a caricature of Marxism. I would not deny this. I would add, however, that one can talk meaningfully of "caricature" only if the caricature resembles the original—as in this case it does. Nor would I deny the obvious fact that Marx's thought was much richer, subtler, and more differentiated than it might seem from the few quotations which are endlessly repeated in Leninist-Stalinist ideology to justify the Soviet system of power. Still, I would argue that these quotations are not necessarily distortions: that the dry skeleton of Marxism adopted by Soviet ideology was a greatly simplified but not a falsified guide to building a new society.

The idea that the whole theory of Communism may be summed up by the single phrase "abolition of private property" was not invented by Stalin. Nor did he come up with the idea that wage labor cannot exist without capital, or that the state must have centralized control over the means of production, or that national hostilities will disappear together with class antagonisms. All these ideas are, as we know, clearly stated in the *Communist Manifesto*. Taken together, they do not merely suggest but logically imply that once the factories and the land are state owned, as was to happen in Russia, society is basically liberated. This was precisely the claim made by Lenin, Trotsky, and Stalin.

The point is that Marx really did consistently believe that human society would not be "liberated" without achieving unity. And there is no known technique apart from despotism whereby the unity of society can be achieved: no way of suppressing the tension between civil and political society except by the suppression of civil society; no means of eliminating the conflicts between the individual and the "whole" except by the destruction of the individual; no way toward a "higher," "positive" freedom—as opposed to "negative," "bourgeois" freedom—except through the suppression of the latter. And if the whole of human history is to be conceived in class terms—if all values, all political and legal institutions, ideas and moral norms, religious and philosophical beliefs, all forms of artistic creativity, etc., are nothing but instruments of "real" class interests (and there are many passages to this effect in Marx's writings)—then it does follow that the new society must start by a violent break in cultural continuity from the old one. (In fact the continuity cannot be entirely broken, and in Soviet society a selective continuity was accepted from the beginning; the radical quest for "proletarian culture" was only a short-lived extravagance sponsored by the leadership. The emphasis on selective continuity grew stronger with the development of the Soviet state, mostly as a result of its increasingly nationalist character.)

I suspect that utopias—visions of a perfectly unified society—are not simply impracticable but become counter-productive as soon as we try to create them by institutional means. This is because institutionalized unity and freedom are opposing notions. A society that is deprived of freedom can be unified only in the sense that the expression of conflicts is stifled: the conflicts themselves do not go away. Consequently, it is not unified at all.

I do not deny the importance of the changes that took place in the socialist countries after Stalin's death, although I maintain that the political constitution of these countries has remained intact. But the main point about them is that, however reluctantly it is done, allowing the market some limited impact on production and abandoning or even just loosening rigid ideological control in certain areas of life amounts to renouncing the Marxist vision of unity. What these changes reveal is the impracticability of that vision; they cannot be interpreted as symptoms of a return to "genuine" Marxism—no matter what Marx "would have said."

An additional—although certainly not conclusive—argument in favor of the above interpretation lies in the history of the problem. It would be utterly false to say that "no one could have predicted" such an outcome of Marxist humanist socialism. Anarchist writers actually did predict it, long before the socialist revolution: they thought that a society based on Marx's ideological principles would produce slavery and despotism. Here, at least, mankind cannot complain that it was deceived by history and surprised by the unpredictable connections of things.

The question discussed here is one of "genetic vs. environmental" factors in social development. Even in genetic enquiry, when the properties under investigation are not precisely definable, or when they are mental rather than physical (like "intelligence," for example), it is very difficult to distinguish the respective roles of these factors; how much more difficult, then, to distinguish between the "genetic" and the "environmental" in our social inheritance—between an inherited ideology and the contingent conditions in which people try to implement it. It is common sense that both factors are at work in any particular case, and that we have no way of calculating their relative importance and expressing it in quantitative terms. To say that "genes" (the inherited ideology) are entirely responsible for how the child turns out is just as silly as saying that the "environment" (contingent historical events) can entirely account for it. (In the case of Stalinism, these two unacceptably extreme positions are expressed respectively as the view that Stalinism was in fact "no more than" Marxism realized and as the view that it was "no more than" a continuation of the czarist empire.) But although we cannot perform a calculation and assign each set of factors its "fair share" of responsibility, we can still reasonably ask whether or not the mature form was anticipated by the "genetic" conditions.

The continuity I have tried to trace back from Stalinism to Marxism appears in still sharper outline when we look at the transition from Leninism to Stalinism. The non-Bolshevik factions (the Mensheviks,* not to mention the liberals) were aware of the general direction Bolshevism was taking, and predicted its outcome fairly accurately, just after 1917; moreover, the despotic character of the new system was soon attacked within the party itself (by the "Workers' Opposition" and then the Left Opposition—e.g., Rakovsky†) long before Stalinism was securely established. The Mensheviks saw all their predictions borne out in the 1930s, and Trotsky's belated rejoinder to their "we told you so" is pathetically unconvincing. They may have predicted what would happen, he argued, but still they were quite wrong, for they believed that despotism would come as a result of Bolshevik rule; it has indeed come, he said, but as a result of a bureaucratic coup. *Qui vult decipi, decipiatur.*‡

---

* Mensheviks. See the note to Martov on page 81.

† Christian Rakovsky was Leon Trotsky's principal collaborator. He was executed by the NKVD during World War II.

‡ *Qui vult decipi, decipiatur.* "Whoever wishes to be deceived, let them be deceived."

11

The Image of the Body and Totalitarianism
(1979)

Claude Lefort

The problem of totalitarianism has long occupied a central position in my thinking and requires, I believe, a new approach to politics. This term has enjoyed a rise in its fortunes recently, at least as applied to regimes described as "socialist." It is true that Hannah Arendt, Raymond Aron and a few, very few others, including myself, made use of it twenty or twenty-five years ago, taking it in its widest sense, to describe its socialist as well as Fascist variants. Each of us was following his or her own course; for my part, I did not know the work of Hannah Arendt when, after devoting a number of studies to the critique of bureaucracy (the first being published in 1948), I began to work out a more clearly political conceptualization in an essay entitled "Totalitarianism without Stalin," which dates from 1956. To speak of totalitarianism in relation to the Soviet Union was regarded as scandalous at the time and continued to be so until fairly recently. Today the term surprises no one. I would even say that it has become worn out before becoming meaningful. What does it signify? It signifies a regime in which state violence is practiced on society as a whole, a system of generalized, detailed coercion—scarcely more than that. It is now becoming the foundation of a new kind of political thinking, a new interpretation of the history of modern societies or of history in general. So I am a little afraid of adding my voice to the concert of those known as "new philosophers." But I have regarded totalitarianism for too long as the major fact of our time, posing an enigma that calls for a reexamination of the genesis of political societies, to give into the fear that I might be following fashion.

Having referred to my earliest work on bureaucracy, I should also indicate or remind the reader that my thinking was carried out at first within the horizons of Marxism. In close collaboration with Castoriadis,* who had at an early stage identified the features of a new social formation in the USSR, I set out to demonstrate the class division that had grown up after the Russian Revolution and the specific character of a state with which the dominant class, the bureaucracy, had become interlocked. The bureaucracy did not find the basis of its power in private property, but collectively, interdependently, in its dependence on state power, the party-state, which possessed all the means of production. This bureaucratic stratum displayed a strength and stability that Trotskyist thought was incapable of grasping; for the Trotskyists continued to imagine that a mere caste, parasitical and transitory, had superimposed itself on a socialist infrastructure and they failed to realize that a new form of domination and exploitation had been established at the expense of the peasantry, the proletariat and the overwhelming majority of the population.

Comparing the bourgeoisie and the bureaucracy, I observed that the latter offered a remarkable contrast between the strength of its constitution as a class and the fragility of the position of its members, who were constantly threatened with annihilation, whatever their rank and authority, on account of their subjection to political power. The great Stalinist purges showed that the bureaucracy was ideally everything and the bureaucrats nothing; the periodic eviction of thousands or tens of thousands of bureaucrats, far from being contrary to the interests of the bureaucracy, seemed to me to be proof of its power, beyond the fate of individuals. I developed these analyses under the aegis of what seemed to me to be authentic Marxism, the Marxism of Marx, which I regarded as having been completely distorted in all the versions of so-called orthodox Marxism. This being the case, I firmly believed, at the time, in the role of the proletariat. It was, in my view, the privileged agent of history. I thought, in short, that the bureaucracy, although it had taken advantage of the modern conditions of industrial society, had been able to constitute itself and develop as a historical force only because the working class had

* Cornelius Castoriadis and Lefort together founded the Trostskyite splinter group called Socialisme ou Barbarie (1949–1966), dedicated to reviving the idea of real workers' self-government as true socialism.

178

been divided, opposed to itself, during its century-long struggles to organize and emancipate itself; because it had given rise to a dominant stratum, it had become alienated from itself in the figure of a Leader, a power that turned out to be an alien force working for its own gain. By virtue of a dialectic, whose resources we know only too well, I concluded that this alienation of the proletariat from itself, this ultimate form of alienation, was necessary, that the proletariat had to go through this experience at the end of which a bureaucracy separated itself off from it and turned against it, so that the need for an abolition of all social division, and not only of private property, would be fully affirmed. Thus the representation of a society delivered from division governed my thinking.

But there are two reasons, it now seems to me, which contradicted that Marxist perspective and prevented me from fully accepting a conception that reduced the creativity of history to that of the proletariat. These two reasons apparently belong to quite different orders. In the first place, at the very moment when I imagined an abolition of social division and found in the proletariat the true agent of history, I was reading Marx in a way which encouraged and facilitated questioning. In terms of my background, I am neither a sociologist nor a political scientist. My training is philosophical, and I acquired it, while still on the lycée benches, from Merleau-Ponty, a thinker who had a gift for breaking certainties, introducing complications where one sought simplification, who refused the distinction between the subject and the object, taught that the true questions were not to be exhausted in the answers, that they come not only from us, but are the sign of our interaction with the world, with others, with being itself. So drawn to, indeed enchanted by Marx, I nevertheless could not read him without satisfying the high standards laid down by the philosophy of Merleau-Ponty. I developed a relation to Marx's work in and through my questioning of it. No doubt what I found there responded to a desire within me whose origin I could not identify, but that is of little significance. The fact is that what attracted me in Marx was the ambiguity of his thinking and, more than that, his opposition to himself, the way in which his thought escapes from itself in the best of his works and from one work to another, the indetermination that undermined what was presented as a system, that undermined the commentary which he himself sometimes gave on his work in order to bring it together in the form of theses.

179

For instance, I very soon became aware of an opposition in Marx between the notions of continuity and discontinuity in history: the idea of an ineluctable movement governed by the growth of productive forces, moving from one mode of production to another, on the one hand, and the idea of a radical break between all precapitalist modes of production and modern capitalism, on the other; or in other words, an opposition between the idea of a dissolution of all restricted social relations and the idea of a force of conservation, of mechanisms of repetition which, even in capitalism, seemed to ensure the permanence of a structure. Similarly, I was very aware of the vacillation of an interpretation that sometimes was concerned solely to discover the material foundations of social life and its evolution, while at others revealed the full weight of the social imaginary, the function of the phantoms that haunt the present or the function of fetishism—an interpretation that was sometimes Darwinian, sometimes Shakespearean in inspiration. In short, while being drawn to the theory of the proletariat or of a classless society, I was no less attracted by the elusive elements in Marx's work. Thus, unknown to myself, the ideal of a complete determination of social reality, of the essence of history, was in contradiction with the discovery of an indetermination proper to thought, of a movement that removed statements from any univocal determination. If I have taken the liberty of referring to this relation to Marx's work, it is in order to make it clear that there could be no full adherence to his thought, no question of resting firmly on his theory, as soon it became apparent that, at one and the same time and somewhat paradoxically, the proletariat provided me with the guarantee of social practice and history while the guarantee of this guarantee—namely, Marx's thought—was the object of my questioning. It was inevitable that the moment would come when my earlier certainties would crumble.

The second reason I referred to concerns my experience, while still very young, as a militant in a small political group. I think a brief mention of this will throw light on what I have to say. I joined the Trotskyist party before the end of the war and remained in it for about four years. This group originated, as is well known, in the condemnation of Stalinism. It presented itself as the legitimate heir of Marxism-Leninism, claimed to be taking up the task initiated by the Russian Revolution and prefigured in the Paris Commune; it denounced the counter-revolutionary role of the Communist parties, seeing them as carrying out, *mutatis mutandis*, the same role once played by the social democrats. Whereas the Third International had condemned the betrayal of the interests of the proletariat by the Second International, the Fourth now condemned the Third International and, in short, demanded a return to primal sources. The Trotskyist party claimed allegiance to a founding hero, Trotsky, a hero who was both dead and immortal, and claimed allegiance more generally to a dynasty; immortality was embodied in the crown that had been worn successively by Marx, Engels, Lenin and Trotsky. And that crown guaranteed the immortality of the "body" of the revolutionaries. Stalin, on the other hand, was represented as the usurper that the body of the revolutionaries would expel. Now it gradually occurred to me that the Trotskyist party functioned like a microbureaucracy, despite the rules of so-called democratic centralism which allowed a conflict of tendencies—a conflict that was intense at times. The power of the apparatus, the division between leaders and followers, the manipulation of meetings, the withholding of information, the separation of activities, the stereotyped character of the dominant discourse in its various forms, the imperviousness to events that might challenge the correctness of practice and theory: innumerable such signs convinced me that, despite the enormous gulf between our group and the Communist Party, one could find in the former a tiny replica of the latter. What concerned me was that this microbureaucracy had no basis of a material kind. The positions of power occupied by a small number of militants were ultimately based on the possession of a certain knowledge, a skill in speaking and, to be more precise, the ability to inscribe every internal or external fact in a mytho-history. Russia provided the privileged context for this. It would be impossible here to enumerate all the sacred episodes that, from the formation of Bolshevism to the Stalinist betrayals, made up the register on which the present acquired its meaning. The function of this mytho-history, of the discourse that found its referent there, profoundly disturbed me. After all, this was precisely how I exercised whatever power I had in the party.

It seems to me that not only are we confronted by the problem of bureaucracy, but that certain elements of totalitarianism are to be found here. I don't mean, of course, that I regard the small party to which I belonged as a totalitarian embryo. That is certainly not the case. Indeed it did not have the means of being so. But what strikes me, and already struck me then, was the closed nature of the party, supported by a discourse that was supposedly scientific, declaring the rationality of the real and governed throughout by the representation of what had taken place— of the already-done, the already-thought, the already-seen. This discourse is fundamentally invulnerable; it is subject to error and rectification in fact, but not in principle. It imprints the signs of the real in a text—that of the great authors, but more usually that of a founding past—and it constantly nourishes the reading of the great text with these signs. And what strikes me no less is that the closed nature of this discourse derives from the fact that it is the discourse of no one person: it is the discourse of the party, the ideal body of the revolutionary, which traverses each of its members. Each individual sees himself caught up in an *us*, a *nous*, which imposes a break with the outside; the things of the world, which everybody talks about so much, can be grasped only by being carried back to the imaginary enclosure of history, of which the party is the trustee. And while the militant is incorporated, the supposed real is destined to be assimilated.

The two experiences that I have described are not unrelated. The first cannot be confined to the sphere of theory, the second to the sphere of practice. Being a militant presupposes a certain relationship to knowledge. Every Communist is a person of knowledge, his identity is bound up with a body of knowledge that enables him to apprehend texts and things. The adventure of interpretation, on the other hand, implies a relation to power. To read a work, and I have experienced this even more in connection with Machiavelli than with Marx, is to allow yourself to lose the bearings which assured you of your sovereign distance from the other, which assured you of the distinction between subject and object, active and passive, speaking and hearing (to interpret is to convert reading into writing), the difference between one time and another, between past and present (the latter can neither be suppressed nor ignored), lastly it is to lose your sense of the division between the space of the work and the world on to which it opens. Thus by different paths, which cross and recross, I was gradually led to carry my questioning to the very center of Marxist certainty.

I have now come to the question that I wanted to pose, after giving a brief indication of how I arrived at it. Why is totalitarianism a major event in our time, why does it require us to probe the nature of modern society? At the foundation of totalitarianism lies the representation of the People-as-One. It is denied that division is constitutive of society.

The Image of the Body and Totalitarianism

In the so-called socialist world, there can be no other division than that between the people and its enemies: a division between inside and outside, no internal division. After the revolution, socialism is not only supposed to prepare the way for the emergence of a classless society, it must already manifest that society which bears within itself the principle of homogeneity and self-transparency. The paradox is the following: division is denied—I say denied, since a new dominant stratum is actively distinguishing itself from the rest of society, since a state apparatus is separating itself off from society—and, at the same time as this denial, a division is being affirmed, on the level of phantasy, between the People-as-One and the Other. This Other is the other of the outside. It is a term to be taken literally: the Other is the representative of the forces deriving from the old society (kulaks, bourgeoisie) and the emissary of the foreigner, the imperialist world. Indeed these two representations converge, for it is always imagined that the representatives of the old society are linked up with foreign centers. So it is understandable that the constitution of the People-as-One requires the incessant production of enemies. It is not only necessary to convert, at the level of phantasy, real adversaries of the regime or real opponents into the figures of the evil Other: it is also necessary to invent them. However, this interpretation can be carried further. The campaigns of exclusion, persecution, and, for quite awhile, terror reveal a new image of the social body. The enemy of the people is regarded as a parasite or a waste product to be eliminated. The documents assembled by Solzhenitsyn, some of which have been known for a very long time, are highly instructive in this regard. The pursuit of the enemies of the people is carried out in the name of an ideal of social prophylaxis, and this has been the case since Lenin's time. What is at stake is always the integrity of the body. It is as if the body had to assure itself of its own identity by expelling its waste matter, or as if it had to close in upon itself by withdrawing from the outside, by averting the threat of an intrusion by alien elements. So there must be no failures in the functioning of institutions, failures that might suggest a relaxation in the monitoring of the mechanism of elimination or an attack from disruptive agents. The campaign against the enemy is feverish; fever is good, it is a signal, within society, that there is some evil to combat.

It should also be observed that in totalitarian ideology, the representation of the People-as-One is in no way contradictory with that of the party. The party does not appear as distinct from the people or from the proletariat, which is the quintessence of it. It does not have a specific reality *within* society. The party *is* the proletariat in the sense that it is identical with it. At the same time, it is the guide or, as Lenin put it, the consciousness of the proletariat; or, as I would say, using an old political metaphor, to which I shall come back, it is its head. And, similarly, the representation of the People-as-One is not in contradiction with that of an omnipotent, omniscient power, with, in the last analysis, that of the *Egocrat* (to use Solzhenitsyn's term), the ultimate figure of that power. Such a power, detached from the social whole, towering over everything, merges with the party, with the people, with the proletariat. It merges with the body as a whole, while at the same time it is its head. A whole sequence of representations is to be found here, the logic of which should not escape us. Identification of the people with the proletariat, of the proletariat with the party, of the party with the leadership, of the leadership with the *Egocrat*. On each occasion, an organ is both the whole and the detached part that makes the whole, that institutes it. This logic of identification, secretly governed by the image of the body, accounts in turn for the condensation that takes place between the principle of power, the principle of law and the principle of knowledge. The denial of social division goes hand in hand with the denial of a symbolic distinction which is constitutive of society. The attempt to incorporate power in society, society in the state, implies that there is nothing, in a sense, that can indicate an externality to the social and to the organ that represents it by detaching itself from it. The dimension of law and the dimension of knowledge tend to be effaced, insofar as they do not, as we know very well, belong to the order of things which are socially (or indeed psychologically) conceivable, insofar as they cannot be located in empirical social life, insofar as they establish the very condition of human sociability. A kind of positivisation of the manifest law takes place through intense legislative, legal activity, at the service of the totalitarian state; and a sort of positivisation of manifest knowledge takes place through intense ideological activity—ideology becoming that enterprise of phantasy which tends to produce and to fix the ultimate foundations of knowledge in every sphere. In fact, what one sees is the attempt by power to appropriate the law and the knowledge of the principles and ultimate goals of social life. But this language is still inadequate, for it would be wrong to attribute power with unbridled freedom; to do so would be to confuse, once again, arbitrary power with totalitarian power. Of course, it is true that in innumerable ways power manipulates and subjugates legal rules and "ideas." But one must also see that it is caught up in ideology: the power of discourse is fully affirmed, while the true discourse becomes a discourse of power.

And we must also see that the law, positivized and reduced to the law of socialism, regulates power and renders it opaque to itself, more opaque than it ever was before.

This very sketchy interpretation is concerned only, I should like to stress, with the aim of totalitarianism. It is not my purpose here to inquire into the facts of social development and change. Were this the case, I would have to try to analyze all the forms of resistance to the totalitarian project—and I am not speaking here of conscious, political resistance, but of the social relations that elude the grip of power. I would also have to try to analyze all the pathological processes of the bureaucratic world, for the perversion of the function of power, of law and of knowledge has effects on the whole of social life—let us be in no doubt—even when there is not, or no longer, any support for the regime. Among others, Alexander Zinoviev is one of the most severe analysts of this pathology.

My purpose is rather to bring out, and to submit to the reader's questioning, the image of the political body in totalitarianism. It is an image which, on the one hand, requires the exclusion of the malevolent Other and which, simultaneously, breaks down into the image of a whole and a part that stands for the whole, of a part that paradoxically reintroduces the figure of the other, the omniscient, omnipotent, benevolent other, the militant, the leader, the Egocrat. This other offers his own body—individual, mortal, endowed with all the virtues—whether he is called Stalin or Mao or Fidel. A mortal body which is perceived as invulnerable, which condenses in itself all strengths, all talents, and defies the laws of nature by his super-male energy.

Of course, I am aware that I am drawing on only one thread of the interpretation. I cannot develop this remark here, but I should like to suggest that we ought to examine another pole of the totalitarian representation—that of the organization. Or, to use another term which is more likely to convey the discordance within the totalitarian representation, I would say that the image of the body is combined with that of the machine. The scientifico-technical model and the model of the production enterprise, governed by the rational division of labor, have not only been imported from Western capitalism, but have in a sense taken hold of the whole society. Socialism seems to be linked, at least in an ideal way, with the formula of a harmonious society, in touch with itself through all its parts, delivered from the dysfunctions of a system in which the various sectors of activity each obeyed specific norms and in which their interdependence remained at the mercy of the vicissitudes of the market. The new society is presented as a single organization comprising a network of micro-organizations; furthermore, it is presented paradoxically as that "great automaton" which Marx claimed to uncover in the capitalist mode of production. It is worth pointing out that such a representation is split in two: the social, in its essence, is defined as organization and as the organizable. From the first point of view, socialist man is the man of the organization, imprinted in it; from the second point of view, he is the constantly working organizer, the social engineer. But it is important above all to note the articulation of the two key images, that of the body and that of the machine. In a sense, they are convergent: they involve an ambiguity of the same kind. In the first case, the political agent is dissolved in an us that speaks, hears, reads reality through him, thus identifying himself with the party, the body of the people and, at the same time, representing himself, through the same identification, as the head of that body, attributing consciousness to himself. In the second case, the same agent proves to be a part of the machine, or one of its organs, or a driving belt—a frequently used metaphor—and at the same time an activist-machinist who makes decisions concerning the functioning and production of society. However, the two images do not fully merge; the image of the body is altered when it comes into contact with that of the machine. The latter contradicts the logic of identification; the Communist "us" is itself dissolved. The notion of the organization, even though it gives rise to that of the organizer, poses a threat to the substance of the body politic, making the social appear at the boundaries of the inorganic.

I shall now dare to ask the question, from where does the totalitarian adventure arise? It is not born out of nothing. It is the sign of a political mutation. But what is that mutation? It seems to me that it would be futile to try to analyze it at the level of the mode of production, as the consequence of a final concentration of capital; but it would be equally futile to treat it, as some have been content to do, as the product of the phantasies of revolutionary intellectuals, seeking to complete the work of the Jacobins of 1793 in order to reconstruct the world on a *tabula rasa*. In my view, totalitarianism can be clarified only by grasping its relationship with democracy. It is from democracy that it arises, even though it has taken root initially, at least in its socialist version, in countries where the democratic transformation was only just beginning. It overturns that transformation, while at the same time taking over some of its features and extending them at the level of phantasy.

In what characteristics can we discern this process? I believe that my brief comments on the image of the body politic indicate the lines of a response. For modern democracy is that regime in which such an image tends to vanish. I say *regime* advisedly. Taken in its conventional sense, this term is inadequate. Beyond a historically determined system of political institutions, I wish to call attention to a long-term process, what de Tocqueville called the democratic revolution, which he saw coming to birth in France under the *ancien régime* and which, since his time, has continued to develop. As we know, this revolution found its motive force in the equalization of *conditions*. However important this phenomenon may be, it does not shed enough light for my purpose and it leaves an essential mutation in the shadows: the society of the *ancien régime* represented its unity and its identity to itself as that of a body—a body which found its figuration in the body of the king, or rather which identified itself with the king's body, while at the same time it attached itself to it as its head. As Ernst Kantorowicz* has shown in a masterly fashion, such a symbolism was elaborated in the Middle Ages and is of theologico-political origin. The image of the king's body as a double body, both mortal and immortal, individual and collective, was initially underpinned by the body of Christ. The important point for my purpose—it would be quite outside the scope of this essay to analyze the many displacements of this representation in the course of history—is that, long after the features of liturgical royalty had died away, the king still possessed the power to incarnate in his body the community of the kingdom, now invested with the sacred, a political community, a national community, a mystical body. I am not unaware of the fact that in the eighteenth century this representation was

---

* See Ernst Kantorowicz, *The King's Two Bodies: A Study in Mediaeval Political Theology* (1957).

187

largely undermined, that new models of sociability emerged as a result of the growth of individualism, progress in the equalization of conditions of which de Tocqueville spoke and the development of the state administration, which tended to make the latter appear as an independent, impersonal entity. But the changes that occurred did not entirely eliminate the notion of the kingdom as a unity which was both organic and mystical, of which the monarch was at the same time the body and the head. It can also be seen that, paradoxically, the growth of social mobility and the increasing uniformity of behavior, customs, opinions and rules had the effect of strengthening rather than weakening the traditional symbolism. The *ancien régime* was made up of an infinite number of small bodies which gave individuals their distinctive marks. And these small bodies fitted together within a great imaginary body for which the body of the king provided the model and the guarantee of its integrity. The democratic revolution, for so long subterranean, burst out when the body of the king was destroyed, when the body politic was decapitated and when, at the same time, the corporeality of the social was dissolved. There then occurred what I would call a "disincorporation" of individuals. This was an extraordinary phenomenon, the consequences of which seemed, in the first half of the nineteenth century, absurd, even monstrous, not only to conservatives, but to many liberals. For these individuals might become entities that would have to be counted in a universal suffrage that would take the place of the universal invested in the body politic. The relentless struggle to combat the idea of universal suffrage is not only the indication of a class struggle. The inability to conceive of this suffrage as anything other than a dissolution of the social is extremely instructive. The danger of numbers is greater than the danger of an intervention by the masses on the political scene; the idea of number as such is opposed to the idea of the substance of society. Number breaks down unity, destroys identity.

But if we must speak of a disincorporation of the individual, we must also analyze the disengagement of civil society from a state, itself hitherto consubstantial with the body of the king. Or, to put it another way, we must examine the emergence of social relations, not only economic ones, but legal, educational, and scientific relations which have their own dynamic; and, more specifically, we must examine the disentangling of the spheres of power, law, and knowledge that takes place when the identity of the body politic disappears. The modern democratic revolution is best recognized in this mutation: there is no power linked to a body. Power appears as an empty place and those who exercise it as mere mortals who occupy it only temporarily or who could install themselves in it only by force or cunning. There is no law that can be fixed, whose articles cannot be contested, whose foundations are not susceptible of being called into question. Lastly, there is no representation of a center and of the contours of society: unity cannot now efface social division. Democracy inaugurates the experience of an ungraspable, uncontrollable society in which the people will be said to be sovereign, of course, but whose identity will constantly be open to question, whose identity will remain latent.

I referred to the experience of an ungraspable society. It is true that this society gives rise to a multilayered discourse which tries to grasp it; and in this sense it emerges as an object, by the very fact that it is no longer imprinted in the order of nature or in some supernatural order. But it seems remarkable to me that the discourse that may be imputed to bourgeois ideology was maintained in the early days of democracy under the threat of a breakup of society as such. The institutions and values proclaimed—Property, the Family, the State, Authority, the Nation, Culture—were presented as bastions against barbarism, against the unknown forces from without that could destroy society and civilization. The attempt to sacralize institutions through discourse is directly related to the loss of the substance of society, to the disintegration of the body. The bourgeois cult of order which is sustained by the affirmation of authority, in its many forms, by the declaration of the rules and the proper distances between those who occupy the position of master, owner, cultivated man, civilized man, normal man, adult and those who are placed in the position of the *other*, this whole cult testifies to a certain vertigo in face of the void created by an indeterminate society.

However, as I have just suggested, we must be attentive to another aspect of the mutation. What emerges with democracy is the image of society as such, society as purely human but, at the same time, society sui generis, whose own nature requires objective knowledge. It is the image of a society which is homogeneous in principle, capable of being subsumed to the overview of knowledge and power, arising through the dissolution of the monarchical focus of legitimacy and the destruction of the architecture of bodies. It is the image of the omniscient, omnipotent state, of a state both anonymous and, as de Tocqueville puts it, tutelary. It is also, insofar as inequality exists within the boundaries of the equality of conditions, the image of a mass that passes the last judgment on good and evil, the true and the false, the normal and the abnormal, the image of sovereign opinion. Lastly, what emerges is the image of the people, which, as I observed, remains indeterminate, but which nevertheless is susceptible of being determined, of being actualized on the level of phantasy as an image of the People-as-One.

From this point of view, may not totalitarianism be conceived as a response to the questions raised by democracy, as an attempt to resolve its paradoxes? Modern democratic society seems to me, in fact, like a society in which power, law, and knowledge are exposed to a radical indetermination, a society that has become the theatre of an uncontrollable adventure, so that what is instituted never becomes established, the known remains undermined by the unknown, the present proves to be undefinable, covering many different social times which are staggered in relation to one another within simultaneity—or definable only in terms of some fictitious future; an adventure such that the quest for identity cannot be separated from the experience of division. This society is *historical* society par excellence. What seems to me to be condensed beneath the paradoxes of democracy is the status of power, for this power is not, as a certain contemporary discourse naïvely repeats, a mere organ of domination: it is the agency of legitimacy and identity. Now, as long as it appears detached from the prince, as long as it presents itself as the power of no one, as long as it seems to move towards a *latent* focus—namely, the people—it runs the risk of having its symbolic function cancelled out, of falling into collective representations at the level of the real, the contingent, when the conflicts are becoming sharper and leading society to the edge of collapse. Political power, as circumscribed and localized in society at the same time as being an instituting moment, is exposed to the threat of falling into particularity, of arousing what Machiavelli regarded as more dangerous than hatred, namely, contempt; and similarly those who exercise it or aspire to it are exposed to the threat of appearing as individuals or groups concerned solely to satisfy their desires. With totalitarianism an apparatus is set up which tends to stave off this threat, which tends to weld power and society back together again, to efface all signs of social division, to banish the indetermination that haunts the democratic experience. But this attempt, as I have suggested, itself draws on a democratic source, developing and fully affirming the idea of the People-as-One, the idea of society as such, bearing the knowledge of itself, transparent to itself and homogeneous, the idea of mass opinion, sovereign and normative, the idea of the tutelary state.

Since the advent of democracy, and in opposition to it, the body is thus revitalized. But it is important to point out that what is revitalized is quite different from what was once torn apart. The image of the body that informed monarchical society was underpinned by that of Christ. It was invested with the idea of the division between the visible and the invisible, the idea of the splitting of the mortal and the immortal, the idea of mediation, the idea of a production which both effaced and reestablished the difference between the producer and that produced, the idea of the unity of the body and the distinction between the head and the limbs. The prince condensed in his person the principle of power, the principle of law and the principle of knowledge, but he was *supposed* to obey a superior power; he declared himself to be both above the law and subjected to the law, to be both the father and the son of justice; he possessed wisdom but he was subjected to reason. According to the medieval formula, he was *major et minor se ipso*, above and below himself. That does not seem to be the position of the Egocrat or of his substitutes, the bureaucratic leaders. The Egocrat coincides with himself, as society is supposed to coincide with itself. An impossible swallowing up of the body in the head begins to take place, as does an impossible swallowing up of the head in the body. The attraction of the whole is no longer dissociated from the attraction of the parts. Once the old organic constitution disappears, the death instinct is unleashed into the closed, uniform, imaginary space of totalitarianism.

Such, then, are a few thoughts which indicate the direction for a questioning of the political. Some readers will no doubt suspect that my reflections are nourished by psychoanalysis. That is indeed the case. But this connection is meaningful only if one asks oneself at which hearth Freud's thought was lit. For is it not true that in order to sustain the ordeal of the division of the subject, in order to dislodge the reference points of the *self* and the *other*, to depose the position of the possessor of power and knowledge, one must assume responsibility for an experience instituted by democracy, the indetermination that was born from the loss of the substance of the body politic?

12

National Socialism as a Political Religion (2000)

MICHAEL BURLEIGH

Fair is foul, and foul is fair.
Hover through the fog and filthy air.
　　　　　　—William Shakespeare, *Macbeth*

In 1920 the philosopher Bertrand Russell went on a five-week British Labor Party junket to Bolshevik Russia, to witness the "promised land" at first hand. Despite the Bolshevik comrades' earthy hospitality, and he was quick to note that the word *tovarich* could have different inflections when the "comrade" was Lenin rather than a boatman, Russell found the trip oppressively dispiriting: "I felt that everything I valued in human life was being destroyed in the interests of a glib and narrow philosophy, and that in the process untold misery was being inflicted upon many millions of people."[1] He spoke prematurely. An hour alone with Lenin depressed Russell's spirits further, not least because Lenin, who reminded him of "an opinionated professor," and it took one to know one, mocked Russell's brand of gradualist socialism. But it was Lenin's strange laugh that offended his sensibilities, emitted whenever Lenin savored the idea of rich peasants who hanged their poorer fellows from the nearest tree.[2]

On a recreational cruise along the Volga, Russell's despondency turned to despair, as the voyage became a diseased nightmare amidst utter desolation. Their destination, Astrakhan, struck Russell as "more like hell than anything I had ever imagined." Once he returned to civilization, Russell turned out an instant book, *The Theory and Practice of Bolshe-*

192

vism, about his adventures. His conviction, expressed in his private journal, that the Bolshevik regime's leading cadres consisted of "Americanized Jews," an idiosyncratic version of a widespread and erroneous view in Europe and North America, and the precise reasons why he had found Lenin's laugh "grim," were omitted from a blander account, which half-heartedly condemned the Bolsheviks even as it claimed residual virtue in Communism; the reason being that Russell had to hedge his bets with progressive circles in Britain.

Russell could not put his finger on what he had witnessed, nor could he find the appropriate analogy. In a few pages, this arch-skeptic compared the Bolsheviks with the French Directory, Cromwell's Puritans, Plato's guardians, and the early followers of Mahomet, before alighting upon the following formula:

> I cannot share the hopes of the Bolsheviks any more than those of the Egyptian anchorites. I regard both as tragic delusions, destined to bring upon the world centuries of darkness and futile violence. . . . The war has left throughout Europe a mood of disillusionment and despair which calls aloud for a new religion, as the only force capable of giving men the energy to live vigorously. Bolshevism has supplied the new religion.[3]

Similar analogies between monotheistic religion, Christian or Islamic, and Communism occurred at much the same time to the economist John Maynard Keynes and the theologian Reinhold Niebuhr, but also to liberal critics of Italian Fascism. In April 1923, Giovanni Amendola, editor of the oppositional newspaper, *Il Mondo,* commented: "To possess power is not enough: [Fascism] wants to own the private conscience of every citizen, it wants the 'conversion' of Italians." He continued: "Conversion to what? . . . Fascism has pretensions to being a religion . . . the overweening ambition and the inhuman intransigence of a religious crusade. It does not promise happiness to those who convert; it allows no escape to those who refuse baptism."[4]

And of course, such notions were pervasive among those who witnessed the rise of Nazism, the primary focus of this essay. In October 1932, that adroit political fixer, Franz von Papen,* contrasted his own Catholic-

---

* Franz von Papen, a member of the Catholic Centre Party, was elevated to the Chan-

conservative "worldview . . . anchored in the divine order of things" with Nazism's "political religion," based on, as he put it, "its axiom of the exclusiveness of the political all or nothing [and] its mystical Messiah-faith in the word-mighty Führer as the only one summoned to control destiny."[5] More casual intuitions can be found in the nowadays famous Klemperer diaries, as when Victor and his wife discussed whether Hitler's was "the voice of a fanatical preacher: Eva says Jan van Leyden. I say Rienzi."[6] Sitting in a cinema watching Leni Riefenstahl's *Triumph of the Will* Klemperer noted the scene where, with much eye contact and manly gripping of hands, Hitler commingled the "blood banner" of the "Movement" with new Storm Troop formation colors. Klemperer wrote:

> This whole National Socialist business is lifted from the political realm to that of religion by the use of a single word. [Blutfahne] And the spectacle and the word undoubtedly work, people sit there piously rapt—no one sneezes or coughs, there is no rustling of sandwich paper, no sound of anyone sucking a sweet. The rally is a ritualistic action, National Socialism is a religion—and I would have myself believe that its roots are shallow and weak?[7]

These observations assumed a more systematic form, as scholars who combined deep thought with physical flight, recognized that "the old [explanatory] keys [mainly involving theories of Fascism] do not fit the new locks."[8] Writing in the moral aftershock of the August 1939 Nazi-Soviet Pact, the heterodox ultra-leftist Franz Borkenau struggled to comprehend the Nazi phenomenon.[9] In his book, *The Totalitarian Enemy,* published in 1940, Borkenau devoted a chapter to what he called "the Nazi mentality," a term he probably owed to the involvement of his wife, Lucie Varga, with the early French Annales scholars. Discounting the idea that the Nazis were latter-day "pagans" Borkenau wrote:

> The pages of Western European history are filled with accounts of outbursts similar to those of the Nazi revolution. It is not, of course, that the most fearful forms of political struggle, with

---

cellorship in 1932 for a brief period and then became Vice Chancellor after Hitler's assumption of that post in 1933.

murder, massacres, and torture, were by any means exclusively characteristic of our own Western world. It is, however, remarkable that in our own Western world they have not only appeared at every really important turning-point of history, but that they have always gone together with the idea that some complete salvation could be worked on this earth through an accumulation of atrocities. The origins of this attitude are not to be discovered in our present age; they belong to the revolutionary sects of the Middle Ages. . . . The essence of these revolutionary creeds is the belief that the final day of salvation has come, that the millennium on this earth is near; that God's chosen instruments must make an end of all the hierarchies and the refinements of civilization in order to bring it about; and that complete virtue, simplicity, and happiness can be brought about by violence . . .

To throw off the burden of the sense of guilt which Christianity has brought to us and humanitarianism has emphasized is what they would like to do. . . . What they really are is negative Christians, men in a state of ferocious revolt against the tenets of Christianity, anti-Christians, and therefore worshippers of all that in the Christian tradition is regarded as Satanic. This Satanic attitude necessarily involves the highest as much as the lowest qualities of mankind. Far from innocent nature and from indifference, it contains all the elements of the religious spirit, turned to a negative end. It implies all the devotion, the abnegation, the self-sacrifice, the merging of the individual into a greater good, which are characteristics of a religious spirit, only they are all diverted to the cause of anti-religion.[10]

Another scholar with his bag ready to go was the Catholic conservative Eric Voegelin (1901–85), though echoing Kierkegaard, Voegelin despised such labels as infantile strategies of intellectual negation. The Gestapo had raided his library, while a major book, exposing Nazism's racial hocus pocus as scientistic manner rather than scientific substance, had been confiscated.[11] His latest work, an essay entitled "The Political Religions," was instantly deleted, for apparently being too subversive to circulate freely in Greater Germany.[12] Commencing with the Pharaoh Akhenaton in about 1376 B.C., and ending a few millennia

195

later with Hitler in about 1938, Voegelin's essay may be too Olympian for contemporary tastes. Like his exemplar, the Viennese satirist Karl Kraus, Voegelin chose not to wallow in merely lurid detail. His essay was an early formulation of what developed into an elaborate theory of history, which involves radically reformulating what historians customarily regard as reality. According to Voegelin, political ideologies were secular, temporal attempts to create a religious sense of community, and to explain that little piece of reality, divorced from the spiritual beyond, to which they reduced the human frame of reference. Pharaoh Akhenaton represented the earliest recorded attempt deliberately to change the old ways so that he became the vade mecum to the mysteries of the gods. Voegelin traced the rise in modern times of what he called "intramundane collectivities," which represented the progressive divorce of a sense of religious community from its divine moorings. A succession of "intramundane collectivities," that is the divination of class, state, race, or nation, represented the displacement of hopes of salvation from eternal life to the present. Evil was externalized as the "anti-idea," namely the Jews in the case of Nazi Germany, or "kulaks" in that of Soviet Russia. Political philosophies which resembled medieval Gnosticism claimed to divine what was real, while simultaneously creating a "dream world" in which all was illusion or the illusory abstraction was made real through massive violence. Since these ideologies were finally detached from anything that might have inhibited their actions or conduct, they could abandon St. Ignatius of Loyola's dictum: "earthly means . . . may contain nothing which is inconsistent with the sacred purpose." Gnostic ideological "insights" became utterly lethal when divorced from any restraining moral or spiritual frame of reference.

So far we have heard several voices, including Catholics and Jews, conservatives, liberals, Communists, skeptics, and so forth, striving to comprehend the dawning of disconcerting political developments. The examples could be easily extended to include such major figures as Raymond Aron.[13] It may be that these men and women were experiencing a collective religious delusion, or exaggerating the significance of one aspect of these complex phenomena, in line with their own predispositions, just as others construed Fascism or Nazism as the offspring of allegedly degenerate late capitalism or as the handiwork of the frenzied mob. But one rather doubts this. Instead, these disparate figures were heroically searching for explanations which rose above the horizons imposed, and often slavishly followed, by the devotees of such counterideologies as Marxism, which they sometimes felt were part of the problem rather than the solution; that is in the sense of narrowing down the fullest meanings of what it is to be human.[14]

Naturally, construing political phenomena in religious terms was no coinage of the inter-war era. Sporadic utterances, for example de Tocqueville comparing the Jacobin regime to Islam, go back as far as the French Revolution, which developed its own public cults, based on reason, or worse, virtue, which in turn were conceived as rivals to the churches for popular affections and enthusiasms.[15] Other countries, notably the United States of America, managed to synthesize the two, with the resulting "civil religion" being complimentary, rather than militantly antagonistic to, the activities of the churches.[16]

The rhetoric of nineteenth-century Romantic nationalism, whether one is thinking of Giuseppe Mazzini,* Henri Michelet† or Adam Mickiewicz,‡ was saturated with religious emotion. Indeed, Michelet regarded Romantic nationalism as a substitute for it, as noted in his journal:

> It is from you that I shall ask for help, my noble country, you must take the place of the God who escapes us, that you may fill within us the immeasurable abyss which extinct Christianity has left there.[17]

Sometimes these nationalistic cults assumed blasphemous forms. For example, an 1864 catechetical poster titled "The Doctrine of Giuseppe Garibaldi," included a parody of the Ten Commandments—"Thou shalt not kill, except those who bear arms against Italy"—and a version of the Lord's Prayer which ran in part: "Give us today our daily cartridges."[18]

---

* Giuseppe Mazzini (1805–1872) was an Italian nationalist who was involved in many plots and uprisings to promote Italian unity.

† Henri Michelet, a French historian best known for his massive, multivolume *History of France* (1833–1867).

‡ Adam Mickiewicz is the father of Polish romanticism and perhaps Poland's greatest poet. His works include *Forefathers' Eve* (1823) and the great epic poem *Pan Tadeusz* (1834).

The late George L. Mosse spent a distinguished career reanimating the symbolic spaces of the nineteenth-century nation-state, or the independently sponsored efforts, which were supposed to quicken the pulse rates of a wider community. The spaces consisted of such things as the giant wedding cake monument to Victor Emmanuel I, near the classical Forum in central Rome; the latter, the figure of Hermann the German, to see which a detour to the otherwise enchanting Teutoburger Forest may be superfluous. Bombastic and pretentious though these things were, none of them involved the transformation of passive spectators into active participants, nor the marginalization of monarchs or traditional religious authorities, let alone anything so overly pretentious *as* defining good and evil or the making and unmaking of humanity. In other words, they were relatively underfreighted with ambition. The symbolic space was not a total assault on the nature of mankind. However, it did provide a sort of altar upon which new idols could be set up.[19]

The First World War gave enormous impetus to the on-going sacralization of politics. God fought on every side, for apparently, He was not just an Englishman, while the war itself was often construed as a great apocalyptic and regenerating moment. As the poet Rupert Brooke had it: "Now God be thanked Who has matched us with His hour, / And caught our youth, and wakened us from sleeping, / With hand made sure, clear eye, and sharpened power, / To turn as swimmers into cleanness leaping."[20]

The agony of mass death amidst mud, barbed wire, shells and clouds of bullets, roughly averaging over six thousand men per day over more than four years, reawakened religious yearnings, a Durkheimian "effervescence," generating new forms of secular religion related to the war experience, even though the postwar cults could not communicate much beyond a sanitized version of it, as Edward Lutyens implicitly realized when he designed Whitehall's Cenotaph, using stone to signify nothingness. The symbolism of death and resurrection, dedication to the nation, the mystic qualities of blood and sacrifice, the cult of heroes and martyrs, and the masculine "communion" of the trenches, led to the diffusion among combatants of political notions as a total religious experience, that would renew all aspects of existence through purifying violence.[21]

If the war produced the social ferment, and hence mass appetency for a compelling new faith, its martyrs, myths, and vocabulary of remembrance were absorbed into the new anti-, or rather, metapolitical creeds of Fascism and Nazism. Not quite so simply, however, because a new generation of political artistes supervened, beginning with the poet D'Annunzio's idiosyncratic experiment in postwar Fiume, and then moving on to the extended melodrama of Mussolini's Italy, and the pseudo-Wagnerian meltdown of Hitler's Germany. This point, however, does not imply that the destruction of liberal democracy in Italy was somehow less serious than in Germany.[22] With terrifying presumption they sought to treat entire societies as a tabula rasa or lumps of clay, to be made and unmade literally at will. Nietzsche anticipated the mindset rather well:

> And if your hardness will not flash and cut and cut to pieces: how can you one day create with me? For creators are hard. And it must seem bliss to you to press your hand upon millennia as upon wax, bliss to write upon the will of millennia as upon metal—harder than metal, nobler than metal. Only the noblest is perfectly hard.[23]

Of course, such vivid characters could only operate in a world perceived as grey, with all the metaphorical undertones of senescence, and none of those associated with wisdom; grey ideas, institutions, men and so forth, which contrasted to ill effect against the garish hues, raucous rhythms and strident youthfulness of every totalitarian movement. Astute observers, like the German-Jewish publisher Ullstein, who made the deceptively flip remark that maybe the Weimar president should at least put in a ceremonial appearance at horse-races like his French confrère, worried that Republican Constitution days might seem colorlessly insipid beside politics as a constant multihued bombardment of the senses. This was a lesson learned very late by intelligent socialists like Carlo Mierendorff, who developed the Left's only potent counter-symbol, for the purchase of the hammer and sickle was limited in comparison to the three diagonal freedom arrows chasing off an up-ended swastika.[24]

As painters know, it is often best to define broad compositional areas, rather than to fiddle around with details. Audaciously and rapidly, these personalities and their propagandists constructed symbolic spaces and symbols, whose content was pillaged eclectically from very remote as well as recent times. The sources included classical antiquity, the northern barbarian cultures, the occult and the Orient, as well as

Roman Catholicism and the "Red Dragon" of the labor movement, both of which pillaged for whatever would enhance Fascism or Nazism's affective potency. Let's just develop the relationship with Christianity, for this had hidden depths which lictorial bundles, runes and swastikas probably lacked.

Both Mussolini and Hitler explicitly, and repeatedly, identified themselves as agents of Providence, dispatched to lead their respective chosen peoples from helotry and ignominy. Here are two examples from 1925, the first from an Italian Fascist newspaper:

> A century from now, history may tell us that after the war a Messiah arose in Italy, who began speaking to fifty people and ended up evangelizing a million; that these first disciples then spread through Italy and with their faith, devotion, and sacrifice conquered the hearts of the masses.[25]

At Christmas later that year, Hitler spoke in Lower Bavaria. The time and context prompted the following blasphemous comparison, although the racist emphases were his own:

> Then too [he meant at the time when Jesus was born] there existed a materialistic world, contaminated by Jews. Then too, victory did not come from state's power, but by means of salvific doctrine whose herald was born under the most wretched circumstances. . . . We, too, have again created today a poisonous period in which the state's power is completely incompetent . . . Christ rose in a rotten world, preached the faith, was at first scorned, and yet out of this faith a great world movement has been made.[26]

The call to faith was reciprocated by many believers, with the dedicated disciples of the early persecuted sects becoming self-confident masses of people. However, through propaganda and the workings of mass consumer-celebrity culture, this call to faith was progressively focused upon the leaders rather than on their respective parties; the latter being rightly perceived as highly corrupt, a perception which, as Ian Kershaw has shown, replicated the venerable tradition of the sacred king being incapable of wrongdoing amidst wicked advisors and counsellors.[27]

The elementary patterns of Fascist and Nazi faiths were similar, namely a form of political eschatology: from perdition to redemption, abject misery to glory, from tiny sect to mighty mass movement, from fractiousness to harmony. All were expressed in a common tone of indignancy, ethnosentimentality, and moralizing self-righteousness, in other words, aspects of this discourse that in the first and last case at least, our time is underequipped to notice without strenuous self-overcoming.

In both countries, the public realm was colonized with ad hoc cults, which often revolved around a bathetic "necropolitics." Here, the pluri- or nonpolitical dead of the Great War were appropriated for narrow ideological purposes, and into which the movements' own casualties were aggregated, for they hovered now among the living. Both movements exploited the memory of their carefully vetted, political martyrs, cynically discarding the drunks who fell into a canal after a brawl with opponents, or those lacking grieving widows and orphans.[28] Winnowing out from the chaff, such latter-day saints as Horst Wessel,* at least by the time Goebbels had finished doctoring his less than pristine image. For, as in the Soviet Union, the values of the "New Man" or "New Woman" were established with the aid of a few moral exemplars: Aleksei Stakhanov[†] and Pavlik Morozov[‡] here; *Hitler Youth Quex*[§] and Horst Wessel there.[29] Both systems also tried to marginalize the traditional religious calendar, and, at least as far as the demonstrably committed were concerned, the customary rites of passage, although the latter seems to have caught on to a greater extent in Bolshevik Russia than in Germany.[30] As well as appropriating such traditions as harvest or labor festivals, which were militarized and adapted to altered purposes, for example, human fertility rather than firm cabbages or plump tomatoes, or uniformed workers saluting with spades, major rallies fused mathematical choreography with liberating paroxysms of mass

---

* Horst Wessel, a young Nazi party member killed by political enemies at the age of 22. He was made a martyr by the party and the "Horst Wessel Lied" became the Nazi party anthem.

† Aleksei Stakhanov, a coal miner who ostensibly over-fulfilled his coal production norm by a vast margin, was made a cult hero by Stalin and the Soviet authorities.

‡ Pavlik Morozov, adopted as a kind of patron saint for the Soviet youth group The Young Pioneers for denouncing his father to the secret police.

§ *Hitler Youth Quex*, a Nazi propaganda novel and film.

rapture, with even British and French ambassadors not impervious to low-grade plangency, one of the essential features, along with sustained brutality, both bureaucratic or visceral, of this excited brand of politics.

For this was politics with a raw edge, a whiff of danger, which George Orwell shrewdly captured in 1940, when in the course of his review of *Mein Kampf* he remarked:

> Hitler . . . knows that human beings don't only want comfort, safety, short working hours, hygiene, birth-control and, in general, common sense; they also, at least intermittently, want struggle and self-sacrifice, not to mention drums, flags and loyalty-parades. . . . Whereas Socialism, and even capitalism in a more grudging way, have said to people "I offer you a good time," Hitler has said to them "I offer you struggle, danger and death," and as a result a whole nation flings itself at his feet."[31]

In this sense, as Fritz Stern noted some time ago, National Socialism was a form of transgressive temptation.[32]

So far, we have touched on emotion (vulgarly conceived) and externalities, without saying much about beliefs, though "struggle, danger and death" were prominent among them. At first sight, even mentioning Nazism in connection with the great transcendental monotheisms seems excessive, like comparing a little brown puddle to a tremulous ocean on the grounds that they both contain water. It also seems to fly in the face of Hitler's public insistence that Nazism should not become a cult, though there was a cult he made an exception for.

Speaking in September 1938 he reminded Himmler and Rosenberg:

> National Socialism is a cool and highly-reasoned approach to reality based on the greatest of scientific knowledge and its spiritual expression. . . . The National Socialist Movement is not a cult movement; rather; it is a völkisch and political philosophy which grew out of considerations of an exclusively racist nature. This philosophy does not advocate mystic cults, but rather aims to cultivate and lead a nation determined by its blood.[33]

Writing in 1934, Christopher Dawson caught both the threat Nazism posed to Christianity and what differentiated it from the Communist creed:

> It is not that the Nazi movement is anti-religious. The danger is rather that it has a religion of its own which is not that of Christian orthodoxy. This religion has not the dogmatic character of the Communist creed, it is a fluid and incoherent thing which expresses itself in several different forms. There is the neo-paganism of the extreme pan-German element, there is the Aryanized and nationalized Christianity of the German Christians, and there is the racial and nationalistic idealism which is characteristic of the movement as a whole, and which, if not religious in the strict sense, tends to develop a mythology and ethic of its own that may easily take the place of Christian theology and Christian ethics.[34]

But there were ways in which these two apparently antagonistic positions could be defused in a deadly synthesis. Nazism was the intellectual legatee of those who had reconciled racial science with the consolations of religion, by ascribing a redemptive mission to the racially defined elective people. It fused bleakly crude biological determinism, designed to reintegrate Man into Nature, with a bowdlerized version of Christianity, a synthesis quite possibly derived in the main, as Saul Friedlander has argued, from the coterie which shaped and tended the dead maestro's legacy at Bayreuth.[35] A vulgarized Nietzscheanism provided the amoral claptrap needed to "liberate" the Nazis from traditional values, as the consequences of the death of God emerged like delayed light rays from a vanished star. The distinguished American writer, Mary McCarthy, made the imaginative connection with Shakespeare's *Macbeth*:

> *Macbeth*, in short, shows life in the cave. Without religion, animism rules the outer world, and without faith, the human soul is beset by hobgoblins. This at any rate was Shakespeare's opinion, to which modern history, with the return of the irrational in the Fascist nightmare and its new specters of Communism, Socialism, etc., lends support.[36]

The failed artist Hitler needed something more boundless than the folk beliefs of peasants, or the arcane, desiccated, involutions of professors whose minds were stuck in the year A.D. 700, as he once sarcastically put it. That sort of thing had all the attraction of a dull afternoon at some interminable scientific conference; precisely the type of academic, *völkisch* politics which Hitler, who was a product of the rougher school of Lueger[*] and Schönerer,[†] eschewed. His experiences and temperament, forged by Viennese flophouses, the wartime trenches, and, last but not least, the hysterical and murderous climate of postwar Munich, adjusted the emphases in ways which differentiated him from his effete exemplars.

Vagueness about the desired dystopia, where the farmer prised the clods apart, the soldier stood sentinel, and mothers produced healthy "Aryan" babies seriatim, contrasted with the "thick description" lavished on the Jews, whose eradication was integral to Hitler's reading of the cycle from perdition to redemption in which he was the moving agent. Now since the power ascribed to the Jews in this pseudocosmology differentiated anti-Semitism from other forms of "racism," for eugenic "burdens" and gypsy "nuisances" were not existentially menacing in the same comprehensive way, it followed that the desired end state was not certain. This was the case even in the assumption that the ultimate hidden desire, and one should not casually discount it, was not to annihilate oneself and everyone else anyway.

Communism too posited the rebirth of a new society and a "new man" from the ashes of the old, a mythology well described in 1932 by the German journalist Klaus Mehnert:

A new mythology has arisen in Russia, a mythology of the creation of the world by human hands. In the beginning there was Chaos-capitalism. The parasites lived in luxury; the slaves were starving. Then came Marx and Lenin and Red October. After violent battles with internal and external foes and at the cost of immense sacrifices made by the chosen Russian proletariat, Chaos was cast out. Now Stalin with the Five Year Plan is building a

---

* Karl Lueger, the demagogic, anti-Semitic mayor of Vienna from 1897–1910.
† Georg Ritter von Schönerer was a supporter of Austria's merger with Germany to promote the racial purity of the Teutonic race.

world of order, harmony and justice, while the remaining five-sixths of the earth, as punishment for their opposition to Communist doctrine, are being smitten with the plague of world crisis and the scourge of unemployment. The nations can never enjoy peace and happiness until the Hammer and Sickle are gleaming over them as well.[37]

Under National Socialism, by contrast, the Jews, or the forces they could allegedly mobilize through "devilish cunning," might just prevail, in ways which the opponents of Communist Utopianism would not, for the latter were never weightier than the iron wheels of history under which they would vanish. The distinguished theologian Reinhold Niebuhr caught this self-confidence very well in a passage from Proudhon* which Trotsky introduced at the end of his autobiography, adding apropos Proudhon, "in spite of their slight savor of ecclesiastical eloquence, these are fine words. I subscribe to them." Proudhon wrote:

> The movement [of history] is no doubt irregular and crooked, but the tendency is constant. What every government dies in turn in favor of revolution becomes inviolable; what is done against it passes over like a cloud. I enjoy watching this spectacle, in which I enjoy every single picture. I observe these changes in the life of the world as if I had received their explanation from above; what oppresses others elevates me more and more, inspires and fortifies me; how can you want me to accuse destiny or to complain about people or curse them? Destiny—I laugh at it; and as for men, they are too ignorant and too enslaved for me to be annoyed by them.[38]

Although Nazism shared with Communism the notion of apocalyptic palingenesis, it was more overtly imbued with the irrational and saturated with doom-laden imaginings, but less confident in its reading of the evolution of the larger picture. The first point is easy to establish. Nazism was born under torchlight, illuminated by burning books and synagogues, and ended, appropriately enough, as Heine† once pre-

---

* Proudhon, see note on page 160.

† Heinrich Heine, the German Romantic poet. Burleigh is alluding to lines from

dicted, with entire cities and millions of people reduced to smoke, ash, and embers. Images so kitschy that they invoke the mindset all too perfectly, for Jamesian artistry is redundant regarding a subject so lacking in the density of finer feeling.[39]

Hitler's own direst prognostications diverged radically from the reactionary aristocrat Gobineau[*] or the Francophone, Germanophile, deracinated English aesthete Houston Stewart Chamberlain,[†] in that both regarded loss of racial élan as the nightmare scenario, though in his dreams at least, Chamberlain was frequently abducted to be tormented by Jews. By contrast, Hitler seems to have envisaged something akin to a nuclear winter in the event that "the Jew" triumphed, for he spoke of the Jews' "crown [being] the funeral wreath of humanity and this planet will, as it did thousands of years ago, move through the ether devoid of human beings," to forestall which dread outcome, only some massive act of purifying violence seemed commensurate, although the reality was impossibly tawdry. Such a view, largely derived from Philippe Burrin, is not incompatible with Christian Gerlach's compelling researches on the exact timing of the "Final Solution," when in early December 1941 a global anti-Hitlerian coalition loomed over the horizon, and the Jews whom Hitler held responsible for the coalition, both before and after it, literally had to perish. Regionally specific mass killing programs in areas such as the Balkans or Soviet Union, where no account had to be taken of local sensibilities, were suddenly escalated into a comprehensive pan-European project.[40]

But we need only intimate the Holocaust in this connection. For there were lower-key moral transformations at work, long before that, which it would be a pity to lose sight of amidst the intense contemporary discussions of the psychological processes of mass killing. This may, in turn, evade more controversial explanations of what drove a society mad in favor

---

Heine's 1821 play *Almansor*: "That was but a prelude; where they burn books, they will ultimately burn people also."

[*] Joseph Arthur Comte de Gobineau (1816–1882), author of *An Essay on the Inequality of the Human Races*.

[†] Houston Stewart Chamberlain (1855–1927) was a well-known advocate of the racial and cultural superiority of "Aryans." British-born, Chamberlain spent much of his life in Germany and was a key influence on Nazi racial theory.

of things that probably apply to the dynamics of any group of warlike men extrapolated from their customary frame of moral and social reference. In other words, perpetrator psychology, that academic by-product of forensic investigations of Nazi crimes against humanity, tells us rather less than is claimed, or intended, for it neglects the deeper metaphysical context which shaped these appalling actions at the highest level.

In 1937, the exiled Social Democrats' Reports on Germany incorporated a lengthy meditative piece that stemmed from confessing church circles. It contained a striking metaphor for the moral transformations, which Nazism appeared to be effecting. The authors imagined a railway bridge undergoing reconstruction. Since engineers could not simply demolish what was there, because of the impact on traffic, they laboriously renewed each bolt, girder, and rail over a protracted period. Passengers on trains crossing this work in progress eventually found the work itself unremarkable. However, one day, if and when they thought to glance up from their newspapers, they would realize that the old bridge had vanished entirely, to be replaced by something which, while being a bridge, no longer resembled the old structure in all but its Platonic essence.[41]

In recent decades, historians have begun to trace the moral erosion which preceded Nazism, part of that great interregnum between universal belief in God and the man-made moralities that are still being formed to suit ever-evolving social circumstances. Many of these trends went back to the 1880s, including the inhuman possibilities opened up by nihilist art, philosophy, or science, or acquaintance with other times, other places and customs; one by-product of European colonialism, which Hannah Arendt imaginatively connected with totalitarianism by invoking the shock and surprise of Europeans encountering Conradian darkness, even if her nineteenth-century examples were of countries which did not engender totalitarian governments in the twentieth century.[42] While in the great metropolises, people were hoovered up from the land in the transformative processes of industrialization and urbanization, to which ideologists in turn gave catastrophist or progressive meanings, and from whose oppressive complexities utopians of various persuasions sought flight by creating some little oasis of happiness, with cooperative housing for the workers, or more sinister, total, instantaneous solutions, in which mere human beings were the raw material of a grotesque experiment. Very often, as the following example of Nazi Germany shows, such experiments combined flight forwards into a brave new world with nostalgia for remoter simplicities.[43]

Even something so outwardly modern and technocratic as the international fad for eugenic solutions to social problems, often reflected the conscious wish to leap back in time over liberal humanitarianism or the Judeo-Christian legacy, to the simpler mores of ancient or primitive societies. Such a desire can also be found within Nazism, which positively reveled in the atavistic world of "healthy instinct," despite its advanced bureaucratic and technological accoutrements. These slower secular changes were accompanied by more immediate disturbances, albeit ones which admitted of an internationalized reading, but which induced their own localized pathologies.

Historians of Weimar Germany such as Richard Bessel or Gerald Feldman, have sensitively studied the ways in which the First World War, and its aftermath of rampant inflation, confused notions of honesty and just reward for a days labor, disorientated many of the young, and affected comfortable people with extreme turbulence as the Reichsmark was rapidly restabilized.[44] The war itself also resulted in the reinjection of brutality into a postwar political climate supercharged by the arbitrary arrangements of Versailles, and the ensuing succession of disasters, one response to which, and first noted by Uriel Tal but recently biographically elaborated by Ulrich Herbert, was a deliberate retreat under a carapace of inhuman hardness on the part of some of the student generation, who thus equipped themselves to deal "objectively" with the nation's problems in future. And of course, the depredations of the Bolshevik Revolution also made their own unique contribution to the cynical creed of the end justifying any means, by butchering obstacles along the shortcut to equality and social justice.[45] Such events were assiduously covered in the conservative, liberal, confessional and socialist press of the period, threatening replication from time to time on the streets of central Europe, in ways which both the bourgeoisie and the established left had no hesitation in cauterizing with considerable violence, and which, however much the facts said otherwise, many on the international right thought amenable to a racial-conspiratorial reading.

If these wider perspectives have to be taken into account in any discussion of events in Italy or Germany, one cannot overlook the transformations which Fascism or Nazism effected itself. *The mis en scène* touched on earlier, was integral in a dynamic way to the process of transforming human beings in the desired direction. The style engendered the substance, though the ambience is exceptionally difficult to recover from the published doxologies and liturgies, just as it is hard to evoke a stirring opera from a tattered program found in the attic.

Let's start with the body language of the zig-zag men, covered in symbols, which at once evoked the pagan past, modern expressionism, and the conventional signs for high-voltage danger. In his subtle study of linguistic contamination, the insistence upon belief, faith, fanaticism and so forth, Victor Klemperer described how the sight of a Nazi drum-major parading in Potsdam forced him "to confront the language of the Third Reich for the first time." Significantly, the Dresden philologist began with the visual vocabulary:

> Marching out in front, he had driven the outstretched fingers of his left hand into his hip, or rather he had arched his body into this supporting hand in an attempt to find his balance, whilst his right arm thrust the baton high up into the air and the tip of his boot appeared to reach up after it with every swing of his leg. The man hung there at an angle in mid-air, a monument without a plinth, mysteriously held erect by a cramp which stretched from head to toe paralyzing his fingers and feet. His performance was not simply a drill, it was as much archaic dance as goose-stepping. . . . Amidst the sober life of the most sober town its impact was that of unalloyed novelty. And it was highly contagious. A bellowing crowd pushed forward until it was almost touching the troops, frantically outstretched arms appeared to want to grab hold of them, a young man in the front row with eyes ablaze bore an expression of religious ecstasy.[46]

At roughly the same time, as part of a project intended to make fat men lean, and thin women fat, and all wired-up, fierce of mien, stepping forth in the martial *passo romano,* the Italian Fascists dispensed with the bourgeois handshake in favor of the Roman salute, replaced the refined *Lei* with *Tu* or *Voi*, and reduced an elegantly sonorous language to harsh metallic barks. The year XI (the year according to the new Fascist calendar), Achille Starace explained in 1932, would be "the twilight of the era of shaking hands."[47] Just as the atheist Bolsheviks underwent a conversion experience, notionally akin to that of monks or nuns, when they became Anvil, Hammer, or Man of Steel, rather than, say Leaf, Rose, or Man of Mush, so their radicalized confrères in Germany or Italy became someone else when they donned the antibourgeois black or brown shirt, and called each other "comrade," which may have been part of the fundamental attraction. Every small-town nobody became a posturing somebody, disguising their inadequate sense of selfhood with uniforms and titles; empty people, filled this way and that, and hence capable of anything. Here is the aristocratic, reactionary diarist Reck Malleczewen, who was eventually shot in the back of the head in Dachau, observing a group of young Schutzstaffel men at play in a Berlin nightclub in early 1939. He did not need to see evidence of their terrifying potentialities; he could sense them:

> The first thing is the frightening emptiness of their faces. Then one observes, in the eyes, a kind of flicker from time to time, a sudden illumination. This has nothing to do with youth. It is the typical look of this generation, the immediate reflection of a basic and completely hysterical savagery . . . woe to Europe if this hysteria that confronts us now gets free rein. These young men would turn the paintings of Leonardo into an ash-heap if their Führer declared them degenerate. They would not hesitate to send cathedrals tumbling into the air, to sue the hellish arts of IG Farben, if this were part of a given situation. Or they will perpetuate still worse things and worst, most dreadful of all, they will be totally incapable of even sensing the deep degradation of their existence.[48]

This proves all too prescient. Of course, these men represented the most radically successful conversion of people into attenuated uniformed symbols. When they stepped over the thresholds of occupied eastern Europe, adorned with their kitschy iconography of adolescent morbidity, and schooled in missionary self-righteousness and unfeeling, literally nothing restrained them. Steeped as they were, they possessed a mindset of beastly fantasies of death, domination, and destruction, and were given increasingly free rein in contexts widely regarded as culturally inferior anyway. They were on the loose, like half-human predators, moving murderously through phantoms who happened to be fellow humans, and very often elated, or intoxicated, by the mounting scale of their own inhuman depredations.

But for most Germans at the time, who were somewhat more than mono-dimensional ideological soldiers, Nazism's transgressive temptations interacted in more subtle ways with received precepts which continued to operate in an attenuated way, just short of civil courage. Few doubt that one can find endless amounts of evidence of cruelty, greed, malice and so forth among the general population, much of it expertly chronicled by, for example, Robert Gellately in his subtle, unlurid studies of delation and the Gestapo. But as William Sheridan Allen showed long ago in an important study of popular reactions to *Reichskristallnacht*, ideology and the various modes of its implementation jostled uncomfortably with a range of normative values, including the feeling of belonging to a civilized Christian country; respect for the elderly and moral concern for the young; the sacrosanctity of life, private property, or sacred places, for churches might soon follow synagogues, as was indicated by sporadic waves of iconoclastic vandalism. Not to speak of the general proprieties of life in the 1930s, which led people to draw the line at the pornographic excess of *Der Sturmer* or bestial mobs rampaging around them.[49] One cannot simply ignore these ambivalences in the interests of ascribing responsibility for the last century's most diabolic crime solely to all those dwelling between the Elbe and Oder, a view which has some peripheral difficulties, moreover, in explaining who annihilated the Jewish population of Odessa, the largest single anti-Semitic massacre of the last World War. For evil snaked through human hearts rather than along formal borders.[50]

Part of the climate of progressive moral breakdown, in Germany rather than the imperial Transnistrian Romania just alluded to above, stemmed from the marginalizing or silencing of traditional sources of authority, which they themselves compromised by putting institutional survival before their own ultimate values. An obvious example of this being the hierarchies of the Christian churches under National Socialism, which, to put it at a minimum, were beset by paralyzing caution and a view of society and time, which in turn sometimes led to the egregious misidentification of the Jews with several untoward contemporary pathologies.

But there was contested terrain between the regime and the churches, beyond the quite successful campaign to repulse the most aggressive manifestations of neopaganism. The most keenly contested field involved young people, who became the sites of contending absolutisms. However, while the churches restrained the beast in man, Nazism deliberately unleashed it. Furthermore, despite being subjected to various forms of totalitarian regimentation, the young were also liberated from traditional sources of moral constraint, whether represented by clerics, teachers, or their own parents. As the chief Nazi pedagogue Ernst Krieck put it:

> Blood and race are the place upon which man attains a consciousness of himself and thus freedom. Race and blood are unavoidable primeval forces with primeval power, and in accepting the yoke of these forces man is liberated from enslavement to reason, logic, and other sterile forms of the human spirit.[51]

By which he presumably meant such inconsequential factors as guilt, pity, or sin, all divorced now from a Christianity cleansed of effeminately "weak" or "Jewish" elements. The result being the delinquency and viciousness which occupy pages of the Reports of the exiled Social Democratic Party; eloquent guides to the ethical wasteland encouraged by National Socialism, whose malign consequences were duly unfolded in occupied Europe, as the logic of constant talk, and practice, of "hardness," and the legalized exclusion of racial minorities from the ambit of human concern, became all too apparent. For, as Omer Bartov has shown in his studies of the German army, this dialectic of constraint and utter license was carried over into military contexts, where normal human sympathies were in any case replaced by the brutality of an exceptionally cruel war, with its cycle of partisan attacks, mutilation, and horrendous reprisals.[52]

But if the young were especially susceptible to the temptations that Nazism offered, the average person was subjected to a confusing message which combined barbarity, often masked by the rhetoric of higher collective necessity, with things which were reassuringly familiar. For bathos and brutality were accompanied by kitsch, that syrupy commodity which permeated this entire enterprise, like a restorative bath in some cheaply lurid substance after a strenuous day at the office. A folksy idyll tailored to Mr. and Mrs. Everyman in their collective, imaginative flight from noticing the realities of life under a pernicious dictatorship. Radical evil came camouflaged in solid, lesser virtues, although never to the exclusion of common or garden vices. Let's introduce the most incongruous element of the title, that is charity, for we have already seen hope and faith aplenty. The discussion is necessarily brief. Let's sample the rhetoric, which is about as inauthentic and unmoving as it could be:

> Sometimes when I see shabbily dressed girls, shivering with cold themselves, collecting with infinite patience for others who are cold, then I have a feeling that they are all apostles of a certain Christianity! This is a Christianity which can claim for itself as no other can: this is the Christianity of a sincere profession of faith, because behind it stands not the word, but the deed! . . . And beyond that: there is a difference between the theoretical knowledge of socialism and the practical life of socialism. People are not born socialists, but first must be taught how to become them.[53]

This is actually Hitler speaking in 1935. And charity, of a sort, was in abundance, with much of it, like Winter Aid, increasingly coercive, while the needy, the beggars or the "anti-social," were tidied away into concentration camps and workhouses for the lethal bouts of reeducation, which as the satirist Karl Kraus noted, could magically transform the grim into happy men between one sunrise and sunset. While the so-called "bossocracy" of organized labor also disappeared into exile or places of confinement, their erstwhile constituency was not simply consoled with employment or organized excursions, but with a rhetoric of vice and virtue they could relate to. That is, they were constantly lauded as God's gift to the productive process, the ethnic acme of craftsmanship, but biologically noble too, even if they had recently experienced a bout of false consciousness induced by their erstwhile leaders.

And all was delivered in a rhetoric which, while allegedly transcending the class struggle, scarcely departed from the Left's own resentful script, in the crude vituperation against the "cowardly" bourgeoisie and "degenerate" upper classes, by political figures drawn from a denatured demimonde. For they were not primarily alluding to the working classes when they denounced the past age of humanitarianism or liberalism, as they knew their workers rather better than many of those who wrote about them.

Now throughout, it has been intimated that the exterior trappings of political religion, if such things can be said to exist, were integral to the

213

reconstruction of man's new moral identity. This did not consist of much, for the process of deconstruction was much more evident than addition, as layers of density and complexity were burned off with the equivalent of a blowtorch. Subsequently, it seems vaguely perverse to then attempt to intellectually reelaborate, for the point of the project was to make beings who in some specific sense were less than fully human; that is, degraded into instruments of ideology, and radically divorced from the plenitude of human spiritual destiny. Outrage, regarding Versailles, the so-called November criminals, and the abused rights of the ethnic German diaspora catered to the self-righteously vengeful, who were keen to lash out against whatever constrained Germany's still-latent power. Mob-like resentments towards the rich, privileged, powerful, intelligent, and successful occurred, with much of it refocused on the Jewish minority, which was caricatured to fit those categories. The sentimentalization of children, mothers, the workers, the Volk, life on the land, and so forth, was overlain with some vague desire to abolish the bewildering present, in favor of a thousand years of stasis, in which the remote past and the far future were blurred and elided into something called eternity, as in eternal German Reich, and so on, for apparently eternity itself had ethno-temporal limits. These were among the necessary consolations for a bleak, barbarous ideology, almost psychologically unbearable in its unalloyed reality, even for those who most deeply espoused it.

That is why the cast of the loved were repeatedly invoked, even as the unloved were being murdered and shoveled underground by men armed with statistical tallies, and maps in which entire Jewish populations were represented by drawings of coffins, the rationalistic paraphernalia that currently over-mesmerizes some of our colleagues, but does not quite account for the compelling necessity to, for example, abduct Jews—and nobody else—from remote Greek islands to kill them in Poland. When the realities of this were addressed without circumlocution, minds constantly sought to re-anchor themselves in the familiar, no doubt to discharge the shock, rather than the shame, of what they were doing. They looked into the moral abyss they had created and scuttled back to the cozy and homely, even if the juxtaposition of the two seems grotesque. For there was no shame regarding this secret page in history. If someone comes to me and says: "I can't build an anti-tank ditch with women and children. This is inhuman because they'll die doing it"—then I have to reply: "You are a murderer of your own blood, for if the anti-tank ditch is not built then German soldiers will die, and these are sons of German mothers. That is our blood."

What is she doing in there, invoked in some all-male hellhole in Russia, except to provide some sheet anchoring to the abnormal?

A little later in the same 1943 speech, "decency" combined with "hardness," something that even the SS had found difficult to routinize, as their weaker vessels cracked under the quotidian strains of ideological soldiery, with a few going mad, many turning to drink, and not just a few becoming raving psychopaths who taunted the Jews with the impotence of their Jehovah, in scenes more redolent of Europe at the long-drawn out dawn of the Christian era. Himmler only revealed emotional animation over the disciplinary issue of stealing cigarettes from the victims, invoking mere crime to obfuscate evil on a scale hard to imagine. Perhaps we should be grateful he did not censure the victims for smoking, in his Pooter-ish substitution of the trivial for the dreadful? Of course, they had been robbed, down to the clothes they wore, which were redistributed to needy ethnic German national comrades, for charity, like faith and hope could be harmonized with murder quite felicitously. For we can turn this quite easily into a very dangerous circle, a witches whirligig, consisting of layer upon layer of moral involution, which may speak to the reality of it, in ways which a more anodyne discourse of division of labor, group psychology, Milgram tests, and so forth, may not, as it disperses evil down more predictable channels, converting such an ontological event into the subject of an essay or seminar.

Most of the themes touched on this essay were present in Himmler's own conclusion. Many of history's murderers, with the exception of the fictional Macbeth, who as Solzhenitsyn remarked, was too recognizably complete to contemplate killing more than a dozen people, for he was not driven by an "idea," have invoked the moral high ground. This was regardless of whether they killed for confession, country, liberation or the omletteless utopia of recent unhappy memory, in which human beings were shoveled beneath the earth in a sort of frenzy. Real lethality is possessed (in the fullest meaning of the word) of a big idea, that gnostic "sixth sense" denied to simple humanity. In this case, Himmler drew upon centuries of theological casuistry deployed to justify slaughtering Moslems, pagans, and sometimes Jews, blended with the

215

exclusionary nationalism and pseudoscientific racism of late modernity, which had settled over the Jews like a shroud. The tone was predictably self-righteous; for in the interim, the dead had been transformed into aggressors.[54] He said:

> We had the moral right, we had the duty towards our people, to destroy this people who wanted to destroy us. . . . All in all, however, we can say that we have carried out this most difficult of tasks in a spirit of love for our people. And we have suffered no harm in our inner being, our soul, our character.[55]

Words which all too well evoke the themes of utopia, good and evil, and the making and unmaking of humanity, not to speak of the deformation and reformation of modern moral identities, which may have more to do with it than accounts, which evince a certain incapacity or unease with more metaphysical questions, suggest.

III
ORIGINS

13

German Nihilism*
(1941)

LEO STRAUSS

I

What is nihilism? And how far can nihilism be said to be a specifically German phenomenon? I am not able to *answer* these questions; I can merely try to *elaborate* them a little. For the phenomenon which I am going to discuss is much too complex, and much too little explored, to permit of an adequate description within the short time at my disposal. I cannot do more than to scratch its surface.

---

* This was a lecture that Strauss delivered in the General Seminar of the Graduate Faculty of Political and Social Science of the New School for Social Research on February 26, 1941. "German Nihilism" was first published in the journal *Interpretation* in the spring of 1999. That edition comes from a typewritten manuscript found in the Leo Strauss papers at the University of Chicago. This manuscript includes Strauss's rather extensive handwritten and typewritten additions and corrections. Professors David Janssens and Daniel Tanguay, in preparing the text for initial publication, incorporated those corrections and added some additional information about names and texts in endnotes. Their endnotes also document precisely where Strauss made changes to his original typescript. I have retained the endnotes that included information about names and texts, but have omitted the notes dealing with Strauss's textual emendations. Those interested in the more extensive editorial apparatus should consult "German Nihilism," *Interpretation* 26:3 (Spring 1999), 352–78. The version published here also includes some minor corrections to this initial publication. See Wiebke Meier, "Corrections to Leo Strauss, 'German Nihilism,'" *Interpretation* 28:1 (Fall 2000).

2. When we hear at the present time the expression "German nihilism," most of us naturally think at once of National Socialism. It must however be understood from the outset that National Socialism is only the most *famous* form of German nihilism—its lowest, most provincial, most unenlightened and most dishonorable form. It is probable that its very vulgarity accounts for its great, if appalling, successes. These successes may be followed by failures, and ultimately by complete defeat. Yet the defeat of National Socialism will not necessarily mean the end of German nihilism. For that nihilism has deeper roots than the preachings of Hitler, Germany's defeat in the World War and all that.

To explain German nihilism, I propose to proceed in the following way. I shall first explain the *ultimate motive* which is underlying German nihilism; this motive is not in itself nihilistic. I shall then describe the *situation* in which that non-nihilistic motive led to nihilistic aspirations. Finally, I shall attempt to give such a *definition* of nihilism as is not assailable from the point of view of the non-nihilistic motive in question, and on the basis of that definition, to describe German nihilism somewhat more fully.

3. Nihilism might mean: *velle nihil*, to will the nothing, the destruction of everything, including oneself, and therefore primarily the will to self-destruction. I am told that there are human beings who have such strange desires. I do not believe, however, that such a desire is the ultimate motive of German nihilism. Not only does the unarmed eye not notice any unambiguous signs of a will to self-destruction. But even if such a desire were *demonstrated* to be the ultimate motive, we still should be at a loss to understand why that desire took on the form, not of the mood called *fin de siècle* or of alcoholism, but of militarism. To explain German nihilism in terms of mental diseases, is even less advisable than it is to explain in such terms the desire of a cornered gangster to bump off together with himself a couple of cops and the fellow who double-crossed him; not being a Stoic, I could not call *that* desire a morbid desire.

The fact of the matter is that German nihilism is not absolute nihilism, desire for the destruction of everything including oneself, but a desire for the destruction of something *specific*: of *modern* civilization. That, if I may say so, limited nihilism *becomes* an *almost* absolute nihilism only for this reason: because the negation of modern civilization, the No, is not guided, or accompanied, by any clear positive conception.

220

German nihilism desires the destruction of modern civilization as far as modern civilization has a *moral* meaning. As everyone knows, it does not object so much to modern *technical* devices. That moral meaning of modern civilization to which the German nihilists object, is expressed in formulations such as these: to relieve man's estate; or: to safeguard the rights of man; or: the greatest possible happiness of the greatest possible number. What is the motive underlying the protest against modern civilization, against the spirit of the *West*, and in particular of the *Anglo-Saxon* West?

The answer must be: it is a *moral* protest. That protest proceeds from the conviction that the internationalism inherent in modern civilization, or, more precisely, that the establishment of a perfectly *open* society which is as it were the goal of modern civilization, and therefore all aspirations directed toward that goal, are irreconcilable with the basic demands of *moral life*. That protest proceeds from the conviction that the root of all moral life is essentially and therefore eternally the *closed* society; from the conviction that the open society is bound to be, if not immoral, at least amoral: the meeting ground of seekers of pleasure, of gain, of irresponsible power, indeed of any kind of irresponsibility and lack of seriousness.[1]

Moral life, it is asserted, means *serious* life. Seriousness, and the ceremonial of seriousness—the flag and the oath to the flag—are the distinctive features of the *closed* society, of the society which by its very nature is constantly confronted with, and basically oriented toward, the *Ernstfall*,* the serious moment, M-day, *war*. Only life in such a *tense* atmosphere, only a life which is based on constant awareness of the *sacrifices* to which it owes its existence, and of the necessity, the *duty* of sacrifice of life and all worldly goods, is truly human: the sublime is unknown to the open society. The societies of the West which claim to aspire toward the open society, actually are closed societies in a state of disintegration: their moral value, their respectability, depends *entirely* on their still being closed societies.

Let us pursue this argument a little further. The open society, it is asserted, is actually impossible. Its possibility is not proved at all by what is called the *progress* toward the open society. For that progress is largely fictitious or merely verbal. Certain basic facts of human nature which have been honestly recognized by earlier generations who used to call a spade a spade, are at the present time verbally denied, superficially covered over

---

* Emergency.

by fictions legal and others, e.g., by the belief that one can abolish war by pacts not backed by military forces punishing him who breaks the pact, or by calling ministries of *war* ministries of *defence*, or by calling punishment sanctions, or by calling capital punishment *das höchste Strafmass*.* The open society is morally inferior to the closed society also because the former is *based* on hypocrisy.

The conviction underlying the protest against modern civilization has *basically* nothing to do with bellicism, with *love* of war; nor with nationalism: for there were closed societies which were not nations; it has indeed something to do with what is called the sovereign state, insofar as the sovereign state offers the best modern example of a closed society in the sense indicated. The conviction I am trying to describe is *not*, to repeat, in its origin a love of war: it is rather a love of morality, a sense of responsibility for endangered morality. The historians in our midst know that conviction, or passion, from Glaukon's, Plato's brother's, passionate protest against the city of pigs, in the name of noble virtue.[2] They know it, above all, from Jean-Jacques Rousseau's passionate protest against the easy-going and somewhat rotten civilization of the century of taste, and from Friedrich Nietzsche's passionate protest against the easy-going and somewhat rotten civilization of the century of industry. It was the same passion—let there be no mistake about that—which turned, if in a much more passionate and infinitely less intelligent form, against the alleged or real corruption of postwar Germany: against "the subhuman beings of the big cities (*die Untermerzschen der Grosstadt*)," against "cultural bolshevism (*Kulturbolschewismus*)," etc. That passion, or conviction, is then not in itself nihilistic, as is shown by the examples of Plato and Rousseau, if examples are needed at all. (One may even wonder whether it has not a sound element, remembering, e.g., the decision of the Oxford students not to fight for king and country and some more recent facts.) While not being nihilistic in itself, and perhaps even not entirely unsound, that conviction *led* however to nihilism in postwar Germany owing to a number of circumstances. Of those circumstances, I shall mention in the survey which follows only those which, to my mind, have not been sufficiently emphasized in the discussions of this seminar nor in the literature on the subject.

---

* The Maximum penalty.

4. One would have to possess a gift which I totally lack, the gift of a lyrical reporter, in order to give those of you who have not lived for many years in postwar Germany an adequate idea of the *emotions* underlying German nihilism. Let me tentatively define nihilism as the desire to destroy the present world and its potentialities, a desire not accompanied by any clear conception of what one wants to put in its place. And let us try to understand how such a desire could develop.

No one could be satisfied with the postwar world. German liberal democracy of all descriptions seemed to many people to be absolutely unable to cope with the difficulties with which Germany was confronted. This created a profound prejudice, or confirmed a profound prejudice already in existence, against liberal democracy as such. Two articulate alternatives to liberal democracy were open. One was simple reaction, as expressed by the Crown Prince Ruprecht of Bavaria in about these terms: "Some people say that the wheel of history cannot be turned back. This is an error." The other alternative was more interesting. The older ones in our midst still remember the time when certain people asserted that the conflicts inherent in the present situation would necessarily lead to a revolution, accompanying or following another World War—a rising of the proletariat and of the proletarianized strata of society which would usher in the withering away of the State, the classless society, the abolition of all exploitation and injustice, the era of final peace. It was this prospect at least as much as the desperate present, which led to nihilism. The prospect of a pacified planet, without rulers and ruled, of a planetary society devoted to production and consumption only, to the production and consumption of spiritual as well as material merchandise, was positively horrifying to quite a few very intelligent and very decent, if very young, Germans. They did not object to that prospect because they were worrying about their own economic and social position; for certainly in that respect they had no longer anything to lose. Nor did they object to it for religious reasons; for, as one of their spokesmen (E. Jünger[*]) said, they *knew* that they were the sons and grandsons and great-grandsons of godless men.[3] What they hated was the very prospect of a world in which everyone would be happy and satisfied, in which everyone would have his little pleasure by day

---

* Ernst Jünger (1895–1998) was an influential and widely read German writer who first attained fame with his account of his experiences in World War I, *Storm of Steel* (1920). His other prominent works include *On Pain* (1934) and *On the Marble Cliffs* (1939).

and his little pleasure by night, a world in which no great heart could beat and no great soul could breathe, a world without real, unmetaphoric, sacrifice, i.e., a world without blood, sweat, and tears. What to the Communists appeared to be the fulfilment of *the* dream of mankind, appeared to those young Germans as the greatest debasement of humanity, as the coming of the end of humanity, as the arrival of the latest man. They did not really know, and thus they were unable to express in a tolerably clear language, what they desired to put in the place of the present world and its allegedly necessary future or sequel: the only thing of which they were absolutely certain was that the present world and all the potentialities of the present world as such, must be destroyed in order to prevent the otherwise necessary coming of the Communist final order: literally anything, the *nothing*, the chaos, the jungle, the Wild West, the Hobbesian state of nature, seemed to them infinitely better than the Communist-anarchist-pacifist future. Their Yes was inarticulate—they were unable to say more than: No! This No proved however sufficient as *the* preface to action, to the action of destruction. This is the phenomenon which occurs to me first whenever I hear the expression German nihilism.

It is hardly necessary to point out the fallacy committed by the young men in question. They simply took over the Communist thesis that the proletarian revolution and proletarian dictatorship is necessary, if civilization is not to perish. But they insisted rather more than the Communists on the conditional character of the Communist prediction (*if* civilization is not to perish). That condition left room for *choice*: they chose what according to the Communists was the only alternative to Communism. In other words: they admitted that all rational argument was in favor of Communism; but they opposed to that apparently invincible argument what they called "irrational decision." Unfortunately, all rational argument they knew of, was *historical* argument, more precisely: statements about the probable future, *predictions*, which were based on analysis of the past and, above all, of the present. For that modern astrology, predicting social science, had taken hold of a very large part of the academic youth.* I have emphasized the fact that the nihilists were *young* people.

---

* Strauss would become a prominent and persistent critic of modern social science. See, for example, chapter 2 of *Natural Right and History* and "An Epilogue," in *Essays on the Scientific Study of Politics*, edited by Herbert Storing. The latter essay can also be found in *An Introduction to Political Philosophy: Ten Essays by Leo Strauss*, edited by Hilail Gildin.

5. One or the other modern pedagogue would perhaps feel that not everything was bad in that nihilism. For, he might argue, it is not unnatural that the intelligent section of a young generation should be dissatisfied with what they are told to believe by the older generation, and that they should have a strong desire for a *new* word, for a word expressing *their* longings, and, considering that moderation is not a virtue of youth, for an *extreme* word. Moreover, he would conceivably say, it is not unnatural that the young people, being constitutionally unable to discover that new word, are unable to express in articulate language more than the negation of the aspirations of the older generation. A lover of paradoxes might be tempted to assert an essential affinity of youth to nihilism. I should be the last to deny the juvenile character of that specific nihilism which I have tried to describe. But I must disagree with the modern pedagogue all the more insofar as I am convinced that about the most dangerous thing for these young men was precisely what is called progressive education: they rather needed *old-fashioned teachers*, such old-fashioned teachers of course as would be undogmatic enough to understand the aspirations of their pupils. Unfortunately, the belief in old-fashioned teaching declined considerably in postwar Germany. The inroads which William II had made on the old and noble educational system founded by great liberals of the early nineteenth century were not discontinued, but rather enlarged by the Republic. To this one may add the influence of the *political* emancipation of youth, the fact frequently referred to as the children's vote. Nor ought we to forget that some of the young nihilists who refused to undergo severe *intellectual discipline*, were sons or younger brothers of men and women who had undergone what may be described as the *emotional discipline* of the youth movement, of a movement which preached the *emancipation* of youth. Our century has once been called the century of the child: in Germany it proved to be the age of the adolescent. Needless to say that not in all cases was the natural progress from adolescence to senility ever interrupted by a period however short of maturity. The decline of reverence for old age found its most telling expression in Hitler's shameless reference to the imminent death of the aged President Hindenburg.

I have alluded to the fact that the young nihilists were *atheists*. Broadly speaking, prior to the World War, atheism was a preserve of the radical Left, just as throughout history atheism had been connected with philosophic materialism. German philosophy was predominantly idealistic, and the German idealists were theists or pantheists. Schopenhauer was, to my knowledge, the first nonmaterialist *and* conservative German philosopher who openly professed his atheism. But Schopenhauer's influence fades into insignificance if compared with that of *Nietzsche*. Nietzsche asserted that the atheist assumption is not only reconcilable with, but indispensable for, a radical antidemocratic, antisocialist, and antipacifist policy: according to him, even the Communist creed is only a secularized form of theism, of the belief in providence. There is no other philosopher whose influence on postwar German thought is comparable to that of Nietzsche, of the *atheist* Nietzsche. I cannot dwell on this important point, since I am not a theologian. A gentleman who is much more versed in theology than I am—Professor Carl Mayer of the Graduate Faculty—will certainly devote to this aspect of German nihilism all the attention which it requires in an article to be published in *Social Research*.[4]

The adolescents I am speaking of were in need of teachers who could explain to them in articulate language the positive, and not merely destructive, meaning of their aspirations. They believed to have found such teachers in that group of professors and writers who knowingly or ignorantly paved the way for Hitler (Spengler,* Moeller van den Bruck,† Carl Schmitt,‡ Bäumler,§ Ernst Jünger,¶ Heidegger). If we want to understand the singular success, not of Hitler, but of those writers, we must cast a quick glance at their opponents who were at the same time the opponents of the young nihilists. Those opponents committed frequently a grave mistake. They believed to have refuted the No by refuting the Yes, i.e., the inconsistent, if not silly, positive assertions of the young men. But

---

* Spengler. See note on page 113.

† Arthur Moeller van den Bruck was a highly influential conservative thinker during the Weimar period. His major work, *The Third Reich*, argued for a conservative National Socialist revolution that would provide a fundamental break with the past and herald the beginning of a new era. He committed suicide in 1924.

‡ Carl Schmitt was a prominent German political philosopher and legal theorist who joined the Nazi party in 1933. Strauss wrote an early review of Schmitt's book *The Concept of the Political*. The review can be found in the University of Chicago Press edition (1996) of Schmitt's book, translated with an introduction by George Schwab.

§ Alfred Bäumler, author of *Nietzsche, der Philosoph und Politiker* (Leipzig 1931).

¶ See note on page 223.

one cannot refute what one has not *thoroughly* understood. And many opponents did not even try to understand the ardent passion underlying the negation of the present world and its potentialities. As a consequence, the very refutations confirmed the nihilists in their belief; all these refutations seemed to beg the question; most of the refutations seemed to consist of *pueris decantata*, of repetitions of things which the young people knew already by heart. Those young men had come to doubt seriously, and not merely methodically or methodologically, the *principles* of modern civilization; the great authorities of that civilization did no longer impress them; it was evident that only such opponents would have been listened to who knew that doubt from their own experience, who through years of hard and independent thinking had overcome it. Many opponents did not meet that condition. They had been brought up in the belief in the principles of modern civilization; and a belief in which one is brought up is apt to degenerate into *prejudice*. Consequently, the attitude of the opponents of the young nihilists tended to become *apologetic*. Thus it came to pass that the most ardent upholders of the principle of progress, of an essentially *aggressive* principle, were compelled to take a defensive stand; and, in the realm of the mind, taking a defensive stand looks like admitting defeat. The ideas of modern civilization appeared to the *young* generation to be the old ideas; thus the adherents of the ideal of progress were in the awkward position that they had to resist, in the manner of *conservateurs*, what in the meantime has been called the wave of the future. They made the impression of being loaded with the heavy burden of a tradition hoary with age and somewhat dusty, whereas the young nihilists, not hampered by any tradition, had complete freedom of movement—and in the wars of the mind no less than in real wars, freedom of action spells victory. The opponents of the young nihilists had all the advantages, but likewise all the disabilities, of the intellectually propertied class confronted by the intellectual proletarian, the sceptic. The situation of modern civilization in general, and of its backbone, which is modern science, both natural and civil in particular, appeared to be comparable to that of scholasticism shortly before the emergence of the new science of the seventeenth century: the technical perfection of the methods and terminology of the old school, Communism included, appeared to be a strong argument *against* the old school. For technical perfection is apt to hide the basic problems. Or, if you wish, the bird of the goddess of wisdom starts its flight only

227

when the sun is setting.* It was certainly characteristic of German post-war thought that the output of technical terms, at no time negligible in Germany, reached astronomic proportions. The only answer which could have impressed the young nihilists had to be given in nontechnical language. Only one answer was given which was adequate and which would have impressed the young nihilists if they had heard it. It was not however given by a German and it was given in the year 1940 only. Those young men who refused to believe that the period following the jump into liberty, following the Communist world revolution, would be the finest hour of mankind in general and of Germany in particular, would have been impressed as much as we were, by what Winston Churchill said after the defeat in Flanders about Britain's finest hour.[5] For one of their greatest teachers had taught them to see in Cannae the greatest moment in the life of that glory which was ancient Rome.[6]

6. I have tried to circumscribe the intellectual and moral situation in which a nihilism emerged which was not in all cases base in its origin. Moreover, I take it for granted that not everything to which the young nihilists objected, was unobjectionable, and that not every writer or speaker whom they despised, was respectable. Let us beware of a sense of solidarity which is not limited by discretion. And let us not forget that the highest duty of the scholar, truthfulness or justice, acknowledges no limits. Let us then not hesitate to look for one moment at the phenomenon which I called nihilism, from the point of view of the nihilists themselves. "Nihilism," they would say, is a slogan used by those who do not understand the new, who see merely the rejection of *their* cherished ideals, the destruction of *their* spiritual property, who judge the new by its first words and deeds, which are, of necessity, a caricature rather than an adequate expression. How can a reasonable man expect an adequate expression of the ideal of a new epoch at its beginning, considering that the owl of Minerva starts its flight when the sun is setting?† The Nazis? Hitler? The less is said about him, the better. He will soon be forgotten. He is merely the rather contemptible *tool* of "History": the midwife who assists at the birth of the new epoch, of a new spirit; and a midwife usually understands

---

* A paraphrase of Hegel's famous lines from the preface to his *Philosophy of Right*, "The owl of Minerva spreads its wings only with the falling of the dusk."

† See preceding footnote.

nothing of the genius at whose birth she assists; she is not even supposed to be a competent gynecologist. A new reality is in the making; it is transforming the whole world; in the meantime there is: nothing, but—a fertile nothing. The Nazis are as unsubstantial as clouds; the sky is hidden at present by those clouds which announce a devastating storm, but at the same time the long-needed rain which will bring new life to the dried-up soil; and (here I am almost quoting) do not lose hope; what appears to you the end of the world, is merely the end of an epoch, of the epoch which began in 1517 or so. I frankly confess, I do not see how those can resist the voice of that siren who expect the answer to the first and the last question from "History," from the future *as such*; who mistake analysis of the present or past or future for philosophy; who believe in a progress toward a goal which is itself progressive and therefore undefinable; who are not guided by a *known* and *stable* standard: by a standard which is stable and not changeable, and which is known and not merely believed. In other words, the lack of resistance to nihilism seems to be due ultimately to the depreciation and the contempt of reason, which is one and unchangeable or it is not, and of science. For if reason is changeable, it is dependent on those forces which cause its changes; it is a servant and slave of the *emotions*; and it will be hard to make a distinction, which is not arbitrary, between noble and base emotions, once one has denied the rulership of reason. A German who could boast of a life-long intimate intercourse with the superhuman father of all nihilism, has informed us as reliably, as we were ever informed by any inspired author, that the originator of all nihilism admitted: "Just despise reason and science, the very highest power of man, and I have got you completely."[7]

7. I had to condense a number of recollections of what I have heard, seen, and read while I was living in Germany, into the foregoing fragmentary remarks, because I had to convey an *impression* of an irrational movement and of the frequently irrational reactions to it, rather than a reasoned argument. I have now, however, reached the point where I can venture to submit a definition of nihilism. I do this not without trepidation. Not because the definition which I am going to suggest does not live up to the requirements of an orderly definition (for I know that sins of that kind are the ones which are most easily forgiven); nor because it is in any way novel, but for precisely the opposite reason. It will seem to most of you that it is a commonplace and that it consists of commonplaces.

The only thing which I can say to justify myself, is this: I expected to find a definition of nihilism as a matter of course in Mr. Rauschning's well-known book.* Only my failure to discover such a definition in that book gives me the courage to indulge in what you will consider a triviality, if a necessary triviality.

I shall then say: Nihilism is the rejection of the principles of civilization as such. A nihilist is then a man who *knows* the principles of civilization, if only in a superficial way. A merely uncivilised man, a savage, is not a nihilist. This is the difference between Ariovistus, the Teutonic chieftain whom Caesar defeated, and Hitler who otherwise have the characteristic qualities of the perfect barbarian (arrogance and cruelty) in common.[8] The Roman soldier who disturbed the circles of Archimedes, was not a nihilist, but just a soldier.[9] I said *civilization*, and not: *culture*. For I have noticed that many nihilists are great lovers of culture, as distinguished from, and opposed to, civilization. Besides, the term *culture* leaves it undetermined what the thing is which is to be cultivated (blood and soil or the mind), whereas the term civilization designates at once the process of making man a citizen, and not a slave; an inhabitant of cities, and not a rustic; a lover of peace, and not of war; a polite being, and not a ruffian. A tribal community may possess a culture, i.e., produce, and enjoy, hymns, songs, ornament of their clothes, of their weapons and pottery, dances, fairy tales and what not; it cannot however be civilised. I wonder whether the fact that Western man lost much of his former pride, a quiet and becoming pride, of his being civilised, is not at the bottom of the present lack of resistance to nihilism.

I shall try to be somewhat more precise. By civilization, we understand the conscious culture of humanity, i.e., of that which makes a human being a human being, i.e., the conscious culture of reason. Human reason is active, above all, in two ways: as regulating human conduct, and as attempting to understand whatever can be understood by man; as practical reason, and as theoretical reason. The pillars of civilization are therefore morals and science, and both united. For science without morals degenerates into cynicism, and thus destroys the basis of the scientific effort itself; and morals without science degenerates into superstition and

---

* Hermann Rauschning, *The Revolution of Nihilism: Warning to the West* (New York: Longmans, Green and Co., 1939).

thus is apt to become fanatic cruelty. Science is the attempt to understand the universe and man; it is therefore identical with philosophy; it is not necessarily identical with *modern* science. By morals, we understand the rules of decent and noble conduct, as a reasonable man would understand them; those rules are by their nature applicable to any human being, although we may allow for the possibility that not all human beings have an equal natural aptitude for decent and noble conduct. Even the most violent sceptic cannot help from time to time despising, or at least excusing, this or that action and this or that man; a complete analysis of what is implied in such an action of despising, or even excusing, would lead to that well-known view of morals which I sketched. For our present purpose it will suffice if I illustrate decent and noble conduct by the remark that it is equally remote from inability to inflict physical or other pain as from deriving pleasure from inflicting pain. Or by the other remark that decent and noble conduct has to do, not so much with the natural *aim* of man, as with the *means* toward that aim: the view that the end sanctifies the means, is a tolerably complete expression of immoralism.

I deliberately excluded "art" from the definition of civilization. Hitler, the best-known champion of nihilism, is famous for his love of art and is even an artist himself. But I never heard that he had anything to do with search for truth or with any attempt to instill the seeds of virtue into the souls of his subjects. I am confirmed in this prejudice concerning "art" by the observation that the founding fathers of civilization who taught us what science is and what morals are, did not know the term art as it is in use since about 180 years, nor the term, and the discipline, aesthetics which is of equally recent origin. This is not to deny, but rather to assert, that there are close relations between science and morals on the one hand, and poetry and the other imitative arts on the other, but those relations are bound to be misunderstood, to the detriment of both science and morals as well as of poetry, if science and morals are not considered *the* pillars of civilization.

The definition which I suggested, has another implication, or advantage, which I must make explicit. I tentatively defined, at the beginning, nihilism as the desire to destroy the present civilization, *modern* civilization. By my second definition I intended to make clear that one cannot call the most radical critic of *modern* civilization as such, a nihilist.

Civilization is the conscious culture of reason. This means that civilization is not identical with human life or human existence. There were,

231

and there are, many human beings who do not partake of civilization. Civilization has a natural basis which it *finds*, which it does not create, on which it is dependent, and on which it has only a very limited influence. Conquest of nature, if not taken as a highly poetic overstatement, is a nonsensical expression. The natural basis of civilization shows itself for instance in the fact that all civilized communities as well as uncivilized ones are in need of armed force which they must use against their enemies from without and against the criminals within.

8. I presume, it is not necessary to prove that nihilism in the sense defined is dominant in Germany, and that nihilism characterizes at present Germany more than any other country. Japan, e.g., cannot be as nihilistic as Germany, because Japan has been much less civilized in the sense defined than was Germany. If nihilism is the rejection of the principles of civilization as such, and if civilization is based on recognition of the fact that the subject of civilization is man as man, every interpretation of science and morals in terms of races, or of nations, or of cultures, is strictly speaking nihilistic. Whoever accepts the idea of a Nordic or German or Faustic science, e.g., rejects *eo ipso* the *idea* of science. Different "cultures" may have produced different types of "science"; but only one of them can be *true*, can be *science*. The nihilist implication of the nationalist interpretation of science in particular can be described somewhat differently in the following terms. Civilization is inseparable from *learning*, from the desire to learn from anyone who can teach us something worthwhile. The nationalist interpretation of science or philosophy implies that we cannot really learn anything worthwhile from people who do not belong to our nation or our culture. The few Greeks whom we usually have in mind when we speak of *the* Greeks, were distinguished from the barbarians, so to speak exclusively by their willingness to learn—even from barbarians; whereas the barbarian, the non-Greek barbarian as well as the Greek barbarian, believes that all his questions are solved by, or on the basis of, *his* ancestral tradition. Naturally, a man who would limit himself to asserting that one nation may have a greater aptitude to understanding phenomena of a certain type than other nations, would not be a nihilist: not the accidental *fate* of science or morals, but its essential *intention* is decisive for the definition of civilization and therewith of nihilism.

9. The nihilists in general, and the German nihilists in particular reject the principles of civilization as such. The question arises, in favor of

what do the German nihilists reject those principles? I shall try to answer that question to begin with on the basis of Mr. Rauschning's book. This will give me an opportunity to elucidate somewhat more the foregoing definition of nihilism.

Mr. Rauschning has called the foreign and domestic policy of the Nazis "the revolution of nihilism." This means: it is not, as it claims to be, "a new order in the making," but "the wasteful and destructive exploitation of irreplaceable resources, material, mental, and moral, accumulated through generations of fruitful labor" (XI). This would mean that N.S. is nihilistic in its effect, but it does not necessarily mean that it is nihilistic in its intention. What Rauschning says in this passage quoted about the Nazis, might conceivably be said of the Communist Revolution as well. And yet, one cannot call Communism a nihilist movement. If the Communist Revolution is nihilist, it is so in its consequences, but not in its intention. This reminds me of another remark of Rauschning's: he identifies nihilism with the "destruction of all traditional spiritual standards" (XII). What I object to, is the use of the term *traditional* in the definition of nihilism. It is evident that not all traditional spiritual standards are, by their nature, beyond criticism and even rejection: we seek what is good, and not what we have inherited, to quote Aristotle.[10] In other words, I believe it is dangerous, if the opponents of National Socialism withdraw to a mere conservatism which defines its ultimate goal by a specific *tradition*. The temptation to fall back from an unimpressive present on an impressive past—and every past is as such impressive—is very great indeed. We ought not, however, cede to that temptation, if for no other reason, at least for this that *the* Western tradition is not so homogeneous as it may appear as long as one is engaged in polemics or in apologetics. To mention one example out of many: the great tradition of which Voltaire is a representative, is hard to reconcile with the tradition of which Bellarmine is a representative, even if both traditions should be equally hostile to National Socialism. Besides, I wish, Mr. Rauschning had not spoken of *spiritual* standards; this savours of the view that materialism is essentially nihilistic; I believe that materialism is an error, but I have only to recall the names of Democritus and Hobbes in order to realize that materialism is not essentially nihilistic. Not to mention the fact that a certain anti-materialism or idealism is at the bottom of German nihilism.

Rauschning operates on somewhat safer ground when he stresses the Nazis' lack of any settled aims. He understands then by German nihilism the "permanent revolution of sheer destruction" for the sake of destruction, a "revolution for its own sake" (248). He stresses the "aimlessness" of the Nazis; he says that they have no program except action; that they replace doctrine by tactics (75); he calls their revolution "a revolution without a doctrine" (55); he speaks of the "total rejection" by the Nazis "of any sort of doctrine" (56). This appears to be an exaggeration. For elsewhere Rauschning says: "One thing National Socialism is not: a doctrine or philosophy. Yet it *has* a philosophy." (23). Or: "the fight against Judaism, while it is beyond question a central element not only in material considerations, but in those of cultural policy, is part of the party doctrine" (22).

Their anti-Jewish policy does seem to be taken seriously by the Nazis. But even if it were true, that no single point of the original party program or party doctrine had a more than provisional and tactical meaning, we still should be at a loss to understand a party, a government, a State—not merely without a program or doctrine—but without any *aims*. For it seems hard to conceive how any human being can act without having an aim. John Dillinger* probably had no program, but he doubtless had an aim. In other words: Rauschning has not considered carefully enough the difference between program and aim. If he defines nihilism as a political movement without aims, then he defines a nonentity; if he defines nihilism as a political movement without a program or doctrine, then he would have to call all opportunists nihilists, which would be too uncharitable to be true.

As a matter of fact, Rauschning does not always deny that the Nazis have aims: "a permanent revolution of sheer destruction by means of which a dictatorship of brute force maintains itself in power" (xif.). Here, Rauschning *states* the aim of the Nazis: that aim is their power, they do not destroy in order to destroy, but in order to maintain themselves in power. Now, to keep themselves in power, they depend, to a certain extent, on their ability to make their subjects, the Germans, happy, on their ability to satisfy the needs of the Germans. This means, as matters stand, that, in order to maintain themselves in power, they must embark upon a policy of aggression, a policy directed toward world dominion.

Rauschning corrects his remark about the aimlessness of the Nazis by saying "the German aims are indefinite to-day only because they are

---

* John Dillinger was an American gangster who went on a spectacular string of bank robberies during 1933.

234

infinite" (275). Their "goal" is "the world-wide totalitarian empire" (58). They have not only aims, their aims form even a hierarchy leading up to a principal aim: "the principal aim, the redistribution of the world" (229). German nihilism, as described by Rauschning, is then the aspiration to world dominion exercised by the Germans who are dominated in their turn by a German *élite*; that aspiration becomes nihilistic, because it uses *any* means to achieve its end and thus destroys everything which makes life worth living for any decent or intelligent being. However low an opinion we may have of the Nazis, I am inclined to believe that they desire German world dominion not merely as a means for keeping themselves in power, but that they derive, so to speak, a disinterested pleasure from the prospect of that glamorous goal "Germany ruling the world." I should even go one step further and say that the Nazis probably derive a disinterested pleasure from the aspect of those human qualities which enable nations to conquer. I am certain that the Nazis consider any pilot of a bomber or any submarine commander absolutely superior in human dignity to any traveling salesman or to any physician or to the representative of any other relatively peaceful occupation. For, a German nihilist much more intelligent and much more educated than Hitler himself has stated: "What kind of minds are those who do not even know this much that no mind *can* be more profound and more knowing than that of *any* soldier who fell anywhere at the Somme or in Flanders? *This* is the standard of which we are in need." ("Was aber sind das für Geister, die noch nicht einmal wissen, dass kein Geist tiefer and wissender sein kann als der jedes beliebigen Soldaten, der irgendwo an der Somme oder in Flandern fiel? Dies ist der Massstab, dessen wir bedürftig sind." Jünger, *Der Arbeiter*, 201.) The admiration of the warrior as a type, the unconditional preference given to the warrior as warrior, is however not only *genuine* in German nihilism: it is even its distinctive feature. Our question: in favor of what does German nihilism reject the principles of civilization as such must therefore be answered by the statement: that it rejects those principles in favor of the military virtues. This is what Mr. Rauschning must have had in mind when speaking of "*heroic* nihilism" (21).

War is a destructive business. And if war is considered more noble than peace, if war, and not peace, is considered *the* aim, the aim is for all practical purposes nothing other than destruction. There is reason for believing that the business of destroying, and killing, and torturing is a source of an almost disinterested pleasure to the Nazis as such, that they derive a genuine pleasure from the aspect of the strong and ruthless who subjugate, exploit, and torture the weak and helpless.

10. German nihilism rejects then the principles of civilization as such in favor of war and conquest, in favor of the warlike virtues. German nihilism is therefore akin to German militarism. This compels us to raise the question what militarism is. Militarism can be identified as the view expressed by the older Moltke in these terms: "Eternal peace is a dream, and not even a beautiful one."[11] To believe that eternal peace is a dream, is not militarism, but perhaps plain commonsense; it is at any rate not bound up with a particular moral taste. But to believe that eternal peace is not a *beautiful* dream, is tantamount to believing that war is something desirable in itself; and to believe that war is something desirable in itself, betrays a cruel, inhuman disposition. The view that war is good in itself, implies the rejection of the distinction between just and unjust wars, between wars of defense and wars of aggression. It is ultimately irreconcilable with the very idea of a law of nations.

11. German nihilism is *akin* to German militarism, but it is not *identical* with it. Militarism always made at least the *attempt* to reconcile the ideal of war with *Kultur*, nihilism however is based on the assumption that *Kultur* is finished. Militarism always recognized that the virtues of peace are of equal dignity, or almost equal dignity, with the virtues of war. When denying that the rules of decency cannot be applied to foreign policy, it never denied the validity of those rules as regards home policy or private life. It never asserted that science is essentially national; it merely asserted that the Germans happen to be the teachers of the lesser breeds. German nihilism on the other hand asserts that the military virtues, and in particular courage as the ability to bear any physical pain, the virtue of the red Indian, is the only virtue *left* (see Jünger's essay on pain in *Blütter and Steine*).[12] The only virtue *left*: the implication is that we live in an age of decline, of the decline of the West, in an age of civilization as distinguished from, and opposed to culture; or in an age of mechanic society as distinguished from, and opposed to, organic community. In that condition of debasement, only the most elementary virtue, the first virtue, that virtue with which man and human society stands and falls, is capable to grow. Or, to express the same view somewhat differently: in an age of utter corruption, the only remedy possible is to destroy the edifice of corrup-

tion—"das *System*"—and to return to the uncorrupted and incorruptible *origin*, to the condition of *potential*, and not actual, culture or civilization: the characteristic virtue of that stage of merely *potential* culture or civilization, of the *state of nature*, is courage and nothing else. German nihilism is then a radicalized form of German militarism, and that radicalization is due to the fact that during the last generation the *romantic* judgment about the whole modern development, and therefore in particular about the present, has become much more generally accepted than it ever was even in nineteenth century *Germany*. By romantic judgment, I understand a judgment which is guided by the opinion that an absolutely superior order of human things existed during some period of the recorded past

12. However great the difference between German militarism and German nihilism may be: the kinship of the two aspirations is obvious. German militarism is the *father* of German nihilism. A thorough understanding of German nihilism would therefore require a thorough understanding of German militarism. Why has Germany such a particular aptitude for militarism? A few, extremely sketchy remarks must here suffice.

To explain German militarism, it is not sufficient to refer to the fact that German civilization is considerably *younger* than the civilization of the Western nations, that Germany is therefore perceivably nearer to barbarism than are the Western countries. For the civilization of the Slavonic nations is still younger than that of the Germans, and the Slavonic nations do not appear to be as militaristic as are the Germans. To discover the root of German militarism, it might be wiser to disregard the *prehistory* of German civilization, and to look at the history of German civilization itself. Germany reached the hey-day of her letters and her thought during the period from 1760 to 1830; i.e., *after* the elaboration of the ideal of *modern* civilization had been finished almost completely, and while a *revision* of that ideal, or a *reaction* to that ideal, took place. The ideal of *modern* civilization is of English and French origin; it is not of German origin. What the meaning of that ideal is, is, of course, a highly controversial question. If I am not greatly mistaken, one can define the tendency of the intellectual development which as it were exploded in the French Revolution, in the following terms: to lower the moral standards, the moral claims, which previously had been made by all responsible teachers, but to take better care than those earlier teachers had done, for the putting into practice, into political and legal practice, of the rules of human conduct. The way in which this was most effectually achieved, was the identification of morality with an attitude of claiming one's *rights*, or with enlightened self-interest, or the reduction of honesty to the best policy; or the solution of the conflict between common interest and private interest by means of industry and trade. (The two most famous philosophers: Descartes, his *générosité*, and no justice, no duties; Locke: where there is no property, there is no justice.) Against that debasement of morality, and against the concomitant decline of a truly philosophic spirit, the thought of Germany stood up, to the lasting honor of Germany. It was however precisely this reaction to the spirit of the seventeenth and eighteenth century which laid the foundation for German militarism as far as it is an intellectual phenomenon. Opposing the identification of the morally good with the object of enlightened self-interest however enlightened, the German philosophers insisted on the *difference* between the morally good and self-interest, between the *honestum* and the *utile*; they insisted on self-*sacrifice* and self-*denial*; they insisted on it so much, that they were apt to forget the natural aim of man which is happiness; happiness and utility as well as commonsense (*Verständigkeit*) became almost bad names in German philosophy. Now, the difference between the noble and the useful, between duty and self-interest is *most* visible in the case of one virtue, courage, military virtue: the consummation of the actions of every other virtue is, or may be, *rewarded*; it actually *pays* to be just, temperate, urbane, munificent etc.; the consummation of the actions of courage, i.e. death on the field of honour, death for one's country, is *never* rewarded: it is the flower of self-sacrifice. Courage is the only unambiguously unutilitarian virtue. In defending menaced morality, i.e., nonmercenary morality, the German philosophers were tempted to overstress the dignity of military virtue, and in very important cases, in the cases of Fichte, Hegel, and Nietzsche, they succumbed to that temptation. In this and in various other ways, German philosophy created a peculiarly German tradition of contempt for commonsense and the aims of human life, as they are visualized by commonsense.

However deep the difference between German philosophy and the philosophy of the Western countries may be: German philosophy ultimately conceived of itself as a *synthesis* of the premodern ideal and the ideal of the modern period. That synthesis did not work: in the second half of the nineteenth century, it was overrun by Western positivism, the natural child of the enlightenment. Germany had been educated by her philosophers in contempt of Western philosophy (*Je méprise Locke*, is a saying of Schelling's); she now observed that the synthesis effected by her philosophers, of the premodern ideal and the modern ideal did not work; she saw no way out except to purify German thought completely from the influence of the ideas of modern civilization, and to return to the premodern ideal. National Socialism is the most famous, because the most vulgar, example of such a return to a pre-modern ideal. On its highest level, it was a return to what may be called the preliterary stage of philosophy, presocratic philosophy. On *all* levels, the pre-modern ideal was not a *real* premodern ideal, but a premodern ideal *as interpreted* by the German idealists, i.e., interpreted with a polemic intention against the philosophy of the seventeenth and eighteenth century, and therefore distorted.

Of all German philosophers, and indeed of *all* philosophers, none exercised a greater influence on postwar Germany, none was more responsible for the emergence of German nihilism, than was Nietzsche. The relation of Nietzsche to the German Nazi Revolution is comparable to the relation of Rousseau to the French Revolution. That is to say: by interpreting Nietzsche in the light of the German revolution, one is very unjust to Nietzsche, but one is not *absolutely* unjust. It may not be amiss to quote one or the other passage from *Beyond Good and Evil*, which are related to our subject: "That is no philosophic race, these Englishmen. Bacon represents an *attack* on the philosophic spirit as such. Hobbes, Hume and Locke are a degradation and debasement of the very concept of 'philosopher' for more than a century. *Against* Hume, Kant stood up and stood out. It was Locke, of whom Schelling was *entitled* to say *Je méprise Locke*. In the fight against English mechanist interpretation of nature [Newton], Hegel and Schopenhauer and Goethe were unanimous." "That what one calls the modern ideas, or the ideas of the 18th century, or even the French ideas, that ideal, in a word, against which the German spirit stood up with profound disgust—it is of *English* origin, there can be no doubt about that. The French have merely been the imitators and actors of those ideas, besides their best soldiers, and also, unfortunately, their first and most complete victims." (aph. 252 f.)[13] I believe that Nietzsche is substantially correct in asserting that *the* German tradition is very critical of the ideals of modern civilization, and those ideals are of *English* origin. He forgets however to add that the English almost always had the very un-German prudence and moderation not to throw out the baby with the bath, i.e., the prudence to conceive of the modern ideals as a reasonable adaptation of the old and eternal ideal of decency, of rule of law, and of that liberty which is not license, to changed circumstances. This taking things easy, this muddling through, this crossing the bridge when one comes to it, may have done some harm to the radicalism of English thought; but it proved to be a blessing to English life; the English never indulged in those radical breaks with traditions which played such a role on the continent. Whatever may be wrong with the peculiarly modern ideal: the very Englishmen who originated it, were at the same time versed in the classical tradition, and the English always kept in store a substantial amount of the necessary counter-poison. While the English originated the modern ideal—the premodern ideal, the classical ideal of humanity, was nowhere better preserved than in Oxford and Cambridge.

The present Anglo-German war is then of symbolic significance. In defending modern civilization against German nihilism, the English are defending the eternal principles of civilization. No one can tell what will be the outcome of this war. But this much is clear beyond any doubt: by choosing Hitler for their leader in the crucial moment, in which the question of who is to exercise planetary rule became the order of the day, the Germans ceased to have any *rightful* claim to be more than a provincial nation; it is the English, and not the Germans, who *deserve* to be, and to *remain*, an *imperial* nation: for only the English, and not the Germans, have understood that in order to *deserve* to exercise imperial rule, *regere imperio populos*, one must have learned for a very long time to spare the vanquished and to crush the arrogant: *parcere subjectis et debellare superbos.*[14]

14

Three Riders of the Apocalypse: Communism, Nazism, and Progressive Democracy* (1950)

Aurel Kolnai

1

Of the three classic types of modern mass regimes, made to fit the body of emancipated Man, one—Nazism—would seem to bear no relevancy except to Germanic mankind alone, and owing to the defeat of Nazi Germany lacks practical support for the time being; another—Progressive Democracy, as I call it for want of a better name—is of manifold appearance, a world hag-ridden with a certain well-identifiable but flexible scheme of "isms" rather than an embodied "ism" proper, and in the sense again not wholly on a footing with that most genuine and powerful brand of totalitarianism which is the Marxist-Leninist one. Progressive Democracy, from which the other two have sprung, may be looked upon as too universal to form a threefold division with these, whereas Nazism may appear disqualified for such a status in view of its being too particular: too limited in space and time. Still, it is not without reason that Christian conservative—or in other words—antitotalitarian writers have again and again emphasized the essential kinship of these three "modes of life" of modern man, adding or not a description of their distinctive marks. Their emphasis may be an overemphasis, their attempt at distinctive characterization may be sketchy or shallow; for we are only too apt to lump together whatever things we dislike and to underestimate their mutual differences,

---

* Originally written in 1950 but first published in 1998.

241

though they were locked in a deadly fight among one another. So also the liberal would assert that Nazism and Communism are "essentially" the selfsame totalitarian "dictatorship" only painted different colors; the "democratic" Socialist, that Bolshevism is really a "reactionary" system; and he in his turn will hear from his Communist rivals that he is nothing but a "Social Fascist" or a "lackey of capitalists and imperialists." And yet, without allowing our *ressentiments* to tempt us into any of these inane simplifications, and aware from the outset that *Communism alone* represents, as it were, the fullness of the Inferno which man in the process of his self-enslavement has vowed to make unto himself for an earthly paradise, we may meaningfully consider the three-headed monster under the aspect of its unitary principle of life as well as under that of the respective contrasts between any two of the three heads or between any pair of them (taken as a unit) and the third. Nazism, indeed, which only yesterday astounded mankind with its tremendous outburst of energy and conquering appetite, is not a wholly parochial affair, nor in all certainty obsolete or irrevocably dead; Progressive Democracy, again, is neither a sheer recusancy from Communism nor perhaps merely its preparatory phase but the primal form of the "Common Man" world, instinct with an "ideology" of its own. In order even to fight Communism intelligently and effectively—which is our one paramount business of supreme urgency—we had better survey all these things, to the best of our ability, in their true proportions. I think the fittest way of procedure to establish and delimit the "three pairs" as against, respectively, the third member of the triad.

2

Nazism and Communism, as contrasted to Progressive Democracy, have in common most of their aspects, down to a great deal of concrete detail, relative to the *technique of government* along with its various mental paraphernalia and psychological accompaniment. They both imply one-part rule, severe dictatorship with deified "leaders" as personal figureheads, a regime of terror in permanence exercised by the secret police, state omnipotence encroaching upon all domains of life including the most intimate ones, the reducing of law and morality to mere functions of state power and of the government's will, the tendency to suppress such social inequality as is

not inherent in the gradation of political power proper, and lastly, the substitution for transcendent religion of political ideology and the self-wor-
ship of society as informed by an exclusive and militant will, implying a
pretension on the government's part to "represent" that will entirely, taken
in its massive self-identity one and indivisible. Besides these basic traits—
an utterly monistic and centralistic conception of social power; terror as
a constitutive element, a mainstay and a cornerstone, of government; the
quasi-religious idea of a limitless self-sovereignty of man, to be made valid
and guaranteed by the total sovereignty of state power—we notice certain
further points of structural similarity between the two systems: extending to the more or less arbitrarily specified objects they mark out for cul-
tic veneration or sustained hatred, to the peculiar cants and styles they
impose in the realms of art, language, science, and so forth, as well as to
other devices for ensuring a trance-like state of high tension, a continually
whipped-up sense of privileged abnormality and a mood of taut militancy.
Compared to this, Progressive Democracy, even in its most advanced and
gravest forms—which are Socialist Party rule on the one hand, American-
ism on the other—unmistakably clings to a kind of continuity with the
normal life of society and the pluralistic landscape of interests, points of
view, and accents which is inherent in the ordinary consciousness of man;
particularly, perhaps, or at least most evidently so as regards the man of
liberal civilization. Progressive Democracy, to be sure, is also informed by
a "secular religion," with its various trappings and the sullen fanaticism
attaching to it; but this false religion intrinsically connotes an element of
tolerance, indetermination, and détente (as an actual state of mind here
and now, not as a chiliastic promise to be redeemed after a world-wide
dictatorship and a reign of terror growing beyond all limits shall have
created human nature anew); indeed, it is incapable of unequivocal definition and its adepts, unable to think except in an idiom of compromise, are
constitutionally precluded from enforcing an un-"constitutional" mode
of life and from claiming a massive totality of uncontrolled power. That,
nevertheless, the goal towards which Progressive Democracy is progressing lies in such a direction, being in fact indistinguishable from that of
Communism, is true enough; yet "Progress," according to our Western
coinage of its idolatry, is conceived of as an "infinite" one, never to be
accomplished definitively, and with its tangible fruits of safety, welfare,
peace, freedom, "culture," and the like being gathered, consumed, and

enjoyed by all of us daily; hence the driving force that makes *our* world go round cannot take body in one omnipotent center of power but remains subject, so far as its actual workings are concerned, to the empirical tests of success and immediate pleasure: to a network of checks and balances, that is, which affords the plain man and even the Christian with some opportunity of making his weight felt. The world of Progressive Democracy, then, is ordered on a dualist and "idealistic" plan, which implies the recognition of a "given" human reality underneath the "ideal," subsisting in its own right and incurably falling short of the "perfection" of utopia it is expected to "approximate" in time, with the division between the two remaining ineliminable; that this world, *so long as it would last*, should never be completely determined by its dominant ideology is part of the ideology itself.

Communism and Nazism, on the other hand, both presuppose the antecedent of Progressive Democracy, from which they both represent a radical new departure, directed to entirely disparate or even antithetic aims but revealing a far-reaching analogy between the two as regards the totalitarian conception of "identity" between the wills of the rulers and the ruled, the long-range program of terroristic dictatorship, and the ingenious idea—thought up in response to the growing sense of emptiness, nihilism, and palsy in liberal society—of a new "meaning of life" provided and imposed by state power.

3

What Nazism and Progressive Democracy have in common is, to put it briefly, the character of *incomplete totalitarianism*. So far as ideological "signs" and "emphases" alone are concerned it would seem, admittedly, that our democratic regimes are not totalitarian at all, whereas Nazism is most noisily and defiantly so, connoting Socialism too and insisting on state omnipotence not a whit less than does Communism. Again, if instead of judging by the sound of party slogans and the demeanor of terroristic gangsters drunk with power we consider the "insidious" totalitarianism inherent in the trend towards equality, uniformity and administrative "planning for welfare," we might on the contrary find that Progressive Democracy really outstrips the totalitarianism not only of the Nazis but even of the Communists, assimilating as it does (under the deceptive verbal cloak of liberalism and tolerance) the thinking, moods, and wills of everybody to a wholesale standard of the "socialized" mind more organically and perhaps more durably; eliminating all *essential* opposition to its own pattern by incomparably milder methods but so much the more effectively and irrevocably. However, both these perspectives, though highly relevant to a full assessment of the objects of our study, are one-sided and liable to make us miss the central point of distinction. Neither our horror of Nazi perversity, cruelty, and vulgarity nor our disgust at the mediocrity and duplicity, the inner unfreedom, the deadening quack rationality and the sickening pseudoculture of Progressive Democracy should blind us to the patent and highly important truth that, in contraposition to the Communist regime bent on determining the whole of human reality according to the pattern of an unnatural utopia and reducing every aspect and detail of men's lives to a function of One all-absorbing political Will, both Nazism and Progressive Democracy represent the maimed forms of normal human society, not integrally suppressed but, respectively, overlaid with a fiendish tyranny totalitarian in temper, and infiltrated by the virus of subversive utopia bound for a totalitarian goal. As regards Progressive Democracy, its essentially curtailed totalitarianism is too obvious to need elaborate treatment. Notwithstanding the subtle expansion of the old concept of political liberty into that of "Freedom from Want" and the surreptitious displacement of citizens' rights by the changeling idol of a "right to security," the elements of the "rights of man" and "the dignity of the individual" cannot be wholly ousted from Progressive Democracy short of a radical overthrow of the system: until that, the bar to keep out tyranny proper continues acting, though there is no denying that the inward logic of the system makes it wear ever thinner and threatens to eat it away altogether. Still, how could a conservative writer call the democratic regime properly tyrannical or actually totalitarian, so long as he is able to get his very accusations into print?—and without on that score coming to immediate and crushing grief, into the bargain!

To deny a genuinely totalitarian character to Nazism may sound a little odder, seeing that not only liberal-democratic but also conservative and Christian authors have betrayed a fondness for arguing glibly from Communism to Nazism and conversely, interpreting Nazism as a "Brown" variety of its "Red" model and Bolshevism as nationalism or imperialism under a Red flag, overworking the term "National Socialism," harping on the disciplinarian and allegedly "nationalistic" traits in Russian Bolshevism, subsuming the two evil things under an identical concept of "Neo-Paganism" and placing the Nazi worship of a "superior race" on a level with the Marxian deity, absolutely different as to its logical structure and historical meaning, of the "class struggle." The truth is that the Nazi order never was, nor was intended to be, a *socialistic* one—in the proper, collectivist sense of that term—and for that reason alone, which is far from being the deepest, could not amount and could never have attained to true totalitarianism. Despite the terrorism of Nazi dictatorship which bore down severely on the noble and wealthy classes as well as on the broad masses (thus connoting, as it were, a kind of new equalitarianism), it was utterly alien to the Nazi conception of society to do away with class distinctions; despite the enmity it had sworn to the "Jewish moneylender," Nazism reserved a high place of honor to the "German entrepreneur"; despite its playing ducks and drakes with the economy of the country and countries it had subjugated, Nazism would not dream of effecting incisive structural changes in the economic system, let alone of seeking them for their own sake; despite its wallowing in the ecstasy of "total state power," Nazism was definitely and consistently hostile to the idea of reducing all social relations of power and dependence to a mere function or expression of that state power, and in fact ultimately aimed at creating a new type of social aristocracy. To be sure, Nazi tyranny was "unlimited" in the sense that it kicked aside constitutional "checks and balances" and even moral restraints just as scornfully as did Bolshevism, but not at all in the sense of claiming, as Bolshevism does claim, a total determination of the order of human life and relationships on behalf of one exclusive political will as actualized by the rulers; to be sure, it ruthlessly trampled under foot all "opposition" but it did not define from the outset everything not of its own making as "opposition"; to be sure, it would order about capitalists perhaps as harshly as workers, but without for a moment entertaining the idea of *"liquidating"* the capitalist class (or, for that matter, the peasantry) and of manufacturing society anew as homogeneous mass of "toilers." It should be added that, if Nazi tyranny was explicitly oppressive and (unlike the old absolutisms at their worst) positively totalitarian in the educational, literary, artistic, and similar fields, the intellectual life of Germany under its heel—and of occupied France as well—still compared as a paradise of freedom and spontaneity with the spiritual cemetery which promptly covers every place where the Bolshevik steam-roller has passed. Could any one imagine, in Soviet Russia or one of her dependences a counterpart to Jünger's *Marble Cliffs*: a nauseating and at the same time wholly unambiguous vision of Stalin as the incarnation of malicious barbarism, published with impunity—or only published; or, indeed, only written—by, say, a Menshevik university professor or an anarchist prince of yesterday, disillusioned with the revolution?

In some respects Progressive Democracy, and in another but not entirely different sense Nazism, might be described as more "progressive," "modern" and "totalitarian" than Communism. Democratic thought is more anxious to be up-to-date and elastic; to scan, to recognize, and to put to the test—rather than merely prescribe and enforce—the new states of mind rising, in society, in a kind of perpetual flux; to effect not only but to undergo a constant change, absorbing as it were all aspects of a "world in change" into the very tissue of its own details and formulations. Nazism, in its turn, views man, his nature and history, in a perspective admitting of a greater manifoldness of dimensions, and thus aspires to a totalitarian determination of man by state power through more numerous channels; through more complex leverage. Biological and eugenic points of view seem to rank higher, not only in Nazi racialism but also in the Progressive Democratic trend towards a medical and psychiatric dictatorship, than in the Communist state-worship with its monomaniac reference to political power and social (in the sense of extra-political) equality. Thus Communism cares less, one might say, about an all-round predetermination of the "human material," including its *natural quality*, on which Society as represented by its central agency of power expects to work. But, on the other hand, all such lines of determination are of a more partial, haphazard, experimental, uncertain kind than is the direct bending of men's wills by an unrestrained and effectively organized power of command; moreover, they leave some space for categories of value—specifications of "good and bad"—not defined in terms of present governmental decision as such: for measures of judgment that lie beyond the one and indivisible political will of man. Communism, then, remains the absolute, classic, and insuperable type of totalitarianism proper.

4

Progressive Democracy and Communism are aligned together as the work-ing out of the *selfsame basic concept of Social Revolution*, whereas Nazism essentially aims at bringing about a Counter-Revolution; a reversal of the trend which White mankind has followed ever since the first steps towards the secularization of Christianity (or, to be more exact, since the adoption of Christianity), and which has led up, itself coming to be more and more consciously experienced in the process and doted upon as "the meaning of history," to the various forms of present modernity. The two first-named "isms" coincide in *"Leftism"*; their Nazi counterpart, however unpleas-ant this may sound to many conservative ears, embodies one extreme (or, rather extremist) type of *"Rightism."* However, "Right and Left" is a highly important but by no means an overwhelmingly sovereign division or test: one may be a Rightist yet an enemy of Nazism just as well as one may be a Left-wing democrat yet rigidly opposed to Communism, or again, an orthodox Communist who by definition is ready to suppress whatever other kinds of Leftists walk abroad; one may certainly be, as I am, a con-firmed Rightist who yet prefers Democracy at its worst to Nazism. What is more, I even prefer the drab but comparatively solid commonplace advocates of the liberal-democratic "middle road" to the flippant aesthetes of conservatism who despise "trivial" facts and obvious "truisms" for their lack of piquancy, twist the truth so as to fit the ideological need of the moment, and reel in skin-deep "depths" such as the analogy between "National Socialism" and Communist imperialism or the violent moods and the patterns of action Nazism had in common with its so-called "Red twin-brother"—labeling, on their strength, Nazism as a "brand Leftism," while the pundits of Labourism and Yankeesism no less libelously tag the terrible epithet "reactionary" to their unloving brothers of Moscow.

This has been the primary, manifest, consistent, and permanent prin-ciple, the set purpose, of Nazism—as, indeed, of all "Fascism," with which Nazism is partly identical but which it transcends *essentially*; to save the national society from annihilation by the Bolshevists and from Social-ist ascendancy; to destroy the Marxian and all independent (including the Christian) labor movement[s] in the world of capitalist economy; to abolish the liberal and democratic framework of bourgeois society itself, which provides Socialist subversion with a thriving-ground and thus dialectically invites its own destruction; reaching out into a vaster historical perspective, to undo the work of the French Revolution, together with the mental atmosphere of rationalism, enlightenment, and progress which bred forth that revolution and again drew new strength from its impetus and achievements; to turn back to, and to revive, autochthonous national traditions, with more stress laid on their political exploitation than on their historic genuineness and therefore a tendency to interpret them in a narrow, aggressive, as it were "tribal" and deliberately mythical sense. True Fascism—that is Mussolini's: the only one that existed—went further along this path than the improperly "Fascist" Right dictatorships— Dollfuss's,* Salazar's,† Franco's‡ and others—and for this reason, being more activistic, more aggressive, more overheatedly "political," more reckless, more totalitarian, more antiliberal, might *so far* be found more antibourgeois, "subversive" and "revolutionary." Nazism again went further; but this time with a decisively greater stride and broader scope, in a unique and incomparable style: negating, over and above liberalism and rationalism, Christian civilization as such (the breeding ground of modernity and progress) as well as the faith which has informed it, together with some if not most of its subsoil in Greco-Roman antiquity; and groping back, in its quest for "rejuvenating" antimodern traditions, across the Prussian glory of yesterday and the more brutal aspects of the German Middle Ages towards the barbarous world of Teutonic heathendom—not without a side-glance, in my opinion at any rate, at Hindu racialism and caste religion. Call, then, Nazism extremistic and totalitarian; call it an archenemy of conservatism proper; call it, if you like, subversive or revolutionary, provided you are clear in your mind what you mean by that: a revolutionist's state of mind, to be sure, afire with the ambitious vision of a vast and

---

* Engelbert Dollfuss was an Austrian politician. Appointed Chancellor in 1933, he allied Austria with Horthy's Hungary and Mussolini's Italy, but opposed the Anschluss with Germany. He was assassinated by Austrian Nazis in July 1934.

† António de Oliveira Salazar became premier of Portugal in 1932 and promptly assumed dictatorial powers and moved the country toward Fascism.

‡ Francisco Franco was proclaimed the head of state in Spain at the conclusion of the civil war in 1939. He led Spain on the model of Mussolini's Italy for many years, utilizing a single political party, the Falange.

perhaps measureless transformation of society; dynamic, petulant, savage, uninhibited, in many a sense not unlike Bolshevism—but setting out in an opposite direction. No sharper contrast could be thought of than the one between the historical locus of Bolshevism and that of Nazism; the concept of history as a dialectical process ordained to the goal of a man-made "rational" utopia, and the paganistic idea of restoring history to its place as an aspect of natural "becoming," a "cosmic wave" of vital ups and downs, an aimless clash and interplay of irrational forces with man as their mere emanation, product, and sport, whose only task is to acknowledge his status as such and to make the most of it by submitting to the mysterious imperatives of that immutable order of everlasting change as reechoed in the "throbbing of this blood," Communism take action so as to bring progress to a head: to institute the world-wide reign of Antichrist—which explicitly presupposes the historical lineage marked by the names of Jahweh, Christ, Luther and Calvin, Rousseau, Kant, Fichte and Hegel—embodied in mankind wholly organized on a unitary plan and wholly master of itself, that is, wholly slave to its center of will. But Nazism would subvert, as it were, the tradition of subversion; break off the beaten track of history and scorn the path of progress struck out by an intelligible formula of the human mind engaged in its dialectical self-creation; though aware of its unavoidable heirship to Christianity also to mass democracy, it would in the final reckoning "cut out" the Christian "episode" altogether and revert to a state of things in which the old daemons dwelling in the hearts and governing the fates of men should again come into their own.

The very immensity of a "counterrevolution on a cosmic scale" as envisioned in Nazism cannot but imply a certain "revolutionary" note peculiar to it, with an emphasis stronger than that of the Communists on the abstract elements of "newness," "youth," "reversal" (*Umbruch*) and similar such notions. Whereas, in the Communist optics, Christianity and feudalism appear to represent a historical "progress" over Paganism and slave economy, the Nazi writers, steeped in a mood of unreal but not wholly irrelevant wistfulness for "Teutonic religion," were fond of vilifying Charlemagne, whom they used to call "Charles the Butcher." But the German *völkish* (ethnic or racialist) conservatives had already indulged in such whims long before the advent of Nazism. From the moment of its birth up to the time when it achieved the uprooting of all the Leftist and "Centrist" forces in Germany, the Nazi movement was developing and maneuvering in constant and organic co-operation—never felt by anybody to be "paradoxical" or "treacherous"—with parties and social groups of the "right." It cannot be mere coincidence nor a matter of mere trickery that von Kahr* should have patronized and encouraged Hitler in 1923 before "betraying" him; that von Papen† and Hugenberg‡ should have prevailed over Hindenburg§ to appoint Hitler chancellor; that Hitler should have started his rule by dissolving the Communist Party and calling Parliament in Potsdam; that he should have obtained full powers from his Rightist allies and the Catholic Center itself over the opposition of the Socialists, to be dissolved in their turn forthwith; that even at the time of his collaboration with Moscow, he should have persistently tried to use Pétain,¶ Franco, Horthy,** Antonescu†† and Mussolini as lieutenants in his campaign against the democracies; that it should have been the conservatives in England (backed by most of the French Right) who endeavored to

---

* Gustav Ritter von Kahr was a powerful conservative, monarchist politician in Bavaria during the 1920s. He fostered a movement for Bavarian secession in defiance of the Weimar government but without success. He helped to suppress Hitler's attempted putsch in November of 1923 and was later murdered by the Nazis in the 1934 Night of the Light Knives.

† von Papen. See note on page 193.

‡ Alfred Hugenberg was a German politician, industrialist, and media mogul who exercised great influence with German public opinion through his newspapers. As a leader of the conservative German National People's Party, he sought to control Hitler by making alliances between the Nazis and his party, only to be outwitted and cast aside.

§ Paul von Hindenburg was a key German military leader during the first world war who was elected president in 1925. He was reelected to that office in 1932, and appointed Adolph Hitler Chancellor in 1933.

¶ Henri Philippe Pétain was a French military hero of WWI. He became head of the Vichy government of occupied France during WWII. He was tried and found guilty of treason after the war.

** Miklós Horthy led a counterrevolution against Bela Kun and the Hungarian Communists in 1920. Horthy ruled Hungary during the interwar years. Horthy and Hungary entered WWII on the side of Nazi Germany, though he maintained ties with the Allies. Horthy unsuccessfully sued for a separate peace with the Soviet Union in 1944.

†† Ion Antonescu was a Romanian dictator during WWII who allied his country with Nazi Germany.

come to an agreement with Hitler up to his conquest of Prague and the relatively Rightist or at least strongly capitalistic circles in America who were busy hindering Roosevelt from opposing Nazi Germany up to Pearl Harbor. To try and discredit Nazism (or else, the Left) by calling it a brand of Leftism is just as absurd as it would be to apply the same epithet to Fascists and Falangists* as well as to all liberals, conservatives and Christian democrats or Catholic People's Parties of the present epoch, seeing that all these represent political forces acting on a mass scale in an "age of the masses." "Leftist" would then be a synonym of the political man as such; "Rightist" a word to designate the solitary thinker with an anarchical turn of mind and a scorn of collective discipline, whatever the content of his ideas may be. Such an utter misuse of current terminology is incompatible with any purposeful political thought, and indeed with intellectual seriousness and honesty.

"We fight the Nazis because we have to; the Socialists are the enemy we fight cheerfully, with joy in our hearts"—thus spoke, in the summer of 1933, Major Fey, a "Rightist" halfway between Fascist and Monarchist, Minister for Public Security under Chancellor Dollfuss in Austria. It is with an even more pitifully bleeding heart than Fey when at war with Rightist "hotspurs" that English Labourites and the like see themselves compelled to take a stand against Soviet Russia, "the greatest hope of the international workers' movement." Nor is the secret of why President Roosevelt offered the Russian Bolsheviks half the world on a silver tray anything other than the simple fact that he loved them; that his heart went out to them as instinctively as he distrusted the English "Tories" whom he was reared, fashioned and taught to regard as the hereditary and natural antagonist. The man of Progressive Democracy is loath to understand that the Communist is not only "also a Leftist" but a *totalitarian* Leftist, who is resolved to devour him lock, stock, and barrel after he has ceased to be useful and "preferable for the moment" or "comparatively progressive." But at a certain juncture, the instinct of self-preservation may prevail in the man of Progressive Democracy; he will then willynilly resist the onslaught of the Communist and, to justify this depressing necessity in his own malformed conscience, come to discover that

* The Falange was founded in 1933 and was the party that dominated Spain under the rule of Franco.

Communism is not really a luminous beacon for the workers of the world but a "reactionary" dictatorship and a reedition of "Tsarism." The typical "rightist" attitude towards Nazism has been closely analogous to this. But, as we shall see, it is easier for a Conservative than for a Progressive thinker to avoid this pitfall; for to be "a Rightist above all"—rather than to measure all political questions by objective moral and religious standards—is itself a mood copied from the Left.

5

The "Riders of the Apocalypse" are nothing but three classic postures, three epiphanies as it were, of *Man at large*: Man first set free from Christianity and lifted above the flats of his fallen nature; Man who then wrenched himself free *from* Christianity and construed the automatic workings of his fallen nature into a mirage of self-made heaven; finally, Man impatiently bent on converting that mirage into a cast-iron reality and thereby stultifying it so as to become in his turn, more than ever before, a house divided in itself, though still afire with the unholy rage of his emancipation and sovereignty.

Our appreciation—from a Christian conservative point of view—of the three great hostile powers of this *saeculum* will, however, differ both in degree and, particularly, in kind. In Communism, the pure embodiment of subversive totalitarianism, we shall see our foe most entirely and unequivocally; in Progressive Democracy, least so. For, although or just because Progressive Democracy enfolds the historical "Left" in its broad and wholesale sense, it also represents in a backwater fashion the obscured, silenced, disfigured, and disinherited remains of true Christian civilization with its timeless standards of right, honor, and wisdom: the precariously surviving body of Christendom in a scene resounding with the slogans of Antichrist; a scant but precious heirloom of common decency and common sense overshadowed by the witless romanticism of its exact opposite—the cult of the Common Man. But nonetheless do we owe a debt of gratitude to the totalitarianisms proper, Communism and Nazism, for being *witnesses* to the truth that the idol of the Common Man cannot indefinitely reign without ruling beyond all restraining and absorbing everything into its hideous texture; for having *exploded* the lying prophecies and fond hopes clustered round the idea of progress and the myths of "social science" about an approaching golden age of sweet silliness and meaningless abundance. This has been and is being done by Communism, itself a victim of the giant imposture of Enlightenment, far more powerfully and definitively than by Nazism. Again, to Nazism we must assign the peculiar merit of having sounded, for once, though in as false a key and with as strident overtones as it possibly could, the bugle-call for a radical revulsion from the sleepwalkers path of progress and thus broken the spell more sharply—in a more direct and positive sense—than Communism, whose infinitely greater terrors are still sweetened by the psychological credentials of a vision, false and self-contradictory as it is, of "ultimate" peace and welfare. But Nazism, with its abstract worship (alien from modernity and Communism) of wickedness, cruelty and deceit for their own sake, with its *en bloc* rejection of the Christian past as a corruptive and lethal blind alley in the life of the race, with its reading of history (no less dogmatic and arbitrary than are the creeds of progress) as a "dynamic" but aimless sequence of biological cycles of blossoming, thriving and decay, with its self-duping trust in the limitless power of human unreason and its calculated underbidding of the progressive cheapjacks in the field of mob-mastery, is scarcely less tainted than are its rivals by the spirit of unnatural utopia and the hypnosis of the "situation" and "opportunity" as present at a given point in the dialectical course of the "age of masses." In opposing the mutilated and debased post-Christianity of Progressive Democracy by its forceful but wholly artificial and unreal evocation of a phantom of inferior paganism (unmistakably doctored in the image of the devil of Christianity), it reveals the character of an "extreme Right" which is anything but conservative; in substituting for the sanctification of the will of Man by Rousseau and—in a more concrete, determined and effective fashion—by Marxian Communism the more modest and less blasphemous but all the more irrational and willful sanctification of one particular human "We" or center of power, it offers in the place of the Leftist misconception of order, not any elements of a true order but the mere lust of disorder.

Nazism, then, has shown—as have also done, less impressively but perhaps more conclusively and fruitfully, the less ambitious but sounder contemporary attempts to ward off the Bolshevist menace, at least on a local scale and for a while, by a Rightist emergency dictatorship cleared of the biases of Progressive Democracy—that powerful spiritual and popular forces *can* be stirred up and made effective against alleged fatality of a historical "logic" by which mankind must drive itself, as a final and total "solution" of its equation into the pen of the Red slaveholders. But Nazism, devoid of patience and wisdom, bent on prompt success, and mesmerized with the idea of taking mankind on the rebound, borrowed its soul from that very experience of an unstable historical situation calling for "activism" and evoking a trance of "dynamism," whose progressive and revolutionary meaning it irrationalized into the sublimely meaningless concept of a "crisis in permanence": the hour of great deeds, the cosmic walpurgis night, its own law and purpose and the object of a morbid mystical worship. In its very negation of the alleged meaning of history as a progressive self-creation of omnipotent human Reason and Will, the Nazi mind kept enslaved to the suasion of the "historical situation" as a supreme political principle and the sovereignty of one human group-will over and above the timeless moral order which genuine conservative statecraft recognizes as the irremovable measure of its designs and acts, discarding it along with the pet concept of Leftism like progress, planning or universal education, as though it too were nothing but a presumptuous and licentious fabrication of human reason. If Leftism means the preposterous endeavor to abolish contingency and man's dependence on an order of things he cannot fathom and an order of right and wrong he can discern but not decree or improve upon, the endeavor in a word to subject all things that affect his condition to a human counterfeit of Providence, the adventurers of Nazism would jump to the opposite "extreme" of erecting brute contingency itself into an all-embracing rule of the universe with nothing beyond it, under which the political agent that "happens to be strongest" may, and is called to, assume an unregulated and irresponsible pragmatic mastery over all men, societies, and domains of life he can bring within his range of power. Though undoubtedly a form of anti-Leftism, this "extreme" Rightism by the same token is an *eccentric* Rightism, which cannot but miss entirely, shooting past it as it were, the vital center of conservative thought: the respect of that which is, *including* its order, manifoldness and various gradations, and therefore also the duty of men and of rulers to use their intelligence, to administer things and effect reforms prudently and in awareness of their limitations, to exercise their freedom of choice in the framework of moral standards not issued from that freedom, to wield power in keeping with rather than in violation of alien spheres of will or traditions of power, to contribute to the shaping of human reality in a state of mind responsible to God the Creator and Legislator (and *therefore* and *inasmuch* also to their fellow man affected by their actions); in other words, in a spirit of *intrinsic* and not merely of tactical moderation. Thus, again, Nazism represents by no means the only Right-tinged political initiative or trend of thought that has pitifully fallen short of essential conservatism. There are many more forms, and less easy to array in a neat order of subdivisions, of "rightism" than of "Leftism," because the Leftist mind is committed to the historically given "trend of progress" as ushered in by the Renaissance "emancipation of Man" and modeled by its successive upshoots, whereas Rightist thought, so far as it outsteps the limits of mere retardation, expediency, or formal traditionalism and to concepts of restoration, may (or, rather, must) choose its actual pivots of orientation and work out its structure of preferences with a broad margin of freedom. The Left expresses the mind of man as a fellow-traveler and interpreter of the movement of the "world spirit" towards the goal of their fusion into one and man's becoming his own universal providence; the Right typifies man's submission to an unchangeable superior order and for that very reason, once it comes to the marking out of his concrete objects as an agent, his consciousness and love of being embedded in a motley world of contingency. That is why, as I hinted earlier, the conservative is better able to disavow and repudiate Nazism, notwithstanding its Rightist sign, than a Leftist to disclaim affinity with anything that smacks of Leftism, but especially of a Leftism more advanced than his own (*"Pas d'ennemis à gauche!"*) and therefore in a significant sense foreshadowing his own motion towards his "truer self."

Here is, in addition to the irremediable absence of effective rulership and the no less organic disease of pacifism, a most essential source of weakness hampering the efforts of Progressive Democracy to parry the menace of Communism. "Fifth columns," "diabolically clever propaganda," and the misuse of liberty by its enemies, are scarcely more than embodied reflections and obvious consequences of the basic fact that Progressive Democracy in its most intimate nerve-centers cannot help being vulnerable to the charms, monstrous though they may seem to its own upper-floor consciousness, of its more "integrated" rival, whose apocalyptic rush it has both set on foot and timidly tried to imitate—both stimulated and lamely attempted to curb—but is unable either to outpace or to *mean* to stop earnestly at the risk of bringing its own movement to a halt and thus perhaps putting an end to the whole nightmare of modernity.

6

Progressive Democracy is, then, neither a spiritually acceptable choice in the teeth of Bolshevism (being too much kin to the foe precisely as regards its innermost substance) nor a safe rampart against the danger (being "dialectically" subject to its attraction). Conservative thought—and, should it exist or were it to rise again, a conservative policy underlain by such thought—must neither identify itself with the principles, habits and fashions of Progressive Democracy, melting as it were into a Right-wing shade thereof; nor forcedly interpret Progressive Democracy in its own likeness; nor even, withdrawing on its part into the secret chambers of a "small elite's" mental inwardness, simply and cheerfully entrust the practical defense of Civilization against Bolshevism to the forces of Progressive Democracy. If only to fight Bolshevism with the utmost rigor and the bitterest determination, with all resources of the mind and the heart human nature can muster, something more unlike Bolshevism and more deeply opposed to it than democracy is required. However, no less a blunder is it for conservatives to observe an attitude of neutrality in the struggle between democracy and Bolshevism, because both are of the Left; as if, for that reason, their fight (wherever democracy puts up a fight, that is) were unreal or its outcome irrelevant to Civilization (and accordingly, to the chances of conservatism). A kindred blunder conservatives may be tempted to commit is that of "unconditional Rightism"; the vice practiced, from the middle of the 1920s well into the middle of the 1930s, by most of them in the central Europe—with consequences I need not stress at length. It can be hardly our ambition to conjure up the ghost of Nazism, were that practicable; nor, generally speaking, to breed or to set loose a fourth rider of the Apocalypse.

It is unworthy of conservatives, indeed a betrayal of the mode of life they stand for, to indulge in any postures of all-round "radicalism," crisis-mongering, or voluptuous visions of a *grand soir* or "twilight of the gods": of a universal catastrophe leaving behind an empty field of ruins, so that kings, nobles and priests may rise again comfortably from the midst of the debris and start building the world anew in the void space. To be sure, the onerous, distasteful, and lopsided partnership—a leonine contract, as it were, to our disadvantage—we may at present alone maintain with Progressive Democracy cannot constitute our final aim; but that does not mean that we should submit to such co-operation with dishonest intentions modeled on the totalitarian cheat of Communist "Popular Front" tactics. To turn on our partner directly after our common enemy has collapsed in order to destroy him likewise is an idea as utterly unconservative as that of establishing a uniformly "Rightist" system of power all over the earth. Although a universal *reference* may properly belong to all serious politics (and particularly so in the present state of communications and interdependence), any world-political "plan" is strictly incompatible with a conservative outlook no matter how "Rightist" the intention in which it be conceived; for all susceptibility to the magic of the "clean sheet" and of "extirpating the evil with the root" or "curing the disease of Civilization by destroying its ultimate causes" is a stigma of the subversive and totalitarian mind bent on tampering with the divine governance of human history and averse to the proper business of man: that of doing what is right—though with an eye on foreseeable consequences and in an intelligent framework of limited perspectives—and entrusting the fruits of his action to providence. A "streamlined" Christian "blueprint" for the construction of the "City of Man," notwithstanding the gilded lettering in honor of God that may be meant to adorn its portals, cannot be Christian except in name; an anaemic ghost of modernity unsuccessfully and unpleasantly trying to outvie its fullblooded daemons. Again, such political thought alone is truly conservative as seeks above all to "conserve," and in the second place to supplement and to perfect as well as to disengage and to revive the existing good rather than to "create" the good out of naught of an a priori scheme embellished with an arbitrary muddle of romantic reminiscences.

According to its dominant signature, its characteristic edge, the mechanism of its march and the appetite of its idols, Progressive Democracy is indeed *the* Rider of the modern Apocalypse rather than merely one among the others, seeing that has sired the rest. But materially, it contains and shelters, it has devalued and impoverished, yet so far guarded against utter peril and extinction, the traditions of civilization and fragments of liberty—the shreds of morality and cells of Christian tissue—which its violent and all-round destruction by *any* opposing force would wipe out, beyond repair, along with the species of evil that forms its more vigorous and more showy reality. Christian conservatives cannot, therefore, aim at anything better than helping and stimulating all anti-Communist action Progressive Democracy may be capable and willing to undertake, though with a full inward detachment and sovereign aloofness from its genius, doctrines, habits, and interests as such, and seeking at the same time (in a spirit of healthy empiricism) to encourage and support the genuinely traditionalist centers of power and types of society—such as, for instance, Spain—which are likely to play an invaluable part both in bolstering the anti-Communist front and in counterbalancing the world supremacy of Progressive Democracy, circumscribing its range of influence and breaking its totalitarian monopoly after the downfall of Communism.

15

The Origins of Totalitarianism[*]
(1953)

ERIC VOEGELIN

The vast majority of all human beings alive on earth is affected in some measure by the totalitarian mass movements of our time. Whether men are members, supporters, fellow-travelers, naïve connivers, actual or potential victims, whether they are under the domination of a totalitarian government, or whether they are still free to organize their defenses against the disaster, the relation to the movements has become an intimate part of their spiritual, intellectual, economic, and physical existence. The putrefaction of Western civilization, as it were, has released a cadaveric poison spreading its infection through the body of humanity. What no religious founder, no philosopher, no imperial conqueror of the past has achieved to create a community of mankind by creating a common concern for all men has now been realized through the community of suffering under the earthwide expansion of Western foulness.

Even under favorable circumstances, a communal process of such magnitude and complexity will not lend itself easily to exploration and theorization by the political scientist. In space the knowledge of facts must extend to a plurality of civilizations; by subject matter the inquiry will have to range from religious experiences and their symbolization, through governmental institutions and the organization of terrorism, to the transformations of personality under the pressure of fear and habituation to

---

[*] Voegelin's review of Arendt's book was published in the journal *The Review of Politics* alongside a reply by Arendt. See *The Review of Politics*, vol. 15, no. 1 (January 1953).

atrocities; in time the inquiry will have to trace the genesis of the movements through the course of a civilization that has lasted for a millennium. Regrettably, though, the circumstances are not favorable. The positivistic destruction of political science is not yet overcome; and the great obstacle to an adequate treatment of totalitarianism is still the insufficiency of theoretical instruments. It is difficult to categorize political phenomena properly without a well-developed philosophical anthropology, or phenomena of spiritual disintegration without a theory of the spirit; for the morally abhorrent and the emotionally existing will overshadow the essential. Moreover, the revolutionary outburst of totalitarianism in our time is the climax of a secular evolution. And again, because of the unsatisfactory state of critical theory, the essence that grew to actuality in a long historical process will defy identification. The catastrophic manifestations of the revolution, the massacre and misery of millions of human beings, impress the spectator so strongly as unprecedented in comparison with the immediately preceding more peaceful age that the phenomenal difference will obscure the essential sameness.

In view of these difficulties the work by Hannah Arendt on *The Origins of Totalitarianism* deserves careful attention. It is an attempt to make contemporary phenomena intelligible by tracing their origin back to the eighteenth century, thus establishing a time unit in which the essence of totalitarianism unfolded to its fullness. And as far as the nature of totalitarianism is concerned, it penetrates to the theoretically relevant issues. This book on the troubles of the age, however, is also marked by these troubles, for it bears the scars of the unsatisfactory state of theory to which we have alluded. It abounds with brilliant formulations and profound insights—as one would expect only from an author who has mastered her problems as a philosopher—but surprisingly, when the author pursues these insights into their consequences, the elaboration veers toward regrettable flatness. Such derailments, while embarrassing, are nevertheless instructive—sometimes more instructive than the insights themselves—because they reveal the intellectual confusion of the age, and show more convincingly than any argument why totalitarian ideas find mass acceptance and will find it for a long time to come.

The book is organized in three parts: Anti-Semitism, Imperialism, and Totalitarianism. The sequence of the three topics is roughly chronological, though the phenomena under the three titles do overlap in time.

Anti-Semitism begins to rear its head in the Age of Enlightenment; the imperialist expansion and the pan-movements reach from the middle of the nineteenth century to the present; and the totalitarian movements belong to the twentieth century. The sequence is, furthermore, an order of increasing intensity and ferocity in the growth of totalitarian features toward the climax in the atrocities of the concentration camps. And it is, finally, a gradual revelation of the essence of totalitarianism from its inchoate forms in the eighteenth century to the fully developed, nihilistic crushing of human beings.

This organization of the materials, however, cannot be completely understood without its emotional motivation. There is more than one way to deal with the problems of totalitarianism; and it is not certain, as we shall see, that Dr. Arendt's is the best. Anyway, there can be no doubt that the fate of the Jews, the mass slaughter and the homelessness of displaced persons, is for the author a center of emotional shock, the center from which radiates her desire to inquire into the causes of the horror, to understand political phenomena in Western civilization that belong to the same class, and to consider means that will stem the evil. This emotionally determined method of proceeding from a concrete center of shock toward generalizations leads to a delimitation of subject matter. The shock is caused by the fate of human beings, of the leaders, followers, and victims of totalitarian movements; hence, the crumbling of old and the formation of new institutions, the life-courses of individuals in an age of institutional change, the dissolution and formation of types of conduct, as well as of the ideas of right conduct, will become topical; totalitarianism will have to be understood by its manifestations in the medium of conduct and institutions just adumbrated. And indeed there runs through the book—as the governing theme—the obsolescence of the national state as the sheltering organization of Western political societies, owing to technological, economic, and the consequent changes of political power. With every change sections of society become "superfluous," in the sense that they lose their function and therefore are threatened in their social status and economic existence. The centralization of the national state and the rise of bureaucracies in France makes the nobility superfluous; the growth of industrial societies and new sources of revenue in the late nineteenth century make the Jews as state bankers superfluous; every industrial crisis creates superfluity of human beings through unemployment; taxation and the inflations of the twentieth century dissolve the middle classes into social rubble; the wars and the totalitarian regimes produce the millions of refugees, slave-laborers, and inmates of concentration camps, and push the membership of whole societies into the position of expendable human material. As far as the institutional aspect of the process is concerned totalitarianism, thus, is the disintegration of national societies and their transformation into aggregates of superfluous human beings.

The delimitation of subject matter through the emotions aroused by the fate of human beings is the strength of Dr. Arendt's book. The concern about man and the causes of his fate in social upheavals is the source of historiography. The manner in which the author spans her arc from the presently moving events to their origins in the concentration of the national state evolves distant memories of the grand manner in which Thucydides spanned his arc from the catastrophic movement of his time, from the great *kinesis*, to its origins in the emergence of the Athenian polis after the Persian Wars. The emotion in its purity makes the intellect a sensitive instrument for recognizing and selecting the relevant facts; and if the purity of the human interest remains untainted by partisanship, the result will be a historical study of respectable rank—as in the case of the present work, which in its substantive parts is remarkably free of ideological nonsense. With admirable detachment from the partisan strife of the day, the author has succeeded in writing the history of the circumstances that occasioned the movements, of the totalitarian movements themselves, and above all of the dissolution of human personality, from the early antibourgeois and anti-Semitic resentment to the contemporary horrors of the "man who does his duty" and of his victims.

This is not the occasion to go into details. Nevertheless, a few of the topics must be mentioned in order to convey an idea of the richness of the work. The first part is perhaps the best short history of the anti-Semitic problem in existence; for special attention should be singled out the sections on the court-jews and their decline, on the Jewish problem in enlightened and romantic Berlin, the sketch of Disraeli,* and the concise account of the Dreyfus Affair.† The second part—on Imperialism—

---

* Benjamin Disraeli, British conservative statesman, born into a Jewish family, twice served as Prime Minister in the latter half of the nineteenth century.

† Alfred Dreyfus, a Jewish officer on the French General Staff, was convicted of espi-

is theoretically the most penetrating, for it creates the type-concepts for the relations between phenomena which are rarely placed in their proper, wider context. It contains the studies on the fateful emancipation of the bourgeoisie that wants to be an upper class without assuming the responsibilities of rulership, on the disintegration of Western national societies and the formation of elites and mobs, on the genesis of race-thinking in the eighteenth century, on the imperialist expansion of the Western national states and the race problem in the empires, on the corresponding continental pan-movements and the genesis of racial nationalism. Within these larger studies are embedded previous miniatures of special situations and personalities, such as the splendid studies of Rhodes* and Barnato,† of the character traits of the Boers and their race policy, of the British colonial bureaucracy, of the inability of Western national states to create an imperial culture in the Roman sense and the subsequent failure of British and French imperialism, of the element of infantilism in Kipling and Lawrence of Arabia, and of the central European minority question. The third part—on Totalitarianism—contains studies on the classless society that results from general superfluity of the members of a society, on the difference between mob and mass, on totalitarian propaganda, on totalitarian police, and the concentration camps.

The digest of this enormous material, well documented with footnotes and bibliographies, is sometimes broad, betraying the joy of skillful narration by the true historian, but still held together by the conceptual discipline of the general thesis. Nevertheless, at this point a note of criticism will have to be allowed. The organization of the book is somewhat less strict than it could be, if the author had availed herself more readily of the theoretical instruments which the present state of science puts at her

---

onage in 1894 and sentenced to lifelong deportation. Evidence then surfaced confirming Dreyfus's innocence, and he was pardoned in 1899. Subsequent trials would follow, and the entire episode inspired political passions on all sides and became an international event.

* Cecil Rhodes, British proponent of imperialism and prime minister of the Cape Colony in South Africa (1890–1896). Rhodes is treated in part two of *The Origins of Totalitarianism*.

† Barney Barnato was a British financier who sought to develop and control the mining industry in South Africa. Barnato is also discussed by Arendt in part 2 of *Origins*.

disposition. Her principle of relevance that orders the variegated materials into a story of totalitarianism is the disintegration of a civilization into masses of human beings without secure economic and social status; and her materials are relevant insofar as they demonstrate the process of disintegration. Obviously this process is the same that has been categorized by Toynbee* as the growth of the internal and external proletariat. It is surprising that the author has not used Toynbee's highly differentiated concepts; and that even his name appears neither in the footnotes, nor in the bibliography, nor in the index. The use of Toynbee's work would have substantially added to the weight of Dr. Arendt's analysis.

This excellent book, as we have indicated, is unfortunately marred, however, by certain theoretical defects. The treatment of movements of the totalitarian type on the level of social situations and change, as well as of types of conduct determined by them, is apt to endow historical causality with an aura of fatality. Situations and changes, to be sure, require, but they do not determine a response. The character of a man, the range and intensity of his passions, the controls exerted by his virtues, and his spiritual freedom, enter as further determinants. If conduct is not understood as the response of a man to a situation, and the varieties of response as rooted in the potentialities of human nature rather than in the situation itself, the process of history will become a closed stream, of which every cross-cut at a given point of time is the exhaustive determinant of the future course. Dr. Arendt is aware of this problem. She knows that changes in the economic and social situations do not simply make people superfluous, and that superfluous people do not respond by necessity with resentment, cruelty, and violence; she knows that a ruthlessly competitive society owes its character to an absence of restraint and of a sense of responsibility for consequences; and she is even uneasily aware that not all the misery of National Socialist concentration camps was caused by the oppressors, but that a part of it stemmed from the spiritual lostness that so many of the victims brought with them. Her understanding of such questions is revealed beyond doubt in the following passage: "Nothing perhaps distinguishes modern masses as radically from those of previous centuries as the loss of faith in a Last Judgment: the worst have lost their fear and

---

* Arnold Toynbee was one of the most influential historians of the twentieth century and author of the twelve-volume *A Study of History* (1934–1961).

the best have lost their hope. Unable as yet to live without fear and hope, these masses are attracted by every effort which seems to promise a man-made fabrication of the paradise they longed for and of the hell they had feared. Just as the popularized features of Marx's classless society have a queer resemblance to the Messianic Age, so the reality of the concentration camps resembles nothing so much as mediaeval pictures of hell" (p. 419). The spiritual disease of agnosticism is the peculiar problem of the modern masses, and the man-made paradises and man-made hells are its symptoms; and the masses have the disease whether they are in their paradise or in their hell. The author, thus, is aware of the problem; but, oddly enough, the knowledge does not affect her treatment of the materials. If the spiritual disease is the decisive feature that distinguishes modern masses from those of earlier centuries, then one would expect the study of totalitarianism not to be delimited by the institutional breakdown of national societies and the growth of socially superfluous masses, but rather by the genesis of the spiritual disease, especially since the response to the institutional breakdown clearly bears the marks of the disease. Then the origins of totalitarianism would not have to be sought primarily in the fate of the national state and attendant social and economic changes since the eighteenth century, but rather in the rise of immanentist sectarianism since the high Middle Ages; and the totalitarian movements would not be simply revolutionary movements of functionally dislocated people, but immanentist creed movements in which mediaeval heresies have come to their fruition. Dr. Arendt, as we have said, does not draw the theoretical conclusions from her own insights.

Such inconclusiveness has a cause. It comes to light in another one of the profound formulations which the author deflects in a surprising direction: "What totalitarian ideologies therefore aim at is not the transformation of the outside world or the revolutionizing transmutation of society, but the transformation of human nature itself" (p. 432). This is, indeed, the essence of totalitarianism as an immanentist creed movement. Totalitarian movements do not intend to remedy social evils by industrial changes, but want to create a millennium in the eschatological sense through transformation of human nature. The Christian faith in transcendental perfection through the grace of God has been converted—and perverted—into the idea of immanent perfection through an act of man. And this understanding of the spiritual and intellectual breakdown

266

is followed in Dr. Arendt's text by the sentence: "Human nature as such is at stake, and even though it seems that these experiments succeed not in changing man but only in destroying him . . . one should bear in mind the necessary limitations to an experiment which requires global control in order to show conclusive results" (p. 433). When I read this sentence, I could hardly believe my eyes. "Nature" is a philosophical concept; it denotes that which identifies a thing as a thing of this kind and not of another one. A "nature" cannot be changed or transformed; a "change of nature" is a contradiction of terms; tampering with the "nature" of a thing means destroying the thing. To conceive the idea of "changing the nature" of man (or of anything) is a symptom of the intellectual breakdown of Western civilization. The author, in fact, adopts the immanentist ideology; she keeps an "open mind" with regard to the totalitarian atrocities; she considers the question of a "change of nature" a matter that will have to be settled by "trial and error"; and since the "trial" could not yet avail itself of the opportunities afforded by a global laboratory, the question must remain in suspense for the time being.

These sentences of Dr. Arendt, of course, must not be construed as a concession to totalitarianism in the more restricted sense, that is, as a concession to National Socialist and Communist atrocities. On the contrary, they reflect a typically liberal, progressive, pragmatist attitude toward philosophical problems. We suggested previously that the author's theoretical derailments are sometimes more interesting than her insights. And this attitude is, indeed, of general importance because it reveals how much ground liberals and totalitarians have in common; the essential immanentism which unites them overrides the differences of ethos which separate them. The true dividing line in the contemporary crisis does not run between liberals and totalitarians, but between the religious and philosophical transcendentalists on the one side, and the liberal and totalitarian immanentist sectarians on the other side. It is sad, but it must be reported, that the author herself draws this line. The argument starts from her confusion about the "nature of man": "Only the criminal attempt to change the nature of man is adequate to our trembling insight that no nature, not even the nature of man, can any longer be considered to be the measure of all things"—a sentence which, if it has any sense at all, can only mean that the nature of man ceases to be the measure, when some imbecile conceives the notion of changing it. The author seems to be impressed by the imbecile and is ready to forget about the nature of man, as well as about all human civilization that has been built on its understanding. The "mob," she concedes, has correctly seen "that the whole of nearly three thousand years of Western civilization . . . has broken down." Out go the philosophers of Greece, the prophets of Israel, Christ, not to mention the Patres and Scholastics; for man has "come of age," and that means "that from now on man is the only possible creator of his own laws and the only possible maker of his own history." This coming-of-age has to be accepted; man is the new lawmaker; and on the tablets wiped clean of the past he will inscribe the "new discoveries in morality" which Burke had still considered impossible.

It sounds like a nihilistic nightmare. And a nightmare it is rather than a well considered theory. It would be unfair to hold the author responsible on the level of critical thought for what obviously is a traumatic shuddering under the impact of experiences that were stronger than the forces of spiritual and intellectual resistance. The book as a whole must not be judged by the theoretical derailments which occur mostly in its concluding part. The treatment of the subject matter itself is animated, if not always penetrated, by the age-old knowledge about human nature and the life of the spirit which, in the conclusions, the author wishes to discard and to replace by "new discoveries." Let us rather take comfort in the unconscious irony of the closing sentence of the work where the author appeals, for the "new" spirit of human solidarity, to Acts 16:28: "Do thyself no harm; for we are all here." Perhaps, when the author progresses from quoting to hearing these words, her nightmarish fright will end like that of the jailer to whom they were addressed.

16

Is Technological Civilization Decadent, and Why?
(1975)

Jan Patočka

The nineteenth and twentieth centuries are the age of an industrial civilization that has swept away—definitively, it now seems—humankind's other, older attempts to shape, even to produce their lives without the help of science and technology (of technology based on science and in a sense even fusing with it). This has carved so vast a cleft across the continuity of human history that some modern Enlightenment thinkers perceive the recent age of barely three hundred years as a timid beginning of the true history of humanity while all else is shunted off to prehistory. The humans of the industrial age are incomparably more powerful and have at their disposal a far greater reservoir of energy than humans of earlier ages, reaching into the subatomic regions which nourish the stars because the earth is no longer enough for them. They live in an incomparably greater social density and can make use of it to intensify their attack on nature to force her to yield ever more of the energy they intend to integrate in the schemata of their calculations and the levers of their hands.

The mighty growth of industrial civilization appears as a trend which no difficulties can hinder, be they external or internal. The external obstacles, reflected in perhaps the sharpest and most modern idiom, physicalistic and quantitative, in the deliberations of the Club of Rome,[1*] concern the exhaustion of the global supply of raw materials, demographic growth,

---

* The Club of Rome was an international organization founded in 1968 to study global environmental issues.

environmental pollution, and the impossibility of expanding the nutritional basis, with the exponential nature of growth trends indicating a possibility of not-too-distant catastrophes. Still, the alarming outlook, against which there are admittedly no incontrovertible arguments so far, has not evoked any fundamental interest in contemporary society, as rationalists were wont to expect. The internal obstacles, resulting from the way this civilization affects the nature of being human as such and which manifests itself in those human hekatombs (myriatombs, actually)[2] that have no analogue, have so far become historically manifest with any clarity only as a motive for seeking and finding as rapid ways of forgetting in further intensification of our achievements. European societies have evidently not only never been as rich but also have never in history carried out so vast a social undertaking as in the "postwar" time (that is, in the era following the Second World War), as if this benefit could make up for the retreat of Europe from the center of history (meaning thereby the old Europe, the European West as it grew out of the western Roman empire). Yet on the whole this unheard-of progress proved unsatisfying and the demands on the world's wealth and therewith on the structure of a society which seems to resist such demands continue to expand. The optimism of this trend, full of vitality, defying attempts to tame it, appears more powerful than any objection that the development itself can provoke. Nor is there any shortage of objections; we could say that an entire scientific scholarly discipline, modern sociology, is basically an outgrowth of an awareness of the danger, or even of a sense of the pathological nature, of the development of the industrial civilization up to now. To some this pathology appeared as something transient, something that future development would itself cure in virtue of the inner logic which they believed they could detect therein; so Auguste Comte saw the crisis of society in a lack of social consensus, of a spontaneous harmony of perspective which, he claimed, would return as the common mode of thought would inevitably become more positive, more scientific.[3] Karl Marx was no less confident, though he trusted in a different evolution: the inevitable disintegration and burial of the mode of industrial production toward which capitalist society is driven by its very functioning. Others, though, believed that they could see evident symptoms of pathology in the increasing incidence of suicides and mental disorders;[4] today we could add drug abuse, the revolt of the young, and the destruction of all social taboos, all of which manifest an evident conversion at anarchy as their limit.

Is Technological Civilization Decadent, and Why?

Yet before we can answer the question posed in our title, we need to agree on a criterion, a standard by which we could judge something decadent or positive. We do not wish at this time to examine the whole question of value judgments and of their relation to the problem of truth. We shall rest content with noting that decadence and its opposite are not mere abstract "values" and "moral concepts" but, rather, are inseparable from human life in its intrinsic nature, its very being. A life can be said to be decadent when it loses its grasp on the innermost nerve of its functioning, when it is disrupted at its inmost core so that while thinking itself full it is actually draining and laming itself with every step and act. A society can be said to be decadent if it so functions as to encourage a decadent life, a life addicted to what is inhuman by its very nature.

What manner of life is it, though, which mutilates itself precisely when it seems full and rich? The answer has to be sought in the question itself.

What would human life have to be if something like that were to be possible—if life were in truth other than as at first it appears to itself? That *things* appear differently than they are is a function of their presenting themselves always one-sidedly, at a distance, in a perspective, and as a result can assume an appearance they share with other things. That we appear to ourselves as other than we are must be based on something else. Humans are not alien to themselves as things and their mode of being appears alien to them. Humans *are* themselves. If they are to appear to themselves as otherwise, they must become estranged from themselves and this process of estrangement must be something intrinsic to their mode of being. Thus there is something about the human way of being that humans find estrangement somehow "more pleasant" or "more natural" than their own being. Being themselves is something that "comes naturally." It is always an achievement. In a sense, we can say that even self-estrangement is in the last instance an achievement. It is a "relief," not a "natural" lightness but the result of a certain "act."

Humans cannot *be with the spontaneity* of nonhuman existents; they must *accomplish* their life, must *lead* it; they must "be done with it," "come to terms" with it. Thus it seems that humans stand ever between two equivalent possibilities. That, though, is not the case. Estrangement means that *there is no* equivalence but, rather, that only one of the possible lives is the "right" one, our own, irreplaceable, the only one that we ourselves can act out in the sense that we truly bear it, that we identify with

271

its burden—while the other is avoidance, escape, deviation into inauthenticity and relief. Thus the perspective of "choice," decisionism, is from the start a false, objectivized, and objectivistic perspective *from without*. The true "perspective" is one of nonequivalence for which there is a fundamental difference between the responsibility which *bears* and "exposes itself" on the one hand and avoidance and escape on the other. Thus the reality of human life does not allow a perspective from without, the perspective of a "disinterested observer."

One other distinction is needed besides this distinction between the authentic and the inauthentic.

The opposition, authentic/inauthentic, is based on the recognition that we can never be not interested in our own being: our own responsibility always captivates us, occupies us: a decision has been made about us before "we have decided." True, authentic being consists in our ability to let all that is be as and how it is, not distorting it, not denying its own being and its own nature to it.

There is, however, also the distinction between the ordinary, the "everyday," and the exceptional, the holiday. The exceptional, the holiday also unburdens, though not by escaping from responsibility but rather by revealing that dimension of life in which the point is not the burden of responsibility and the *escape* from it but where, rather, we are *enraptured*, where something more powerful than our free possibility, our responsibility, seems to break into our life and bestow on it meaning which it would not know otherwise. It is the dimension of the demonic and of passion. In both, humans are placed at risk; however, they are not simply escaping from themselves into the "public realm," into the ordinary everyday, into "objectivity," they do not become estranged in the everyday manner. It is not a self-estrangement but rather being swept along, enraptured. Here we are not escaping from ourselves but, rather, we are surprised by something, taken aback, captivated by it, and that something does not belong among things and in the ordinary day in which we can lose ourselves among the things that preoccupy us. Here we experience the world not only as the region of what is in our power but also as what opens itself to us *of itself* and, as experience (for instance of the erotic, of the sexual, of the demonic, of the dread of the holy), is then capable of penetrating and transforming our life. Face to face with this phenomenon we tend to *forget* the entire dimension of the struggle for ourselves, forget responsibility and escape, letting ourselves be drawn into a new, open dimension as if only now true life stood before us, as if this "new life" had no need to care for the dimension of responsibility.

Thus the distinction of the sacred and the profane is distinct from that of authenticity-responsibility and escape. It has to be related to responsibility by means other than escape, it cannot be simply overpowered, it has to be grafted on to responsible life.

The distinction sacred/profane is important also because the profane is essentially the realm of work and of the self-enslavement of life, of its bondage to itself. The demonic, orgiastic dimension is fundamentally opposed to the sense of enslavement experienced by humans alone and expressed most powerfully by the need to work. Work is always forced labor. Work is concern for oneself, the demonic is heedless. To the life which is bound to itself, to the self-bondage of life, there belongs an orgiastic pendant, life engendering what we cannot procure and what is not at our disposal. For that reason the orgiastic dimension is not absent simply because responsibility as such is not discovered or taken into account, where we avoid it, but, rather, there it becomes pressing. Its inevitability and its rule extend from the "primitive" natural peoples to our own day.

Thus the sacred, the domain of the holy, represents an other, different counterpart to the everyday. Durkheim's sociology stresses, for instance, that in totemic societies such as he studied in Australia, reality breaks down into two basic categories, that of the profane with which humans deal "economically" and that of the sacred, including totems, their symbols, their representatives among humans.

For anyone familiar with Durkheim's analyses, the description of the orgiastic scene of the explorers Spencer and Gillen, as Durkheim interprets it, is unforgettable.

> It is easy to imagine that on this level of exaltation people lose all self-consciousness. Since they feel ruled, drawn along by some external power which makes them think and act otherwise than in ordinary times, they have understandably the feeling of being themselves no longer. It seems to them that they have been made anew: the decorations with which they drape themselves, the masks covering their faces, express this inner transformation outwardly more than they help bring it about. And since all of a com-

pany feel transformed at the same time and in the same way . . . it appears to all as if they really had been carried over into a special world, quite different from the one in which they normally live. How could such experiences, especially when repeated daily for weeks on end, help but convince the experiencers that there really exist two diverse and incompatible worlds? In one of them they laboriously carry out their everyday life; the other they need but enter to stand in relation to extraordinary powers which galvanize them to the point of frenzy. One is profane, the other is the world of the sacred.[5]

The positivist prejudice that attributes to the everyday world a primacy over the other world cannot keep us from recognizing in this interpretation a sharp, precise presentation of a phenomenon.

The demonic needs to be brought into a relation with responsibility as originally and primarily it is not. The demonic is demonic precisely in its ability to deepen the self-estrangement to which, on the other hand, it points: humans estrange themselves by becoming bound to life and its objects, losing themselves among them. Ecstasy is an *ekstasis* from this bondage, but it is not yet freedom. Ecstasy can pretend to be freedom and at times it does—from the perspective of overcoming this orgiastic sacredness it is precisely then that it is seen as *demonic*.

No special proof is needed that sexuality belongs to this dimension of the demonic opposition to the profane everydayness—orgiastic cults almost always have a sexual aspect; on the other hand sexuality contains within it the same differentiation of two worlds, of a double reality which is the characteristic consequence of an orgy as Spencer and Gillen describe it.

At the same time, sexuality illustrates how inevitably the orgiastic realm is brought into a relation to the sphere of responsibility. This bringing into relation to responsibility, that is, to the domain of human authenticity and truth, is probably the kernel of the history of all religions. Religion is not the sacred, nor does it arise directly from the experience of sacral orgies and rites; rather, it is where the sacred qua demonic is being explicitly overcome. Sacral experiences pass over religious as soon as there is an attempt to introduce responsibility into the sacred or to regulate the sacred thereby.

All that originally takes place and can take place ever again without any explicit clarity about the mode of being of the responsible beings that humans are. Explicit clarity about humans cannot be achieved without an explicit relation to being. Religious and sacred forms of experience do not always include such clarity. They are experiences of breaks, of inversions and conversions in which the being of humans asserts itself without explicit clarity, without a fundamental criterion of what is and what is not. For that reason, in the question of being human religious conversions (and all that goes with them, for instance artistic experience) do not have the fundamental importance of the *ontological* experience of philosophy. Perhaps for that reason, too, it may turn out that religion is subject to temporary obscurity until its problems have been resolved philosophically.

The opposition of the sacred and the profane, of the feast and the workday, of the exceptional and the ordinary is not the opposition of the authentic and the inauthentic but rather belongs among the problems responsibility has yet to master. Every form of humanity on whatever "level" recognizes some form of the opposition between the ordinary and the exceptional, but not everyone also seeks to rise above decadence. The ordinary and the special can mean simply that we are rid of the ordinary; does that, though, mean that we have thereby also achieved our inmost, full and irreplaceable being at which the word "I" points with its mysterious hint? We believe that I in this sense emerges at the dawn of history and that it consists in not losing ourselves in the sacred, not simply surrendering our selves within it, but rather in living through the whole opposition of the sacred and the profane with the dimension of the problematic which we uncover in the responsible questioning in a quest for clarity with the sobriety of the everyday, but also with an active daring for the vertigo it brings; *overcoming* everydayness without collapsing in self-forgetting into the region of darkness, however tempting. Historical life means, on the one hand, a differentiation of the confused everydayness of prehistoric life, of the division of labor and functionalization of individuals; on the other, the inner mastering of the sacred through its interiorization, by not yielding to it externally but rather confronting internally its essential ground to which human unclarity, that refuge of our life's routines, opens the way when it has been shaken to the very foundations. That is why the emergence of epic and especially of dramatic poetry is so important among the foundations of the historical process, since here humans follow first with the inner and then the outer eye the events in which they can participate only by yielding to the orgiastic. History originates as a rising above decadence, as the realization that life hitherto had been a life in decadence and that there is or that there are possibilities of living differently than by toiling for a full stomach in misery and need, ingeniously tamed by human technologies—or, on the other hand, by striving for private and public orgiastic moments, sexuality and cult. The Greek polis, epos, tragedy, and philosophy are different aspects of the same thrust which represents a rising above decadence.

Precisely because history first means this inner process, the emergence of humans who master the original dilemma of human possibilities by discovering the authentic, unique *I*, that history is foremost a history of the soul. For that reason history is almost from the beginning accompanied by a reflection on history; for that reason Socrates designated the polis, which is the proper place of history, as also the proper place of the care for the soul. For that reason already earlier Heraclitus, angered that his polis destroys the best, those who alone are capable of rising above decadence in defiance both of everydayness and of the orgiastic leap into darkness, spoke of the bounds of the soul (that which gives it its form) which cannot be found along any (ordinary) path, for its logos, the expression for it, is too deep.[6] For that reason, the central theme of Plato's thought is the state, which for him was at the same time the model by which it is possible to reveal externally the structure of the individual soul. For that reason Plato's philosophy is at its core focused on the soul as that which first makes it something firm and definite. We might suppose that the special character of ancient society favored the special character of ancient philosophy in its classical phase. Plato's thought, decisive for the ontological character of this philosophy as a metaphysics, is, according to Eugen Fink's apt description,[7] an attempt to think light without shadow (in the last instance, to be sure, because there can be no doubt about the duality of reason and necessity in the world of fact as Plato sees it). That means that philosophy can dedicate itself to its inmost life's task, that of being the nonecstatic, nonorgiastic counterpart and inmost resolution of the problem posed by everydayness, regardless of the structure of the society—reason, understanding, has here only this function and can find its fulfillment in it since in living reality there is so much that is nonordinary that there need be no fear that the pathos of the everyday might overwhelm and choke out its opposite. This ontology is for that reason a philosophy of the soul which, by *perceiving* that authentic, transcendent being differs from our reality of mere transient, changing opinion by virtue of its character of eternally immovable being, first gains its own unitary core, capable of resisting the pressure of various questions and problems which would otherwise drive the soul hither and yon. Unity is the essence of the soul, achieved by thought, an inner dialogue, a dialectic which is the proper method of insight and the essence of reason. That is why philosophy must be at the same time the care for the soul (*epimeleia tēs psuchēs*), ontology and theology—and all that in the care for the polis, for the optimal state. It retains this structure even when the nature of its proper object shifts from *idea* to *energeia* (in Aristotle) and transcendence shifts from the world of ideas to god or gods. Here philosophical theory still lives up to its calling to be the realm in which our I arrives at itself as well as at the lived experience its being which it has grasped at last. (The transcendence of the divine part of the world is then made more emphatic by the inability of the world to reach the divine and of the divine to think the world—this transcendence is an expression precisely of that "spiritual" overcoming of everydayness to which philosophy fundamentally contributes.)

Plato's doctrine of the soul has still other aspects. Eugen Fink calls attention to one of the most important in his analysis of Plato's allegory of the cave.[8] This presentation, especially in its dramatic part, is a reversal of the traditional mysteries and of their orgiastic cults. Those cults already aimed if not at a fusion, then at least at a confrontation of the responsible and the orgiastic. The cave is a remnant of the subterranean gathering place of the mysteries; it is the womb of Earth Mother. Plato's novel idea is the will to leave the womb of Earth Mother and to follow the pure "path of light," that is, to subordinate the orgiastic entirely to responsibility. Hence the path of the Platonic soul leads directly to eternity and to the source of all eternity, the sun of "The Good."

There is another aspect linked to this. The Platonic "conversion" makes a vision of the Good itself possible. This view is as unchanging and eternal as the Good itself. The journey after the Good, which is the new *mystery* of the soul, takes the form of the soul's internal dialogue. Immortality, inseparably linked with this dialogue, is thus different from the immortality of the mysteries. For the first time in history it is individual immortality, individual because inner, inseparably bound up with its own achievement. Plato's doctrine of the immortality of the soul is the result of the confrontation of the orgiastic with responsibility. Responsibility

277

triumphs over the orgiastic, incorporates it as a subordinate moment, as *Eros* which cannot understand itself until it understands that its origin is not in the corporeal world, in the cave, in the darkness, but rather that it is only a means for the ascent to the Good with its absolute claim and its hard discipline.

As a result of this conception, in Neoplatonism the demonic—*Erōs* is a great *daimōn*—becomes a subservient realm in the eyes of the philosopher who has overcome all its temptations. Hence a somewhat unexpected outcome: the philosopher is at the same time a great *thaumaturge*. The Platonic philosopher is a magician—a Faustus. The Dutch historian of ideas, Gilles Quispel, derives from this one of the principal sources of the Faust legend and of Faustianism in general, that "endless striving" which makes Faust so dangerous but which ultimately can save him.[9]

Another important moment is that the Platonic philosopher overcame death fundamentally by not fleeing from it but by facing up to it. This philosophy was *meletēthanatou*, care for death; care for the soul is inseparable from care for death which becomes the true care for life; life (eternal) is born of this direct look at death, of an overcoming of death (perhaps it is nothing but this "overcoming"). That, however, together with the relation to the Good, identifying with the Good while breaking free of the demonic and the orgiastic, means the rule of responsibility and so of freedom. The soul is absolutely free, that is, it chooses its destiny.

So a new, light mythology of the soul grows on the basis of the duality of the authentic/responsible and the exceptional/orgiastic: the orgiastic is not removed but is disciplined and made subservient.

It is understandable that this entire complex of motifs could not but acquire a global significance in the moment when the end of the polis/*civitas* in the form of the Roman principality posed the problem of a new responsibility founded on the transcendent even within the framework of the social, in relation to a state which could no longer be a community of equals in freedom. Freedom is no longer defined in terms of a relationship to equals (other citizens) but to a transcendent Good. That also poses new questions and makes new solutions possible. The social problem of the Roman empire is ultimately acted out on a foundation made possible by the Platonic conception of the soul.

The Neoplatonic philosopher Julian the Apostate on the imperial throne represents—as Quispel saw, probably rightly[10]—an important turn in the relation between the orgiastic and the discipline of responsibility. Christianity could overcome this Platonic solution only by an about-face. Responsible life was itself presented as a gift from something which ultimately, though it has the character of the Good, has also the traits of the inaccessible and forever superior to humans—the traits of the *mysterium* that always has the final word. Christianity, after all, understands the Good differently than Plato—as a self-forgetting goodness and a self-denying (not orgiastic) love. It is not the orgiastic—that remains not only subordinated but, in certain respects, suppressed to the limit—yet it is still a *mysterium tremendum*. *Tremendum*, for responsibility is now vested not in a humanly comprehensible essence of goodness and unity but, rather, in an inscrutable relation to the absolute highest being in whose hands we are not externally, but internally. The freedom of the wise man who has overcome the orgiastic can still be understood as demonic, as a will to separation and autonomy, a resistance to total devotion and self-forgetting love in which the true image of God consists. The soul now does not simply seek itself in the ascent of an inner dialogue but also senses its danger. In the final analysis, the soul is not a relation to an object, however noble (like the Platonic Good) but rather to a Person who sees into the soul without being itself accessible to view. What a Person is, that really is not adequately thematized in the Christian perspective. However, it is powerfully presented in images and "revelations," especially in the form of the problem of divine love and of the God-Human who takes our transgressions unto godself. Transgression, too, acquires a new meaning: it is an offense against the divine love, a dishonoring of the Highest, which is a personal matter and demands a personal solution. The responsible human as such is *I*; it is an individual that is not identical with any role it could possibly assume—in Plato this is expressed in the myth of the drawing of life's lot; it is a responsible I because in the confrontation with death and in coming to terms with nothingness it takes upon itself what we all must carry out in ourselves, where no one can take our place. Now, however, individuality is vested in a relation to an infinite love and humans are individuals because they are guilty, and *always* guilty, with respect to it. We all, as individuals, are defined by the uniqueness of our individual placement in the universality of sin.

Nietzsche coined the saying that Christianity is Platonism for the people and there is this much truth in it, in that the Christian God took over the transcendence of the onto-theological conception as a matter of course.[11] In the Christian conception of the soul, though, there is a fundamental, profound difference. It is not just that, as St. Paul would have it, the Christian rejects the Greek *sophia tou kosmou*[12](metaphysics) and its method of inner dialogue—eidetic intuition—as the way to that being which belongs inseparably to the discovery of the soul. The chief difference appears to be that it is only now that the inmost content of the soul is revealed, that the truth for which the soul struggles is not the truth of intuition but rather the truth of its own destiny, bound up with eternal responsibility from which there is no escape *ad secula seculorum*. The intrinsic life of the soul, its essential content, comes not from seeing ideas and so from its bond to the being, which agelessly, eternally is, but rather in an openness to the abyss in the divine and the human, to the wholly unique and so definitively self-determining bond of divinity and humanity, the unique drama to which the fundamental content of the soul relates throughout. The transcendent God of antiquity combined with the Old Testament Lord of History becomes the chief personage in the inner drama which God makes into the drama of salvation and grace. The overcoming of everydayness assumes the form of the care for the salvation of the soul which won itself in a moral transformation, in the turn in the face of death and death eternal; which lives in anxiety and hope inextricably intertwined, which trembles in the knowledge of its sin and with its whole being offers itself in the sacrifice of penance. Implied, though never explicitly thematized and never grasped philosophically as a central question, is the idea that the soul is by nature wholly incommensurate with all eternal being, that this nature has to do with its care for its own being in which, unlike all other existents, it is infinitely interested; and that an essential part of its composition is responsibility, that is, the possibility of choice and, in this choosing, of arriving at its own self—the idea that the soul is nothing present *before, only afterwards*, that it is historical in all its being and only as such escapes decadence.

By virtue of this foundation in the abysmal deepening of the soul, Christianity remains thus far the greatest, unsurpassed but also unthought-through human outreach that enabled humans to struggle against decadence. The actual forms of life in the Christian era, both external (social) and internal (conceptual), are, however, linked with the problems of the Roman empire (originally analogous to the Greek polis, though thanks to its own success gradually transformed from a mere res publica into an imperium, alienating the masses of its citizens whose lives that change stripped of content) and with its downfall. This downfall, however, was not only something negative, the destruction of an elitist civilization, dependent on an increasingly oppressive and crisis-prone slave system, and the transformation of its economic and social order. It represents at the same time the *birth* of Europe in the present sense of the word. For us, a revolutionary philosophy of economic dialectics has obscured the reality that the foundations of our revolutionary epoch lie in a transformation brought about by an external destruction and not by an internal eruption; the internal social transformation was largely a peaceful one, consisting in a progressive shift of the burden of labor from a *thing*, which is what a slave was, a being denied moral standing, to a being who, in family and property, however exploited, however modest, had an autonomous, potentially free character, the standing of a person. (Still the Hegelian and Comtean philosophies of history remained aware of the significance of this transformation and were fully conscious of its central significance.) It was thanks to this transformation that, after centuries of confusion, the European and especially the Western European social mass reappeared as an awesome expansive power, that the potentials therein contained found expression in new social and political structures with immense impact: in internal colonization of the land, in the rise of cities wholly different from the ancient polis, cities where labor is guided by the idea of a tool and its perfecting, thus shifting the *burden* of labor from persons to things; in the expansion into the regions lost by the Roman Empire—the Mediterranean and the East—as well as into those which it never possessed: central and northeastern Europe.

What, however, interests us most in our context is that an entire school of modern sociology, inspired by de Tocqueville, insisted and still insists that the modern development tends towards a democratic equalization, an equality of opportunity, preferring well-being to "greatness." What is the basis of this trend? Medieval society was hierarchical in origin, resting on the remnants of Roman municipal organization and Germanic conquest, but its real basis was the new attitude toward work, one based on rural colonization and urban production. The ecclesiastical hierarchy served the function of transcending the tedium of everydayness by introducing a dimension of authenticity, at times dissolving orgiastic tendencies, at other times (as in the Crusades) channeling them. Understandably, the urban element proved the bearer of some new possibilities in the process. Its new attitude to work and the skeptical use it made of ancient rationalism helped generate a new conception of knowledge as ultimately practical and mastering nature. That was echoed by a distinctly practical tendency of Christian theology which emphasized that humans are not on this earth only or primarily to contemplate it but rather to serve and act. European expansion shifted from the form of Crusades to exploration beyond the seas and in the grasp for the wealth of the world; simultaneously, the internal development of production, of technologies, of commercial and financial practices led to the rise of an entirely new kind of rationalism, the only one we know today: a rationalism that wants to master things and is mastered by them (by the desire for gain).

The origin of this modern (non-Platonic) rationalism is complex. A moment of far-reaching significance in it is the unresolved problem which the Christian era took over from antiquity: transcending the everyday and the orgiastic. Christian theology rejected the Platonic solution, though this theology did accept extensive elements of a solution launched along Platonic lines.

Platonic rationalism, the Platonic effort to subject even responsibility itself to the objectivity of knowledge, continues to affect the nether layers of the Christian conception. Theology itself rests on a "natural" foundation, understanding "the supernatural" as a fulfillment of "the natural."

The distancing of humans from "nature," which is no longer the locus of being human but rather something from which humans are separated by their unique unmediated relation, their relation to God, now enables them to perceive this "nature" as an "object."

Within the framework of nature so conceived, humans then strive for their freedom—understood Platonically as that over which they stand because they grasp it in eidetic insight. Hence the "mathematical" conception of nature and its new appearance, in the making since the fourteenth century and definitively triumphing in the seventeenth, when it achieves its main interpretive successes. Galileo is, notoriously, a Platonist. It is Plato's metaphysics of the immortal soul that makes it possible for the domination of nature by the human soul to find a place in the Christian world with its unresolved problem of metaphysical philosophy and Christian theology.

Thaumaturgy, astrology, alchemy, and the Paracelsian[13] medicine of the Renaissance are likewise Platonic. Faustian tendencies claim their own and tempt humans to break the bond with the divine by the demonic.

On the other hand, the Christian attitude to life's practice, its valorization of practical life against theory, makes it possible to integrate even the Platonic "mastery" of nature into practical contexts and so to create a truly effective knowledge that is technique and science in one—modern natural science.

Transformations in the Christian spiritual core itself, the transition first from a Christianity of and for the nobility to an ecclesiastical autonomy and then to a lay Christianity, made it possible for Christianity—with Reformation's ascetic attitude to the world, and with the pathos of personal certification by economic blessings—to contribute to the rise of that autonomy of the productive process that characterizes modern capitalism. That capitalism quickly sheds the constraints of its religious impetus and allies itself fundamentally with a superficial modern rationalism, estranged from any personal and moral vocation. It comes to be characterized by an immensely successful mathematical formalism. Its most successful aspect focuses on a mastery of nature, of movement, and of force. That is the modern mechanism which capitalism was only too glad to turn into a cult of the mechanical, so contributing to what came to be known as the Industrial Revolution. This revolution then penetrates throughout and ever more completely determines our lives. Given its differentiation of vocations and interdependence of interests, European humanity and by now already humanity as such simply are no longer capable of physically surviving but for the mode of production that rests increasingly on science and technology (and, of course, increasingly devastates the global, planetary store of energy), so that rational domination, the cold "truth" of that coldest of cold monsters, today wholly obscures to us its origin, eliminating our traditional ways of overcoming everydayness in a nonorgiastic and so truthful mode (a deeper form of truth which pays heed not only to the formal guise assumed by dominable nature but also to humans in their uniqueness and profound individuality) while posing as the All in All, the steward of the cosmos.

So many spiritual themes ultimately conjoined in giving rise to an unspiritual, wholly "practical," secular and material conception of reality as an object to be mastered by our mind and hands.

What had originally in Plato been a bulwark against orgiastic irresponsibility has now passed into the service of everydayness. Therein humans flatter themselves that they are taking their lives into their own hands, and can indeed make use of causes they discovered to generate means for the facilitation and external multiplication of life and of its goods. In the process, work itself does at first enslave them more than once it did, then, though, it gradually "liberates" them until humans see the possibility of being "liberated" from it altogether.

One of the consequences which presents itself at first inconspicuously, then ever more insistently, is boredom. Boredom is not something negligible, a "mere mood," a private disposition, but rather the ontological condition of a humanity which has wholly subordinated its life to everydayness and its anonymity.

Already in the nineteenth century Kierkegaard identified boredom as the root of the aesthetic stage, of that inconstancy which cannot become rooted in what there is because boredom drives it out of it. In the seventeenth century, in Pascal, we can already find similar themes, conceived in the face of the mechanistic conceptions advancing across the board at the time.[14]

Durkheim noted that certain phenomena of the Great Revolution manifest a spontaneous renewal of the sacred. At the time of the Revolution humans seemed seized by something like a "religious" fervor. "This ability of the society to posit itself as divine or to found divinities was never as evident as in the first years of the Revolution. Under the impact of the common wave of enthusiasm, matters wholly secular by nature were transformed into sacred, as Fatherland, Liberty, Reason . . ."[15] That, to be sure, is an enthusiasm which, for all the cult of Reason, has an orgiastic cast, either undisciplined or insufficiently disciplined by a link to personal responsibility. Here a danger of a new decline into the orgiastic is acutely evident.

A new flood of the orgiastic is an inevitable appendage to addiction to things, to their everyday procurement, to bondage to life.

The more modern technoscience asserts itself as the true relation to what is, the more it draws everything natural and then even everything human into its orbit, the more the ageless traditions of balancing the authentic and the captivating are set aside and condemned as unrealistic, untrustworthy, and fantastic, the more cruel will the revenge of orgiastic fervor be. It makes itself felt already in the "wars of liberation" and the revolutionary crises of the nineteenth century.[16] It is exacerbated by their commonly cruel repression. The entire earnestness of life, its entire interest in its own being, becomes compressed into the realm of social conflict. Everydayness and the fervor of the fight to the finish, without quarter, belong together. Throughout the nineteenth century this link remains largely latent, the forces of inertia remain highly powerful. However, in the twentieth century, which is something like the "truth" of the nineteenth, this contradiction clearly becomes so dominant a motive as to require no proof.

In this century, war is the full fruition of the revolt of the everyday. A growing laxness in all things and random "happening"[17] go hand in hand with it, as the new manifestation of the orgiastic. Not just the outbreak of wars and revolutions, but the disintegration of old forms of ethos, the insistence on the "right to one's body" or to "a life of my own," the universal spread of "happenings" and so on attest to this linkage. War as a global "anything goes," a wild freedom, takes hold of states, becoming "*total*." The same hand stages orgies and organizes everydayness. The author of the five-year plans is at the same time the author of orchestrated show trials in a new witch hunt. War is simultaneously the greatest undertaking of industrial civilization, both product and instrument of total mobilization (as Ernst Jünger rightly saw[18]), and a release of orgiastic potentials which could not afford such extremes of intoxication with destruction under any other circumstances. Already at the dawn of modernity, at the time of the wars of religion in the sixteenth and seventeenth centuries, that kind of cruelty and orgiasm emerged. Already then it was the fruit of a disintegration of traditional discipline and demonization of the opponent—though never before did the demonic reach its peak precisely in an age of greatest sobriety and rationality.

Boredom, naturally, does not retreat but rather forces its way to the forefront. Nor does it assume only the refined forms of the aesthetic and of romantic protest, but also the clear form of consumer offerings and the end of utopia (brought about by "positive" means). In the form of compulsory recreation, it becomes one of the characteristic collective metaphysical experiences of our age (while others include the experience of combat or Hiroshima).

What else does it mean, this gigantic Boredom which cannot be covered up even by the immense ingenuity of modern science and technology which it would be naïve and cynical to underestimate or ignore? The most sophisticated inventions are boring if they do not lead to an exacerbation of the Mystery concealed by what we discover, what is revealed to us. The powerful penetrating ability of the human mind uncovers with an undreamed-of insistence, yet what it uncovers is right away seized by the everyday and by understanding of being as in principle already fully uncovered and cleared, that understanding which at a stroke turns today's mystery into tomorrow's common gossip and triviality.

The problem of the individual, the problem of the human person, was from the start the problem of transcending the ordinary and the orgiastic. It implied simultaneously that humans cannot be identified with any role they may assume in the world. Modern individualism, as it stretches from the Renaissance on (according to Burckhardt and many others[19]), was an attempt not to penetrate beyond and beneath every role but rather to play an *important* role. Bourgeois revolutions battle over roles (equality is equality of roles! and freedom is the possibility to choose whatever role suits us!). Modern individualism is increasingly being unmasked as a collectivism (universalism), and collectivism as this false individualism. Thus the real question concerning the individual is not at issue between liberalism and socialism, between democracy and totalitarianism, which for all their profound differences equally overlook all that is neither objective nor a role. For the same reason, a resolution of their conflicts cannot resolve the problem of setting humans in their place, resolving their wandering alienated from themselves and from the place that belongs to them.

This bewildered wandering is manifest, among other things, in modern homelessness. For all the vast production of the wherewithal of living, human life remains homeless. Home is understood ever more as a shelter, a place to sleep over so we can return to work the next day, the place where we store the fruits of our labor and lead our "family life" of which there is ever less. That humans, unlike all other animals, build dwellings, because they are not at home in the world, because they lean out of the world and for that reason are charged with a calling within and towards it, anchored in deep layers of the past which have not passed as long as they live on in them—all that vanishes in the face of modern voluntary and enforced mobility, the gigantic migrations which by now affect nearly all the continents. The greatest homelessness, however, is in our relation to nature and to ourselves: Hannah Arendt used to point out that humans no longer

286

understand what it is they do and calculate. In their relation to nature, they are content with mere practical mastery and predictability without intelligibility. In a sense, in their natural sciences they left the earth long before cosmic flights and so have in reality lost contact with that ground beneath their feet to which they had been called. Thereby, though, they also gave up their own selves, their distinctive place among all that is, which consists in being the living beings we know who relate to their being, who really are this relation. Being ceased to be a problem once all that is was laid out before us as obvious in its quantifiable meaninglessness.

Humans have ceased to be a relation to Being and have become a force, a mighty one, one of the mightiest. Especially in their social being, they became a gigantic transformer, releasing cosmic forces accumulated and bound over the eons. It seems as if humans have become a grand energy accumulator in a world of sheer forces, on the one hand making use of those forces to exist and multiply, yet on the other hand themselves integrated into the same process, accumulated, calculated, utilized, and manipulated like any other state of energy. At first sight, this image seems mythological: what is force if not a concept for the human mode of predicting and controlling reality? Yet that precisely is the crucial point, that understanding the world as Force makes mere forces something more than a correlate of human activities. Hidden within Force there is being which has not ceased to be that light which lights up the world, though now only as a malevolent light. If we understand being merely from the perspective of the existents among which it belongs, and we do so understand it because being for us is what is forever, radically and agelessly ruling over all, what is thus contingent on the primordial beginnings which to master means to master all, then in present day understanding Force is the Highest Being which creates and destroys all, to which all and everyone serve.

Thus a metaphysics of force is fictitious and inauthentic, an anthropomorphism, and yet this criticism does not do it justice. For precisely this practical deification of force makes it not only a concept but a reality, something which, through our understanding of things, frees up all the effectiveness potentially contained in things; makes it an actualization of all potentials. Thus force becomes not only something that is but all of reality: everything is only in its functioning, in the accumulation and discharge of potentials, while all other reality dissolves, qualities, comprehension for things (for the knowing subjects who themselves no longer "comprehend" but only transform) . . . Thus force manifests itself as the highest concealment of Being which, like the purloined letter in E. A. Poe's familiar story, is safest where it is exposed to view in the form of the totality of what is; that is, of forces that organize and release one another, not excluding humans who, like all else, are stripped of all mystery.

A great contemporary thinker presented this vision of being absorbed in what is in his work without being trusted or noted.[20] The next and last chapter of our essay about history will seek to show how this is reflected in contemporary historical events and the alternatives they present.*

As to the question whether the industrial civilization is decadent (as a whole and in its character as a scientific and technological revolution), the answer now seems easy. Still, we hesitate about it. It is true that it did not resolve the great, principal human—and so also its own—problem, namely, not only to live but to live in a humanly authentic way, as history shows we can, but that it has actually made the situation more difficult because the matrix of its possibilities does not include the relation of humans to themselves and so also to the world as a whole and to its fundamental mystery. Its concepts encourage superficiality and discourage thought in a deeper, fundamental sense of the word. They offer substitutes where the original is needed. They alienate humans from themselves, depriving them of dwelling in the world, submerging them in the everyday alternative which is not so much toil as boredom, or in cheap substitutes and ultimately in orgiastic brutality. The age reduces understanding to the monotonous model of applied mathematics. It generates a conception of a force ruling over all and mobilizes all of reality to release the bound forces, a rule of Force actualized through global conflicts. Humans are thus destroyed externally and impoverished internally, deprived of their "ownness," of that irreplaceable I, they are identified with their roles, standing and falling with them.

On the other hand, it is also true that this civilization *makes possible* more than any previous human constellation: a life without violence and with far-reaching equality of opportunity. Not in the sense that this goal would anywhere be actual, but humans have never before found the means of struggle with external misery, with lack and want, which this

---

* The next essay is called "Wars of the Twentieth Century and the Twentieth Century as War."

civilization offers. Not that this struggle with external want could be resolved by those social ways and exclusive means which the age offers. Even the struggle with *outer* need is an inner struggle. The chief possibility, however, which emerges for the first time in history with our civilization, is the *possibility* of a turn from accidental rule to the rule of those who understand what history is about. It would be a tragic *guilt* (not a misfortune) of the intelligentsia if it failed to comprehend and grasp this opportunity. History is nothing other than the shaken certitude of pre-given meaning. It has no other meaning or goal. For the bad infinity of the precarious human existence in the world, however, complicated today by a global emergence of the masses, accustomed to flattery and escalating their expectations, such a goal and meaning will largely do to make them facile victims of manipulative demagogues.

The second main reason why the technological civilization cannot be simply labeled decadent is that the manifestations of decadence which we have noted and described in it are not simply its own work but a bequest of preceding ages out of whose spiritual problems and themes it made up its dominant matrix. Our sketch of the rise of the modern age and of its fundamental metaphysical character was intended to show as much. Modern civilization suffers not only from its own flaws and myopia but also from the failure to resolve the entire problem of history. Yet the problem of history may not be resolved, it must be preserved as a problem. Today the danger is that knowing so many particulars we are losing the ability to see the questions and that which is their foundation.

Perhaps the entire question about the decadence of civilization is incorrectly posed. There is no civilization as such. The question is whether historical humans are still willing to embrace history.

17

Politics and Conscience*
(1984)

Václav Havel

I

As a boy, I lived for some time in the country and I clearly remember an experience from those days: I used to walk to school in a nearby village along a cart track through the fields and, on the way, see on the horizon a huge smokestack of some hurriedly built factory, in all likelihood in the service of war. It spewed dense brown smoke and scattered it across the sky. Each time I saw it, I had an intense sense of something profoundly wrong, of humans soiling the heavens. I have no idea whether there was something like a science of ecology in those days; if there was, I certainly knew nothing of it. Still that "soiling of the heavens" offended me spontaneously. It seemed to me that, in it, humans are guilty of something, that they destroy something important, arbitrarily disrupting the natural order of things; and that such things cannot go unpunished. To be sure, my revulsion was largely aesthetic; I knew nothing then of the noxious emissions which would one day devastate our forests, exterminate game, and endanger the health of people.

If a medieval man were to see something like that suddenly on the horizon—say, while out hunting—he would probably think it the work of the Devil and would fall on his knees and pray that he and his kin be saved.

---

* This was a speech Havel wrote for the occasion of his acceptance of an honorary degree from the University of Toulouse. Havel was denied travel and was represented at the occasion by the English playwright Tom Stoppard.

Politics and Conscience

What is it, actually, that the world of the medieval peasant and that of a small boy have in common? Something substantive, I think. Both the boy and the peasant are far more intensely rooted in what some philosophers call "the natural world," or *Lebenswelt,* than most modern adults. They have not yet grown alienated from the world of their actual personal experience, the world which has its morning and its evening, its *down* (the earth) and its *up* (the heavens), where the sun rises daily in the east, traverses the sky and sets in the west, and where concepts like "at home" and "in foreign parts," good and evil, beauty and ugliness, near and far, duty and rights, still mean something living and definite. They are still rooted in a world which knows the dividing line between all that is intimately familiar and appropriately a subject of our concern, and that which lies beyond its horizon, that before which we should bow down humbly because of the mystery about it. Our "I" primordially attests to that world and personally certifies it; that is the world of our lived experience, a world not yet indifferent since we are personally bound to it in our love, hatred, respect, contempt, tradition, in our interests and in that pre-reflective meaningfulness from which culture is born. That is the realm of our inimitable, inalienable, and nontransferable joy and pain, a world in which, through which, and for which we are somehow answerable, a world of personal responsibility. In this world, categories like justice, honor, treason, friendship, infidelity, courage, or empathy have a wholly tangible content, relating to actual persons and important for actual life. At the basis of this world are values which are simply there, perennially, before we ever speak of them, before we reflect upon them and inquire about them. It owes its internal coherence to something like a "prespeculative" assumption that the world functions and is generally possible at all only because there is something beyond its horizon, something beyond or above it that might escape our understanding and our grasp but, for just that reason, firmly grounds this world, bestows upon it its order and measure, and is the hidden source of all the rules, customs, commandments, prohibitions, and norms that hold within it. The natural world, in virtue of its very being, bears within it the presupposition of the absolute which grounds, delimits, animates, and directs it, without which it would be unthinkable, absurd, and superfluous, and which we can only quietly respect. Any attempt to spurn it, master it, or replace it with something else, appears, within the framework of the natural world, as an expression of hubris for which humans must pay a heavy price, as did Don Juan and Faust.

To me, personally, the smokestack soiling the heavens is not just a regrettable lapse of a technology that failed to include "the ecological factor" in its calculation, one which can be easily corrected with the appropriate filter. To me it is more, the symbol of an age which seeks to transcend the boundaries of the natural world and its norms and to make it into a merely private concern, a matter of subjective preference and private feeling, of the illusions, prejudices, and whims of a "mere" individual. It is a symbol of an epoch which denies the binding importance of personal experience—including the experience of mystery and of the absolute—and displaces the personally experienced absolute as the measure of the world with a new, man-made absolute, devoid of mystery, free of the "whims" of subjectivity and, as such, impersonal and inhuman. It is the absolute of so-called objectivity: the objective, rational cognition of the scientific model of the world.

Modern science, constructing its universally valid image of the world, thus crashes through the bounds of the natural world, which it can understand only as a prison of prejudices from which we must break out into the light of objectively verified truth. The natural world appears to it as no more than an unfortunate leftover from our backward ancestors, a fantasy of their childish immaturity. With that, of course, it abolishes as mere fiction even the innermost foundation of our natural world; it kills God and takes his place on the vacant throne so that henceforth it would be science which would hold the order of being in its hand as its sole legitimate guardian and be the sole legitimate arbiter of all relevant truth. For, after all, it is only science that rises above all individual subjective truths and replaces them with a superior, suprasubjective, suprapersonal truth, which is truly objective and universal.

Modern rationalism and modern science, though the work of people that, as all human works, developed within our natural world, now systematically leave it behind, deny it, degrade and defame it—and, of course, at the same time colonize it. A modern man, whose natural world has been properly conquered by science and technology, objects to the smoke from the smokestack only if the stench penetrates his apartment. In no case, though, does he take offense at it metaphysically since he knows that the factory to which the smokestack belongs manufactures things that he needs. As a man of the technological era, he can conceive of a remedy only within the limits of technology—say, a catalytic scrubber fitted to the chimney.

Lest you misunderstand: I am not proposing that humans abolish smokestacks or prohibit science or generally return to the Middle Ages. Besides, it is not by accident that some of the most profound discoveries of modern science render the myth of objectivity surprisingly problematic and, via a remarkable detour, return us to the human subject and his world. I wish no more than to consider, in a most general and admittedly schematic outline, the spiritual framework of modern civilization and the source of its present crisis. And though the primary focus of these reflections will be the political rather than ecological aspect of this crisis, I might, perhaps, clarify my starting point with one more ecological example.

For centuries, the basic component of European agriculture had been the family farm. In Czech, the older term for it was *grunt*—which itself is not without its etymological interest. The word, taken from the German *Grund,* actually means ground or foundation and, in Czech, acquired a peculiar semantic coloring. As the colloquial synonym for "foundation," it points out the "groundedness" of the ground, its indubitable, traditional and prespeculatively given authenticity and credibility. Certainly, the family farm was a source of endless and intensifying social conflict of all kinds. Still, we cannot deny it one thing: it was rooted in the nature of its place, appropriate, harmonious, personally tested by generations of farmers and certified by the results of their husbandry. It also displayed a kind of optimal mutual proportionality in extent and kind of all that belonged to it; fields, meadows, boundaries, woods, cattle, domestic animals, water, roads, and so on. For centuries no farmer made it the topic of a scientific study. Nevertheless, it constituted a generally satisfactory economic and ecological system, within which everything was bound together by a thousand threads of mutual and meaningful connection, guaranteeing its stability as well as the stability of the product of the farmer's husbandry. Unlike present-day "agribusiness," the traditional family farm was energetically self-sufficient. Though it was subject to common calamities, it was not guilty of them—unfavorable weather, cattle disease, wars, and other catastrophes lay outside the farmer's province.

Certainly, modern agricultural and social science could also improve agriculture in a thousand ways, increasing its productivity, reducing the amount of sheer drudgery, and eliminating the worst social inequities. But this is possible only on the assumption that modernization, too, will be guided by a certain humility and respect for the mysterious order of nature and for the appropriateness which derives from it and which is intrinsic to the natural world of personal experience and responsibility. Modernization must not be simply an arrogant, megalomaniac, and brutal invasion by an impersonally objective science, represented by a newly graduated agronomist or a bureaucrat in the service of the "scientific world view."

That, however, is just what happened to our country: our word for it was "collectivization." Like a tornado, it raged through the Czechoslovakian countryside thirty years ago, leaving not a stone in place. Among its consequences were, on the one hand, tens of thousands of lives devastated by prison, sacrificed on the altar of a scientific utopia offering brighter tomorrows. On the other hand, the level of social conflict and the amount of drudgery in the countryside did in fact decrease while agricultural productivity rose quantitatively. That, though, is not why I mention it. My reason is something else: thirty years after the tornado swept the traditional family farm off the face of the earth, scientists are amazed to discover what even a semiliterate farmer previously knew—that human beings must pay a heavy price for every attempt to abolish, radically, once for all and without trace, that humbly respected boundary of the natural world, with its tradition of scrupulous personal acknowledgment. They must pay for the attempt to seize nature, to leave not a remnant of it in human hands, to ridicule its mystery; they must pay for the attempt to abolish God and to play at being God. This is what in fact happened. With hedges plowed under and woods cut down, wild birds have died out and, with them, a natural, unpaid protector of the crops against harmful insects. Huge unified fields have led to the inevitable annual loss of millions of cubic yards of topsoil that have taken centuries to accumulate; chemical fertilizers and pesticides have catastrophically poisoned all vegetable products, the earth, and the waters. Heavy machinery systematically presses down the soil, making it impenetrable to air and thus infertile; cows in gigantic dairy farms suffer neuroses and lose their milk while agriculture siphons off ever more energy from industry—manufacture of machines, artificial fertilizers, rising transportation costs in an age of growing local specialization, and so on. In short, the prognoses are terrifying and no one knows what surprises coming years and decades may bring.

It is paradoxical: people in the age of science and technology live in the conviction that they can improve their lives because they are able to grasp and exploit the complexity of nature and the general laws of its functioning. Yet it is precisely these laws which, in the end, tragically catch up with them and get the better of them. People thought they could explain and conquer nature—yet the outcome is that they destroyed it and disinherited themselves from it. But what are the prospects for man "outside nature"? It is, after all, precisely the sciences that are most recently discovering that the human body is actually only a particularly busy intersection of billions of organic microbodies, of their complex mutual contacts and influences, together forming that incredible mega-organism we call the "biosphere" in which our planet is blanketed.

The fault is not one of science as such but of the arrogance of man in the age of science. Man simply is not God, and playing God has cruel consequences. Man has abolished the absolute horizon of his relations, denied his personal "pre-objective" experience of the lived world, while relegating personal conscience and consciousness to the bathroom, as something so private that it is no one's business. Man rejected his responsibility as a "subjective illusion"—and in place of it installed what is now proving to be the most dangerous illusion of all: the fiction of objectivity stripped of all that is concretely human, of a rational understanding of the cosmos, and of an abstract schema of a putative "historical necessity." As the apex of it all, man has constructed a vision of a scientifically calculable and technologically achievable "universal welfare," that need only be invented by experimental institutes while industrial and bureaucratic factories turn it into reality. That millions of people will be sacrificed to this illusion in scientifically run concentration camps is not something that concerns our modern man unless by chance he himself lands behind barbed wire and is thrown drastically back upon his natural world. The phenomenon of empathy, after all, belongs with that abolished realm of personal prejudice which had to yield to science, objectivity, historical necessity, technology, system, and the apparat—and those, being impersonal, cannot worry. They are abstract and anonymous, ever utilitarian, and thus ever a priori innocent.

And as for the future, who, personally, would care about it or even worry about it when the perspective of eternity is one of the things locked away in the bathroom, if not expelled outright into the realm of fairy tales? If a contemporary scientist thinks at all of what will be in two hundred years, he does so solely as a disinterested observer who, basically, could not care less whether he is doing research on the metabolism of the flea, on the radio signals of pulsars, or on the global reserves of natural gas. And a modern politician? He has absolutely no reason to care, especially if it might interfere with his chances in an election, as long as he lives in a country where there are elections.

II

The Czech philosopher Václav Bělohradský has persuasively developed the thought that the rationalistic spirit of modern science, founded on abstract reason and on the presumption of impersonal objectivity, has its father not only in the natural sciences—Galileo, but also a father in politics—Machiavelli, who first formulated (albeit with an undertone of malicious irony) a theory of politics as a rational technology of power. We could say that, for all the complex historical detours, the origin of the modern state and of modern political power may be sought precisely here, that is, once again in a moment when human reason begins to "liberate" itself from the human being as such, from his personal experience, personal conscience, and personal responsibility and so also from that to which, within the framework of the natural world, all responsibility is uniquely related, his absolute horizon. Just as the modern scientists set apart the actual human being as the subject of the lived experience of the world, so, ever more evidently, do both the modern state and modern politics.

To be sure, this process by which power becomes anonymous and depersonalized, and reduced to a mere technology of rule and manipulation, has a thousand masks, variants, and expressions. In one case it is covert and inconspicuous, while in another case it is entirely overt; in one case it sneaks up on us along subtle and devious paths, in another case it is brutally direct. Essentially, though, it is the same universal trend. It is the essential trait of all modern civilization, growing directly from its spiritual structure, rooted in it by a thousand tangled tendrils and inseparable even in thought from its technological nature, its mass characteristics, and its consumer orientation.

Rulers and leaders were once personalities in their own right, with particular human faces, still in some sense personally responsible for their deeds, good and ill, whether they had been installed by dynastic tradition, by the will of the people, by a victorious battle, or by intrigue. But they have been replaced in modern times by the manager, the bureau-crat, the apparatchik—a professional ruler, manipulator, and expert in the techniques of management, manipulation, and obfuscation, filling a depersonalized intersection of functional relations, a cog in the machinery of state caught up in a predetermined role. This professional ruler is an "innocent" tool of an "innocent" anonymous power, legitimized by sci-ence, cybernetics, ideology, law, abstraction, and objectivity—that is, by everything except personal responsibility to human beings as persons and neighbors. A modern politician is transparent: behind his judicious mask and affected diction there is not a trace of a human being rooted in the order of the natural world by his loves, passions, interests, personal opin-ions, hatred, courage, or cruelty. All that he, too, locks away in his private bathroom. If we glimpse anything at all behind the mask, it will be only a more or less competent technician of power. System, ideology, and apparat have deprived us—rulers as well as the ruled—of our conscience, of our common sense and natural speech and thereby, of our actual humanity. States grow ever more machinelike; people are transformed into statistical choruses of voters, producers, consumers, patients, tourists, or soldiers. In politics, good and evil, categories of the natural world and therefore obsolete remnants of the past, lose all absolute meaning; the sole method of politics is quantifiable success. Power is a priori innocent because it does not grow from a world in which words like "guilt" and "innocence" retain their meaning.

This impersonal power has achieved what is its most complete expres-sion so far in the totalitarian systems. As Bělohradský points out, the depersonalization of power and its conquest of human conscience and human speech have been successfully linked to an extra-European tradi-tion of a "cosmological" conception of the empire (identifying the empire, as the sole true center of the world, with the world as such, and consid-ering the human as its exclusive property). But, as the totalitarian sys-tems clearly illustrate, this does not mean that modern impersonal power is itself an extra-European affair. The truth is the very opposite: it was precisely Europe, and the European West, that provided and frequently forced on the world all that today has become the basis of such power: natural science, rationalism, scientism, the Industrial Revolution, and also revolution as such, as a fanatical abstraction, through the displacement of the natural world to the bathroom down to the cult of consumption, the atomic bomb, and Marxism. And it is Europe—democratic western Europe—which today stands bewildered in the face of this ambiguous export. The contemporary dilemma, whether to resist this reverse expansionism of its erstwhile export or to yield to it, attests to this. Should rockets, now aimed at Europe thanks to its export of spiritual and technological potential, be countered by similar and better rockets, thereby demonstrating a determination to defend such values as Europe has left, at the cost of entering into an utterly immoral game being forced upon it? Or should Europe retreat, hoping that the responsibility for the fate of the planet demonstrated thereby will infect, by its miraculous power, the rest of the world?

I think that, with respect to the relation of western Europe to the totalitarian systems, no error could be greater than the one looming largest: that of a failure to understand the totalitarian systems for what they ultimately are—a convex mirror of all modern civilization and a harsh, perhaps final call for a global recasting of how that civilization understands itself. If we ignore that, then it does not make any essential difference which form Europe's efforts will take. It might be the form of taking the totalitarian systems, in the spirit of Europe's own rationalistic tradition, for a locally idiosyncratic attempt at achieving general welfare, to which only men of ill-will attribute expansionist tendencies. Or, in the spirit of the same rationalistic tradition, though this time in the Machiavellian conception of politics as the technology of power, one might perceive the totalitarian regimes as a purely external threat by expansionist neighbors who can be driven back within acceptable bounds by an appropriate demonstration of power, without having to be thought about more deeply. The first alternative is that of the person who reconciles himself to the chimney belching smoke, even though that smoke is ugly and smelly, because in the end it serves a good purpose, the production of commonly needed goods. The second alternative is that of the man who thinks that it is simply a matter of a technological flaw, which can be eliminated by technological means, such as a filter or a scrubber.

The reality, I believe, is unfortunately more serious. The chimney "soiling the heavens" is not just a technologically corrigible flaw of design, or a tax paid for a better consumerist tomorrow, but a symbol of a civilization which has renounced the absolute, which ignores the natural world and disdains its imperatives. So, too, the totalitarian systems warn of something far more serious than Western rationalism is willing to admit. They are, most of all, a convex mirror of the inevitable consequences of rationalism, a grotesquely magnified image of its own deep tendencies, an extreme offshoot of its own development and an ominous product of its own expansion. They are a deeply informative reflection of its own crisis. Totalitarian regimes are not merely dangerous neighbors and even less some kind of an avant-garde of world progress. Alas, just the opposite: they are the avant-garde of a global crisis of this civilization, first European, then Euro-American, and ultimately global. They are one of the possible futurological studies of the Western world, not in the sense that one day they will attack and conquer it, but in a far deeper sense—that they illustrate graphically the consequences of what Bělohradský calls the "eschatology of the impersonal."

It is the total rule of a bloated, anonymously bureaucratic power, not yet irresponsible but already operating outside all conscience, a power grounded in an omnipresent ideological fiction which can rationalize anything without ever having to come in contact with the truth. Power as the omnipresent monopoly of control, repression, and fear; power which makes thought, morality, and privacy a state monopoly and so dehumanizes them; power which long since has ceased to be the matter of a group of arbitrary rulers but which, rather, occupies and swallows up everyone so that all should become integrated within it, at least through their silence. No one actually possesses such power, since it is the power itself which possesses everyone; it is a monstrosity which is not guided by humans but which, on the contrary, drags all persons along with its "objective" self-momentum—objective in the sense of being cut off from all human standards, including human reason, and hence entirely irrational—toward a terrifying, unknown future.

Let me repeat: totalitarian power is a great reminder to contemporary civilization. Perhaps somewhere there may be some generals who think it would be best to dispatch such systems from the face of the earth and then all would be well. But that is no different from an ugly woman trying to get rid of her ugliness by smashing the mirror that reminds her of it. Such a "final solution" is one of the typical dreams of impersonal reason—capable, as the term "final solution" graphically reminds us, of transforming its dreams into reality and thereby reality into a nightmare. It would not only fail to resolve the crisis of the present world but, assuming anyone survived at all, would only aggravate it. By burdening the already heavy account of this civilization with further millions of dead, it would not block its essential trend to totalitarianism but would rather accelerate it. It would be a Pyrrhic victory, because the victors would emerge from a conflict inevitably resembling their defeated opponents far more than anyone today is willing to admit or able to imagine. Just a minor example: imagine what a huge Gulag Archipelago would have to be built in the West, in the name of country, democracy, progress, and war discipline, to contain all who refuse to take part in the effort, whether from naïvete, principle, fear, or ill will!

No evil has ever been eliminated by suppressing its symptoms. We need to address the cause itself.

III

From time to time I have a chance to speak with Western intellectuals who visit our country and decide to include a visit to a dissident in their itinerary—some out of genuine interest, or a willingness to understand and to express solidarity, others simply out of curiosity. Beside the Gothic and Baroque monuments, dissidents are apparently the only thing of interest to a tourist in this uniformly dreary environment. Those conversations are usually instructive: I learn much and come to understand much. The questions most frequently asked are these: Do you think you can really change anything when you are so few and have no influence at all? Are you opposed to socialism or do you merely wish to improve it? Do you condemn or condone the deployment of the Pershing II and the Cruise missiles in western Europe?* What can we do for you? What drives you to do what you are doing when all it brings you is persecution, prison—and no visible results? Would you want to see capitalism restored in your country?

Those questions are well intentioned, growing out of a desire to understand and showing that those who ask do care about the world, what it is and what it will be.

Still, precisely these and similar questions reveal to me again and again how deeply many Western intellectuals do not understand—and in some

---

* The missiles placed by the United States and its allies in western Europe to counter the threat of the Soviet missiles deployed in eastern Europe.

respects, cannot understand—just what is taking place here, what it is that we, the so-called dissidents, are striving for and, most of all, what the overall meaning of it is. Take, for instance, the question: "What can we do for you?" A great deal, to be sure. The more support, interest, and solidarity of free-thinking people in the world we enjoy, the less the danger of being arrested, and the greater the hope that ours will not be a voice crying in the wilderness. And yet, somewhere deep within the question there is built-in misunderstanding. After all, in the last instance the point is not to help us, a handful of "dissidents," to keep out of jail a bit more of the time. It is not even a question of helping these nations, Czechs and Slovaks, to live a bit better, a bit more freely. They need first and foremost to help themselves. They have waited for the help of others far too often, depended on it far too much, and far too many times came to grief: either the promised help was withdrawn at the last moment or it turned into the very opposite of their expectations. In the deepest sense, something else is at stake—the salvation of us all, of myself and my interlocutor equally. Or is it not something that concerns us all equally? Are not my dim prospects or, conversely, my hopes *his* dim prospects and hopes as well? Was not my arrest an attack on him and the deceptions to which he is subjected an attack on me as well? Is not the suppression of human beings in Prague a suppression of all human beings? Is not indifference to what is happening here or even illusions about it a preparation for the kind of misery elsewhere? Does not their misery presuppose ours? The point is not that some Czech dissident, as a person in distress, needs help. I could best help myself out of distress simply by ceasing to be a "dissident." The point is what that dissident's flawed efforts and his fate tell us and mean, what they attest about the condition, the destiny, the opportunities, and the problems of the world, the respects in which they are or could be food for thought for others as well, for the way they see their, and so our, shared destiny, in what ways they are a warning, a challenge, a danger, or a lesson for those who visit us.

Or the question about socialism and capitalism! I have to admit that it gives me a sense of emerging from the depths of the last century. It seems to me that these thoroughly ideological and often semantically confused categories have long since been beside the point. The question is wholly other, deeper and equally relevant to all: whether we shall, by whatever means, succeed in reconstituting the natural world as the true terrain of politics, rehabilitating the personal experience of human beings as the initial measure of things, placing morality above politics and responsibility above our desires, in making human community meaningful, in returning content to human speech, in reconstituting, as the focus of all social action, the autonomous, integral, and dignified human "I," responsible for ourselves because we are bound to something higher, and capable of sacrificing something, in extreme cases even everything, of his banal, prosperous private life—that "rule of everydayness," as Jan Patočka used to say—for the sake of that which gives life meaning. It really is not all that important whether, by accident of domicile, we confront a Western manager or an Eastern bureaucrat in this very modest and yet globally crucial struggle against the momentum of impersonal power. If we can defend our humanity, then perhaps there is a hope of sorts—though even then it is by no means automatic—that we shall also find some more meaningful ways of balancing our natural claims to shared economic decision-making and to dignified social status, with the tried-and-true driving force of all work: human enterprise realized in genuine market relations. As long, however, as our humanity remains defenseless, we will not be saved by any technical or organizational trick designed to produce better economic functioning, just as no filter on a factory smokestack will prevent a general dehumanization. To what purpose a system functions is, after all, more important than how it does so. Might it not function quite smoothly, after all, in the service of total destruction?

I speak of this because, looking at the world from the perspective which fate allotted me, I cannot avoid the impression that many people in the West still understand little of what is actually at stake in our time.

If, for instance, we take a second look at the two basic political alternatives between which Western intellectuals oscillate today, it becomes apparent that they are no more than two different ways of playing the same game, proffered by the anonymity of power. As such, they are no more than two diverse ways of moving toward the same global totalitarianism. One way of playing the game of anonymous reason is to keep on toying with the mystery of matter—"playing God"—inventing and deploying further weapons of mass destruction, all, of course, intended "for the defense of democracy" but in effect further degrading democracy to the "uninhabitable fiction" which socialism has long since become on our side of Europe. The other form of the game is the tempting vortex that draws so many good and sincere people into itself, the so-called struggle for peace.

Certainly it need not always be so. Still, often I do have the impression that this vortex has been designed and deployed by that same treacherous, all-pervasive impersonal power as a more poetic means of colonizing human consciousness. Please note, I have in mind impersonal power as a principle, globally, in all its instances, not only Moscow—which, if the truth be told, lacks the capability of organizing something as widespread as the contemporary peace movement. Still, could there be a better way of rendering an honest, free-thinking man (the chief threat to all anonymous power) ineffectual in the world of rationalism and ideology than by offering him the simplest thesis possible, with all the apparent characteristics of a noble goal? Could you imagine something that would more effectively fire a just mind—preoccupying it, then occupying it, and ultimately rendering it intellectually harmless—than the possibility of "a struggle against war"? Is there a more clever means of deceiving men than with the illusion that they can prevent war if they interfere with the deployment of weapons (which will be deployed in any case)? It is hard to imagine an easier way to a totalitarianism of the human spirit. The more obvious it becomes that the weapons will indeed be deployed, the more rapidly does the mind of a person who has totally identified with the goal of preventing such deployment become radicalized, fanaticized and, in the end, alienated from itself. So a man sent off on his way by the noblest of intentions finds himself, at the journey's end, precisely where anonymous power needs to see him: in the rut of totalitarian thought, where he is not his own and where he surrenders his own reason and conscience for the sake of another "uninhabitable fiction"! As long as that goal is served, it is not important whether we call that fiction "human well-being," "socialism," or "peace."

Certainly, from the standpoint of the defense and the interests of the Western world, it is not very good when someone says "Better Red than dead." But from the viewpoint of the global, impersonal power, which transcends power blocs and, in its omnipresence, represents a truly diabolical temptation, there could be nothing better. That slogan is an infallible sign that the speaker has given up his humanity. For he has given up the ability personally to guarantee something that transcends him and so to sacrifice, *in extremis,* even life itself to that which makes life meaningful. Patočka once wrote that a life not willing to sacrifice itself to what makes it meaningful is not worth living. It is just in the world of such lives and of such a "peace"—that is, under the "rule of everydayness"—that wars happen most easily. In such a world, there is no moral barrier against them, no barrier guaranteed by the courage of supreme sacrifice. The door stands wide open for the irrational "securing of our interests." The absence of heroes who know what they are dying for is the first step on the way to the mounds of corpses of those who are slaughtered like cattle. The slogan "Better Red than dead" does not irritate me as an expression of surrender to the Soviet Union, but it terrifies me as an expression of the renunciation by Western people of any claim to a meaningful life and of their acceptance of impersonal power as such. For what the slogan really says is that nothing is worth giving one's life for. However, without the horizon of the highest sacrifice, all sacrifice becomes senseless. Then nothing is worth anything. Nothing means anything. The result is a philosophy of sheer negation of our humanity. In the case of Soviet totalitarianism, such a philosophy does no more than offer a little political assistance. With respect to Western totalitarianism, it is what constitutes it, directly and primordially.

In short, I cannot overcome the impression that Western culture is threatened far more by itself than by SS-20 rockets.* When a French leftist student told me with a sincere glow in his eyes that the Gulag was a tax paid for the ideals of socialism and that Solzhenitsyn is just a personally embittered man, he cast me into a deep gloom. Is Europe really incapable of learning from its own history? Can't that dear lad ever understand that even the most promising project of "general well-being" convicts itself of inhumanity the moment it demands a single involuntary death—that is, one which is not a conscious sacrifice of a life to its meaning? Is he really incapable of comprehending that until he finds himself incarcerated in some Soviet-style jail near Toulouse? Did the newspeak of our world so penetrate natural human speech that two people can no longer communicate even such a basic experience?

IV

I presume that after all these stringent criticisms, I am expected to say just what I consider to be a meaningful alternative for Western humanity today in the face of political dilemmas of the contemporary world.

---

* The missiles deployed by the Soviet Union in eastern Europe.

Politics and Conscience

As all I have said suggests, it seems to me that all of us, East and West, face one fundamental task from which all else should follow. That task is one of resisting vigilantly, thoughtfully, and attentively, but at the same time with total dedication, at every step and everywhere, the irrational momentum of anonymous, impersonal, and inhuman power—the power of ideologies, systems, apparat, bureaucracy, artificial languages, and political slogans. We must resist its complex and wholly alienating pressure, whether it takes the form of consumption, advertising, repression, technology, or cliché—all of which are the blood brothers of fanaticism and the wellspring of totalitarian thought. We must draw our standards from our natural world, heedless of ridicule, and reaffirm its denied validity. We must honor with the humility of the wise the limits of that natural world and the mystery which lies beyond them, admitting that there is something in the order of being which evidently exceeds all our competence. We must relate to the absolute horizon of our existence which, if we but will, we shall constantly rediscover and experience. We must make values and imperatives the starting point of all our acts, of all our personally attested, openly contemplated, and ideologically uncensored lived experience. We must trust the voice of our conscience more than that of all abstract speculations and not invent responsibilities other than the one to which the voice calls us. We must not be ashamed that we are capable of love, friendship, solidarity, sympathy, and tolerance, but just the opposite: we must set these fundamental dimensions of our humanity free from their "private" exile and accept them as the only genuine starting point of meaningful human community. We must be guided by our own reason and serve the truth under all circumstances as our own essential experience.

I know all that sounds very general, very indefinite, and very unrealistic, but I assure you that these apparently naïve words stem from a very particular and not always easy experience with the world and that, if I may say so, I know what I am talking about.

The vanguard of impersonal power, which drags the world along its irrational path, lined with devastated nature and launching pads, is composed of the totalitarian regimes of our time. It is not possible to ignore them, to make excuses for them, to yield to them or to accept their way of playing the game, thereby becoming like them. I am convinced that we can face them best by studying them without prejudice, learning from them, and resisting them by being radically different, with a difference born of a continuous struggle against the evil which they may embody most clearly, but which dwells everywhere and so even within each of us. What is most dangerous to that evil are not the rockets aimed at this or that state but the fundamental negation of this evil in the very structure of contemporary humanity: a return of humans to themselves and to their responsibility for the world; a new understanding of human rights and their persistent reaffirmation, resistance against every manifestation of impersonal power that claims to be beyond good and evil, anywhere and everywhere, no matter how it disguises its tricks and machinations, even if it does so in the name of defense against totalitarian systems.

The best resistance to totalitarianism is simply to drive it out of our own souls, our own circumstances, our own land, to drive it out of contemporary humankind. The best help to all who suffer under totalitarian regimes is to confront the evil which a totalitarian system constitutes, from which it draws its strength and on which its "vanguard" is nourished. If there is no such vanguard, no extremist sprout from which it can grow, the system will have nothing to stand on. A reaffirmed human responsibility is the most natural barrier to all irresponsibility. If, for instance, the spiritual and technological potential of the advanced world is spread truly responsibly, not solely under the pressure of a selfish interest in profits, we can prevent its irresponsible transformation into weapons of destruction. It surely makes much more sense to operate in the sphere of causes than simply to respond to their effects. By then, as a rule, the only possible response is by equally immoral means. To follow that path means to continue spreading the evil of irresponsibility in the world, and so to produce precisely the poison on which totalitarianism feeds.

I favor "antipolitical politics," that is, politics not as the technology of power and manipulation, of cybernetic rule over humans or as the art of the utilitarian, but politics as one of the ways of seeking and achieving meaningful lives, of protecting them and serving them. I favor politics as practical morality, as service to the truth, as essentially human and humanly measured care for our fellow humans. It is, I presume, an approach which, in this world, is extremely impractical and difficult to apply in daily life. Still, I know no better alternative.

V

When I was tried and then serving my sentence, I experienced directly the importance and beneficial force of international solidarity. I shall never cease to be grateful for all its expressions. Still, I do not think that we who seek to proclaim the truth under our conditions find ourselves in an asymmetrical position, or that it should be we alone who ask for help and expect it, without being able to offer help in the direction from which it also comes.

I am convinced that what is called "dissent" in the Soviet bloc is a specific modern experience, the experience of life at the very ramparts of dehumanized power. As such, that "dissent" has the opportunity and even the duty to reflect on this experience, to testify to it and to pass it on to those fortunate enough not to have to undergo it. Thus we too have a certain opportunity to help in some ways those who help us, to help them in our deeply shared interest, in the interest of mankind.

One such fundamental experience, that which I called "antipolitical politics," *is* possible and can be effective, even though by its very nature it cannot calculate its effect beforehand. That effect, to be sure, is of a wholly different nature from what the West considers political success. It is hidden, indirect, long-term, and hard to measure; often it exists only in the invisible realm of social consciousness, conscience, and subconsciousness, and it can be almost impossible to determine what value it assumed therein and to what extent, if any, it contributes to shaping social development. It is, however, becoming evident—and I think that is an experience of an essential and universal importance—that a single, seemingly powerless person who dares to cry out the word of truth and to stand behind it with all his person and all his life, ready to pay a high price, has, surprisingly, greater power, though formally disfranchised, than do thousands of anonymous voters. It is becoming evident that even in today's world, and especially on this exposed rampart where the wind blows most sharply, it is possible to oppose personal experience and the natural world to the "innocent" power and to unmask its guilt, as the author of *The Gulag Archipelago* has done. It is becoming evident that truth and morality can provide a new starting point for politics and can, even today, have an undeniable political power. The warning voice of a single brave scientist, besieged somewhere in the provinces and terrorized by a goaded community, can be heard over continents and addresses the conscience of the mighty of this world more clearly than entire brigades of hired propagandists can, though speaking to themselves. It is becoming evident that wholly personal categories like good and evil still have their unambiguous content and, under certain circumstances, are capable of shaking the seemingly unshakable power with all its army of soldiers, policemen, and bureaucrats. It is becoming evident that politics by no means need remain the affair of professionals and that one simple electrician with his heart in the right place, honoring something that transcends him and free of fear, can influence the history of his nation.

Yes, "antipolitical politics" is possible. Politics "from below." Politics of man, not of the apparatus. Politics growing from the heart, not from a thesis. It is not an accident that this hopeful experience has to be lived just here, on this grim battlement. Under the "rule of everydayness" we have to descend to the very bottom of a well before we can see the stars.

When Jan Patočka wrote about Charter 77, he used the term "solidarity of the shaken." He was thinking of those who dared resist impersonal power and to confront it with the only thing at their disposal, their own humanity. Does not the perspective of a better future depend on something like an international community of the shaken which, ignoring state boundaries, political systems, and power blocs, standing outside the high game of traditional politics, aspiring to no titles and appointments, will seek to make a real political force out of a phenomenon so ridiculed by the technicians of power—the phenomenon of human conscience?

18

Letters to Olga*
(1982)

Václav Havel

May 22, 1982

Dear Olga,

Birth from the maternal womb—as the moment one sets out on one's journey through life—presents a telling image of the initial condition of humanity: a state of separation. Of release. Of breaking away. The human race becomes distinct from the animal kingdom; a living cell comes into being in a dead ocean; a planet that will one day be occupied by man becomes self-sustaining: in these events can be read the history, or the prehistory, of a constant, and constantly recurring, state of separation. The idea that the human spirit and reason are constituted by a severing of something from the hidden spirit and reason of Being is one that is constantly occurring to us in one form or another, and at the very least, it suggests that "separation" is a fundamental experience that man has of himself and his existence in the world. With the advent of humanity, how-

---

* In October of 1979 Havel, along with Václav Benda and four other defendants, were tried and found guilty of the crime of subversion of the republic. Havel was sentenced to four years in prison. Shortly after he was released from prison in 1983, Havel's letters to his wife Olga were circulated as a book in samizdat. The final sixteen letters, from which the letters included in this volume are taken, were also published separately in samizdat as Havel meant them to be read as a unit.

ever, something intrinsically new has appeared, something that ultimately is not referable to anything else, something that is, but is no longer spontaneously in "Being as such"; something that is, but somehow "otherwise," that stands against everything, even against itself.

The miracle of the subject is born. The secret of the "I." The awareness of self. The awareness of the world. The mystery of freedom and responsibility. Man as a being that has fallen out of Being and therefore continually reaches toward it, as the only entity by which and to which Being has revealed itself as a question, as a secret and as meaning.

It seems to me that the notion of separation as humanity's starting point helps us establish our bearings when we explore the stage on which human existence is constituted and its drama unfolded.

Separation creates a deeply contradictory situation: man is not what he has set out into, or rather, he is not his experience of what he has set out into. To him, this terrain—the world—is an alien land. Every step of the way, he comes up against his own "otherness" in the world and his otherness vis-à-vis himself. This terrain is essentially unintelligible to man. He feels unsettled and threatened by it. We experience the world as something not our own, something from which meaning must first be wrested and which, on the contrary, is constantly taking meaning away from us. No longer protected and hidden by spontaneous, unseparated participation in Being, we are exposed to what Being, for us, has become by virtue of our separation—the world of existing entities. Exposed and vulnerable to it. On the other hand, we are no longer what we have become separated from, either: we lose the certitude of Being, of our former rootedness in its integrity, totality, and universality, of our involvement in its general "identity." In other words, we are no longer identical with Being. We do not experience it simply, from "inside," but only as our own alienation from it. The certitude of our being in Being has irredeemably become a thing of the past, clouds have darkened the sky and we are flung into the uncertainty of the world. A recollection of this past, its birthmark and the ineradicable seal of our origins in it, go with us every step we take. But even that, to a considerable extent, is alienated from us (if only because we reflect upon it) and as such, it is in fact a part of what we have been thrown into or what we have fallen into and what drives us—in the alienness of the world—into situations we do not fully understand, which we suffer, but cannot avoid.

This inner echo of a home or a paradise forever lost to us—as a constitutive part of our "I"—defines the extent of what we are destined to lack and what we therefore cannot help but reach toward: for does not the hunger for meaning, for an answer to the question of what—in the process of becoming ourselves—we have become, derive from the recollection of a separated being for its state of primordial being in Being? From the other side, the alien world into which we are thrown beckons to us and tempts us. On the one hand we are constantly exposed to the temptation to stop asking questions and adapt ourselves to the world as it presents itself to us, to sink into it, to forget ourselves in it, to lie our way out of our selves and our "otherness" and thus to simplify our existence-in-the-world. At the same time we are persuaded over and over again that we can only reach toward meaning within the dimensions of this world, as it lies before us, by being open to the opening out of meaning within the world.

Thus is man alienated from Being, but precisely because of this he is seared by longing for its integrity (which he understands as meaningfulness), by a desire to merge with it and thus to transcend himself totally. As such, however, he is also alienated from the world in which he finds himself, a world that captivates and imprisons him. He is an alien in the world because he is still somehow bound up in Being, and he is alienated from Being because he has been thrown into the world. His drama unfolds in the rupture between his orientation "upward" and "backward" and a constant falling "downward" and into "now." He is surrounded by the horizon of the world, from which there is no escape, and at the same time, consumed by a longing to break through this horizon and step beyond it.

The absurdity of being at the intersection of this dual state of "thrownness," or rather this dual expulsion, can understandably give a person a reason (or an excuse) for giving up. He may also, however, accept it as a unique challenge enjoined upon his freedom, a challenge to set out—by virtue of all his thrownnesses—on a multisignificational journey between Being and the world (and thus, at the same time, to establish the outlines of his identity); to undertake it, aware that his goal lies beyond his field of vision, but also that precisely and only that fact can reveal the journey, make it possible and ultimately give it meaning; to fulfill uniquely the enigmatic mission of humanity in the history of Being by submitting to his destiny in an authentic, thoughtful way, a way that is faithful to everything originally good and therefore effective, and to make this entirely lucid acceptance of his entirely obscure task a source of sage delight to him.

I kiss you,
Vašek

May 29, 1982

Dear Olga,

Several days ago, during the weather report (it precedes the news on television each day, so I see it regularly), something went wrong in the studio and the sound cut out, though the picture continued as usual (there was neither the announcement "Do not adjust your sets" nor landscape photographs, as there usually is in such cases). The employee of the Meteorological Institute who was explaining the forecast quickly grasped what had happened, but because she was not a professional announcer, she didn't know what to do. At this point a strange thing happened: the mantle of routine fell away and before us there suddenly stood a confused, unhappy, and terribly embarrassed woman: she stopped talking, looked in desperation at us, then somewhere off to the side, but there was no help from that direction. She could scarcely hold back her tears. Exposed to the view of millions, yet desperately alone, thrown into an unfamiliar, unexpected and unresolvable situation, incapable of conveying through mime that she was above it all (by shrugging her shoulders and smiling, for instance), drowning in embarrassment, she stood there in all the primordial nakedness of human helplessness, face-to-face with the big bad world and herself, with the absurdity of her position, and with the desperate question of what to do with herself, how to rescue her dignity, how to acquit herself, how to be. Exaggerated as it may seem, I suddenly saw in that event an image of the primal situation of humanity a situation of separation, of being cast into an alien world and standing there before the question of self. Moreover, I realized at once that with the woman, I was experiencing—briefly—an almost physical dread; with her, I was overwhelmed by a terrible sense of embarrassment; I blushed and felt her shame; I too felt like crying. Irrespective of my will, I was flooded with an absurdly pow-

312

erful compassion for this stranger (a surprising thing here, of all places, where in spite of yourself you share the general tendency of the prisoners to see everything related to television as a part of the hostile world that locked them up): I felt miserable because I had no way of helping her, of taking her place, or at least of stroking her hair.

Why did I suddenly—and quite irrationally—feel such an overwhelming sense of responsibility for someone whom I not only did not know, but whose misery was merely transmitted to me via television? Why should I care? Does it even distantly concern me? Am I any more observant or sensitive than others? (Perhaps, but does that explain anything?) And if I am, why was I so affected by this, of all things; when today and every day, I see incomparably worse forms of suffering all around me?

After having read only one short excerpt in Ivan's* letter, I don't feel I can judge the breadth and depth of meaning that the idea of responsibility has in Levinas's† philosophical work. But if Levinas is claiming that responsibility for others is something primal and vitally important, something we are thrown into and by virtue of which we transcend ourselves from the beginning, and that this sense of responsibility precedes our freedom, our will, our capacity to choose and the aims we set for ourselves, then I share his opinion entirely. In fact I've always felt that, though I didn't put it to myself that way. Yes, a boundless and unmotivated sense of responsibility, that "existence beyond our own existence," is undoubtedly one of the things into which we are primordially thrown and which constitutes us. That responsibility—authentic, not yet filtered through anything else, devoid of all speculation, preceding any conscious "assumption," nontransferable to anything else, inexplicable in psychological terms—exists, as it were, before the "I" itself: first I find myself in it, and only then—having in one way or another either accepted or rejected this thrownness—do I constitute myself as the person I am.

In itself, the incident with the weatherwoman was insignificant, yet it vividly confirmed all of this within my own tiny frame of reference—not only because it happened in the atmosphere evoked by my having read that excerpt from Levinas, but mainly, I think, because it was such an incisive representation of human vulnerability. And if, in that moment, I

---

* Havel's brother Ivan.

† The Lithuanian born French philosopher Emmanuel Levinas (1906–1995).

felt such a powerful sense of responsibility for this particular woman and felt so entirely on her side (though common sense tells me she is doubtless better off than I am and probably never gives me a thought, if she knows about me at all), then this was likely because the more transparently vulnerable and helpless humanity is, the more urgently does its misfortune cry out for compassion. This dramatic exposure of another, void of all obfuscating detail and all "appearances," reveals and presents to man his own primordial and half-forgotten vulnerability, throws him back into it, and abruptly reminds him that he, too, stands alone and isolated, helpless and unprotected, and that it is an image of his own basic situation, that is, a situation we all share, a common isolation, the isolation of humanity thrown into the world, and that this isolation injures us all the same way, regardless of who, concretely, happens to be injured in a given instant.

Just as there is no escape from the world we are condemned to live in, so there is no escape from our unfulfilled connection with the universality of Being, from the painful presence of its absence in us, from this constant appeal to transcend ourselves, from the beckoning of our source and our destination. Speculating about where that endless, boundless and unreserved, prerational and prerationalized responsibility for another and for others comes from, I realize that it can only be one of the ways that separated being remembers its ancient being-in-Being, its presubjective state of being bound to everything that is, its intrinsic urge to break out of its self-imprisonment, step outside itself and merge once more with the integrity of Being. The vulnerability of another person, therefore, touches us not only because in it we recognize our own vulnerability, but for reasons infinitely more profound: precisely because we perceive it as such, the "voice of Being" reaches us more powerfully from vulnerability than from anything else: its presence in our longing for Being and in our desire to return to it has suddenly, in a sense, encountered itself as revealed in the vulnerability of another. This cry from the depths of another's fate arouses and excites us, mobilizes our longing to transcend our own subjectivity, speaks directly to the latent memory of our "prenatal" state of being-in-Being; it is, so to speak, stronger than everything else ("rational") within us—we suddenly find ourselves compelled to identify with Being, and we fall into our own responsibility. From this point of view, responsibility for others manifests itself as a revitalized or actualized responsibility "for everything," for Being, for the world, for its meaning. It is a revitalized involvement in Being, or rather an identification with what we are not and what does not touch us; it is the manifestation of a primordial experience of the self in Being and Being in us; the expression of a deep-seated intention to cover the world with our own subjectivity. Compassion, love, spontaneous help to our neighbors, everything that goes beyond speculative concern for our own being-in-the-world and what precedes it, these genuine "depths of the heart" can thus be understood as a unique part of what the world of human subjectivity becomes, evolves toward, and how it flourishes when it is thrown into its source in the integrity of Being, and of how that subjectivity constantly strives toward and returns to that integrity—while at the same time being astonished by it—just as I was astonished at the sympathy I felt for the meteorologist, caught unaware by the sudden breakdown of television technology.

I kiss you,
Vašek

July 3, 1982

Dear Olga,

The emerging "I" gains its first experiences when its longing for the lost fullness of Being collides with the barrier of its own state of separation. Through these experiences, both what is experienced (the world and the "I" in it) and that which experiences (the "I" that knows of itself and of the world) are established. The "I" begins to exist as a subject—that is, as the subject of those experiences—and becomes "an existence," i.e., separated being that is aware of itself and its own state of separation. In the beginning, therefore, there is unfreedom, dependency; blind (or rather still blinded) thrownness; the "I" as an object of its own thrownness and as a milieu from which it will arise (i.e., the stage of its own self-constitution). Obviously its initial experiences—in fact its first "existential" experiences—are what first fully transform it into "an existence," primarily by awakening the consciousness, the ability to reflect, mind. This means that the "I"—already aware that it exists—is continually stepping outside itself in order to return to itself once more and, through this "circulation," it inevitably matures—becomes itself. The existential experience—which

315

opens the spatiotemporal world to the "I"—also opens up the "inner world" as the proper stage for the activity that the "I" represents, and it sets this activity in motion: the "I" begins to understand its own thrown-ness, and thus it extricates itself from blind dependence on it; it becomes free, begins to "make itself up," to choose, to want, to write its own history and thus to define its own identity.

The intrinsic orientation of the "I" toward Being means, of course, a will to be. As the "I" begins to take stock of its situation and understand its separation, it begins to understand as well that "to be" means "to be in the world," that is, to exist in it. And here we encounter, in a new form, the profoundly paradoxical nature of human existence: the "I" can only approach the kind of Being it longs for (i.e., in the fullness of Being) through its own existence-in-the-world, and the manner of that existence. It can neither skip over that existence, nor get around it, nor avoid it, nor ignore it. On the other hand, however, to focus one's attention exclusively on existence-in-the-world as such and thus substitute the means for the end means inevitably to reject the fullness of Being. To succumb entirely to existence-in-the-world means to block entirely any chance of coming in contact with Being; it means a loss of Being, not to be. Existence, therefore, is a kind of permanent balancing act between the unattainability of Being and succumbing to existence in-the-world. A constant search for what can never completely be found: a way of best achieving all the demands of that existence-in-the world without, at the same time, ever succumbing to it, of constantly striving toward Being, not to the detriment of one's existence-in-the world, or by denying it, but through and by it. Existence-in-the-world is, *after all, a temptation and* a seduction: it drags one down into the world of things, surfaces, frantic consumption and self-absorption; it offers, as the most advantageous alternative, a kind of "setting up shop" among the demands of one's "existence-in-the-world"; it offers identifica-tion with them, a chance to forget oneself among them—and thus, it constantly distracts the "I" from itself, from its orientation toward Being. It manages, therefore, successfully to conceal precisely the goal to which it is supposed to lead one and, creating the illusion that it is assuring his passage toward Being, it leads him in precisely the opposite direction: toward meaninglessness, nothingness, and non-Being. For succumbing to existence-in-the-world is in fact surrendering to the "non-I." In renounc-ing the transcendental dimensions of his "I," man renounces its paradoxi-

cal essences, disrupts that fundamental tension from which its very existence, subjectivity, and ultimately its identity all stem, dissolves himself in
aims and matters that he himself has defined and created, and finally loses
himself in them entirely. He becomes a mechanism, a function, a frantic
consumer, a thing, manipulated by his own manipulations. At the same
time, the most treacherous and insidious form of this descent into the
"non-I" is the one that appears most effective in overcoming the alienation
of the world: the one that drives man to take the world—as the milieu of
his existence and therefore as the only proper object of his attention—"by
storm," as it were, to overpower it and rule it. At the end of this apparent
control of the world lies self-enslavement, nothing more: in assuming that
he rules the world and has thus liberated himself, man—dominated by his
own "dominion"—loses his freedom: he becomes a prisoner of his own
"worldly" schemes, dissolves himself in them and ultimately discovers that
by apparently eliminating the barriers to his existence-in-the-world, he has
merely succeeded in losing himself. The integrity of the free "I," always
open to the fullness of Being and—in all the freshness of its "preoriginal"
intentions and despite their ultimate futility—constantly striving toward
it, has vanished. Continuity and identity have vanished. The subject, its
freedom and its will, have been lost and all that remains is an intersection
of different aspects of the "non-I": "the subject no longer belongs to the
category of reasons," "man is outside" (Levinas), the "I," in a roundabout
way, has returned to its initial unfreedom and has become the alienness of
the world (few things can make me feel more anxious and alienated than a
scientific "explanation" of my "I"—whether as a biological, psychological
or political phenomenon).

As man becomes a full existence, he is confronted with the central
task of coming to terms with his own thrownnesses—both into an orientation toward Being and into his Being-in-the-world. And each moment,
he is confronted with two basic alternatives: he can seek a way of living out
his Being-in-the-world in such a way that he might touch Being, not turn
away from it, listen, as a matter of course, to "what is unexpressed in the
language of the world" and thus accept the world permanently as a partly
opened doorway to Being; or he can simply turn away from Being, accept
his existence-in-the-world as his ultimate direction and meaning (in reality a pseudomeaning), enter fully into its service and thus give up on the
difficult and demanding "voice of Being" in himself and in the world, i.e.,

to give up on himself as a subject and as "separated Being," to alienate himself from his own most proper, enigmatic essence.

These alternatives, of course, are also the alternatives of human responsibility: either the primordial, "irresponsible" "responsibility for everything" gradually takes on—through its existence-in-the-world, space and time—the dimensions of the responsibility of the "I" for itself and responsibility "toward" (in other words, becomes "the responsibility of man for his own responsibility") and thus leads man to a permanent, and permanently deepening, relation with the integrity of Being—or else man devalues such responsibility, retreats from it, renounces it (with the help of a wide range of self-deceptions) and replaces it with a utilitarianism that is completely tied to the demands of his existence-in-the-world. His morality is then the morality of the "hypothetical imperative" (for instance, he cares for others—including those who have yet to come—only to the extent that is useful and practical within the terms of his own existence-in-the-world), or it is a "reified" morality, that is, a morality whose measure is no longer a fresh, radical ongoing confrontation with his own source in Being and with the experience of contact with its integrity, but one that is measured only by its fidelity to itself as a human creation, which, though it may originally have come out of a genuine transcendence toward Being, has for a long time now only been living the autonomous life of something man accepts as one of the accessories of his existence-in-the-world. As I will try to show, by conserving the now distant intention of the "pre-I," such a morality creates the illusion that the original intention is still alive and, in the process, deludes man so profoundly that it ultimately makes it possible for him to commit any evil whatsoever in the name of good.

I kiss you,
Vašek

July 10, 1982

Dear Olga,

Orientation toward Being leads to that central existential quest, the quest for meaning. It is not a quest after the purpose or function of one particular entity in relation to another particular entity within the framework of a world constituted in any particular way, but a quest that goes beyond the horizon of all entities and beyond the horizon of the world as well. In this matter, man treats both the world and himself as the subject of his quest. He seeks with his entire being, and in that quest, his being is entirely transformed, as the world is entirely transformed in it as well. The object of the quest is Being itself. As an existential experience, this quest cannot be "answered," not in any specific way. The only possible response to it is another experience—the experience of meaningfulness as a joyful encounter with the unity between the voice of Being within us and the voice of Being in the world, an encounter that first gives both these voices a full voice, as it were, and thus opens the Being of the world up to us at the same time as it opens us up to that Being. In other words: the world becomes genuinely meaningful to one who is questing for meaning—and not just as that part of his experience which is still waiting to be assimilated, but also as that very process of assimilation, that is, as a result of the active entry of the "I" into the primordial alienness of the world and an image of its Being in that world.

And indeed: the world of an "I" that is oriented toward Being is different from the world of an "I" that has succumbed to its existence-in-the-world. Nothing in the former world is entirely defined by its function; everything, in a way that is unclear, somehow transcends both its function and itself as well; everything in it seems turned toward Being, its harmony, its infinitude, its totality, and its mystery; everything mirrors the openness of the subject that is assimilating itself into this world, mirrors its humble wonder—and terror—at the sovereignty of Being, its longing for Being's touch and its irrepressible hope.

Precisely these hard-to-grasp but vitally important dimensions are fatally lacking in the world of the "I" that has settled for mere existence-in-the-world: this is a world of functions, purposes and functioning, a world focused on itself, enclosed within itself, barren in its superficial variety, empty in its illusory richness, ignorant, though awash in information, cold, alienated, and ultimately absurd. (It is eloquently symbolized by high-rise housing, which guarantees accommodation by denying a real home: without a genius loci to transcend its function as a source of accommodation, it transforms the mystery of the city into something that merely complicates life: there is no adventure in trying to find someone in a high-rise complex, it is merely a tiresome process.) It is a world of exte-

319

riority, extension, and expansion, a world of taking power, of ruling and conquering: we conquer continents, mineral resources, the air, the energy trapped in matter, outer space. The aim, however, is simple conquest, and when it is all over the familiar scenery of the conquered territory emerges: continents are turned upside down, the bowels of the earth plundered, the atmosphere polluted, the energy trapped in matter released in the form of thousands of atomic warheads capable of destroying civilization and the surface of the planet ten times over. And having successfully conquered outer space, we now have a junkyard on the moon, a small prefiguration of what this civilization is preparing to make of the planet on which it arose.

Surrender to existence-in-the-world means the creation of an imbalance in the intrinsic intentions of existence and thus a denial of its dramatically contradictory essence, a contradiction that could be— if acknowledged—the mainspring of a flourishing of existence becomes, when banished beyond its borders, its graveyard. Thus the world constituted by this surrender grows out of a crisis of human integrity, a crisis of the inner world, a crisis of the subject as subject. It is an expression of the crisis of human responsibility, and at the same time it continues to deepen that crisis. Surrendering to existence-in-the-world, therefore, means falling into a vicious circle in which helplessness, seeking compensation in orgies of power, increases by degrees until at last man—like Goethe's sorcerer's apprentice*—can merely gape uncomprehendingly at what has come from his high and mighty illusion of understanding.

How can this vicious circle be broken? There would seem to be only one way: a revolutionary turning toward Being. The first condition for such an about-face, of course, is a recognition of the viciousness of this circle. Modern man has already, I think, come to just such a recognition: it is contained in the experience of absurdity.

A flower, a fish, a galaxy, a neutrino, man's nervous system—anything that is not the work of man—can awaken in us feelings of amazement, horror, joy and a whole range of other emotions, but they cannot, in themselves, awaken a sensation of absurdity. That feeling is always evoked by something man does, by human institutions, thoughts, products, relation-

---

* Goethe's poem of 1797, The Sorcerer's Apprentice, recounts the follies of an apprentice who summons magical powers which he cannot control.

ships, actions, etc. Absurdity is the experience that something that has, should, or could have aspired to meaning—that is, something intrinsically human—does not do so at all, or else has lost it. It is, therefore, the experience of losing touch with Being, the experience of a disintegration of the power to confer meaning, the experience of a humanity that has discovered it has defrauded itself, "lost its way"—and which, for that reason, turns back to its proper track: in the awareness of meaning's absence, the longing for meaning announces its presence again. If "meaning" is an entirely human category, then this is doubly true of "non-meaning": it is a human experience not just because man has it, but also because man only has it when confronted with what he has already done. It is the experience of the "I" oriented toward Being with the "I" that has surrendered to existence-in-the-world; it is the experience of man alone with himself. And even if that experience revives, or is reminiscent of, that primordial experience of the alienness of the world, the experience of absurdity—as a relatively late experience of the "mature I"—is far from being identical with that recollection: for in absurdity, the alienness of the world is not something that needs to be there; it is not something into which we have been "preprimordially" thrown; on the contrary, it is something that does not have be there, and into which, in a sense, we throw ourselves. For isn't this precisely the point where true absurdity begins?

The moon is not absurd. What is absurd is the junkyard man has left on it: it is not the moon, but the junkyard that lacks the slightest transcendence toward Being and its mysterious order, or the slightest reflection of the wonder, the humility, and the hope of someone who aspires to Being. There is in it only the desolation of things torn from their context, the arrogance of conquerors who expect that the captives and the vanquished will clean up after them, the despair of those who do not relate to eternity, but only to the present day. The absurd—because in its pride it is ludicrously inappropriate—expansion of mere occupancy, paid for by a loss of the capacity to make oneself at home. Man here enters the universe not as a wise participant in its order but as its arrogant destroyer, carrying into space only unbelonging, disorder, and futility. It is the calling card of fallen humanity, which has ejected from the module of its existence in the world—as something too heavy and no longer necessary—the most important thing of all: its meaning—and thus, to its belated astonishment, it has placed that existence-in-the-world face-to-face with the threat of extinction. Thus a turning away from Being in the philosophical sense of the word points ultimately to a non-Being that is terrifyingly nonphilosophical.

I kiss you,
Vašek

July 17, 1982

Dear Olga,

For many years now, whenever I have thought about responsibility or discussed it with someone, a trivial illustration has come to mind: at night, I board the rear car of a tram to go one stop. The car is empty, and since the fare is paid by dropping a crown into a box, not even a conductor is present (this self-service system, as far as I know, is no longer used on Prague streetcars). So I have the option of throwing the fare into the box or not: if I don't, no one will see me, or ever find out; no witnesses will ever be able to testify to my misdemeanor. So I'm faced with a great dilemma, regardless of how much money I happen to have with me: to pay or not to pay? From the point of view of my existence-in-the-world, it clearly makes sense not to pay, since putting a crown in the box amounts to throwing it down the drain. Still, it troubles me; I hesitate, think about it; in fact I might even be said to agonize over it. Why? What, after all, is compelling me to pay? Certainly not fear of the consequences if I don't—for my misdemeanor will never be discovered, nor will I ever be brought to trial. It is not even a desire to demonstrate my sense of civic duty, for there is no one either to condemn me for cheating or commend me for paying. My friends, fellow citizens, the public, society, the transport commission and the state itself are all, at this moment, sound asleep, quite outside my dilemma, and any instrumental regard for their opinion would be obvious nonsense. The conflict is entirely my own, and my concern, or lack of it, for opinion is simply not a factor. But more than that: in this dispute, not even the extent of my concern, or lack of it, for the general good is germane: clearly, my night ride in the streetcar will cost society what it will cost whether I pay or not, and clearly it is of no concern to the transport commission whether my crown shows up in their ledgers or not. Why, then, does something urge me to pay? Or conversely, why does the thought of not paying make me feel guilty?

The problem is deeper than it would seem at first. I know I should behave as everyone should; I know it's right to pay, that one should pay; that is how I was taught, and I accept that; I respect those who so taught me and who so behave. My upbringing, my sense of propriety, my habits, my sense of duty and responsibility to the whole, instilled in me throughout my life—all of these are certainly factors in my dilemma, but merely background factors, as external, essentially, as matters such as the amount of the fare, how much money I have with me, how far I am going, the chances of someone seeing me, etc. etc. The influence of my upbringing or the extent to which I accept the general moral norms explains the nub of my dilemma as little as all the other external factors, which together bear somewhat the same relationship to it as the scenery, the stage, and the lights bear to the drama that unfolds with their help.

Let us examine, then, the structure of this drama: I think everyone must realize, from his own experience, that what is going on here is a dialogue. A dialogue between my "I," as the subject of its own freedom (I can pay or not), of its ability to reflect (I give thought to what I should do) and of its choice (I will pay or I won't) and something that is outside this "I," separated from it and not identical with it. This "partner," however, is not standing beside me; I can't see it, nor can I quit its sight: its eyes and its voice follow me everywhere; I can neither escape it nor outwit it: it knows everything. Is it my so-called "inner voice," my "superego," my "conscience"? Certainly, if I hear it calling me to responsibility, I hear this call within me, in my mind and my heart; it is my own experience, profoundly so, though different from the experiences mediated to me by my senses. This, however, does nothing to alter the fact that the voice addresses me and enters into conversation with me, in other words, it comes to my "I"—which I trust is not schizoid—from the outside.

Who, then, is in fact conversing with me? Obviously someone I hold in higher regard than the transport commission, than my best friends (this would come out when the voice would take issue with their opinions), and higher, in some regards, than myself, that is, myself as subject of my existence-in-the-world and the carrier of my "existential" interests (one of which is the rather natural effort to save a crown). Someone who "knows everything" (and is therefore omniscient), is everywhere (and therefore omnipresent) and remembers everything; someone who, though infinitely understanding, is entirely incorruptible; who is, for me, the highest and utterly unequivocal authority in all moral questions and who is thus Law itself; someone eternal, who through himself makes me eternal as well, so that I cannot imagine the arrival of a moment when everything will come to an end, thus terminating my dependence on him as well; someone to whom I relate entirely and for whom, ultimately, I would do everything. At the same time, this "someone" addresses me directly and personally (not merely as an anonymous public passenger, as the transport commission does).

But who is it? God? There are many subtle reasons why I'm reluctant to use that word; one factor here is a certain sense of shame (I don't know exactly for what, why, and before whom), but the main thing, I suppose, is a fear that with this all-too-specific designation (or rather assertion) that "God is," I would be projecting an experience that is entirely personal and vague (never mind how profound and urgent it may be), too single-mindedly "outward," onto that problem-fraught screen called "objective reality," and thus I would go too far beyond it. Whether God exists or not—as Christians understand it—I do not and cannot know; I don't even know if that word is an appropriate label for the call to responsibility I hear. I know only this: that Being (which is, after all, easier to posit than the being of God) in its integrity, fullness, and infinity, as the principle, direction, and meaning of everything that is, and as the most profound and, at the same time, the broadest "innerness" of everything that exists (I intend to write about this in more detail) takes on, in the sphere of our inner experience that I am writing about here, an expressly personal outline: its voice, as we receive it—because we are "tuned in to its wavelength" (i.e., because of our source in it and our orientation toward it)—seems to emerge from a particularly "unseparated" subjective aspect of Being, with its own infinite memory, an omnipresent mind and an infinitely large heart. In other words: the Being of the universe, at moments when we encounter it on this level, suddenly assumes a personal face and turns this, as it were, toward us. The extent to which it acquires this face from our limited and deeply anthropomorphic imaginations, or, to be more precise, how much of this experience can be attributed to the one who is having it and how much to what causes it, is of course impossible to judge, nor does it make sense to try: to ascertain that would require climbing above the particular experience and all our other experiences too, that is, it would mean abandoning oneself, one's state of separation and one's humanity, to become God. But however it is, one thing seems certain to me: that our "I"—to the extent that it has not been entirely successful in suppressing its orientation toward Being, and becoming completely absorbed in its existence-in-the-world—has a sense of responsibility purely and simply because it relates intrinsically to Being as that in which it feels the only coherence, meaning and the somehow inevitable "clarification" of everything that exists, because it relates and aspires toward Being with all its being, because it hears within and around itself the "voice" in which this Being addresses and calls out to it, because in that voice it recognizes its own origin and its purpose, its true relevance and its true responsibility, and because it takes this voice more seriously than anything else.

I kiss you,
Vašek

IV
SEDUCTION

19

The Pill of Murti-Bing*
(1953)

Czeslaw Milosz

It was only toward the middle of the twentieth century that the inhabitants of many European countries came, in general unpleasantly, to the realization that their fate could be influenced directly by intricate and abstruse books of philosophy. Their bread, their work, their private lives began to depend on this or that decision in disputes on principles to which, until then, they had never paid any attention. In their eyes, the philosopher had always been a sort of dreamer whose divagations had no effect on reality. The average human being, even if he had once been exposed to it, wrote philosophy off as utterly impractical and useless. Therefore the great intellectual work of the Marxists could easily pass as just one more variation on a sterile pastime. Only a few individuals understood the causes and probable consequences of this general indifference.

A curious book appeared in Warsaw in 1932. It was a novel, in two volumes, entitled *Insatiability*. Its author was Stanislaw Ignacy Witkiewicz, a painter, writer, and philosopher, who had constructed a philosophical system akin to the monadology of Leibnitz.** As in his earlier novel, *Farewell to Autumn,* his language was difficult, full of neologisms. Brutal descriptions of erotic scenes alternated with whole pages of

---

* This is the first chapter of Milosz's classic work *The Captive Mind* (1953).
** Gottfried Wilhelm Leibnitz (1648–1716) was a German mathematician and philosopher.

discussions on Husserl,* Carnap,† and other contemporary philosophers. Besides, one could not always tell whether the author was serious or joking; and the subject matter seemed to be pure fantasy.

The action of the book took place in Europe, more precisely in Poland, at some time in the near future or even in the present, that is, in the thirties, forties, or fifties. The social group it portrayed was that of musicians, painters, philosophers, aristocrats, and higher-ranking military officers. The whole book was nothing but a study of decay: mad, dissonant music; erotic perversion; widespread use of narcotics; dispossessed thinking; false conversions to Catholicism; and complex psychopathic personalities. This decadence reigned at a time when western civilization was said to be threatened by an army from the East, a Sino-Mongolian army that dominated all the territory stretching from the Pacific to the Baltic.

Witkiewicz's heroes are unhappy in that they have no faith and no sense of meaning in their work. This atmosphere of decay and senselessness extends throughout the entire country. And at that moment, a great number of hawkers appear in the cities peddling Murti-Bing pills. Murti-Bing was a Mongolian philosopher who had succeeded in producing an organic means of transporting a "philosophy of life." This Murti-Bing "philosophy of life," which constituted the strength of the Sino-Mongolian army, was contained in pills in an extremely condensed form. A man who used these pills changed completely. He became serene and happy. The problems he had struggled with until then suddenly appeared to be superficial and unimportant. He smiled indulgently at those who continued to worry about them. Most affected were all questions pertaining to unsolvable ontological difficulties. A man who swallowed Murti-Bing pills became impervious to any metaphysical concerns. The excesses into which art falls when people vainly seek in form the wherewithal to appease their spiritual hunger were but outmoded stupidities for him. He no longer considered the approach of the Sino-Mongolian army as a tragedy for his own civilization. He lived in the midst of his compatriots like a

---

* Edmund Husserl (1859–1938) was one of the most influential philosophers of the twentieth century, best known as the founder of a philosophical school called "phenomenology."

† Rudolf Carnap (1891–1970) was a German-born philosopher and a major exponent of a philosophical school called "logical positivism."

healthy individual surrounded by madmen. More and more people took the Murti-Bing cure, and their resultant calm contrasted sharply with the nervousness of their environment.

The epilogue, in a few words: the outbreak of the war led to a meeting of the armies of the West with those of the East. In the decisive moment, just before the great battle, the leader of the Western army surrendered to the enemy; and in exchange, though with the greatest honors, he was beheaded. The Eastern army occupied the country and the new life, that of Murti-Bingism, began. The heroes of the novel, once tormented by philosophical "insatiety," now entered the service of the new society. Instead of writing the dissonant music of former days, they composed marches and odes. Instead of painting abstractions as before, they turned out socially useful pictures. But since they could not rid themselves completely of their former personalities, they became schizophrenics.

So much for the novel. Its author often expressed his belief that religion, philosophy, and art are living out their last days. Yet he found life without them worthless. On September 17, 1939, learning that the Red Army had crossed the eastern border of Poland, he committed suicide by taking veronal and cutting his wrists.

Today, Witkiewicz's vision is being fulfilled in the minutest detail throughout a large part of the European continent. Perhaps sunlight, the smell of the earth, little everyday pleasures, and the forgetfulness that work brings can ease somewhat the tensions created by this process of fulfillment. But beneath the activity and bustle of daily life is the constant awareness of an irrevocable choice to be made. One must either die (physically or spiritually), or else one must be reborn according to a prescribed method, namely, the taking of Murti-Bing pills. People in the West are often inclined to consider the lot of converted countries in terms of might and coercion. That is wrong. There is an internal longing for harmony and happiness that lies deeper than ordinary fear or the desire to escape misery or physical destruction. The fate of completely consistent, nondialectical people like Witkiewicz is a warning for many an intellectual. All about him, in the city streets, he sees the frightening shadows of internal exiles, irreconcilable, nonparticipating, eroded by hatred.

In order to understand the situation of a writer in a people's democracy, one must seek the reasons for his activity and ask how he maintains his equilibrium. Whatever one may say, the New Faith affords great possibilities for an active and positive life. And Murti-Bing is more tempting to an intellectual than to a peasant or laborer. For the intellectual, the New Faith is a candle that he circles like a moth. In the end, he throws himself into the flame for the glory of mankind. We must not treat this desire for self-immolation lightly. Blood flowed freely in Europe during the religious wars, and he who joins the New Faith today is paying off a debt to that European tradition. We are concerned here with questions more significant than mere force.

I shall try to grasp those profound human longings and to speak about them as if one really could analyze what is the warm blood and the flesh, itself, of man. If I should try to describe the reasons why a man becomes a revolutionary I would be neither eloquent nor restrained enough. I admit that I have too much admiration for those who fight evil, whether their choice of ends and means be right or wrong. I draw the line, however, at those intellectuals who *adapt* themselves, although the fact that they are adapted and not genuine revolutionaries in no way diminishes their newly acquired zeal and enthusiasm.

There are, I believe, a few key concepts which may lead us to understand why they accept Murti-Bing.

THE VOID

The society portrayed by Witkiewicz is distinguished by the fact that in it religion has ceased to exist as a force. And it is true that religion long ago lost its hold on men's minds not only in the people's democracies, but elsewhere as well. As long as a society's best minds were occupied by theological questions, it was possible to speak of a given religion as the way of thinking of the whole social organism. All the matters which most actively concerned the people were referred to it and discussed in its terms. But that belongs to a dying era. We have come by easy stages to a lack of a common system of thought that could unite the peasant cutting his hay, the student poring over formal logic, and the mechanic working in an automobile factory. Out of this lack arises the painful sense of detachment or abstraction that oppresses the "creators of culture." Religion has been replaced by philosophy which, however, has strayed into spheres increasingly less accessible to the layman. The discussions of Husserl by Witkiewicz's heroes can scarcely interest a reader of even better-than-average education; whereas the peasants remained bound to the Church, be it only emotionally and traditionally. Music, painting, and poetry became something completely foreign to the great majority of people. A theory developed that art should become a substitute for religion: "metaphysical feelings" were to be expressed in the "compression of pure form"; and so form soon came to dominate content.

To belong to the masses is the great longing of the "alienated" intellectual. It is such a powerful longing that, in trying to appease it, a great many of them who once looked to Germany or Italy for inspiration have now become converted to the New Faith. Actually, the rightist totalitarian program was exceptionally poor. The only gratification it offered came from collective *warmth:* crowds, red faces, mouths open in a shout, marches, arms brandishing sticks; but little rational satisfaction. Neither racist doctrines, nor hatred of foreigners, nor the glorification of one's own national traditions could efface the feeling that the entire program was improvised to deal with problems of the moment. But Murti-Bing is different. It lays scientific foundations. At the same time, it scraps all vestiges of the past. Post-Kantian philosophy, fallen into disrepute because of its remoteness from the life of men; art designed for those who, having no religion, dare not admit that to seek the "absolute" through a juxtaposition of colors and sounds is cowardly and inconclusive thinking; and the semimagic, semireligious mentality of the peasants—these are replaced by a *single* system, a single language of ideas. The truck driver and elevator operator employed by a publishing firm now read the same Marxist classics as its director or staff writers. A day laborer and a historian can reach an understanding on this basis of common reading. Obviously, the difference that may exist between them in mental level is no smaller than that which separated a theologian from a village blacksmith in the Middle Ages.

But the fundamental principles are universal; the great spiritual schism has been obliterated. Dialectical materialism has united everyone, and philosophy (i.e., dialectics) once more determines the patterns of life. It is beginning to be regarded with a respect one reserves only for a force on which important things depend: bread and milk for one's children, one's own happiness and safety. The intellectual has once more become *useful*. He who may once have done his thinking and writing in his free moments away from a paying job in a bank or post office, has now found his rightful place on earth. He has been restored to society, whereas the businessmen, aristocrats, and tradespeople who once considered him a harmless blunderer have now been dispossessed. They are indeed delighted to find work as cloakroom attendants and to hold the coat of a former employee of whom they said, in prewar days, "It seems he writes." We must not oversimplify, however, the gratifications of personal ambition; they are merely the outward and visible signs of social usefulness, symbols of a recognition that strengthens the intellectual's feeling of *belonging*.

THE ABSURD

Even though one seldom speaks about metaphysical motives that can lead to a complete change of people's political opinions, such motives do exist and can be observed in some of the most sensitive and intelligent men. Let us imagine a spring day in a city situated in some country similar to that described in Witkiewicz's novel. One of his heroes is taking a walk. He is tormented by what we may call the suction of the absurd. What is the significance of the lives of the people he passes, of the senseless bustle, the laughter, the pursuit of money, the stupid animal diversions? By using a little intelligence he can easily classify the passersby according to type; he can guess their social status, their habits and their preoccupations. A fleeting moment reveals their childhood, manhood, and old age, and then they vanish. A purely physiological study of one particular passer-by in preference to another is meaningless. If one penetrates into the minds of these people, one discovers utter nonsense. They are totally unaware of the fact that nothing is their own, that everything is part of their historical formation—their occupations, their clothes, their gestures and expressions, their beliefs and ideas. They are the force of inertia personified, victims of the delusion that each individual exists as a self. If at least these were souls, as the Church taught, or the monads of Leibnitz! But these beliefs have perished. What remains is an aversion to an atomized vision of life, to the mentality that *isolates* every phenomenon, such as eating, drinking, dressing, earning money, fornicating. And what is there beyond these things? Should such a state of affairs continue? Why should it continue? Such questions are almost synonymous with what is known as hatred of the bourgeoisie.

Let a new man arise, one who, instead of submitting to the world, will transform it. Let him create a historical formation, instead of yielding to its bondage. Only thus can he redeem the absurdity of his physiological existence. Man must be made to understand this, by force and by suffering. Why shouldn't he suffer? He ought to suffer. Why can't he be used as manure, as long as he remains evil and stupid? If the intellectual must know the agony of thought, why should he spare others this pain? Why should he shield those who until now drank, guffawed, gorged themselves, cracked inane jokes, and found life beautiful?

The intellectual's eyes twinkle with delight at the persecution of the bourgeoisie, and of the bourgeois mentality. It is a rich reward for the degradation he felt when he had to be part of the middle class, and when there seemed to be no way out of the cycle of birth and death. Now he has moments of sheer intoxication when he sees the intelligentsia, unaccustomed to rigorously tough thinking, caught in the snare of the revolution. The peasants, burying hoarded gold and listening to foreign broadcasts in the hope that a war will save them from collectivization, certainly have no ally in him. Yet he is warm-hearted and good; he is a friend of mankind. Not mankind as it is, but as it *should* be. He is not unlike the inquisitor of the Middle Ages; but whereas the latter tortured the flesh in the belief that he was saving the individual soul, the intellectual of the New Faith is working for the salvation of the human species in general.

NECESSITY

His chief characteristic is his fear of thinking for himself. It is not merely that he is afraid to arrive at dangerous conclusions. His is a fear of sterility, of what Marx called the misery of philosophy. Let us admit that a man is no more than an instrument in an orchestra directed by the muse of History. It is only in this context that the notes he produces have any significance. Otherwise even his most brilliant solos become simply a highbrow's diversions.

We are not concerned with the question of how one finds the courage to oppose the majority. Instead we are concerned with a much more poignant question: can one write well outside that one real stream whose vitality springs from its harmony with historical laws and the dynamics of reality? Rilke's* poems may be very good, but if they are, that means there must have been some reason for them in his day. Contemplative poems, such as his, could never appear in a people's democracy, not only because it would be difficult to publish them, but because the writer's impulse to write them would be destroyed at its very root. The objective conditions for such poetry have disappeared, and the intellectual of whom I speak is not one who believes in writing for the bureau drawer. He curses and despairs over the censorship and demands of the publishing trusts. Yet at the same time, he is profoundly suspicious of unlicensed literature. The publishing license he himself receives does not mean that the editor appreciates the artistic merits of his book, nor that he expects it to be popular with the public. That license is simply a sign that its author reflects the transformation of reality with scientific exactness. Dialectical materialism in the Stalinist version both reflects and directs this transformation. It creates social and political conditions in which a man ceases to think and write otherwise than as necessary. He accepts this "must" because nothing worthwhile can exist outside its limits. Herein lie the claws of dialectics. The writer does not surrender to this "must" merely because he fears for his own skin. He fears for something much more precious—the significance of his work. He believes that the by-ways of "philosophizing" lead to a greater or lesser degree of graphomania. Anyone gripped in the claws of dialectics is forced to admit that the thinking of private philosophers, unsupported by citations from authorities, is sheer nonsense. If this is so, then one's total effort must be directed toward following the line, and there is no point at which one can stop.

The pressure of the state machine is nothing compared with the pressure of a convincing argument. I attended the artists' congresses in Poland in which the theories of socialist realism were first discussed. The attitude of the audience toward the speakers delivering the required reports was decidedly hostile. Everyone considered socialist realism an officially imposed theory that would have, as Russian art demonstrates, deplorable results. Attempts to provoke discussion failed. The listeners remained silent. Usually, however, one daring artist would launch an attack, full of restrained sarcasm, with the silent but obvious support of the entire audi-

* Rainer Maria Rilke (1875–1926) was a Bohemian poet and essayist whose major works include *Duino Elegies* and *Letters to a Young Poet*.

ence. He would invariably be crushed by superior reasoning plus practicable threats against the future career of an undisciplined individual. Given the conditions of convincing argument plus such threats, the necessary conversion will take place. That is mathematically certain.

The faces of the listeners at these congresses were not completely legible, for the art of masking one's feelings had already been perfected to a considerable degree. Still one was aware of successive waves of emotion: anger, fear, amazement, distrust, and finally thoughtfulness. I had the impression that I was participating in a demonstration of mass hypnosis. These people could laugh and joke afterwards in the corridors. But the harpoon had hit its mark, and henceforth wherever they may go, they will always carry it with them. Do I believe that the dialectic of the speakers was unanswerable? Yes, as long as there was no fundamental discussion of methodology. No one among those present was prepared for such a discussion. It would probably have been a debate on Hegel, whose reading public was not made up of painters and writers. Moreover, even if someone had wanted to start it, he would have been silenced, for such discussions are permitted—and even then, fearfully—only in the upper circles of the Party.

These artists' congresses reveal the inequality between the weapons of the dialectician and those of his adversary. A match between the two is like a duel between a foot soldier and a tank. Not that every dialectician is so very intelligent or so very well educated, but all his statements are enriched by the cumulated thought of the masters and their commentators. If every sentence he speaks is compact and effective, that is not due to his own merits, but to those of the classics he has studied. His listeners are defenseless. They could, it is true, resort to arguments derived from their observations of life, but such arguments are just as badly countenanced as any questioning of fundamental methodology. The dialectician rubs up against his public at innumerable meetings of professional organizations and youth groups in clubs, factories, office buildings, and village huts throughout the entire converted area of Europe. And there is no doubt that he emerges the victor in these encounters.

It is no wonder that a writer or painter doubts the wisdom of resistance. If he were sure that art opposed to the official line could have a lasting value, he probably would not hesitate. He would earn his living through some more menial job within his profession, write or paint in his spare time, and never worry about publishing or exhibiting his work. He believes, however, that in most cases such work would be artistically poor, and he is not far wrong. As we have already said, the objective conditions he once knew have disappeared. The objective conditions necessary to the realization of a work of art are, as we know, a highly complex phenomenon, involving one's public, the possibility of contact with it, the general atmosphere, and above all freedom from involuntary subjective control. "I can't write as I would like to," a young Polish poet admitted to me. "My own stream of thought has so many tributaries, that I barely succeed in damming off one, when a second, third, or fourth overflows. I get halfway through a phrase, and already I submit it to Marxist criticism. I imagine what X or Y will say about it, and I change the ending."

Paradoxical as it may seem, it is this subjective impotence that convinces the intellectual that the one Method is right. Everything proves it is right. Dialectics: I predict the house will burn; then I pour gasoline over the stove. The house burns; my prediction is fulfilled. Dialectics: I predict that a work of art incompatible with socialist realism will be worthless. Then I place the artist in conditions in which such a work *is* worthless. My prediction is fulfilled.

Let us take poetry as an example. Obviously, there is poetry of political significance. Lyric poetry is permitted to exist on certain conditions. It must be: 1) serene; 2) free of any elements of thought that might trespass against the universally accepted principles (in practice, this comes down to descriptions of nature and of one's feelings for friends and family); 3) understandable. Since a poet who is not allowed to *think* in his verse automatically tends to perfect his form, he is accused of formalism.

It is not only the literature and painting of the people's democracies that prove to the intellectual that *things cannot be different*. He is strengthened in this belief by the news that seeps through from the West. The Western world is the world of Witkiewicz's novel. The number of its aesthetic and philosophical aberrations is myriad. Disciples imitate disciples; the past imitates the past. This world lives as if there had never been a Second World War. Intellectual clans in eastern Europe know this life, but know it as a stage of the past that isn't worth looking back on. Even if the new problems are so oppressive that they can break a great many people, at least they are contemporary. And mental discipline and the obligation to be clear are undoubtedly precious. The work of really

338

fine Western scholars and artists escapes notice. The only new names that are known are those of "democrats"—a delicate circumlocution for a non-pagan. In short, the recompense for all pain is the certainty that one belongs to the new and conquering world, even though it is not nearly so comfortable and joyous a world as its propaganda would have one think.

SUCCESS

Mystery shrouds the political moves determined on high in the distant Center, Moscow. People speak about prominent figures in hushed voices. In the vast expanses of Euro-Asia, whole nations can vanish without leaving a trace. Armies number into the millions. Terror becomes socially useful and effective. Philosophers rule the state—obviously not philosophers in the traditional sense of the word, but dialecticians. The conviction grows that the whole world will be conquered. Great hordes of followers appear on all the continents. Lies are concocted from seeds of truth. The philosophically uneducated bourgeois enemy is despised for his inherited inability to think. (Classes condemned by the laws of history perish because their minds are paralyzed.) The boundaries of the Empire move steadily and systematically westward. Unparalleled sums of money are spent on scientific research. One prepares to rule all the people of the earth. Is all this too little? Surely this is enough to fascinate the intellectual. As he beholds these things, historical fatalism takes root in him. In a rare moment of sincerity he may confess cynically, "I bet on this horse. He's good. He'll carry me far."

A patient has a hard time, however, when the moment comes for him to swallow Murti-Bing in its *entirety*. He becomes such a nervous wreck that he may actually fall ill. He knows it means a definitive parting with his former self, his former ties and habits. If he is a writer, he cannot hold a pencil in his hand. The whole world seems dark and hopeless. Until now, he paid a minimal tribute: in his articles and novels, he described the evils of capitalist society. But after all, it isn't difficult to criticize capitalism, and it can be done honestly. The charlatans of the stock exchange, feudal barons, self-deluding artists, and the instigators of nationalistic wars are figures who lend themselves readily to his pen. But now he must begin to approve. (In official terminology this is known as a transition from the stage of critical realism to that of socialist realism. It occurred in the newly-established people's democracies about the year 1950.) The operation he must perform on himself is one that some of his friends have already undergone, more or less painfully. They shake their heads sympathetically, knowing the process and its outcome. "I have passed the crisis," they say serenely. "But how he is suffering. He sits at home all day with his head in his hands."

The hardest thing to conquer is his feeling of *guilt*. No matter what his convictions, every man in the countries of which I speak is a part of an ancient civilization. His parents were attached to religion, or at least regarded it with respect. In school, much attention was devoted to his religious upbringing. Some emotional traces of this early training necessarily remain. In any case, he believes that injury to one's fellow-man, lies, murder, and the encouragement of hatred are evil, even if they serve to accomplish sublime ends. Obviously, too, he studied the history of his country. He read its former poets and philosophers with pleasure and pride. He was proud of its century-long battle to defend its frontiers and of its struggle for independence in the dark periods of foreign occupation. Consciously or unconsciously, he feels a certain loyalty to his forefathers because of the history of toil and sacrifice on their part. Moreover, from earliest childhood, he has been taught that his country belongs to a civilization that has been derived from Rome rather than Byzantium.

Now, knowing that he must enter a gate through which he can never return, he feels he is doing *something wrong*. He explains to himself that he must destroy this irrational and childish feeling. He can become free only by weeding out the roots of what is irretrievably past. Still the battle continues. A cruel battle—a battle between an angel and a demon. True, but which is the angel and which the demon? One has a bright face he has known since his childhood—this must be the angel. No, for this face bears hideous scars. It is the face of the old order, of stupid college fraternities, of the senile imbecility of politicians, of the decrepitude of western Europe. This is death and decadence. The other face is strong and self-contained, the face of a tomorrow that beckons. Angelic? That is doubtful.

There is a great deal of talk about patriotism, about fine, progressive, national traditions, about veneration of the past. But no one is so naïve as to take such talk seriously. The reconstruction of a few historical monuments, or a reediting of the works of·former writers cannot change certain revealing and important facts. Each people's democracy becomes a province of the Empire, ruled by edicts from the Center. It retains some autonomy, but to an ever-diminishing degree. Perhaps the era of independent states is over, perhaps they are no more than museum pieces. Yet it is saddening to say good-bye to one's dreams of a federation of equal nations, of a United States of Europe in which differing languages and differing cultures would have equal status. It isn't pleasant to surrender to the hegemony of a nation which is still wild and primitive, and to concede the absolute superiority of its customs and institutions, science and technology, literature and art. Must one sacrifice so much in the name of the unity of mankind? The nations of western Europe will pass through this phase of integration later, and perhaps more gently. It is possible that they will be more successful in preserving their native language and culture. By that time, however, all of eastern Europe will be using the one universal tongue, Russian. And the principle of a "culture that is national in form, socialist in content" will be consummated in a culture of monolithic uniformity. Everything will be shaped by the Center, though individual countries will retain a few local ornaments in the way of folklore. The Universal City will be realized when a son of the Kirghiz steppes waters his horses in the Loire, and a Sicilian peasant plants cotton in Turkmen valleys. Small wonder the writer smiles at propaganda that cries for a freeing of colonies from the grasp of imperialistic powers. Oh, how cunning dialectics can be, and how artfully it can accomplish its ends, degree by degree!

All this is bitter. But what about the harbinger of the Springtime of Nations, and Karl Marx, and the visions of the brotherhood of mankind? After all, nothing can be accomplished without the iron rule of a single Master. And what about this Master? A great Polish poet, describing his journey to the East—where he went in 1824 as a political prisoner of the Tsar—compared the soul of the Russian nation to a chrysalis. He wondered anxiously what would emerge when the sun of freedom shone: "Then will a shining butterfly take flight, or a moth, a sombre creature of the night?" So far, nothing prophesies a joyous butterfly.

The writer, in his fury and frustration, turns his thought to Western Communists. What fools they are. He can forgive their oratory if it is necessary as propaganda. But they believe most of what they proclaim about

341

the sacred Center, and that is unforgivable. Nothing can compare to the contempt he feels for these sentimental fools.

Nevertheless, despite his resistance and despair, the crisis approaches. It can come in the middle of the night, at his breakfast table, or on the street. It comes with a metallic click as of engaged gears. *But there is no other way.* That much is clear. There is no other salvation on the face of the earth. This revelation lasts a second; but from that second on, the patient begins to recover. For the first time in a long while, he eats with relish, his movements take on vigor, his color returns. He sits down and writes a "positive" article, marveling at the ease with which he writes it. In the last analysis, there was no reason for raising such a fuss. Everything is in order. He is past the "crisis."

He does not emerge unscathed, however. The aftereffects manifest themselves in a particular kind of extinguishment that is often perceptible in the twist of his lips. His face expresses the peaceful sadness of one who has tasted the fruit from the Tree of the Knowledge of Good and Evil, of one who knows he lies and who feels compassion for those who have been spared full knowledge. He has already gone through what still awaits so many others.

In 1945, an eminent Soviet journalist came to Poland. He was an elderly gentleman, who looked like a middle-class lawyer. That he was an extremely clever and rather unscrupulous person was evidenced by the tenacity with which he had maintained his position—and by his advanced years. After his return to Warsaw from a tour of several provincial Polish towns, he laughingly recounted an incident that had occurred in Silesia. Someone had spread the report that a delegation of foreigners from the West had arrived. The journalist (whose round belly and honest expression were inducive to such effusive manifestations of confidence) was seized and embraced on the street by a man crying: "The English have come." "That's just how it was in the Ukraine in 1919," was the journalist's comment on the incident. This recurrence of sterile hopes amused him and he was flattered to be the representative of a country ruled according to infallible predictions; for nation after nation had indeed become part of its Empire, according to schedule. I am not sure that there wasn't in his smile something of the compassionate *superiority* that a housewife feels for a mouse caught in her trap.

The "post-crisis" writer may well expect one day to be sent on a similar journalistic mission to some newly acquired Western country. Such a prospect is not altogether distasteful. To observe people who know nothing, who still have everything to learn, must undoubtedly afford moments of unadulterated sweetness. The master knows that the trap in which the mouse has been caught is not an entirely agreeable place to live in. For the moment, however, the citizens of these newly converted countries will understand little of their new situation. They will be exhilarated at first by the flutter of national banners, the blare of marching bands, and the proclamations of long-awaited reforms. Only he, the observer, will see into the future like a god; and know it to be hard, necessarily hard, for such are the laws of History.

In the epilogue of Witkiewicz's novel, his heroes, who have gone over to the service of Murti-Bing, become schizophrenics. The events of today bear out his vision, even in this respect. One can survive the "crisis" and function perfectly, writing or painting as one must, but the old moral and aesthetic standards continue to exist on some deep inner plane. Out of this arises a split within the individual that makes for many difficulties in his daily life. It facilitates the task of ferreting out heretical thoughts and inclinations; for thanks to it, the Murti-Bingist can feel himself into his opponent with great acuteness. The new phase and the old phase exist simultaneously in him, and together they render him an experienced psychologist, a keeper of his brother's conscience.

One can expect that the new generation, raised from the start in the new society, will be free of this split. But that cannot be brought about quickly. One would have to eradicate the Church completely, which is a difficult matter and one that demands patience and tact. And even if one could eliminate this reverenced mainstay of irrational impulses, national literatures would remain to exert their malignant influence. For example, the works of the greatest Polish poets are marked by a dislike of Russia, and the dose of Catholic philosophy one finds in them is alarming. Yet the state must publish certain of these poets and must teach them in its schools for they are the classics, the creators of the literary language, and are considered the forerunners of the Revolution. To place them on the index would be to think nondialectically and to fall into the sin of "leftism." It is a difficult dilemma, more difficult in the converted countries than in the Center, where the identification of national culture with the interests of humanity has been achieved to a great degree. Probably, therefore, the schizophrenic as a type will not disappear in the near future.

Someone might contend that Murti-Bing is a medicine that is incompatible with human nature. That is not a very strong argument The Aztecs' custom of offering human sacrifices to their gods, or the mortification of the flesh practiced by the early Christian hermits scarcely seem praiseworthy. The worship of gold has become a motive power second to none in its brutality. Seen from this perspective, Murti-Bing does not violate the nature of humankind.

Whether a man who has taken the Murti-Bing cure attains internal peace and harmony is another question. He attains a relative degree of harmony, just enough to render him active. It is preferable to the torment of pointless rebellion and groundless hope. The peasants, who are incorrigible in their petty bourgeois attachments, assert that "a change must come, because *this can't go on*." This is an amusing belief in the natural order of things. A tourist, as an anecdote tells us, wanted to go up into the mountains, but it had been raining for a week. He met a mountaineer walking by a stream, and asked him if it would continue to pour. The mountaineer looked at the rising waters and voiced the opinion that it would not. When asked on what basis he had made his prediction, he said, "Because the stream would overflow." Murti-Bing holds such magic judgments to be phantoms of a dying era. The "new" is striving to overcome the "old," but the "old" cannot be eliminated all at once.

The one thing that seems to deny the perfection of Murti-Bing is the apathy that is born in people, and that lives on in spite of their feverish activity. It is hard to define, and at times one might suppose it to be a mere optical illusion. After all, people bestir themselves, work, go to the theater, applaud speakers, take excursions, fall in love, and have children. Yet there is something impalpable and unpleasant in the human climate of such cities as Warsaw or Prague. The collective atmosphere, resulting from an exchange and a recombination of individual fluids, is bad. It is an aura of strength and unhappiness, of internal paralysis and external mobility. Whatever we may call it, this much is certain: if hell should guarantee its lodgers magnificent quarters, beautiful clothes, the tastiest food, and all possible amusements, but condemn them to breathe in this aura forever, that would be punishment enough.

No propaganda, either pro or con, can capture so elusive and little-known a phenomenon. It escapes all calculations. It cannot exist on paper. Admitting, in whispered conversation, that something of the sort does exist, one must seek a rational explanation for it. Undoubtedly the "old," fearful and oppressed, is taking its vengeance by spilling forth its inky fluid like a wounded octopus. But surely the socialist organism, in its growth toward a future of guaranteed prosperity, is already strong enough to counteract this poison; or perhaps it is too early for that. When the younger generation, free from the malevolent influence of the "old," arises, everything will change. Only, whoever has observed the younger generation in the Center is reluctant to cast such a horoscope. Then we must postpone our hopes to the remote future, to a time when the Center and every dependent state will supply its citizens with refrigerators and automobiles, with white bread and a handsome ration of butter. Maybe then, at last, they will be satisfied.

Why won't the equation work out as it should, when every step is logical? Do we have to use non-Euclidian geometry on material as classic, as adaptable, and as plastic as a human being? Won't the ordinary variety satisfy him? What the devil does a man need?

20

The Smatterers*
(1975)

ALEKSANDR I. SOLZHENITSYN

The fateful peculiarities of the educated stratum of Russians before the revolution were thoroughly analyzed in *Vekhi (Landmarks)*—and indignantly repudiated by the entire intelligentsia and by all political parties from the Constitutional Democrats to the Bolsheviks. The prophetic depth of *Vekhi* failed (as its authors knew it would fail) to arouse the sympathies of the Russian reading public; it had no influence on the development of the situation in Russia and was unable to avert the disastrous events which followed. Before long the very title of the book, exploited by another group of writers with narrowly political interests and low standards *(Smena Vekh—New Bearings),* was to grow blurred and dim and to disappear entirely from the memory of new generations of educated Russians, as the book itself inevitably disappeared from official Soviet libraries. But even after sixty years its testimony has not lost its brightness:

---

* This essay was first published in Paris in 1974 in a volume called *From Under the Rubble* shortly after Solzhenitsyn was arrested and preparing for his exile. Edited by Solzhenitsyn, the volume contains eleven essays by seven authors (three essays by Solzhenitsyn himself). It is modeled on the 1909 collection *Vekhi* (or *Landmarks*) in which prominent formerly radical intellectuals repudiated the reigning atheistic, revolutionary, intellectual atmosphere. The version of the essay published here is significantly abridged. The title refers to a section of Russian society. The "smatterers" retain the outward polish of the old intelligentsia and do not hesitate to refer to themselves as such, but Solzhenitsyn calls them "the semieducated estate."

Vekhi today still seems to us to have been a vision of the future. And our only cause for rejoicing is that now, after sixty years, the stratum of Russian society able to lend its support to the book appears to be deepening.

We read *Vekhi* today with a dual awareness, for the ulcers we are shown seem to belong not just to an era that is past history, but in many respects to our own times as well. That is why it is almost impossible to begin talking about today's intelligentsia (a problematical term which for the moment, in this first part, we shall take as referring to "that mass of people who call themselves by this name," and an intellectual—an "*intelligent*"— "any person who demands that he be regarded as such"), without drawing a comparison between its present attributes and the conclusions of *Vekhi*. Historical hindsight always offers a better understanding.

However, being in no way obliged to preserve the comprehensive structure of *Vekhi's* analysis, we shall for the limited purposes of the present survey take the liberty of summarizing and regrouping *Vekhi's* conclusions into the following four categories:

(1) *Faults of the old intelligentsia* which were important in the context of Russian history but which today have either faded away, or still exist in a much weaker form, or have become diametrically reversed:

Clannish, unnatural disengagement from the general life of the nation. (Today there is a considerable feeling of involvement by virtue of the intelligentsia's employed status.) Intense opposition to the state as a matter of principle. (Today it is only in its private thoughts and among small circles of friends that the intelligentsia draws a distinction between its own interests and those of the state, delights in any failure on the part of the state, and passively sympathizes with any show of resistance; in all else it is the loyal servant of the state.) Individual moral cowardice in the face of "public opinion," mental mediocrity at the individual level. (Now far outstripped by total cowardice when confronted by the will of the state.) Love of egalitarian justice, the social good and the material well-being of the people, which paralyzed its love of and interest in the truth; the "temptation of the Grand Inquisitor": let the truth perish if people will be the happier for it. (Nowadays it has no such broad concerns. Nowadays it is "let the truth perish if by paying that price I can preserve myself and my family.") Infatuation with the intelligentsia's general credo; ideological intolerance of any other; hatred as a passionate ethical impulse. (All this bursting passion has now disappeared.) Fanaticism that made the intelligentsia deaf to the voice of life. (Nowadays: accommodation and adaptation to practical considerations.) There was no word more unpopular with the intelligentsia than "humility." (Now they have humbled themselves to the point of servility.) Daydreaming, a naïve idealism, an inadequate sense of reality. (Today they have a sober, utilitarian understanding of it.) A nihilistic attitude to labor. (Extinct.) Unfitness for practical work. (Fitness.) A strenuous, unanimous atheism which uncritically accepted the competence of science to decide even matters of religion—once and for all and of course negatively; dogmatic idolatry of man and mankind; the replacement of religion by a faith in scientific progress. (The atheism has abated in intensity, but is still as widespread among the mass of the educated stratum; by now it has grown traditional and insipid, though unconditional obeisance is still made to scientific progress and the notion that "man is the measure of all things.") Mental inertia; the feebleness of autonomous intellectual activity and even hostility to autonomous spiritual claims. (Today, on the contrary, there are some educated people who make up for their withdrawal from public passion, faith, and action by indulging at their leisure, in their closed shell and among their circle of friends, in quite intensive intellectual activity, although usually with no relevance to the outside world—sometimes by way of anonymous, secret appearances in *samizdat.**)

In the main *Vekhi* was critical of the intelligentsia and set down those of its vices and inadequacies that were a danger to progress in Russia. It contains no separate analysis of the virtues of the intelligentsia. Yet looking at *Vekhi* comparatively from an angle of vision that enables us to take account of the qualities of the educated stratum of the present time, we find that, among its faults, the authors of *Vekhi* also list features which today cannot be viewed otherwise than as

(2) *Virtues of the prerevolutionary intelligentsia:* A universal search for an integral worldview, a thirst for faith (albeit secular), and an urge to subordinate one's life to this faith. (Nothing comparable exists today, only tired cynicism.) Social compunction, a sense of guilt with regard to the people. (Nowadays the opposite is widely felt: that the people is guilty toward the intelligentsia and will not repent.) Moral judgments and moral considerations occupy an exceptional position in the soul of the Russian

---

* *Samizdat* refers to self or underground publishing.

348

intellectual: all thought of himself is egoism; his personal interests and very existence must be unconditionally subordinated to service to society; puritanism, personal asceticism, total selflessness, even abhorrence and fear of personal wealth as a burden and a temptation. (None of this relates to us—we are quite the reverse!) A fanatical willingness to sacrifice oneself—even an active quest for such sacrifice; although this path is trodden by only a handful of individuals, it is nevertheless the obligatory and only worthy ideal aspired to by all. (This is unrecognizable, this is not us! All that remains in common is the word "intelligentsia," which has survived through force of habit.)

The Russian intelligentsia cannot have been so base if *Vekhi* could apply such lofty criteria in its criticism of it. This will strike us even more-forcibly when we look at the group of characteristics depicted by *Vekhi* as

(3) *Faults at the time,* which in our topsy-turvy world of today have the *appearance almost of virtues*:

The aim of universal equality, in whose interests the individual must be prepared to curtail his higher needs. The psychology of heroic ecstasy, reinforced by state persecution; parties are popular in proportion to their degree of fearlessness. (Today the persecution is crueler and more systematic, and induces depression instead of ecstasy.) A personal sense of martyrdom and a compulsion to confess; almost a death wish. (The desire now is for self-preservation.) The heroic intellectual is not content with the modest role of worker and dreams of being the savior of mankind or at least of the Russian people. Exaltation, an irrational mood of elation, intoxication with struggle. He is convinced that the only course open to him is social struggle and the destruction of society in its existing form. (Nothing of the kind! The only possible course is subservience, sufferance, and the hope of mercy.)

But we have not lost all of our spiritual heritage. We too are recognizably there.

(4) *Faults inherited in the present day:*

Lack of sympathetic interest in the history of our homeland, no feeling of blood relationship with its history. Insufficient sense of historical reality. This is why the intelligentsia lives *in expectation of a social miracle* (in those days they did a great deal to bring it about; now they make it less and less possible for the miracle to happen—but hope for it all the same!). All that is bad is the result of outward disorganization and consequently all that is needed are external reforms. Autocracy is responsible for everything that is happening, therefore the intellectual is relieved of all personal responsibility and personal guilt. An exaggerated awareness of their rights. Pretentiousness, posturing, the hypocrisy of constant recourse to "principles"—to rigid abstract arguments. An overweening insistence on the opposition between themselves and the "philistines." Spiritual arrogance. The religion of self-deification—the intelligentsia sees its existence as providential for the country.

This all tallies so perfectly that it needs no comment.

Let us add a dash of Dostoyevsky (from *The Diary of a Writer)*:

Faintheartedness. A tendency to jump to pessimistic conclusions.

And many more qualities of the old intelligentsia would have survived in the present one if the *intelligentsia itself* had remained in existence.

—

It is all very well to charge the working class at the present time with being excessively law-abiding, uninterested in the spiritual life, immersed in philistinism and totally preoccupied with material concerns—getting an apartment, buying tasteless furniture (the only kind in the shops), playing cards and dominoes or watching television and getting drunk—but have the smatterers, even in the capital, risen all that much higher? Dearer furniture, higher-quality concerts, and cognac instead of vodka? But it watches the same hockey matches on television. On the fringes of smatterdom an obsession with wage-levels may be essential to survival, but at its resplendent center (in sixteen republican capitals and a handful of closed towns) it is disgusting to see all ideas and convictions subordinated to the mercenary pursuit of bigger and better salaries, titles, positions, apartments, villas, cars (Pomerants:* "A dinner service is compensation for lost nerves"), and—even more—trips abroad! (Wouldn't this have amazed the prerevolutionary intelligentsia! It needs explaining: new impressions, a gay time, the good life, an expense account in foreign currency, the chance to buy gaudy rags. . . . For this reason I think even the sorriest member of the prerevolutionary intelligentsia would refuse to shake hands with the most

---

* Pomerants. Solzhenitsyn comments extensively on his work (essays published in *samizdat*) in other sections of the essay not reproduced here.

illustrious of our metropolitan smatterers today.) But what distinguishes the mentality of the Moscow smatterers more than anything else is their greed for awards, prizes and titles far beyond the reach of the working class or the provincial smatterers—the prize money is higher, and what resounding titles they are: "People's Artist (Actor, etc.) . . . Meritorious Practitioner . . . Laureate . . ."! For all this people are not ashamed to toe the line punctiliously, break off all unapproved friendships, carry out all the wishes of their superiors and condemn any one of their colleagues either in writing or from a public platform, or simply by refusing to shake his hand, if the party committee orders them to.

If all these are the qualities of the *intelligentsia,* who are the *philistines?*

People whose names we used to read not so long ago on our cinema screens and who passed for members of the intelligentsia if anyone did, who recently left this country for good, saw no shame in taking eighteenth-century escritoires to pieces (the export of antiques is prohibited), nailing the pieces to some ordinary planks of wood to make grotesque "furniture," and exporting them in that form. Can one still bring oneself to utter the word "intelligentsia"? It is only a customs regulation that prevents icons older than the seventeenth century from leaving the country. Whole exhibitions of later icons are at this very moment being staged in Europe—and not only the state has been selling abroad. . . .

Everybody who lives in our country pays dues for the maintenance of the obligatory ideological lie. But for the working class, and all the more so for the peasantry, the dues are minimal, especially now that the financial loans which used to be extorted annually have been abolished (it was the fake voluntariness of these loans that was so perfidious and so distressing: the money could have been appropriated by some other means); all they now have to do is vote every so often at some general meeting where absenteeism is not checked with particular thoroughness. Our state bailiffs and ideological inculcators, on the other hand, sincerely believe in their ideology, many of them having devoted themselves to it out of long years of inertia or ignorance, or because of man's psychological quirk of liking to have a philosophy of life that matches his basic work.

But what of our central smatterers? Perfectly well aware of the shabbiness and flabbiness of the party lie and ridiculing it among themselves, they yet cynically repeat the lie with their very next breath, issuing "wrathful" protests and newspaper articles in ringing, rhetorical tones, and expanding and reinforcing it by their eloquence and style! Where did Orwell light upon his *doublethink,* what was his model if not the Soviet intelligentsia of the 1930s and 1940s? And since that time this doublethink has been worked up to perfection and become a permanent part of our lives.

Oh, we crave *freedom,* we denounce (in a whisper) anyone who ventures to doubt the desirability and necessity of total freedom in our country. (Meaning, in all probability, not freedom for everyone but certainly for the central smatterers. Pomerants, in a letter to the twenty-third Party Congress, proposes setting up an association of the "nucleus of the intelligentsia," which would have a free press at its disposal and be a theoretical center giving advice to the administrative and party centers.). But we are waiting for this freedom to fall into our lap like some unexpected miracle, without any effort on our part, while we ourselves do nothing to win this freedom. Never mind the old traditions of supporting people in political trouble, feeding the fugitive, sheltering the pass-less or the homeless (we might lose our state-controlled jobs)—the central smatterers labor day after day, conscientiously and sometimes even with talent, to strengthen our common prison. And even for this they will not allow themselves to be blamed! A multitude of excuses has been primed, pondered and prepared. Tripping up a colleague or publishing lies in a newspaper statement is resourcefully justified by the perpetrator and unanimously accepted by his associates: If I (he) hadn't done it, they would have sacked me (him) from my (his) job and appointed somebody worse! So in order to maintain the principle of what is *good* and for the benefit of all, it is natural that every day you will find yourself obliged to harm the few ("honorable men play dirty tricks on their neighbors only when they have to"). But the few are *themselves* guilty: why did they flaunt themselves so indiscreetly in front of the bosses, without a thought for the *collective*? Or why did they hide their questionnaires from the personnel department and thus *lay the entire collective open to attack*? Chelnov (in the *Vestnik RSKD,** No. 97) wittily describes the intelligentsia's position as *standing crookedly—"from which position the vertical seems a ridiculous posture."*

But the chief justifying argument is: *children!* In the face of this argu-

---

* *Vestnik RSKD* (Russkogo Khristianskogo Studencheskogo Dvizhenia—Herald of the Russian Student Christian Movement) was a Russian journal published in Paris by the YMCA Press—an outlet for the publication and circulation of Russian *samizdat* essays.

ment everyone falls silent: for who has the right to sacrifice the material welfare of his children for the sake of an *abstract* principle of truth?! That the moral health of their children is more precious than their careers does not even enter the parents' heads, so impoverished have they themselves become. And it is reasonable that their children should grow up the same: pragmatists right from their school days, first-year students already resigned to the lie of the political education class, already shrewdly weighing their most profitable way into the competitive world of science. Theirs is a generation that has experienced no real persecution, but how cautious it is! And those few youths—the hope of Russia—who turn and look truth in the face are usually cursed and even persecuted by their infuriated, affluent parents.

And you cannot excuse the central smatterers, as you could the peasants in former times, by saying that they were scattered about the provinces, knew nothing of events in general, and were suppressed on the local level. Throughout the years of Soviet power the intelligentsia has been well enough informed, has known what was going on in the world, and *could* have known what was going on in its own country, but it looked away and feebly surrendered in every organization and every office, indifferent to the *common* cause. For decade after decade, of course, it has been held in an unprecedented stranglehold (people in the West will never be able to imagine it until their turn comes). People of dynamic initiative, responsive to all forms of public and private assistance, have been stifled by oppression and fear, and public assistance itself has been soiled by a hypocritical state-run imitation. Finally, they have been placed in a situation where there appears to be no third choice: if a colleague is being hounded no one dares to remain neutral—at the slightest evasion he himself will be hounded too. But there is still a way out for people, even in this situation, and that is to let themselves be hounded! Let my children grow up on a crust of bread, so long as they are honest! If the intelligentsia were like *this,* it would be invincible.

There is also a special category of distinguished people whose names have become so firmly and inviolably established and who are so protectively cloaked in national and sometimes international fame that, in the post-Stalin period at least, they are well beyond the reach of the police, which is plain as plain could be from both near and far; nor do they fear need—they've put plenty aside. Could not *they* resurrect the honor and independence of the Russian intelligentsia? Could not *they* speak out in defense of the persecuted, in defense of freedom, against rank injustices and the squalid lies that are foisted upon us? Two hundred such men (and they number half a thousand altogether) by coming forward and taking a united stand would purify the public air in our country and all but transform our whole life! The prerevolutionary intelligentsia did this in their thousands, without waiting for the protection of fame. But can we find as many as ten among our smatterers? The rest feel no such *need*! (Even a person whose father was shot thinks nothing of it, swallows the fact.) And what shall we say about our prominent men at the top? Are they any better than the smatterers?

In Stalin's day, if you refused to sign some newspaper smear or denunciation, or to call for the death or imprisonment of your comrade, you really might have been threatened with death or imprisonment yourself. But today—what threat today induces our silver-haired and eminent elders to take up their pens, obsequiously asking "where?", and sign some vile nonsense concocted by a third person about Sakharov?* Only their own worthlessness. What force impels a great twentieth-century composer to become the pitiful puppet of third-rate bureaucrats from the Ministry of Culture and at their bidding sign any contemptible piece of paper that is pushed at him, defending whoever they tell him to abroad and hounding whoever they want him to at home? (The composer's soul has come into direct and intimate contact—with no screen in between—with the dark, destructive soul of the twentieth century. He has gripped—no, it has gripped him with such piercing authenticity that when—if!—mankind enters upon a more enlightened age, our descendants will hear from Shostakovich's[†] music how we were in the devil's clutches, utterly in its possession, and that we found beauty in those clutches and in that infernal breathing.)

Was the behavior of the great Russian scholars in the past ever so wretched? Or the great Russian artists? Their tradition has been broken: we are the smatterers.

What is triply shameful is that now it is not fear of persecution, but devious calculations of vanity, self-interest, personal welfare, and tranquil-

* Andrei Sakharov (1921–1989) was an eminent Russian physicist and dissident who won the Nobel Peace Prize in 1975.

† Dmitri Shostakovich (1906–1975) was a celebrated Russian composer.

ity that make the "Moscow stars" among the smatterers and the middle stratum of "moderates" so pliant. Lydia Chukovskaya[1] is right: the time has come to count *some* people out of the intelligentsia. And if that doesn't mean all *these,* then the meaning of the word has been irretrievably lost.

Oh, there have been fearless people! Fearless enough to speak up for an old building that was being demolished (as long as it wasn't a cathedral), and even the whole Lake Baikal area.[2] And we must be thankful for that, of course. One of the contributors to the present anthology was to have been an exceptionally distinguished person with a string of ranks and titles to his name. In private conversations his heart bleeds for the irrevocable ruin that has befallen the Russian people. He knows our history and our culture through and through. But—he declined: *What's the use? Nothing will come of it* . . . the usual good excuse of the smatterers.

We have got what we deserve. So low have we sunk.

When they jerked the string from on top and said we could be a little bolder (1956, 1962) we straightened our numbed spines just a trifle. When they jerked "quiet!" (1957, 1963) we subsided at once.* There was also the spontaneous occurrence of 1967–1968, when *samizdat* came pouring out like a spring flood, more and more names appeared, new names signed protests and it seemed that only a little more was needed, only a tiny bit more, and we should begin to breathe. And did it take all that much to crush us? Fifty or so of the most audacious people were deprived of work in their professions. A few were expelled from the party, a few from the unions, and eighty or so protest signers were *summoned for discussions* with their party committee. And they came away from those "discussions" pale and crestfallen.

And the smatterers took flight, dropping in their haste their most important discovery, the very condition of continued existence, rebirth and thought—*samizdat.* Was it so long ago since the smatterers had been in hot pursuit of the latest items of *samizdat,* begging for extra copies to

---

* The 20th Congress of the Communist Party of 1956 was the site of Khrushchev's famous denunciation of Stalin. This coincided with a continuing "thaw" in Soviet control of cultural life that had begun with Stalin's death. The year 1962 brought the publication, with Khrushchev's approval, of Solzhenitsyn's own *One Day in the Life of Ivan Denisovich.* The years 1957 and 1963 included attempts by the regime to reassert stricter control after moments of liberalization.

be typed, starting to collect *samizdat* libraries or sending *samizdat* to the provinces? Now they began to burn those libraries and cherish the virginity of their typewriters, only occasionally borrowing a forbidden leaflet in some dark passageway, snatching a quick look at it and returning it at once as if they had burned their fingers.

Yes, in the course of those persecutions a definite *core of the intelligentsia* did take shape and emerge into view, consisting of people who continued to risk their necks and make sacrifices—by openly or in wordless secrecy keeping dangerous materials, by fearlessly helping prisoners or by paying with their own freedom.

But there was another "core" that also came to light and discovered an ingenious alternative: to flee the country! Thereby preserving their own unique individuality (*"over there* I shall be able to develop Russian culture in peace and quiet"). Or saving those whom they had left behind ("from *over there* we shall be better able to defend your rights here"). Or, finally, saving their children, who were more precious than the children of the rest of their compatriots.

Such was the "core of the Russian intelligentsia" that came to light and that could exist even without Russia. But all this would be forgiven us, would arouse only sympathy—our downtrodden degradation and our subservience to the lie—if we meekly confessed to our infirmity, our attachment to material prosperity, our spiritual unpreparedness for trials too severe for us to bear: we are the victims of history that happened before our time, we were born into it, and have tasted our fair share of it, and here we are, floundering and not knowing how to escape from it.

But no! We contrive in this situation to find tortuous excuses of stunning sublimity as to why we should "become spiritually aware of ourselves without abandoning our scientific research institutes" (Pomerants)—as if "becoming spiritually aware" were a matter of cozy reflection, not of harsh ordeal and merciless trial. We have not renounced our arrogance in the least. We insist on the noble, inherited title of intelligentsia, on the right to be the supreme arbiters of every spiritual manifestation in our own country and of mankind: to make peremptory judgments about social theories, trends, movements, historical currents and the activities of prominent individuals from the safety of our burrows. Even as we put on our coats in the lobbies of our institutes we grow a head taller, and by the evening over the tea table we are already pronouncing the supreme judgment and deciding which actions and which of their perpetrators the "intelligentsia will forgive" or "not forgive."

Observing the pitiful way the central smatterers actually behave in the service of the Soviet state, it is impossible to believe the high historical pedestal they see themselves as occupying—each placing himself, his friends, and his colleagues on that pedestal. The increasingly narrow specialization of professional disciplines, which enables semi-ignoramuses to become doctors of science, does not bother the smatterer in the slightest.

—

But the picture Pomerants paints of the people is, alas, to a large extent true. Just as we are probably mortally offending him now by alleging that there is no longer an intelligentsia in our country, and that it has all disintegrated into a collection of smatterers, so he too mortally wounds us by his assertion that neither is there a *people* any longer.

"The people no longer exists. There is the mass, with a dim recollection that it was once the people and the bearer of God within itself, but now it is utterly empty. . . . The people in the sense of a Chosen People, a source of spiritual values, is nonexistent. There are the neurasthenic intellectuals—and the masses. . . . What do the collective farm workers sing? Some remnants of their peasant heritage" and whatever is drilled into them "at school, in the army and on the radio. . . . Where is it, this 'people'? The real native people, dancing its folk dances, narrating its folktales, weaving its folk-patterned lace? In our country all that remains are the vestiges of a people, like the vestiges of snow in spring. . . . The people as a great historical force, a backbone of culture, a source of inspiration for Pushkin and Goethe, no longer exists. . . . What is usually called the people in our country is not the people at all but a petit bourgeoisie."

Gloom and doom. And not far from the truth either.

Indeed, how *could* the people have survived? It has been subjected to two processes both tending toward the same end and each lending impetus to the other. One is the universal process (which, if it had been postponed any longer in Russia, we might have escaped altogether) of what is fashionably known as *massovization* (an abominable word, but then the process is no better), a product of the new Western technology, the sickening growth of cities, and the general standardization of methods of information and education. The second is our own special Soviet process, designed to rub off the age-old face of Russia and rub on another, synthetic one, and this has had a still more decisive and irreversible effect.

How could the people possibly have survived? Icons, obedience to elders, bread-baking, and spinning wheels were all forcibly thrown out of the peasants' cottages. Then millions of cottages—as well-designed and comfortable as one could wish—were completely ravaged, pulled down or put into the wrong hands and five million hardworking, healthy families, together with infants still at the breast, were dispatched to their death on long winter journeys or on their arrival in the tundra. (And our *intelligentsia* did not waver or cry out, and its *progressive* part even assisted in driving them out. *That* was when the intelligentsia ceased to be, in 1930; and is that the moment for which the people must beg its forgiveness?) The destruction of the remaining cottages and homesteads was less trouble after that. They took away the land which had made the peasant a peasant, depersonalized it even more than serfdom had, deprived the peasant of all incentive to work and live, packed some off to the Magnitogorsks,[3] while the rest—a whole generation of doomed women—were forced to feed the colossus of the state before the war, for the entire duration of the war and after the war. All the outward, international successes of our country and the flourishing growth of the thousands of scientific research institutes that now exist have been achieved by devastating the Russian village and the traditional Russian way of life. In its place they have festooned the cottages and the ugly multistory boxes in the suburbs of our cities with loudspeakers, and even worse, have fixed them on all the telegraph poles in city centers (even today they will be blaring over the entire face of Russia from six in the morning until midnight, the supreme mark of culture, and if you go and shut them off it's an anti-Soviet act). And those loudspeakers have done their job well: they have driven everything individual and every bit of folklore out of people's heads and drilled in stock substitutes, they have trampled and defiled the Russian language and dinned vacuous, untalented songs (composed by the intelligentsia) into our ears. They have knocked down the last village churches, flattened and desecrated graveyards, flogged the horse to death with Komsomol zeal, and their tractors and five-ton lorries have polluted and churned up the centuries-old roads whose gentle tracery adorns our countryside. Where is there left, and who is there left to dance and weave lace? Furthermore, they have visited the village youth with specially juicy tidbits in the form of quantities of drab, idiotic films (the intellectual: "We have to release them—they are *mass-circulation* films")—and the same rubbish is crammed into school textbooks and slightly more adult books (and you know *who* writes them, don't you?), to prevent new growth from springing up where the old timber was felled. Like tanks they have ridden rough-shod over the entire historical memory of the people (they gave us back Alexander Nevsky without his cross,[4] but anything more recent—no), so how *could* the people possibly have saved itself?

And so, sitting here in the ashes left behind by the conflagration, let us try to work it out.

The people does not exist? Then it's true that there can be no national revival? But what's that gap there? I thought I glimpsed something as a result of the collapse of universal technological progress, in line with the transition that will be made to a stable economy, there will be a restoration everywhere of the primeval attachment of the majority of the people to the land, to the simplest materials and tools, and to physical labor (which many satiated town-dwellers are even now instinctively seeking for themselves). Thus in every country, even the highly developed ones, there will inevitably be a restoration of some sort of successor to the peasant multitudes, something to fill the vacuum left by the people, an agricultural and craftsman class (naturally with a new, but decentralized, technology). But what about us; can the "operatic" peasant return no more?

But then the intelligentsia doesn't exist either, does it? Are the smatterers dead wood for development?

Have *all* the classes been replaced by inferior substitutes? And if so how can we develop?

But surely *someone* exists? And how can one deny human beings a future? Can *human beings* be prevented from going on living? We hear their weary, kindly voices sometimes without even seeing their faces—as they pass by us somewhere in the twilight, we hear them talking of their everyday concerns, which they express in authentic—and sometimes still very spontaneous—Russian speech, we catch sight of their faces, alive and eager, and their smiles, we experience their good deeds for ourselves, sometimes when we least expect them, we observe self-sacrificing families with children undergoing all kinds of hardships rather than destroy a soul—so how can one deny them all a future?

It is rashness to conclude that the people no longer exists. Yes, the village has been routed and its remnants choked, yes, the outlying suburbs are filled with the click of dominoes (one of the achievements of universal literacy) and broken bottles, there are no traditional costumes and no folk dances, the language has been corrupted and thoughts and ambitions even more deformed and misdirected; but why is it that not even these broken bottles, nor the litter blown back and forth by the wind in city courtyards, fills one with such despair as the careerist hypocrisy of the smatterers? It is because *the people* on the whole *takes no part in the official lie,* and this today is its most distinctive feature, allowing one to hope that it is not, as its accusers would have it, utterly devoid of God. Or at any rate, it has preserved a spot in its heart that has still not been scorched or trampled to death.

It is also rashness to conclude that there is no intelligentsia. Each one of us is personally acquainted with at least a handful of people who have resolutely risen above both the lie and the pointless bustle of the smatterers. And I am entirely in accord with those who want to see, who want to believe that they can already see the *nucleus of an intelligentsia,* which is our hope for spiritual renewal. Only I would recognize and distinguish this nucleus by other signs: not by the academic qualifications of its members, nor the number of books they have published, nor by the high educational level of those who "are accustomed to think and fond of thinking, but not of plowing the land," nor by the scientific cleverness of a methodology which so easily creates "professional subcultures," nor by a sense of alienation from state and people, nor by membership in a spiritual diaspora ("nowhere quite at home"). I would recognize this nucleus by the purity of its aspirations, by its spiritual selflessness in the name of truth, and above all for the sake of *this* country, in which it lives. This nucleus will have been brought up not so much in libraries as on spiritual sufferings. It is not the nucleus that wishes to be regarded as a nucleus without having to forego the comforts of life enjoyed by the Moscow smatterers. Dostoyevsky dreamed in 1877 of the appearance in Russia of a generation of "modest and valiant young people." But on *that* occasion it was the "demons" ("the possessed") who appeared—and we can see where that got us. I can testify, however, that during the last few years I have seen these modest and valiant young people with my own eyes, heard them with my own ears; it was they who, like an invisible film, kept me floating in air over a seeming void and prevented me from falling. Not all of them are still at liberty today, and not all of them will preserve their freedom tomorrow. And far from all of them are evident to our eyes and ears—like spring streams they trickle somewhere beneath the dense, gray, hard-packed snow.

It is the method that is at fault: to reason along the lines of "social strata" and accept no other basis. If you take social strata you will end in despair (as did Amalrik).[5] The intelligentsia as a vast *social stratum* has ended its days in a steaming swamp and can no longer become airborne again. But even in the intelligentsia's former and better times, it was incorrect to include people in the intelligentsia in terms of whole families, clans, groups and strata. There might well have been particular families, clans, groups and strata that were intelligentsia through and through, but even so it is as an individual that a man becomes a member of the intelligentsia in the true sense of the word. If the intelligentsia was a stratum at all, it was a psychological, not a social, one; consequently entrance and exit always depended upon individual conduct, not upon one's occupation or social standing.

A stratum, a people, the masses, the smatterers—they all consist of *human beings,* and there is no way in which the future can be closed to human beings: human beings determine their future themselves, and whatever point has been reached on the crooked, descending path, it is never too late to take a turn for the good and the better.

The future is indestructible, and it is in our hands. If we make the right choices.

—

People will laugh at us from outside: what a timid and what a modest step we regard as *sacrifice.* All over the world students are occupying universities, going out into the streets and even toppling governments, while our students are the tamest in the world: tell them it's time for a political education lecture, refuse to let them take their coats out of the cloak room, and nobody will leave. In 1962 the whole of Novocherkassk was in tumult,* but at the Polytechnic Institute they simply locked the door of

---

* Following price increases in retail goods such as meat and poultry, steelworkers in

361

the students' quarters and nobody jumped out the windows! Or take the starving Indians, who liberated themselves from British domination by nonviolent, passive resistance and civil disobedience: but we are incapable of even this desperate bravery, neither the working class nor the smatterers, for we have been terrorized for three generations ahead by dear old Uncle Joe: how can you *not carry out* an order of the authorities? That would be the ultimate in self-destruction.

And if we set out in capital letters the nature of the examination we are going to set our fellowmen: DO NOT LIE! DO NOT TAKE PART IN THE LIE! DO NOT SUPPORT THE LIE!—it is not only the Europeans who are going to laugh at us, but also the Arab students and the ricksha-drivers in Ceylon: is this all that is being asked of the Russians? And they call that a *sacrifice,* a bold step, and not simply the mark that distinguishes an honest man from a rogue?

But it is all very well for the apples in another barrel to laugh: those being crushed in ours know that it is indeed a bold step. Because in our country the daily lie is not the whim of corrupt natures but a mode of existence, a condition of the daily welfare of every man. In our country the lie has been incorporated into the state system as the vital link holding everything together, with billions of tiny fasteners, several dozen to each man.

This is precisely why we find life so oppressive. But it is also precisely why we should find it natural to straighten up. When oppression is not accompanied by the lie, liberation demands political measures. But when the lie has fastened its claws in us, it is no longer a matter of politics! It is an invasion of man's moral world, and our straightening up and *refusing to lie* is also not political, but simply the retrieval of our human dignity.

Which is the *sacrifice?* To go for years without truly breathing, gulping down stench? Or to begin to breathe, as is the prerogative of every man on this earth? What cynic would venture to object aloud to such a policy as *nonparticipation in the lie?*

Oh, people will object at once and with ingenuity: what *is* a lie? Who can determine precisely where the lie ends and truth begins? In every

---

a factory in the northern Caucasus city of Novocherkassk went on strike on June 1. Marches and demonstrations followed the next day, the crowd reaching nearly 10,000 as it reached Lenin square in the city. Twenty-three people were killed and eighty-seven more wounded as the Red Army put down the uprising.

historically concrete dialectical situation, and so on—all the evasions that liars have been using for the past half century.

But the answer could not be simpler: decide *yourself,* as *your* conscience dictates. And for a long time this will suffice. Depending upon his horizons, his life experience and his education, each person will have his own perception of the line where the public and state lie begins: one will see it as being altogether remote from him, while another will experience it as a rope already cutting into his neck. And *there,* at the point where *you yourself* in all honesty see the borderline of the lie, is where you must refuse to submit to that lie. You must shun *that part* of the lie that is clear and obvious to you. And if you sincerely cannot see the lie anywhere at all, then go on quietly living as you did before.

What does it mean, *not to lie?* It doesn't mean going around preaching the truth at the top of your voice (perish the thought!). It doesn't even mean muttering what you think in an undertone. It simply means: *not saying what you don't think,* and that includes not whispering, not opening your mouth, not raising your hand, not casting your vote, not feigning a smile, not lending your presence, not standing up, and not cheering.

We all work in different fields and move in different walks of life. Those who work in the humanities and all who are studying find themselves much more profoundly and inextricably involved in lying and participating in the lie—they are fenced about by layer after layer of lies. In the technical sciences it can be more ingeniously avoided, but even so one cannot escape daily entering some door, attending some meeting, putting one's signature to something or undertaking some obligation which is a cowardly submission to the lie. The lie surrounds us at work, on our way to work, in our leisure pursuits—in everything we see, hear, and read.

And just as varied as the forms of the lie are the forms of rejecting it. Whoever steels his heart and opens his eyes to the tentacles of the lie will in each situation, every day and every hour, realize what he must do.

Jan Palach burned himself to death.* That was an extreme sacrifice. Had it not been an isolated case it would have roused Czechoslovakia to action. As an isolated case it will simply go down in history. But not so

* On January 16, 1969, Palach, a student at Charles University, committed suicide through self-immolation in Wenceslas Square to protest the Soviet invasion of Czechoslovakia in August of 1968.

much is demanded of everyone—of you and me. Nor do we have to go out and face the flamethrowers breaking up demonstrations. All we have to do is *breathe*. All we have to do is not lie.

And nobody need be "first," because there are already many hundreds of "firsts," it is only because of their quietness that we do not notice them (especially those suffering for their religion, and it is fitting that they work as cleaners and caretakers). I can point to several dozen people from the very nucleus of the intelligentsia who have been living this way for a long time, for *years!* And they are still alive. And their families haven't died out. And they still have a roof over their heads. And food on the table.

Yes, it is a terrible thought! In the beginning the holes in the filter are so narrow, so very narrow: can a person with so many needs really squeeze through such a narrow opening? Let me reassure him: it is only that way at the entrance, at the very beginning. Very soon, not far along, the holes slacken and relax their grip, and eventually cease to grip you altogether. Yes, of course! It will cost you canceled dissertations, annulled degrees, demotions, dismissals, expulsions, sometimes even deportations. But you will not be cast into flames. Or crushed by a tank. And you will still have food and shelter.

This path is the safest and most accessible of all the paths open to us for the average man in the street. But it is also the most effective! Only we, knowing our system, can imagine what will happen when thousands and tens of thousands of people take this path—how our country will be purified and transformed without shots or bloodshed.

But this path is also the most moral: we shall be commencing this liberation and purification with *our own souls*. Before we purify the country we shall have purified ourselves. And this is the only correct historical order: for what is the good of purifying our country's air if we ourselves remain dirty?

People will say: how unfair on the young! After all, if you don't utter the obligatory lie at your social science exam, you'll be failed and expelled from your institute, and your education and life will be disrupted.

One of the articles in the present collection discusses the problem of whether we have correctly assessed the best directions to take in science and are doing what is necessary to follow them. Be that as it may, educational damage is not the greatest damage one can suffer in life. Damage to the soul and corruption of the soul, to which we carelessly assent from our earliest years, are far more irreparable.

Unfair on the young? But whose is the future if not theirs? Who do we expect to form the sacrificial elite? For whose sake do we agonize over the future? We are already old. If they themselves do not build an honest society, they will never see it at all.

21

Aleksandr Solzhenitsyn
and European "Leftism"
(1976)

RAYMOND ARON

S ome time ago I read three articles in the *Nouvel Observateur* in which Jean-Paul Sartre gave what seemed to be a self-portrait in the form of answers to questions put by his friend Contat; I also read, more or less simultaneously, Solzhenitsyn's *The Oak and the Calf.* In the book Solzhenitsyn refers to an encounter, which in the event did not take place, between the greatest contemporary Russian writer and the man whom he calls the "ruler of minds" in the West. I trust the reader will forgive me for reproducing Solzhenitsyn's account of this episode word for word:

> Six months later the man whose canvassing obtained the prize for Sholokhov[*] (and inflicted the most hurtful insult imaginable on Russian literature)—Jean Paul Sartre—was in Moscow, and through his interpreter expressed a wish to see me. I met the interpreter on Mayakovsky Square, and she told me that "the Sartres were expecting me to dine with them at the Peking Hotel." At first sight it might seem well worth my while to meet Sartre: here was a "master of men's minds" in France and throughout Europe, an independent writer with a worldwide reputation. There was no reason why we should not be sitting together around a table in ten minutes' time: I could complain about all the things that had been

---

[*] Mikhail Sholokhov, winner of the Nobel Prize for Literature in 1965 and author of *And Quiet Flows the Don*, was an ardent supporter of the Soviet regime.

done to me, and this wandering minstrel of humanism would alert all Europe. If only it had been someone other than Sartre. Sartre needed me partly to satisfy his curiosity, partly so that he would have the right later on to talk about our meeting, perhaps to criticize me—and I would have no means of defending myself. I said to the interpreter: "What's the good of two writers meeting if one of them is gagged and has his hands tied behind his back?"

"Aren't you interested in meeting him?"

"It would be unbearably painful. My head is barely above water. Let him help us to get published first."

I drew an analogy between Russian literature and the deformed boy in *Cancer Ward*. It seemed to me just as twisted and one-sided when viewed from Europe. The undeveloped potential of our great literature has remained completely unrecognized there.

I wonder whether Sartre discerned in my refusal the depth of our aversion to him?[1]

For an answer to this question we have only to open Simone de Beauvoir's latest book. Lena reports to the "Sartres" that Solzhenitsyn does not wish to meet them. "Why not?" asks Simone de Beauvoir. Solzhenitsyn had not made himself clear. And she adds: "We are surprised at his reaction. There can be no doubt that Sartre knew him better than he knew Sartre."

Which of them knew the other better? Sartre, who leads the life of a student loafer in Paris, drifting from café to café, and who travels the world unhindered and esteemed? Or Solzhenitsyn, hounded by the police, after years in camp, years of exile? The one has at his disposal all the information which press and radio deliver to Western homes. The other used to be hard pressed to hear the broadcasts of the BBC or Voice of America. In Moscow Solzhenitsyn saw in Sartre, who was a guest of the Writers' Union, the accomplice of his persecutors. When Solzhenitsyn reached Switzerland it may well be that he became, in Sartre's eyes, an ally of the hated enemy. Beyond their mutual noncomprehension we can discern two quite alien worlds, the world of the Russian dissident and the world of the "European Leftist."

A Western writer who is officially received by an authoritarian or totalitarian regime finds himself in an awkward position—a fact of which he cannot but be aware if he has the slightest intelligence and capacity for self-criticism. I for my part have never been disconcerted by this. In Moscow I took part in a congress organized by UNESCO where in the course of the sessions, and to the considerable delight of the younger Soviet delegates, I several times clashed with an old Stalinist, the vice-president of the Academy of Sciences. In Spain I consistently refused to lecture whenever my hosts demanded to see a synopsis of my speech in advance. Incidentally, in my conversations with Spanish intellectuals and with bank officials too I more than once ran up against the Marxist "Vulgate." The higher the positions which these dissidents occupied in the present system, the more radical their views tended to be. In Mexico my main discussions were with intellectuals sympathetic to Fidel Castro but who conformed to the regime in their country. When I went to Brazil, President Goulart had not yet been overthrown by the military. It was in my journalistic capacity that I traveled to Cuba: I was not received by Fidel Castro, but had a long talk with Rafael Carlos Rodriguez, Head of the Cuban Communist Party, who explained to me in Marxist Spanish how a proletarian revolution could have been brought about by members of the petty bourgeoisie.

Sartre and Simone de Beauvoir enjoyed privileges of quite a different order. Their fame has allowed them to pass the frontiers even of countries ruled by rightist military regimes. In Cuba they were able to approach that historic hero who was to remain friendly towards Sartre as long as he sang the praises of Castroism and remained ignorant of the fate of the dissidents (already present in their thousands in Cuban prisons at the time he made friends with Castro). The day that Sartre signed a document in support of an imprisoned Cuban writer (who, incidentally, was set free after acknowledging the error of his way, if my memory serves me well), the Supremo thundered out against these petty bourgeois and their scrupulous consciences. The Sartres lost interest in Cuba and the Cubans.

The Sartres really do have something of a gay-Parisian background: they are litterateurs first and foremost and for them their works are just as important as people are. Sometimes they bring off the difficult trick—he despite his genius, she despite her education and intelligence—of seeming simple-minded. How can Simone de Beauvoir possibly fail to understand Solzhenitsyn's rebuff? How can she possibly fail to envisage the anger or hilarity with which Soviet dissidents greet a statement such as the following, from *The Critique of Dialectical Reason:* "Marxism is the unsurpassable philosophy of our era"? A statement, by the way, which one could not but describe as plain stupid if it stemmed from the pen of a lesser figure than Jean-Paul Sartre. A more temperate Western author might perhaps have said that Marxism remains at the center of philosophical inquiry, while Solzhenitsyn calmly writes that "Marxism has fallen so low that it can now arouse only contempt. No one in our country who wishes to be taken seriously, not even a schoolboy, can talk about Marxism today without a smile."

Marxism (and Solzhenitsyn is not interested in distinguishing between Marxism and Marxism-Leninism, between ordinary Marxism and subtle Marxism) is quite simply the doctrine in whose name the Bolsheviks seized power, destroyed first political parties, then the peasantry, set up concentration camps and murdered millions upon millions of ordinary citizens. More than this: in Solzhenitsyn's eyes Marxism as an ideology is the root of all ill, the source of falsehood, the principle of evil:

> Fortunately, it is in the nature of the human being to seek a *justification* for his actions.
>
> Macbeth's self-justifications were feeble—and his conscience devoured him. Yes even Iago was a little lamb too. The imagination and spiritual strength of Shakespeare's evildoers stopped short at a dozen corpses. Because they had no *ideology*.
>
> Ideology—that is what gives evildoing its long-sought justification and gives the evildoer the necessary steadfastness and determination. That is the social theory which helps to make his acts seem good instead of bad in his own and others' eyes, so that he won't hear reproaches and curses, but will receive praise and honors. That was how the agents of the Inquisition fortified their wills: by invoking Christianity; the conquerors of foreign lands, by extolling the grandeur of their Motherland; the colonizers, by civilization; the Nazis, by race; the Jacobins (early and late), by equality, brotherhood, and the happiness of future generations.
>
> Thanks to *ideology* the twentieth century was fated to experience evildoing on a scale calculated in the millions?[2]

I have chosen this passage from *The Gulag Archipelago* for two reasons. Firstly because it goes to the very heart of the question, to the ideology which alone can give the criminal a clear conscience. In addition it mentions other doctrines besides Marxism—those of Hitler, of the colonists, of the nationalists. Nor does Solzhenitsyn, a Christian himself, forget that Christianity can serve to bolster up the inquisitors. He tends to afford Marxists, if not Marxism itself, a special place, rather as if the quantitative difference brought with it a corresponding modification in quality (he will, I trust, forgive this reference to one of the laws of Engels' and Hegel's dialectic). During the eighty years preceding the Revolution of 1917 there were seventeen executions a year. When the Spanish Inquisition was in full swing the figure was ten per month. In the first years of Bolshevik rule it ran at one thousand a month. At the height of Stalin's Terror the monthly total of executions reached forty thousand. Evil needs an ideology before it can operate in millions. And this need is all the more urgent if the Terror is to remain unrecognized or even acclaimed. But the Sartres, more than other Western writers, justify Evil by justifying the justification of it. They are not Marxists—they have no wish to give up any of *their* freedom, but by philosophical means they justify other men's deprivation of liberty at the hands of totalitarianism and terror. Sartre is the philosopher of ideological thinking.

I do not wish to trace Sartre's political and philosophical career, beginning with *Nausea* in which he makes of the humanist a figure of fun, through to his dialogues with Left extremists. Favorably disposed towards the Munich agreement* before 1938 because of his pacifism, after the liberation he adopted positions which can be reconciled only with the greatest difficulty. Among this long series of attitudes, however, certain postulates and maxims are to be found which one would be inclined to ascribe to a somewhat degenerate practical sense. The most important ones are: that anti-Communists are blackguards; that the only people who have the right to criticize Communism are those who become involved in the movement; that it is impossible not to be a Marxist since Marxism sets its indelible stamp upon our age. These postulates have consequences which Sartre has strictly observed. At a time when people in the West were discussing the fact that there were concentration camps in the Soviet

---

* The Munich agreement was the settlement reached on September 30, 1938, by Germany, Great Britain, France and Italy that permitted the German annexation of the Sudetenland in western Czechoslovakia.

Union, he directed his anger not so much against the Soviet authorities who had established these camps, nor against the Communists who had denied their existence, but against the anti-Communists and the so-called Rightists who were suspected of rejoicing in the fact.

At no time did the philosopher of peace stand closer to the Communists than in the period of the peace movement, in other words in the Stalin era. Indefatigable defender of the persecuted, so long as their hangmen did not appeal to Marx or other acceptable doctrines, actively, passionately interceding for the release of Henry Martin* (does anyone still remember that sailor?), or against the execution of the Rosenbergs,† he belonged to the front organizations along with Communists and fellow-travelers, and without any perceptible conflict with his conscience. In a word, he provides the perfect example of that Western "Leftism" which Solzhenitsyn repeatedly pillories in his book. "Leftism" is, so to speak, the elaboration of the principle according to which everything is measured by two different scales. It matters little what a man of the Right actually says, his views will be rejected in advance. If he mentions Soviet concentration camps, then it is not because he loves freedom and loathes the repression of one man by his fellows, but because for reasons which he cannot admit he has chosen the camp of the "Rightists" (or the conservatives, or the reactionaries); he is looking for reasons which he *can* own to for a choice to which he cannot own. A Rightist, authoritarian, or moderate regime without any concentration camps must be condemned by the same token, and more fiercely than a Soviet regime which bears the responsibility for tens of millions of deaths within the space of sixty years.

Nor does it help to appeal to those texts in which Sartre at long last comes to grips with Stalinism. After the suppression of the Hungarian revolution he wrote *The Ghost of Stalin,* but without expressing the slightest regret for his former views and activities. Nor did he question the fundamentals of "Leftism," for this bloody monster was once again none other than Socialism. In other words he disavowed neither his "Leftism"

---

* Henry Martin was a French Communist who was arrested for sabotage during the French war in Indochina. Sartre joined a defense committee for Martin and in 1953 published a book called *The Henry Martin Affair.*

† Julius and Ethel Rosenberg were American Communists who were executed in 1953 for conspiracy to commit espionage.

nor his affiliation with the Communists. Nor did he come any nearer to doing so in his *Socialism That Came in from the Cold:* in between the lines he foisted the blame for "inhuman socialism" upon the Russian influence, upon fortuitous factors. The Czechs' humane socialism lay in the camp of the Left and of Marxism. The ideology was intact.

The Critique of Dialectical Reason lends itself both to a Marxist-Leninist and a Leftist *(gauchiste)* interpretation. According to Maurice Merleau-Ponty* ultra-Bolshevism expresses itself in a breakdown, in a revolt, in action, but doubts remain. Is it really the Party which with its merciless discipline *(fraternité-terreur)* takes it upon itself to wrench men locked in "practico-inertia" out of this state? Or is it rather the spontaneity of the group symbolized by the masses in the exalted days of Revolution, the fusion of the individual's consciousness with that of the others, which furnishes the model for the future society, for the truly liberated consciousness, transparent to all? Whatever the answer may turn out to be, Leftism remains, remains intact and, one may say, is still gaining in intensity. Ultra-Bolshevism demands revolt or, to put it more clearly, the categorical imperative of violence.

After 1968 Sartre discovered that ultimately his philosophy was more likely to culminate in anarchy than in Sovietism. But why hesitate between the one and the other? Why justify that total power, that cruelest of powers in our century, the power which enables us to do anything at all out of revulsion at the power of the state? Marxism itself explains nothing.

Much as Sartre may have busied himself with the writings of Marx, there is barely a trace of this reading to be found. Sartre alludes to the first volume of *Capital* and the theory of surplus value, but this is grist to his mill since it seems to show that the entrepreneur exploits the employee and the capitalist the wage-earner. There are no grounds for suspecting that he is even remotely interested in the relations between Ricardo[†] and Marx or in Marx's place in the history of political economy. As for the unsurpassable philosophy of our epoch, which has incidentally been essentially sterile for more than half a century now, Sartre summarizes it in vague, indeed almost meaningless phrases, such as, "Men make their own history but on the basis of the given material conditions." Putting it differently:

---

* Maurice Merleau-Ponty. See note on page 52.

† David Ricardo (1772–1823) was a very influential English political economist to whom Marx was indebted.

it was not Marxism which brought this by nature anarchistic man to the point of sympathizing with Stalin's Terror, but, on the contrary, his inclination towards anarchy induced him to accept Marxism, which remains alien to him or of which he retains only the negations and the utopia.

What has produced the vacillation between the two extremes of anarchy and totalitarianism, what has made of Sartre a philosopher of ideology instead of a mere ideologist, is the cult of violence turned moralism, the sternness of a Protestant moralism swung round into rejection of the social order. But what is staggering is that on this long path Sartre expresses a moral condemnation of those who think differently from himself. Who accords him the right to mount the throne of Jupiter or Jehovah, to sound the hearts of men?

How, one may ask, are we to know since after all there is no possibility of distinguishing between Good and Evil, between good and evil conduct, except within history, and since after all we must wait for a social order free from exploitation and repression before we can begin to write our ethics? It is enough to call for the categorical imperative of Revolt (or even the categorical imperative of violence) and the game is won. How quickly it goes! A few thousand students occupy the Sorbonne, rebuild the University and the world from scratch, sleep with one another and talk, talk, talk. . . .

Since neither Sartre's Marxism nor his Existentialism has a clearly delineated political content, he can pass from the *Rassemblement démocratique révolutionnaire* to fraternizing with Stalinism, can admit that there are millions of labor-camp prisoners in the Soviet Union without this causing him to break with the Communists, he can condemn the suppression of the Hungarian revolution as if it were separate from the whole of that which he approves of or puts up with. He can write that the dictatorship of the proletariat is a contradictory concept while simultaneously describing himself as a Marxist, and that without his conscience experiencing the slightest trouble; and finally he can distance himself from the Communists because a few thousand students or workers have had the experience of his *groupe en fusion* and have dreamed of his anarchy. He can even muster a degree of sympathy for the left-wing extremists of the Baader-Meinhof gang,* and he who loses no sleep over millions of concen-

---

* Baader-Meinhof Gang or the Red Army Faction was a West German terrorist organization founded in 1970. Though the principals such as Andreas Baader and Ulrike Mein-

tration camp inmates, holds press-conferences to expose the misery and loneliness to which Baader and his companions are condemned (he probably does not know that Ulrike Meinhof originally received money from the East German Secret Service).

The fact that he has pilgrimaged in undiscriminating succession to Belgrade, Havana, Moscow or Peking bothers him not at all; evidently, he feels responsible for all men, but not for his previous conduct. It may be that he feels more at ease in the company of Victor[3] than of Stalin (whom he has probably never seen) or even Fidel Castro (in whom he believed he had found a friend). Nevertheless, he has not dissociated himself from his earlier positions. Here is the Right and here the Left. Here are the concentration camps which one does not accept and here the ones which one does. There are good murderers and evil ones. Marxism remains the unsurpassable philosophy of our epoch, and those who base themselves upon it are always on the right side, while those who defend freedom against the advocates of that philosophy are in the wrong.

In a certain sense Simone de Beauvoir is right in saying that Aleksandr Solzhenitsyn does not know Sartre well (although he knows him better than Sartre knows Solzhenitsyn). And yet she is wrong about the main point: if the *zek*[*] had known the "ruler of minds" better, he would have still seen no sense in talking to him. As a personality Sartre embodies everything which Solzhenitsyn loathes: the rejection of moral guidelines, the refusal to accept the age-old distinction between good and evil, the sacrifice of men's lives and the justification of crimes by appeals to an indefinite future ("indefinite" in all its senses), in short, the evil of ideology—a kind of evil which in Sartre's case takes on a pure form—indirect, delegated evil. He kills nobody; he would not hurt a fly and his only participation in history is through his pen. Now he gives Stalin his half-hearted applause, now Castro his unreserved though short-lived, greeting, but never does he condemn the practice which Solzhenitsyn finds detestable: the practice of committing crimes in the name of ideology. "Ruler of minds" in the West, Solzhenitsyn writes. Although even in his own lifetime Sartre's only place is in the past, he is still, if not the "ruler," then at least the most

---

hof were captured in 1972 and committed suicide in prison, the group continued its terrorist activity under successive generations of members in the late 1970s and 1980s.

* Zek is a Russian slang term for an inmate of the camps.

representative figure (if only in caricature) of the European intelligentsia, or of the intellectual Left, whichever description is preferable. It matters little that nowadays few of them still read *Being and Nothingness* or *The Critique of Dialectical Reason,* or that Foucault, Deleuze or Althusser* have supplanted him; he is the one who more than any other has made "Leftism" respectable, indeed obligatory. To a Solzhenitsyn and to other Soviet dissidents none of the Rightist authoritarian regimes, neither the Greek military junta nor Franco† in Spain, seemed comparable with the tyranny which weighs upon the peoples of the Soviet Union. Not one of them has perpetrated so many crimes; not one has so enslaved free thought. But the Sartres and all their disciples forbid us to condemn the Soviet Union unless we first embrace Leftism and join the Socialist movement.

What would have come of a dialogue between Solzhenitsyn and Sartre? Nothing. Each of them would have rejected any comparison of respective number of victims under one form of despotism or another, albeit for quite different reasons: Sartre—because under certain kinds of despotism men were ostensibly liberated, whereas under others hereditary injustice and disorder were upheld; Solzhenitsyn—because, over and above the number of victims, the Soviet regime seems of its very nature perverse, for it lies and compels others to lie. The Greek Colonels "saved" Greece; Franco "saved" Christian Spain; neither of them created a world of mandatory falsehood. In Spain censorship was called censorship, not "the leading role of the Party." In the universities and in the streets everyone could speak his own language; all books, or nearly all, could be translated and published. The regime, born in a brutal revolution, remained brutal till the end; it was neither democratic, nor liberal; but it was not totalitarian, and crimes there were not sanctified by ideology.

Compared with Stalin's regime, that of Franco may justly have been regarded as liberal. A pious man of the Left holds such a view to be scandalous and monstrous. Solzhenitsyn holds it to be true and evident. It takes the whole "Leftism" of the Western intelligentsia to doubt it.

---

* Michel Foucault (1926–1984), Gilles Deleuze (1925–1995), and Louis Althusser (1918–1990) were prominent French philosophers in the latter half of the twentieth century.

† Franco. See note on page 249.

My friend Manès Sperber* joined the Communist Party in Vienna after the First World War. Had I, like him, witnessed the collapse of a world, I might perhaps have succumbed to the same temptation. But never since the day in the mid-thirties when I first met him in Andre Malraux's home have I seen his disillusionment cloud the sobriety of his judgment. We have not always agreed in our assessment of this or that event; no one can claim the truth for his own. If the past can of its very nature be subjected to legitimate reinterpretation, how then can history as it evolves and shapes itself in the present lend itself to unerring diagnosis?

Our friendship has survived forty years without a setback; this is due not only to the fact that he broke with a revolution betrayed, with a totalitarian regime, with an ideology which henceforth served to justify the unjustifiable, but also to the fact that his view of the Marxist tragedy coincided both with my own instinctive liberalism and with the faith of the Soviet dissidents.

Solzhenitsyn's message can be summarized, it seems to me, in two fundamental sentences: there is something worse than poverty and repression—and that something is the Lie; the lesson this century teaches us is to recognize the deadly snare of ideology, the illusion that men and social organizations can be transformed at a stroke.

Solzhenitsyn does not call for a crusade against Soviet totalitarianism; he does not wish upon his country a revolution which could cause chaos and bring bloodshed. The writer, his country's greatest and perhaps the greatest of our time, takes, and will continue to take, offense at the conspiracy of unrepentant ideologues which more than ever dominates the press, radio and television of the West. But he will gather about him in a vast silent mass all those who see no other defense against the raging of fanaticism and who have no other hope for the future than in respect for moral laws and the rejection of ideological knavery. He had nothing to say to Sartre and his like; in Manès Sperber he encountered a brother.

---

* Manès Sperber (1905–1984) was a prominent ex-Communist, much like Arthur Koestler, whose anti-Communist autobiographical writings and essays were influential during the Cold War. His three-volume memoir, *All Our Yesterdays,* was published between 1974 and 1977.

22

A Treatise on Ticks*
(1979)

PIOTR WIERZBICKI

DEFINITION OF THE TICK

Ticks are something between the new masters of Poland and opposition activists, like the majority of the Polish nation, forced into at least passive participation in the socialist-Soviet Vistula spectacular. Is a tick therefore simply a gray citizen of Poland? Is a peasant a tick if he thinks that things were better in Bierut's** time, or a worker if he commits himself to labor emulation, or a clerk sent out with a banner into the streets of Warsaw to welcome the beloved leader of the land of the Soviets? Is everyone a tick who bows down obsequiously to the new masters? No, if tickery were simply a synonym for submissiveness, there would be nothing to discuss. Submissiveness is a banal phenomenon, existing in all places and as old as the world. Tickery is something rather special. It is, a phenomenon characteristic not of society as a whole but only of the upper intellectual levels. We do not

---

* This and the following essay by Michnik were first published in *Zapis*, a literary journal founded by KOR (see note on page 393).

** Bolesław Bierut became president of Poland in July 1944 after having served as Chair of the National People's Council (the Soviet-controlled alternative to the Polish Underground). After 1948 Bierut was a zealous promoter of the Sovietization of Poland and sought to stamp out any deviations from orthodox Soviet Communism. He died in Moscow in 1956 where he was to attend the 20th Congress of the Communist Party of the Soviet Union.

seek ticks among peasant-workers, booking clerks, and charwomen. We seek them among rectors of colleges, journalists, and artists. Would a rector be a tick then, if, on orders from someone in the government or Party, he found a place in his college for the son of some dignitary? Is a journalist, if, in fear of the censorship, he describes only half of what he sees, or an artist if, for pay, he paints a certain head with a pointed beard? No, these again are symptoms of pure submissiveness, not worth writing about. Tickery depends on something different. The tick serves his masters in a highly specific and refined manner. He serves them by the quiet work of his grey matter. A tick stands erect on his two hind legs and thinks. About what? About how to justify the idea that that which is, must be. Justification is not the strongest point of the new masters. In the task of justification, the ticks fill in for them. When a rector finds a place for some dignitary's son at the behest of someone on high, this is simply an ordinary case of bowing one's head. When a professor writes a text indicating that from ages past intellectuals have been eager for power for reasons of ambition, and publishes this precisely when the security police are holding discussions with those intellectuals, the situation is more refined. Here it is not the body but the spirit that stands up on its hind legs. Here the grey matter is put into service.

Are they then cynics, refined swindlers, out for profit? Really! A tick a cynic! If a tick were a cynic, then this sketch would have been finished long ago. If a tick had the ability to be a cynic, such a great tick ulcer would never have arisen to poison Polish culture. But the tick does not know how to be a cynic. A cynic is someone who has the courage to lie brazenly. Brazenly, but once only! A cynic does not do and say what he thinks, but he does think for himself. His words and deeds may be called deceitful, but the sphere of his thought is free from deceit. A cynic is in conflict with life. A tick is not. A tick, then, while laboring to find some justification for the various deeds of the new masters of Poland must also toil at talking himself into these deeds. The tick does violence to his own spirit.

GENEALOGY OF THE TICK

We shall leave to the historian the discovery of the forefathers of ticks in past ages. Being concerned with the present, we shall point out only their immediate ancestors. The tick directly traces his descent from the "positive non-

Party" type who inhabited Poland in Bierut's day. The "positive non-Party" type was a citizen of the People's Poland, concerned with the reconstruction of the country, supporting the general line of the Party, sympathetic to the Soviet Union, honest, active, disciplined but having in his ideological ballast small accretions of the "old," a dubious social origin, a certain intellectual way of expressing himself, a certain tendency to fall into aestheticism. Precisely as a result of this small accretion of foreign matter, the "positive non-Party" type did not belong to any militant organization. But he played a very active role in organizations of a general humanitarian character such as the Polish-Soviet Friendship Society, the League of Women, the Committee for the Defense of Peace, the Popular Front and the Polish Red Cross. The "positive non-Party" type was generally a middle-aged professor who looked with warm sympathy on the execution carried out on Polish learning by the Party, security police, and Communist youth, or a grey-haired writer of an aesthetic type who granted the Stalinist activists absolution from the uplands of Bach and Chopin, or a prewar engineer who was an enthusiast for the rationalization movement. The "positive non-Party" type was a person well-known in his own environment. He was distinguished therefore by a certain positive character; he diligently approached everyone personally when there was a meeting, and sometimes even sat on the presidium.

The positive non-Party type played rather a passive role in the class struggle then being waged in our country. He did not unmask enemies of the people; only rarely did he speak up sharply at meetings, he emphasized what was humanistic in the new system, rather than its revolutionary character. Obviously there was nothing remarkable in this. And yet it was necessary. The Stalin-Bierutite functionaries valued him and cherished him more than one of their own. Sometimes he even drove a "Demokratka."* Every union of creative artists, every academic discipline, every place of work had a very essential educational function; it showed that truly the best Poles were members of the PUWP† and employees of the security service, but that the non-Party citizen, if he so wished, could stand, perhaps not in the first but anyway in the second rank.

---

* A luxury car driven by Poland's elite.

† The Polish United Workers Party (PUWP) was created in 1948 at the onset of the Sovietization of Poland. It would remain the principal Communist organ until its dissolution in 1990.

Types of Tick

Ticks live mostly in the capital of Poland or in some of the larger administrative centers. The biggest concentrations are in Warsaw and Krakow. Ticks congregate in the universities and in other types of institutes of higher learning, in the presidium, committees, departmental secretariats and institutes of the Polish Academy of Sciences, in the scientific institutes of individual ministries, in unions of creative artists and the press, particularly in the editorial boards of literary social weeklies or monthlies. Ticks appear among the young, the middle aged, the old, among Aryans and among Jews, Catholics, and atheists. Ticks—from a certain intellectual level upwards—appear everywhere, in every generation, in every social, racial, and ideological group. The multitude of their varieties is thus impressive.

But let us consider, first of all, the artistic tick, principally of the literary kind. It seems that there are at least three varieties:

1. *The grey-haired creative type, the humanist and aesthete.* Ticks of this variety are extremely well known and popular in society; they have received from the new masters of Poland the right to carry on in their old-fashioned, prewar, European style. In return, all that is demanded of them is that every so often they should, with an understanding smile, do homage to the socialist-Soviet crudeness flooding into Poland. Their mouths are full of Bach, Chopin, Leonardo, and Tolstoy; sometimes they sit on some presidium or other and utter beautiful speeches to suit the occasion.

2. *The young creative type, the avant-gardist.* Ticks of this kind are particularly cunning. They know that under Bierut avant-garde creative artists were treated frostily by the *crème de la crème*. And they know quite well too that today, (under Gierek*), the avant-gardist is treated warmly by the people's government, because, today, the threat for that government is not the form but the content. So let him jabber, screech, and use a

---

* Edward Gierek succeeded Władysław Gomułka as First Secretary of the Central Committee of the PUWP in 1970. Gomułka was forced out of office after he suppressed workers' strikes in the Baltic coast region. Gierek found himself facing similar strikes in 1980, but refused to use force. He was removed from power after signing an agreement with strike committees.

donkey's tail as a paintbrush—just so long as he does not describe what is actually going on in Poland. They hope, however, that the public at large will not notice this turnabout in the government's attitude to the donkey's tail. And so, dressed-up in the plumage of nonconformists, they soar on the fumes of pure form. The task assigned by their masters is exceptionally modest: not to see what is going on in Poland. And, to the best of their strength and ability, they do not see.

3. *The middle-aged creative type, the petty realist.* The masters of Poland do allow these ticks to look at the country, but subject to a certain condition, that out of it comes a twisted, trifling, old-womanish "tut-tut." The petty realist, who in his mind has chopped Poland up into tiny pieces so that the censorship can swallow it, gains from the authorities the right to work, publish, and even to criticize individual errors and shortcomings. In exchange, he supplies the reading public with proof that it is possible to write as he wishes, provided that it is done skillfully so as not to irritate the censor.

We now have to analyze how the tick reveals himself in his political attitude, in his actions and towards his environment. And here again we are struck by the considerable diversity of ticks. We can distinguish— from the point of view of political attitude—at least four varieties of tick.

1. *Party ticks.* There must be some misunderstanding here. A red tick? Not at all. The Party, although continually criticized for its dogmatism and rigidity is nevertheless at bottom extremely elastic and tolerates in its ranks some extremely atypical citizens. If then it is possible to be a member of the Party while going to church and conforming to a fideist outlook (recognizing, of course, its inferiority to Marxism-Leninism), why should it be impossible to be a member of the Party and also a tick? And, in fact, there are quite a few ticks in the Party. In the coffee house or the literary salon, the Party tick is absolutely indistinguishable from the non-Party tick. If he practices the profession of writer or journalist, he becomes increasingly absorbed with cultivating the most enlightened and humanistic traditions of socialism and fighting the most hard-headed groups within the bosom of the Party. The Party tick rails against any Party hard-liner, and, out of his experience forged by polemics against idiocy, can without fear for his reputation publish every couple of years an article justifying the necessity for successive price rises and how absolutely essential they are for further increases in the standard of living. The Party tick functions daily as if certi-

fied. He can specialize in criticism and polemics, and is not obliged to write every day about love for the Soviet Union. Once in several years, however, he behaves like a completely normal person; he receives an assignment, he fulfils obligations, he does his duty. Some Party ticks have long since become ripe for the change into non-Party ticks and remain in the Party organization only out of inertia and fear of the face which the *apparatchik* pulls when he sees returned to him forever the tickish party card which is so valuable for the organization.

2. *Ticks of the center.* These make up a definite majority of the tick population. The tick of the center (non-Party, obviously), is a loyal citizen of the country; except for certain reservations regarding the conduct of current politics, he never comes into conflict with the government; he supports that government with learned works demonstrating the incompetence of the government of prewar Poland and the growth of Fascist trends at that time by articles on the denaturalization of the consumer lifestyle in Western countries, reports of Nazi war criminals who have escaped punishment, and books on the positive changes which, in spite of errors, are taking place in our country. It is only rarely that the tick of the center receives an assignment to defend the progressive system, only at difficult moments and in drastic situations. He does not play a fundamental role in political campaigns, he does not write manifestos, he does only as much as he has to, and so, for example, if he works for a newspaper he does not on his own initiative write an attack on the workers of Radom and Ursus.* If, however, the Editor in Chief asks him to write an anonymous editorial on that subject, he does so, trying though to make the text as cultural as possible, and is very proud that, instead of the word "bandits" which someone proposed, he used only the milder designation of "hooligans" to refer to the demonstrators. The tick of the center is sure that somewhere on the political map of the country is to be found a mean between the opposition and the government, and that the stance which he adopts is the most natural, normal, and justified for an intelligent person under Polish conditions.

3. *Nonconformist ticks.* The nonconformist tick is encountered only rarely. He is a tick who has won for himself the status of a notorious and incorrigible fighter, battling against the nonsense which surrounds us on all sides. The nonconformist tick does not deliver laudatory speeches, he

---

* Radom and Ursus were the sites of major workers' strikes in 1976.

does not write propaganda, no one proposes to him that he should write some introductory article justifying some thing or other. He holds views which are honest, bold, and incorruptible. And these are his text. There is only one threshold that the nonconformist tick will not cross. He will not associate himself with any opposition activity. Provided that he does not sign protest letters or go to illegal meetings, he is allowed to act and function as public figure. In fact, not much is demanded of him. But if he wants to remain a nonconformist tick, he will have to work at it systematically, since few people are able to remain one. It is necessary to hold some trump card, for example, an unquestioned talent, or an especially influential job. Nonconformist ticks who are honest, talented, critical of the reality about them, and who do not come into conflict with the government are valuable to the latter, provided that they stay under control. From time to time a nonconformist tick actually does get out of control, signs a round-robin or a protest, and moves on into the category of enemies of the people.

4. *Ticks who are victims of oppression.* This would appear to be a contradiction in terms: a victim of oppression can surely not be tick, a victim of oppression is surely an undaunted opposition activist, prepared to make the greatest sacrifices. And yet there do exist ticks who are victims of oppression. How? Because a progressive system wages war against the enemy within in a very specific manner. In reactionary social systems the state dealt with its enemies by striking at them alone. This constitutes a serious breach of the principles of dialectics, forbidding the separation of anything or anyone from their socioeconomic base. Hence in the Soviet Union and later in People's Poland and the other socialist countries the method adopted was to deal with the enemy by striking not only at him but also at his children, great-grandmothers, aunts-in-law, neighbors, acquaintances, and anyone else who might know him, when possible, and also at those who might not know him, but who independently are enemies, or at least potential ones. Ninety-nine point something or other percent of the tens of millions of inhabitants of the Gulag Archipelago are people who never themselves raised a hand against the land of the Soviets. In People's Poland this phenomenon occurred on a scale that was incomparably smaller but sufficient, with the additional refinement that there were to be found in prison or simply on the pavement a few random individuals who not only were not enemies of the people (or who fought

against the Germans in the Home Army*), but, on the contrary, intended merely to honor that people or to offer it support with advice and a timely word, or even had already begun to support it, but of course it is impossible to check this. Thus we come to the position that certain actual or potential ticks did become victims of oppression. In 1956, the ticks came out of prison, were rehabilitated, and began their great careers as ticks. They ran like the wind into collaboration with their masters. Forthwith, too, they began to lead the way in sycophancy, sycophantic intrigue, and semideviationist pretence at opposition. Their busy goings on would have been suspect to anyone who drew a distinction between liberal-humanist slogans and the moral and political content of concrete actions. But their goings on were not suspect to everyone. For they had their past of suffering. They were victims of oppression. They had passed their practical examination with flying colors. No one reminded these martyrs why they had been persecuted. Human memory is short. He was in prison, therefore he is a hero.

In fact, there was not such a great number of ticks who went to prison by chance. But is prison necessary for a tick to parade in the plumage of a martyr? All he needs is a far milder form of persecution, such as dismissal from work, demotion, no promotion, censorship of a "sharp" article, suspension of the publication of a novel. A progressive system creates unlimited possibilities for this type of persecution. In a country where one's job, pension, and possibilities of promotion are partially decided by one's moral-political stance (i.e., degree of submission to the authorities) there is no constant and rational criterion for evaluating performance, and it can be very easy to lose your position without having first made some mistake, without having first taken some risk, but by the purest chance, just because someone higher up has lost his job (likewise by chance). The tick who has been sacked assumes the plumage of a martyr and becomes sacrosanct. In a country in which the First Secretary of the Party is subject to censorship, in which everyone and everything is subject to censorship, if someone writes an article or story, he has to deal with the censorship, even if he only writes about Lenin, humanism, and peace. Sooner or later

---

* The Home Army was formed in February 1942 to fight the Nazis in German-occupied Poland and was the principle organizer of the famous Warsaw Uprising in the fall of 1944. It was loyal to the Polish government-in-exile in London.

he will make a mistake and, for example, use a name which has been anathema since yesterday, or, conversely, forget something which became obligatory from today. No one in Poland has yet puzzled out every intention of the censorship. The fact that the censorship stops something is evidence of absolutely nothing and, in particular, is not evidence that this was a "sharp" text. It is by no means impossible that, quite on the contrary, it was not that it was too "sharp," but, for example, too anti-American, just at a moment when the Polish People's Republic is seeking a new hand-out of dollars from the USA. Obviously the tick counts on the fact that the public does not know how the censorship works and wears his confiscation like a wound from a famous victory.

MECHANISM OF FORMATION OF THE TICK

A citizen of the Polish People's Republic, we may say, is not born a tick. At some period in his life, some process takes place in him or there appears in him some tickogenic element. There are various ways of turning into a tick. We have been able to identify and distinguish four.

1. *Bad social origin.* A progressive system is so perfect and so morally elevated that it constantly produces complexes in people. In Bierut's time, one such very typical complex was the social origin complex. The social origin of highest renown in People's Poland is obviously a working class origin. In second place comes a peasant origin, and here it is preferable to be the child of a poor peasant than a rich one (in Bierut's time, this was applied with greater consequence than today: the children of poor peasants were made much of, the children of middle peasants less so, while the brood of kulaks, owning farms of say, fifteen hectares, could not even dream of getting a place in higher education). In third place comes intellectual origin (here in Bierut's time two possibilities were distinguished, the "work-log intelligentsia," a more positive group, and the "intelligentsia", a decidedly suspect group). In fourth place, came "private enterprise" origin, which was obviously fatal. And what then? A great big gap, and then came the worst thing under the sun: origin among the prewar landowners, aristocrats, and factory owners. If—speaking about Bierut's time—it was difficult to be the child of parents owning more than two cows, how was one to bear the burden of being the child of a banker, a

squire, an aristocrat, in short, of an exploiter and enemy of the people who in collusion with foreign capital had pushed Poland towards the calamitous precipice of September 1939? For some people this was past endurance. They created for themselves, against the background of their inappropriate social origin, a guilt complex and made an all out effort somehow to wipe out their guilt and to beseech the favor of the people's government. A Party career was closed to them, but the career of a tick lay open. And they became ticks. A count for hire; a positive count is an important sociological element for present-day Poland. He is living proof of the humanitarian tolerance of the proletarian avant-garde which, rather than breaking his bones, cossets him, and also of the patriotic unity of all Poles, concentrated, in spite of the differences which divide them, around the Party and its leaders.

2. *The desire to be someone.* This is at once the most universal and most banal tickogenic mechanism. In a country where to become not only a director but even some subordinate boss or department head, it is desirable and usually obligatory to belong to the PUWP, the road to a career and a life of success lies open only to those who rule and those who toady to them. If one is not very gifted or indispensable as an engineer, mathematician, physicist, chemist, astronomer, etc., then to carve out a career for oneself one must either join the Party or become a tick. Some jobs are simply closed to other citizens. For example, that of journalist. In a progressive system a journalist is not just an expert in transmitting and commenting on information; he is a "worker on the ideological front," a petty clerk with the task of carrying out propaganda instructions. A journalist in People's Poland has the responsibility of defending and praising the current team of the PUWP to the last hour it holds office, even if (as in December 1970[*]) it sends out machine guns against the workers, and then to criticize it and thunder without mercy the instant that it has been ousted by another PUWP team. Only Party members and ticks are fit for this task.

3. *Total loyalty.* A celebrated Polish composer found himself one day (during the 1970s) among a group of his fellow musicians in the presence of one of the deputy ministers of culture and art. During the course of a discussion on the problems of music, someone drew the attention of the Deputy Minister to the fact that there were two gifted Polish compos-

---

[*] In December of 1970 the first great workers' strikes took place on the Baltic coast in the shipyards of Gdańsk.

ers living abroad, Andrzej Panufnik and Roman Palester, and that it was many years since their music had been performed on Polish platforms. The Deputy Minister replied: "I don't see any objections: if you want to play them, then play them!" At this the celebrated Polish composer burst out: "But, Mr. Minister, haven't you seen the anti-Soviet implication on the sleeve of the Panufnik record?" (he meant the composition dedicated to the memory of the victims of Katýn*). The Minister had not seen it, he was put out of countenance and said that since the musicians themselves had reservations concerning the matter, he did not want to have to deal with it. Thus the question of the blocking of Panufnik and Palester was deferred for a certain time. The question now arises: what did the celebrated composer achieve by making this denunciation of his émigré colleague? We would propose the hypothesis: loyalty. The celebrated composer, winner of a state prize, esteemed by ministers and deputy ministers, constantly able to travel abroad, simply does not know how to behave disloyally. If one Minister let him travel abroad, if a second pays him compliments, a third gives him a prize, if the Party accepts his slightly suspect aesthetics, how can he have the right to behave as a Judas? No, from the Deputy Minister who favored him with his trust he could not hide anything. The Deputy Minister was quite ready to agree to Panufnik, because he obviously had not seen this anti-Soviet sleeve. If the celebrated composer did not have the duty of informing the Minister, then who did? Obviously he had a moral duty. The total loyalist wants to be in good standing with everyone. And since the thing which surrounds every citizen of the Polish People's Republic the most closely and tightly on all sides is the government, the loyalist, wanting to be in good standing with everyone, is loyal first and foremost to the government. There is not, in fact, too great a number of total loyalists in Poland.

4. *The truth lies somewhere in between.* There exists, as indeed is all too well known, a type of character and intellect trained to the formula "the truth lies somewhere in between." These are the compromisers, the people

---

* The victims of Katýn were the nearly 22,000 Poles (mostly military and police officers) murdered by the Soviet NKVD during April and May of 1940. The bodies of the victims were tossed into large graves in the Katýn forest near the city of Smolensk in Western Russia. The execution of these Poles was a closely guarded secret in Soviet circles and for many years the Soviet government blamed the massacre on the Nazis.

who never clearly commit themselves to any one side because they have a soft character and intellect. In any situation they have a simply infinite battery of arguments for and against. They are of the opinion that the government in Poland is bad, but there are certain positive features, that in Sweden the government is better, but . . . that dependence on Russia is a very bad thing but, on the other hand, however. . . . Ticks of the "truth lies somewhere in between" type perhaps lack the essential quality of the tick: they do not have to do much work on themselves to become muddle-headed; they already are muddle-headed, they get their heads at birth already infected with compromise and halfway-itis. There are grounds for assuming that if the system changed, these "ticks by birth" would behave in the new anti-Communist system just as they do today, namely, with reserve and hesitation, while all the other ticks would obviously immediately don the plumage of indefatigable anti-Communists. Ticks from birth, less hypocritical than the rest, nevertheless fulfill the same tickish function and are, moreover, fairly numerous, especially in university circles.

LIFE OF THE TICK IN SOCIETY

The tick is a citizen who is active professionally. Just active? Unusually active, committed, even a fighter. Against whom does the tick fight? Surely against the dictator Somoza,* the revisionist Strauss, the hawk Brzezinski.† Stop, don't show that we know nothing about ticks. They fight against symptoms of evil appearing not somewhere abroad but here in Poland. The tick, generally speaking, cannot come to terms with the fact that roses still do not grow everywhere around the prisons and jails. So the tick fights for flower beds and herbaceous borders. He dedicates his working life to this cause. He speaks out and writes articles and letters to the

---

* The Samoza family ruled Nicaragua by military dictatorship for most of the latter half of the twentieth century before being overthrown by the Sandinista National Liberation Front in 1979.

† Zbigniew Brzezinski, scholar and United States government official, born in Poland, worked with Carl Friedrich to develop the concept of totalitarianism in the 1950s. He later became extensively involved in foreign policy and politics in the United States. He served as National Security Adviser to President Jimmy Carter.

editor. Just pick up the annual index for any newspaper from 1956, 1968, 1970 and 1976.* There we can see numerous ticks in action. One devotes a series of articles to an incompetently restored apartment house in Gdańsk, a second rages about the neglected grave of some poet, a third considers that it would be possible to build a funfair in Radom, a fourth states that he will not rest until they repaint the fence of the children's playground at Ursus, a fifth is of the opinion that sugar coupons could be ornamented with some pretty design. And so, according to the ticks, the unwearying improvement of our reality continues.

THE TICK AND HIS COMPANIONS

A tick normally associates with ticks. There are obviously exceptions to this rule. These relate to contacts both with Party members and members of the opposition. In the case of a Party member, the tick generally contents himself with a single representative of this variety, a single one but not a random match. Who is this person? He is the tick's immediate superior, his boss, chairman, or professor. The contact which the tick maintains with the Party member, his superior (very cordial, marked by a somewhat intimate respect, but not too frequent), is usually concealed from the rest of his acquaintances. The tick fears that his superior, the Party members, might not take the fancy of some of his companions, that indeed this group of companions might think evil of him. What does it mean, evil? That he is a red. To a tick—this must be plainly understood—it matters considerably that those around him should not confuse him with the Party riff-raff. Some ticks are prepared to distance themselves from Party members to the extent that they maintain contacts with members of the opposition. Perhaps "members of the opposition" is too strong—such a tick generally has one member of the opposition in his circle of acquaintances. As a result he suffers agonies of fear (when they bundle off to jail the member of the opposition who has the tick's telephone number in his diary), but still it makes him feel heroic, courageous,

---

* The years of significant anti-Communist revolts: the Hungarian revolution (1956), the Prague Spring (1968), and workers strikes and uprisings in Poland (1970 and 1976).

and antistate. The majority of ticks, however, keep clear of the opposition, and when one of their nonopposition acquaintances becomes a dissident they sever relations with him.

Ticks congregate in coffee houses, inciting people against the system, rooting for enemies of the people and intriguers. They read the opposition press (ah, what dissidents it makes them feel), but still, they will never sign any protest letters, never write an antistate text, and never meddle in anything which might cost them their job. If at their place of work, for example, in an editorial office, some conflict of a political nature breaks out in the Union of Creative Artists, the tick tries to settle it. When there is a drive against Solzhenitsyn, Kołakowski* or Sakharov,† the tick is bold enough to point out that while it is possible, even necessary, to write polemics against them, this must be done in a skilful and cultured manner; that assaults which are too sharp and unwarranted have the reverse effect. When the Party members launch a political attack on some celebrated artist or other, the tick does not join the offensive, but expresses a skeptical or downright negative opinion on the purely artistic values of his work.

THE INNER LIFE OF THE TICK

We now come to the most important part of our text. Now follows something much more fundamental than deliberations on the genesis, types, and education of the tick; an attempt to present his system of thought, an attempt to describe the tick's intellectual structure. How could one dream of omitting this section? Leaving it out would be blatantly injurious to the ticks. For it is this system of thought, this intellectual structure which is precisely the achievement which the tick in the course of his quiet intellectual work on himself has arrived at painfully in the course of the thirty odd years of the existence of the Polish People's Republic, worked out by the joint efforts of the tick's grey matter, and their shield and defense. So let us have a proper look at it.

---

* Kołakowski. See the notes on contributors to this volume.

† Sakharov. See note on page 354.

A. Arguments for not signing a protest letter

Ding-dong! A visitor he hasn't seen for ever so long, tea, chat, and more chat. The tick's acquaintance from opposition circles has come to see him. They wax indignant together over some new police roundup, massacre, or amendment to the constitution imbued with warm sentiment towards the USSR. The doors and windows are tightly shut, one can frolic at will. Suddenly the visitor goes to his coat pocket and takes out a sheet of typing. He gives it to the tick, who quickly skims through the closely typed text of the latest protest letter. The tick stops reading and begins to ask factual questions about the present range of actions. The visitor replies, the tick listens. But only on the surface. In reality, he is busy with another matter, figuring out how to explain that he cannot sign. At this point the reader will surely feel disgust. This figuring out is the thing ticks have been exerting their grey matter on for the last thirty years of quiet conceptual work, and now their representative is unexpectedly driven to the wall, he has to wait and think out arguments against signing. Patience, good reader, have a little more trust in the ticks. For, of course, they have these arguments figured out, on call and ready drilled for all occasions. But it is one thing to know theoretically how to behave when someone gives you a paper to sign, and another to find oneself face to face with a paper and a member of the opposition. The tick must decide, according to the circumstances and the person of his interlocutor, what line of argument to use. This is the repertoire at his disposal.

(a) *Duty to the family.* The tick cannot sign a protest letter because the tick is a person with duties and responsibilities. It is not oneself, of course; the tick cannot allow that certain definite consequences of signing should affect his family. It is rather a matter of wife, husband, aunt, and grandmother. Most of all, the children. It would be easy to get the impression that no one in the world has ever loved or will love their children like this Polish-People's-Republic tick. The thought that his children might have to eat brawn instead of frankfurters, or apples instead of bananas, that they might be expelled from the crèche, not admitted to kindergarten, won't get exemplary conduct badges in school, is unbearable to him. Protest letters are all right for bachelors and unmarried women, and also for basically irresponsible people. His hands are tied. One day, when the child has his school leaving certificate, his MA, and his Doctorate, then maybe, maybe providing of course that no grandchildren have appeared. For the good of his grandson, the tick will have to restrain himself even more. But in heaven, he will protest for sure, with all his might.

(b) *Love of his job.* The tick cannot join in the protest because his professional work plays a simply enormous role in his life. Without his editorial board, his theatre, his film crew, his union of creative writers, without the responsibility of publishing his books, life would be simply unimaginable. Singing a protest would mean dismissal from work, a ban on publication, annihilation of his career. The tick can't do this to himself. Of course, he would sign at once if he were in as strong a position as N. N. cannot be touched. If N. signs no one will do anything to him. In general, it is people like N. who should sign, those who cannot be touched. Here the tick calls to mind the million-fold ranks of pensioners. That's who should be the army of the opposition. What can they do to pensioners? They won't cut off their pensions. Why does no one go to the pensioners with protest letters? And the chronically ill—the tick begins to dream—the incurables, the cancer patients, those to whom the Polish People's Republic can do nothing more, why do they not sign? Go and seek your signatories in the hospitals, and don't expose people who are already exposed to repression. Go to the hospitals and old people's homes.

(c) *The wrong moment.* The tick has been thinking about taking part in some protest action, but just now it is quite the wrong moment. Why did no one come to him with a protest letter last September. September was the time to protest, and to protest sharply, not now: The action is simply too late. Too late, and in another sense, too early. This is too important a question to be played about with in an incompetent matter. Think about what you're doing! I'm warning you!

B. Provocation

And are these three arguments all one has to protect oneself from the intriguer who wants a signature to a letter? Ah, have more trust in the ticks, more faith in their wisdom, more esteem for their achievements. These three arguments are only, as it were, the first and most distant line of defense. They are the methods which the tick, forced to the wall, most probably uses as a first reaction. But in addition there exists a whole battery of intellectual achievements ready for more complicated scenarios, capable of being deployed in a situation which has been analyzed somewhat more profoundly. And in addition to these reserve arguments there is the whole interior make-up of the tick, his whole intellectual world, from which you can grab whole handfuls of arguments. Surely, isn't it true in a certain sense, that everything which the tick has at the center, has been amassed, as a result of quiet conceptual work, to serve as a reason for refusing to sign a protest? Let us try to reveal something new about this inner make-up.

The tick possesses an irresistible, powerful, and all-embracing tendency to see provocation in everything that goes on around him. Provocation, of course, by the Party or the security police. The mouse lashes its tail against the cat. The naïve person thinks that this is an anticat action. The tick knows better: it is not an anticat action but a cat action. The cat had a hand in it, inspired it, and lets the mouse come closer, to get its hands on the evidence. Evidence of what? That the mouse doesn't like it. The students have taken to the streets—provocation. The workers of Radom and Ursus protested against the decision to raise prices—provocation. The setting up of KOR*—provocation. Setting up the Movement for the Defense of Human and Civil Rights—obviously provocation. How does the tick know that these are all provocations? Why, because if the security police did not have a hand in it, no one would have taken to the streets, no one would have protested against anything, no one would have been able to found anything. The very success of the action is evidence of its provocative character. The security police doesn't let anything happen without its approval. If a certain grade of tick were to wake up and find Poland swept clean of Party organizations, Soviet troops, police, security forces, the Polish-Soviet Friendship Society, and the Volunteer Auxiliary Police, and Poland ruled by the London government-in-exile, he would certainly go on maintaining for a long time that this was a new provocation by the government of the Polish People's Republic, and would refuse to acknowledge that there was no longer any need to sign anything.

---

* KOR (Komitet Obrany Robotników) is a Polish acronym for Workers' Defense Committee. This group was founded in 1976 to assist the prisoners and families involved in the labor strikes. It was a precursor to the more well-known group Solidarity.

For what purpose—according to the tick—does the government of the Polish People's Republic burn down regional Party headquarters, get students and workers on to the streets, and induce naïve intellectuals to organize protest actions? Obviously to trap those opponents of the regime who have not yet been trapped and to have an excuse for turning the screw still further.

The tick has seen the authorities' deceit, and does not let himself be maneuvered and will not let himself become involved in suspicious goings on.

C. Liberals and hardheads

The tick is an expert in a certain field of knowledge, to which one would have thought he would not have access. Namely, he has a perfect knowledge of the faction fights within the PUWP. In knowledge on this subject the tick surpasses not only the rank-and-file members of the Party but also a great many members of the Central Committee, and maybe even of certain secretaries, not to speak of members of the secretariat. The tick knows the Party set-up, and nobody knows it better than him, or maybe only the CIA. This knowledge includes the view that members of the Politburo and their deputies, secretaries, and members of the secretariat, heads of Party sections, and first secretaries of regional committees can be divided into two categories of activists: liberals and hardheads or hardliners. The liberals try all they can (unfortunately, it is not much) to make the economic policy more rational, to have greater freedom prevailing in matters of culture, and to see that the police and security authorities dealing with dissidents use as gentle methods as possible. The hardheads or hardliners strive (and unfortunately they succeed) to tighten the belt of the economy, to turn the screw on culture and to use the sharpest means possible in the struggle against the opposition. To this intra-party front must be added—in the opinion of the ticks—another conflict which divides the whole government apparatus: the conflict between the Party as a whole and the security apparatus. The security apparatus—in the opinion of the ticks—is an independent force, which implements its own policies. Some hardheads within the Party possess certain contacts with security. However, the Party as a whole, its First Secretary included, has only a limited influence on the doings of security. The police in Radom tortured the workers—Gierek knew nothing about it. The security hounds the members of KOR, gifted intellectuals and artists—Minister of Culture Tejchma, who is a member of the Politburo, knows nothing about it. The Party liberals in general know very little and can do even less. But why can they do so little? And here we come to perhaps the greatest achievement of the ticks' grey matter, because the opposition has weakened their position.

What this liberal Tejchma builds up, what steps he takes to loosen the screw on culture, is immediately undone by some letter from writers about the fate of Poles in the USSR or on the amendments to the constitution. For the hardliners say at once: "You want to loosen the screw a bit, Comrade, you feel sure that they'll be good now, but what does this letter say?" and Minister Tejchma cannot find an answer, the protest letter has knocked the arguments out of his hands.

The program of action which results from the ticks' diagnosis: the sensible citizen must act in such a way as to enhance the power of the liberal wing of the Party. What weakens that wing? Letters, protests, strikes, demonstrations, and uncensored books. What strengthens it? The absence of letters, strikes, demonstrations and uncensored books. You want liberalization—avoid all ill-considered actions, don't protest, don't make demands, don't take to the streets, don't take part in producing provocative literature—only censor it carefully at home yourself. Be present at the Meeting of the Union of Polish Writers. After the meeting, somewhere upstairs, there will obviously be a dogged battle between the liberal minister Tejchma and the hardline secretary Lukasiewicz. The meeting elects an executive committee from writers guided by the party, the opposition doesn't get to vote. "Victory for Tejchma," the ticks say with relief in their voice. In a literary weekly there appears—surely by chance—a cartoon against anti-Semitism and so antistate. The editorial ticks express their profound sorrow: "something terrible has happened, we have given a pretext to the hardheads; now they will grab our journal, now we shall have to take great care that these idiots (the bosses) don't let something through again." You want liberalization, you don't want the hotheads to carry the vote, then be on your guard, take action against irresponsible behavior, censor your own work and other people's (for it could happen, by chance that something could get past the censorship, and then the hard heads will notice it). You want liberalization, then fight against freedom. Why? Because otherwise the hardliners will come and grab you by the throat.

D. Someone worse will come

Let us for a moment take a closer look at the soul of a tick in a middle or high position in the social hierarchy, for example, the head of a section of a socio-literary weekly, or the director of a scientific institute. Isn't he full up to the nostrils with these ultraloyal leading articles, this scolding from under-educated apparatchiks from the Central Committee? He's fed up to the back teeth and even higher; ten times over he's been ripe to chuck the job and do anything else. But if he's a true tick, then he'll never actually do it. Why? Because if he leaves, someone worse will come in his place. And that our tick can't allow. Someone will come, and will call the workers of Radom, not just hooligans, as before, but bandits, someone will come and will attack idealistic scholars not for idealism but for subjectivism, someone will come and throw out the book, standing ready in type, which the censor did not pass, crudely and with insults, instead of sending it back after half a year of delay and smiling conversations. Everyone must—in the opinion of the ticks—stick to his job, bear the heavy burden of responsibility, even humiliation, for the sake of higher reasons. Such as? The good of Polish culture, obviously. The good of Polish culture is the supreme value. One must be able to sacrifice one's personal interests for it. The ticks make this sacrifice. They serve, they offer incense to the censor, they kick out, even make denunciations—all for the good of Polish culture.

E. The world through the eyes of a tick

How does the contemporary world appear through the eyes of a tick? It is obviously a world divided into two blocs, American and Soviet. Poland is dependent on the Soviet Union, which is obviously a totalitarian state. Indeed, today there are not more than two or three completely independent states in the world. The struggle for the complete independence of Poland is an unreal one. The West is obviously better than the Soviet Union, but it to has various deeds on its conscience. Radio Free Europe sometimes gives interesting news but it is generally biased. The BBC is better. Nationalism, national fervor is a bad thing; the best stance is that shown by mildly leftish intellectual centers in the West: humanism, progress, common human values. Liberalization is a good thing. The struggle for the complete independence of Poland smells of must and obscurantism.

F. The ticks' authorities

Ticks consider themselves to be morally pure individuals, untainted by any dirty or, God forbid, nasty business. They are humanists and moralists against the brutal reality of the Polish People's Republic and Party, they wear a coat of moral principles and higher culture. What plays the fundamental role in tick morality and culture? Obviously, the examples of actual people. For a tick to feel good and to be himself, he needs a compass in the person of some coryphaeus, some individual of renown and moral purity, acknowledged for his higher culture. This is usually a professor, cosseted and promoted by the Polish People's Republic, but for some period subjected to mild repression, prosecuted, or in any case put out of his job, but afterwards gloriously restored to favor. Such a professor, armed with the reputation of indomitable courage, afterwards delivers an innumerable number of fine speeches, sits on innumerable presidiums, is spoken of as a great scholar and is quoted in the press by every second journalist. And a great tick or quasi tick like this is chosen by the ordinary tick as his compass. Above the tumult of opposition blusterers, he rises like a great statue, imparting spirit, support, and warmth.

G. The tick wants to be loved

Being related spiritually and socially to the liberal opposition, but a comrade after the flesh to the Party masters of the Polish People's Republic, the tick tries to be on good terms with everyone and wants to be loved by everyone. In an opposition milieu, he strives to pass as truly committed to opposition activity, morally pure, indomitably brave, nonconformist. In institutions of the Polish People's Republic, he wants to appear truly apolitical, dutiful, devoted to his work, loyal. From the members of the opposition he looks for acceptance, from the Polish People's Republic, prizes, promotions, awards, and orders. And usually, it must be recognized, he is successful. The opposition is exceptionally forbearing, the People's Government is extraordinarily generous. When one side ceases to accept the tick, he raises hell. Some ticks are temporarily betrayed by their People's Republic masters. They are martyrs under the clause which we have discussed in a previous section; they fall into disgrace by the laws of chance, without any previous lapse into opposition activity; they are then swiftly restored to the bosom of the Polish People's Republic in the fraudulent plumage of indomitable victims of repression. Ticks who really try to put on the skin of the opposition can be counted on the fingers of one hand. A compromised tick, caught out in servility, usually falls into a great panic. He mobilizes his acquaintances, who have influence with the opposition, he runs around town offering profuse explanations. His advocates quickly come forward, showing that a righteous man has been wronged, that he is in a very specific situation, that he cannot be put on the same plane as patent conformists, that he has suffered so much. . . . A tick caught in *flagrante* snatches at the most fantastic means of defense. These depend principally on the attribution of hidden antistate intentions to visibly progovernment deeds and actions. For example, a journalist who specializes in praising the world revolution, caught between two fires and driven to the wall, will try to show that under the guise of criticism of presidents and kings, he is really criticizing the leaders of totalitarian states such as the Soviet Union and the Polish People's Republic.

Who Has the Right to Write about Ticks?

In concluding this sketch, let us ask ourselves, formally, but not just formally, the question: who should write about ticks, who has the right to do so? The answer seems simple—the non-ticks should write about ticks. But this answer is simple only on the surface; who can say of himself with a clear conscience that he is not a tick? Who, indeed? It is the tragedy of the Polish intelligentsia, Polish culture, and simply of Poland, and the reason that this text has been written, that all or almost all of us are, in whole or in part, or have been to a certain degree, ticks.

23

Ticks and Angels
(1979)

ADAM MICHNIK

Wierzbicki says: "We shall leave to the historians the task of discovering the forefathers of ticks in past ages." Since I feel that I have connections with the profession of historian, I shall allow myself to make a few remarks by way of a supplement.

The genealogy of the "tick " phenomenon must be sought in political situations where foreign domination of the Polish people assumed a chronic character and any hope of armed defense for our national values was totally illusory, when compromise with the conqueror had become inevitable to preserve the very existence of the nation. The problem of the permissible limits of compromise was then a daily challenge to the minds and consciences of people who, in a conquered country, wanted to live and act. Total acceptance of the formula of compromise was the road to becoming morally compromised and to spiritual capitulation; total rejection of the formula of compromise was the road to a more or less heroic isolation. During the years of the partition of Poland, attitudes of compromise and situations of difficult choice were our daily bread.

There were violent disagreements and fundamental differences between the supporters and opponents of accommodation, between the legalists and the conspirators, between those who advocated special betterment and the insurrectionists. The supporters of radical action in the heat of their polemics always glossed over the differences between betrayal of the nation, accommodation, and work for social improvement, but tended to reduce all these different patterns of behavior to a common denominator: a desire for personal gain. Only when time had rubbed off the corners and leveled out the contours did it become possible to evaluate the effectiveness of different forms of resistance to the fate of foreign domination and to see the complementary nature of these opposites.

To put it clearly: there were different ways of fighting for the Polish cause and these were effective in different ways. It was not only those who took part in armed uprisings who fought for the existence of the nation. Sometimes accommodation was effective, sometimes legal opposition, and sometimes society was simply forced to strive for social betterment. If there was some sense (and I myself think there was, though even today it is open to doubt) in resorting to insurrection tactics in the time of Kościuszko,[*] the Legions[†] or the [1830] "November Night,"[‡] it quite clearly made political nonsense to plot insurrections in the puppet-kingdom of Poland under the governorship of [the Russian General] Paskevich.

I want to recall that time, now far in the past, because it makes it easier, I think, to master our emotions and to think things over calmly.

We may note, therefore, that an active member of the opposition views reality in one way and an intellectual writing a commentary in another, while a moralist, trying to dispense justice to the "visible world" will view things in yet a third way. Each of these views has it own lights and shades. The perspective of the member of the opposition is inevitably forced to be one-sided. This helps him to reshape the world, but makes it difficult for him to perceive the many dimensions involved. Moralism lets one perceive the snares which lie in wait for everyone who assumes an active responsibility, but fosters the aesthetic cult of "clean hands." The stance of the spectator makes it easier to understand the complexity of the human con-

---

* Tadeusz Kościuszko (1746–1817) was a Polish-Lithuanian general who led the uprising against the Russian Empire and Prussia in 1794.

† In the wake of the French Revolution and the rise of Napoleon, the recently partitioned Poland (1795) turned to France for help in its fight for independence. The Polish *Legions* were created in 1797 in Italy from Poles who deserted the Austrian army. They believed that by serving with Napoleon as he moved through central Europe they could advance the cause of Polish independence.

‡ On November 29, 1830, young Polish cadets at the Russian Empire's military academy seized arms from the military garrison and attacked the palace of the Grand Duke. The November Night uprising was suppressed by the Russian general Ivan Paskevich.

dition but makes it no easier to answer the "question what is to be done?" nor the question " what is good and what is evil?"

One looks upon the world one way if one wants to change it, another if one wants to understand it, and yet another if one wants to pass moral judgment upon it. I am convinced that I will not change this state of affairs by my article. Anyway, that is not my ambition. I simply want to try to convince my opponent that if he totally commits himself to thinking in moralistic or current-opposition terms (which comes to the same thing), then he will lose a certain essential part of reality from his field of vision.

It is important to remember these shamefully banal observations when taking up the question of the attitude of the Polish intelligentsia under the governments of the former regime. The picture drawn by Wierzbicki is clear and unambiguous. At that time, Poland was under the rule of Stalinist-Bierutist functionaries and Party Young Communist troops carried out the execution of Polish learning. And that's all. Somewhere the whole dramatic quality of social and political reality has been lost; lost too somewhere the whole impassioned picture of the mingling of disaster and hope, understanding and naïvety, fear and gallant courage, the dynamism of society and the behind the scenes actions of the Soviet advisers. It is as if in answer to the Stalinist primer on which we were reared at the time we had been given a primer *à rebours* where the colors were equally compressed and glaring and the picture of the world equally infantile.

The reality of the early postwar years was—in my opinion—incomparably more complicated than would appear from the ultrasimplistic formula of the "reds" and their intellectual lackeys, the "ticks."

This period is among the most painful in our history and among the most hypocritical. It may even be that it is because it is so painful that it is hypocritical. Putting aside the general discussion, which cannot but be painful, to another occasion, we shall make only a few fragmentary remarks.

At that time, the country was drained of blood and the fortune of war determined by the Yalta Conference.* The form of postwar reality had been determined not by the blood which had been shed and the heroism of the anti-Nazi resistance but by the international balance of power.

---

* The Yalta conference took place in February 1945. Roosevelt, Churchill, and Stalin met to discuss the postwar organization of Europe.

The Western allies abandoned Poland. What way forward was left to our society?

Many a time I have dwelt on this problem. So many times have I striven to find, in the not too far distant history, the point at which an error or false choice in Polish policy sealed the unhappy fate of the Polish nation. And I could not find one. Following through the history of the Polish cause during and after the war, I have the feeling that Clio, the muse of history, has turned her back on the Poles, so as not to give them even the shadow of a chance to break the bonds of misfortune and to find a way out of national oppression. Every direction of Polish policy was a losing one.

Time went by, the Stalinist noose was drawn even tighter around the neck of a nation oppressed and drained of blood. Everyone was faced with the question: where is the limit of permissible compromise? What price can be paid for the chance of lecturing, publishing, pursuing one's profession? For in a totalitarian system it is always necessary to pay an admission fee, and this has become ever more exorbitant: the conditions laid down are always accompanied by more or less veiled threats and blackmail.

I do not remember such times, I know them only from various reports and documents. Today, years later, it is difficult to evaluate the actual choices which were made at that time. It is even more difficult to find a measure out of the context of that time. He who knows of such a measure is simply to be envied. If Nadezhda Mandelstam* is right when she asserts that silence in the face of totalitarian domination is a "true crime against the human race," then almost everyone is guilty of that crime. Even the noblest have been forced into passivity and silence. Only those in the prisons and labor camps are free from this. "Blessed prisons," wrote Solzhenitsyn, "only there can a man achieve freedom from participation in this accursed machine of lies."

Aleksander Wat† wrote somewhere that there is only one answer to the question of how intellectuals should behave in the lands where Stalin ruled. It is the Shakespearean answer: "They must die."

Perhaps this is the true answer. But still, I consider this answer can be made only for oneself, this measure meted out only to oneself, this sacrifice demanded only from oneself. Anyone who demands this answer from

---

* Nedezhda Mandelstam. See note on page 149.

† Aleksander Wat (1900–1967) was a renowned Polish poet and essayist.

another is arbitrarily arrogating to himself the right of determining the life of another. And this, in general, leads to nothing good.

In spite of what we read in the "Treatise on Ticks" no rectors or editors who were outwardly obedient but "pro-Western" and "counterrevolutionary "in the depths of their soul had an easy life, by any means, in Stalin's time. Fingers were constantly pointed at them. They were constantly suspected of the "taint of bourgeois consciousness." Over-zealous agitators saw in them camouflaged defenders of the past. To such juvenile agitators the world appeared grossly simple. The capitalist system—the cradle of Fascism—was enemy number one of human happiness. Anyone who decided to make even the least compromise with the dying culture of the capitalist West was, for them, the principal adversary.

The simplicity of this view of the world, the ease of passing judgments, the highly intolerant political fanaticism of these years dictated to a young writer, even if he already had recognized productions to his credit, lampoon-formulae such as "for bourgeois writers the fight against German Fascism became an escape from political decision, or even worse, became a cover-up for imperialist ideology! . . . It is necessary to reassess actions which in the years of nationalist deviation were termed 'anti-Fascist' and 'righteous,' thinking that this would suffice for ever."

Please believe me. I really do understand Wierzbicki's anger and his opposition to the process which Milosz, some years ago, called "moral decay" and "Pétainism." I understand too, however, the bitterness of people who, through all this, often clenching their teeth and enduring humiliations, created a morsel of our own mental reality, preserved and restored old values, and built up new ones, and now, today, are called " ticks."

It is senseless to demand careful and balanced appraisals from a lampoonist. The very technique of the lampoonist's art makes an opinion more radical. I do not make the claim that Wierzbicki, by employing the definition "tick" is sharpening the outlines of reality, but that his anti-tick passion makes it impossible for him to understand them.

For—although this does not emerge from Wierzbicki's text—the reality of our country differs considerably from the reality of those countries which are our neighbors. We are less receptive to the process of Sovietization. Why?

There are various factors which make us different, historical tradition, the Catholic Church, and the brave though so very realistic line taken by the Episcopate, the countryside which has defended itself in the face of collectivization; finally, unremitting social pressure. This has manifested itself sometimes in violent explosions (Poznan 1956, March 1968, December 1970, Radom 1976), but generally in quiet, daily, dogged resistance. A resistance which is, as it were, incompatible with denunciation. The mental atmosphere of a part of the intellectual environment, lectures and seminars in institutions of higher learning, the carrying out of doctoral research and the publication of learned communications, novels, slim volumes of poetry, essays, meetings of the Union of Writers or the P.E.N. Club, films and theatrical presentations, museums, concerts, and vernissages. And this comes largely from the work of people who sign no protests and perform no spectacular deeds of opposition. Yet it is equally due to them that we now breathe a different air in Poland. A spiritual air. And this daily creation of an invisible but fundamental strand in the culture and consciousness of the nation is not simply the result of reading *Zapis* or the *Biuletyn Informacyjny* or the publications of the Independent Publishing House.* It is a result of the totality of Polish achievements.

This totality is becoming an object of envy to visitors who are citizens of other nations of the "camp." They do not envy us just for KOR, SAC, and uncensored publications, but also for journals which are published officially. And not only for *Tygodnik Powszechny* or *Więź* but also for *Twórczość, Pamiętnik Literacki* and even for *Polityka.*† They envy us our full churches and our fully operational catechetical centers, the theatrical productions of Diemek‡ and the films of Wajda,§ the appearance of our streets and our attractively dressed girls. Thanks then to all this we are preserving our identity and a capacity to keep up a resistance to the Sovietization process.

I should be the last to claim that our situation is satisfactory and that our aspirations have been pacified. I am constantly writing on this theme in the uncensored press. Sometimes, however, one must look at our situation,

---

* *Zapis* was a literary journal and *Biuletyn Informacyjny* was a news bulletin—both founded by KOR, the Workers Defense Committee (see note on page 393).

† *Tygodnik Powszechny* and *Więź* were lay Catholic journals. *Twórczość* and *Pamiętnik Literacki* were literary journals. *Polityka* was a political weekly (see the next chapter).

‡ Kazimierz Diemek was a prominent theatre director.

§ Andrej Wajda is a world-renowned film director. His films include *Ashes and Diamonds, Man of Iron,* and *Katyn.*

at our ills and misfortunes, not only from the viewpoint of aspirations and misfortunes, but also from the viewpoint of threats. Among those threats I include the picture of the fate of a nation which we see in our eastern neighbors, the Lithuanians, Belorussians, and Ukrainians. They have to fight for their existence at the elementary level: it is a struggle for language, religion, the treasury of national culture. Let us evaluate these differences. Let us evaluate how different is the fate of nations under a Communist system. It is also worth considering circumstances which are taken for granted concerning the most essential differences between the Russian and Polish defenders of human rights. In short: although the political police make life difficult for us, we feel that we are strong, since we have the support—moral and material—of broad sections of our society. We have the support of people who are not by temperament either politicians or heroes, who do not want to have to give up their comparatively stabilized family life, who certainly rarely decide to sign a protest letter, and who—I must say—actually take for granted the success of the campaign in defense of the workers of Radom and Ursus. Without the support of such people, independent publishing work would be hard to imagine.

I have a different outlook from Wierzbicki concerning the "people between the government and opposition." When a learned professor of sociology reacts to the protests of intellectuals against torture in Radom by writing a refined theoretical study in which the protest of these individuals is depreciated, then my anger resembles that of the author of the "Treatise on Ticks," and it is with satisfaction that I read the keen riposte of Jacek Bocheński[*] to these lucubrations. But when a professor, instead of making a comparative psychoanalysis of the protesting individuals decides to use his parliamentary immunity and go to Radom for one of the trials, to see for himself how the functionaries were meting out justice, if then, without in the least involving himself in the cases that were being fought, he makes a report to the government about what he has seen there—why does Wierzbicki call his action "tickish"? I do not consider it so. I would rather rejoice that in the bosom of the governing elite rational attitudes are beginning to take shape, that the ruling strata are beginning to define correctly their own proper interest, that I can recognize in the circle of my opponents at least a shadow of political culture. So far there have not

* Jacek Bocheński was a well-known writer and journalist—editor of *Zapis*.

been many such symptoms. I think, however, that if we abandon hope of such an evolution, then the alternative scenario must include a sequence of violent confrontations between the authorities and society. Any one of these confrontations can give rise to a national tragedy. It is our common duty to avoid such situations, since it could turn out that the whole nation and every Pole, not excluding the government, would pay an inordinately high price for their lack of responsibility in this matter.

This conclusion does not mean simply that anyone should be persuaded to take part in intra-Party intrigues. On this point I share Wierzbicki's skepticism. It is important, however, to remember that we live in a society where hundreds of thousands of active people belong to the Communist Party. Membership is the price which has to be paid for taking part in public life, for the chance of a job at management level, and so forth. Maybe Wierzbicki considers (and I myself am of that opinion) that the price is too high, that it is a price not worth paying and is unseemly. Nevertheless, we live and we shall continue to live among people who think otherwise. We must learn how to coexist with them and to teach them to coexist with us. We must learn the difficult art of compromise without which true pluralism is impossible. Furthermore, we must observe in the face of the authorities the standards of political culture, even when the authorities do not preserve these standards. Only then shall we manage to set dignity against totalitarian brutishness.

I am not an aesthete, and I do not suppose that everybody, one and all, could live in a state of uninterrupted friendship. I do, however, believe in the creative power of our actions. I believe that it is possible to increase or decrease the amount of hatred and intolerance in our public life. I believe, finally, that the shape of an independent and democratic Poland is even now being hammered out. I should wish to see it based on tolerance and political culture, but I know that it will require long years of work to make these values universal. Hence it is necessary to make them universal even today, and not in verbal declarations but in daily action.

That is why I am so afraid of a certain type of reaction to Wierzbicki's essay. For the "Treatise on Ticks" is an extremely evocative text in its passion for unmasking the essential diseases of Polish intellectual and civil life. It is a continuation of the great tradition of Polish lampoons on society. Wierzbicki does not flatter the reader; he accuses and overturns. Such a stance in an author earns respect.

Nevertheless, the "Treatise" will not be a bucket of cold water on the intelligentsia, but a nice simple reader confined to cheering the hearts of the dissidents, unless it is supplemented by a "Treatise on Angels." For among us, angels are doomed to criticism, which they are bound to scorn, especially if it comes from the pen of Gontarz or Kłodzińska.* But an angel who is not criticized, an angel confirmed in his angelicness can turn into a devil. Don't you believe it? Read that book about the most noble and valiant people in Russia, a book which I have hated for years, yet to which I return again and again, like an addict to cocaine, a book which is a curved mirror in which every angel sees his disgustingly distorted face, a book which is antipathetic and penetrating to the point of cruelty. Read *The Devils* by Dostoyevsky.

I know that whenever a tick wants to justify his "tickery," he takes down from the shelf this very book, nicely bound in morocco, and reads out to his interlocutor choicer and choicer extracts. I know, too, however, that if the experience of the "devils" is not thought over and internalized by the Polish democratic opposition, then that opposition will be menaced not so much by secret policemen with scarred faces, and dead eyes, but by Stavrogin's and Verkhovensky's *à la polonaise.*†

For a movement which does not perceive what is an unacceptable value in society is not sufficiently mature to reform it.

---

* Gontarz and Kłodzińska were journalists loyal to the PUWP.

† Stavrogin and Verkhovensky are characters from Dostoyevsky's novel *The Devils*.

24

The Hair Styles of Mieczysław Rakowski (1983)

Leopold Tyrmand

I no longer believe that the revolution should sit in judgment on the world. I believe only in the revolution which transforms us.
—Henri de Man, *The Psychology of Socialism*

And quite right, too. However, I shall use de Man's proposition in a sense different from the one in which he intended it. The verb "to transform" de Man uses in its positive and directional sense, as if to say: "Let us, instead of making revolution, transform ourselves, become better people." Fine, but isn't it more interesting to consider how a successful revolution transforms us all, different people that we are? Were I determined to seek out finer details, I might easily run the risk of producing truisms. I propose instead to let the brilliant plurality of metamorphoses, their richness and diversity, spread themselves before us in a startling array like an Op Art painting. This way we shall have no difficulty in avoiding vulgarizations.

I introduce Mieczysław Rakowski with a feeling of emotional neutrality. Life has never brought us close to one another. He has always greeted me politely, if without interest, as I have him. What we knew about each other and what we thought has remained unchanged over the years. We were ideological enemies, but there was no hatred between us. I even regarded him with a certain degree of pleasure, despite the general sense of revulsion I felt. There was something vaguely amusing about him which confirmed my more general assumptions, and it is always agreeable to be proved right.

The Hair Styles of Mieczysław Rakowski

In 1958 the International Press Club asked me to take part in a public discussion of my article in *Tygodnik Powszechny* in which I had suggested that a revision of our concepts of postwar Germany was necessary—the first time this had been attempted in Poland since the end of the war. It provoked a wave of indignant slogans from the Communist press, as well as insults from émigré Poles, and *Tygodnik* skillfully dissociated itself from me. I accepted the invitation with the masochistic pleasure of a suicide who becomes ecstatic at the thought of being publicly torn to pieces. In the event, it wasn't quite as bad as that. True, the Nationalist-Communist coalition sank its teeth into me, but the university students and other youngish people responded with a remarkably pragmatic approach and applauded loudly my most provocative excursions. Rakowski was in the chair, and one had to admit that he performed his duty with the forced but obvious neutrality of a referee who desperately wants his own eleven to win but never for a moment forgets his position as umpire.

Some years later I suggested to Rakowski that he should print the first part of my unpublished novel. It was a tactical move: the publication of my novel in his journal *Polityka* would be a surrealist event and neither of us took the possibility seriously. In my battle for a passport and for the publication of my book, I wanted to be able to say: "*Polityka* is considering publishing a novel of mine." This throw-away remark, skillfully dropped in various offices in the course of various conversations, made a certain impression. Sometime later, Rakowski telephoned and returned my typescript (which he certainly had not read) and we parted with great affability, smiles, and *bonhomie* all around. We both understood very well what the game was about. The fact was that Rakowski had also scored a few points in his own game—at that time he was immensely keen to appear as liberal an editor as possible who gave due consideration to every manuscript on its merits. So, even if in his opinion I was too extreme even for a' liberal editor, he could not refuse to have a look at my typescript; for then I would have gone around Warsaw with new evidence of persecution, this time from *Polityka*.

Rakowski is a syndrome, like Kott,* Comrade Blatmanowa,† and Mr.
Bolo, about whom more later. You may ask why, when attacking other
syndromes, I consider Rakowski with a degree of neutrality. The answer
isn't simple. Although they represent a dangerously prolific species, Kott,
Comrade Blatmanowa, and Mr. Bolo are just nauseating. Rakowski is a
more complex phenomenon. Of course, one could make him into a convenient stereotype, but to what end? Individualization and incarnation
better convey the horrors of the transformations which de Man was not
himself able to know.

The history of the hair styles of Mieczysław Rakowski is the history of victorious Polish Communism. Rakowski's social credentials are
of the best: he is the son of a Pomeranian peasant. At the beginning,
the Communists loved nothing so much as authentic peasant progeny; in
anticipation, they had prepared little verses about the Slavonic and truly
Aryan sons of the soil, who fought bravely against the deluge of German
imperialism, in poverty but unswervingly. The product was consequently
healthy, well built, fair-haired, and fetching. When I first saw Rakowski,
he had on his head what one might call a shock, an enormous crop of
blond curls, a veritable thatch of hair. The result was undistinguished, or
so it seemed at first, but in fact it was a carefully studied exercise in style.
This was the heyday of Stalinism, and Rakowski, together with a pal of
his, a certain Wysznacki (later editor of *Stolica*), was apprenticed to learn
the trade of Communist executioner of the printed word, under the then-
famous butcher Stefan Staszewski, head of the press section of the Central
Committee, and later a rebel. I had been told about Staszewski many
years before by Immanuel Birnbaum, of *Süddeutsche Zeitung*, the doyen
of European wit. He once remarked, when we were both living in the
Warsaw YMCA among the Christian youth: "Staszewski? Take care! A
blond Jew—it goes against nature—you can never tell what he'll do next"

* Jan Kott was a writer, translator, and critic who after WWII joined the Polish Workers'
Party and became a proponent of Socialist Realism. He was the type of learned, cultured
figure whom the Communists loved to have in their camp (somewhat like Maxim Gorky
in the Soviet Union). In 1957 he renounced his membership in the Communist Party.
† Comrade Blatmanowa is a composite character, a general pseudonym for an intelligent, well-mannered, and cultured Communist who serves in editorial offices and
cultural ministries.

The Hair Styles of Mieczysław Rakowski

... "In the light of the October 1956 events, this proved prophetic. At the time of which I am speaking, Staszewski had not yet become a noncon-formist rebel, but was a stooge, while Rakowski called himself an instruc-tor in the press section of the Party's Central Committee—a title whose significance was lost in the maze of Communist euphemisms. His appear-ance was stylized, with discernment and precision: an effect of unobtru-sive "ruralness" was achieved by means of the hair style and clothes, while the face was designed to radiate the intellectual ardor of a nascent class and Party-consciousness. Much, sometimes a career, depended on the adroit use of such devices—Rakowski hit upon the right solution. His hair was flaxen, curly yet wiry, bouffant in effect, and it never failed to produce a feeling of solidarity in those with new positions in the Party and the government, whose birth certificates were to be found in the reg-istries of the smaller towns of the Republic. He dressed neatly, although he wore shapeless anoraks and overcoats, with padded shoulders, which came down to his ankles. Never a tie. From a distance, his appearance was no different from that of the village youth, who looks the same whether in the volunteer militia, a cooperative society, at a Service to Poland meet-ing in the village hall, in the Corpus Christi procession, or at a village dance, always associated in one's mind with canoes on the Vistula sands, smoked bacon, Double-Double beer, and the slushy tune they play under the paper lanterns which hang among the posters extolling Stakhanovite[*] workers. At that time, the young were thought to personify the beauty of the socialist body; they were much relied upon. It was they who were to Polonize the Russian-Jewish, intelligentsia-ridden Party cadre, and bring it closer to the populist image. The cadre, just then, was engaged in lay-ing the foundations of the system amid dialectical traps. The less gifted among them went into the army and joined the security police as officers; the brighter ones were made to learn about materialism and the theory of surplus value, with much sweating of brow and grinding of teeth. It was very much in vogue to stress the importance of the psycho-physical traits of country bumpkins in the development of the intellect, of cul-ture, and of the new Poland. Nevertheless, a certain smile played over the peasant-fresh lips of Instructor Rakowski, unobtrusively supported by a steely glance, from which it seemed that the instructor knew all too well

---

[*] Stakhanovite. See note on page 201.

the theory of the intensification of the class struggle with the progress of socialism. Iosif Vissarionovich* could rest assured that the peasant masses of Polish Pomerania would do all that was necessary to raise themselves higher according to dialectical precepts.

At the time of the debate in the International Press Club, Rakowski's hair was shorter but still flaxen, like a golden fleece, and crew-cut so as not to put off the new administration with an excess of dandyism. He was now wearing a double-breasted, off-the-rack suit bought from a big department store, and a tie. He laughed a lot, mostly at the more radical attacks on official policy. He was most charming and carefully avoided causing me any embarrassment. Despite the surface ease, one could detect an underlying anxiety. It grew from years of failure and turned into the pliability of one who realized early on that a different approach was needed now. He, and others like him, still dressed modestly and with sobriety, but now with a socialist urbanity which somehow protected them from shafts of irony, and made it possible for them to laugh at things to which five years earlier they would have taken a gun. In the extreme complexity of the situation, Comrade Rakowski managed to demonstrate, with grace and to the best of his abilities, something which was difficult to grasp but which it was essential to understand in order to survive. And, moreover, he did this more adroitly and with more tact than most. At that time, of course, it was the editor of *Polityka* and the future chairman of the Polish Journalists' Association that I had the pleasure of meeting.

A historical sketch from memory: When Gomułka† came to power, he immediately ordered a retreat from liberalism. But he did it so quietly that only the cleverest noticed it. The less clever, with their ears still buzzing with the music of jazz festivals, failed to notice it (some are still vegetating at a table shared with Janusz Minkiewicz‡ in the Actors' Club; others are enjoying great respect in the town of Lomza, where they now hold an extremely useful position in the local library). Rakowski picked up the

---

* Iosif Vissarionovich Stalin.

† Władysław Gomułka was an early member of the Communist Party of Poland. After demonstrating his differences with Stalin in the late 1940s, he was arrested in 1951. After Stalin's death he was released and then rehabilitated, becoming First Secretary to the PUWP in 1956, holding that post until 1970. Also see note on page 380.

‡ Janusz Minkiewicz (1914–1981) was a Polish writer and satirist.

directive instantly; he has an extraordinarily sensitive ear. It is by no means out of the question, however, that Gomułka himself whistled the new tune to him from close at hand, since at that time, it was said, they were on closer terms than is usual even within a family. I do not know all the details of the steps in Rakowski's career, but the fact is that immediately after October 1956 he found himself in the limelight and at the hub of national politics. Everyone drew attention to the intimacy between the new Boss and the press instructor of the Bierut era. As I said, I don't know for sure how it came about, but I do know that the new job fitted Rakowski to a T.

A very special periodical was needed. And a very special formula to justify the ideological-political swindle which had stripped the Poles of what they thought they had won. It had to be done delicately, with great finesse and with due regard to the latest achievements, in a style which in no way recalled the prehistoric primitivism of a Jakub Berman.* This journal would have to forge a new path of novel concepts; it would have to become a super-laundry for old wangles and tricks which have failed so many times in the course of the revolutionary "unfolding" and the building of socialism, and which have still to be constantly cleaned, turned, dyed, and used anew. Who would be able to think up a new version of the old tricks? That was the message, and the prize would be sizable. *Trybuna Literacka* was already in existence; this was a Sunday supplement to *Trybuna Ludu*,† in which Putrament,‡ Żukrowski,§ and a few others busied themselves trying to salvage Things Eternal and Things of Value from the previous era, as if anything other than their own salaries were worth salvaging. The one genuine journal, *Po Prostu*,¶ had been abolished: the only true agent of change and

---

* Jakub Berman was a member of the Politburo of the PUWP and served as the head of the Polish State Security Service. Until 1956 he was one of the key leaders in Stalinist-era Poland.

† *Trybuna Ludu* was the main newspaper of the PUWP.

‡ Jerzy Putrament was a Polish writer and editor and member of the Central Committee of the PUWP. He had significant influence in the regime's cultural policies. Czeslaw Milosz provided a sketch of Putrament as Gamma in *The Captive Mind*.

§ Wojciech Żukrowski (1916–2000) was a prolific Polish author who wrote many novels and film scripts.

¶ *Po Prostu* was shut down during the cultural and intellectual chill of the late 1950s and early 1960s (after the brief thaw of 1955–1957).

focus of effort to develop something worthwhile in Polish socialist thought since the days of Rosa Luxemburg. The bankrupt stock was there for the taking; all that was needed was a receiver. But why Rakowski? What were his qualifications, his merits, his abilities? Again I must plead ignorance. I know him only by his fruits. He was given quite a base of operations: *Trybuna Literacka* was merged with *Trybuna Wolności,* the theoretical organ of the Central Committee of the Polish Communist Party, with a circulation well into the six-figure bracket and much appreciated by the private sector, whose shopkeepers considered its paper ideal for wrapping pickled herring. Apparently no one found another use for it during the twenty years of its existence. Another paper which was incorporated in the merger was a periodical with the somewhat megalomaniac title *Świat i Polska (The World and Poland),* known to have been read exclusively by the editor, the proofreader, and their respective families. The resulting amalgam was accommodated in great comfort in a building which survived the war because the Germans had used its walls as a backdrop against which to shoot Poles, lined up in rows. It took the name *Polityka.*

I do not intend to write a critical analysis or study of *Polityka.* I have not the time, qualifications, or, above all, interest. But I do know, instinctively and for practical purposes, what *Polityka* is. First, it is an attempt at theft which did not come off. It was intended to steal the position of *Po Prostu* and it failed to do so. Nonetheless, it is not an imitation. It carved out its own image, distinctive if not very pretty. Its original purpose was to rescind the ideas of the Polish October, a program terrifying in its simplicity. The Poles, according to this program, had achieved *politically* everything it was possible to achieve; to have gone further would have meant abandoning socialism and that could not have been allowed, not only because the Russians might feel hurt, but because of the incontrovertible fact that socialism was axiomatically a good thing per se. Not yet perfect, of course. Therefore we must improve it. But the theory is okay, to be subjected neither to revision nor to improvement. Practice is another matter, and the main accomplishment of October, which itself was an Enormous and Splendid Achievement, was that we will now be able to discuss it. To discuss, but not necessarily to change. The social model was also okay, there was no question of change there. But in places the implementation was not quite up to the mark, and in such cases we will send our reporters to write extensive reports. The economic model was also okay and correct, but, here and there, there were certain faulty details of implementation which we will bring out into the open and analyze. Our foreign policy was correct, we were on the right side and we will look among our brothers for those whose sentiments were closest to ours, be it even Togliatti,* for what he said was true and beautiful, even if it is impracticable from our point of view. We were deeply concerned about social injustice and would expose it without fail. We will pinpoint corruption, dogmatism, nepotism, abuse of authority, stupidity, selfishness, and mutual backscratching, all of which were covered up in the previous period for the sake of a falsely conceived *raison d'état*. Socialism is openness, light, thought, rationalization, science, sociology, public-opinion polls, modernity, and the inviolably *correct principles* of social existence. From time to time and here and there, these principles have been broken by weak, inadequate, and narrow-minded people, sometimes through lack of understanding and sometimes out of malice. There were occasions when this happened as a result of the complicated interplay of social interdependence and class-conditioning, but the complexity and the mysterious impenetrability of such situations were bound to yield to the rays of the only modern scientific and progressive ideology known to man. That was how, by the circuitous route of the October revelation and enlightened absolutism, *Polityka* returned to the obscurantist intellectual hotchpotch in which, as experience has shown us, it was impossible to build for the future or even to breathe. However, anyone who has lived through the past twenty years, from the village simpleton to Professor Infeld, has it ingrained on his mind once and for all that:

It is the *system* that is bad and rotten, the people who live under it become corrupt, it contaminates anyone within its orbit, while the untainted are condemned to be crushed and go under.

Communism equals humanity deceived. All that generations of dreamers, ideologists, and writers proclaimed about it (before it acquired its earthly form) amounted to the abuse of public confidence. They said, poor innocents:

---

* Palmiro Togliatti (1893–1964) was one of the principal founders of the Italian Communist Party. During the Cold War years he argued for a more gradualist approach to Communism and more independence from the Soviet Union.

415

1. That it would be based on truth. It brought about a sanctification of lies on a scale never known before.

2. That it would be based on justice. It became a gigantic incubator of large and small injustices.

3. That it would bring true freedom. It brought about the best-organized slavery in every walk of life and every social institution to a degree unknown in the tyrannies of old.

4. That it would ennoble man, who would be free from exploitation. It degraded man, placed him under the power of stupidity, cupidity, and the basest of instincts; it led him to destroy others in the most sophisticated way yet invented.

None of these are, however, problems with which *Polityka* would concern itself, even by way of the most recondite allusion. Socialism is a sacred cow; it is not to be eaten. But one must eat to live. Therefore, everyone under the Red Star has to rely on contrivance of some sort in order to survive. As these things go, *Polityka's* contrivance was simple: substitute a mock problem for a genuine one, or a pseudo-solution where no real one was acceptable, and you're off. As with Orwell, everyone is equal, some more than others, so with matters of concern, "objective" concern being superior to all others. *Polityka's* "objective" concerns were wide-ranging: Poland and socialism and the human condition and distribution and hooliganism, traffic regulations and midwives and the quantum theory and the quality of lubricants and the health service and some unknown aspects of Pilsudski's rule. "Objective" concern meant that *Polityka* was not to be concerned with *Ding an Sich** (that would be subjectivism at its worst), only with its place in Gomułka's Communism. Viewed from the perspective of fifty years of Leninist–Stalinist Communism, it represented a kind of achievement: the cult of the individual and the dogmatism of the past disallowed all such concerns en bloc on the premise that all was for the best in the best of all countries. The simplest empiricism indicates, of course, that morally and socially *Polityka's* kind of concern amounts to

---

* *Ding an Sich* or the thing-in-itself.

one Great Big Nothing, in the words of Winnie-the-Pooh. The men of *Polityka* will read these words with bitter resentment: they alone know how many of their initiatives were stopped, how they had to fight for every word, and how difficult it was to achieve even that which someone like myself ("bastard") can so easily squash, besmear, and make into a mockery. The trouble with their superhuman efforts and their bitterness remains the same: they amount to precisely nothing. They have no moral or social significance. It is an essential quality of Communism that everyone struggles, panting for breath, with someone more stupid and more vile than himself, but the very universality of the struggle does not make it of value in itself. It is only its direction and quality that place it in some hierarchy of values and meaning. *Polityka* displays positive concern (already emancipated from the constraints of Socialist Realism) for the man-in-the-street, the grey cooperative, the average machine tool, and the post-October mill girl, a girl who uses Lechia cosmetics and Przemyslawka eau de cologne, a girl who "poses" a problem—is she, in fact, correctly fulfilled sexually and technologically? This pseudofactual, pseudosocial, pseudoresponsible substitute for involvement in reality led to *Polityka* becoming the favorite reading matter and the mini-Bible of Mr. Bolo. But *Polityka* dreamed of fulfilling another role: it wanted to be the forum and the font of wisdom for the Gomułka-style progressive intelligentsia, the technological new class, and the neopositivists of the petrochemical industry.

Mr. Bolo presents quite a problem: it is difficult to produce a Bolo synthetic portrait, if only because he comes from such a range of social backgrounds. In the early days of our People's Democracy he walked around in a cashmere overcoat, was scented with lavender, and tended to be involved in Silesian or Cracovian private enterprise. The private-enterprise band is, of course, the most heroic social group in Poland; its superhuman struggle with Communism, bureaucracy, and the exterminating effect of the tax system surpasses the Greek myths, the battle of sailors with the elements, the pioneers' efforts to combat the cruelty of desert and forest. Such a proud and admirable stance in the war with Public Enemy No. 1 should, should it not, assure the private entrepreneurs of the love and respect of the rest of society. Not a bit of it! Someday soon I intend to devote more time and attention to the problem. Mr. Bolo must not, however, be identified with private enterprise alone: there are numerous Mr. Bolos among the ranks of doctors, lawyers, technicians, and civil servants, especially those engaged in foreign trade. The beaches of the Baltic and the Tatra resorts were once full of Mr. Bolos, but no longer: they now spend their holidays in other People's Democracies, or, quite simply, in Paris. Mr. Bolo never has any trouble obtaining a passport, foreign currency, or anything else one would need for these occasions. Since October 1956 Mr. Bolo has driven a Wartburg, then a Skoda, then a Fiat, and so on—no public-transport nightmares for Mr. B. since the Polish October, Mr. Bolo has also changed his style of dress: his inspiration derives from Western films, now more widely available. Mr. Bolo changed to synthetics, nylon, Orlon, and, of course, to suede jackets.

I think Mr. Bolo must, in fact, be a son of August Bec-Walski from the 1940s cartoon, a stereotype of a reactionary, an ex-landowner and bigot; but he was flattened by the Stalinist steamroller and is now a thoroughly reformed and perfectly well-adapted individual. After October, Mr. Bolo became a kingpin in the so-called small stabilization. Ideologically and socially his background is socialist, and it follows that he is an anti-Semite by tradition, but his snobbery has overridden even his anti-Semitism and in his dreams he often sees himself walking arm-in-arm with Adolf Rudnicki* along a crowded resort promenade. In short, Mr. Bolo is a wheeler-dealer, one of those who couldn't care less and who knows nothing because he has no wish to know. He could not care less; he would get on just as well in Pilsudki's Poland as in a Communist Australia. People of that type silently ducked down for a time during the [1939–45] war, for it was too risky a game and the price one might have had to pay was too high, but they rose to the surface again in excellent form under Communism, and the species is flourishing in numerous varieties. Were one to tell them the truth about themselves, they would feel deeply hurt. They do not do any harm to anyone, they criticize things as much as anyone else, they tell political jokes and get on with everyone, don't they? And if they are friends with one or another notorious member of the apparat, does it matter? What's wrong with that? That's the way it always has been and always will be: the strong get to the top and the wise stick with them. I have been told that I myself infuriated one of the Bolo tribe by openly describing in a book my own stratagems when dealing

---

* Adolf Rudnicki was a Polish-Jewish author and essayist. He participated in the Warsaw Uprising in 1944 and is best known for his writings on the Holocaust.

with the bigwigs of the Security Services. Thus, I apparently "spoiled" the efforts and chances of others. How unethical. Humanism, freedom, and principles are all "bullshit" to Mr. Bolo, but even so he fails to see that crooked dealing is so much a permanent function of a totalitarian system that, even if I tried, I couldn't have spoiled any other "deals." On the weekends Mr. Bolo buys his *Przekroj** and his *Polityka,* slips them both into the door pocket of his new BMW, and drives off to Zalew, the newest spot. *Przekroj* makes him feel "in"; *Polityka* absolves him. Thanks to *Polityka,* Mr. Bolo feels politically involved, socially concerned. Thanks to Mr. Bolo, *Polityka's* circulation swells.

It is the silent tragedy of *Polityka* that it sees itself as the organ of the descendants of Zeromski's[†] self-sacrificing heroes (now armed with a television set and a motorbike). In reality, it is the organ of the Bolos of this world.

I suspect that the fundamental watershed in the life of Mieczysław Rakowski occurred in the early 1960s. As before, he responded instantly to a new variation on the theme of Polish Communism. The time of conditioning and instrumentalism was over; we were entering the era of personalities. Everyday history was no longer to be governed by the iron laws of science, by the letter of the Leninist gospel, by the political textbooks, but by a series of trials of strength among the people in power. The personality of the Boss was always dominant, but others were now emerging. There was Kliszko,[‡] the Harlequin Confessor; Moczar,[§] the small-town bully who managed to rise to the provincial level and then higher still; there was Cyrankiewicz,[¶] the old snooker player and cardsharp who had a way of marking the cards in such a manner that they still looked clean. There was Gierek,[**] the King of Silesia, a specially guarded region, gener-

---

* *Przekroj* is a Polish weekly news magazine.

† Stefan Zeromski (1864–1925) was a Polish writer known for his depictions of Polish resistance to Russian domination.

‡ Zenon Kliszko was a central figure in the PUWP who also served as speaker of the Sejm.

§ Mieczysław Moczar was a Polish Communist leader known for his severe repression of anti-Communist activity. Also a political rival of Gierek.

¶ Józef Cyrankiewicz presided over the formation of the PUWP and then served as Prime Minister. He was forced out of office with Gomułka in 1970.

** Gierek. See note on page 380.

ally known as "Katanga." There were the momentary, short-lived successes of Zambrowski* and Strzelecki,† but the message was filtering through: in order to get anywhere, you had to be a somebody. This was the present rule of the game. Best of all, you should be someone in your own right, someone unique, an exceptional individual all around. The difficult part was hitting on the right sort of individual characteristics.

I saw Rakowski again, this time at the premiere of the student cabaret STS in Warsaw. The venue itself was significant: a favorite of Gomułka's in one of the few remaining shelters of the surviving revisionists, very much emasculated but still rather dicey. This was a completely new-style Rakowski, and the change seemed, frankly, fascinating to me. All in beige, enveloped in Western wools, suedes, leathers, and olive-toned shoes, the editor shone, distributing smiles, gracious glances, bon mots. Instant ripostes made him a full-fledged member of that particular milieu where baroque bitterness and razor-sharp conversation reigned. There was nothing of Mr. Bolo in all this. On the contrary, Rakowski represented Mr. Bolo's natural adversary: a swinging beatnik, a rock 'n' roller, a frustrated existentialist with a penchant for the chic, and, with sufficient foreign currency, he modeled himself on the style of Saint-Germain de Pres and the heroes of New Wave films. But the hair style, the hair style above all! It was the keynote of the whole effect, giving it an absolutely up-to-the-minute slant: the hair was cut short and combed forward at the front, not, however, in bangs, but in the newest French fashion introduced by Maurice Ronet. How impressive it was! I instantly understood the difficulties which had had to be overcome, and the strength of character required to overcome them in the process of straightening those curly ringlets of yore. But the clothes? The clothes! My God, how did he get hold of them? "Quite simple," said the girl I was with. "Through Wikomirska, of course."

I don't know exactly when Rakowski married Wanda Wiłkomirska. I do know, however, that the famous violinist really came into her own at the time I am referring to, when the uniqueness of personality acquired overall importance. The sobriety of village jerkins was left behind: playing

* Roman Zambrowski was extremely active in Polish Communism in its various incarnations. He was removed from the PUWP in 1968.
† Ryszard Strzelecki, an active leader in the PUWP—member of the Central Committee and briefly responsible for the supervision of cultural affairs in the early 1960s.

the peasant and donning the appearance of a puritan in rustic clothing was now part of the dim and distant past; wealth and its appurtenances became the symbol of achievement. Now it was permitted to have one's own villa furnished with antiques, a small yacht on the lakes, and wallpaper from Hamburg—all this underlined the correctness of development. Obviously, in the circumstances, Wiłkomirska was worth her weight in gold. I am told that she is a distinguished violinist, recognized on both sides of the Great Divide. This may well be the case, I know nothing about it, but I couldn't help noticing that no other musician went abroad quite so often, especially during the Stalinist era. It is no secret that Wiłkomirska is from a well-known Party family and that from childhood she was the delight of various Komsomols. Under Communism, as elsewhere, some are better than others, and a good violinist will be a *better* violinist for being the daughter of old Communists, who made her first appearance on stage in a pretty red Pioneer's kerchief; just as under feudalism, a poet who was also a count was a *better* poet than a poet who was only a villein. The Party had molded her, she owed everything to the Party, the Party was proud of her. No wonder, then, that she was so often to be found on the lists of artists representing Polish art in the West, that it was easier for her to travel abroad, to buy a car in West Germany and bring it back into Poland without paying duty on it, to exchange it for another model when the fashion changed, and so on and so forth.

The Rakowski-Wiłkomirska marriage seemed to me to throw a very interesting light on the mores of our time and constituted the successful attempt by an individual to become financially independent under Communism, an attempt worthy of a character in a Balzac novel. It should be made clear that in the Warsaw of Comrade Rakowski, as much as in the Paris of Monsieur de Rastignac, political independence and freedom of maneuver, the ability to think for oneself and to commit acts of real and not-so-real nonconformism, are a direct function of financial independence and of being freed from the worries of tomorrow's bread-and-butter. And how all this helps in building up the personality! I'm inclined to think that, without the Wiłkomirska investment, Rakowski would never have managed that astounding transformation into a *Przekrój* playboy, despite the fact that the sensational new hair style revealed certain attractive features which had been unnoticeable in the past. There he was, quite a lad, an open smile, strong manly features, a kind of Pomeranian Steve

McQueen. It is a fact that middle-aged farmers and such-like, suitably emancipated and coiffed, always had a charm of their own, much sought after in the capitals of the world. Some circles in Poland simply adore having Gramsci* read aloud to them by just such a product of *Przekrój*, and Rakowski, dressed to the nines, mastered the style to perfection. It is worth noting, just for the record, that in the past Rakowski the Central Committee instructor, Rakowski the editor, and Rakowski the chairman of the Journalists' Association, hated *Przekrój* and all it stood for, and was the first to demand that anyone who followed the *Przekrój* recipe for dress or coiffure be burned at the stake. What caused him to change so? Why such a turnaround? Was this change visceral in nature or cosmetic only?

In the mid-1960s, the situation (very much telescoped) looked something like this: Gomułka and Kliszko were out on a limb, Cyrankiewicz was still available, Ochab† was in retirement, and around them bubbled molten magma from which the occasional cry could be heard: "Moczar!" "Gierek!" "the young secretaries!" This last was often interpreted as "Rakowski!" particularly among the Americans, who take with a childlike innocence to anything and everything they are told in Warsaw. The Americans evolved a theory. As the secretaries to the secretaries of the Central Committee were only taken on after thorough testing, and as it was possible to get a lot done with their help, it followed that they probably formed a definite political force, a potential partnership perhaps: the Young Turks, the Young Secretaries. Rakowski was therefore invited to America, where he spent a few months, was given the red-carpet treatment, and was allowed to talk to President Kennedy. There is no end to the naïveté of the Americans. It seems they are still living under the spell of Scheherazade;‡ it is difficult to imagine what they were hoping to achieve with this visit. In any case, at the beginning they were charmed by the swinging appearance and hair style number three, and swallowed

---

* Antonio Gramsci (1891–1937) was a founding member of the Italian Communist Party who was imprisoned under Mussolini. He was also an influential Marxist thinker, noted for his *Prison Notebooks*.

† Edward Ochab served at First Secretary of the PUWP briefly in 1956 prior to the ascension of Gomułka.

‡ Scheherazade is the legendary queen in *One Thousand and One Nights* who tells beguiling stories to the king to keep herself alive.

politely the banal slogans about coexistence, which were slightly adjusted for different audiences (be it the Department of State or the American left). They got their just deserts when Rakowski, on his return to Warsaw, published a book with the title *Multi-Story America,* which he wrote in a style quite different from that which he had adopted in his conversations in America. The book was essentially a pack of lies, gross oversimplifications, and an insult to the reader's intelligence. But it won't do any good to accuse Rakowski of writing a bad and silly book: he was not, after all, a genuine writer or journalist, but only a press instructor, an editor and chairman of the Journalists' Association. However, the Americans will never learn that it is not important what a political sponger says when he is in America, that it is what he says at home that matters. They won't learn, and that is why they may well lose the battle for the world. Heaven help us if they do. The only beneficiary of the whole expedition was, of course, Rakowski: his American grant and the bit of globe-trotting created, in Warsaw and elsewhere, an aura of tolerance and accessibility about him. And that was just what he was after.

Social position, a Party post (Rakowski became a deputy member of the Central Committee), financial security, exotic sex appeal, and the fashionable appearance of a swinging Marxist are trump cards in the formation of a personality with a view to a great career. But there was still something missing, the mixture did not quite gel; the format, the caliber were not quite there. There was, however, the tried-and-tested technique: if not quite up to the job yourself, join forces with others in the same position. Thus a triumvirate was born: Starewicz,* Żółkiewski, Rakowski. They came together, reached an understanding, and hung up their sign: "Liberalism."

What did this liberalism amount to? Everything and nothing at all. Each of the triumvirate, until the moment when he revealed himself to be a neoliberal, had behind him the beautiful and richly illustrated dossier of a totalitarian bully, a Stalinist hireling, a cynical hypocrite, a servile flunky. Starewicz and Żołkiewski need no introduction: their names speak for themselves, one in the field of administration, the other in the realm of culture. For twenty years they played out their roles with the ruthlessness of Nazi *Gauleiters,* leaving behind a trail of cruelty by com-

---

* Władysław Starewicz (1882–1965) was a filmmaker and animator.

mand. The liberalism of ideas, conduct, and principle was the subject of their lifelong contempt. As young men, they prostrated themselves before violence executed against truth and goodness; it had become their life-blood to worship brute force, which they called reason or necessity, and which they made into an absolute value. In the Communist decalogue, liberalism is a mortal sin; the word is a stench to the nostrils, it is associated with mental and physical decay, the putrescence of the body cells and psychological disintegration. What, then, prompted the triumvirs to take such a hazardous step? What provoked their chief instrument, Alicja Lisiecka, to use the term "liberal" in a place as full of malicious gossip as the canteen of the Writers' Association? A term which, if repeated to Gomułka or Kliszko, carried with it the risk of bloody reckonings behind closed doors. They took this risk openly and deliberately. What made them endorse such words? What made them raise the cursed word, like a reptile, above their heads and hold it there for all to see, despite the revulsion they must have felt?

The fight for Gomułka's inheritance was on. There were a number of challengers. The small-town giant Moczar bulges at the security police headquarters (now computerized), the power rooted in the provincial miasma, heading a force of butchery cooperatives, small fruit-growers, allotment holders, and the barmaids from Zamosc, where during the war everyone had someone in the Underground, only nobody now knows what kind of Underground it was. Moczar forges ahead under the banner of patriotism; others fight behind a veil of economics, using truncheons but with the promise of a higher standard of living, fridges for all; some even attack the feudal privilege of the apparat. There isn't much room at the top, it's difficult to get in, yet they have to produce an alternative that will be attractive enough. What about freedom, then? What about liberty and slogans, which always go down well among people in Poland who have lost their political bearings, and among the "wet pragmatists" in the intelligentsia who still believe in barter politics: buy here, sell there, give support to one, put pressure on another. The triumvirs' past is, of course, a bit of a drawback. Żółkiewski, an old campaigner of repression, makes you want to throw up when he starts talking about freedom. Among the non-Party members of the Sejm, Starewicz is known as the Flunky: it is well known that he is prepared to act the executioner as and when required by the Master. As for Rakowski . . . how then should they set

424

about it? There is a way, though. If all else fails, there is always the way of Konrad Wallenrod,* who acted as a double agent among the Prussian Knights. The Poles love it. No one has written better on the subject than Adam Mickiewicz,† and in no other country do poetry-reading teenagers so admire the biography of a noble double agent. Perhaps it is just because they have no idea of how to play the double game that the Poles admire it; the presence of Wallenrod looms large in Polish literature, but Polish history has no Talleyrand. Yet it is Talleyrand who appeals to many among the intellectual elite, who prefer him to their own relatively simple and straightforward collaborators of the past, the Drucki-Lubeckis‡ and the Wielopolskis.§ Under Communism, with its plethora of moral imbroglios, tolerance of the double game has grown, and its social prestige has grown with it. It seems that it is enough for a Party member to have his child baptized in secret for him to feel that he is a latter-day heroic little Wallenrod. Communism, particularly its Polish version, is, of course, ideally suited to Talleyrand-like practices. That is why so often two members of the Party, who are as like as twins, can be regarded in a totally different light by public opinion. In a democracy, people's moral qualities are tested only on special occasions, but under Communism this tired litmus paper never has a break; it is put to work day in and day out to make new assessments, always depending on the facts of a particular case, always from the perspective of other people's interests, filtered through the sieve of constantly changing norms of behavior. Moral ambivalence reigns and no universal norms apply. A person is good for a day, good for a purpose, good for now. Under Communism, a politician is not judged by his political program but by the decency of his day-to-day behavior. In the eyes of the people, decency is odds in his favor, which, one must admit, is an odd paradox.

---

* *Konrad Wallenrod* (1828) is a narrative poem by Adam Mickiewicz. The poem is thought to have inspired the Polish uprising against the Russian Empire in November 1830.

† Mickiewicz. See note on page 197.

‡ Franciszek Drucki-Lubecki (1778–1846) held various governmental posts in partitioned Poland. He represented a political faction called the conciliators who spoke out against military resistance to Russian domination.

§ Aleksander Wielopolski (1803–1877) was a member of the Polish nobility. He served in the administration of partitioned Poland. His attempt to derail the Polish national movement in 1863 ended up provoking of the famous January Uprising in that year.

Elections under Communism are highly amusing, not because the whole thing is a sham, but because the voters in all seriousness consider and devoutly hope that the candidate, if elected, will be a decent enough man *not* to do what he promised in his manifesto. The variations on the Wallenrod or Talleyrand theme are infinite, but our triumvirs have gone one better and have thought up an improved scheme.

Nothing new, however. The magic formula used to justify the implementation of sixty years of Communism in practice—"He meant well!"—has been tried before. It was first used when it became necessary to explain away the chasm between what Marx and Engels wanted and what was done in their name in the process of carrying out their ideas in real life. Lenin and Dzerżhińsky also "meant well" at a time when one could have washed one's hands in the blood running down the gutters of Lubyanka.* "He meant well," said the cretins collecting money for International Red Aid before the last war, whenever anyone dared to criticize Stalin for finishing off his closest henchmen. After the war, Hilary Minc† applied this formula—this dialectical gadget—with consummate skill. Half of Poland was still repeating "He means well" as the economic magician pushed on toward total collectivization, grinding the peasants into the ground. Cyrankiewicz's factotums have been telling us for twenty years that "he meant well," but time passes and the formula is wearing a little thin. Nowadays, they often add that things would have been much worse without him, but of this we cannot be sure: we have never yet been without him. We know all too well, however, what it is like with him. Gomułka managed to keep his popularity up after October, his tired lieutenants whispering "He means well" at the celebratory banquets, while to anyone with a pair of eyes in his head it was obvious that he in fact meant as ill as possible. The tune, then, has been tried out extensively and the triumvirs' acolytes were able to play an even more complicated version of it with all the exultation and wild excitement brought out by careful rehearsal: "They mean well, they cannot show it at the moment, but if you help them and back them in their struggle with the dark butcher from the

* Lubyanka was the popular name for the headquarters of the Soviet secret police and the site of a notorious prison.

† Hilary Minc was a Communist leader who served in a number of ministries during the Stalinist regime of Bolesław Bierut.

Lodz security police [Moczar], the boorish illiterate, they will rise to the top and practice what they are now preaching."

The physiology of lying and the function of distortion under Communism are governed by their own peculiar laws. The totalitarian lie comes effortlessly, it is resilient and full of life like a toxin; the serum has to be new each time, the difficulties in producing it are considerable. How easily lying came to the SS men at their trials: it was an order, they had to, they did not know. We know that they were turning the truth inside out, but do we know how to disinfect, delouse, filter, and unravel what remains of reality? On Gomułka's orders Żołkiewski liquidated the bestially revisionist *Nowa Kultura*—did he mean well then, just "could not do otherwise, but had to do it"? Why couldn't he have gone away for a slimming cure, giving as an explanation that obesity would shorten his life? Why did he accept the commission, and now hints that he did not want to do it, and anyway that he meant well? After "the protest of the 34,"* Rakowski wrote an obnoxious article in *Polityka* full of stereotyped accusations taken straight out of the Leninist catechism. Now, courting some of the thirty-four with his supposedly alternative program, he gives one to understand that "he had to, it was necessary, superior force, that he didn't mean it, did not want it, that he meant well," and that the rest was just tactics and rules of the game. The myth of the game is one of the most serviceable devices, one of the better gadgets. An entire machinery of false images and carefully planted rumors serves to create the myth of struggle where there is no real struggle. We witness a game played for high stakes when the stakes are sham, there are no conflicting programs, and not one job will be lost over the whole thing. Of course, it does not follow from this that there is no conflict between factions. There is, but this is a totally different kettle of fish: genuine gangs fighting for genuine power stick genuine knives into their opponents' genuine backs, but in public they hug one another, they bill and coo, providing the press with lovely pictures of brotherly slap and tickle. The more someone whispers into your ear how much he is against something, the greater is the likelihood that he is for it. And if he privately lets it be known that he means well, you can be sure that his plans are very nasty indeed. And, anyway, where are

---

* In March of 1964 a group of Polish writers and academics wrote a letter to the Communist authorities protesting censorship.

the guarantees that they have changed at all? We have known the three of them for twenty years: is there anything in their past to suggest that they really mean well now? Why didn't they show it before? Why is it that for the last twenty years they meant so very ill? Why have they never, at any time, done anything whatsoever which might indicate an inkling of good-will? And finally, where are the people to look for the difference between tactics and common sense? The Polish Stalinist school of psychology has considerable achievements to its credit, quite unknown in the West. It has made a very detailed study of the correlation between action, thought, and speech in the "real" man. It appears that the truth about a person bears no close causal relation to his actions, speech, and thought. Moreover, it seems that actions, speech, and thought are not themselves related to one another. Dostoyevsky has already shown quite satisfactorily that a person's actions do not reveal the truth about him to any significant degree. Nor is this truth revealed by speech; we all know that an orator speaking from a tribune draped in red does not believe in even a fraction of his own words. Yet the circumstances in which one can carry out a series of wicked deeds, while thinking that perhaps they are not quite decent, or, better still, com-municating one's doubts to friends around a café table, no—this doesn't count. No, *this* is no justification. This sensational discovery is a revelation and a triumph for the Polish psychological school of morality. It poses a nice problem for traditional Christian attitudes toward these matters: Christianity was always inclined to absolve those who were unaware of what they were doing; but to be told that someone was innocent because he fully understood the moral error of his ways at the time of committing them, and, even in a state of super-consciousness, discussed them in detail with his friends over a glass of vodka, is really quite a blow. Unfortunately, the cognitive achievements of this particular school of moral philosophy have become part and parcel of the way of thinking of quite a number of Poles. Sufficiently so for our triumvirs and their like to build on them false hopes and use them to diffuse and sublimate their own shabby villainy.

Nowadays in Poland one often hears that so-and-so is "having dif-ficulties." It usually means that a man who, until recently, was our mortal enemy, who was ready to annihilate our physical or spiritual existence with the soulless automatism of a programmed mechanism, who was planning it with cold premeditation, while calling it a public duty, social progress, or historical necessity, now fawns like a dog, gazing into our eyes in search of understanding and an uneasy false camaraderie. We have seen so many of them. They often succeed in winning our compassion, sometimes even a kind of admiration. Only they never manage to convince us that when their difficulties come to an end (for, obviously, "they meant well") they will change, become different, better. For we have also seen those who did overcome their little difficulties, who have returned to grace and favor, to power and influence, to new possibilities of action. Yes, we have seen them, and they remained just as they were before—hypocritical worshippers of abominable iniquities.

I heard lately that Rakowski is having some *contretemps*. Difficult to say. I would have to see him. The hair style would reveal all.

(October 1967)

POSTSCRIPTUM

I had a brief glimpse of Rakowski on one later occasion, several years after I left Poland. It was in 1973, or thereabouts, and I was living in Connecticut, within easy reach of New York. My friend Jerzy Turowicz, editor of the Catholic journal *Tygodnik Powszechny,* was over from Poland, and I had been invited to the private viewing of an exhibition of paintings by the famous painter Jan Lebenstein, also from Poland. This was opening in one of the more prestigious galleries on Madison Avenue.

Accordingly, I drove into Manhattan with my American wife, Mary Ellen, and after collecting Turowicz from the Kosciuszko Foundation, we walked from there to the gallery. Inside, I saw a crowd of people at the center of the gallery, one of whom held out his arms to welcome Turowicz. Turowicz was pulling me along with him, and so it was that I suddenly found myself face-to-face with Rakowski in the thick of the crowd. The memory of my article, which *Kultura* had published six years earlier, on "The Hair Styles of Mieczysław Rakowski," flashed through my mind like a red alert. Without a second's hesitation, however, I held out my hand to him. He wavered, turned red, changed expression, but then shook hands. Immediately afterwards, he turned his back on me, and that was the end of our social encounter.

As we drove back, Mary Ellen asked me why that particular individual had so ostentatiously shown his disapproval of my person. I told her who Rakowski was, explained the whole political, social, and moral background, and gave her an outline of what I had written about him and why. Her comment was: "It's odd, but at this moment I wouldn't be able to describe his hair style. It was somehow neutral and unremarkable. Perhaps you made him into too much of a mythological figure in your article, for metaphorical purposes?"

I thought to myself that I, too, had suddenly become less observant. Could I really not have noticed his hair style, such an important element in my assessments of him? "That is ominous," I said. "The fact that one hour after seeing Rakowski I don't really know what hair style he had, doesn't augur well. . . ."

In 1981, when I read in the newspapers that he had been appointed deputy prime minister with the task of negotiating with Solidarity, I remembered my remark. A feeling of sadness and discomfort came over me, as it does on each occasion when I see a glint of sin in people's faces, or the shadow of evil among the events of everyday life.

When Rakowski, on behalf of the government, severed negotiations with Solidarity, it was a preliminary step to General Jaruzelski's coup in December 1981. His subsequent role as the general's right-hand man during the period of repressions and the delegalization of Solidarity confirmed the pattern of his previous behavior. It also confirmed my observation that his hair style is no longer of any significance. He can now afford to be unconcerned about it. And so can we.

(1983)

Editor's Postscriptum

Leopold Tyrmand died in 1985. Mieczysław Rakowski was made prime minister in 1988 and later, in the summer of 1989, first secretary of the Polish Communist Party.

(1989)

V
Dissent

25

Man, This Enemy[*]
(1953)

CZESLAW MILOSZ

Whoever reads the public statements of the four writers discussed in the previous chapters might say that they sold themselves.[**] The truth is, however, more involved. These men are, more or less consciously, victims of a historic situation. Consciousness does not help them to shed their bonds; on the contrary, it forges them. At the very best, it can offer them the delights of Ketman[†] as a consolation: Never before has there been such enslavement through consciousness as in the twentieth century. Even my generation was still taught in school that reason frees men.

In the people's democracies, a battle is being waged for mastery over the human spirit. Man must be made to understand, for then he will accept. Who are the enemies of the new system? The people who do not understand. They fail to understand because their minds work feebly or else badly.

---

[*] This is chapter 8 of Milosz's classic work *The Captive Mind*.

[**] Chapters 4–7 of the book are profiles or character studies of four writers, whom Milosz knew in Poland, all of whom were seduced by Communism to varying degrees.

[†] Ketman is a concept Milosz discusses at length in chapter 3 of his book. It is a phenomenon described by the nineteenth-century French philosopher Gobineau, who observed it in his travels to Persia. A person utilizing Ketman gives the outward appearance of complete orthodoxy while harboring deeply heterodox beliefs. Milosz draws the analogy from the Persians giving the appearance of being orthodox Muslims to those individuals of central Europe appearing as orthodox Communists.

In every capital of central and eastern Europe the windows in the Central Committee buildings are illuminated late into the night. Behind their desks sit men well-versed in the writings of Lenin and Stalin. Not the least of their tasks is to define the position of the enemy. As the situation changes, this military staff pins another little flag on the battle map. Data from each country then aid the supreme command in Moscow to establish an overall strategy.

Different groups of people are the main object of study. The least important is the propertied class which was dispossessed by the national-ization of factories and mines and by the agricultural reform. Their num-ber is insignificant; their way of thinking amusingly old-fashioned. They are no problem. In time they will die off—if need be, with a little help.

The petty bourgeoisie, that is the small merchants and craftsmen, cannot be taken so lightly. They constitute a powerful force, one that is deeply rooted in the masses. Hardly is one clandestine workshop or store liquidated in one neighborhood or city than another springs up elsewhere. Restaurants hide behind a sliding wall of a private house; shoemakers and tailors work at home for their friends. In fact, everything that comes under the heading of speculation sprouts up again and again. And no wonder! State and municipal stores consistently lack even the barest essentials. In the summer, one can buy winter clothes; in the winter, summer wear—but usually of the wrong size and of poor quality. The purchase of a spool of thread or a needle is a major problem, for the one state store in the town may not carry them for a year. Clothes that are given to be mended are held by the local crafts' cooperative for six months. The inns ("Points of Collec-tive Nourishment") are so crowded that people lose the desire to drink with their friends. They know they will have to sit down at a table with strangers and wait, sometimes as long as an hour, before the waiter appears.

All this creates a field for private services. A worker's wife goes to a nearby town, buys needles and thread, brings them back and sells them: the germ of capitalism. The worker himself of a free afternoon mends a broken bathroom pipe for a friend who has waited months for the state to send him a repair man. In return, he gets a little money, enough to buy himself a shirt: a rebirth of capitalism. He hasn't time to wait in line on the day that the state store receives a new shipment of goods, so he buys his shirt from a friend. She has cleverly managed to buy three, let us say, through her friendship with the salesgirl and now she resells them at a small profit. She is speculating. What she earns as a cleaning-woman in a state factory is not enough to support her three children since her husband was arrested by the security police. If these manifestations of human enterprise were not wiped out it is easy to guess what they would lead to. A worker would set up a plumbing repairs shop. His neighbor, who secretly sells alcohol to people who want to drink in relative privacy, would open a café. The cleaning-woman would become a merchant, peddling her goods. They would gradually expand their businesses, and the lower middle class would reappear. Introduce freedom of the press and of assembly, and publications catering to this clientele would spring up like mushrooms after the rain. And there would be the petty bourgeoisie as a political force.

What is worse, this matter involves the peasant problem. Peasants, who make up the majority of the population of the country, have a middle-class mentality. They are more deeply attached to their few little hectares of field than the storekeepers are to their little shops. As late as the nineteenth century they were still living in bondage. They oppose collectivization because they see it as a return to a state their fathers found unbearable. To leap out of bed at the signal of an official on a collective farm is just as hateful as to do so at the sound of a gong rung by the overseer of an estate. The peasants' blind hatred worries the Party. Its more sensitive members secretly bow to the necessity of making concessions. They believe that collectivization should be preceded by cooperative use of machinery on private fields, and that it can come only after a long introductory phase of education, extending possibly over decades. This temporizing spirit breeds trouble; that is why the whispered slogans of the "national Communists" are always so popular. But the Center exacts a certain tempo. The structure of every dependent country must be brought to resemble that of Russia as quickly as possible.

This problem, in turn, affects the cities. Peasants are divided into three categories—"poor," "middle," and "kulak"—in an effort to break their solidarity by engendering mutual antagonisms. A peasant's wealth is rated not only by the amount of land he holds, but by how many horses, cows, and pigs he owns, how he lives, eats, and dresses. Lest he fall into an uncomfortable classification, he drops farming and flees to the city; or else he keeps only a minimum amount of livestock and pretends to be poor. As a result, the city suffers from a lack of provisions.

But the peasants are not dangerous. They may beat up a Party boss or even kill him in a burst of desperation, but nothing more. When the state is the sole buyer of their produce, and when they cannot voice their protest at the amount of tribute the state demands of them, they are powerless. The security police can easily handle recalcitrants, especially since it can complain of no lack of informers, now that informing has become an excellent means of saving oneself. The peasants are a leaderless mass. History shows few instances when they seriously threatened the rulers. The term "peasant revolt" sounds nice in textbooks and has a certain propaganda value, but only for the naïve. In reality, the peasants have almost always served as a tool; their leaders, most often of nonpeasant origin, have used them for their own ends. The power of the peasants lies in their number; it is a power only when a man like Lenin comes along and throws the weight of their numbers into the scale of events. Obviously, peasants can cause trouble in such moments of upheaval as wars. As long as a private peasant economy exists it acts as a natural base for partisan operations. A peasant hut is the ideal place for partisans to eat, sleep, and work out plans of action. Therefore, a collective farm, where a man's every step is easy to trace, guarantees a degree of control that is indispensable if one wants to preclude hostile underground activity.

Workers are far more important than peasants. Most of them are antagonistic to the new system. That is understandable. They resent the norms they must fill. Those norms are constantly rising. Though the "solidarity of the workers" makes a fine slogan, it does not mean that the solidarity of the crews in a factory is to be tolerated. Their ranks are split by the institution of "shock-workers" which is fostered by an appeal to ambition and enforced by pressure from members of the Party cell. A man may at first refuse to become a shock-worker. But gradually he learns it does not pay to be stubborn; because when workers are being chosen for a course in bookkeeping, for instance, his application is rejected, or when his turn comes for a free vacation he is declared ineligible, etc.

The attitude of the workers toward the regime is ambivalent. On the one hand, they prize its positive contributions. Unemployment is a thing of the past; in fact, there is a constant lack of skilled labor. Not only the head of a family but most of its members are employed. This accumulation of wages means that a family would be able to live better than ever before if only the stores were fairly well stocked; but given the shortage of food and consumer goods, this is rarely, if ever, the case. For workers' children, social advancement is easy because the Party must recruit the cadres of the new intelligentsia from their ranks. The worker can educate himself by attending countless evening courses. If he stands in good favor with the Party he can enjoy a vacation in a rest home, all expenses paid. On the other hand, he cannot defend himself against exploitation by his employer, the state. His trade union representatives are Party tools. They team together with the factory managers for one purpose: to raise production. Workers are told that a strike is a crime. Against whom are they to strike? Against themselves? After all, the means of production belong to them, the state belongs to them. But such an explanation is not very convincing. The workers, who dare not state aloud what they want, know that the goals of the state are far from identical with their own.

Central and eastern Europe produce in order to raise the military and economic potential of the Center and to compensate for the industrial backwardness of Russia. Workers and their needs have no influence on production plans. Most of the goods produced ebb away to the East. Besides, every product of a worker's hands is the object of innumerable bookkeeping operations. A whole staff of functionaries sits in every factory, counting, writing reports, compiling statistics; the same thing happens on every rung of the state hierarchy, right through to the state wholesale houses and retail stores. If, at last, the article reaches the consumer, it is very expensive; into its cost are counted the salaries of the swarms of bureaucrats through whose hands it must pass. Factory machines are overaged; there is a scarcity of essential spare parts. So workers are ordered to replace broken parts by whatever homemade means they can devise. Production comes first, even at the price of using up the machines. Discipline is severe; negligence or even a few minutes' lateness are strictly punished. No wonder, then, that the bad side of the system outweighs the good in the worker's mind. Still, he dares not complain. If he betrays any signs of discontent the security police, whose secret agents are his coworkers and sometimes his friends, takes care of him.

The wildcat strikes that break out from time to time are no threat in themselves, for peace returns quickly after mass arrests of all participants. They are, however, ominous signs that discontentment has reached a tension that can find release only in desperate acts. A strike requires a certain minimum of organization. That is why nothing else makes Party

437

dialecticians so uneasy. The workers are the only class capable of organized action—that Marxist principle has never been forgotten. No action, however, is possible without leaders. If the leaders reason correctly, that is, if they understand the necessities of the historic process, then the workers as a mass will be unable to protest.

Everything, thus, takes us back to the question of mastery over the mind. Every possible opportunity for education and advancement is offered to the more energetic and active individuals among the workers. The new, incredibly extensive bureaucracy is recruited from among the young people of working-class origin. The road before them is open, open but guarded: their thinking must be based on the firm principles of dialectical materialism. Schools, theaters, films, painting, literature, and the press all shape their thinking.

We should also call attention to a new institution, the "club," whose significance is comparable to that of the chapel in the Middle Ages. It exists in every factory, every school, every office. On its walls hang portraits of Party leaders draped with red bunting. Every few days, meetings following pre-arranged agendas take place, meetings that are as potent as religious rites. The Catholic Church wisely recognized that faith is more a matter of collective suggestion than of individual conviction. Collective religious ceremonies induce a state of belief. Folding one's hands in prayer, kneeling, singing hymns *precede* faith, for faith is a psycho-physical and not simply a psychological phenomenon. Edward Gibbon, describing the effects of Theodosius's decrees forbidding pagan rites *(The Decline and Fall of the Roman Empire,* chapter 28), says:

> The devotion of the poet, or the philosopher, may be secretly nourished by prayer, meditation, and study; but the exercise of public worship appears to be the only solid foundation of the religious sentiments of the people, which derive their force from imitation and habit. The interruption of that public exercise may consummate, in the period of a few years, the important work of a national revolution. The memory of theological opinions cannot long be preserved, without the artificial helps of priests, of temples, and of books. The ignorant vulgar, whose minds are still agitated by the blind hopes and terrors of superstition, will be soon persuaded by their superiors to direct their vows to the

reigning deities of the age; and will insensibly imbibe an ardent zeal for the support and propagation of the new doctrine, which spiritual hunger at first compelled them to accept."

The Party has learned this wise lesson from the Church. People who attend a "club" submit to a collective rhythm, and so come to feel that it is absurd to think differently from the collective. The collective is composed of units that doubt; but as these individuals pronounce the ritual phrases and sing the ritual songs, they create a collective aura to which they in turn surrender. Despite its apparent appeal to reason, the "club's" activity comes under the heading of collective magic. The rationalism of the doctrine is fused with sorcery, and the two strengthen each other. Free discussion is, of course, eliminated. If what the doctrine proclaims is as true as the fact that 2 x 2 equals 4, to tolerate the opinion that 2 x 2 equals 5 would be indecent.

From his first day in school, the young citizen receives an education based on this truth. There is a great difference between schools in the people's democracies and schools in the West, for example the schools I attended in prewar Poland. My friends and I were exposed to a dual system of values. Mathematics, physics, and biology taught us scientific laws, and inculcated respect for a materialistic outlook inherited from the nineteenth century. History and Letters seemed to elude scientific laws, while the history of the Catholic Church and Apologetics cast doubt, though often naïvely, on what physics and biology taught. In the people's democracies, the materialistic outlook of the nineteenth century has been extended consistently to every subject; history and every branch of human creativity are presented as governed by unshakeable and *already known* laws.

In the nineteenth century, with the rise of literacy, brochures popularizing scientific theories made their appearance. Regardless of the intrinsic worth of these theories, we must grant that from the moment they take on a popular form they become something other than what they were as hypotheses of scientific research. For example, the simplified and vulgarized version of Darwin's theory of the origin of species and the struggle for existence is not the same concept that it was for Darwin or for his scholarly opponents. It takes on emotional coloration, and changes into an important sociological element. The leaders of the twentieth century, like Hitler for instance, drew their knowledge from popular brochures, which explains the incredible confusion in their minds. Evidently, there is no place in such digests for the humble remarks of true scientists who assure us that the laws discovered are hypothetical and relative to the method chosen and the system of symbols used. Vulgarized knowledge characteristically gives birth to a feeling that *everything* is understandable and explained. It is like a system of bridges built over chasms. One can travel boldly ahead over these bridges, ignoring the chasms. It is forbidden to look down into them; but that, alas, does not alter the fact that they exist.

Once the science of nature taught that a forest was a collective of trees governed by a few elementary laws. It seemed that if one cut out the forest and replanted it, after a definite period of years a new forest, exactly like the old, would appear. Today we know this is not so; a forest is an organism arising out of complicated interactions of mosses, soil, fungi, trees, and grasses. The moment these mosses and fungi are destroyed by the cutting out of the forest, the symbiotic pattern is disturbed and the new forest is a completely different organism from what might be expected by someone who ignored the sociology of plants. Stalinists have no knowledge of the conditions human plants need in order to thrive. Forbidding any research in this direction because such study contradicts orthodoxy, they bar mankind from the possibility of acquiring fuller knowledge of itself.

Dialectical materialism, Russian-style, is nothing more than nineteenth-century science vulgarized to the second power. Its emotional and didactic components are so strong that they change all proportions. Although the Method was scientific at its origins, when it is applied to humanistic disciplines it often transforms them into edifying stories adapted to the needs of the moment. But there is no escape once a man enters upon these convenient bridges. Centuries of human history, with their thousands upon thousands of intricate affairs, are reduced to a few, most generalized terms. Undoubtedly, one comes closer to the truth when one sees history as the expression of the class struggle rather than a series of private quarrels among kings and nobles. But precisely because such an analysis of history comes closer to the truth, it is more dangerous. It gives the illusion of *full knowledge;* it supplies answers to all questions, answers which merely run around in a circle repeating a few formulas. What's more, the humanities get connected with the natural sciences thanks to the materialistic outlook (as, for example, in theories of "eternal matter"), and so we see the circle closing perfectly and logically. Then, Stalin becomes the crowning point of the evolution of life on our planet.

The son of a worker, subjected to such an education, cannot think otherwise than as the school demands. Two times two equals four. The press, literature, painting, films, and theater all illustrate what he learns, just as the lives of saints and martyrs serve as illustrations of theology. It would be wrong to assert that a dual set of values no longer exists. The resistance against the new set of values is, however, emotional. It survives, but it is beaten whenever it has to explain itself in rational terms. A man's subconscious or not-quite-conscious life is richer than his vocabulary. His opposition to this new philosophy of life is much like a toothache. Not only can he not express the pain in words, but he cannot even tell you which tooth is aching.

Thanks to excellent means of vulgarization, unprepared people (i.e., those whose minds work feebly) are taught to reason. Their training convinces them that what is happening in the people's democracies is necessary, even if temporarily bad. The greater the number of people who "participate in culture"—i.e., pass through the schools, read books and magazines, attend theaters and exhibitions—the further the doctrine reaches and the smaller grows the threat to the rule of philosophers.

But some people, even with sufficient education, reason "badly." They are impervious to the influence of Hegelian philosophy. A chicken cannot be taught to swim; just so, those who belong to the social groups condemned to disappear cannot be convinced of the truth of dialectics. According to the Party, if these people were clearly aware of their situation, they would have to confess that there is no hope for them. Therefore they look for mental subterfuges. Those people are enemies. They must be ejected to the margins of society not because of what they do, but because of what they *are*. Despite the fact that their intentions may be subjectively good, their guilt has an *objective* character.

Dialecticians have to know the enemy's mentality. Studying the reactionary as a social type, they establish certain features by which he can be recognized. The reactionary, they argue, even though he be an educated man, is incapable of grasping the concept of the interdependence of phenomena. Therefore his political imagination is limited. A man who has been trained sociologically can deduce a whole line of reasoning as to the causes and consequences of every phenomenon. Like a paleontologist, he can divine a whole formation from a single fossil. Show him the verse of a poet from any country, a picture, even an item of clothing and he immediately fits it into a historical context. His line of reasoning may be false; nonetheless he sees everything within the sphere of a given civilization as a symptom, not an accident. The reactionary, incapable of this type of thinking, sees the world as a series of unrelated, parallel occurrences.

Thus, Nazism was for the reactionary merely the result of the activity of Hitler and his clique; revolutionary movements are the effects of Moscow's machinations, etc. All the changes occurring in the people's democracies seem to him to resolve themselves into a question of superior force; if some miraculous accident were to remove this force, everything would return to "normal." He is like a man whose garden has been inundated by a raging river, and who expects to find his old flower beds intact after the waters subside. But a flooding river does not merely *exist;* it tears up and carries away whole banks of soil, fells trees, piles up layers of mud, overturns stones, until the garden of old becomes nothing more than a given number of square meters of unrecognizable land. The reactionary cannot grasp movement. His very language is static; his concepts, unchangeable, never renewed by observation. Laurel and Hardy once made a film in which Laurel, an American soldier in the First World War, is ordered to remain in the trench at his machine-gun post when the company moves to attack. Immediately thereafter the Armistice is signed, and in the resultant confusion he is forgotten. They find him twenty years later, his trench surrounded by a mountain of empty cans. He is still at his post, shooting at every commercial airplane that flies by. The reactionary, like Laurel, knows he must shoot, and he cannot realize that the plane is no longer what it was when he got his orders.

No matter how many books the reactionary reads about the dialectical method, he cannot understand its essence. Some little spring is missing in his mind. As a result he cannot properly evaluate human psychology. Dialecticians work on the premise that a man's mental and emotional life is in constant motion, that it is senseless to treat individuals as if they retained a certain stable, innate character in all circumstances. They know that by changing living conditions they change people's beliefs and reflexes. The reactionary is amazed by the changes people undergo. He awkwardly explains his friends' gradual conversion to the system as "opportunism," "cowardice," "treachery." Without such labels he feels lost. Reasoning on

442

the principle of "either—or," he tries to divide the people about him into "Communists" and "non-Communists"; but such a differentiation loses all meaning in a people's democracy. Where dialectics shapes life, whoever tries to resort to old-world logic must feel completely out of his depth.

Such misfortune always befalls the reactionary. The content suddenly flees from his concepts, and all he has left are empty words and phrases. His friends, who only a year ago used these words and phrases fondly, have rejected them as too general, too ill-defined, too remote from reality. He despairingly repeats "honor," "fatherland," "nation," "freedom," without comprehending that for people living in a changed (and daily changing) situation these abstractions take on a concrete and totally different meaning than before.

Because they so define a reactionary, dialecticians consider him a mentally inferior, and therefore not very dangerous, creature. He is no match for them. Once the propertied class is liquidated, the old intelligentsia (which was reactionary in these terms) can be brought to heel with no great difficulty. Its more vigorous representatives cross over to new ideological positions, while the rest lag further and further behind the transformations occurring all about them and so sink ever lower both socially and mentally.

The new and the old intelligentsia no longer speak a common language. Reactionary tendencies exist in the peasants and the former petty bourgeoisie, but they are unexpressed. The masses are being educated by their new living conditions, and though they are discontented, with every month the mental distance between them and the program of the reactionaries increases. Émigré politicians help greatly to facilitate the work of the government. Ninety percent of them are, according to the above definition, reactionaries. Their appeals and radio talks resemble poor Laurel's barrages at the airplanes. Their listeners are not displeased to hear them abuse a government they, too, dislike; still they cannot treat their formulations seriously. The discrepancy between these politicians' favorite words and the real situation is too clear; the superiority of the dialecticians, whose reasoning is always adapted to actuality, is too obvious. The reactionaries always lose by such comparison; the people's instinctive judgment is tinged with something like embarrassment, with shame that those who oppose dictatorship are not mentally up to its stature. Because man instinctively senses weakness, the people become ever more reluctant to side with the reactionaries. Thus, the feeling of fatalism grows stronger.

Rule over the minds of the masses, therefore, is not seriously threatened. Wherever it appears, intellectual energy can find only one outlet. It is a different matter, however, when one considers the emotional life of the masses and the terrible hatred that dominates it. This hatred cannot be explained on purely economic grounds. The Party senses that in this realm, which Marxism has studied least, surprises and real threats lie hidden.

Above all, there exists the question of religion. This problem still persists despite the many weak points in Christianity that can be attacked successfully. Not without reason did the Catholic Church defend the feudal structure against nascent capitalism during the Reformation. Capitalism created scientific thinking and dealt a powerful blow to religion in Europe by removing the best minds from the confines of theology. Modern society reveals how swiftly ideas that were at first the property of the intellectual few can spread; to discover along what lines society will develop, it is sometimes useful to trace the trend in the thinking of a small number of clear-sighted sensitive people. What is on the surface at a given moment, e.g., a literary style, gives way to new elements, though it may survive for a long time on a second or third level. (Revivals are, of course, possible.) This is what happened to theology in Europe. The Church lost its top-level position when, during the industrial upheavals, it lost the intellectuals and failed to win the new class of workers. And these are the two groups to which the Party attaches most importance. Today, the intellectual life of Christianity grows on the outer fringes of the Church, in little circles that are trying to adapt Christian philosophy to the new needs of the century.

Still, religious needs exist in the masses and it would be a mistake, from the Party's point of view, to deny them. Perhaps they will disappear once the entire population has been transformed into workers; but no one knows when that will happen. We are dealing here with imponderable elements. Mysterious, indeed, is the instinct which makes man revolt against a reasonable explanation of all phenomena. Christianity's armor is so thin in the twentieth century, a child in school is so deeply immersed in the new way of thinking, and yet the zone of shadow eludes the light of reason. We suddenly stumble upon puzzles. Professor Pavlov, who originated the theory of conditioned reflexes, was a deeply religious man. Moscow caused him no trouble over this because he was an eminent scientist and because he was old. The creator of the theory of conditioned reflexes—the very theory that constitutes one of the strongest arguments against the existence of some sort of constant called "human nature"! The defenders of religion maintain that this "human nature" cannot change completely; that gods and churches have existed over thousands of years and in all kinds of civilizations, and that one can expect this to be true of the future as well. What went on in Professor Pavlov's head if two systems of concepts, one scientific and one religious, existed simultaneously there?

The Party teaches that "existence shapes consciousness," that circumstances alter men. But it matters little whether religious drives result from "human nature" or from centuries of conditioning; they exist. During the war against Hitler, the Soviet Union had to dust off its priests as well as appeal to nationalistic feelings. When imminent death brings that moment of absurd revelation that *everything is senseless,* dialectical materialism suddenly discloses its mathematical structure. Man falls from the industriously built bridges. He prefers to surrender to the magic of icons.

In its own fashion, the Party too is a church. Its dictatorship over the earth and its transformation of the human species depend on the success with which it can channel irrational human drives and use them to its own ends. No, logical arguments are not enough. "Club" ceremonies, poetry, novels, films are so important because they reach deeper into the stratum on which the emotional conflict rages. No other church can be tolerated; Christianity is Public Enemy No. 1. It fosters all the skepticism of the masses as to the radical transformation of mankind. If, as the gospel teaches, we must not do harm unto others, then perhaps we must not harm kulaks? If the highest glory does not belong to man, then perhaps worship of Lenin and Stalin is idolatry?

I have known many Christians—Poles, Frenchmen, Spaniards—who were strict Stalinists in the field of politics but who retained certain inner reservations, believing God would make corrections once the bloody sentences of the all-mighties of History were carried out. They pushed their reasoning rather far. They argue that history develops according to immutable laws that exist by the will of God; one of these laws is the class struggle; the twentieth century marks the victory of the proletariat, which is led in its struggle by the Communist Party; Stalin, the leader of the Communist Party, fulfills the law of History, or in other words acts by the will of God; therefore one must obey him. Mankind can be renewed only on the Russian pattern; that is why no Christian can oppose the one—cruel, it is true—idea which will create a new kind of man over the entire planet. Such reasoning is often used by clerics who are Party tools. "Christ is a new man. The new man is the Soviet man. Therefore Christ is a Soviet man!" said Justinian Marina, the Romanian patriarch.

In reality, such Christians (even omitting men like Marina) perpetuate one of the greatest lies of all centuries. They renounce their faith but are ashamed to admit it. The contradiction between Christianity and Stalinist philosophy cannot be overcome. Christianity is based on a concept of *individual* merit and guilt; the New Faith, on *historical* merit and guilt. The Christian who rejects individual merit and guilt denies the work of Jesus, and the God he calls upon slowly transforms himself into History. If he admits that only individual merit and guilt exist, how can he gaze indifferently at the suffering of people whose only sin was that they blocked the path of "historical processes"? To lull his conscience he resorts to the thesis that a reactionary cannot be a good man.

Who is the reactionary? Everyone who opposes the inevitable historical processes, i.e., the Politburo police. The thesis of the "sin of the reactionary" is argued very cleverly: every perception is "oriented," i.e., at the very moment of perceiving we introduce our ideas into the material of our observations; only he sees reality truly who evaluates it in terms of the interests of the class that is the lever of the future, i.e., the proletariat. The writings of Lenin and Stalin teach us what the interests of the proletariat are. Whoever sees reality otherwise than as the proletariat sees it falsely; in other words, his picture of reality is deformed by the pressure of the interests of classes that are backward and so destined to disappear. Whoever sees the world falsely necessarily acts badly; whoever acts badly is a bad man; therefore the reactionary is a bad man, and one should not feel sorry for him.

This line of reasoning has at least one flaw—it ignores the facts. The pressure of an all-powerful totalitarian state creates an emotional tension in its citizens that determines their acts. When people are divided into "loyalists" and "criminals" a premium is placed on every type of conformist, coward, and hireling; whereas among the "criminals" one finds a singularly high percentage of people who are direct, sincere, and true to themselves. From the social point of view these persons would

446

constitute the best guarantee that the future development of the social organism would be toward good. From the Christian point of view they have no other sin on their conscience save their contempt for Caesar, or their incorrect evaluation of his might.

The assertion that historical guilt is individual guilt per se is nothing more than the subterfuge of a guilty and lying conscience. This does not mean that one can put off the problem of historical guilt with easy generalizations. Stupidity, i.e., inability to understand the mechanism of events, can cause tremendous suffering. In this sense, the Polish commanders who gave the order to start the Warsaw uprising in 1944 are guilty of stupidity, and their guilt has an individual character. Another individual guilt, however, weighs upon the command of the Red Army which refused to aid the insurgents—not out of stupidity, but on the contrary out of a full understanding of "historical processes," i.e., a correct evaluation of power.

One more example of guilt through stupidity is the attitude of various societies toward thinkers, writers, or artists whose vision reached into the future and whose works were largely incomprehensible to their contemporaries. The critic who denied the value of these works might have acted in good faith, but by his stupidity he condemned men of incomparably greater worth than himself to poverty, even persecution. The specific trick of the Christian-Stalinists is to lump these two concepts of guilt, individual and historical, together, while it is only in a few instances that these concepts coincide.

Catholics who accept the Party line gradually lose everything except the phraseology of their Christian metaphysics. The true content of their faith becomes the Method by a psychological process well-known to Christians in the people's democracies. The existence of a large number of loyal half-Christians in the subjugated part of Europe could have a tremendous effect on the Imperium's political plans. Toleration and even support of these "Christian-patriots," as they are called, enables the Center to avoid a dangerous conflict. The transition from Christianity to a cult of History takes place imperceptibly. Without doubt, the greatest success of the Imperium would come if it could install a Party-line pope in the Vatican. A mass in the Basilica of St. Peter in Rome performed by such a pope, with the assistance of dignitaries from those subjugated countries which are predominately Catholic, would be one of the most important steps toward the consolidation of the world empire.

447

Christians who serve the Eastern Imperium ingeniously resolve the problem posed by Jesus's words "Render therefore unto Caesar the things that are Caesar's; and unto God the things that are God's." Until now the contrast between the ordinary man and Caesar has never been effaced. Christianity guaranteed this division by teaching that every man had his own history, distinct from the history of the social group or the nation to which he belonged. If, as is taught today from the Elbe to Vladivostok, the history of every man is nothing more than the reflection of the history of his class, and if his class is personified in Caesar, then it is clear that the man who rebels against Caesar rebels against himself. Christians who agree to this thesis prove they no longer believe in God's judgment of each man's acts. Fear that History will damn them eternally motivates their submission.

The Party knows that the conflict between true Christianity and the Revolution is fundamental. The Revolution aims at the highest goal the human species has ever set for itself on earth, the end of "man's exploitation of man." To do this, it must replace man's desire for profit with a feeling of collective responsibility as a motive for action. This is a distant and honorable goal. Probably it will not be reached quickly; and probably, too, for a long period it will be necessary to maintain a constant terror in order to instill that feeling of responsibility by force. But Christianity contains a dual set of values; it recognizes man to be a "child of God" and also a member of society. As a member of society, he must submit to the established order so long as that order does not hinder him in his prime task of saving his soul. Only by effacing this dualism, i.e., raising man as a purely social creature, can the Party release the forces of hatred in him that are necessary to the realization of the new world.

The masses in highly industrialized countries like England, the United States, or France are largely de-Christianized. Technology, and the way of life it produces, undermines Christianity far more effectively than do violent measures. The erosion of religious beliefs is also taking place in central and eastern Europe. There, the core of the problem is to avoid galvanizing the forces of Christianity by some careless misstep. It would be an act of unforgivable carelessness, for example, to close the churches suddenly and prohibit all religious practice. Instead, one should try to split the Church in two. Part of the clergy must be compromised as reactionaries and "foreign agents"—a rather easy task, given the utterly conservative mentality of many priests. The other part must be bound to the state as closely as the Orthodox Church is in Russia, so that it becomes a tool of the government. A completely submissive Church—one that may on occasion collaborate with the security police—loses authority in the eyes of the pious. Such a Church can be preserved for decades, until the moment when it dies a natural death due to a lack of adherents.

So there are measures that can be taken even against the Church, this last stronghold of opposition. Nevertheless, the masses in the people's democracies behave like a man who wants to cry out in his sleep and cannot find his voice. They not only dare not speak, they do not know *what* to say. Logically, everything is as it should be. From the philosophical premises to the collectivization of the farms, everything makes up a single closed whole, a solid and imposing pyramid. The lone individual inevitably asks himself if his antagonism is not wrong; all he can oppose to the entire propaganda apparatus are simply his irrational desires. Should he not, in fact, be ashamed of them?

The Party is vigilantly on guard lest these longings be transmuted into new and vital intellectual formulas adapted to new conditions and therefore capable of winning over the masses. Neither the reaction nor the Church are as great a menace as is *heresy*. If men familiar with dialectics and able to present dialectical materialism in a new light appear, they must be rendered harmless at once. A professor of philosophy who clings to obsolete "idealistic" concepts is not particularly dangerous. He loses his lectureship, but he is allowed to earn a living by editing texts, etc., whereas a professor who, using the names of Marx and Engels, permits himself departures from orthodoxy sows seeds from which alarming crops may grow.

Only the bourgeois persists in thinking that nothing results from these nuances of thought. The Party knows that much can come of them: there was a time when the Revolution was merely a nuance in the thinking of a little group of theoreticians led by Lenin, quarreling around a café table in Switzerland. The most neuralgic points of the doctrine are philosophy, literature, the history of art, and literary criticism; those are the points where man in his unfortunate complexity enters the equation. The difference of a tiny fraction in the premises yields dizzying differences after the calculation is completed. A deviation from the line in the evaluation of some work of art may become the leaven of a political upheaval. The Party rightly and logically condemned the foremost Marxist literary scholar of the twentieth century, the Hungarian professor Lukács.* Deep, hidden reasons lay behind the enthusiasm his works aroused in the Marxists of the people's democracies. They saw in him the harbinger of a new philosophy and a new literature. The dislike of "socialist realism" that he betrayed corresponded to the belief, prevalent in the first years after the Second World War, that in the people's democracies the science of Marx and Engels would blaze new paths, unknown in Russia. Because Lukács expressed this belief in his books, the Party had no course but to stigmatize him.

When one considers the matter logically, it becomes obvious that intellectual terror is a principle that Leninism-Stalinism can never forsake, even if it should achieve victory on a world scale. The enemy, in a potential form, will *always* be there; the only friend will be the man who accepts the doctrine 99 percent. If he accepts only 99 percent, he will necessarily have to be considered a foe, for from that remaining 1 percent a new church can arise. The explanation Stalinists often advance, that this is only a *stage* resulting from "capitalist encirclement," is self-contradictory. The concept of a *stage* presupposes planning from the top, absolute control now and always. Eastern rulers are aware of this contradiction. If they were not, they would not have to present forced participation in clubs and parades, forced voting for a single list, forced raising of production norms, etc., as spontaneous and voluntary acts. This is a dark, unpleasant point for even the most passionate believers.

This way of posing the problem discloses the madness of the doctrines. Party dialecticians know that similar attempts on the part of other orthodoxies have always failed. In fact, History itself exploded one after another the formulas that have been considered binding. This time, however, the rulers have mastered dialectics so, they assert, they will know how to modify the doctrine as new necessities arise. The judgments of an individual man can always be wrong; the only solution is to submit unreservedly to an authority that claims to be unerring.

But what can the doctrine do about the unformulated longings of men? Why does a good Communist, without any apparent reason, suddenly put a pistol to his head? Why does he escape abroad? Isn't this one

* Georg Lukács (1885–1971) was a Hungarian Marxist philosopher who also served as a minister in the Communist governments of Béla Kun and Imre Nagy.

of those chasms over which the scientifically constructed bridges pass? People who flee from the people's democracies usually give as their chief motive the fact that life in these countries is psychically unbearable. They stammer out their efforts to explain: "The dreadful sadness of life over there"; "I felt I was turning into a machine." It is impossible to communicate to people who have not experienced it the undefinable menace of total rationalism.

To forestall doubt, the Party fights any tendency to delve into the depths of a human being, especially in literature and art. Whoever reflects on "man" in general, on his inner needs and longings, is accused of bourgeois sentimentality. Nothing must ever go beyond the description of man's behavior as a member of a social group. This is necessary because the Party, treating man exclusively as the by-product of social forces, believes that he becomes the type of being he pictures himself to be. He is a social monkey. *What is not expressed does not exist.* Therefore if one forbids men to explore the depths of human nature, one destroys in them the urge to make such explorations; and the depths in themselves slowly become unreal.

I should like to clear up in advance a possible misunderstanding. Personally, I am not in favor of art that is too subjective. My poetry has always been a means of checking on myself. Through it I could ascertain the limit beyond which falseness of style testifies to the falseness of the artist's position; and I have tried not to cross this line. The war years taught me that a man should not take a pen in his hands merely to communicate to others his own despair and defeat. This is too cheap a commodity; it takes too little effort to produce it for a man to pride himself on having done so. Whoever saw, as many did, a whole city reduced to rubble—kilometers of streets on which there remained no trace of life, not even a cat, not even a homeless dog—emerged with a rather ironic attitude toward descriptions of the hell of the big city by contemporary poets, descriptions of the hell in their own souls. A real "wasteland" is much more terrible than any imaginary one. Whoever has not dwelt in the midst of horror and dread cannot know how strongly a witness and participant protests against himself, against his own neglect and egoism. Destruction and suffering are the school of social thought.

Yet, if the literature of socialist realism is useful, it is so only to the Party. It is supposed to present reality not as a man *sees* it (that was the trait of the previous realism, the so-called "critical"), but as he *understands* it. Understanding that reality is in motion, and that in every phenomenon what is being born and what is dying exist simultaneously—dialectically speaking, this is the battle between the "new" and the "old"—the author should praise everything that is budding and censure everything that is becoming the past. In practice, this means that the author should perceive elements of the class struggle in every phenomenon. Carrying this reasoning further, the doctrine forces all art to become didactic. Since *only* the Stalinists have the right to represent the proletariat, which is the rising class, everything that is "new" and therefore praiseworthy results from Party strategy and tactics. "Socialist realism" depends on an identification of the "new" with the proletariat and the proletariat with the Party. It presents model citizens, i.e., Communists, and class enemies. Between these two categories come the men who vacillate. Eventually, they must—according to which tendencies are stronger in them—land in one camp or the other. When literature is not dealing with prefabricated figures of friends and foes, it studies the process of metamorphosis by which men arrive at total salvation or absolute damnation in Party terms.

This way of treating literature (and every art) leads to absolute conformism. Is such conformism favorable to serious artistic work? That is doubtful. The sculptures of Michelangelo are completed acts that endure. There was a time when they did not exist. Between their nonexistence and existence lies the creative act, which cannot be understood as a submission to the "wave of the future." The creative act is associated with a feeling of freedom that is, in its turn, born in the struggle against an apparently invincible resistance. Whoever truly creates is alone. When he succeeds in creating, many followers and imitators appear; and then it seems that his work confirms the existence of some sort of "wave of history." The creative man has no choice but to trust his inner command and place everything at stake in order to express what seems to him to be true. This inner command is absurd if it is not supported by a belief in an order of values that exists beyond the changeability of human affairs, that is by a metaphysical belief. Herein lies the tragedy of the twentieth century. Today, only those people can create who still have this faith (among them are a certain number of Stalinists who practice Ketman), or who hold a position of lay Stoicism (which, after all, is probably another form of faith). For the rest there remains the sorry lie of a safe place on the "wave of the future."

This is the framework within which life develops in the people's democracies; but it is a life that moves at a frenzied tempo. "Socialist construction" is not merely a slogan; it is taken in a quite literal sense. The observer's eye meets scaffolding everywhere; new factories, offices, and government buildings spring up almost overnight; production curves rise; the masses change character with unheard-of rapidity; more and more persons become state functionaries and acquire a certain minimum of "political education." The press, literature, films, and theater magnify these attainments. If a man from Mars, knowing nothing of earthly affairs, were to judge the various countries of the world on the basis of Soviet books, he would conclude that the East is inhabited by rational, intelligent beings, while the West is peopled by dwarfs and degenerates. Small wonder that so many intelligent Westerners, for whom the Soviet Union and its satellites are the legendary isles of happiness, arrive at a similar conclusion.

The citizen of the people's democracies is immune to the kind of neurosis that takes such manifold forms in capitalist countries. In the West a man subconsciously regards society as unrelated to him. Society indicates the limits he must not exceed; in exchange for this he receives a guarantee that no one will meddle excessively in his affairs. If he loses, it's his own fault; let psychoanalysis help him. In the East there is no boundary between man and society. His game, and whether he loses or wins, is a public matter. He is never alone. If he loses it is not because of indifference on the part of his environment, but because his environment keeps him under such minute scrutiny. Neuroses as they are known in the West result, above all, from man's aloneness; so even if they were allowed to practice, psychoanalysts would not earn a penny in the people's democracies.

The torment of a man in the East is, as we have seen, of a new, hitherto unknown variety. Humanity devised effective measures against smallpox, typhus, syphilis; but life in big cities or giant collectives breeds new diseases. Russian revolutionists discovered what they claimed were effectual means of mastering the forces of History. They proclaimed they had found the panacea for the ills of society. But History itself repays them in jeers.

The supreme goal of doing away with the struggle for existence— which was the theoretician's dream—has not been and cannot be achieved while every man fears every other man. The state which, according to Lenin, was supposed to wither away gradually is now all-powerful. It holds a sword over the head of every citizen; it punishes him for every careless word. The promises made from time to time that the state will begin to wither away when the entire earth is conquered lack any foundation. Orthodoxy cannot release its pressure on men's minds; it would no longer be an orthodoxy. There is always some disparity between facts and theories. The world is full of contradictions. Their constant struggle is what Hegel called dialectic. That dialectic of reality turns against the dialectic fashioned by the Center; but then so much the worse for reality. It has been said that the twentieth century is notable for its synthetic products—synthetic rubber, synthetic gasoline, etc. Not to be outdone, the Party has processed an artificial dialectic whose only resemblance to Hegel's philosophy is purely superficial. The Method is effective just so long as it wages war against an enemy. A man exposed to its influence is helpless. How can he fight a system of symbols? In the end he submits; and this is the secret of the Party's power, not some fantastic narcotic.

There is a species of insect which injects its venom into a caterpillar; thus inoculated, the caterpillar lives on though it is paralyzed. The poisonous insect then lays its eggs in it, and the body of the caterpillar serves as a living larder for the young brood. Just so (though Marx and Engels never foresaw this use for their doctrine), the anaesthetic of dialectical materialism is injected into the mind of a man in the people's democracies. When his brain is duly paralyzed, the eggs of Stalinism are laid in it. As soon as you are a Marxist, the Party says to the patient, you *must* be a Stalinist, for there is no Marxism outside of Stalinism.

Naïve enemies of the poison may think that they can rid themselves of the danger by locking up the works of Marx and Engels in burglar-proof safes and never allowing anyone to read them. They fail to consider that the very course of history leads people to think about the subject matter of these works. Those who have never personally experienced the magnetic attraction and force of the problems posed in these books can count themselves lucky. Though that does not necessarily mean that they should feel proud of themselves.

Only the blind can fail to see the irony of the situation the human species brought upon itself when it tried to master its own fate and to eliminate accident. It bent its knee to History; and History is a cruel god. Today, the commandments that fall from his lips are uttered by clever chaplains hiding in his empty interior. The eyes of the god are so constructed that they see wherever a man may go; there is no shelter from them. Lovers in bed perform their amorous rites under his mocking glance; a child plays in the sand, not knowing that his future life has been weighed and written into the general account; only the aged, who have but a few days left before they die, can justly feel that they have to a large extent escaped his rule.

The philosophy of History emanating from Moscow is not just an abstract theory, it is a material force that uses guns, tanks, planes, and all the machines of war and oppression. All the crushing might of an armed state is hurled against any man who refuses to accept the New Faith. At the same time, Stalinism attacks him from within, saying his opposition is caused by his "class consciousness," just as psychoanalysts accuse their foes of wanting to preserve their complexes.

Still, it is not hard to imagine the day when millions of obedient followers of the New Faith may suddenly turn against it. That day would come the moment the Center lost its material might, not only because fear of military force would vanish, but because success is an integral part of this philosophy's argument. If it lost, it would prove itself wrong by its own definition; it would stand revealed as a false faith, defeated by its own god, reality. The citizens of the Imperium of the East long for nothing so much as liberation from the terror their own thought creates.

In the Central Committee buildings, strategists move the little flags on the battle map of the war for men's minds. They can pinpoint ever greater successes; the red color, which in 1944 and 1945 was limited to a handful of believers coming from the East, spreads farther every day. But even sages are men, and even they fall prey to anxiety and dread. They compare themselves to the early Christians; they liken the march of the New Faith over the planet to the march of Christianity throughout the decaying Roman empire. But they envy the apostles their gift of reaching deep into the human heart. *"They* knew how to make propaganda! How can we compare ourselves with them?" mourned a certain Party dignitary hearing the gospel read over the radio. The new (anti-) religion performs miracles. It shows the doubters new buildings and new tanks. But what would happen if these miracles suddenly stopped? Knives and pistols would appear in the hands that applaud today. The pyramid of thought would topple. For a long time, on the ground where once it stood there would be nothing save blood and chaos.

455

26

What Charter 77 Is and What It Is Not*
(1977)

JAN PATOČKA

Mankind today, torn apart by ideologies, discontented amid the conditions of prosperity, is looking feverishly and with yearning to ever-new technical recipes for solutions. One of these hopes rests in relying on political power and the state. Does not the state appear with ever-increasing clarity to be a huge manufactory and storehouse of strength, which has at its disposal all the powers that otherwise exist, both physical and spiritual?

Thinkers, however, look around and observe that a *morality*, a truly convincing study of principles and secure inner *dispositions*, has not been created, *because it can't be done*. Nor can habit be trusted, the idea that an order that has come to be de facto will become second nature; nor can trust be placed in the power of coercion without the people's inner conviction.

In order that mankind develop in keeping with the possibilities of technical and instrumental reason, in order that *progress* of knowledge and ability be made possible, mankind must be convinced of the absoluteness of principles that are, in this sense, "holy," principles that are binding on

---

* The arrest and subsequent trial of members of the underground rock band The Plastic People of the Universe in 1976 was a catalyst for the formation of Charter 77. Signatories were gathered in late 1976 and the Charter's founding declaration was issued on January 1, 1977. Patočka was one of the original spokesmen for the Charter. He died on March 13, 1977 from a cerebral hemorrhage after extensive interrogation by the StB (the ministry of state security in Czechoslovakia).

everyone and are capable of limiting ends. In other words it is necessary to have something basically nontechnical, something that has to do not merely with means; there must be an unswerving morality, one that is not occasional, but rather an *absolute* morality.

That means that salvation *in these matters* cannot be expected from the state, from a production-based society, from strength and power.

How pleased all the proponents of the dictatorship of facts as a means to arbitrary ends, how delighted they would be to relinquish some of their overly evident "truths" for a single, solitary, internally binding, practical truth of morality. But that is not possible. Never before have accumulations of power been given the opportunity to assert themselves as has been the case in this century. Yet the result—as far as convincing people—is the exact opposite, as should be clear already.

No society, no matter how good its technological foundation, can function without a moral foundation, without conviction that has nothing to do with opportunism, circumstance, and expected advantage. Morality, however, does not exist just to allow society to function, but simply to allow human beings to be human. Man does not define morality according to the caprice of his needs, wishes, tendencies, and cravings; it is morality that defines man.

That is why we feel that it is time that these axioms, simple yet so painfully confirmed over the decades, sensed one way or another by everyone, it is high time indeed that they penetrate clearly into the consciousness of all of us. Why?

The concept of *human rights* is nothing but the conviction that states and society as a whole also consider themselves to be subject to the sovereignty of moral sentiment, that they recognize something unqualified above them, something that is bindingly sacred and inviolable even for them, and that they intend to contribute to this end with the power by which they create and ensure *legal* norms.

The same conviction exists in individuals as well, and is the basis for the fulfillment of their obligations in their private lives, their work and their public lives. Only in keeping with this conviction is there any true guarantee that people are not acting only for advantage to themselves or out of fear, but rather freely, willingly, and responsibly.

This conviction is voiced in Charter 77, which is the expression of the joy of the citizenry that their country, by signing a document confirming human rights, a signature that made this act a part of Czechoslovakian law, avows the supreme moral foundation of all things political. At the same time, Charter 77 is the public expression of the will of the selfsame citizens to make their own contribution to the implementation of the principles publicly proclaimed in this act.

For that reason, the signatories of Charter 77 feel that this act is far more significant than run-of-the-mill international agreements which are a matter of state power opportunism, because this one touches on the moral, spiritual aspect. That and nothing else is why the signatories feel that the time is right, and the opportunity is at hand, for them to show that they know what is at stake, and for that reason are taking the initiative.

The aforementioned relationship between the realms of morality and state power indicate that Charter 77 is not an act that is political in the narrow sense, that it is not a matter of competing with or interfering in the sphere of any function of political power. Nor is Charter 77 an association or an organization, but it is based on personal morality, and the obligations implicit in it have the same character.

It does recall, however, quite expressly, that 180 years ago, by means of a precise conceptual analysis, it was stressed that all moral obligations rest on what may be referred to as *man's obligation to himself*, which includes his obligations to protect himself from any injustice committed against his own person.

In sum that means that the participants in Charter 77 are not acting out of any interest, but solely out of *obligation*, following a command that stands above political obligations and rights and is their true and only reliable foundation.

Participants in Charter 77 do not take upon themselves any political rights or functions, nor do they want to be a moral authority or "the conscience" of society; they do not raise themselves above anyone or pass judgment on anyone; their effort is aimed exclusively at cleansing and reinforcing the awareness that a *higher authority does exist*, to which they are obligated, individually, in their conscience, and to which states are bound by their signatures on important international covenants; that they are bound not only by expediency, according to the rules of political advantage and disadvantage, but that their signatures there mean that they accept the rule that politics are indeed subject to law and that law is not subject to politics.

458

An evident corollary to this point of view is the conclusion that part of the duty to defend oneself from injustice involves also the possibility to inform any and all of an injustice committed against an individual, and that doing so is within the bounds of one's duty to oneself; it does not mean that anyone is being maligned, whether it be an individual or society.

Moreover it is important that everyone know that in order to defend one's moral rights, that is, one's duty to oneself and others, one need not belong to any association, because here the only thing that is expressed is the respect for man as such inherent in every individual, and the sense that makes a man human, his sense of the common good.

Therefore no individual who is truly oppressed should feel isolated and at the mercy of the superior forces of circumstance, if he himself is determined not to surrender the obligation to stand up for himself, an obligation he holds towards the society of which he is in fact a member.

Thus the aim of Charter 77 is the spontaneous and unbounded solidarity of all who have come to understand how significant a moral way of thinking is for a real society and its normal functioning.

For all these reasons, we consider the time when the signing of the Declaration of Human Rights has become possible to be a new era in history, an era of immense significance, because it means a decisive turn in people's consciousness, in their relationship towards themselves and society. Today it is a matter of seeing that motivations for action need no longer be exclusively, or for the most part, grounded in fear or personal advantage, but rather in respect for what is highest in man, in his understanding of his obligations and of the common weal, of the need to take upon oneself even some discomfort, misunderstanding and a certain risk.

Professor Jan Patočka, DSc, Dr (*hon. causa*)
Spokesman for Charter 77
Prague

459

27

The Parallel Polis[*]
(1978, 1987)

Václav Benda

Charter 77 has at least two remarkable achievements to its credit: it has gathered together a broad spectrum of political opinion and civic attitudes; and it has managed to remain legal. It has paid for these achievements by finding itself, from the outset, in a rather schizophrenic situation. On the one hand, despite deep differences in the principles behind their criticism and even deeper ones in their notions about how

---

[*] This essay (the first part of the text reproduced here) was circulated in samizdat in early 1978. Benda was arrested shortly thereafter for his involvement with VONS (The Committee for the Defense of the Unjustly Persecuted), an organization founded to aid those persecuted by state authorities (modeled on the Polish KOR). The second part of this essay (as the well the essay by Kantůrková) was written in response to inquiries by the scholar Gordon Skilling. In preparing his book *Samizdat and an Independent Society in Central and Eastern Europe*, Skilling asked a number of the prominent signatories of Charter 77 and other dissidents to respond to a series of questions related to themes raised in Benda's original essay. These questions included: (1) Do you think the term "independent society" is relevant and meaningful under present conditions in your country? (2) If so, what would you include as being essential features of an "independent society"? (3) What are the immediate purposes of the independent activities and organizations thus conceived? and (4) What are the implications and possible consequences of such an independent society? The responses were received during 1986–87. Along with the responses reproduced here by Benda and Kantůrková, the sixteen additional responses can be found in *Civic Freedom in Central Europe: Voices from Czechoslovakia*, edited by H. Gordon Skilling and Paul Wilson.

change might be brought about, everyone takes a very dim view of the present political system and how it works. On the other hand, we behave as though we had failed to notice that the claims the regime makes about its own good intentions, and the laws that appear to limit its totality, are merely propagandistic camouflage. This tactic of taking the authorities at their word is, in itself, a shrewd ploy. Nevertheless, with all due respect to shrewdness, such an approach cannot bridge the gap between the positions mentioned above.

Charter 77 managed, at least temporarily and quite effectively, to eliminate this schism by stressing moral and ethical attitudes over political ones. Today this solution no longer works, and the original dilemma has returned in an even more pressing form. The reasons for this are roughly the following:

1. The death of Professor Patočka, who was unquestionably the *spiritus movens* of this solution.

2. The regime has finally realised that its virulent campaign has transformed a political problem into a moral one and that it has thus unwittingly accepted our choice of weapons. From that moment on the official media have fallen silent on the subject of the Charter, and the regime has limited itself to acts of strangulation in the dark. The official term for it is "whittling away at the edges."

3. The moral attitude was postulated abstractly, without raising any concrete issues or aims. An abstract moral stance, however, is merely a gesture; it may be terribly effective at the time, but it cannot be sustained for more than a few weeks or months. Proof of this is a phenomenon familiar to Charter signatories: the ecstatic sensation of liberation caused by signing the Charter gradually gave way to disillusionment and deep skepticism.

Without underestimating the importance of the first two points, I feel that the third is decisive, and sufficient in itself to create a problem. I am therefore suggesting a strategy that should gradually lead us out of the blind alley we are in today. This strategy can be summarized in two phrases: what unifies and drives us must continue to be a sense of *moral commitment and mission;* and this drive should be given a place and a perspective in the creation of a *parallel polis.*

The moral justification of a citizen's right and duty of a citizen to participate in the affairs of a community (affairs that are "political" in the broadest sense of the word) is beyond all doubt. This was the source of the Charter's public mandate, and at first, it was enough to overcome the differences of opinion within the Charter. It was a guarantee of unity, tolerance, cooperation, and, to a certain extent, persistence. Moreover this moral stance is so closely associated with the Charter in the eyes of the public and most of the signatories that any other formula could legitimately lay claim to continuity only with great difficulty. I am not asking, therefore, *whether* we should proceed from a moral basis, but *how* to make that aspect inspiring and mobilizing once more, and how to ensure that its influence will persist. I am asking what *kind* of specific efforts or "positive" program can derive its energy from that morality in the future.

A citizen may certainly see there is a moral commitment involved in challenging an evil political power and trying to destroy it. Nevertheless, in the circumstances, such a commitment is suicidal, and cannot hope for public support in any rational ethical system. Likewise, a citizen may feel morally obliged to size up the situation realistically and try to bring about at least partial improvements through compromise and reform. But given the ethics of the present regime, we cannot expect that the moral motivations of such behaviour will generally be appreciated, or be in any way morally appealing.

There is a third way of ameliorating conditions in the community (*obec*). Most structures that are connected, in one way or another, with the life of the community (i.e., to political life) are either inadequate or harmful. I suggest that we join forces in creating, slowly but surely, parallel structures that are capable, to a limited degree at least, of supplementing the generally beneficial and necessary functions that are missing in the existing structures, and where possible, to use those existing structures, to humanize them.

This plan will satisfy both the "reformists" and the "radicals." It need not lead to a direct conflict with the regime, yet it harbors no illusions that "cosmetic changes" can make any difference. Moreover it leaves open the key question of the system's viability. Even if such structures were only partially successful, they would bring pressure to bear on the official structures, which would either collapse (if you accept the view of the radicals) or regenerate themselves in a useful way (if you accept the reformist position).

462

Both wings will object because this plan reeks of the movement to "enlighten the masses" and it is politically naïve. Yet here we all are in the Charter, and the Charter is an undeniably naïve act, politically speaking, as are all attempts to base one's actions on morality. In any case my suggestion comes directly from the present form of Charter 77, which grew out of actions taken to defend parallel structures that already existed (the Second Culture), and which devotes much of its efforts to "humanizing" existing official structures (like the legislative system) by reinterpreting their meaning. Official politicians should recall that it was they, in the end, who brought the community to its present state and that the decent thing to do would be to rethink either their political beliefs, or their notion of what is and what is not politically naïve. There is no third way.

Perhaps it is beyond our powers to implement this plan. Nevertheless it is realistic in the sense that it has already worked. Here are two examples that are at once remarkable, and yet very different. Parallel cultural structures today undeniably exist, and they are a positive phenomenon. In some areas, like literature, and to some extent in popular music and the plastic arts, the parallel culture overshadows the lifeless, official culture. A phenomenon just as undeniable (and negative, though more functional and more human) is the parallel economy, based on systematic theft, corruption, and "favors." Under the shiny surface of official economics this parallel economy is a factor in most consumer relations, and also in industrial and trade relations as well.

Here, in brief and in no particular order, are the details of my plan:

(a) This point is the preamble to all the others. Our legal system is one of the worst in the world, because it exists solely for propagandistic purposes and for that reason is extremely vague and completely lacking in any legal guarantees. At the same time, and for the very same reasons, this allows it to be interpreted in a very liberal way. We must systematically exploit this discrepancy, and we must be prepared at any time for it to be used systematically against us. The transition from a totalitarian to a liberal system would mean a transition from the principle of "whatever is not expressly permitted is forbidden" to the principle of "whatever is not expressly forbidden is permitted." This can be accomplished only by continually testing the limits of what is permitted, and by occupying the newly won positions with great energy.

(b) So far, the Second Culture is the most developed and dynamic parallel structure. It should serve as a model for other areas and, at the same time, all available means must be deployed to support its development, especially in neglected areas like literary criticism, cultural journalism, theater, and film.

(c) A parallel structure of education and scientific and scholarly life has already established a certain tradition, although in the past two years it has tended to stagnate. I consider the organization of a parallel educational system to be of utmost importance, both for personal reasons (I cannot harbor too many illusions about the chances of my children getting an official education) and for more general reasons. The "underground," which is by far the most numerous element in the Charter, has been able to overcome sectarianism and become political; but if this change is to last, we will clearly have to do "educational" work in these circles. I feel that here in particular there is room for us to aim high with a "maximalist" program.

(d) In its early stages the Charter was able to create a parallel information network that was functional and prompt and involved at least several tens of thousands of people. The gradual degeneration of that network, which unfortunately occurred faster than could be explained by the waning of the Charter's initial sensational impact, is considered one of the greatest failures of the Charter and one of the most critical symptoms, so far, of a crisis in its development.

The most important materials from Charter 77 were disseminated by direct, internal circulation (i.e., not via foreign radio broadcasts) to an estimated tens of thousands or even, in the case of the original declaration, to several hundred thousand people. Recently the number of those receiving Charter material has shrunk to hundreds, or at best to some thousands of citizens.

The contents and form of the information circulated will obviously be of key significance. The circulation of information must be considered as important as the actual preparation of the material. Everyone who complains today about the lack of information should feel obliged to circulate the information they do receive more effectively.

The informational network so created must be used regularly. Long periods of inactivity are more dangerous than overloading it, because this leads to loss of interest and the stagnation of connections already established.

Close to the sources, effectiveness is more important than politeness. It is essential to pass information on to places where its further dissemination is assured. I would rather see some "prominent" person informed of something second hand than have the flow of information clogged, thus limiting it to a narrow circle of people.

There is an urgent need to improve the flow of information to groups outside Prague. It is even more urgent for these groups to establish mutual connections and create autonomous information networks of their own. Here, too, the most important factor in deciding who shall be given the information is whether or not that person can type.

In the future, we will have to consider using other means of reproduction besides the typewriter. A thorough analysis of the legal aspects of this problem should be prepared, and the possibilities of using such technologies as photocopying should be explored.

At the moment, the tasks facing us in the parallel economy are unimaginable, but though our opportunities are limited, the need to exploit them is urgent. The regime treats the economy as a key means of arbitrarily manipulating citizens and, at the same time, it regulates it as strictly as possible. We therefore have to rely on strictly confidential accounting practices (any other kind would cross the line into illegal activity), and we must develop a wide base for charitable and other support activities. Our community ought to be based on a system of mutual guarantees that are both moral and material. To demonstrate the morality and disinterestedness of our own motives by ostentatiously ignoring material factors is, in such circumstances, just as naïve and dangerous as informing the State Security forces about the details of our lives because we consider what we do to be honest and legal. We must resist this pressure by consistently turning to international solidarity for help, starting with support from individuals and organizations and ending with far more effective forms of scientific and cultural cooperation that would assure our relative independence from official economic structures (i.e., honoraria for works of art or scientific articles, stipends, etc.).

(e) The ground must be prepared for the creation and encouragement of parallel political (in the narrow sense of the word) structures. This would include a wide range of activities, from raising people's awareness of their civic responsibilities, to creating the proper conditions for political discussion and the formulation of theoretical points of view. It would also include support for concrete political currents and groupings.

As regards a parallel foreign policy, my premise is that the internationalization of any problem, though it may stand little chance of success, can do no harm. Some of the parallel structures I have mentioned here, in economics and education, for instance, cannot hope to function, in the beginning at least, without support from abroad. Publicity for our efforts will provide protection against arbitrary actions by the regime and, for the majority of citizens, it is also the main source of information (foreign radio and TV).

No less important is mutual cooperation between related trends in other eastern bloc countries. In decades past almost every country in that bloc has paid dearly for the lack of such cooperation. At the moment publicity for what we are doing is quite insignificant and our cooperation with parallel movements inside the bloc has always been painfully inadequate. We must immediately create a team to investigate the reasons for such inadequacies and propose specific remedies.

The individual parallel structures will be connected with the Charter in varying degrees. Some will become an integral part of it; others will be midwived and wetnursed by the Charter; yet others the Charter will provide with a guarantee of legality. The parallel structures so formed will go beyond the framework of the Charter in various ways and sooner or later they must become autonomous, not only because they don't fit into the Charter's original form and mission, but because were they not to become autonomous, we would be building a ghetto rather than a parallel polis.

Even so, the Charter ought not to limit its involvement in such initiatives in any fundamental way, for by doing so, it would shift its focus from civic activity to merely monitoring such activity, and it would thus lose most of its moral energy. For the future, we will have to accept the fact that we will probably find it easier to agree on a common starting point for our efforts than on any external limitations to them. A citizens' initiative like the Charter will inevitably overflow into related initiatives and, because it is a free association, it has no means authoritatively to establish its own limits. The Charter was, is, and will continue to be based on the confidence that individual groups of signatories will responsibly avoid actions unacceptable to other groups, or that would undermine the original unity and solidarity in the Charter.

Charter 77 must continue to fulfill its proper purpose, namely to compile basic documents which draw attention to denial of human rights and suggest ways of correcting the situation. Documents should appear at the very least at two-month intervals. They ought to be addressed not only to the authorities, but also—and above all—to our fellow citizens. They should therefore deal with genuinely urgent problems. They should not be inordinately long and they should be sufficiently comprehensible even for a lay public, avoiding legal or specialist jargon.

If our aim is to combat the general feeling of futility and hopelessness, rather than contributing to it, we must try to learn from our failure to hold a dialogue with the regime. That means going even further. There is nothing to stop us from presenting, in addition to our usual demands for institutional change, proposals for parallel civic activities that would enable improvements to be made in the given state of affairs. If producing documents ceases to be the sole aim and comes to be considered as merely one aspect of a more persistent effort to investigate the causes of the our present misery and to suggest ways of rectification, the Charter 77 is really in no danger of degenerating and becoming a mere producer of dry, rustling papers. Such an approach would represent the most natural transition to the plan, here presented, to create a parallel polis.

—

I shall begin with a personal reminiscence. None of my essays has been so frequently quoted, both approvingly and polemically, and none has been the source of so many inspired slogans, as the one entitled "The Parallel Polis." At the same time, none of my essays was more improvised. When the "second crisis" of Charter 77 took place (the first, in the spring of 1977, was related to Patočka's death and other events, and the rest, from the third to the nth, happen with iron regularity almost every year without arousing much attention) I was given the honor of taking part in a meeting of the Charter 77 "brain trust" which met to study further opportunities and outlooks for the movement. With the zeal of a newcomer, I complied with the general instructions (I was the only one who did, as it turned out) and prepared a discussion paper, which was essentially the text now known as "The Parallel Polis." At the same time the need to face up to a real crisis and real doubts led me to adopt an unambiguously optimistic outlook. Because my contribution to Charter 77 at the time was largely technical and only incidentally intellectual, my paper was by and large a report on very down-to-earth possibilities.

In the . . . years since then, even my most audacious expectations have been considerably surpassed. Thank God for that, although it is also true that for the most part we are only limping far behind the far more impressive developments in Poland. Today it is perhaps no longer necessary to show that the parallel polis is possible: time has shown that even in the spheres of "parallel foreign policy" (which most of my critics considered an arbitrary hypothesis introduced more for the sake of logical completeness) and of "parallel economics" (which even I conceived in a largely negative sense, in terms of the black market, theft, bribery and other phenomena that go along with a centrally directed economy) many things are realizable that neither we nor the Poles even dared dream about ten years ago.

I don't want to turn this essentially positive answer to the question: "Is it possible?" into a celebration of my own foresight and our mutual merits. There have been successes and failures; there was progress and regression. We wasted our energies almost everywhere, naïvely allowing ourselves to be outflanked by repressions or to be bogged down in internal controversies. In almost every sphere, we remained far behind what was possible, even considering all the unfavorable conditions that prevailed. In one area we failed catastrophically: independent education. There were and still are different attempts to do something about it, but all of them have been marred by an excessive exclusivity (not only regarding the circle of participants, but chiefly in the form and content of the courses of study), considerable vulnerability to repressions and a lack of clear-sighted, responsible generosity.

Perhaps this last failure was inevitable. Young people are caught in the tough totalitarian network of predetermined possibilities, obligations to work from a tender age and compulsory military service (for men). Given the total destruction of the family, there is not really a great deal of space for maneuvering here. Let us take a closer look at our school system—and at the educational system in general, where systematic regression is taking place far more rapidly than in any other sphere of social life, and where even the basic totalitarian principle of dispensing advantages and discrimination is becoming largely imaginary, because there are hardly any real advantages left to dispense, and where discrimination is beginning to function as a defense against infection by stupidity. (Here is persuasive proof of the interdependence of education and tradition: as soon as fools are artificially included in the chain of tradition, nothing but stupidity can any longer be passed down). This failure may prove to be a fateful one both for citizens or oppositional movements, and for our whole national community.

Even today bitter problems related to the changing generations are arising in the Charter, in the Church and in independent culture. Unfortunately these problems differ from the ancient generational conflicts in that the rising generation is not marked by a healthy, or even an unhealthy self-confidence, a desire to rebel and take its proper place, but rather by a tendency to declare itself inadequate and place all the blame for that inadequacy on the preceding generation (a conclusion that in a practical respect is just, but in its rejection of the human condition and shared responsibility, deeply godless).

Then, of course, the future presents us with the threat of absolute destruction in a nuclear catastrophe, in economic or ecological collapse, in the perfect and ultimate triumph of totalitarianism. I personally think that a no less effective, exceptionally painful and in the short term practically irreparable way of eliminating the human race or of individual nations would be a decline into barbarism, the abandonment of reason and learning, the loss of traditions and memory. The ruling regime—partly intentionally, partly thanks to its essentially nihilistic nature—has done everything it can to achieve that goal. The aim of independent citizens movements that try to create a parallel polis must be precisely the opposite: we must not be discouraged by previous failures, and we must consider the area of schooling and education as one of our main priorities.

And now some terminological clarifications, and concretely, an explanation of why I used the term "parallel polis" and why I consider this term even today as much more appropriate than "the underground," the "Second Culture," "independent culture," "alternative culture" or whatever other terms have been suggested. My arguments are directly related to both elements of the phrase. The program I once sketched out consisted neither in some sectarian or elitist exclusivity of a group or ghetto of people who "live in truth," nor in a one-sided attempt to preserve some preferred values, whether they be literary, musical, philosophical or religious. If this program gave unequivocal priority to something, it was the preservation or the renewal of the national community (*společenství*) in the widest sense of the word—along with the defense of all the values, institutions and material conditions to which the existence of such a community is bound. This, then, is where the word *"polis"* comes in, or perhaps "structures." It is also where doubts come in about whether terms like "underground" or "culture" represent an excessive narrowing of the intellectual, social, or thematic perspective.

As far as the appropriate adjective is concerned, it is obvious that a community (*obec*) created with such universal claims cannot completely ignore the official social structures and systematically remain separate from them (this is reflected in the more extreme aspects of the ideology of the underground) nor can it merely reject them and be their negative image (as the words "opposition," "second" and to a certain extent even "alternative" and "independent" suggest). The adjective "parallel" seemed, and still seems, more appropriate than other, more categorical solutions. It stresses variety, but not absolute independence, for a parallel course can be maintained only with a certain mutual respect and consideration. Furthermore it does not rule out the possibility that parallel courses may sometimes converge or cross each other (in geometry only at infinity, in practical life, however, much more frequently). Finally, it is a global characteristic, not merely local. For example, there is obviously no relevant official counterweight to parallel philosophy or theology, just as in the foreseeable future there is not likely to be a parallel counterweight to military power. The global nature of "parallelness," in my opinion, bridges over these disproportions and opens the door to a merging of both communities (*obcí*), and even more, to the peaceful dominance of the community anchored in truth over the community based on the mere manipulation of power.

As I have already said, all concrete, tactical tasks, all "small-scale work" involved in creating the "parallel polis" are, for me, connected with the renewal of the national community (*společenství*) in the widest sense of the word. For the main principle of totalitarian control is the utter destruction, the atomization of this and every other community (*společenství*)— replacing them with a paramilitary pseudoparty or, more probably, with a perfectly subordinated, perfectly sterile life-threatening party apparatus. The iron curtain does not just exist between the East and the West: it also separates individual nations in the East, individual regions, individual towns and villages, individual factories, individual families, and even the individuals within those entities from each other. Psychologists might even study the extent to which such an iron curtain has artificially divided various spheres of consciousness within each individual. In any case it is clear that we have far more precise and up-to-date information available about Australia than we do about events in a neighboring part of the city.

To tear down or corrode these miniature iron curtains, to break through the communications and social blockade, to return to truth and justice, to a meaningful order of values, to value once more the inalienability of human dignity and the necessity for a sense of human community (*pospolitost*) in mutual love and responsibility—these, in my opinion, are the present goals of the parallel polis. In concrete terms this means taking over for the use of the parallel polis every space that state power has temporarily abandoned or which it has never occurred to it to occupy in the first place. It means winning over for the support of common aims (taking great care, however, to insure that the usual proscriptions of state power are not only not brought down on it prematurely, but that they are held off for as long as possible) everything alive in society and its culture in the broadest sense of the word. It means winning over anything that has managed somehow to survive the disfavor of the times (e.g., the Church) or that was able, despite the unfavorable times, to come into being (e.g., various youth movements, of which the most articulate is the underground).

The point is that the totalitarian regime is subject to a strange dialectic. On the one hand, its claim is total—i.e., it absolutely denies freedom and tries systematically to eliminate every sphere where freedom exists. On the other hand it has proved incapable, in practical terms, (those who believe in the divine creation, or who at least give precedence to the richness of life as against the poverty of ideology, consider this incapacity to be intrinsic and irremediable) of realizing this claim—that is, of permanently preventing the constant creation of new centers of freedom.

There is, however, a fundamental difference between the natural resistance of life to totalitarianism, and the deliberate expansion of the space in which the parallel polis can exist. The former is a cluster of flowers that has grown in a place accidentally sheltered from the killing winds of totalitarianism and easily destroyed when those winds change direction. The latter is a trench whose elimination depends strictly on a calculated move by the state power to destroy it. Given the time and the means available, only a certain number of trenches can be eliminated. If, at the same time, the parallel polis is able to produce more such trenches than it loses, a situation arises that is mortally dangerous for the regime: it is a blow at the very heart of its power—that is, the possibility of intervening anywhere, without limitations. The mission of the parallel polis is constantly to conquer new territory, to make its parallelness constantly more substantial and more present. Politically, this means to stake out clear limits for totalitarian power, to make it more difficult for it to maneuver.

Even in the apparent nonhistoricity of the Czechoslovakian situation, much has changed [since 1978]. State power has not lost any of its will to totality and the repressions have certainly not become milder, but their psychological effect has essentially changed. In the mid-1970s the persecution of a handful of people was enough to frighten and warn off thousands of others. Today every political trial is a moral challenge for dozens of other citizens who feel a responsibility for taking the place of those who are temporarily silenced. As soon as this reaches a certain level, the parallel polis can obviously be eliminated only by totally destroying it, or at least by decimating the entire nation: a perfect example of this is the evolution of the Polish situation after the declaration of the state of war.

At the same time, however, we come to the first paradox here, connected with the basic and, so far, little understood mysteries of totality. From the other side, it is probably impossible for the parallel polis to destroy, replace or peacefully transform (humanize, democratize, reform, or whatever the other terms for it are) totalitarian power. I have no intention here of analyzing the obvious theological aspects of the problem. I would emphasize most strongly that this has nothing to do with the fact that we are unanimous in preferring nonviolent forms of struggle. Every antitotalitarian tendency worthy of the name (that is, that offers more than just another version of totalitarianism) is, in essence, aiming at the good of the polis, at genuine community (*společenství*), at justice and freedom.

Totalitarianism devotes all its strength, all its technical know-how, towards a single goal: the unimpeded exercise of absolute power. It is capable of the most bizarre tactical somersaults imaginable, but it can never, under any circumstances, admit that anything is more important, more sacrosanct, than "the leading role of the party." In August 1968, after the enemy invasion, there was a great deal of radicalism inside the Communist Party of Czechoslovakia, and a lot of heresy, but on one question an almost pathetic agreement prevailed: no matter what happened, and no matter if all the previous values were suddenly turned inside out, the party must under no circumstances go underground, become an opposition, give up its position of power.

Looking merely at the completely different set of values each side prefers, antitotalitarianism and totalitarianism are not equal adversaries in the struggle for power. Totalitarianism, concentrating all its efforts on this struggle, must always win. The more headway the threats to it make, the more drastic means it chooses from its repertoire, which knows no limitations, to suppress that threat. There is no systematic doctrine capable of liquidating totalitarian power from within, or replacing it. That power, however, works consciously at the outer limits of its own possibilities: a single loose pebble can cause an avalanche, an accidental outburst of discontent in a factory, at a football match, in a village pub, is capable of shaking the foundations of the state. The important thing is the chance factor: totalitarian power can successfully block any apparent adversary, but it is almost helpless against its own subjects who foolishly and infectiously start working to bring about in practice the notion that they need not go on being mere subjects.

Even more important, however, is the social situation, the level to which the parallel polis has built itself up, in which these accidental (chance) events take place. Neither the Committee for Social Self-Defense (KOR) nor the Catholic Church brought the Polish Solidarnosc into being, but to a significant degree they shared in the formation of that movement.* Regarding Charter 77, I doubt that anyone thinks we are capable of starting a revolution. I suspect, however, that everyone realizes that should a revolutionary, or shall we merely say a dramatic situation arise, our voice—"where do we go from here and how?"—will not be insignificant and that we will have to discharge our responsibility (which we, after all, voluntarily assumed) in something more than mere idle chatter and vague declarations.

Which brings me to what I consider the long-range or strategic mission of the parallel polis, the one genuine way of evaluating and justifying this type of "small-scale work." My conclusion is based on several loosely related assumptions. Totalitarian power has extended the sphere of politics to include everything, including the faith, the thinking, and the conscience of the individual. The first responsibility of a Christian and a human being is therefore to oppose such an inappropriate demand of the political sphere, ergo to resist totalitarian power.

Turning to local conditions, the greatest amount of ingenuity, courage, or willingness to make sacrifices has so far not been enough to emancipate us from the sphere of totalitarian power. Afghanistan might become a turning point, yet precisely because of this infectious example, it is highly

---

* KOR/Solidarity. See note on page 393.

unlikely that the occupation armies will soon withdraw from that country. I am aware, and all of us here in central and eastern Europe are more or less aware that the possibilities of a parallel polis and of any other kind of opposition are strictly limited, and that successfully overcoming those limits is conditional upon the world situation. Totalitarian power is a part of our fate (and perhaps God's punishment for our sins), and not just a mere parasite that can be eliminated by decisive action on our part.

At the same time, however, history teaches us that irregularly, but with iron necessity, those "favorable global constellations" come about, in which even small nations cease to be mere vassals of their fate and have the opportunity to become its active captains. In this century such an opportunity has presented itself to Czechoslovakia at least three times: in 1938, 1948 and 1968. Each of these historical opportunities were different, but in each case they were lost or squandered in the most painful and lamentable ways. Despite the situational differences, I observe a common factor in all of them: not once could the failure be blamed on our peoples who, on the contrary, demonstrated an exceptional amount of civic responsibility and willingness to sacrifice themselves. The failure was always that of their political (and military) leadership. We can be certain that we will find ourselves in similar suspicious situations in the future, and it is only a guess whether this will be tomorrow or in twenty years. Given the profound deterioration of our political leadership and of civic culture in general, we may with some reason predict that the next chance will be missed and lost as well. My private opinion is that the cardinal, strategic or long-term task of the parallel polis is to prove this gloomy prediction wrong.

In the diction of our opponents, this task will consist in the "formation of cadres": people who are sufficiently well-known and who enjoy sufficient authority to be able, in a crisis, to take the place of the degenerate political leadership and who will be capable of presenting, and consistently defending, a program that will liquidate the principles of totality. This last statement, which is perhaps too simplified and declarative, requires more detailed commentary. It is in no way to be interpreted as a scheme, either hidden or overt, for seizing power. From what I have said before, it should be clear enough why the parallel polis would be incapable of carrying out anything like that, and why it would not even try.

As for the changes in personnel suggested by my references to "cadres," I see a far greater likelihood of difficulties than success. If by some miracle my good friend Václav Havel were to become General Secretary of the Central Committee of the Communist Party, I would immediately become his toughest opponent. Ontologically, because freedom granted on the installment plan, and as a favor by the totalitarian regime, would have little to do with real freedom; practically, because miracles are a mere exception to the orderly course of things in the world. Hence Václav Havel would either very quickly lose his position as general secretary, or he would equally quickly adapt to the modus operandi of the totalitarian system, even though he might introduce many interesting and dramatic new features. Given his human decency, I have no doubt that his would be the former case. I shall, however, let this remark stand as an answer to the constant speculations about Gorbachev and the tiresome, often capricious questions on that theme.

As I see it, the strategic aim of the parallel polis should be rather the growth, or the renewal, of civic and political culture—and along with it, an identical structuring of society, creating bonds of responsibility and fellow-feeling. The issue is no more and no less that this: when the next crisis comes, the next moment of decision about the future of our nations, the good will of most of society (and I repeat: this has so far been incredibly good and always brutally disappointed) will find a sufficiently clear and a sufficiently authoritative articulation. In other words our political leadership should be at the same level of thinking as society, and if it is not, so much the worse for the leadership.

Let me give an example that is now ancient and has ceased to be painful. The proclamation: "Give us arms, we paid for them!" in 1938 is mere propaganda if it is not followed up with a concrete plan as to where these arms are to be distributed and under whose command they are to be used. If there is any justification for the existence of an army, then their leadership, at a moment when the civilian politicians have betrayed their trust and the nation is in mortal danger, will not resort to theatrical suicides, but to a military coup—which is my answer to the question regarding *what* arms and under *whose* leadership.

Modern totalitarianism is held in check by two great limitations: it is intrinsically suspicious of, and even hostile to, any genuine authority, and it is capable of decisive action only in defense of its own power prerogatives. It is this that gives the parallel polis its strategic location and its long-range task: at a moment of crisis, it is our clear, unequivocal words that will be heard, not the confused and defensive stammerings of the government. For the sake of completeness, I should add that the appropriate clarity, courage, and authority is not something automatic, or a gift from heaven; it must be earned in hard, "small-scale work" and also with the appropriate sacrifices. And if, in the next moment of potential choice we should fail, this would be far more at the expense of Charter 77 and the parallel polis than it would be at the expense of our miserable government. We have taken up arms; now we shall have to fight!

28

The Power of the Powerless[*]
(1978)

Václav Havel

To the memory of Jan Patočka

I

A specter is haunting eastern Europe: the specter of what in the West is called "dissent." This specter has not appeared out of thin air. It is a natural and inevitable consequence of the present historical phase of the system it is haunting. It was born at a time when this system, for a thousand reasons, can no longer base itself on the unadulterated, brutal, and arbitrary application of power, eliminating all expressions of nonconformity. What is more, the system has become so ossified politically that there is practically no way for such nonconformity to be implemented within its official structures.

Who are these so-called dissidents? Where does their point of view come from, and what importance does it have? What is the significance of the "independent initiatives" in which "dissidents" collaborate, and what real chances do such initiatives have of success? Is it appropriate to refer to "dissidents" as an opposition? If so, what exactly is such an opposition within the framework of this system? What does it do? What role does it play in society? What are its hopes and on what are they based? Is it

---

[*] See note on page 26. Two excerpts from this essay appear in this volume. Part II appears in Section I. Parts I and III–XII appear here.

within the power of the "dissidents"—as a category of subcitizen outside the power establishment—to have any influence at all on society and the social system? Can they actually change anything?

I think that an examination of these questions—an examination of the potential of the "powerless"—can only begin with an examination of the nature of power in the circumstances in which these powerless people operate. . . .

III*

The manager of a fruit-and-vegetable shop places in his window, among the onions and carrots, the slogan: "Workers of the world, unite!" Why does he do it? What is he trying to communicate to the world? Is he genuinely enthusiastic about the idea of unity among the workers of the world? Is his enthusiasm so great that he feels an irrepressible impulse to acquaint the public with his ideals? Has he really given more than a moment's thought to how such a unification might occur and what it would mean?

I think it can safely be assumed that the overwhelming majority of shopkeepers never think about the slogans they put in their windows, nor do they use them to express their real opinions. That poster was delivered to our greengrocer from the enterprise headquarters along with the onions and carrots. He put them all into the window simply because it has been done that way for years, because everyone does it, and because that is the way it has to be. If he were to refuse, there could be trouble. He could be reproached for not having the proper decoration in his window; someone might even accuse him of disloyalty. He does it because these things must be done if one is to get along in life. It is one of the thousands of details that guarantee him a relatively tranquil life "in harmony with society," as they say.

Obviously the greengrocer is indifferent to the semantic content of the slogan on exhibit; he does not put the slogan in his window from any personal desire to acquaint the public with the ideal it expresses. This, of course, does not mean that his action has no motive or significance at all, or that the slogan communicates nothing to anyone. The slogan is

---

* Section II appears in the first section of this volume.

really a sign, and as such it contains a subliminal but very definite message. Verbally, it might be expressed this way: "I, the greengrocer XY, live here and I know what I must do. I behave in the manner expected of me. I can be depended upon and am beyond reproach. I am obedient and therefore I have the right to be left in peace." This message, of course, has an addressee: it is directed above, to the greengrocer's superior, and at the same time it is a shield that protects the greengrocer from potential informers. The slogan's real meaning, therefore, is rooted firmly in the greengrocer's existence. It reflects his vital interests. But what are those vital interests?

Let us take note: if the greengrocer had been instructed to display the slogan "I am afraid and therefore unquestioningly obedient," he would not be nearly as indifferent to its semantics, even though the statement would reflect the truth. The greengrocer would be embarrassed and ashamed to put such an unequivocal statement of his own degradation in the shop window, and quite naturally so, for he is a human being and thus has a sense of his own dignity. To overcome this complication, his expression of loyalty must take the form of a sign which, at least on its textual surface, indicates a level of disinterested conviction. It must allow the greengrocer to say, "What's wrong with the workers of the world uniting?" Thus the sign helps the greengrocer to conceal from himself the low foundations of his obedience, at the same time concealing the low foundations of power. It hides them behind the facade of something high. And that something is ideology.

Ideology is a specious way of relating to the world. It offers human beings the illusion of an identity, of dignity, and of morality while making it easier for them to part with them. As the repository of something suprapersonal and objective, it enables people to deceive their conscience and conceal their true position and their inglorious *modus vivendi,* both from the world and from themselves. It is a very pragmatic but, at the same time, an apparently dignified way of legitimizing what is above, below, and on either side. It is directed toward people and toward God. It is a veil behind which human beings can hide their own fallen existence, their trivialization and their adaptation to the status quo. It is an excuse that everyone can use, from the greengrocer, who conceals his fear of losing his job behind an alleged interest in the unification of the workers of the world, to the highest functionary, whose interest in staying in power can be cloaked in phrases about service to the working class. The primary excusatory function of ideology, therefore, is to provide people, both as victims and pillars of the post-totalitarian system, with the illusion that the system is in harmony with the human order and the order of the universe.

The smaller a dictatorship and the less stratified by modernization the society under it, the more directly the will of the dictator can be exercised. In other words, the dictator can employ more or less naked discipline, avoiding the complex processes of relating to the world and of self-justification which ideology involves. But the more complex the mechanisms of power become, the larger and more stratified the society they embrace, and the longer they have operated historically, the more individuals must be connected to them from outside, and the greater the importance attached to the ideological excuse. It acts as a kind of bridge between the regime and the people, across which the regime approaches the people and the people approach the regime. This explains why ideology plays such an important role in the post-totalitarian system: that complex machinery of units, hierarchies, transmission belts, and indirect instruments of manipulation which ensure in countless ways the integrity of the regime, leaving nothing to chance, would be quite simply unthinkable without ideology acting as its all-embracing excuse and as the excuse for each of its parts.

IV

Between the aims of the post-totalitarian system and the aims of life there is a yawning abyss: while life, in its essence, moves toward plurality, diversity, independent self-constitution, and self-organization, in short, toward the fulfillment of its own freedom, the post-totalitarian system demands conformity, uniformity, and discipline. While life ever strives to create new and improbable structures, the post-totalitarian system contrives to force life into its most probable states. The aims of the system reveal its most essential characteristic to be introversion, a movement toward being ever more completely and unreservedly itself, which means that the radius of its influence is continually widening as well. This system serves people only to the extent necessary to ensure that people will serve it. Anything beyond this, that is to say, anything which leads people to overstep their predetermined roles, is regarded by the system as an attack upon itself.

And in this respect it is correct: every instance of such transgression is a genuine denial of the system. It can be said, therefore, that the inner aim of the post-totalitarian system is not mere preservation of power in the hands of a ruling clique, as appears to be the case at first sight. Rather, the social phenomenon of self-preservation is subordinated to something higher, to a kind of blind automatism which drives the system. No matter what position individuals hold in the hierarchy of power, they are not considered by the system to be worth anything in themselves, but only as things intended to fuel and serve this automatism. For this reason, an individual's desire for power is admissible only insofar as its direction coincides with the direction of the automatism of the system.

Ideology, in creating a bridge of excuses between the system and the individual, spans the abyss between the aims of the system and the aims of life. It pretends that the requirements of the system derive from the requirements of life. It is a world of appearances trying to pass for reality.

The post-totalitarian system touches people at every step, but it does so with its ideological gloves on. This is why life in the system is so thoroughly permeated with hypocrisy and lies: government by bureaucracy is called popular government; the working class is enslaved in the name of the working class; the complete degradation of the individual is presented as his ultimate liberation; depriving people of information is called making it available; the use of power to manipulate is called the public control of power, and the arbitrary abuse of power is called observing the legal code; the repression of culture is called its development; the expansion of imperial influence is presented as support for the oppressed; the lack of free expression becomes the highest form of freedom; farcical elections become the highest form of democracy; banning independent thought becomes the most scientific of world views; military occupation becomes fraternal assistance. Because the regime is captive to its own lies, it must falsify everything. It falsifies the past. It falsifies the present, and it falsifies the future. It falsifies statistics. It pretends not to possess an omnipotent and unprincipled police apparatus. It pretends to respect human rights. It pretends to persecute no one. It pretends to fear nothing. It pretends to pretend nothing.

Individuals need not believe all these mystifications, but they must behave as though they did, or they must at least tolerate them in silence, or get along well with those who work with them. For this reason, however, they must live within a lie. They need not accept the lie. It is enough for them to have accepted their life with it and in it. For by this very fact, individuals confirm the system, fulfill the system, make the system, *are* the system.

V

We have seen that the real meaning of the greengrocer's slogan has nothing to do with what the text of the slogan actually says. Even so, this real meaning is quite clear and generally comprehensible because the code is so familiar: the greengrocer declares his loyalty (and he can do no other if his declaration is to be accepted) in the only way the regime is capable of hearing; that is, by accepting the prescribed ritual, by accepting appearances as reality, by accepting the given rules of the game. In doing so, however, he has himself become a player in the game, thus making it possible for the game to go on, for it to exist in the first place.

If ideology was originally a bridge between the system and the individual as an individual, then the moment he steps on to this bridge it becomes at the same time a bridge between the system and the individual as a component of the system. That is, if ideology originally facilitated (by acting outwardly) the constitution of power by serving as a psychological excuse, then from the moment that excuse is accepted, it constitutes power inwardly, becoming an active component of that power. It begins to function as the principal instrument of ritual communication *within* the system of power.

The whole power structure (and we have already discussed its physical articulation) could not exist at all if there were not a certain metaphysical order binding all its components together, interconnecting them and subordinating them to a uniform method of accountability, supplying the combined operation of all these components with rules of the game, that is, with certain regulations, limitations, and legalities. This metaphysical order is fundamental to, and standard throughout, the entire power structure; it integrates its communication system and makes possible the internal exchange and transfer of information and instructions. It is rather like a collection of traffic signals and directional signs, giving the process shape and structure. This metaphysical order guarantees the inner coherence of the totalitarian power structure. It is the glue holding it together, its binding principle, the instrument of its discipline. Without this glue the structure as a totalitarian structure would vanish; it would disintegrate into individual atoms chaotically colliding with one another in their unregulated particular interests and inclinations. The entire pyramid of totalitarian power, deprived of the element that binds it together, would collapse in upon itself, as it were, in a kind of material implosion.

As the interpretation of reality by the power structure, ideology is always subordinated ultimately to the interests of the structure. Therefore, it has a natural tendency to disengage itself from reality, to create a world of appearances, to become ritual. In societies where there is public competition for power and therefore public control of that power, there also exists quite naturally public control of the way that power legitimates itself ideologically. Consequently, in such conditions there are always certain correctives that effectively prevent ideology from abandoning reality altogether. Under totalitarianism, however, these correctives disappear, and thus there is nothing to prevent ideology from becoming more and more removed from reality, gradually turning into what it has already become in the post-totalitarian system: a world of appearances, a mere ritual, a formalized language deprived of semantic contact with reality and transformed into a system of ritual signs that replace reality with pseudoreality.

Yet, as we have seen, ideology becomes at the same time an increasingly important component of power, a pillar providing it with both excusatory legitimacy and an inner coherence. As this aspect grows in importance, and as it gradually loses touch with reality, it acquires a peculiar but very real strength. It becomes reality itself, albeit a reality altogether self-contained, one that on certain levels (chiefly inside the power structure) may have even greater weight than reality as such. Increasingly, the virtuosity of the ritual becomes more important than the reality hidden behind it. The significance of phenomena no longer derives from the phenomena themselves, but from their locus as concepts in the ideological context. Reality does not shape theory, but rather the reverse. Thus power gradually draws closer to ideology than it does to reality; it draws its strength from theory and becomes entirely dependent on it. This inevitably leads, of course, to a paradoxical result: rather than theory, or rather ideology, serving power, power begins to serve ideology. It is as though ideology had appropriated power from power, as though it had become dictator itself. It then appears that theory itself, ritual itself, ideology itself, makes decisions that affect people, and not the other way around.

If ideology is the principal guarantee of the inner consistency of power, it becomes at the same time an increasingly important guarantee of its continuity. Whereas succession to power in classical dictatorship is always a rather complicated affair (the pretenders having nothing to give their claims reasonable legitimacy, thereby forcing them always to resort to confrontations of naked power), in the post-totalitarian system power is passed on from person to person, from clique to clique, and from generation to generation in an essentially more regular fashion. In the selection of pretenders, a new "king-maker" takes part: it is ritual legitimation, the ability to rely on ritual, to fulfill it and use it, to allow oneself, as it were, to be borne aloft by it. Naturally, power struggles exist in the post-totalitarian system as well, and most of them are far more brutal than in an open society, for the struggle is not open, regulated by democratic rules, and subject to public control, but hidden behind the scenes. (It is difficult to recall a single instance in which the First Secretary of a ruling Communist Party has been replaced without the various military and security forces being placed at least on alert.) This struggle, however, can never (as it can in classical dictatorships) threaten the very essence of the system and its continuity. At most it will shake up the power structure, which will recover quickly precisely because the binding substance—ideology—remains undisturbed. No matter who is replaced by whom, succession is only possible against the backdrop and within the framework of a common ritual. It can never take place by denying that ritual.

Because of this dictatorship of the ritual, however, power becomes clearly anonymous. Individuals are almost dissolved in the ritual. They allow themselves to be swept along by it and frequently it seems as though ritual alone carries people from obscurity into the light of power. Is it not characteristic of the post-totalitarian system that, on all levels of the power hierarchy, individuals are increasingly being pushed aside by faceless people, puppets, those uniformed flunkeys of the rituals and routines of power?

The automatic operation of a power structure thus dehumanized and made anonymous is a feature of the fundamental automatism of this system. It would seem that it is precisely the diktats of this automatism which select people lacking individual will for the power structure, that it is precisely the diktat of the empty phrase which summons to power people who use empty phrases as the best guarantee that the automatism of the post-totalitarian system will continue.

Western Sovietologists often exaggerate the role of individuals in the post-totalitarian system and overlook the fact that the ruling figures, despite the immense power they possess through the centralized structure of power, are often no more than blind executors of the system's own internal laws—laws they themselves never can, and never do, reflect upon. In any case, experience has taught us again and again that this automatism is far more powerful than the will of any individual; and should someone possess a more independent will, he must conceal it behind a ritually anonymous mask in order to have an opportunity to enter the power hierarchy at all. And when the individual finally gains a place there and tries to make his will felt within it, that automatism, with its enormous inertia, will triumph sooner or later, and either the individual will be ejected by the power structure like a foreign organism, or he will be compelled to resign his individuality gradually, once again blending with the automatism and becoming its servant, almost indistinguishable from those who preceded him and those who will follow. (Let us recall, for instance, the development of Husák[*] or Gomułka.[†]) The necessity of continually hiding behind and relating to ritual means that even the more enlightened members of the power structure are often obsessed with ideology. They are never able to plunge straight to the bottom of naked reality, and they always confuse it, in the final analysis, with ideological pseudoreality. (In my opinion, one of the reasons the Dubček[‡] leadership lost control of the situation in 1968 was precisely because, in extreme situations and in final questions, its members were never capable of extricating themselves completely from the world of appearances.)

---

[*] Gustáv Husák replaced Alexander Dubček as First Secretary of the Central Committee of the Communist Party of Czechoslovakia (CPC) in April 1969 in the wake of the Soviet suppression of the Prague Spring. He is closely associated with the so-called normalization period of the 1970s and 1980s.

[†] Gomułka. See notes on pages 380 and 412.

[‡] Alexander Dubček replaced Antonín Novotný as First Secretary of the Central Committee of the CPCz in 1968. He quickly became the symbol of the reform movement that had been developing throughout the 1960s. He was pressured by the Soviets and the Communist governments of other Warsaw Pact countries to crush the reform movement. After the Soviets invaded on August 21, 1968, he was arrested and taken to the USSR.

It can be said, therefore, that ideology, as that instrument of internal communication which assures the power structure of inner cohesion is, in the post-totalitarian system, something that transcends the physical aspects of power, something that dominates it to a considerable degree and, therefore, tends to assure its continuity as well. It is one of the pillars of the system's external stability. This pillar, however, is built on a very unstable foundation. It is built on lies. It works only as long as people are willing to live within the lie.

VI

Why in fact did our greengrocer have to put his loyalty on display in the shop window? Had he not already displayed it sufficiently in various internal or semipublic ways? At trade union meetings, after all, he had always voted as he should. He had always taken part in various competitions. He voted in elections like a good citizen. He had even signed the "anti-Charter." Why, on top of all that, should he have to declare his loyalty publicly? After all, the people who walk past his window will certainly not stop to read that, in the greengrocer's opinion, the workers of the world ought to unite. The fact of the matter is, they don't read the slogan at all, and it can be fairly assumed they don't even see it. If you were to ask a woman who had stopped in front of his shop what she saw in the window, she could certainly tell whether or not they had tomatoes today, but it is highly unlikely that she noticed the slogan at all, let alone what it said.

It seems senseless to require the greengrocer to declare his loyalty publicly. But it makes sense nevertheless. People ignore his slogan, but they do so because such slogans are also found in other shop windows, on lampposts, bulletin boards, in apartment windows, and on buildings; they are everywhere, in fact. They form part of the panorama of everyday life. Of course, while they ignore the details, people are very aware of that panorama as a whole. And what else is the greengrocer's slogan but a small component in that huge backdrop to daily life?

The greengrocer had to put the slogan in his window, therefore, not in the hope that someone might read it or be persuaded by it, but to contribute, along with thousands of other slogans, to the panorama that everyone is very much aware of. This panorama, of course, has a subliminal meaning as well: it reminds people where they are living and what is expected of them. It tells them what everyone else is doing, and indicates to them what they must do as well, if they don't want to be excluded, to fall into isolation, alienate themselves from society, break the rules of the game, and risk the loss of their peace and tranquility and security.

The woman who ignored the greengrocer's slogan may well have hung a similar slogan just an hour before in the corridor of the office where she works. She did it more or less without thinking, just as our greengrocer did, and she could do so precisely because she was doing it against the background of the general panorama and with some awareness of it, that is, against the background of the panorama of which the greengrocer's shop window forms a part. When the greengrocer visits her office, he will not notice her slogan either, just as she failed to notice his. Nevertheless, their slogans are mutually dependent: both were displayed with some awareness of the general panorama and, we might say, under its diktat. Both, however, assist in the creation of that panorama, and therefore they assist in the creation of that diktat as well. The greengrocer and the office worker have both adapted to the conditions in which they live, but in doing so, they help to create those conditions. They do what is done, what is to be done, what must be done, but at the same time—by that very token—they confirm that it must be done in fact. They conform to a particular requirement and in so doing they themselves perpetuate that requirement. Metaphysically speaking, without the greengrocer's slogan the office worker's slogan could not exist, and vice versa. Each proposes to the other that something be repeated and each accepts the other's proposal. Their mutual indifference to each other's slogans is only an illusion: in reality, by exhibiting their slogans, each compels the other to accept the rules of the game and to confirm thereby the power that requires the slogans in the first place. Quite simply, each helps the other to be obedient. Both are objects in a system of control, but at the same time they are its subjects as well. They are both victims of the system and its instruments.

If an entire district town is plastered with slogans that no one reads, it is on the one hand a message from the district secretary to the regional secretary, but it is also something more: a small example of the principle of social autototality at work. Part of the essence of the post-totalitarian system is that it draws everyone into its sphere of power, not so they may realize themselves as human beings, but so they may surrender their human identity in favor of the identity of the system, that is, so they may become agents of the system's general automatism and servants of its self-determined goals, so they may participate in the common responsibility for it, so they may be pulled into and ensnared by it, like Faust by Mephistopheles. More than this: so they may create through their involvement a general norm and, thus, bring pressure to bear on their fellow citizens. And further: so they may learn to be comfortable with their involvement, to identify with it as though it were something natural and inevitable and, ultimately, so they may—with no external urging—come to treat any non-involvement as an abnormality, as arrogance, as an attack on themselves, as a form of dropping out of society. By pulling everyone into its power structure, the post-totalitarian system makes everyone an instrument of a mutual totality, the autototality of society.

Everyone, however, is in fact involved and enslaved, not only the greengrocers but also the prime ministers. Differing positions in the hierarchy merely establish differing degrees of involvement: the greengrocer is involved only to a minor extent, but he also has very little power. The prime minister, naturally, has greater power, but in return he is far more deeply involved. Both, however, are unfree, each merely in a somewhat different way. The real accomplice in this involvement, therefore, is not another person, but the system itself. Position in the power hierarchy determines the degree of responsibility and guilt, but it gives no one unlimited responsibility and guilt, nor does it completely absolve anyone. Thus the conflict between the aims of life and the aims of the system is not a conflict between two socially defined and separate communities; and only a very generalized view (and even that only approximative) permits us to divide society into the rulers and the ruled. Here, by the way, is one of the most important differences between the post-totalitarian system and classical dictatorships, in which this line of conflict can still be drawn according to social class. In the post-totalitarian system, this line runs de facto through each person, for everyone in his own way is both a victim and a supporter of the system. What we understand by the system is not, therefore, a social order imposed by one group upon another, but rather something which permeates the entire society and is a factor in shaping it, something which may seem impossible to grasp or define (for it is in the nature of a mere principle), but which is expressed by the entire society as an important feature of its life.

The fact that human beings have created, and daily create, this self-directed system through which they divest themselves of their innermost identity is not therefore the result of some incomprehensible misunderstanding of history, nor is it history somehow gone off its rails. Neither is it the product of some diabolical higher will which has decided, for reasons unknown, to torment a portion of humanity in this way. It can happen and did happen only because there is obviously in modern humanity a certain tendency toward the creation, or at least the toleration, of such a system. There is obviously something in human beings which responds to this system, something they reflect and accommodate, something within them which paralyzes every effort of their better selves to revolt. Human beings are compelled to live within a lie, but they can be compelled to do so only because they are in fact capable of living in this way. Therefore not only does the system alienate humanity, but at the same time alienated humanity supports this system as its own involuntary master-plan, as a degenerate image of its own degeneration, as a record of people's own failure as individuals.

The essential aims of life are present naturally in every person. In everyone there is some longing for humanity's rightful dignity, for moral integrity, for free expression of being and a sense of transcendence over the world of existence. Yet, at the same time, each person is capable, to a greater or lesser degree, of coming to terms with living within the lie. Each person somehow succumbs to a profane trivialization of his inherent humanity, and to utilitarianism. In everyone there is some willingness to merge with the anonymous crowd and to flow comfortably along with it down the river of pseudolife. This is much more than a simple conflict between two identities. It is something far worse: it is a challenge to the very notion of identity itself.

In highly simplified terms, it could be said that the post-totalitarian system has been built on foundations laid by the historical encounter between dictatorship and the consumer society. Is it not true that the far-reaching adaptability to living a lie and the effortless spread of social autototality have some connection with the general unwillingness of consumption-oriented people to sacrifice some material certainties for the sake of their own spiritual and moral integrity? With their willingness to surrender higher values when faced with the trivializing temptations of modern civilization? With their vulnerability to the attractions of mass indifference? And in the end, is not the grayness and the emptiness of life in the post-totalitarian system only an inflated caricature of modern life in general? And do we not in fact stand (although in the external measures of civilization, we are far behind) as a kind of warning to the West, revealing to its own latent tendencies?

VII

Let us now imagine that one day something in our greengrocer snaps and he stops putting up the slogans merely to ingratiate himself. He stops voting in elections he knows are a farce. He begins to say what he really thinks at political meetings. And he even finds the strength in himself to express solidarity with those whom his conscience commands him to support. In this revolt the greengrocer steps out of living within the lie. He rejects the ritual and breaks the rules of the game. He discovers once more his suppressed identity and dignity. He gives his freedom a concrete significance. His revolt is an attempt to live within the truth.

The bill is not long in coming. He will be relieved of his post as manager of the shop and transferred to the warehouse. His pay will be reduced. His hopes for a holiday in Bulgaria will evaporate. His children's access to higher education will be threatened. His superiors will harass him and his fellow workers will wonder about him. Most of those who apply these sanctions, however, will not do so from any authentic inner conviction but simply under pressure from conditions, the same conditions that once pressured the greengrocer to display the official slogans. They will persecute the greengrocer either because it is expected of them, or to demonstrate their loyalty, or simply as part of the general panorama, to which belongs an awareness that this is how situations of this sort are dealt with, that this, in fact, is how things are always done, particularly if one is not to become suspect oneself. The executors, therefore, behave essentially like everyone else, to a greater or lesser degree: as components of the post-totalitarian system, as agents of its automatism, as petty instruments of the social autototality.

Thus the power structure, through the agency of those who carry out the sanctions, those anonymous components of the system, will spew the greengrocer from its mouth. The system, through its alienating presence in people, will punish him for his rebellion. It must do so because the logic of its automatism and self-defense dictate it. The greengrocer has not committed a simple, individual offense, isolated in its own uniqueness, but something incomparably more serious. By breaking the rules of the game, he has disrupted the game as such. He has exposed it as a mere game. He has shattered the world of appearances, the fundamental pillar of the system. He has upset the power structure by tearing apart what holds it together. He has demonstrated that living a lie is living a lie. He has broken through the exalted facade of the system and exposed the real, base foundations of power. He has said that the emperor is naked. And because the emperor is in fact naked, something extremely dangerous has happened: by his action, the greengrocer has addressed the world. He has enabled everyone to peer behind the curtain. He has shown everyone that it is possible to live within the truth. Living within the lie can constitute the system only if it is universal. The principle must embrace and permeate everything. There are no terms whatsoever on which it can co-exist with living within the truth, and therefore everyone who steps out of line denies it in principle and threatens it in its entirety.

This is understandable: as long as appearance is not confronted with reality, it does not seem to be appearance. As long as living a lie is not confronted with living the truth, the perspective needed to expose its mendacity is lacking. As soon as the alternative appears, however, it threatens the very existence of appearance and living a lie in terms of what they are, both their essence and their all-inclusiveness. And at the same time, it is utterly unimportant how large a space this alternative occupies: its power does not consist in its physical attributes but in the light it casts on those pillars of the system and on its unstable foundations. After all, the greengrocer was a threat to the system not because of any physical or actual power he had, but because his action went beyond itself, because it illuminated its surroundings and, of course, because of the incalculable consequences of that illumination. In the post-totalitarian system, therefore, living within the truth has more than a mere existential dimension (returning humanity to its inherent nature), or a noetic dimension (revealing reality as it is), or a moral dimension (setting an example for others). It also has an unambiguous political dimension. If the main pillar of the system is living a lie, then it is not surprising that the fundamental threat to it is living the truth. This is why it must be suppressed more severely than anything else.

In the post-totalitarian system, truth in the widest sense of the word has a very special import, one unknown in other contexts. In this system, truth plays a far greater (and, above all, a far different) role as a factor of power, or as an outright political force. How does the power of truth operate? How does truth as a factor of power work? How can its power—as power—be realized?

VIII

Individuals can be alienated from themselves only because there is something in them to alienate. The terrain of this violation is their authentic existence. Living the truth is thus woven directly into the texture of living a lie. It is the repressed alternative, the authentic aim to which living a lie is an inauthentic response. Only against this background does living a lie make any sense: it exists *because* of that background. In its excusatory, chimerical rootedness in the human order, it is a response to nothing other than the human predisposition to truth. Under the orderly surface of the life of lies, therefore, there slumbers the hidden sphere of life in its real aims, of its hidden openness to truth.

The singular, explosive, incalculable political power of living within the truth resides in the fact that living openly within the truth has an ally, invisible to be sure, but omnipresent: this hidden sphere. It is from this sphere that life lived openly in the truth grows; it is to this sphere that it speaks, and in it that it finds understanding. This is where the potential for communication exists. But this place is hidden and therefore, from the perspective of power, very dangerous. The complex ferment that takes place within it goes on in semidarkness, and by the time it finally surfaces into the light of day as an assortment of shocking surprises to the system, it is usually too late to cover them up in the usual fashion. Thus they create a situation in which the regime is confounded, invariably causing panic and driving it to react in inappropriate ways.

It seems that the primary breeding ground for what might, in the widest possible sense of the word, be understood as an opposition in the post-totalitarian system is living within the truth. The confrontation between these opposition forces and the powers that be, of course, will obviously take a form essentially different from that typical of an open society or a classical dictatorship. Initially, this confrontation does not take place on the level of real, institutionalized, quantifiable power which relies on the various instruments of power, but on a different level altogether: the level of human consciousness and conscience, the existential level. The effective range of this special power cannot be measured in terms of disciples, voters, or soldiers, because it lies spread out in the fifth column of social consciousness, in the hidden aims of life, in human beings' repressed longing for dignity and fundamental rights, for the realization of their real social and political interests. Its power, therefore, does not reside in the strength of definable political or social groups, but chiefly in the strength of a potential, which is hidden throughout the whole of society, including the official power structures of that society. Therefore this power does not rely on soldiers of its own, but on the soldiers of the enemy as it were—that is to say, on everyone who is living within the lie and who may be struck at any moment (in theory, at least) by the force of truth (or who, out of an instinctive desire to protect their position, may at least adapt to that force). It is a bacteriological weapon, so to speak, utilized when conditions are ripe by a single civilian to disarm an entire division. This power does not participate in any direct struggle for power; rather, it makes its influence felt in the obscure arena of being itself. The hidden movements it gives rise to there, however, can issue forth (when, where, under what circumstances, and to what extent are difficult to predict) in something visible: a real political act or event, a social movement, a sudden explosion of civil unrest, a sharp conflict inside an apparently monolithic power structure, or simply an irrepressible transformation in the social and intellectual climate. And since all genuine problems and matters of critical importance are hidden beneath a thick crust of lies, it is never quite clear when the proverbial last straw will fall, or what that straw will be. This, too, is why the regime prosecutes, almost as a reflex action preventively, even the most modest attempts to live within the truth.

Why was Solzhenitsyn driven out of his own country? Certainly not because he represented a unit of real power, that is, not because any of the regime's representatives felt he might unseat them and take their place in government. Solzhenitsyn's expulsion was something else: a desperate attempt to plug up the dreadful wellspring of truth, a truth which might cause incalculable transformations in social consciousness, which in turn might one day produce political debacles unpredictable in their consequences. And so the post-totalitarian system behaved in a characteristic way: it defended the integrity of the world of appearances in order to defend itself. For the crust presented by the life of lies is made of strange stuff. As long as it seals off hermetically the entire society, it appears to be made of stone. But the moment someone breaks through in one place, when one person cries out, "The emperor is naked!"—when a single person breaks the rules of the game, thus exposing it as a game—everything suddenly appears in another light and the whole crust seems then to be made of a tissue on the point of tearing and disintegrating uncontrollably.

When I speak of living within the truth, I naturally do not have in mind only products of conceptual thought, such as a protest or a letter written by a group of intellectuals. It can be any means by which a person or a group revolts against manipulation: anything from a letter by intellectuals to a workers' strike, from a rock concert to a student demonstration, from refusing to vote in the farcical elections to making an open speech at some official congress, or even a hunger strike, for instance. If the suppression of the aims of life is a complex process, and if it is based on the multifaceted manipulation of all expressions of life, then, by the same token, every free expression of life indirectly threatens the post-totalitarian system politically, including forms of expression to which, in other social systems, no one would attribute any potential political significance, not to mention explosive power.

The Prague Spring* is usually understood as a clash between two groups on the level of real power: those who wanted to maintain the system as it was and those who wanted to reform it. It is frequently forgotten, however, that this encounter was merely the final act and the inevitable consequence of a long drama originally played out chiefly in the theater of the spirit and the conscience of society. And that somewhere at the beginning of this drama, there were individuals who were willing to live within the truth, even when things were at their worst. These people had no access to real power, nor did they aspire to it. The sphere in which they were living the truth was not necessarily even that of political thought.

---

* The Prague Spring refers to the eight months of reforms undertaken in 1968 when Czechoslovakia attempted to fashion, in the popular slogan, "socialism with a human face." The movement was crushed in August of 1968 when the Soviet Union, East Germany, Poland, Bulgaria, and Hungary sent troops to invade the country.

They could equally have been poets, painters, musicians, or simply ordinary citizens who were able to maintain their human dignity. Today it is naturally difficult to pinpoint when and through which hidden, winding channel a certain action or attitude influenced a given milieu, and to trace the virus of truth as it slowly spread through the tissue of the life of lies, gradually causing it to disintegrate. One thing, however, seems clear: the attempt at political reform was not the cause of society's reawakening, but rather the final outcome of that reawakening.

I think the present also can be better understood in the light of this experience. The confrontation between a thousand Chartists and the post-totalitarian system would appear to be politically hopeless. This is true, of course, if we look at it through the traditional lens of the open political system, in which, quite naturally, every political force is measured chiefly in terms of the positions it holds on the level of real power. Given that perspective, a mini-party like the Charter would certainly not stand a chance. If, however, this confrontation is seen against the background of what we know about power in the post-totalitarian system, it appears in a fundamentally different light. For the time being, it is impossible to say with any precision what impact the appearance of Charter 77, its existence, and its work has had in the hidden sphere, and how the Charter's attempt to rekindle civic self-awareness and confidence is regarded there. Whether, when, and how this investment will eventually produce dividends in the form of specific political changes is even less possible to predict. But that, of course, is all part of living within the truth. As an existential solution, it takes individuals back to the solid ground of their own identity; as politics, it throws them into a game of chance where the stakes are all or nothing. For this reason it is undertaken only by those for whom the former is worth risking the latter, or who have come to the conclusion that there is no other way to conduct real politics in Czechoslovakia today. Which, by the way, is the same thing: this conclusion can be reached only by someone who is unwilling to sacrifice his own human identity to politics, or rather, who does not believe in a politics that requires such a sacrifice.

The more thoroughly the post-totalitarian system frustrates any rival alternative on the level of real power, as well as any form of politics independent of the laws of its own automatism, the more definitively the center of gravity of any potential political threat shifts to the area of the existential and the prepolitical: usually without any conscious effort, living within the truth becomes the one natural point of departure for all activities that work against the automatism of the system. And even if such activities ultimately grow beyond the area of living within the truth (which means they are transformed into various parallel structures, movements, institutions, they begin to be regarded as political activity, they bring real pressure to bear on the official structures and begin in fact to have a certain influence on the level of real power), they always carry with them the specific hallmark of their origins. Therefore it seems to me that not even the so-called dissident movements can be properly understood without constantly bearing in mind this special background from which they emerge.

IX

The profound crisis of human identity brought on by living within a lie, a crisis which in turn makes such a life possible, certainly possesses a moral dimension as well; it appears, among other things, as a deep moral crisis in society. A person who has been seduced by the consumer value system, whose identity is dissolved in an amalgam of the accouterments of mass civilization, and who has no roots in the order of being, no sense of responsibility for anything higher than his own personal survival, is a demoralized person. The system depends on this demoralization, deepens it, is in fact a projection of it into society.

Living within the truth, as humanity's revolt against an enforced position, is, on the contrary, an attempt to regain control over one's own sense of responsibility. In other words, it is clearly a moral act, not only because one must pay so dearly for it, but principally because it is not self-serving: the risk may bring rewards in the form of a general amelioration in the situation, or it may not. In this regard, as I stated previously, it is an all-or-nothing gamble, and it is difficult to imagine a reasonable person embarking on such a course merely because he reckons that sacrifice today will bring rewards tomorrow, be it only in the form of general gratitude. (By the way, the representatives of power invariably come to terms with those who live within the truth by persistently ascribing utilitarian motivations to them—a lust for power or fame or wealth—and thus they try, at least, to implicate them in their own world, the world of general demoralization.)

If living within the truth in the post-totalitarian system becomes the chief breeding ground for independent, alternative political ideas, then all considerations about the nature and future prospects of these ideas must necessarily reflect this moral dimension as a political phenomenon. (And if the revolutionary Marxist belief about morality as a product of the "super-structure" inhibits any of our friends from realizing the full significance of this dimension and, in one way or another, from including it in their view of the world, it is to their own detriment: an anxious fidelity to the postulates of that worldview prevents them from properly understanding the mechanisms of their own political influence, thus paradoxically making them precisely what they, as Marxists, so often suspect others of being—victims of "false consciousness.") The very special political significance of morality in the post-totalitarian system is a phenomenon that is at the very least unusual in modern political history, a phenomenon that might well have—as I shall soon attempt to show—far-reaching consequences.

X

Undeniably, the most important political event in Czechoslovakia after the advent of the Husák leadership in 1969 was the appearance of Charter 77. The spiritual and intellectual climate surrounding its appearance, however, was not the product of any immediate political event. That climate was created by the trial of some young musicians associated with a rock group called "The Plastic People of the Universe." Their trial was not a confrontation of two differing political forces or conceptions, but two differing conceptions of life. On the one hand, there was the sterile puritanism of the post-totalitarian establishment and, on the other hand, unknown young people who wanted no more than to be able to live within the truth, to play the music they enjoyed, to sing songs that were relevant to their lives, and to live freely in dignity and partnership. These people had no past history of political activity. They were not highly motivated members of the opposition with political ambitions, nor were they former politicians expelled from the power structures. They had been given every opportunity to adapt to the status quo, to accept the principles of living within a lie and thus to enjoy life undisturbed by the authorities. Yet they decided on a different course. Despite this, or perhaps precisely because of it, their case had a very special impact on everyone who had not yet given up hope. Moreover, when the trial took place, a new mood had begun to surface after the years of waiting, of apathy, and of skepticism toward various forms of resistance. People were "tired of being tired"; they were fed up with the stagnation, the inactivity, barely hanging on in the hope that things might improve after all. In some ways the trial was the final straw. Many groups of differing tendencies which until then had remained isolated from each other, reluctant to cooperate, or which were committed to forms of action that made cooperation difficult, were suddenly struck with the powerful realization that freedom is indivisible. Everyone understood that an attack on the Czech musical underground was an attack on a most elementary and important thing, something that in fact bound everyone together: it was an attack on the very notion of living within the truth, on the real aims of life. The freedom to play rock music was understood as a human freedom and thus as essentially the same as the freedom to engage in philosophical and political reflection, the freedom to write, the freedom to express and defend the various social and political interests of society. People were inspired to feel a genuine sense of solidarity with the young musicians and they came to realize that not standing up for the freedom of others, regardless of how remote their means of creativity or their attitude to life, meant surrendering one's own freedom. (There is no freedom without equality before the law, and there is no equality before the law without freedom; Charter 77 has given this ancient notion a new and characteristic dimension, which has immensely important implications for modern Czech history. What Sladeček,* the author of the book *Sixty-eight,* in a brilliant analysis, calls the "principle of exclusion," lies at the root of all our present-day moral and political misery. This principle was born at the end of the Second World War in that strange collusion of democrats and Communists and was subsequently developed further and further, right to the bitter end. For the first time in decades this principle has been overcome, by Charter 77: all those united in the Charter have, for the first time, become equal partners. Charter 77 is not merely a

---

* Sladeček is a pseudonym for the Petr Pithart, who was active in reform circles during the Prague Spring and a signatory of Charter 77. His book *Sixty-eight* is a study of the Prague Spring. After the fall of Communism, Pithart served as Prime Minister of the Czech Republic and as a member of the Senate.

coalition of Communists and non-Communists—that would be nothing historically new and, from the moral and political point of view, nothing revolutionary—but it is a community that is a priori open to anyone, and no one in it is a priori assigned an inferior position.) This was the climate, then, in which Charter 77 was created. Who could have foreseen that the prosecution of one or two obscure rock groups would have such far-reaching consequences?

I think that the origins of Charter 77 illustrate very well what I have already suggested above: that in the post-totalitarian system, the real background to the movements that gradually assume political significance does not usually consist of overtly political events or confrontations between different forces or concepts that are openly political. These movements for the most part originate elsewhere, in the far broader area of the "prepolitical," where living within a lie confronts living within the truth, that is, where the demands of the post-totalitarian system conflict with the real aims of life. These real aims can naturally assume a great many forms. Sometimes they appear as the basic material or social interests of a group or an individual; at other times, they may appear as certain intellectual and spiritual interests; at still other times, they may be the most fundamental of existential demands, such as the simple longing of people to live their own lives in dignity. Such a conflict acquires a political character, then, not because of the elementary political nature of the aims demanding to be heard but simply because, given the complex system of manipulation on which the post-totalitarian system is founded and on which it is also dependent, every free human act or expression, every attempt to live within the truth, must necessarily appear as a threat to the system and, thus, as something which is political par excellence. Any eventual political articulation of the movements that grow out of this "prepolitical" hinterland is secondary. It develops and matures as a result of a subsequent confrontation with the system, and not because it started off as a political program, project, or impulse.

Once again, the events of 1968 confirm this. The Communist politicians who were trying to reform the system came forward with their program not because they had suddenly experienced a mystical enlightenment, but because they were led to do so by continued and increasing pressure from areas of life that had nothing to do with politics in the traditional sense of the word. In fact, they were trying in political ways to solve the social conflicts (which in fact were confrontations between the aims of the system and the aims of life) that almost every level of society had been experiencing daily, and had been thinking about with increasing openness for years. Backed by this living resonance throughout society, scholars and artists had defined the problem in a wide variety of ways and students were demanding solutions.

The genesis of Charter 77 also illustrates the special political significance of the moral aspect of things that I have mentioned. Charter 77 would have been unimaginable without that powerful sense of solidarity among widely differing groups, and without the sudden realization that it was impossible to go on waiting any longer, and that the truth had to be spoken loudly and collectively, regardless of the virtual certainty of sanctions and the uncertainty of any tangible results in the immediate future. "There are some things worth suffering for," Jan Patočka wrote shortly before his death. I think that Chartists understand this not only as Patočka's legacy, but also as the best explanation of why they do what they do.

Seen from the outside, and chiefly from the vantage point of the system and its power structure, Charter 77 came as a surprise, as a bolt out of the blue. It was not a bolt out of the blue, of course, but that impression is understandable, since the ferment that led to it took place in the "hidden sphere," in that semidarkness where things are difficult to chart or analyze. The chances of predicting the appearance of the Charter were just as slight as the chances are now of predicting where it will lead. Once again, it was that shock, so typical of moments when something from the hidden sphere suddenly bursts through the moribund surface of living within a lie. The more one is trapped in the world of appearances, the more surprising it is when something like that happens.

XI

In societies under the post-totalitarian system, all political life in the traditional sense has been eliminated. People have no opportunity to express themselves politically in public, let alone to organize politically. The gap that results is filled by ideological ritual. In such a situation, people's interest in political matters naturally dwindles and independent political thought, insofar as it exists at all, is seen by the majority as unrealistic, farfetched, a kind of self-indulgent game, hopelessly distant from their everyday concerns; something admirable, perhaps, but quite pointless, because it is on the one hand entirely utopian and on the other hand extraordinarily dangerous, in view of the unusual vigor with which any move in that direction is persecuted by the regime.

Yet even in such societies, individuals and groups of people exist who do not abandon politics as a vocation and who, in one way or another, strive to think independently, to express themselves and in some cases even to organize politically, because that is a part of their attempt to live within the truth.

The fact that these people exist and work is in itself immensely important and worthwhile. Even in the worst of times, they maintain the continuity of political thought. If some genuine political impulse emerges from this or that "prepolitical" confrontation and is properly articulated early enough, thus increasing its chances of relative success, then this is frequently due to these isolated generals without an army who, because they have maintained the continuity of political thought in the face of enormous difficulties, can at the right moment enrich the new impulse with the fruits of their own political thinking. Once again, there is ample evidence for this process in Czechoslovakia. Almost all those who were political prisoners in the early 1970s, who had apparently been made to suffer in vain because of their quixotic efforts to work politically among an utterly apathetic and demoralized society, belong today—inevitably— among the most active Chartists. In Charter 77, the moral legacy of their earlier sacrifices is valued, and they have enriched this movement with their experience and that element of political thinking.

And yet it seems to me that the thought and activity of those friends who have never given up direct political work and who are always ready to assume direct political responsibility very often suffer from one chronic fault; an insufficient understanding of the historical uniqueness of the post-totalitarian system as a social and political reality. They have little understanding of the specific nature of power that is typical for this system and therefore they overestimate the importance of direct political work in the traditional sense. Moreover, they fail to appreciate the political signifi-cance of those "prepolitical" events and processes that provide the living humus from which genuine political change usually springs. As political actors—or, rather, as people with political ambitions—they frequently try to pick up where natural political life left off. They maintain models of behavior that may have been appropriate in more normal political circumstances and thus, without really being aware of it, they bring an outmoded way of thinking, old habits, conceptions, categories, and notions to bear on circumstances that are quite new and radically different, without first giving adequate thought to the meaning and substance of such things in the new circumstances, to what politics as such means now, to what sort of thing can have political impact and potential, and in what way. Because such people have been excluded from the structures of power and are no longer able to influence those structures directly (and because they remain faithful to traditional notions of politics established in more or less democratic societies or in classical dictatorships) they frequently, in a sense, lose touch with reality. Why make compromises with reality, they say, when none of our proposals will ever be accepted anyway? Thus they find themselves in a world of genuinely utopian thinking.

As I have already tried to indicate, however, genuinely far-reaching political events do not emerge from the same sources and in the same way in the post-totalitarian system as they do in a democracy. And if a large portion of the public is indifferent to, even skeptical of, alternative political models and programs and the private establishment of opposition political parties, this is not merely because there is a general feeling of apathy toward public affairs and a loss of that sense of higher responsibility; in other words, it is not just a consequence of the general demoralization. There is also a bit of healthy social instinct at work in this attitude. It is as if people sensed intuitively that "nothing is what it seems any longer," as the saying goes, and that from now on, therefore, things must be done entirely differently as well.

If some of the most important political impulses in Soviet bloc countries in recent years have come initially—that is, before being felt on the level of actual power—from mathematicians, philosophers, physicians, writers, historians, ordinary workers, and so on, more frequently than from politicians, and if the driving force behind the various dissident movements comes from so many people in nonpolitical professions, this is not because these people are more clever than those who see themselves primarily as politicians. It is because those who are not politicians are also not so bound by traditional political thinking and political habits and therefore, paradoxically, they are more aware of genuine political reality and more sensitive to what can and should be done under the circumstances.

There is no way around it: no matter how beautiful an alternative political model can be, it can no longer speak to the "hidden sphere," inspire people and society, call for real political ferment. The real sphere of potential politics in the post-totalitarian system is elsewhere: in the continuing and cruel tension between the complex demands of that system and the aims of life, that is, the elementary need of human beings to live, to a certain extent at least, in harmony with themselves, that is, to live in a bearable way, not to be humiliated by their superiors and officials, not to be continually watched by the police, to be able to express themselves freely, to find an outlet for their creativity, to enjoy legal security, and so on. Anything that touches this field concretely, anything that relates to this fundamental, omnipresent, and living tension, will inevitably speak to people. Abstract projects for an ideal political or economic order do not interest them to anything like the same extent—and rightly so—not only because everyone knows how little chance they have of succeeding, but also because today people feel that the less political policies are derived from a concrete and human here and now and the more they fix their sights on an abstract "someday," the more easily they can degenerate into new forms of human enslavement. People who live in the post-totalitarian system know only too well that the question of whether one or several political parties are in power, and how these parties define and label themselves, is of far less importance than the question of whether or not it is possible to live like a human being.

To shed the burden of traditional political categories and habits and open oneself up fully to the world of human existence and then to draw political conclusions only after having analyzed it: this is not only politically more realistic but at the same time, from the point of view of an "ideal state of affairs," politically more promising as well. A genuine, profound, and lasting change for the better—as I shall attempt to show—can no longer result from the victory (were such a victory possible) of any particular traditional political conception, which can ultimately be only external, that is, a structural or systemic conception. More than ever before, such a change will have to derive from human existence, from the fundamental reconstitution of the position of people in the world, their relationships to themselves and to each other, and to the universe. If a better economic and political model is to be created, then perhaps more than ever before it must derive from profound existential and moral changes in society. This is not something that can be designed and introduced like a new car. If it is to be more than just a new variation of the old degeneration, it must above all be an expression of life in the process of transforming itself. A better system will not automatically ensure a better life. In fact, the opposite is true: only by creating a better life can a better system be developed.

Once more I repeat that I am not underestimating the importance of political thought and conceptual political work. On the contrary, I think that genuine political thought and genuinely political work is precisely what we continually fail to achieve. If I say "genuine," however, I have in mind the kind of thought and conceptual work that has freed itself of all the traditional political schemata that have been imported into our circumstances from a world that will never return (and whose return, even were it possible, would provide no permanent solution to the most important problems).

The Second and Fourth Internationals, like many other political powers and organizations, may naturally provide significant political support for various efforts of ours, but neither of them can solve our problems for us. They operate in a different world and are a product of different circumstances. Their theoretical concepts can be interesting and instructive to us, but one thing is certain: we cannot solve our problems simply by identifying with these organizations. And the attempt in our country to place what we do in the context of some of the discussions that dominate political life in democratic societies often seems like sheer folly. For example, is it possible to talk seriously about whether we want to change the system or merely reform it? In the circumstances under which we live, this is a pseudoproblem, since for the time being there is simply no way we can accomplish either goal. We are not even clear about where reform ends and change begins. We know from a number of harsh experiences that neither reform nor change is in itself a guarantee of anything. We know that ultimately it is all the same to us whether or not the system in which we live, in the light of a particular doctrine, appears changed or reformed. Our concern is whether we can live with dignity in such a system, whether it serves people rather than people serving it. We are struggling to achieve this with the means available to us, and the means it makes sense to employ. Western journalists, submerged in the political banalities in which they live, may label our approach as overly legalistic, as too risky, revisionist, counterrevolutionary, bourgeois, Communist, or as too right-wing or left-wing. But this is the very last thing that interests us.

XII

One concept that is a constant source of confusion chiefly because it has been imported into our circumstances from circumstances that are entirely different is the concept of an opposition. What exactly is an opposition in the post-totalitarian system?

In democratic societies with a traditional parliamentary system of government, political opposition is understood as a political force on the level of actual power (most frequently a party or coalition of parties) which is not a part of the government. It offers an alternative political program, it has ambitions to govern, and it is recognized and respected by the government in power as a natural element in the political life of the country. It seeks to spread its influence by political means, and competes for power on the basis of agreed-upon legal regulations.

In addition to this form of opposition, there exists the phenomenon of the "extra-parliamentary opposition," which again consists of forces organized more or less on the level of actual power, but which operate outside the rules created by the system, and which employ different means than are usual within that framework.

In classical dictatorships, the term "opposition" is understood to mean the political forces which have also come out with an alternative political program. They operate either legally or on the outer limits of legality, but in any case they cannot compete for power within the limits of some agreed-upon regulations. Or the term "opposition" may be applied to forces preparing for a violent confrontation with the ruling power, or who feel themselves to be in this state of confrontation already, such as various guerrilla groups or liberation movements.

An opposition in the post-totalitarian system does not exist in any of these senses. In what way, then, can the term be used?

1. Occasionally the term "opposition" is applied, mainly by Western journalists, to persons or groups inside the power structure who find themselves in a state of hidden conflict with the highest authorities. The reasons

for this conflict may be certain differences (not every sharp differences naturally) of a conceptual nature, but more frequently it is quite simply a longing for power or a personal antipathy to others who represent that power.

2. Opposition here can also be understood as everything that does or can have an indirect political effect in the sense already mentioned, that is, everything the post-totalitarian system feels threatened by, which in fact means everything it is threatened by. In this sense, the opposition is every attempt to live within the truth, from the greengrocer's refusal to put the slogan in his window to a freely written poem; in other words, everything in which the genuine aims of life go beyond the limits placed on them by the aims of the system.

3. More frequently, however, the opposition is usually understood (again, largely by Western journalists) as groups of people who make public their nonconformist stances and critical opinions, who make no secret of their independent thinking and who, to a greater or lesser degree, consider themselves a political force. In this sense, the notion of an opposition more or less overlaps with the notion of dissent, although, of course, there are great differences in the degree to which that label is accepted or rejected. It depends not only on the extent to which these people understand their power as a directly political force, and on whether they have ambitions to participate in actual power, but also on how each of them understands the notion of an opposition.

Again, here is an example: in its original declaration, Charter 77 emphasized that it was not an opposition because it had no intention of presenting an alternative political program. It sees its mission as something quite different, for it has not presented such programs. In fact, if the presenting of an alternative program defines the nature of an opposition in post-totalitarian states, then the Charter cannot be considered an opposition.

The Czechoslovakian government, however, has considered Charter 77 as an expressly oppositional association from the very beginning, and has treated it accordingly. This means that the government—and this is only natural—understands the term "opposition" more or less as I defined it in point 2, that is, as everything that manages to avoid total manipulation and which therefore denies the principle that the system has an absolute claim on the individual.

If we accept this definition of opposition, then of course we must, along with the government, consider the Charter a genuine opposition, because it represents a serious challenge to the integrity of post-totalitarian power, founded as it is on the universality of living with a lie.

It is a different matter, however, when we look at the extent to which individual signatories of Charter 77 think of themselves as an opposition. My impression is that most base their understanding of the term "opposition" on the traditional meaning of the word as it became established in democratic societies (or in classical dictatorships); therefore, they understand opposition, even in Czechoslovakia, as a politically defined force which, although it does not operate on the level of actual power, and even less within the framework of certain rules respected by the government, would still not reject the opportunity to participate in actual power because it has, in a sense, an alternative political program whose proponents are prepared to accept direct political responsibility for it. Given this notion of an opposition, some Chartists—the great majority—do not see themselves in this way. Others—a minority—do, even though they fully respect the fact that there is no room within Charter 77 for "oppositional" activity in this sense. At the same time, however, perhaps every Chartist is familiar enough with the specific nature of conditions in the post-totalitarian system to realize that it is not only the struggle for human rights that has its own peculiar political power, but incomparably more "innocent" activities as well, and therefore they can be understood as an aspect of opposition. No Chartist can really object to being considered an opposition in this sense.

There is another circumstance, however, that considerably complicates matters. For many decades, the power ruling society in the Soviet bloc has used the label "opposition" as the blackest of indictments, as synonymous with the word "enemy." To brand someone "a member of the opposition" is tantamount to saying he is trying to overthrow the government and put an end to socialism (naturally in the pay of the imperialists). There have been times when this label led straight to the gallows, and of course this does not encourage people to apply the same label to themselves. Moreover, it is only a word, and what is actually done is more important than how it is labeled.

The final reason why many reject such a term is because there is something negative about the notion of an "opposition." People who so define themselves do so in relation to a prior "position." In other words, they relate themselves specifically to the power that rules society and through it, define themselves, deriving their own position from the position of the regime. For people who have simply decided to live within the truth, to say aloud what they think, to express their solidarity with their fellow citizens, to create as they want and simply to live in harmony with their better self, it is naturally disagreeable to feel required to define their own original and positive position negatively, in terms of something else, and to think of themselves primarily as people who are against something, not simply as people who *are* what they are.

Obviously, the only way to avoid misunderstanding is to say clearly—before one starts using them—in what sense the terms "opposition" and "member of the opposition" are being used and how they are in fact to be understood in our circumstances.

29

Thoughts on "The Parallel Polis"* (1987)

Eva Kantůrková

It is important to know what "independent societies" (*společností*) or activities are independent of, what they are separating themselves from, and what the *theme* of their independence is. The regime's claim to have a monopoly on politics, economics, and ideology creates an artificial reality that stands above our society, and it is on that artificiality that the regime establishes its power. In the attempt to create an integrated "Communist civilization"—that is, something unnaturally onesided—something almost grandiose can be contemplated; but we who have to breathe in this world know where and how its unnaturalness stinks, and we also perceive this artificiality with all our senses. In the hectic political somersaulting that goes on, every word officially uttered about society loses its meaning. Even "socialism" in the mouths of officials has become a dead expression. Nothing of what is said, nothing of what society is "trained for"—as officials arrogantly declare—is the real issue. The only issue is staying in power. The absolutization of power, the shameless hegemony of the state, and the artificiality of society that follows from this has different intensities at various times and in various countries of the eastern bloc, depending on how the vitality of reality defends itself and disrupts the lifeless ideological canon when it is applied in practice. When I was a child, the small shops on the outskirts of town sold Olomouc cheese, and because they smelled badly they were kept under hemispherical glass bells.

---

* The title for this essay is the editor's, not Kantůrková's. See note on page 460.

We used to say that when the smell became thick enough, it would lift the lid off. We find ourselves in a similar situation: public mendacity has become unbearable even to those who rule with its help: the stench has become powerful enough to lift the lid off artificiality.

People who live in the West and who have a different experience of life have a hard time imagining the concrete details of a reality described in general terms. I shall try, giving two examples, to create a picture of our lives.

Just after receiving these questions I happened, by sheer coincidence, to talk to two people who work in what we call "the structures"—that is, people who have managed to keep their official positions. The first of them was a gentle, educated woman who teaches medieval studies at a university. I won't be more specific than that, for obvious reasons. This woman has a black mark in her book going back to the Prague Spring. Specifically, she is known to be a Christian, and consequently, despite her erudition and ability she was not allowed to qualify as a lecturer. On the other hand, because her black mark was not that large and her specialization allowed her to keep her opinions to herself, she did not have to leave the university. She told me that the past fifteen years—which for us was an increasingly dense vacuum—seemed to have vanished in time. It was as though those years had never occurred; there were no real events to mark their passage, no living possibilities realized to give it a name; it was as though the period had become invisible. She feels this part of her life as a hole, as unreality. At the same time, given her age and profession, it was a time when she should have matured as a scholar.

My second encounter was with a man who is a theater director who, like the woman, is half permitted to work and half not. He is one of our best theoreticians of the theater, yet he works in a small provincial theatre and is not allowed to direct in Prague. He characterized this vacuum of artificial reality around us not in terms of his own personal feelings, but in the wider cultural context. He doesn't think that the official, permitted culture is exclusively dominated by the uncultural. He even thinks it is imprecise to use the term "Second Culture" or "parallel culture" to describe what is not officially permitted, because he believes that there is only one culture, regardless of where it is. Occasionally a marvelous film gets made in the state studios. Excellent theatrical productions are not entirely rare, especially in the small theaters. Sometimes an outstanding book is published. These exceptions clearly represent a kind of conquest over the artificial world; they happen in spite of it, not because of it. At the same time, however, because the public media do not take proper critical note of them, society has no opportunity to absorb or digest them, and because they are not connected with anything else, they stand poised for their brief existence over the abyss and then tumble into the monopoly vacuum, leaving behind them in society almost the same kind of emptiness as my friend described in her personal life.

Such isolated achievements are not able to create a general cultural awareness, not because they are exceptional—outstanding achievements are rare in any society—but because in a society without a structure they do not belong anywhere. They have no chance of becoming standards of excellence because the structural ladder, with its different stages of value, has been destroyed. Society at large knows about them, but it has no means of classifying them, absorbing them, and preserving them as criteria, so they are sucked into the vacuum. In practice, the public rushes out to see movies that have been attacked in the press. There is even a certain critic to whose opinions they react in a way precisely opposite to his intentions. On the other hand, even excellent Soviet films regularly draw only a handful of people per showing. Monopoly, in the imbecilic form that impinges on us, destroys the natural tendency of society to structure itself, and it destroys this so profoundly that it absorbs anything of value into its vacuum, excluding it from a share in the creation of a value system. In its place, monopoly installs a universal system of pseudovalues.

Seen in this context, "independent activity" has its own plan. It is a precursor, or perhaps even the creator, of natural social structures and hierarchies of value. It is a form of social self-defense, a barrier against complete degeneration. The writer who is not allowed to publish in state-controlled publishing houses and "publishes" his work himself in typewritten form; the actress who puts on a performance for her friends in her own flat; artists who hold shows in the courtyards of old tenement houses—these people are hounded by the regime, but they do not suffer from the vacuum. The unofficial magazines, copied on typewriters, if they have the spiritual strength to reflect our world truthfully, are an embryonic structure upon which a new cultural awareness can be established. For the same reason there is not an impassible barrier between this so-called Second Culture—works of art or scholarship published in *samizdat* or in exile—and those excellent works that arise inside the space

controlled by officialdom. The power of the intellect and the spirit trans-
poses everything of quality into a single denominator: culture, and the
authors and their readers, the actors and their audience, the creators and
their consumers, are all shaped into a single cultural milieu that escapes
the official vacuum. At the same time, the standards are set as objectively
as possible; not everything that is created unofficially, "independently,"
bears, *eo ipso* the hallmark of authenticity.

I have taken an example from culture, but the living desire for natu-
ralness penetrates into other realms of public life too. For example, over
the . . . years of its existence Charter 77 has established a remarkable social
position that one may or may not add to; but in any case, it is already one
of the valid structures and public life now reflects this. Some examples of
this are almost anecdotal. When a member of VONS* (The Committee to
Defend the Unjustly Persecuted) arrived in a small town to determine why
a young person had been taken into police custody, the police preferred to
let him go rather than risk a VONS communique being published about
the arrest. Another Chartist told of how in a large town, some local ecolo-
gists decided to hand over some of their critical material to the Charter
for publication, but when word of this got out, the local authorities very
quickly began trying to rectify matters. And one highly placed official
apparently became very exercised about something stupid the regime had
done, and was heard to remark: "Perhaps the Charter should take a look
at that!" Although Charter rules only by words, the word is a power here.
We can never be grateful enough to our friends in exile who broadcast our
material over the air, or publish it in magazines and books.

But another description of the state of our society, from a different
point of view, is valid as well. A young woman lawyer from Belgium came
to observe a trial of some members of VONS, and we gave her a demonstration of how Western radio stations were jammed. When the room
filled with the ghastly noise of artificial static, the young woman, who had
just come back from Africa, cried, "It's Biafra all over again!"† We nod-

---

* VONS. See note on page 460.

† Biafra was part of the eastern region of Nigeria that formally and unilaterally declared
its independence from that country in 1967. A particularly brutal civil war followed.
As the statement from the lawyer from Belgium attests, these events galvanized the
international human rights community.

ded, but at the same time we knew that it was hardly accurate to call our reality "Biafran." The regime's immobility is breathtaking, but at the same time the conditions after the defeat of the Prague Spring stabilized within limits that are more bearable than those we experienced right after the coup d'état of 1948.* The power elite of today, of course, fully endorses the results of the February coup, but it did not introduce the bloody terror of the years that followed. It is true that dissidents, especially those lesser known, are continually threatened with prison, but they don't face the possibility of execution.

The dictatorship in Czechoslovakia has a rather complex face. Though it considers itself exclusively Communist, it feels somehow bound by the principles of European political and social culture. In its central principle, that "all power comes from the people"—in other words that power derives from society and not society from power—our constitution does not stand apart from the norms of democratic thought in Europe. Our dictatorship is constantly hiding its true face behind democratic forms: we have elections; we have a parliament to which the government is responsible; we have a National Front system with different political parties; we have a democratic rhetoric that, when the situation demands it, comes pouring out of the mouths of even the most left-wing tyrant. After the socialist coups d'état, eastern Europe did not completely separate itself from the European context, and both for external and internal reasons, the governments of these countries cannot permit themselves the luxury of a permanent and open dictatorship. That is an objective fact which modifies the potential and the activities of the "independent society." Charter 77, for example, thanks to certain objective conditions which it seeks out and exploits (it was established *after* the ratification of the codex on human rights by the Czechoslovakian parliament) can afford to be an open movement, a movement with no aspirations to political power.

That is the source of Charter 77's strength vis-à-vis the regime. It works on territory given by the regime; it respects the laws and the constitution; it appeals to them and has no hidden intention to prepare for an eventual takeover of power. Therefore it cannot be apprehended by force, and because it eschews manipulatory methods, it cannot itself be manipulated. It is not one-sided, it is alive. The struggle it is waging is not

---

* The Communist Party of Czechoslovakia seized power in a coup d'état in 1948.

for power, but for rights, and within the limits it has created by its own activity, it observes these rights.

In a way, the powers that be have even got used to it. When the Charter 77 spokesmen tried to deliver their first petition to parliament, the police arrested them on the way and put them in jail. Now, during interrogations, the security officers ask that the Charter documents be presented via parliament; they say they do not want to hear about them first over the radio from abroad.

Charter activities take place in the open on principle. Conspiracy is foreign to it. It has no intention of using, or advocating the use of, violence. It is not engaged in a struggle with the government, but merely criticizes it or takes it at its word. And whenever they are cleverly done, the Charter documents have a profound influence on the public. This position also gives Charter 77 an inner strength. Because it is not competing for power, it can gather to itself a wide variety of opinion, sometimes even antipathetical groups and tendencies. It is a practical realization of pluralism, on a small scale, yes, but this is not the same as saying that the cause is small.

If one speaks of "independence" in this context, I would characterize it as a choice: one chooses and is willing to speak the truth about conditions in the country. It is a truth that most of society knows already, but it has no chance or compelling reason or desire to express it out loud. Thus Charter 77 goes halfway to meet a certain suspicion of empty, megalomaniac gestures that is deeply engrained in the Czech character.

Thus all unofficial activities tend to imbue the rest of society with their values; they resist being cut off from it, they respect what is good in it and try to make their own good as widely available as possible. It is not unusual for a writer to publish books both officially and in the independent publishing series *Petlice,* and *Petlice* is glad to accept their unpublishable manuscripts. The authors who publish in *samizdat* form would be happy to offer their work to state houses if they would publish them uncut. As for Charter 77 documents, they could, figuratively speaking, be written by a government minister if his text were truthful.

What I wish to say is this: independent activities are prosecuted, those who undertake them are, in various ways, harassed and persecuted, but even so—of their own will and according to the possibilities accorded to them—they do not vegetate on the edge of a hostile system. The power structure is hostile to them, but that is far from being the whole of society. The national collectivity, let us hope, will eventually persuade itself that it deserves more than hopelessness and life on one's knees.

I would say that the basic characteristic of changeable and varied range of opinion to be found in the community of independent societies and activities is the search for a point of view. At the time of the founding of Charter 77, Jan Patočka called this remarkably heterogeneous movement, which included former Communists, various shades of socialists, Christians from different churches, liberals and conservatives—in other words the whole spectrum of opinion across the nation—"the solidarity of the shaken." "Shakenness" is the source of the solidarity and it concerns everyone, each for his own reason, whether it be personal dissatisfaction or the intrinsic need to oppose the destruction around one. In essence it is a shakenness emanating from the world, of power manipulation and purely utilitarian behavior. As individuals and as a nation, we feel that we are at the breaking point. The longing for something essential is not something that is just part of the era we live in: we feel it as an inner need. It is related to the sense of a vacuum in the atmosphere, but not just with that. Here in Bohemia, we have had experience both with the futility of both liberal and pragmatic utilitarianism, and with the total utilitarianism of Communism. Both have failed us at a decisive moment in our national history.

A change of mind is taking place. The urgency of the pressures on us had led to the knowledge that in order for man to liberate himself, he must stop thinking and acting only within the dimensions of superficial manipulation and of issues raised by the political agenda. He frees himself by grasping the meaning of what is happening to him and around him. This provokes a quick, sharp sense of what is true, a desire to understand the essence of things. Not ends, but meaning: this might stand as a slogan for our activities. And it is no accident that the main philosophical trend in this community is phenomenology, or that it derives its ethics from Christianity. Nor was it simply a gesture of political cleverness that Charter 77 established itself as a defender of human rights. Here it can be shown how a subject of political sleight of hand—for what government cannot accuse another of not completely observing the codex of human rights—can become an ethical norm in politics, valid in all regimes without distinction.

In this quest, two basic postulates stand out: identity and integrity. Independent activities seek out, raise, and defend the inner "I" and its right to authentic expression against all forms of enforced coordination (*zglajchšaltování*). Perhaps for this reason one of the trends in unofficial Czech literature is diary-writing. For opposite reasons, the authorities persecute musical groups that express, through their music and their texts, the feelings and attitudes of young people. But the authentic expression of one's identity is only half of what is required. The spirit of integrity is also strengthened, undoubtedly under the influence of a revitalized Christianity and its sense of the transcendent. It is sought, in ethical and philosophical integrity, in other words, in an inner, personal integrity, but also in the creation of communities (*obcí*) and societies (*společenství*). An individualistic act is not worth much; from the most enlightened minds come appeals for tolerance, and for the possibility that both you and I will find a piece of the truth. I, for example, am not religiously inclined, but this is not an insuperable barrier between me and my Catholic and Protestant friends. Our values, the shades of difference in our opinions, the degrees of our erudition, our different cultural points of departure—none of these are of primary importance. What is primary is a sensitivity to the meaning of things and of our behavior. Even though some of the disputes that take place inside our independent societies are rather passionate, partisan particularism or religious intolerance have become not only a faux pas socially, but are felt to be as threatening as manipulation from outside by empty ideologies that long to rule over us. In a divided Bohemia, where partisanship has always been a higher prerogative than truth, this new tendency is more than praiseworthy.

In an integrated identity, freedom is the awareness of freedom with others; it is a lifestyle that puts the main stress not on one's personal interest, but on one's claim to oneself. Responsible freedom is not only creatively positive; it is also, at the same time, a way of experiencing the world: my behavior, the behavior I am courageous enough to indulge in, provides me with a picture of what the world is. Placing consistently high demands before others seems to be a decent way out of our rather complex situation, but also a good defense against the destructive influence of power.

I would say that the meaning and the goal of the "independent societies" is that they *exist*. Another dynamism appears here, different from one that is linearly "progressive": in a vacuum-like society, to be somehow *for* something and to *be* someone is, in itself, a good goal, both for today and for tomorrow. It means setting meaning against nonsense, creativity against destruction, content against emptiness. The fact that independent activities *exist* and *how* they exist puts pressure on power and narrows the limits of what is forbidden and punishable. Five years ago, people were locked up for copying books; today, far more books are copied and in far more "workshops," and the punishments for doing it are simply not commensurate. It is the same with putting out magazines, or the work of VONS. In this sense, too, we can talk about aims to enlarge the possibilities and the space for independent activity.

At the same time, these goals cannot be attained other than right now, and through the work itself. We cannot talk about being prepared to occupy "positions." The paradoxical aim of Charter 77 is to create the conditions for its own demise. Unofficial magazines are not "bothered" by the presence of official magazines that are churned out in enormous numbers. In the first place, very few read them; in the second place, they too participate in creating a picture of the world. The only pity is that it seems a great waste of paper. When I think of aims, I say that looking for new ways of self-expression, new solutions to various problems and situations, the contention of opinion and of course all the scientific, scholarly, and artistic work done—all this creates and preserves culture in the nation. But it is difficult to talk of that culture as a mere "aim." It is the very meaning of our national existence.

I see independent society and activities as a dynamic process, a search in which there is a healthy tendency to penetrate into all the cracks and test the extent to which the power structure is willing to defend its own vacuum. At the same time, it is quite possible that in some absurd political convolution they might suddenly lock us all up and perhaps even kill some of us. But I can just as easily imagine that someone clumsy might drop the vacuum pump and break it. As acts, both would touch the independent activities only indirectly: they would lose or gain social space. But they would certainly lose their independence the moment they tried to govern anything themselves.

At the same time, it would make no sense whatever to imagine a savior riding up on a white horse (or on a war steed) to establish freedom and democratic order for us. The longing for freedom is more a constant hope than it is a concrete goal. I would say that we here—who live in fear of persecution and imprisonment—create democratic attitudes and space for freedom ourselves, by being what we are. Nothing can be given to us. Knowing this may be the source of the self-assurance behind independent activities.

30

Jan Patočka versus Václav Benda
(1989)

MARTIN PALOUŠ

I

Independent citizens' initiatives, independent culture, independent church structures, and so on, represent a radically new phenomenon which in the past twelve years has become a part of the Czechoslovakian reality that cannot be overlooked. Even if much of what we would include in this category—a wide range of cultural activity, for instance—has a prehistory of its own, it is undeniable that the declaration of Charter 77 in January 1977 was the decisive impulse towards independent activity of all kinds. In Czechoslovakian society—which at that time had been controlled by a Communist regime for almost thirty years and had been paralyzed since the late 1960s by the "normalization process"*—the emergence of the Charter was extremely important: it meant the restoration of a certain public space that was independent of the ruling power and unmanipulated by it. A "parallel polis" was constituted within a society that had been formed by totalitarianism.

Against the expectations of the skeptical, this community has proven to be an unusually vigorous social phenomenon. It has managed, so far, to defend its own existence, in the face of almost overwhelming odds,

---

* The stale, repressive period under Husák following the Prague Spring became known as the period of "normalization." For a powerful evocation of this time, see Havel's essay "Dear Dr. Husák," originally published in 1975.

against the attempt by the organs of power to destroy, or at least curtail it. Vasil Bil'ák* for all his talk about "the rubbish heap of history" and the express train that would crush the legs of those foolish enough it get in its way, has finally had to retire without seeing the "final solution" of the dissident question. It is highly probable that neither his colleagues who are still in power, nor their eventual replacements, will ever see their dream of crushing dissent come true. The fact is that the cause for which this parallel community came into being in the first place, and which remains its fundamental raison d'être—the defence of human rights and freedoms—has taken on an unexpected urgency. Regardless of the reasons for this—whether it was the activities of those in the parallel communities, or the fact that at the same time, the Americans elected President Reagan to a second term and Mikhail Gorbachev assumed power in Moscow, or simply because of the logic of historical development—the question of human rights is no longer just the concern of isolated groups of eccentric individuals and the humanitarian problems that constantly arise around them, but it is a domestic political question of the first order, and therefore one of the key elements on the agenda of international politics.

II

The philosopher Jan Patočka, one of the prime movers and ultimately one of the first spokesmen of Charter 77, wrote several texts in which he outlined what, in his opinion, the activity of Charter 77 was based on, what goals it ought to set for itself, and what means it ought to use to achieve those ends; in other words, "what the Charter is and what it is not." Patočka's exegesis seems to me the best place to start if we wish to find our bearings in the independent community that the Charter opened up.

According to its original declaration, Charter 77 saw itself as a "loose, informal, and open community of people of different convictions, different faiths, different professions, who are joined together by the determination to work, as individuals and together, for the respecting of civic and

---

* Vasil Bil'ák was a member of the Central Committee of the CPC. He supported the Soviet invasion of 1968, signed a letter inviting the Warsaw Pact countries to send military forces, and was closely associated with the "normalization" process that followed.

human rights both in our own country and in the world." But the appearance of Charter 77 cannot be understood as a political act, and therefore its significance cannot be measured by the usual political measurements. According to Patočka, what its signatories had in common was not anything political, but a certain *moral stance,* the conviction that human society cannot function satisfactorily if it does not rest on a moral foundation. Not only that, but without this moral foundation, society finds itself in danger of losing its integrity altogether, of losing that from which springs the very meaning of its existence. The point is, Patočka said, that morality "is not here to make society work, but so that *man can be man* [my emphasis]. It does not define man according to the whims of his wants and needs, his tendencies, and his longings, because morality itself is the very thing that defines man."

In Patočka's conception, the citizens who sign the Charter declaration are saying to those who run the state: "Govern, make sure the vital functions of the social organism run smoothly, but on one condition: that you unconditionally subordinate the exercise of that power to morality! Do not infringe upon the legal rights of those who, from your point of view, are powerless! And you must maintain this stance even when, and especially when, it is not in 'the interests of the state' to do so. You must recognize, at last, that the supremacy of morality over power is what makes human society human; it is the state's most elementary raison d'etre; it represents the only possible basis for that 'social contract' posited by the founders of modern political theory."

Patočka's conception of Charter 77, which in my opinion is generally accepted as "canonical" to this day, has left something essential unsaid, for obvious reasons, since Jan Patočka died in March of 1977, and therefore could not have analyzed the experiences undergone by Chartists in their effort to live out the consequences of this "moral stance" under totalitarian conditions. What is missing is an answer to the question: in what new situation does this event place both those who take direct part in it, and the rest of society, particularly the power structure, which was compelled to respond in some way to the existence of Charter 77, and still has to?

One of the first to attempt such a response was Václav Benda, who in 1978 published his essay on the parallel polis.

Benda argues that Patočka was right in pointing out the absolute preference for a moral stance over practical political considerations: a demand to act not opportunistically, but *sub speciae aeterni,* was the basis on which the Charter stands. If, however, the Chartists, now that their cause is in motion, wish to find a guide that would allow them to keep their bearings and to act and make responsible decisions in the new situation, then Patočka's point of departure—because of its timeless abstraction from a concrete temporal horizon—is inadequate. According to Benda the task of the Chartists, and of all like-thinking people regardless of whether they signed the Charter or not, is this: to continue building the independent community that has thus come into being, to defend in every possible way the space it has managed to wrest for itself from the powers that be, and not to waste a single opportunity to expand it. How can this be achieved? By creating all kinds of independent parallel structures—that is, structures unmanipulated by totalitarian power: parallel information networks, cultural and educational institutions, parallel foreign contacts.

On the one hand, therefore, we have Patočka's perspective: the Charter is purely apolitical, a matter for *inner* decision of all those who take part; it appeals to something elementary and prepolitical, something that forms a basis for political behavior, but which is not in itself political. On the other hand we have Benda's point of view: in signing the Charter, each signatory in effect joins *other* signatories, and this, in effect, is a political act. Even though the Charter entered the world with unpolitical assumptions, it established a parallel polis, which is a political community, and this fact cannot simply be ignored or glossed over. Moreover, the intrinsically political nature of the Charter represents its most powerful weapon, enabling it to confront totalitarian power and realize its moral ideals even in unfavorable circumstances.

III

Patočka's exegesis of the Charter is strongly reminiscent of the Socratic point of view, of Socrates's way of coming to terms with social and political crisis in the Athens of his time. Before concerning yourself with public matters, Socrates urged his fellow citizens, pay heed to "reason and truth and the soul, so that they will be the best they can."[*] His concern for

---

[*] See Plato's *Apology of Socrates,* 29d–30a.

prepolitical matters is, in a certain sense, more important than political activity. According to Socrates, only a man alert to the truth, a man of inner discipline, integrity and responsibility, is capable of being a good citizen, or rather a politician.

It seems to me that something quite similar echoes from the words of Patočka's conversations on the nonpolitical character of Charter 77. Anyone who publicly supports the Charter with his or her signature has, in effect, sent this message to those who hold power: I hereby retire from the game you've been forcing on the people of this country. It is a false and immoral game, and I've simply had enough.

Just as Socrates did not take part in the degenerate political life in Athens, but instead spent his time talking with his fellow citizens, mainly the young, examining the assumptions on which some future political action might be based, so Patočka claimed that the Chartists have nothing to do with politics, as it is generally understood, a politics that thinks only of power and acts from motives of success and fear. "Those who participate in the Charter," Patočka wrote, "are not only not taking unto themselves any political right or function; they are not even attempting to be a moral authority or the 'conscience' of society. They are not placing themselves over others, nor judging anyone. Their only effort is to purify and strengthen their awareness that a higher authority exists, in which individuals are bound by their consciences, and states by their signatures, on important international agreements; and that they are so bound not in any opportunistic sense, according to the rules of political advantage and disadvantage, but their signature here means a commitment to see that politics is subordinate to law, and not law to politics."

But let us carry the analogy a step further. The figure of Socrates is far more paradoxical, for although he refuses to take part in politics, although he, figuratively speaking, retreats from the public square of Athens into the back streets, where he carries on conversations that have nothing to do with the political agenda of the day, it is he who, in the end, comes to embody Athenian virtues that are, in the true sense of the word, political. Such virtues had been gradually disappearing from Athenian public life. Socrates towers above the grey Athenians around him because he has an active interest not just in private matters, but also in matters he believes to be important to the community. It is Socrates, and not those who condemn him, who is capable of the activity which puts him in danger of losing his life. Nor does he retreat, but prefers death to giving up his cause. "Citizens of Athens," says this apolitical philosopher before the court, "either you believe Anytus or you believe me; and either you free me or you don't, but I can assure you that I would not change what I have done even if I were to die a hundred times for it."

Perhaps it will not sound like an exaggeration if I say that Jan Patočka, too, ended his life as a philosopher in the Socratic mould; as a philosopher who withdrew from the *Agora,* from the place that represented the center of political life, not because he surrendered it to irresponsible usurpers and politicians blinded by power, so he could go on philosophizing somewhere in peace, but in order to reveal, and even at the cost of his life, once more to make public the meaning of political activity, the only thing that can become the cornerstone of any future political sphere.

There is only one sense in which our analogy falters. Whereas Socrates was unsuccessful in his political reform of Athens, and instead became the founder of a European philosophical tradition, Patočka's philosophical act changed the public face of his society in a genuinely essential way. Within a community that had been paralyzed for decades by totalitarian mechanisms, and whose citizens appeared to be asleep, enchanted by some black magic, a new community was awakened, independent of the first one. It is this fact, this heritage, left behind by the philosopher, to which Václav Benda turns his attention with such urgency.

IV

Regardless of how influential Patočka's thinking was, the independent community that arose from it is in no sense a community of philosophers. On the contrary, the great majority of those who live in it don't think philosophically, nor are they in any particular way interested in philosophy. To the question what is keeping them together, then, despite vast individual differences, a single answer may be given: it is precisely what the totalitarian system denies them in the first place—freedom.

Are we not offered a prototype, through which we can come close to the events in that polis which Benda described by the adjective "parallel," precisely in the polis of ancient times, in the ideal of civil freedom on which it is based, and in the political action for which it opens up space?

But today there is one basic difference. If we mention freedom, we almost automatically assume that it means *freedom of will,* that quality of an individual who is free to the extent that he acts according to his own lights, his own decisions, and, on the contrary, resists submitting to arbitrary decisions forced on him from outside. Whether this will is conceived of as mere willfulness (i.e., the power to do whatever one wants), or whether one sees it as the capacity to submit voluntarily to a higher principle and act in accord with one's responsibilities, either to God, or to oneself, or to one's humanity—in one aspect the same thing is always involved.

For man to be free, he must disengage himself from all external things, the course of which he cannot influence anyway, and withdraw into himself: this is what the Stoic philosopher advises.

Do not love this world, take no care for its fleeting glories, rewards or wisdom, and cleave entirely to eternal truths, to one's God, in expectation of His Kingdom. Only that will make you free: this is what Christian faith says.

Freedom is primarily freedom from politics, and consists in the guarantees that every individual must have, so that he may in peace and security devote his energies to his private affairs: this is what the theoreticians of liberalism claim.

Don't get mixed up in anything and look out for yourself: this is the decadent opinion of modern bourgeois man.

However different these points of view are, the point on which they agree is obvious: freedom is something that is directed inwards, away from a world that has succumbed to vanity, from the labyrinth of the world to the paradise of the heart, to the cultivation of one's immortal soul, from public affairs towards private interests.

I would say that the Greek notion of freedom was just the opposite. The citizen of Athens was not free when he was by himself, his own master, among his possessions, in private, where, in our modern view of things, he could do what he wanted. On the contrary, he became free the moment he left this private space and went out into the community—when he spent his time, not among those whom the gods had endowed with power over him, but among his equals, his fellow citizens, with those who were as free as he was. It was important not just that he had the right to take part in public affairs, that he could speak in the *agora* or do what he thought was for the good of the community, but also the fact that he did so in the presence of others, who at the same time could see him and hear him, and judge his actions and his words, who could either agree with him, or oppose him, yet always recognizing him as a free person capable of free action.

Unlike our conception, this notion of freedom was essentially political. It was not free will, but rather free *initiative*. It did not depend merely on the abilities or qualities of isolated individuals, on their private possibilities or outlooks, but it was conditional on the freedom of others around him. It was not a matter of the state of one's soul, but rather on the state of the world.

It seems to me that precisely here is the core of the argument that Benda opposes to Patočka's conception of Charter 77. For Benda, what creates the identity of the "dissident," what differentiates the citizen of the independent community from the other members of society, does not consist in any higher morality or greater love of truth, nor in his ability to carry on a philosophical dialogue, but in his conception of freedom. There are people who have ceased to perceive freedom, as those around them do, as free will (which one can cultivate in private) and have once again begun to understand it in the Greek way: as something essentially political, as initiative. These are not apolitical people, as Patočka stressed; far from it. On the contrary, they are people who, thanks to their experience with totalitarianism, which utterly deprived them of a political dimension to their lives, have rediscovered and are now experiencing that which politics originally was. They have experienced the meaning of free behavior.

In this situation, the decision to create a parallel polis cannot be understood as a step away from the world, as an escape from the contemporary crisis, which is first and foremost a political crisis. On the contrary, it is a step into the world, to the very focus of what is happening, into politics, a step taken in the belief that it is only personal risk and personal initiative, regardless of how meaningless and unimportant it may seem to the powers that rule this world, that can bring about a cure.

The place of the independent community in the wider context of Czech history can be determined only by the future. Perhaps much of what today seems important and fascinating to us, the things we talk and worry about, will prove to be merely marginal and will, in time, be forgotten. And on the contrary, perhaps something we are overlooking, something that is quietly and secretly at work among us, may with the distance of time become apparent. But there is one thing I believe can be said with certainty now: that the motives which brought the parallel polis into existence and thanks to which those who live in it have been moved to action, which changed the course of their lives in decisive ways, will certainly remain. For I believe that these motives are, at least from the human perspective, eternal.

VI
Lessons

31

Letters to Olga
(1982)

VÁCLAV HAVEL

August 14, 1982

Dear Olga,

Orientation toward Being as a state of mind can also be understood as faith: a person oriented toward Being intrinsically believes in life, in the world, in morality, in the meaning of things, and in himself. His relationship to life is informed by hope, wonder, humility, and a spontaneous respect for its mysteries. He does not judge the meaning of his efforts merely by their manifest successes, but first of all by their "worth in themselves" (i.e., their worth against the background of the absolute horizon). In this general sense, however, believers are all those who do not surrender to their existence-in-the-world, regardless of whether or not they acknowledge a God, a religion, or an ideology, and even regardless of whether they admit or deny that there is a transcendental dimension to their way of existence-in-the-world. The state of mind that has given in to existence-in-the-world is, on the contrary, a state of total resignation (regardless of how it disguises itself). Somewhere in the depths of his spirit, man feels that nothing matters. He is concerned for nothing but his purely "worldly" interests, which are his sole responsibility, and he behaves morally only insofar as, and only when and where, it is expedient to do so, when his actions are visible, for instance. (He would certainly not pay his fare in the night streetcar were he alone.)

When I wrote that human identity is not a path that is chosen once and for all but rather must be constantly reestablished and that a person is in fact always "naked," I had in mind, among other things, the fact that faith, as a state of mind, cannot be "reified" into something complete, something given for all time and no longer problematic, which then requires only to be served, without constantly having to go back over elementary questions. Such a reification ceases to be faith as an orientation toward Being and becomes a mere clinging, an orientation toward entities, things, and objects (however abstract) and thus ultimately only a covert way of surrendering to existence-in-the-world. "Responsibility for everything," that intrinsic intention of the "pre-I" (i.e., the "I" that has not yet managed to "forget" entirely its source in the fullness of Being and its belonging to everything that exists), is precisely the disposition that, primordially, renders one open to the "voice of Being" and permits one "subsequently"—as an "I" that is already maturing into itself—to hear this voice in the first place, to understand, respect, and begin to take it into account. For this reason, "responsibility for everything" is not only the starting point for all future ("mature") responsibility, but is also an inseparable and constant aspect or dimension of it in the present. Constantly reflected upon, developed, controlled, and projected by the mind into the spatiotemporal reality of human duties, it also constantly controls the outbursts and tricks of the mind and through its authenticity, measures, criticizes, and provides direction; and if the mind keeps it on a tight "leash of reality," responsibility also holds the mind on the same leash (because a mind unhitched from its existential context can easily end up in the same timelessness and unreality as a "responsibility for everything" that has not been developed by the mind). The maturing or self-discovery of responsibility is not, therefore, a gradual distancing from its original source rooted in the "prenatal" experience of the integrity of Being, nor an emancipation from it, but on the contrary, an increasingly profound, conscious, and thoughtful drawing on that source. And our permanent "nakedness" before fundamental questions (which goes along with being exposed to a parting of the ways, the wonder of our "I" at its own freedom and undoubtedly as well that primordial shame that Levinas talks about) is in fact only an injunction to pay constant attention (or constantly return) to that "pre-mental" source of our self-transcendence. It is only by constantly giving those roots their due, by being mindful of them, faithful to them, prepared to confront them and measure ourselves by them, that we are capable at all of

seeking our own absolute horizon, relating to it with the same élan, tireless-
ness, and "youthful" seriousness and listening, with the same enthusiasm,
to the "voice of Being." And it is only a constantly open view, unobstructed by
our former successes, into the primordial absoluteness of those demands that
keeps us from every temptation on the part of worldly interests to drown out
that voice, falsify it, replace it with a stage prop or, instead of listening to it, to
become its prompters. In general, then: the precondition for genuine responsibility and thus for genuine identity, and the condition of alert choice and
self-choice that keeps to the proper path is something that might be called a
constant, deepening turbulence of the mutual illumination, verification, and
augmentation of everything primordial, everything that has been achieved,
everything intended and acted upon, spontaneously felt and worked out by the
mind; a kind of unceasing dramatic confrontation between primordial vulnerability and achieved experience, between the primordial limitlessness
of self-transcendence and the reflected limitations of separation, between
the primordial radicalism of the unbridled intentions of the "pre-I" and the
deliberation and stability of their self-aware projections into the world of our
earthly "existential praxis."

I speak of this because it might throw some light on the essence of a
very dangerous way of—almost inadvertently—tragically ruining everything:
fanaticism.

What is fanaticism? I would say it is nothing other than this reified, mys-
tified, fetishized, and thus self-alienated faith (with consequences—at
least in terms of the immediate human suffering it causes—essentially worse
than all the direct ways of surrendering to existence-in-the-world). At the
beginning of fanaticism—as in the case of a genuine orientation toward
Being, perhaps even more limitlessly—is a feeling that one is "responsible
for everything," and this feeling is all the more boundless, of course, the
more one feels threatened by the shock of alienation from the freshly perceived world. The emerging mind reflects on the situation and latches onto
this expansive intention of the "pre-I" in an effort to provide quick protection against imminent collapse (the fall into hopelessness), and tries, come
what may, to give it a fixed form, for all time, on the projecting screen
of the reality of human separation. But precisely at this moment, the "I"
commits a fatal error, which is extraordinarily seductive to a lazy mind, a
weak character and everyone who, though he may be intrinsically and almost
physically averse to turning away from Being, at the same time suffers a fatal

lack of the intellectual and moral courage (including the courage to go it alone against everyone and deny oneself the advantages of mob possession of ideas) which, in extreme circumstances, a true orientation toward Being cannot get along without; in other words everyone who cannot resist the attractive force of self-deception, the kind that hides surrender to existence-in-the-world beneath the illusion that it is a particularly radical form of orientation toward Being. The essence of this error is the notion that transferring primordial self-transcendence from the boundlessness of the dream to the reality of human actions is a one-shot affair, that all you have to do is "come up with an idea" and then blindly serve it—that is, create some intellectual project that permanently fixes and fulfills the original intention—to be relieved of the duty and effort of constantly aspiring toward Being: for in its place there is a handy substitute—the relatively undemanding duty of devoted service to a given project. Being is thus, in fact, represented by a maquette of itself: by a thesis; that is, by an entity among entities, a thing among things, which can then be made to serve one as easily and mindlessly as one's car or cottage and which—if it fails or does not work out—can just as easily be traded in for another. (Indeed, the more fanatical a person is, the easier it is for him to transfer his "faith" to another object: Maoism can be exchanged overnight for Jehovahism or vice versa, while the intensity of the dedication remains unaltered.) In this case, surrendering to existence-in-the-world is obviously masked by the illusion that one is serving an intellectualized point of contact with Being. All of this, however, hopelessly disrupts and even stops outright that essential and life-giving turbulence of the "pre-I"'s intentions, which mutually check each other, and the alert reflection on them: both the truths that are "preprimordially" and "prementally" perceived and the truths arrived at by insight and experience. Fanaticism inevitably stunts them and eventually they both die out: the monster of the constructed project—by its very nature—rapidly evicts them both from the soul of the "believer" and ultimately eliminates them in reality as well, and in the end, it can only persecute genuine morality and ban genuine thinking because it feels threatened and condemned by both of them, and with good reason. "Responsibility for everything" and human rationality have snapped the chain that kept them both under control, and thus they lose touch both with reality and with Being—and lumped together in a rational (or "rationally mythological") plan for general salvation, they career through the world, wiping out everything alive and living, true and truthful, lopping off the head and limbs of everything that transcends or eludes the given project, that resists it or that simply can't be explained in terms of it. In the name of universal salvation (no one is asked, of course, if they care to be saved) the doors are ultimately opened—because the means justify the ends and self-control has perished—to all the horrors of bureaucracy, repression, high-handedness, violence, terror, and terrorism. (The connection between childish enthusiasm, mindless rationalism, and merciless violence is, of course, familiar enough: the dreamer becomes the worst bureaucrat and the bureaucrat the most conscientious organizer of mass extermination, because rigid rationalism is the most accessible substitute for living thought, so difficult of access to the "pre-I"'s one-dimensional thought.)

In other words, a fanatic is someone who, without realizing it, replaces the love of God with the love of his own religion; the love of truth, freedom, and justice with the love of an ideology, doctrine, or sect that promises to guarantee them once and for all; love of people with love of a project claiming that it—and it alone, of course—can genuinely serve them. To put it in general terms, it replaces a difficult orientation toward Being with a more facile orientation toward the human product, claiming exclusive rights—as a representative of the human "I"—to mediate contact with Being. Thus wrapping its existential nakedness, and its exhausting, lifelong openness to questions, in the flag of its own responses, fanaticism may make life simpler—but at the cost of hopelessly destroying it. Its tragedy lies in the fact that it takes the beautiful and profoundly authentic longing of the human "pre-I" to take the suffering of the world upon itself and transforms it into something that merely multiplies that suffering: an organizer of concentration camps, inquisitions, massacres, and executions. By the time one finally realizes what has happened, it is usually too late. The danger that flows from this "tiny flaw" in the mechanism of how the "I" is constituted is as old as human history and is certainly not the main danger in the world today (even though it has something in common with it). Nevertheless, it is especially relevant now: the general turning away from Being so typical of contemporary civilization provides fertile soil indeed for various forms of fanaticism, which are short-circuited responses to that turning away.

I kiss you,
Vašek

August 21, 1982

Dear Olga,

We live in an age in which there is a general turning away from Being: our civilization, founded on a grand upsurge of science and technology, those great intellectual guides on how to conquer the world at the cost of losing touch with Being, transforms man its proud creator into a slave of his consumer needs, breaks him up into isolated functions, dissolves him in his existence-in-the-world and thus deprives him not only of his human integrity and his autonomy but ultimately any influence he may have had over his own "automatic responses." The crisis of today's world, obviously, is a crisis of human responsibility (both responsibility for oneself and responsibility "toward" something else) and thus it is a crisis of human identity as well. But a warning here: all this does not mean in the least that the experience of Being and the orientation toward it have vanished entirely from the structure of contemporary humanity. On the contrary: as that which in humanity is failing and breaking down, and which is constantly betrayed, duped, and deluded by humanity, they are both, in fact, latently present in the structure of humanity, be it only in the form of fissures and faults that must be filled at all costs to preserve appearances—both on the surface and "inside." The point is that morality seldom sees itself as purely utilitarian, and even less would it admit publicly to this. It always pretends, or tries to persuade itself, that its roots go deeper, even in matters less extreme than fanaticism. Would anyone, for example, dare to deny that he had a conscience? There are no two ways about it: the "voice of Being" has not fallen silent—we know it summons us, and as human beings, we cannot pretend not to know what it is calling us to. It is just that these days, it is easier to cheat, silence, or lie to that voice (think of the many ways science gives us to do this!). The source of this latent regard for Being, therefore, is not merely convention (that is, a reified morality of traditions which, from the point of view of our existence-in-the-world, it would be a pointless faux pas to ignore publicly) but rather it lies deeper: in our thrownness into our source in Being from which—so long as we remain people and do not become mere robots—we cannot extricate ourselves and which—though it might exist merely as "memories of memories," "homesickness for homesickness," or "longing for long-

536

ing"—exposes us to that voice. And regardless of how selfishly we act, of how indifferent we remain to everything that does not bring us immediate benefit (the kind that is fully rooted in the world of phenomena), regardless of how exclusively we relate to our utilitarian "here" and "now," we always feel, in some corner of our spirit at least, that we should not act that way and that therefore we must find a way to defend and justify our actions, and by some "mental trick," gloss over its disaccord with something we are simply no longer capable of striving toward. It makes no difference whether, to that end, we invoke the somewhat mystical claim that "all is lost anyway" or on the contrary, the illusion that our bad behavior serves a good cause.

All of this—the turning away from Being, the crisis of the absolute horizon, of genuine responsibility, and thus of genuine identity as well, along with heightened efforts to "satisfy" the betrayed "voice of being" by mystification—is transferred or projected, understandably, into the behavior of various "interexistential" formations as well: society, nations, classes, social strata, political movements and systems, social power groups, forces and organisms, and ultimately even states and governments themselves. For not only do all these formations shape and direct contemporary humanity, humanity shapes and directs them as well, since they are ultimately the product and image of humanity. And just as man turns away from Being, so entire large social organisms turn away from it—if I may put it that way—having surrendered to the same steadily increasing temptation of existence-in-the-world, of entities, aims, and "realities" (whose attractions are merely strengthened by surrendering to them). And just as man conceals his turning away from the world and himself by pretending that it is not a turning away at all, so these social organisms hide their turning away from the world and themselves in an analogical fashion. For this reason, we may observe how social, political, and state systems, and whole societies, are inevitably becoming alienated from themselves. The difficult and complex task of serving primary moral ideals is reduced to the less demanding task of serving projects intended to fulfill those ideals in a concrete way; and, when such projects have won the day, there is a further reduction to the even more comfortable task of serving systems allegedly designed to carry these projects out; and finally, it degenerates into a situation, common enough now, in which the power that directs these systems (or more precisely "possesses" them) simply looks out for its own interests, or else the systems, in a purely utilitarian fashion, adapt themselves to the demands of that power. By now, the behavior of social power, of various establishments, and finally of whole societies (which either identify with the given power, or adapt to it, or simply surrender to it) has become utterly self-serving, alienated many times over from the original ideals, and has degenerated into the "realities of existence-in-the-world," and at the same time, of course, it still persists in operating in the name of the morality of the original—and long since betrayed—ideals. One consequence of this alienating process is the enormous conflict between words and deeds so prevalent today: everyone talks about freedom, democracy, humanity, justice, human rights, universal equality and happiness, about peace and saving the world from nuclear apocalypse, and protecting the environment and life in general—and at the same time, everyone—more or less, consciously or unconsciously, in one way or another—serves those values and ideals only to the extent necessary to serve himself, i.e., his "worldly" interests—personal interests, group interests, power interests, property interests, state or great-power interests. Thus the world becomes a chessboard for this cynical and utterly self-serving "interplay of interests," and ultimately there are no practices, whether economic, political, diplomatic, military, or espionage, which, as means sanctified by an allegedly universal human end, are not permissible if they serve the particular interests of the group that carries them out. Under the guise of the intellectually respectable notion of "responsibility for everything" (i.e., for the "welfare of mankind")—that is, pretending to relate to the absolute horizon—huge and uncontrollable forces and powers are in fact responsible only to the particular horizon from which they derive their power (e.g., to the establishment that put them in power). Pretending to serve the "general well-being of mankind," they serve only their own pragmatic interests, and they are oriented exclusively toward "doing well in the world" and expanding and proliferating further—wherein that very expansion and proliferation which flows directly from the expansive essence of focusing on existence-in-the world is interpreted as service to "higher things"—to universal freedom, justice, and well-being. This entire mendacious "world of appearances," of grandiose words and phraseological rituals is, again, merely the tax that one who has surrendered to existence-in-the-world pays—on the social level this time—to his "recollection of conscience," i.e., to his duty to respond, in this formal and ritualistic fashion, at least, to the languishing "voice of Being" in his indolent heart.

The tension between the world of words and the real practices of those in power is not just directly experienced by millions of ordinary, powerless people, nor thought about only by intellectuals, whose voices those in power either ignore (in some places) or pay "too much" attention to (in others), nor is it pointed out only by minorities in revolt. The power in society can actually see it better than anyone else, but only in others, never in itself. In such circumstances, however, it is not surprising that no one believes anyone and that everyone uses the contradiction between someone else's words and deeds to justify a deepening of the same contradictions in himself. It may even appear that those with fewer inhibitions in this regard will ultimately triumph and crush the others. So the power structures apparently have no other choice than to sink deeper and deeper into this vicious maelstrom, and contemporary people—if they take any interest at all in such "great matters"—apparently have no other choice than to wait around until the final inhibition drops away.

Naturally I am not underestimating the importance of international talks on arms limitation. I'm afraid, however, that we will never attain a peace that will permanently eliminate the threat of a nuclear catastrophe as long as mutual trust among people, nations, and states is not revitalized to a degree far greater than has been the case at any time in the past. And that, of course, won't happen until the terrifying abyss between words and deeds is closed. And that, in turn, won't happen until something radical—I would even say revolutionary—changes in the very structure and "soul" of humanity today. In other words, until man—standing on the brink of the abyss—recovers from the massive betrayal he commits every day against his own nature, and goes back to where he has always stood in the good moments of his history: to that which provides the foundations for that dramatic essence of his humanity (as "separated being"), that is, to Being as the firm vanishing point of his striving, to that absolute horizon of his relating.

But who should begin? Who should break this vicious circle? I agree with Levinas* when he says that responsibility cannot be preached, but only borne, and that the only possible place to begin is with oneself. It may sound strange, but it is true: it is I who must begin. One thing about it, however, is interesting: once I begin—that is, once I try—here and now, right where I am, not excusing myself by saying that things would be easier elsewhere, without grand speeches and ostentatious gestures, but all the more persistently—to live in harmony with the "voice of Being," as I understand it within myself—

* Levinas. See note on page 313.

as soon as I begin that, I suddenly discover, to my surprise, that I am neither the only one, nor the first, nor the most important one to have set out upon that road. For the hope opened up in my heart by this turning toward Being has opened my eyes as well to all the hopeful things my vision, blinded by the brilliance of "worldly" temptations, could not or did not wish to see, because it would have undermined the traditional argument of all those who have given up already: that all is lost anyway. Whether all is really lost or not depends entirely on whether or not I am lost.

I kiss you,
Vašek

32

We have ceased to see the Purpose*
(1993)

Aleksandr I. Solzhenitsyn

Each time I arrive in the principality of Liechtenstein, I recall with emotion that outstanding lesson in courage which this tiny country and its esteemed prince, the late Franz Joseph II, presented to the world in 1945: standing up to the relentless menace of the Soviet military machine, they did not hesitate to shelter a detachment of Russian anti-Communists seeking refuge from Stalin's tyranny.

This example is all the more instructive because in those same months the mighty democratic powers, authors of the Atlantic Charter, with its ringing promise of freedom for all the oppressed of the earth, sought to ingratiate themselves with the victorious Stalin by yielding up into slavery all of eastern Europe, and turning over—from the West's own territory!— hundreds upon hundreds of thousands of Soviet citizens, against their expressed will, disregarding the suicides of some right there on the spot. With base force, these people were literally prodded with bayonets into Stalin's murderous reach, towards the torments of concentration camp and death. It was appropriate that the Soviet people lay down their lives by the millions for the common victory with the West, but, it turned out, they themselves did not have the right to freedom. (And it is astonishing that the free Western press helped to cover up this crime for twenty-five years. No one, either at the time or later, has called those British and

---

* Solzhenitsyn delivered this speech to the International Academy of Philosophy in Liechtenstein on September 14, 1993.

541

American generals and administrators *war criminals* for their deeds, much less brought them to trial.)

POLITICS AND ETHICS

This contrast between the courageous act of little Liechtenstein and the act of betrayal in the halls of the Great Powers naturally leads us further: What is the role, the justifiable and necessary share of morality in politics?

Erasmus[*] believed politics to be an ethical category, and called on it to manifest ethical impulses. But that, of course, was in the sixteenth century.

And then came our Enlightenment, and by the eighteenth century we had learned from John Locke that it is inconceivable to apply moral terms to the state and its actions. Politicians, who throughout history were so often free of burdensome moral constraints, had thus obtained something of an added theoretical justification. Moral impulses among statesmen have always been weaker than political ones, but in our time the consequences of their decisions have grown in scale.

Moral criteria applicable to the behavior of individuals, families, and small circles certainly cannot be transferred on a one-to-one basis to the behavior of states and politicians; there is no exact equivalence, as the scale, the momentum, and the tasks of governmental structures introduce a certain deformation. States, however, are led by politicians, and politicians are ordinary people, whose actions have an impact on other ordinary people. Moreover, the fluctuations of political behavior are often quite removed from the imperatives of State. Therefore, any moral demands we impose on individuals, such as understanding the difference between honesty, baseness, and deception, between magnanimity, goodness, avarice, and evil, must to a large degree be applied to the politics of countries, governments, parliaments, and parties.

In fact, if state, party, and social policy are not based on morality, then mankind has no future to speak of. The converse is true: if the politics of a state or the conduct of an individual is guided by a moral compass, this turns out to be not only the most humane but, in the long run, the most prudent behavior for one's own future.

---

[*] Desiderius Erasmus (1466–1536), the Dutch Catholic priest and humanist.

Among the Russian people, for one, this concept—understood as an ideal to be aimed for, and expressed by the word *truth* (*pravda*) and the phrase *to live by the truth* (*zhit' po pravde*) has never been extinguished. And even at the murky end of the nineteenth century, the Russian philosopher Vladimir Solovyov insisted that, from a Christian point of view, moral and political activity are tightly linked, that political activity must a priori be *moral service*, whereas politics motivated by the mere pursuit of interests lacks any Christian content whatsoever.

Alas, in my homeland today these moral axes have fallen into even greater disuse than in the West, and I recognize the present vulnerability of my position in passing such judgments. When, in what had been the USSR, seven decades of appalling pressure were followed by the sudden and wide-open unchecked freedom to act, in circumstances of all-around poverty, the result was that many were swept down the path of shamelessness, unrestrainedly adopting the worst features of human behavior. It must be noted here that, for seventy years, annihilation was visited upon people in our country not in a purely random fashion but was directed at those with outstanding mental and moral qualities. And so the picture in Russia today is bleaker and more savage than if it were simply the result of the general shortcomings of our human nature.

But let us not partition the misfortune between countries and nations: The misfortune is for all of us to share, as we stand at the end of Christianity's second millennium. Moreover, should we so lightly fling about this term—morality?

BENTHAM'S BEHEST

The eighteenth century left us the precept of Jeremy Bentham[*]: Morality is that which gives pleasure to the greatest number of persons; man can never desire anything except that which favors the preservation of his own existence. And the eagerness with which the civilized world took up so convenient and precious an advice was astonishing! Cold calculation holds sway in business relations, and has even become accepted as normal

---

[*] Jeremy Bentham (1748–1832) was an English philosopher known primarily for his moral philosophy of utilitarianism.

behavior. To yield in some way to an opponent or competitor is considered an unforgivable blunder for the party having an advantage in position, power, or wealth. The ultimate measure of every event, action, or intention is a purely legalistic one. This was designed as an obstacle to immoral behavior, and it is often successful; but sometimes, in the form of "legal realism," it facilitates precisely such behavior.

We can only be grateful that human nature resists this legalistic hypnosis, that it does not allow itself to be lulled into spiritual lethargy and apathy towards the misfortunes of others: for many in the well-to-do West respond with spirit and warmth to far-off pain and suffering by donating goods, money, and not infrequently expending significant personal effort.

Infinite Progress

Human knowledge and human abilities continue to be perfected; they cannot, and must not, be brought to a halt. By the eighteenth century this process began to accelerate and grew more apparent. Anne-Robert-Jacques-Turgot* gave it the sonorous title of Progress, meaning that Progress based on economic development would inevitably and directly lead to a general mollification of the human temperament.

This resonant label was widely adopted and grew into something of a universal and proud philosophy of life: we are *progressing!* Educated mankind readily put its faith in this Progress. And yet somehow no one pressed the issue: progress yes, but *in what*? And *of what*? And might we not lose something in the course of this Progress? It was enthusiastically assumed that Progress would engulf all aspects of existence and mankind in its entirety. It was from this intense optimism of Progress that Marx, for one, concluded that history will lead us to justice without the help of God.

Time passed, and it turned out that Progress is *indeed* marching on, and is even stunningly surpassing expectations, but it is doing so only in the field of technological civilization (with especial success in creature comforts and military innovations).

Progress has indeed proceeded magnificently, but has led to consequences which the previous generations could not have foreseen.

---

* Turgot (1727–1781) was a French economist and statesman.

PROGRESS IN CRISIS

The first trifle which we overlooked and only recently discovered is that unlimited Progress cannot occur within the limited resources of our planet; that nature needs to be supported rather than conquered; that we are successfully *eating up* the environment allotted to us. (Thank heaven the alarm has been sounded, especially in developed countries, and rescue operations have begun, although on much too small a scale. And one of the most positive consequences of Communism's collapse is the disintegration of the world's most senseless, recklessly wasteful economy, a tempting model for so many nations.)

The second misjudgment turned out to be that human nature did not become gentler with Progress, as was promised. All we had forgotten was the human soul.

We have allowed our wants to grow unchecked, and are now at a loss where to direct them. And with the obliging assistance of commercial enterprises, newer and yet newer wants are concocted, some wholly artificial; and we chase after them en masse, but find no fulfillment. And we never shall.

The endless accumulation of possessions? That will not bring fulfillment either. (Discerning individuals have long since understood that possessions must be subordinated to other, higher principles, that they must have a spiritual justification, a mission; otherwise, as Nikolai Berdyaev put it, they bring ruin to human life, becoming the tools of avarice and oppression.)

Modern transportation has flung the world wide open to people in the West. Even without it, modern man can all but leap out beyond the confines of his being; through the eyes of television he is present throughout the whole planet all at the same time. Yet it turns out that from this spasmodic pace of technocentric Progress, from the oceans of superficial information and cheap spectacles, the human soul does not grow, but instead grows more shallow, and spiritual life is only reduced. Our culture, accordingly, grows poorer and dimmer, no matter how it tries to drown out its decline with the din of empty novelties. As creature comforts continue to improve for the average person, so spiritual development grows stagnant. Surfeit brings with it a nagging sadness of the heart, as we sense that the whirlpool of pleasures does not bring satisfaction, and that, before long, it may suffocate us.

No, all hope cannot be pinned on science, technology, or economic growth. The victory of technological civilization has also instilled in us a spiritual insecurity. Its gifts enrich, but enslave us as well. All is *interests*; we must not neglect our *interests*, all is a struggle for material things; but an inner voice tells us that we have lost something pure, elevated, and fragile. We have ceased to see *the purpose*.

Let us admit, even if in a whisper and only to ourselves: In this hustle of life at breakneck speed—*what* are we living for?

THE ETERNAL QUESTIONS REMAIN

It is up to us to stop seeing Progress (which cannot be stopped by anyone or anything) as a stream of unlimited blessings, and to view it rather as a gift from on high, sent down for an extremely intricate trial of our free will.

The gifts of the telephone and television, for instance, when used without moderation, fragment the wholeness of our time, jerking us from the natural flow of our life. The gift of lengthened life expectancy has, as one of its consequences, made the elder generation into a burden for its children, while dooming the former to a lingering loneliness, to abandonment in old age by loved ones, and to an irreparable rift from the joy of passing on their experience to the young.

Horizontal ties between people are being severed as well. With all the seeming effervescence of political and social life, alienation and apathy towards others have grown stronger in human relations. Consumed in their pursuit of material interests, people find only an overwhelming loneliness. (It is this that gave rise to the howl of existentialism.)

We must not simply lose ourselves in the mechanical flow of Progress, but strive to harness it in the interests of the human spirit; not to become the mere playthings of Progress, but rather to seek or expand ways of directing its might towards the perpetration of good.

Progress was understood to be a shining and unswerving vector, but it turned out to be a complex and twisted curve, which has once more brought us back to the very same eternal questions which loomed in earlier times, except that facing these questions then was easier for a less distracted, less disconnected mankind.

We have lost the harmony with which we were created, the internal harmony between our spiritual and physical being. We have lost that clarity of spirit which was ours when the concepts of Good and Evil had yet to become a subject of ridicule, shoved aside by the principle of fifty-fifty.

And nothing so bespeaks the current helplessness of our spirit, our intellectual disarray, as the loss of a clear and calm attitude towards *death*. The greater his well-being, the deeper the chilling fear of death cuts into the soul of modern man. This mass fear, a fear the ancients did not know, was born of our insatiable, loud, and bustling life. Man has lost the sense of himself as a limited point in the universe, albeit one possessed of free will. He began to deem himself the center of his surroundings, adapting not himself to the world but the world to himself. And then, of course, the thought of death becomes unbearable: it is the extinction of the entire universe at a stroke.

Having refused to recognize the unchanging Higher Power above us, we have filled that space with personal imperatives, and suddenly life has become a harrowing prospect indeed.

AFTER THE COLD WAR

The middle of the twentieth century passed for all of us under the cloud of the nuclear threat, a menace fierce beyond the limits of imagination. It seemed to blot out all the vices of life. Everything else seemed insignificant: we are lost for anyhow, so why not live as we please? And this great threat also served both to halt the development of the human spirit and to postpone our reflection on the meaning of our life.

But paradoxically, this same danger temporarily gave Western society something of a unifying purpose of existence: to withstand the lethal menace of Communism. By no means did all fully understand this threat, and in no sense was this firmness equally absorbed by all in the West; there appeared not a few faint hearts thoughtlessly undermining the West's stand. But the preponderance of responsible people in government preserved the West and allowed for victory in the struggles for Berlin and Korea, for the survival of Greece and Portugal. (Yet there was a time when the Communist chieftains could have delivered a lightning blow, probably without receiving a nuclear one in return. It may be that only the hedonism of those decrepit chieftains served to postpone their scheme, until President Reagan derailed them with a new, spiraling, and ultimately unbearable arms race.)

And so, at the end of the twentieth century there burst forth a sequence of events, expected by many of my countrymen but catching many in the West by surprise: Communism collapsed due to its inherent lack of viability and from the weight of the accumulated rot within. It collapsed with incredible speed, and in a dozen countries at once. The nuclear threat suddenly was no more.

And then? A few short months of joyful relief swept over the world (while some bemoaned the death of the earthly Utopia, of the Socialist Paradise on Earth). It passed, but somehow the planet did not grow calmer; it seems instead that with a greater frequency something flares up here or explodes there; even scraping together enough UN forces for peacekeeping has become no easy task.

Besides, Communism is far from dead on the territory of the former USSR. In some republics, its institutional structures have survived in their entirety, while in all of them millions of Communist cadres remain in reserve, and its roots remain embedded in the consciousness and the daily life of the people. At the same time, under the nascent savage nonproducing capitalism, ugly new ulcers have surfaced from years of torment, ushering in such repulsive forms of behavior and such plunder of the nation's wealth as the West has not known. This, in turn, has even brought an unprepared and unprotected populace to a nostalgia for the "equality in poverty" of the past.

Although the earthly ideal of Socialism-Communism has collapsed, the problems which it purported to solve remain: the brazen use of social advantage and the inordinate power of money, which often direct the very course of events. And if the global lesson of the twentieth century does not serve as a healing inoculation, then the vast red whirlwind may repeat itself in its entirety.

The Cold War is over, but the problems of modern life have been laid bare as immensely more complex than what had hitherto seemed to fit into the two dimensions of the political plane. That earlier crisis of the meaning of life and that same spiritual vacuum (which during the nuclear

548

decades had even deepened from neglect) stand out all the more. In the era of the balance of nuclear terror this vacuum was somehow obscured by the illusion of attained stability on the planet, a stability which has proved only transitory. But now the former implacable question looms all the clearer: What is our destination?

On the Eve of the Twenty-First Century

Today we are approaching a symbolic boundary between centuries, and even millennia: less than eight years separate us from this momentous juncture (which, in the restless spirit of modern times, will be proclaimed a year early, not waiting until the year 2001).

Who among us does not wish to meet this solemn divide with exultation and in a ferment of hope? Many thus greeted the twentieth, as a century of elevated reason, in no way imagining the cannibalistic horrors that it would bring. Only Dostoyevsky, it seems, foresaw the coming of totalitarianism.

The twentieth century did not witness a growth of morality in mankind. Exterminations, on the other hand, were carried out on an unprecedented scale, culture declined sharply, the human spirit waned. (The nineteenth century, of course, did much to prepare this outcome.) So what reason have we to expect that the twenty-first century, one bristling with first-class weaponry on all sides, will be kinder to us?

And then there is environmental ruin. And the global population explosion. And the colossal problem of the Third World, still called so in quite an inadequate generalization. It constitutes four-fifths of modern mankind, and soon will make up five-sixths, thus becoming the most important component of the twenty-first century. Drowning in poverty and misery, it will, no doubt, soon step forward with an ever-growing list of demands to the advanced nations. (Such thoughts were in the air as far back as the dawn of Soviet Communism. It is little known, for example, that in 1921 the Tatar nationalist and Communist Sultan-Galiev called for the creation of an International of colonial and semicolonial nations, and for the establishment of its dictatorship over the advanced industrial states.) Today, looking at the growing stream of refugees bursting through all European borders, it is difficult for the West not to see itself as something of a fortress—a secure one for the time being, but clearly one besieged. And in the future, the growing ecological crisis may alter the climatic zones—leading to shortages of fresh water and arable land in places where they were once plentiful. This, in turn, may give rise to new and menacing conflicts on the planet, wars for survival.

A complex balancing act thus arises before the West. While maintaining full respect for the entire precious pluralism of world cultures and for their search for distinct social solutions, the West cannot at the same time lose sight of its own values, its historically unique stability of civic life under the rule of law—a hard-won stability which grants independence and space to every private citizen.

SELF-LIMITATION*

The time is urgently upon us to limit our wants. It is difficult to bring ourselves to sacrifice and self-denial, because in political, public, and private life we have long since dropped the golden key of self-restraint to the ocean floor. But self-limitation is the fundamental and wisest step of a man who has obtained his freedom. It is also the surest path towards its attainment. We must not wait for external events to press harshly upon us or even topple us; we must take a conciliatory stance and through prudent self-restraint learn to accept the inevitable course of events.

Only our conscience, and those close to us, know how we deviate from this rule in our personal lives. Examples of deviations from this course by larger entities—parties and governments—are in full view of all.

When a conference of the alarmed peoples of the earth convenes in the face of the unquestionable and imminent threat to the planet's environment and atmosphere, a mighty power (one consuming not much less than half of the earth's currently available resources and emitting half of its pollution) insists, because of its present-day internal interests, on lowering the demands of a sensible international agreement, as though it does not itself live on the same earth. Then other leading countries shirk from

---

* Solzhenitsyn explores this concept of *self-limitation* in an essay called "Repentance and Self-limitation in the Life of Nations," originally published in *From Under the Rubble.*

fulfilling even these reduced demands. Thus, in an economic race, we are poisoning ourselves.

Similarly, the breakup of the USSR along the fallacious Lenin-drawn borders has provided striking examples of newborn formations, which, in the pursuit of great-power imagery, rush to occupy extensive territories that are historically and ethnically alien to them—territories containing tens of thousands, or in some cases millions, of ethnically different people—giving no thought to the future, imprudently forgetting that taking never brings one to any good.

It goes without saying that the application of the principle of self-restraint to groups, professions, parties, or entire countries raises difficult questions which outnumber the answers already found. On this scale, all commitments to sacrifice and self-denial will have repercussions for multitudes of people who are perhaps unprepared for or opposed to them. (And even the personal self-restraint of a consumer will have an effect on producers somewhere.)

And yet, if we do not learn to limit firmly our desires and demands, to subordinate our interests to moral criteria—we, humankind, will simply be torn apart, as the worst aspects of human nature bare their teeth.

It has been pointed out by various thinkers many times (and I quote here the words of the twentieth century Russian philosopher Nikolai Lossky): If a personality is not directed at values higher than the self, corruption and decay inevitably take hold. Or, if you will permit me to share a personal observation: We can only experience true spiritual satisfaction not in seizing, but in refusing to seize. In other words: in self-limitation.

Today it appears to us as something wholly unacceptable, constraining, and even repulsive, because we have over the centuries grown unaccustomed to what for our ancestors had been a habit born of necessity. They lived with far greater external constraints, and had far fewer opportunities. The paramount importance of self-restraint has only in this century arisen in its pressing entirety before mankind. Yet, taking into account even the various mutual links running through contemporary life, it is nonetheless only through self-restraint that we can gradually cure both our economic and political life, albeit with much difficulty.

Today, not many will readily accept this principle for themselves. However, in the increasingly complex circumstances of our modernity, to limit ourselves is the only true path of preservation for us all.

And it helps bring back the awareness of a Whole and Higher Authority above us—and the altogether forgotten sense of humility before this Entity.

There can be only one true Progress: the sum total of the spiritual progresses of individuals; the degree of self-perfection in the course of their lives.

We were recently entertained by a naïve fable of the happy arrival at the "end of history,"* of the overflowing triumph of an all-democratic bliss; the ultimate global arrangement had supposedly been attained.

But we all see and sense that something very different is coming, something new, and perhaps quite stern. No, tranquility does not promise to descend upon our planet, and will not be granted us so easily.

And yet, surely, we have not experienced the trials of the twentieth century in vain. Let us hope: we have, after all, been tempered by these trials, and our hard-won firmness will in some fashion be passed on to the following generations.

---

* The reference is to Francis Fukuyama's famous article and subsequent book *The End of History and the Last Man* (1992).

33

Moral Destruction
(1998)

ALAIN BESANÇON

The physical destruction—the vast loss of life and demolition of the earth that constitute the most obvious aspect of the century's ideological disasters—tends to be the focus of the studies and statistics. But surrounding this is an invisible sphere where the damage is probably more extensive, affects more people, and will take even longer to repair: the destruction of minds and souls.

INEPTITUDE

The intellectual genealogy of the two main ideologies that engulfed part of humanity in the twentieth century can be traced—and this has been done. The danger is that one might come to believe that the vast, deep-seated ideas upon which these ideologies drew live on in those ideologies. But this would grant them a dignity and nobility they do not deserve, would play their game—for this is the genealogy to which they lay claim. Marxism-Leninism proclaimed itself heir to a tradition stretching back to Heraclitus and Democritus.* It claimed to descend from Lucretius,† the Enlightenment, Hegel, and the entire scientific movement. It claimed

---

* Heraclitus and Democritus were pre-Socratic philosophers.

† Titus Lucretius Carus (first century B.C.) was a Roman poet and philosopher and author of *On the Nature of Things*.

to be a synthesis and a fulfillment of these movements. Nazism found its predecessors in Greek tragedy, Herder,* Novalis,† a different reading of Hegel, and Nietzsche; and naturally, it based its legitimacy on the scientific movement since Darwin. Yet these claims must not be believed. They constitute an illusion entailing the further danger of compromising the lineage to which they lay claim: there is a risk of criticizing Hegel—or any other philosopher or scholar—for having begotten such descendants.

This illusion wears off when we observe how the Nazi and Communist leaders truly operated intellectually. Their thinking was completely governed by an extraordinarily impoverished system of interpreting the world. It saw classes or races as engaged in a dualistic struggle. The definition of these classes or races makes sense only within the system, with the result that any objectivity that could exist in the notion of classes or races vanishes. These notions gone awry explain the nature of the struggle; they justify it and, in the mind of the ideologist, guide the actions of enemies and allies. The means used to reach the goal can be cunning and shrewd (and in fact, with Lenin, Stalin, Mao, and Ho Chi Minh, Communism benefited from agents more capable than Hitler). But the logic of the system as a whole remains absurd, and its goal unattainable.

The psychological state of the militant is distinguished by his fanatical investment in the system. This central vision reorganizes his entire intellectual and perceptual field, all the way to the periphery. Language is transformed: it is no longer used to communicate or express, but to conceal a contrived continuity between the system and reality. Ideological language is charged with the magical role of forcing reality to conform to a particular vision of the world. It is a liturgical language for which every utterance points to its speaker's adherence to the system, and it summons the interlocutor to adhere as well. Code words thus constitute threats and figures of power.

It is not possible to remain intelligent under the spell of ideology. Nazism seduced some great minds (Heidegger, Carl Schmitt‡), but these

* Johann Gottfried von Herder (1744–1803) was a German poet and philosopher closely associated with Romanticism.
† Novalis, a pseudonym for Georg Philipp Friedrich Freiherr von Hardenberg (1772–1801), a German philosopher also associated with Romanticism.
‡ Carl Schmitt. See note on page 226.

projected onto Nazism foreign ideas of their own: a profound antimodern-
ism and antidemocratism, and nationalism transformed into metaphysics. Nazism seemed to take on all these elements—but not the reflection,
depth, and metaphysics that made them of value to the intellectual lives of
these philosophers. They, too, had succumbed to the illusion of genealogy.

Marxism-Leninism recruited only second-rate minds (Georg Lukács,
for example): men who lost their talent rather quickly. Communist parties could boast a number of illustrious members: Louis Aragon,* Brecht,†
Picasso, Paul Langevin,‡ Pablo Neruda.§ The party made a point of keeping these members on the sidelines in order to confine their adherence to
chance, mood, interest, or circumstance. But despite the superficial nature
of these artists' adherence, the painting of Picasso (see *The Massacres of
Korea*) and the poetry of Neruda and Aragon suffered because of it. Artistically, adherence could survive in a style of provocation. The embrace of
ideology by superior minds came about through a random confluence of
diverse nonideological passions. But as these passions came closer to the
heart of the ideology, they faded. Sometimes, a residue of ineptitude was
all that remained.

In the Communist zone, leaders sometimes took it upon themselves
to collect and publish the basic tenets of their ideology under their own
names. Such was the case with Stalin and Mao. These basic outlines
amount to a few pages containing the entire doctrine: no treatise was
deemed superior to these manuals, which were sometimes described as
"elementary" to make people believe that more scholarly ones also existed.
Although these longer works were no more than expanded and diluted
versions of the same, this did not prevent them from being imposed as
objects of "study"—which means that their subjects were required to
spend hundreds of hours reviewing and mindlessly repeating their les-

---

* Louis Aragon (1897–1982), the French poet and novelist and member of the French
Communist Party.

† Bertolt Brecht (1898–1956) was a German playwright and poet who was a committed Marxist, though he never joined a Communist Party.

‡ Paul Langevin (1872–1946) was a renowned French physicist and member of the
French Communist Party.

§ Pablo Neruda (1904–1973) was a Chilean poet and member of the Chilean Communist Party.

sons. In the Nazi zone, such compendia did not exist. All thinking was supposed to hinge on that of the leader, who presented himself as oracular and inspired. In analyzing the substance of Nazism, one finds a miserable blend of social Darwinism, eugenics, a vaguely Nietzschean hatred for Christianity, a religion of "resentment," and pathological anti-Semitism.

The Nazi or Communist presents a clinical case for psychiatric examination. He seems imprisoned, cut off from reality, capable of arguing indefinitely in circles with his interlocutor, obsessed. Yet he is convinced he is rational. This is why psychiatrists have established a link between this state of chronic systematized delirium and such conditions as schizophrenia and paranoia. If one ventures further into the examination, it becomes clear that this characterization is metaphorical. The most obvious sign that ideological insanity is artificial is that it is reversible: when the pressure ceases and circumstances change, one gets out all at once, as if from a dream. But it is a waking dream—one that does not block motility and maintains a certain apparently rational coherence. Outside the affected area, which is the superior part of the mind in a healthy person—the part that articulates religion, philosophy, and the "governing ideas of reason," as Kant would say—the comprehensive functions seem intact but focused on and enslaved by the surreal object. When one wakes, one's mind is empty; one's life and knowledge must be entirely relearned. Germany, which for a century had been the Athens of Europe, woke up stupefied by twelve years of Nazism. And how to describe Russia, which was subjugated to this pedagogy of the absurd far more systematically for seventy years, and where intellectual foundations were less established and more fragile?

These artificial mental illnesses were also epidemic and contagious. They have been compared to a sudden outbreak of the plague or the flu. Formally, the Nazification of Germany in 1933 and the Chinese Cultural Revolution indeed developed like a contagious disease. But such comparisons probably have only metaphorical value while we await a better understanding of these psychological pandemics.

The backdrop of moral destruction is ineptitude. It is its condition. Natural and shared awareness can be distorted only if one's conception of the world, one's link to reality, has first been disrupted. Whether this blindness is an extenuating circumstance or an integral part of the evil, I will not debate here. In any case, it does not suspend moral judgment.

THE NAZI FALSIFICATION OF THE GOOD

When we attempt to examine closely all that was done to people at the six camps listed in the first chapter, words do not suffice, concepts fail, imagination refuses to conceive, and memory refuses to retain. We are outside of the human realm here, as though standing before a negative transcendence. The idea of the demonic arises irresistibly.

What suggests the demonic is that these acts were carried out in the name of a good, under the guise of a moral code. The instrument of moral destruction is a falsification of the good that allows the criminal—to an extent impossible to describe—to sweep aside any sense that he is doing evil.

During the war, Heinrich Himmler* delivered several speeches to high-ranking officers and section leaders of the SS.[1] His tone was always one of moral exhortation.

The following passage rises above the contingent circumstances of the era, above even the immediate interests of the Reich, to touch the universal:

> All that we do must be justified in relation to our ancestors. If we do not find this moral connection, which is the deepest and best connection because it is the most natural, we will never rise to the level necessary to defeat Christianity and to constitute this German Reich, which will be a blessing to the entire world. For thousands of years, it has been the duty of the blond race to rule the world and always to bring it happiness and civilization. (June 9, 1942).

The good, according to Nazism, consisted in restoring a natural order that history had corrupted. The proper hierarchical organization of races had been overturned by the harmful influences of Christianity ("this plague, the worst sickness that has affected us throughout our history"), democracy, the rule of gold, Bolshevism, and the Jews. The German Reich was the apex of the natural order, but it made room for the other Germanic peoples—the Scandinavians, the Dutch, and the Flemish. Even

---

* Himmler. See note on page 22.

the British empire, "a worldwide empire created by the white race," could be left intact. The French and Italians were next in the hierarchy. Further down were the Slavs, who would be enslaved and reduced in number: Himmler contemplated a "reduction" of thirty million. The natural order, according to which the best, the most hardened, the purest, and the most chivalrous rule, would also be restored within the German society. The living examples of men of this nature were the elite of the Waffen-SS. By the time Himmler made this speech, the incurable and disabled—those alienated from the German "race"—had already been secretly euthanized in hospitals and asylums.

All of this would not take place, Himmler continued, without an extremely hard fight. In his speeches, he constantly invoked heroism, going beyond oneself, and a sense of the higher duty his listeners owed towards the Reich, especially when it concerned carrying out difficult orders. "We must tackle our ideological duties and answer to destiny, no matter what the situation is; we must always stand tall and never fall or falter, but be ever present until our life comes to an end or our task is accomplished."

From a certain standpoint, then, the "Final Solution" was only a technical problem, like delousing when there is a danger of typhus: "Destroying lice is not a question of world view. It is a question of cleanliness. . . . Soon there will be no more lice" (April 24, 1934). The metaphor of the insect that must be destroyed turns up regularly in the discourse of ideological extermination. Lenin had already used it. But Himmler, good leader that he was, said this to reassure and encourage his audience. He knew that it was not easy, that false scruples could arise. But to accomplish a certain type of task, "it is always necessary to be aware of the fact that we are caught up in a primitive, natural, original, and racial battle" (December 1, 1943). These four adjectives appropriately describe the Nazi ethic.

In an October 6, 1943, address, Himmler stated his view of the Final Solution:

> The phrase "the Jews must be exterminated" consists of few words; it is quickly said, gentlemen. But what it requires for those who carry it out is the hardest and most difficult thing in the world. Naturally, these are Jews, just Jews, of course; but think of all those—even friends of the Party—who have made the famous request to some department or to myself saying, "Of course, all

Jews are swine, except Mr. So-and-so, who is a decent Jew and should not be harmed." I dare say that judging by the number of these requests and the number of these opinions in Germany, there were more decent Jews than existed nominally. . . . I insist that you simply listen to what I am saying here in this meeting and never speak of it. We were asked the following question: what are we to do with the women and children? I have come to a decision and have found an obvious solution for this matter also. I did not feel I had the right to exterminate the men—in other words, to kill them or have them killed—while allowing their children to grow up, children who would take revenge on our children and our descendants. It was necessary to make the serious decision to eliminate this people from the earth. For the organization that had to accomplish this task, it was the hardest thing it had done. I think I can say that this was accomplished without our men or our officers suffering because of it in their hearts or in their souls. Even so, this was a real danger. The path lies between the two possibilities: become too hardened, become heartless, and no longer respect human life; or else become too soft and lose one's mind to the point of having fits of hysterics—this path between Scylla and Charybdis is hopelessly narrow.

This virtuous golden mean that Himmler called for was occasionally attained: several great executioners were indeed loving fathers and sensitive husbands. The "task" had to be performed without the intervention of "selfish" motives—calmly, without nervous weakness. Indulging in drinking, raping a young girl, robbing the prisoners for one's profit, or stooping to pointless sadism showed a lack of discipline, disorder. Such actions marked a forgetting of Nazi idealism; they were blameworthy and had to be punished.

Nazi morality demanded that one follow the order that nature had established. But this natural order was not a matter of contemplation; it was deduced from ideology. With the pole of good represented by the "blond race" and that of evil by the "Jewish race," the cosmic battle was to end with the victory of one or the other.

But the whole thing was false. There are no "races" in the sense intended by the Nazis. The tall blond Aryan did not exist, even if there were Germans who were tall and blond. The Jew as represented by Nazism did not exist, because the racial representation that Nazism made of the Jews had only coincidental connections with the real identity of the people of the biblical covenant. The Nazi thought he saw nature, but nature was dissimulated by his interpretive grid. Nor did he perceive the historical and military situation without distortion. Because of his "Nazism," Hitler went to war, and because of his same Nazism, he lost that war. The superiority of Stalin was that he was able to set his ideology aside long enough to prepare for victory. The Leninist ideology was "better" because it allowed for such pauses and authorized a political patience of which Nazism—impulsive and convulsive—was incapable.

The Nazi ethic manifested itself as a negation of the ethical tradition of all humanity. Only a few marginal thinkers had dared to advance some of its themes, but only as an aesthetic provocation. In fact, the kind of naturalism that it proposed—the superman, the subhuman, the will to power, nihilism, irrationalism—places it more in the domain of aesthetics. It is the artistic kitsch that intoxicates, the staging of Nuremberg, the colossal architecture à la Speer,* the dark splendor of brute force. As a morality, the Nazi ethic cannot gain serious support in history. Its perversity easily becomes evident and it cannot be universalized.

The Communist ethic, by contrast, can be universalized and its perversity is not readily evident. This explains why Nazi morality was less contagious than Communist morality and why the moral destruction it engendered was more limited in scope. The "inferior" "subhuman" races saw an imminent deadly threat in this doctrine and could not be tempted. As for the German people themselves, to the extent that they followed Hitler, they did so out of nationalism rather than Nazism. Nationalism, a natural passion that has been particularly aroused during the last two centuries, supplied the Nazi regime's artificial constructs with energy and fuel, just as it supplied these for the Communist regime. Although some members of the German elite had supported the chancellor's coming to power, the vulgar elitism of Hitler's troops had nothing to do with the old elite. Those who claimed to follow Nietzsche were caught in the trap like everyone else. As for the loyalty of the officer corps, it can be explained by

* Albert Speer was Hitler's chief architect and served as Minister of Armaments and War Production during WWII.

military tradition, reinforced on occasion by a little Kantianism or Hegelianism. The soldiers obeyed simply as soldiers do.

That is why the theoretical crux of Nazism—the physical destruction of the Jewish people, then of other peoples in hierarchical order—was one of the best-kept secrets of the Reich. *Kristallnacht** was a test, an attempt to invite and rally the German people behind the great plan, but it was not a political success. Thus, Hitler decided to build the six major extermination camps outside the historical borders of Germany.

The moral damage of Nazism can be described in terms of concentric circles moving around the central core suggested by the passage quoted from Himmler. The central core consists of those who were converted to the fullness of Nazism. Few in number, these were the heart of the party, the heart of the Waffen-SS and the Gestapo. The practitioners of extermination were even fewer. They did not have to be numerous: the high level of German industrial and technological development made it possible to economize on manpower. The few hundred SS who controlled the death camps delegated the "manual" tasks to the victims themselves. The *Einsatzgruppen*[†] were recruited without preliminary qualifications. It has been noted that, theoretically, members were allowed to leave these corps of murderers. But major troubles awaited them, the first of which was fighting on the Soviet front. The men of the *Einsatzgruppen* were—or became—monsters. Whether they were all converted to the Nazi ideology is still an open question. But in every population, it is easy to recruit as many torturers and murderers as are needed. The ideological veneer only made it easier for some to accept such a vocation; it allowed this vocation to flourish.

It has been noted that the Wehrmacht could not have been ignorant of the activity of the *Einsatzgruppen* that operated behind its lines. The destination of the convoys and liquidation of the ghettos did not leave much room for doubt; despite the no-man's-land surrounding the death camps,

---

* *Kristallnacht,* or the Night of Broken Glass, refers to a series of attacks on Jews in Germany and Austria on November 9–10, 1938.

† *Einsatzgruppen* were the paramilitary death squads who followed the advance of the Wehrmacht and were responsible for mass killings such as Babi Yar. They operated primarily in the territory seized after the Nazi-Soviet pact of August 1939 and continued their operations after the Nazi invasion of the Soviet Union in June of 1941.

something eventually had to leak out. Hilberg writes that the secret was "a secret that everyone knew." That is probably true, but two points must be considered.

First, a secret that everyone knows is not the same thing as a proclaimed policy or a public fact. The Germans followed out of military and civic discipline, nationalism, fear, and the inability to devise or carry out an act of resistance. The secret—despite being out—released them from immediate moral responsibility, or at least allowed them to hedge, to look the other way, and to act as though it all did not exist. Under Nazism, German society still had remnants of law. The officer corps included a number of men who remained loyal to the canons of war and strove—with greater or lesser success—to maintain a certain honor. Because private property had not yet been abolished, civil society thrived. The film *Schindler's List* is built around the fact that a business owner was still able to recruit and house a Jewish workforce in Germany. From the first year of Communism, such a thing was no longer conceivable in Russia.

Second, the contents of the secret were not believable for a normal mind. Much of Germany still lived in a natural society governed by a natural morality, and did not size up what was in store for it. This fact made it harder to believe that reality was being hidden from it, that the suspicions were well founded and the various clues obvious. Even Jews—who underwent expropriation, concentration, and deportation—did not always believe it when they arrived at the gas chambers.

Nazi pedagogy was practiced for only a few years. When Germany was occupied, Nazism disappeared immediately—at least in the Western Zone (in the East, it was put in part to new use). It disappeared, first, because it was tried and sentenced at all levels under German and international law. Another reason was that the majority of the population had not been deeply saturated with it. Finally, Nazism disappeared because even the Nazis, once awakened, did not clearly see the link between what they had been under the ideology's magic spell and what they were now that this spell had worn off. Eichmann's fundamental nature was that of a middle-class bureaucrat; he had been this before and would have become again had he not been captured and punished. He greeted this punishment passively, in keeping with his bland character. As Hannah Arendt rightly pointed out, the crimes Eichmann was accused of were incommensurable with the limited consciousness of this banal being.

THE COMMUNIST FALSIFICATION OF THE GOOD

Communism was moral. A moral imperative underlay the entire prehistory of Bolshevism (French and German socialism, Russian populism), and the victory of Bolshevism was celebrated as a victory of the good. Aesthetics did not take precedence over ethics. The Nazi considered himself an artist; the Communist, a virtuous man.

The foundation of Communism's morality lay in its interpretive system, one deduced from knowledge. Primitive nature, the system taught, was not the hierarchical, cruel, implacable nature in which the superior Nazi man rejoices, but resembled the goodness of nature according to Rousseau. Nature had been lost, but socialism would re-create it by lifting it to a higher level. There, man would be completely fulfilled. Trotsky claimed that such exemplars as Michelangelo and da Vinci would mark the base level of the new humanity. Communism democratized the superman.

Natural progress was regarded as historical progress, since historical and dialectical materialism unifies nature and history. Communism appropriated progress, that great theme of the Enlightenment, in contrast with the theme of decadence that haunted Nazism; but in this case, dramatic progress included tremendous and unavoidable destruction. One recognizes here bits of Hegelian pantragism[2] and particularly the hardcore Darwinism of the struggle to survive applied to society. The "social relations of production" ("slavery," "feudalism," "capitalism") succeeded one another like the various reigns in the animal kingdom, as when the mammals took over from the reptiles. Such progressivism was a secret point of agreement between Nazism and Communism: you don't cry over spilled milk; you can't make an omelet without breaking eggs; when you chop wood, the chips fly—all these expressions were familiar to Stalin. On both sides, history was the master. Nazism would restore the world in its beauty; Communism, in its goodness.

The Communist restoration depended on the human will enlightened by ideology. Even more clearly than Nazism, Leninism followed the gnostic blueprint of two antagonistic principles and three periods. In the beginning, there was the primitive commune; in the future, there would be Communism; today, there was the period of the battle between the two principles. The forces that furthered "progress" were deemed good and those that hindered it were bad. The scientifically guaranteed ideology designated the bad principle. Not a biological entity in the sense of an inferior race, that principle was a social entity seen to grow like a cancer throughout society: it was property, capitalism, and the complex of mores, law, and culture summed up in the expression "the spirit of capitalism." Those who had understood the three periods and two principles, who were acquainted with the essence of the naturo-historical order, who knew both the direction of its evolution and the means to hasten it—these people came together and formed the party.

All means that would bring about the end as foreseen by the revolutionary were considered good. Since the process was as natural as it was historical, destruction of the old order would in itself bring about the new order. Bakunin's expression, summarizing what he had understood from Hegel, was the maxim of Bolshevism: the spirit of destruction is the same as the spirit of creation. In Bolshevism's prehistory, the *Narodnik*[*] heroes were conscious of the moral revolution that followed from these ideas. Chernyshevsky,[†] Nechayev,[‡] and Tkachyov[§] developed a literature of "the new man," one Dostoyevsky satirized and whose metaphysical meaning he grasped. The new man appropriated the new morality of an absolute devotion to the ends. This new morality required one to drive out the remnants of the old morality, which "class enemies" advanced in order to perpetuate their rule. Lenin canonized Communist ethics. Trotsky wrote a pamphlet whose title says it all: *Their Morality and Ours*.

THEIR MORALITY AND OURS

What is amazing is that not everyone outside of this revolutionary milieu was aware of this moral rupture. In fact, Communism used words from

---

* *Narodnik*, a member of the nineteenth-century socialist movement in Russia.

† Nikolay Chernyshevsky (1828–1889) was a radical Russian journalist whose novel *What Is to Be Done?* (1863) was very influential with figures such as Lenin.

‡ Sergey Nechayev (1847–1882) was a Russian revolutionary perhaps best known for his advocacy of a professional, militant, revolutionary party.

§ Peter Tkachyov (1844–1886) was another Russian radical and Marxist who favored the seizure of state power by an elite party.

the old morality—justice, equality, liberty, etc.—to describe the new one. It is true that the world Communism planned to destroy was full of injustice and oppression. Virtuous men had to acknowledge that the Communists denounced these evils with extreme vigor. Everyone agreed that distributive justice was not upheld. The good man, guided by a sense of justice, attempted to promote a better distribution of wealth. The Communist, by contrast, saw the idea of justice consisting not in a "fair" distribution of wealth, but in the establishment of socialism and suppression of private property—this consequently voided all standards of fairness, fairness itself, and ultimately the right of individuals. The Communist commitment to creating an awareness of inequality did not aim to call attention to a defect of law, but to elicit desire for a society in which regulation would not be a matter of law. Similarly, the Communist idea of liberty aimed to arouse the awareness of oppression in circumstances in which the individual—a victim of capitalist alienation—believed he was free. Finally, all the words that were used to express modalities of the good—justice, liberty, humanity, goodness, generosity, achievement— were directed towards a single goal that encompassed and fulfilled them all: Communism. In the Communist perspective, these words were no more than homonyms of the old words.

Yet some simple criteria should have cleared up this confusion. By natural or common morality I mean the morality referred to by the sages not only of antiquity, but also of China, India, and Africa. In the world of the Bible, this morality is summed up in the second table of the commandments of Moses. Communist ethics opposed common morality head-on, and very consciously. The Communist ethic sought to destroy ownership—and the laws and liberty connected to it—and to reform the order of the family. By permitting itself all manner of lies and violence in order to overcome the old order and call forth the new, it openly and fundamentally infringed upon the fifth commandment ("Honor thy father and thy mother"), the sixth ("Thou shalt not kill"), the seventh ("Thou shalt not commit adultery"), the eighth ("Thou shalt not steal"), the ninth ("Thou shalt not bear false witness against thy neighbor"), and the tenth ("Thou shalt not covet that which is thy neighbor's"). It is not at all necessary to believe in biblical revelation to accept the spirit of these precepts, which are found throughout the earth. The majority of mankind honors the idea that certain behaviors are true and good because they correspond to what we know of the structure of the universe. Communism, which conceived of another universe, derived its morality from that. This is why Communism challenged not only the precepts, but also their foundation: the natural world. Although I said previously that Communist morality was based on nature and history, this in fact was not true: it was based on a super-nature that never existed and on a history devoid of truth.

In *Democracy and Totalitarianism*, Raymond Aron argues that

> the Soviet regime came from a revolutionary will inspired by a humanitarian ideal. The goal was to create the most humane regime history had ever known, the first regime in which everyone could achieve humanity, where classes would disappear, and where the homogeneity of society would allow for the mutual recognition of citizens. But this movement aiming at an absolute goal did not shrink from any means: according to the doctrine, only violence could create this absolutely good society, and the proletariat was involved in a ruthless war with capitalism. From this combination of a sublime goal and ruthless methods, the different phases of the Soviet regime arose.[3]

These lines reflect, with all possible clarity, the ambiguity and illusion of Communism. What it labeled the human and the humanitarian was really the superhuman and superhumanitarian promised by the ideology. The human and the humanitarian had neither rights nor a future. Classes were not reconciled; they were to disappear. Society did not become homogeneous; its autonomy and its proper dynamic were destroyed. The war against capitalism was waged not by the proletariat, but by the ideological sect that spoke and acted in its name. Finally, capitalism existed solely in opposition to a socialism that existed nowhere but in the ideology; consequently, the concept of capitalism was inadequate to describing the reality that had to be brought down. The goal was not sublime: it took on the colors of sublimity. The means, which was killing, became the only possible end.

After drawing a long and admirable parallel between Nazism and Communism, Raymond Aron writes:

> I will maintain to the end that the difference between these two phenomena is an essential one, whatever the similarities may be.

566

The difference is essential because of the idea that drives each of the two enterprises. In one case, the final outcome is the labor camp; in the other, it is the gas chamber. In the one case, there is at work a will to build a new regime—and perhaps a new man—using any means; in the other, what is at work is a properly demonic will to destroy a pseudo-race.[4]

I, too, acknowledge the difference, but on the basis of arguments I will expound below. I am not convinced by those Aron presents here. Nazism also planned for a new regime and a new man using any means. It is impossible to decide which is more demonic: destroying a pseudorace and then successively destroying the other pseudoraces—including the "superior" one—because they are all polluted, or destroying a pseudoclass and then successively destroying the others, which are all contaminated by the spirit of capitalism.

Raymond Aron concludes:

If I had to summarize the meaning of each of the two enterprises, I think these are the phrases I would suggest: concerning the Soviet enterprise, I would quote the trite expression "he who wants to play the angel plays the beast." Concerning the Hitlerian enterprise, I would say: "it would be wrong for man to set a goal to become like a beast of prey: he pulls it off too well."

Is it better to be a beast that plays the angel or a man that plays the beast—given that both are beasts "of prey"? This is indeterminable. In the first case, the degree of the lie is stronger and the appeal is greater. The Communist falsification of the good went deeper, since the crime more closely resembled the good than the naked crime of the Nazi. This trait allowed Communism to expand more widely and to work on hearts that would have turned away from an SS calling. Making good men bad is perhaps more demonic than making men who are already bad worse. Raymond Aron's argument boils down to a difference of intentions: the Nazi intention contradicted the universal idea of the good, whereas the Communist intention perverted it, because it had the appearance of good. But it tricked many more inattentive souls to go along with it as a result. Because the Communist project was unattainable, we are left to judge only the means; but because these means were incapable of attaining their end, they became the real end. The lie overlaid the crime, making it all the more tempting and dangerous.

Leninist Communism is more tempting because it appropriates an ancient ideal—albeit by removing it from its heritage. At the time they became adherents, many were unable to discern the corruption brought about by Leninism. Some people remained Communists for a long time, even all their lives, without realizing it. The confusion of the old (common) morality with the new morality was never completely dispelled. Thus, a number of "decent people," those whose moral decay was delayed, remained in Communist parties. Their presence counts in favor of granting collective amnesty. The former Communist has been more easily forgiven than the former Nazi, who was suspected of having consciously broken with common morality from the time of his joining.

Communism is more dangerous because its education is insidious and gradual; it disguises the evil acts it causes as good acts. It is also more dangerous because it is unpredictable to its future victims: anyone can potentially assume enemy status from one moment to the next. Nazism designated its enemies in advance. True, it endowed them with a fantastical nature bearing no relation to reality. But behind the subhuman, there was a real Jew, behind the despicable Slav, a Pole or a Ukrainian in flesh and blood. Those who were neither Jewish nor Slavic got a reprieve. The same universalism that had represented the great superiority of Communism over Nazi exclusiveness before the Communists' seizure of power became a universal threat once the Communists were in power. Capitalism, as the word was employed, existed only ideologically. No category of humanity was spared the curse it bore: whether the "middle" and "poor" peasantry, the intelligentsia, the "proletariat," or the party itself. Because anyone could be contaminated by the spirit of capitalism, no one was safe from suspicion.

With a certain realism, Nazi leaders promised blood and tears and anticipated a fight to the death to restore humanity to its proper racial order. Lenin, on the contrary, thought that the time was right and the eschatology would be realized as soon as "capitalism" was overthrown. The revolution was going to sweep over the entire world. Once the expropriators were expropriated, socialist administration would spontaneously move into position. But nothing happened on the day following November 7, 1917: the curtain rose on an empty stage. Where did the proletariat, the poor and middle peasantry, and proletarian internationalism all go? Lenin was alone with his party (and a few Red Guards) in a hostile or indifferent world.

Still, because Marxism-Leninism was "scientific," experience had to validate the theory. With capitalism overthrown, socialism had to take over. But since this did not seem to be happening, socialism had to be constructed along the lines indicated by the theory and each step had to be verified to ensure that the result would be true to the prediction. Piece by piece, a universe of lies was constructed to replace the truth. An atmosphere of widespread lies thickened as the facts increasingly diverged from the words that were supposed to describe them. The good asserted itself frenetically in order to deny the reality of evil.

This, mainly, is how moral destruction occurs in the Communist regime. As in the Nazi regime, it expands in concentric circles around an initial core.

At the center lies the party, and in the party, its ruling circle. When the party first comes to power, it is still completely in the grip of ideology. This is the time when it makes every effort to eliminate "the class enemy." Its moral conscience completely poisoned, the party destroys entire categories of human beings in the name of its utopia. A retrospective view shows that, in the cases of Russia, Korea, China, Romania, Poland, and Cambodia, the initial slaughters were some of the most significant in the history of these regimes—their toll was something on the order of 10 percent or more of the population.

When it turns out that the utopian dream is still not being realized, that the propitiatory decimation has been useless, there is a gradual shift from seeking a utopia to merely preserving power. Given that the objective enemy has already been exterminated, vigilance is now required. It must not be allowed to regroup, let alone to rise up in the very ranks of the party. A second terror arises, a time that seems absurd because it corresponds to no social and political resistance, but aims at a total control of all human beings and all thought. Fear then becomes universal: it spreads within the party itself, and every member feels threatened by it. Everyone denounces everyone else, and all are caught in a chain reaction of betrayal.

Next comes the third stage. Taking precautions against a permanent purge, the party now contents itself with a routine management of power and security. It no longer believes in the ideology, but continues to speak its language. The party sees that this language, which it knows to be a lie, is the only one spoken because it is the mark of the party's domination. The party accumulates privileges and advantages; it becomes a caste. Corruption within the party becomes widespread. The people compare its members no longer to wolves, but to swine.

The periphery is composed of the rest of the population, which is immediately summoned and mobilized for the building of socialism. The entire periphery is threatened, fed lies, and solicited to participate in the crime.

The first step of the mobilization process is to seal off the periphery. As one of its first acts, every Communist government closes its borders. Until 1939, the Nazis authorized departures in exchange for ransom—this served the "purity" of Germany. But the Communists never did this: they needed their borders completely sealed off to protect the secret of their slaughter, of their failure. But they especially needed such isolation because the country was supposed to become an extensive school where all would receive the education that would eradicate the spirit of capitalism and instill the socialist spirit in its place.

The second step is to control information. The population must not know what goes on beyond the socialist camp. It must not know what goes on inside either. Indeed, it must not know its past or its present—only its radiant future.

The third step is to replace reality with a pseudoreality. To this end, a whole corps specializes in the production of false journalists, false historians, a false literature, and a false art that pretends to reflect a fictitious reality as in a photograph. A false economy produces imaginary statistics. Sometimes, the need for cosmetic retouches led to Nazi-style measures. In the USSR, for example, disabled ex-servicemen and workers were removed from the public eye and taken to remote asylums where they could no longer spoil the picture. It has been reported that, in Korea, a decision has been made that the dwarf "race" must disappear; thus, dwarves are deported and prevented from procreating. Millions are involved in the construction of this immense stage production. What is its purpose? To prove that socialism is not only possible, but under construction, that it is growing stronger—or, better, that it has already been realized. There is a new, free, self-regulating society where "new human beings" think and act

570

spontaneously within this fictitious reality. The strongest tool fabricated by this power is a new language in which existing words take on a meaning that differs from the common usage. The diction and special vocabulary of this new language endow it with the quality of a liturgical language; it denotes the transcendence of socialism and indicates the omnipotence of the party. Its popular use is the obvious sign of the people's servitude.

At first, a significant portion of the population welcomes the teaching of the lie in good faith. It enters into the new morality, taking along its old moral heritage. These people love the leaders who promise them happiness and they believe that they are happy. They think that they are living in a just order. Hating the enemies of socialism, they denounce them and approve of having them robbed and killed. They join in their extermination and lend their strength to the endeavor. Inadvertently, they take part in the crime. Along the way, ignorance, misinformation, and faulty reasoning numb their faculties and they lose their intellectual and moral bearings. When their sense of justice is offended, their inability to distinguish Communism from the common moral ideal causes them to attribute the offense to the external enemy. Until the collapse of Communism, people who were mistreated by the police or by militants in Russia commonly called them "Fascists." It did not occur to them to call them by their true name: Communists.

But life on this socialist stage—instead of becoming "more cheerful and happier," as Stalin said in the middle of the Great Purge—became grimmer, more dismal. Fear was everywhere and people had to fight to survive. The moral degradation that had been subconscious to that point now crept into consciousness. The socialist people, who had committed evil believing they were doing good, now knew what they were doing. They denounced, stole, and degraded themselves; they became evil and cowardly and they were ashamed. The Communist regime did not hide its crimes as Nazism did; it proclaimed them and invited the population to join in. Each condemnation was followed by a meeting at which the accused was publicly cursed by his friends, his wife, his children. These yielded to the ceremony out of fear or out of self-interest. The enthusiastic Stakhanovite of an earlier era—if he had ever existed as anything but a prop—revealed himself to be a lazy, servile, idiotic *Homo Sovieticus.* The women came to loathe the men and the children their parents—even though they sensed that they, in turn, were becoming like them.

The last stage is described for us by the writers of the end of Soviet-ism: Erofeev* and Zinoviev.† The most widespread feelings were despair and self-disgust. What remained was to take advantage of the specific pleasures this regime procured: irresponsibility, idleness, and vegetative passivity. One no longer made the effort to practice double-thought; one attempted simply to stop thinking entirely. One withdrew. As with the drunkard, tearful sentimentality and self-pity were a way to call others to witness one's degradation. In Zinoviev's "ratorium" one was still involved in the Hobbesian struggle of all against all, but with very little energy. Zinoviev considered *Homo Sovieticus* to be the product of an irreversible mutation of the species—fortunately, he was probably wrong.

There was no safe haven where one could escape the teaching of the lie. The social structures of the old society had been destroyed along with private property, and had been replaced by new ones that were at once schools and places of surveillance: the *kolkhoz*, the Chinese popular com-mune for the peasant, the "trade union" for the worker, the "unions" for writers and artists. The history of these regimes can be described as a continuous race for universal control. From the standpoint of the subjects, it was a frantic race for places of refuge, or at the very least, for places to hide. And there were always places of refuge. In Russia, a few families of the old intelligentsia were able to preserve their traditions—an Andrei Sakharov‡ emerged from this class. In the universities, there were more or less untroubled chairs of Assyriology or Greek philology, and in the subservient churches there were pockets of fresh air. At the end of the regime, small groups of young people could be found in Moscow. Having recovered their moral and intellectual lives, these people chose to live by their wits, not taking on any work or seeking any position, and minimized their contact with the external Soviet world. In this way, they were able to hold on until the very end.

In the Soviet empire, the Communist zeal to reeducate stopped at the gate of the camp. For the Nazis, there was no need to convert subhu-

---

* Venedikt Erofeev was a Russian writer best known for his prose poem *Moscow Sta-tions* (1969).

† Alexander Zinoviev was a Russian writer best known for his mocking, satirical works *The Yawning Heights* (1976) and *Homo Sovieticus* (1982).

‡ Sakharov. See note on page 354.

mans, and the Bolsheviks practically abandoned the idea of converting prisoners. Solzhenitsyn could therefore state that the camp, in spite of its horrors, was a place of intellectual freedom and fresh spiritual air. Asian Communism, on the contrary, made the camp the place where teaching was practiced in the most obsessive and cruel way. Authorities noted the progress of the prisoners. No one but the dead or the reeducated ever left.

ASSESSMENT

Within the limits imposed by the historical perspective adopted here, let us attempt a comparative assessment of the moral destruction wrought by Nazism and Communism in the twentieth century.

By moral destruction, I do not mean the breakdown of mores in the sense of the age-old grumbling of the elderly as they examine the mores of the youth. Nor do I wish to pass judgment on this century compared to others. There is no philosophical reason to think that man was either more or less virtuous during this period. Still, Communism and Nazism set out to change something more fundamental than mores—that is, the very rule of morality, of our sense of good and evil. And in this, they committed acts unknown in prior human experience.

Even though the Nazis carried crime to a level of intensity perhaps unequaled by Communism, one must nevertheless affirm that Communism brought about a more widespread and deeper moral destruction. There are two reasons for this.

First, the obligation to internalize the new moral code extended to the entire population subjected to reeducation. Accounts tell us that this compulsory internalization was the most unbearable part of Communist oppression: all the rest—the absence of political and civil liberties, police surveillance, physical repression, and fear itself—was nothing compared to this mutilating pedagogy. Having driven its victims mad because it contradicted what was obvious to the senses and understanding, it did so all the more because the whole range of "measures" and "organs" were ultimately subjected to this indoctrination. Communism, unlike Nazism, had the time to pursue its pedagogy, and it did so to the full extent. Its collapse or retreat has left behind a disfigured humanity. The poisoning of souls is more difficult to purge from the former Communist bloc than it was from Germany. The latter nation, stricken with a temporary insanity, awoke from its nightmare ready for work, self-examination, and a purifying repentance.

Next, the moral destruction of Communism was worse because the confusion between common morality and Communist morality remains deep rooted. With the latter hiding behind the former, it is parasitical and polluting, using common morality to spread its contagion. Here is a recent example: in the discussions that followed the publication of *The Black Book of Communism*, an editorial writer at the French Communist newspaper *L'Humanité* announced on television that 85 million deaths did not in any way tarnish the Communist ideal. They represented only a very unfortunate deviation. After Auschwitz, he continued, one can no longer be a Nazi, but one can remain a Communist after the Soviet camps. This man, who spoke in good conscience, did not realize at all that he had just articulated his own most fatal condemnation. He could not see that the Communist idea had so perverted the principles of reality and morality that it could indeed outlive 85 million corpses, whereas the Nazi idea had succumbed under its dead. He thought he had spoken as a great and decent man, idealistic and uncompromising, without realizing that he had uttered a monstrosity. Communism is more perverse than Nazism because it does not ask man consciously to take the moral step of the criminal, and because it uses the spirit of justice and goodness that abounds throughout the earth to spread evil over all the earth. Each Communist experience begins anew in innocence.

34

The Return of Political Philosophy
(2000)

PIERRE MANENT

It could be said that the twentieth century has witnessed the disappearance, or withering away, of political philosophy. An old-fashioned empirical proof of this statement is easy to produce: certainly no Hegel, no Marx, even no Comte, has lived in our century, able to convey to the few and the many alike a powerful vision of our social and political statics and dynamics.

However highly we might think of the philosophical capacities and results of Heidegger, Bergson,* Whitehead,† or Wittgenstein,‡ we would not single out any of them for his contribution to *political* philosophy. Heidegger, it is true, ventured into some political action, including speeches, but it is a matter for deep regret. Heidegger's was the steepest fall; on a much lower level, there was Sartre's indefatigable vituperation against anything rational or decent in civic life.

It is true that contrariwise, authors like Sir Karl Popper§ and Ray-

---

* Henri-Louis Bergson (1859–1941) was a French philosopher whose best known work is *The Two Sources of Morality and Religion* (1932).

† Alfred North Whitehead (1861–1947) was an English philosopher and mathematician—very influential in analytic philosophy.

‡ Ludwig Wittgenstein (1889–1951) was an Austrian-born philosopher whose work focuses on logic and language.

§ Sir Karl Popper (1902–1994) was an Austrian-born philosopher of science who also wrote extensively on political themes. He taught for many years in London and his most

mond Aron have been worthy contributors to both general epistemology and political inquiry, always in a spirit of sturdy and humane citizenship. And some modern representatives of that venerable tradition of thought, Thomism, have offered serious reflection on moral, social, and political problems within a comprehensive account of the world. But despite such countervailing considerations, the general diagnosis seems to me to be inescapable: no modern original philosopher has been willing or able to include a thorough analysis of political life within his account of the human world, or, conversely, to elaborate his account of the whole from an analysis of our political circumstances.

To be sure, the effort to understand social and political life did not cease in this century. It even underwent a huge expansion through the extraordinary development of the social sciences, which have increasingly determined the self-understanding of modern men and women. It might be asserted that the collective and multifaceted work of all those sociologists, anthropologists, psychologists, economists, and political scientists has shed more light on our common life than could the exertions of any individual mind, however gifted; that, when it comes to understanding our social and political life, this "collective thought" is necessarily more impartial than even a mind as impartial as Hegel's; that in this sense political philosophy, including democratic political philosophy, has an undemocratic character since it cannot be so collectivized; and that accordingly its withering away is a natural accompaniment to the consolidation and extension of democracy.

As is the case with all collective enterprises, the social sciences have many more practitioners than they do ideas and principles. I would even argue that they rest upon one sole principle, the separation of facts and values, which sets them apart from philosophy and testifies to their scientific character. The demise of political philosophy is of a piece with the triumph of this principle. I admit that generally such sweeping statements are better avoided. Nevertheless it is a fact that the fact/value distinction has become not only the presupposition of present-day social science but also the prevalent opinion in society at large. In present conditions, a teenager proves his or her coming of age, a citizen proves his or her competence and loyalty, by making use of this principle. Nowhere has the prin-

---

prominent political work is the two-volume *The Open Society and Its Enemies* (1945).

ciple been set forth with more power and brilliance than in the work of Max Weber. The limitless and tormented landscape of twentieth-century social and political thought is commanded by Weber's towering presence and overwhelming influence.

Speaking before students just after the end of World War I, Weber asks about his duty as a teacher, about what his audience, and the public at large, can legitimately require of him. He answers, in reflections later published as *Science as a Vocation*, that they have a claim on his *intellectual probity*: the teacher, as a scientist, has the obligation to acknowledge that to establish the intrinsic structures of cultural values and to evaluate those values constitute two totally distinct tasks. Weber rigorously distinguishes between *science*, which ascertains facts and relations between facts, and *life*, which necessarily involves evaluation and action.

This proposition has become commonplace today, yet it is difficult to understand what exactly it means. To give an example that is more than an example, how does one describe what goes on in a concentration camp without evaluating it? As some commentators have pointed out, Weber, in his historical and sociological studies, does not tire of evaluating even when establishing the facts; no, he ceaselessly evaluates so as to be able to establish the facts. Otherwise how could he tell a "prophet" from a "charlatan"?

However that may be, it is clear that for Weber, intellectual honesty necessarily prevents us from believing or teaching that science can show us how we ought to live; and that this same intellectual probity necessarily prevents us from believing, for instance, that a thing is good because it is beautiful, or the other way around. But what are the causes of his peculiar preoccupation with intellectual probity? In Weber's opinion, modern science exposes it to a specific danger.

Modern science exhibits a singular trait: it is necessarily unfinished—it can never be completed. It is open-ended, since there is always more to be known. Weber asks why human beings devote themselves to an activity that can never be completed, why they ceaselessly try to know what they know they will never completely know. The meaning of modern science is to be meaningless. Thus intellectual honesty requires that we not confer an arbitrary meaning on science, that we be faithful to its meaninglessness by fearlessly carrying on its enterprise. This necessary virtue is at the same time inhuman, or superhuman; indeed it is heroic. Since heroism, however necessary, is rare, many so-called scholars or teachers succumb to the temptation to confer arbitrarily some human meaning on science, or its provisional results. Weber believed that the scientist who thus lapses from his duty transforms himself into a petty demagogue or a petty prophet.

What characterizes the modern situation is that only science can be the object of public affirmation or approbation. Other "values"—for instance, esthetic or religious "values"—cannot be publicly expressed with enough sincerity to hold their own in the public square. At the end of *Science as a Vocation*, we read:

> The fate of an epoch characterized by rationalization, intellectualization, most of all by the disenchantment of the world, led human beings to expel the most sublime and supreme values from public life. They found refuge either in the transcendent realm of mystical life or in the fraternity of direct and reciprocal relationships among isolated individuals. There is nothing fortuitous in the fact that the most eminent art of our time is intimate, not monumental, nor in the fact that nowadays it is only in small communities, in face-to-face contacts, in pianissimo, that we are able to recover something that might resemble the prophetic pneuma that formerly set whole communities ablaze and welded them together. . . . For those who are unable to bear this present fate with manliness, there is only this piece of advice: go back silently—without giving to your gesture the publicity dear to renegades, but simply and without ceremony—to the old churches who keep their arms widely open.

This eloquent conclusion bears, and needs, rereading today. There is nothing antiquated or quaint about it. On the contrary, the stripping down of the public square and the flight into private realms have continued apace, coupled with the ever growing power of science to mold every aspect of our lives, including the most intimate. As a consequence, public life is more and more exclusively filled with private lives: what remains of "the public" is nothing but the publicization of "the private"—or so it seems.

Of course, this assessment could be said to miss the fundamental fact of modern society which, under the appearance of meaninglessness, is the coming-into-being of the noblest principles of all, democracy and self-determination. There is no doubt that Weber, however friendly to its political institutions, underestimates the strength and resilience of democracy, perhaps its human meaning and range. In his eyes democracy is no match—no remedy—for the disenchantment of the world, and for a good reason: it results from it. It is unable to reunify modern human beings since it ratifies and, so to speak, institutionalizes their intimate divisions.

If we take seriously *Science as a Vocation*, we will say that there is a gaping hole, a void, a meaninglessness at the heart of modern life since science, the highest and sole truly public activity, is meaningless. At the same time, if modern man wants to be equal to the task of science, he ought to look this nothingness in the face without blinking. In this sense, nihilism, at least this nihilism, is not only our curse but also our duty. Weber's eloquence aimed at keeping us awake and forcing our gaze toward this central nothingness. Thus the most authoritative, nay, the only authoritative voice in the realm of social and political thought in this century was a desperate voice.

It is impossible to put Max Weber behind us. Because he looms so large, it is difficult for us to see how the human phenomenon appeared before he separated science and life. But let us be alert enough to realize how strange and lopsided our intellectual and moral life currently is. Each and every human thing is fair game for science. Through separating facts from values we are able to divert the mighty flow of reality into the bottles of science.

But there is no reciprocity: science is never allowed to come back to illuminate reality and life. Democracy is predicated on the basic intelligence of the common man, which in turn is predicated on the inherent intelligibility of life, at least of the current occurrences of life. As a result, democracy is the regime that has the least tolerance for nihilism. (And nihilism breeds contempt for democracy.) To say that life is intelligible is not to say that it is unproblematic or without mystery. It is only to say that what we do is naturally accompanied by what we think and say, or that we ordinarily give some account of what we do. Our actions are many, and our accounts often conflicting, and so we reflect and deliberate and debate. The life of the mind is inherently dialectical—although, through the separation of facts and values, we have often lost sight of that reality.

Weber well understood that the separation between life and science was in some sense unbearable for ordinary mankind, and he rightly

579

noticed that the attendant discomfort gave rise to fake monumentalism, spurious prophesying, and pedantic fanaticism. Certainly Europe would soon experience all those ugly phenomena on a scale that the desperate Weber had not anticipated even in his most desperate mood. Very roughly, we could say that totalitarianism was the attempt to fuse together science and life. In Communism, the fusion was forced through the despotism of "science"—understood vulgarly. In Nazism, the fusion came through the despotism of "life"—again, understood in an utterly vulgar way.

Totalitarianism was the *experiment crucis* for political philosophy in our century. Through it political philosophy was radically tested, and was found wanting. The mere fact that such terrible enterprises could arise was proof that European thinkers had not developed and spread a rational and humane understanding of modern political circumstances. This claim does not presuppose the proposition, abstract to the point of meaninglessness, that "ideas govern the world"—only the sound observation that human beings are thinking animals who need tolerably accurate ideas and evaluations to orient themselves in the world. This truism is the truer the more intellectually active and able the person concerned. It would be unfair to extend culpability for this century's crimes into the past indefinitely, but it is true that, after Hegel elaborated his synthesis, no other philosopher was able to give a satisfactory, that is, an impartial, account of the modern state and society. Political philosophy after Hegel was not able to give a nearly satisfactory account of totalitarianism during and even *after* the fact.

Michael Oakeshott* once remarked that great political philosophies are generally answers to specific political predicaments. It is easy to document this proposition from Plato and Aristotle, through Machiavelli and Hobbes, to Rousseau and Hegel. As I observed at the outset, the twentieth century did not elicit such comprehensive answers from political reflection, and this despite the fact that its predicament was of the most extreme sort: devastating world wars, murderous revolutions, beastly tyrannies. If there ever was a time for writing a new *Leviathan*, that was it.

But our most impressive documents are novels: which political treatise on Communism is a match for *1984* or *Animal Farm* or *One Day in the Life*

---

* Michael Oakeshott (1901–1990) was an English philosopher who is regarded as one of the seminal conservative thinkers of the latter half of the twentieth century.

of Ivan Denisovich or *The Yawning Heights?*[*] And what a strange commentary on this situation that, for some readers at least, the most suggestive introduction to Nazi tyranny to be found in *On the Marmor Cliffs* (1939), a fable whose author, Ernst Jünger, was a soldier and adventurer with more than a passing complicity with the nihilistic mood that fomented Hitler's rise to power. Some will object that this indictment is unfair, that many penetrating books on Communism, Fascism, and Nazism have been written by historians, social scientists, and political philosophers; indeed, that the notion of totalitarianism itself got its currency and credit more from philosophy than from literature; and that at least one philosophical book on the subject—Hannah Arendt's *The Origins of Totalitarianism* (1951)— won a fame and exercised a power of fascination comparable to those of the literary works I have just mentioned. The objection is valid as far as it goes. We need to take stock of this momentous debate.

For political philosophers, dealing with Nazism and Communism was difficult. These unprecedented *political* phenomena required a specific effort of analysis, yet most of the interpreters no longer had much place in their thought for political categories, especially the notion of *regime*. Their natural reaction was to make sense of these new forms of politics by subsuming them under nonpolitical categories with which they were more familiar. For instance, Communism came to be understood as the domination of "bureaucracy," or as "bureaucratic state capitalism," a Trotskyist mantra widely used in France and elsewhere. As for Nazism, not a few on the left would see in it the instrument of "the most reactionary strata of financial capital," while many on the right saw just another avatar of "eternal Germany."

Of course these definitions, however fashionable for a time, could not long satisfy honest or discerning people, who eventually elaborated and gave credit to the notion of totalitarianism as a new and specific regime. We can be grateful to those who introduced this notion, because more than any other it helped us to look at the facts, to "save the phenomena," so to speak, and accordingly to evaluate more adequately the thorough ugliness of the whole thing. At the same time, however, totalitarianism remained an ad hoc construct. The discussion of it mainly concerned the marks, or criteria, of totalitarianism: whether "ideology" or "terror" or

---

[*] *The Yawning Heights.* See note on page 572.

both together were principal or necessary components of any "totalitarian" regime. The proponents of the notion were prone to try to outbid one another by concentrating attention on the most extreme characteristics of these regimes, with the result that, as in Hannah Arendt's case, the notion is not even applicable to Nazism and Communism except in their most extreme fits of terror and murder. This bidding war induced the mainstream of political scientists to renounce the notion completely, or to dilute it until it became unrecognizable and useless.

The facts of Nazism and Communism obliged honest and discerning observers to elaborate the notion of a new regime. At the same time, this "regime" was the opposite of a regime. The classical regime, harking back to Plato's and Aristotle's first elaboration of political philosophy, is what gives political life its relative stability and intelligibility. The totalitarian "regime," on the contrary, was characterized first of all by its instability and its formlessness. It described itself, accurately, as essentially a *movement*: the "international Communist movement," or *die NZ-Bewegung* (Munich was called by the Nazis *die Hauptstadt der Bewegung* [the capital of the movement]). Arendt herself was acutely aware of the paradoxical character of totalitarianism. In a piece titled "Ideology and Terror,"* Arendt borrows from Montesquieu's analysis and classification of regimes to try to categorize the totalitarian regime. For Montesquieu, each regime has a nature and a principle. The principle is the more important, since it is the "spring" that "moves" the regime. Now, explains Arendt, totalitarianism has no principle, not even fear—which is the principle of "despotism" according to Montesquieu. For fear to be a principal motive of action, the individual would need to think or feel that he is able to escape danger through his own actions; under totalitarianism, on the other hand, where the killings wax and wane without any discernible reason, this sense cannot be sustained. Raymond Aron's commentary on Arendt's analysis is severe but illuminating:

> One cannot help asking oneself whether Mrs. Arendt's thesis, thus formulated, is not contradictory. A regime without a principle is not a regime. . . . As a regime, it exists solely in its author's imagination. In other words, when Mrs. Arendt elaborates some aspects

---

* See part 2, chapter 2 of this volume.

of Hitlerite and Stalinist phenomena into a regime, a political essence, she brings out and probably exaggerates the originality of German or Russian totalitarianism. Mistaking this admittedly real originality for a fundamentally new regime, she is induced to read into our epoch the negation of classical philosophies and thus to slide into a contradiction: defining a working regime by an essence which so to speak implies the impossibility of its working.

This sharp criticism undoubtedly hits the mark. But Arendt would probably hit back that the "contradiction" is not of her making: it belongs to the "contradictory essence" of totalitarianism.

It is interesting to note that Alain Besançon, a distinguished French historian who studied with Aron, rediscovered and trenchantly brought out this difficulty twenty years later. In an article aptly titled "On the Difficulty of Defining the Soviet Regime,"* Besançon tries and exhausts Aristotle's and Montesquieu's classifications of regimes, concluding that the Soviet regime does not fit into any of them. In his eyes it is an "absolutely new" regime, and its newness lies in the part played by "ideology." Besançon proposes that instead of "totalitarianism" we simply classify Communism as an "ideological regime." In their different ways, Arendt, Aron, and Besançon all draw our attention to the problem of relating totalitarianism to the tradition of political philosophy. The totalitarian regime seems to be the regime embodying the negation of the idea of regime, and accordingly the irrelevance of classical political philosophy.

More than any other thinker in this century, Leo Strauss tried to recover the genuine meaning of political philosophy. Indeed, political philosophy as originally understood owes its bare survival—fittingly unobtrusive to the point of secretiveness—to Leo Strauss's sole and unaided efforts. Without him, the philosophy of history, or historicism of any stripe, would have swallowed political philosophy completely. For Strauss, in seeming contradiction to what I have just said, twentieth-century experiences were motives for going back to political philosophy, specifically to *classical* political philosophy: "When we were brought face to face with tyranny—with a kind of tyranny that surpassed the boldest imagination of the most powerful thinkers of the past—our political science failed to

---

* See part 1, chapter 4 of this volume.

recognize it. It is not surprising then that many of our contemporaries . . . were relieved when they rediscovered the pages in which Plato and other classical thinkers seemed to have interpreted for us the horrors of the twentieth century." Thus modern tyranny—Strauss carefully avoids the word "totalitarianism"—brings us back to ancient tyranny as described and understood by Plato and other Greek thinkers.

At the same time, Strauss makes clear that there is in modern tyranny something specific, and terrible, that eludes the grasp of classical categories. The return to the Greeks can only be a "first step toward an exact analysis of present-day tyranny," he argued, for contemporary tyranny is "fundamentally different" from the tyranny analyzed by the ancients. How could Strauss offer such a proposition? Recall that he devoted his life to establishing that classical philosophy elaborated the true understanding of the world, founded on nature which does not change, and that accordingly it does not need to be superseded or improved upon by a new "historical" understanding. Given that, how could Leo Strauss admit that Communism and Fascism are *fundamentally* new? How could the political life of man undergo a fundamental change? He answers: "Present-day tyranny, in contradistinction to classical tyranny, is based on the unlimited progress in the 'conquest of nature' which is made possible by modern science, as well as on the popularization or diffusion of philosophic or scientific knowledge."

Strauss was perfectly aware that such a change, or at least the possibility of such a change, needs to have been taken into account by Greek philosophy if the claim he raises on its behalf is to be upheld. He affirms that that is the case: "Both possibilities—the possibility of a science that issues in the conquest of nature and the possibility of the popularization of philosophy or science—were known to the classics. . . . But the classics rejected them as 'unnatural,' i.e., as destructive of humanity. They did not dream of present-day tyranny because they regarded its basic presuppositions as so preposterous that they turned their imagination in entirely different directions." Thus, the Greek thinkers did not imagine modern tyranny because they understood its principles and saw that they would be so much against nature that there was no use dwelling on them.

However galling the affirmation that the Greeks understood us better than we understand them, and ourselves, it is not what most impresses us in Strauss' assessment. It is rather that the two principles that make for the specific evil of modern tyranny are part and parcel of the foundation on which modern democracy was built. If this is true, modern tyranny would have as much in common with modern democracy as with ancient, i.e., "natural," tyranny.

We must not forget that these rare propositions of Strauss on contemporary political circumstances were formulated in the context of an exchange with Alexandre Kojève, one of the most influential interpreters of Hegel in this century. The Russian-born philosopher and French civil servant held that the conceptions of classical political philosophy have lost their relevance because the modern regime, or rather state, precisely through the transformation of nature and the reciprocal recognition implied in democratic citizenship, has basically solved the human problem. The unpalatable traits of modern "tyranny" must not blind us to the fact that "history has come to its end."

Thus Kojève is not much interested in the totalitarian phenomenon, the ugliness of which disappears against the big picture. However shocking Kojève's benign neglect, even favor, toward Communist totalitarianism, he does draw our attention to the disturbing fact that modern democracy shares with totalitarianism the claim to have solved the human problem. Modern democracy understands itself not as a regime among others, not even as the best regime, but as the only legitimate regime: it embodies the final, because rational, state of humanity.

Here we encounter a topic as difficult and intricate as it is important. In the classical understanding, the plurality of regimes was rooted in the intrinsic diversity of human nature, in the heterogeneity of its parts: human beings were soul and body, and the life of the human soul had its springs in the specific motions of its different parts. In the modern democratic understanding, a human being is first and foremost a self, and mankind as a whole is simply the fulfilled self writ large, which is to say, considered universally. This generalization is valid only if all the selves of all the human beings are in some important sense the same. The affirmation of the self, or the self-affirmation of humankind as composed of selves, thus presupposes the homogeneity of human nature. For the modern understanding, the solution of the human problem is one with the homogenization of human life.

A mighty task—an indefinite one—is contained herein, because that homogeneity can never be complete, or it will be so only "at the end of history," when nature, human as well as nonhuman, will have been mastered.

But in some sense, and this is Kojève's point, we have already reached a sufficient level of mastery. The science necessary for the conquest of nature is without end, it is true, but that means that its power is destined to grow without end, which means that reason allows us to imagine ourselves all-powerful already. As for human life proper, oppressive differences will long continue to arise, but they are in principle already vanquished by the declaration and institutionalization of the equality of rights. In brief, the miracles of science and the good works of democracy are attested enough to legitimate faith that liberal democracy has answered all the big questions of politics.

Of course faith can be lost. When the good works of democracy are less apparent, or when the delicate mechanisms of constitutional government, necessary for guaranteeing rights, are not available in a certain situation, the temptation arises to make good on the promises of democracy by every means available, that is, even or especially by antidemocratic means, to bring science to completion and achieve human homogeneity by overturning democracy.

Herein lies what has been aptly called the "totalitarian temptation." In this sense, as the French philosopher Claude Lefort has pointed out in *L'invention dinsocratique* (1981), his acute analysis of democracy, totalitarianism is the attempt to "embody" or "incorporate" democracy, to transform "indeterminate" democracy into a visible "body." Democracy is "indeterminate" because, in the democratic dispensation, the "seat of power" is "void"—occupied only provisionally by succeeding representatives. The king's presence was overwhelming; the democratic statesmen's is ordinarily underwhelming. As long as the citizens have not accustomed themselves to the worthy but modest function of choosing their representatives, the representatives will not be a match for the majesty of the people. Some demagogue will explain to the people that he will lead them to the empty place so that they themselves will occupy the seat of power: "Totalitarianism establishes a mechanism which . . . aims to weld anew power and society, to obliterate all the signs of social division, to banish the indetermination which haunts democratic experience. . . . From democracy and against it a body is thus made anew." When writing those lines, Lefort had principally in mind the Soviet regime, but it is clear that "race," no less than "class," can offer the basis for the building of this new homogeneous body.

Thus Lefort, drawing part of his inspiration from the phenomenological tradition, brings to our attention the bodily character of the political, or the political character of the body. This close relationship, although coming to the surface of speech in common expressions like "political body" or "body politic," has long been obscured in our democratic dispensation. Our forefathers, on the contrary, were well aware of it. Indeed how best to define the predemocratic order? If we look for one synthetic trait, then we will define it as an order founded on *filiation*. Everyone's place in society was in principle determined by his or her "birth." One's name and estate were determined through heritage. There were only families, poor or rich, common or noble, but each one governed by the head of family.

In contradistinction to ancient cities, in which heads of families were roughly equal politically and participated in the same "public space," in Western predemocratic societies there was no public space. Or rather, what was public was the family analogy, the logic of filiation and paternity, the fact that the same representation of the human ties or bonds circulated throughout the whole. Ultimately, what was public, that is, what was sacred, was the person of the king, that is, *the king's body*.

This familial order, based as it was on the fecundity of the body and on accidents of birth, strikes us today as bizarre and even disgusting. If we are sophisticated enough, we will say with cool competence: it was the value system of our forefathers, ours is different, and our grandchildren's will again be different from it and ours. I'm afraid I am not so sophisticated. This familial order was not just a value system or a cultural construct. It drew its strength, its durability, its quasi-universal validity (before democracy) from the general awareness that it was rooted not only in an undoubtedly natural fact, but in the fact that, so to speak, sums up "nature," that is, birth and filiation.

Even among scholars, it is a common mistake to confuse any political reference to "the body" with "organicism." It is then seen either as a mere figure of speech, or, more ominously, as a "holistic" representation fraught with oppressive potentialities. As a matter of fact, a "body" is very different from what is generally understood by "organism." In the latter, the part is strictly subordinated to the whole. In the former, the whole is present and active in each part. Thus the idea of the body is not at all a mechanical, or even a physical, idea. It is, on the contrary, a spiritual idea:

each part is at the same time itself and the whole. In this sense, every society, every polity, is a body.

These very sketchy observations help us to understand the meaning and strength of the order of the body, and by the same token to wonder at its swift and nearly complete demise. Lefort describes the nature, and appreciates the enormity, of the process as follows:

> The *ancien régime* was made up of innumerable little bodies that provided people with their bearings. And those little bodies disposed themselves within a huge imaginary body of which the King's body offers a replica and the token of its integrity. The democratic revolution, long underground, blows up when the King's body is destroyed, when the head of the body politic falls to the ground, when accordingly the corporeity of society dissolves. Then something happens which I would dare to call the disincorporation of individuals. Extraordinary phenomenon. . . .

Why was it such an "extraordinary phenomenon"? To put it in a nutshell: while previous societies organized themselves so as to bind their members together, while they extolled the ideas of concord and unity, our democratic society organizes itself so as to untie, even to separate, its members, and thus guarantee their independence and their rights. In this sense, our society proposes to fulfill itself as a dis-society. An extraordinary phenomenon indeed!

But will not a society thus dissociating be unable to carry on, to say nothing of prospering? That is the recurrent fear in modern society, voiced by conservatives and socialists alike, with even a few liberals joining in at times. But as a matter of fact, belying all the prophets of doom, democratic societies have maintained their cohesion, they have prospered; indeed, they offer today—the vast bulk of mankind agrees on this point—the only viable and desirable way of organizing a decent common life. So we must infer that their continuous decomposition has been accompanied by a continuous recomposition. What is the principle of this recomposition? To cut a very long story short: it is the principle of *representation*. As Lefort emphasizes, the order of representation has succeeded the order of incorporation. And the principle behind the principle of representation is the *will*—the will of people—a purely spiritual principle. The ultimate mainspring of democratic society is the fecundity of human will, or rather the capacity of the will to produce desirable effects.

Let us retrace our journey so far. I have argued that totalitarianism has been the *experimentum crucis* for political philosophy in this century, and that political philosophy, thus tested, was found wanting. We are able now to give a more precise assessment. The perplexities that attend the inquiry into the nature of totalitarian regimes do not arise solely from the peculiarly enigmatic essence of those regimes. Or rather, their enigmatic essence derives from another enigma or uncertainty, one that also concerns democracy. The uncertainty is this: where, and what, is the people's will? How can a purely spiritual principle give form and life to a body politic? The "totalitarian temptation" is made possible by, and takes place in, the uncharted territory between the "body" of predemocratic society and the "soul" of democratic politics. There is much more here than a glib metaphor. Indeed, we are at the heart of our practical and theoretical difficulties: herein lies the task of political philosophy, if it cares to have one.

We need to return again and again to the contrast between predemocratic and democratic societies, and to the dialectics between the two. This insistence may seem odd to Americans, since the U.S. had no real experience of predemocratic society and does not seem to be worse off for it: as Tocqueville so memorably said, "Americans are born equal, instead of becoming so." But my proposal is for a philosophical inquiry, not a historical one.

We begin with a paradox. We instinctively think that predemocratic societies gave an advantage to the soul as opposed to the body, even as we instinctively suppose that democratic societies have rejected the excessive pretensions of the soul and have "liberated the body," or, in Saint-Simonian parlance, "rehabilitated the flesh." These impressions are not simply erroneous; there is much truth in them. But at the same time we could say that the opposite also is true. We have seen that predemocratic societies were "incorporated" societies, rooted in the fecundity of the body, culminating in the king's body. As for democratic societies, while they are not particularly religious, they are politically and morally spiritualist, even otherwordly. Electing a representative, unlike begetting an heir, is the work of the will—of the mind or the soul.

That spirituality holds true not only in political relations, but in social and moral life as well. Democratic societies typically insist that all our bonds, including our bodily ones, have their origin in a purely spiritual decision, a decision reached in full spiritual sovereignty. We reject any suggestion that the body could create bonds by itself, that there could be ties rooted essentially in the "flesh." The "new family" results from the growing understanding of marriage and parenthood as "continuous choice." Even bodily intercourse is no longer supposed to create bonds by itself, to have meaning by itself: it does so only as far, and as long, as the will makes it so. Such meaning the will is free to confer and withdraw "at will." We increasingly behave, and we increasingly interpret our behavior, as if we were angels who happen to have bodies. Carnal *knowledge* is no longer such.

No wonder, then, that what goes by the name of political philosophy or theory today is rather angelology. In an otherwordly space—perhaps separated from this earth by a "veil of ignorance"—beings who are no longer, or not yet, truly human deliberate over the conditions under which they would consent to land on our lowly planet and don our "too solid flesh." They hesitate a lot, as well they might, and their abstract reasonings are complex and multifarious, if so hypothetical that they carry little weight. Political thought cannot indulge indefinitely to live in an atmosphere that is at the same time rarefied and vulgar. Totalitarianism, it is true, has been defeated without much contribution from political philosophy, and democracy seems to sail on unchallenged. But even in practical terms, it is not prudent to lean exclusively on the workaday virtues of the democratic citizenry.

We need to recapture something of what democracy left behind in its march to supremacy. Modern democracy has successfully asserted and realized the homogeneity of human life, but it is now required to try to recover and salvage the intrinsic heterogeneity of human experiences. The experience of the citizen is different from that of the artist, which in turn is different from that of the religious person, and so on. These decisive articulations of human life would be hopelessly blurred if the current conceit prevailed that every human being, as "creator of his or her own values," is at the same time an artist, a citizen, and a religious person—indeed, all these things and more. Against this conceit, political philosophers should undertake to bring to light again the heterogeneity of human life.

It might be argued that this heterogeneity is adequately taken care of through the public acknowledgment of the legitimate plurality of human values. Nothing could be more mistaken. As Leo Strauss once tersely remarked, pluralism is a monism, being an -ism. The same self-destructive quality attaches itself to our "values." To interpret the world of experience as constituted of admittedly diverse "values" is to reduce it to this common genus, and thus to lose sight of that heterogeneity we wanted to preserve. If God is a value, the public space a value, the moral law within my heart a value, the starry sky above my head a value . . . what is not? At the same time, for this is confusion's great masterpiece, the "value language" makes us lose the unity of human life—this necessary component of democratic self-consciousness—just as it blurs its diversity: you don't argue about values since their value lies in the valuation of the one who puts value on them. Value language, with the inner dispositions it encourages, makes for dreary uniformity and unintelligible heterogeneity at the same time.

Certainly Max Weber would look with consternation on a state of things he unwillingly did so much to advance. As *Science as a Vocation* makes clear, he devoted his uncommon strength of mind and soul to the task for which I have just entered my feeble plea: to recover, or to salvage, the genuine diversity of human experiences. He was undoubtedly right to underline that the Beautiful is not the same as the Good or the True. But then, or so it seems to me, he crossed the line. Why interpret this internal differentiation of human life as a conflict, even as a "war"—the "war of the gods" attendant to the "polytheism" of human "values"? Why say that we know that some things are beautiful *because* they are not good? Why say that we know that some beings are good or holy *because* and *inasmuch* as they are not beautiful? It seems that Weber here let himself be carried away by the restlessness of his spirit. How impatient we moderns have become! If two things don't match exactly, then they must be enemies.

Perhaps we have been impatient and restless from the beginning. Was not Descartes, the father of Enlightenment, as well the father of our impatience when he deliberately equated what is doubtful with what is false? How much wiser in my opinion was Leibniz,* who tranquilly countered that what is true is true, what is false is false, and what is doubtful is . . . well, it is doubtful. We need Leibniz's equanimity more than Descartes' impatience, so that we may sojourn within our different experiences, and draw from each its specific lesson.

------

* Leibnitz. See note on page 329.

The same human being, after all, admires what is beautiful, is motivated by what is good, and pursues the truth. Sometimes he comes across a "brave bad man," as it befell Lord Clarendon;* or he meets a fair treacherous woman. These complexities, sometimes even incongruities, of human experience need to be described accurately. Generally, the more bold the colors, the less exact the drawing. Human life does not warrant despair, and the social sciences do not warrant nihilism, because human life is humanly intelligible.

It is possible, even probable, that the democratic regime could not have come into being without the impatience of Descartes and others; it is possible as well that democratic citizens would have fallen asleep if not for the strident clarion calls of Weber and others. But victorious and mature democracy would do well to temper these extreme moods and open itself to the inner diversity of human experience as it claims to be open to the outer diversity of the human species. This would seem to be a tall order: for now, at least, few political philosophers have given it heed.

---

* In his *History of the Rebellion and Civil Wars in England*, Edward Hyde, the First Earl of Clarendon, says posterity will look upon Oliver Cromwell as a "brave bad man."

35

The Traces of a Wounded Animal
(2000)

CHANTAL DELSOL

The dissidents of the Soviet bloc, especially in central Europe, have analyzed the meaning of their struggle with precision and depth, and through them comes to us a plea to safeguard the world of being.

What is the meaning of their struggle? They struggled against a power structure, supported by official and secret police, against a ruling caste, and against a certain form of despotism—and so they appear to have been freedom fighters. But that is nothing. Or rather, it is only the tip of the iceberg, the political consequence of a philosophical situation that extends infinitely beyond it. The dissidents struggled much more against the will to make man live in a way that is not his, to re-create him in a way he cannot be; they struggled against the systematic destruction of man's reality.

Western public opinion has not understood a thing when it considers Havel or Wałęsa* to be simple descendants of the first Brutus: their aim was not only to dethrone a tyrannical power and to liberate speech and political, educational, and economic activity; they were concerned with reestablishing the rights of man as he actually is. The combat of the dissident is philosophical because beyond tyrannical politics lies a human truth that was crushed and rejected. This is why the revolutions of 1989 aimed to restore being to its true place.

---

* Lech Wałęsa was the co-founder of the independent Polish trade union Solidarity. In 1983 he won the Nobel Peace Prize and would later serve as the President of Poland.

The Marxist ambition to reinvent man established a separation between the world *before* and the world *after*. The separation naturally turned out to be brutal, since it was, after all, a question of fabricating a new species. Entry into the new world was to occur through a sort of asceticism that was at once personal and social. In this process, each individual was to rid himself of the old man within. Each was to struggle against the temptation to return to the safe haven of received ideas. The communist makes himself out to be a man of the open seas: he burns his bridges behind him and rushes headlong into the absolutely new.

The dissident says that he wants to save what remains of these bridges. He regards this debris as "tracks,"[1] or "traces." The question is why he wishes to rescue a world that has almost disappeared, a world that our era has consciously tried to erase. This might look like the pathetic nostalgia of someone who cannot stop mourning the past, like the attachment to the old-fashioned that characterizes reactionaries, who are actually on the same side as the Communists: the former point to oldness as the absolute criterion of the good, the latter to newness. But for the dissident, the yardstick of *when* something happened is of no importance. The "good" is that which suits man, that which makes him happy.

In Kundera's[*] short story, "Edward and God,"[2] the hero is accused by his colleagues of going to church: how could a young man believe in God? Edward acknowledges all the theoretical reasons for abandoning belief in God: faith is a vestige, it takes us back to prehistoric times, it is not worthy of the new humanity. However, he shamefacedly says, "'I recognize that faith in God will lead us to obscurantism. I recognize that it would be better if He didn't exist. But when here inside I . . .' he pointed with his finger to his heart, 'feel that He exists . . .'" And a colleague concludes, "The struggle between the old and the new goes on not only between classes, but also within each individual man. Just such a struggle is going on inside our comrade here. With his reason he knows, but feeling pulls him back. We must help our comrade in this struggle, so that reason may triumph."

In Bulgaria in the 1950s, for the great feast of Orthodox Easter the regime did not actually close the churches but rather allowed only old

---

* Milan Kundera, the prominent Czech novelist whose works include *The Joke* (1967), *The Book of Laughter and Forgetting* (1978), and *The Unbearable Lightness of Being* (1984).

women to go in. A little boy who had accompanied his grandmother came out of the church with a candle in his hand and was beaten by the police in the street. The older women were confirming the order of the past. The little boy was committing an offense against the future.

Whether it makes itself manifest through Sovietism or in contemporary democracies, the ideology of progress always expresses a rejection of, even an accusation against, humanity, fallen from its throne because of "backwardness of conscience" or "mental immaturity." What is called "maturity" here is a purely rational age, as defined by elite opinion: "In periods of maturity it is the duty and the function of the opposition to appeal to the masses. In periods of mental immaturity, only demagogues invoke the 'higher judgment of the people.'"[3] In the France of the 1990s, objective and respectful mention was made of a survey indicating the indulgence the French showed toward soft drugs, but if a majority were to call for a return to capital punishment, the mood would turn to indignation over the reactionary character of our compatriots. Majority rule has its limits under an ideology of progress sui generis, as dictated by politically correct opinion, that functions as though it were an enlightened elite. What does the development of social maturity mean anyway, and with respect to what points of reference? "Questions of personal pride; prejudices such as exist everywhere against certain forms of self-abasement; personal feelings of tiredness, disgust, and shame—are to be cut off root and branch."[4] It means, wrote Koestler,* that man is to be torn away from his narrow world where he finds attention, remorse, and forgiveness. Today this would probably translate into tearing man away from his guilty past, from his heteronomous beliefs, from his backward behavior patterns of respect and trueness to himself. In either case, it means tearing down the meanings by which man establishes his bearings, finds his identity, and engages his future.

If it is indeed possible to speak of the development of individual conscience in history, it is nevertheless inappropriate to think of this development as a movement from childhood to adulthood. Soviet man and the individual of late modernity play a character who has exited history, the role of an invented mature adult. Neither is an adult in this sense. Nothing

---

* Arthur Koestler (1905–1983) was a Hungarian-born novelist, essayist, and influential anti-Communist. He is best known for his novel *Darkness at Noon* (1940).

allows us to believe that they are free of prejudices; they simply re-create other prejudices. Each, in his own way, lives on the sidelines of life. The ideology of progress equates happiness with "maturity," or replaces happiness with "maturity" as a criterion of the good. Maturity means a distancing from childhood. The more society differentiates itself from the past, the better it will be.

Dissidence is devoted to preserving human unity over time. It refuses to relegate our predecessors to the shadows of the past, to the realm of "societies in their infancy." It believes that they participate in the same condition as do we. In reality, it is possible that although they are dead, they are also more alive than we are. It is possible that in order to distance ourselves from them, we have buried ourselves alive. What binds us to them are the "traces."

These "traces," or vestiges, are nocturnal remains, aspects of man's dependence. The dissident seeks to rescue a truth about man, the kind of truth from which man is entirely liberated only at the cost of self-destruction. That is how the persistence, even the obstinate survival, of these traces, these remnants, is explained. They are what is left of reality when one attempts to dismantle it, and manages then only to live in an unreal world: "Reality is a wounded animal that drags itself around in search of a place to hide, leaving behind a trail of blood."[5] The trail is what lingers of the truth, if what one means by truth is consistency with present and living reality, not consistency with a supposed future reality. "The dissident," writes Predrag Matvejević,[*] "is a hostage of truth."[6] The dissident volunteers to keep watch over this exposed and threatened truth, to remain vigilant so that it does not entirely disappear.

The world of the Soviets and the world of the West both have their roots in the sacralization of progress, or in the certitude according to which the sole criterion of the good is liberation from previously held beliefs. The France of today would concur with the reproach Edward's colleagues in communist Bohemia leveled at him: how indeed can a young man possibly do something like go to church? A large number of reforms are rationalized as progress defined in terms of liberation. Those who dissociate

---

[*] Predrag Matvejević, a writer born in 1932 in Bosnia Herzegovinia, has lived and taught in France and Italy. His book *Mediterranean Breviary: A Cultural Landscape* (1987) has been translated into many languages.

progress and the good, who suggest that progress be judged in light of the good and not the contrary, are accused of being reactionaries. In other words, to better society is increasingly to extract man from his habitat, to disentangle him from all the networks of meaning that imprison and shape him. But this process alienates him. Like totalitarian ones, Western societies also attempt, and for the very same reasons, methodically to reconstruct cultural reality. But in order to do this, they use derision instead of terror, which is merely another way of practicing exclusion. As a replacement for physical constraint, verbal contempt is an extreme measure, one that marks the uninterrupted continuation of hatred.

The conscious will to nullify the religious question and keep man apart from God was solemnly proclaimed in the Universal Declaration of Human Rights of 1948. The Preamble states: "Whereas disregard and contempt for human rights have resulted in barbarous acts which have outraged the conscience of mankind, and the advent of a world in which human beings shall enjoy freedom of speech and belief and freedom from fear and want has been proclaimed as the highest aspiration of the common people. . . ." Thus, in an authoritarian fashion and by decree, the highest aspiration to which we can lay claim was assigned to the temporal realm. The heavens were closed by magistrate's order! The term "proclaimed" indicates officiality, ultimately in a comical way since it is rather difficult to decree an aspiration. We know that the declaration was written with a view to universality and owes much of its shape to concessions made to the Soviet regime, which never did sign it. Nevertheless, since 1989 no attempt has been made to rework this proclamation—on this point or on any other.[7]

Social aspirations are not everything there is to humanity. Today we live in a truncated world. To treat lightly grave questions, those which weigh heavily upon existence, is to show contempt for the human beings who ask them. Religious questions cannot be rubbed out like punctuation errors. They are our heritage, they characterize and differentiate us: "The absolute cannot be eradicated, it can only be degraded."[8] To deprive humanity of a dimension of existence, whether it be religious, moral, or aesthetic, amounts to an abduction of being—a philosophical crime even if it is no longer a political one. He who is made uneasy by questions of good and evil becomes neither a noble savage nor a neutral and colorless being, for such a being does not exist: any passing cruelty, if it is the least bit persuasive or appealing, attaches itself to his amorphous conscience

597

and conquers it. He who no longer sees the necessity of discerning the boundary separating truth from falsehood will not take on the peaceful countenance of a newborn child but will rather be receptive to every passing bit of nonsense, willing to believe the assertions of any guru. The abduction of being is a violent story in which we have perhaps not yet witnessed the worst chapter.

Nietzsche described the great questions about which humanity wondered as illusions. In fact it is the will to deny them that has turned out to be an illusion. In a wild maelstrom of irrationality, late modernity simultaneously derides spirituality and bemoans the triumph of materialism, proclaims moral relativism and becomes indignant over the spread of pedophilia, claims that all is in vain and deplores a society where boredom can lead to suicide. Every society expresses what it has been given. Even though they are always debatable, answers to the eternal questions of mankind are all that can raise barriers, however fragile, against the chaos of meaninglessness. One might argue that our answers will be insufficient and prone to pretension, or that suffering will reappear along with hope. Supervielle,* speaking of human faces, described them as being "awkwardly immortal." Seeking to avoid, out of pride, the label "awkwardly," modernity preferred to abandon religious questions altogether. The inhabitants of late modernity need to reconnect with their humanity.

Many ways of being and thinking, say the dissidents, have been decreed old-fashioned and yet have survived in secret. It is possible that these remnants represent in fact an imposing proportion of the structures of existence, even though we view them as old foolishness, or as foolishness because they are old. It is possible, too, that they are not mere residue that the winds of history are destined to erode, but structures without which we could not live.

Of course, these pesky remnants remind us of our dependence, but to forbid their recognition would be to accept a lesser way of being. It is true that, in a way, man is alienated from the very habitat that nourishes him. Yet can one deprive him of it for that reason and then call such deprivation alienation? Am I alienated by that which enables me to live? Dissidence emphasizes two aspects of this underground world which obstinately resists all attempts at systematic eradication: prejudice and scruples.

---

* Jules Supervielle (1884–1960), a French poet.

Prejudice takes root in specific times and places and reflects an era's genealogies of thought. Prejudice has often lost its justification through overuse, long use, and habituation. Modernity hunts down prejudice, often for good reason, because it is a conduit for errors that have never been challenged. Modernity detests prejudice to the point that it seeks a kind of crystal-clear reasoning, based on pure objectivity. Ultimately it demands a form of reasoning that for man is unattainable. For what is human thought stripped of the impressions, moods, and passions that history leaves in its wake like so many layers of sediment? Kundera's hero describes belief in God as a feeling. "No one has ever yet proved that God exists," insists his interlocutor. Indeed. This prejudice nevertheless forces itself upon the character's mind like a kind of extension of the self, its inner structure, and the atmosphere in which the self thrives. It is easy to see the danger prejudice poses. But what should also be seen is the danger of a life without a history, a life deprived of its unfounded fears, its secret venerations, and its indescribable superstitions. A man who was able to know the world by objective reason alone would be deprived of any personal ways of thinking: modernity depersonalizes by rationalizing. To want to rescue prejudice, therefore, does not mean to defend obscurantism, but rather to defend the shadowy side of man that makes of him an individual being through his complex relationships to time and to inner and outer events.

It is quite possible that what is most important for us is precisely what cannot be proved: for example, the intrinsic dignity of every human being. This paradox becomes clearly visible when the rational systems of modernity give rise to acts that we cannot help but see as human catastrophes. This tendency leads us to take up the defense of scruples (from the Latin *scrupulous*, or little pebble), which bother the moral conscience like pebbles lodged in a shoe. Such doubts about the rightness of an action to be undertaken reveal the difficulty of embodying moral precepts in concrete existence. They may, as is true in the case in point, represent the last remnants of conscience after customary or historical morality has been, or is about to be, thrown out the window. Scruples are what resist the will to transform or destroy morality. They show up in the writings of Darwin and the first advocates of eugenics at the end of the nineteenth century: basic reason, they say, would have us not prolong or even destroy the lives of "undesirables," and yet our scruples keep us from doing so; thus, civilization is rushing toward its ruin.[9] Scruples here rest on no clear foundation, the thinking of the time rejects them, and social analysis demolishes them. They represent a tiny and contemptible obstacle to grandiose undertakings. But it is precisely these seemingly insignificant objections which must be listened to, for they are bearers of the meaning—albeit sometimes unfathomable and irrational—of our common existence. The one who sweeps away our last scruples, the one who presides over the auto-da-fé of scruples, is Hitler.

Today we are inundated with reasons to go ahead with human cloning and to create genetically perfect children; we are restrained from indulging these ambitions solely by scruples, which stand in the way with all the insolence of a pebble in a shoe. Any ninth grade student could come up with the necessary arguments to junk these scruples, which grate upon the conscience and paralyze it without any serious reason, since they come from a morality we are determined to reshape according to our needs. These bothersome remnants are perhaps more than just remainders of an ancient world to be eradicated: they are perhaps the ultimate and persistent traces of a human truth that we rashly wish to efface.

The untiring defense of these traces, which are visible in prejudices and scruples, is in no way similar to defending traditional values or tradition as a value. Although the defense of these traces does claim that the future is not necessarily better with respect to the idea of progress, it does not claim that the past was necessarily better either. That question is beyond this debate. In this regard, the defense offered by the dissident contests not progress, but rather the ideology of progress. It wishes to put its finger on what deserves to endure, because there are things the absence of which is much worse than their presence. Defending these traces can only be undertaken at a time of decisive tabula rasa. It is when human existence has been thrown into complete disarray that the ineffaceable becomes fully visible.

Just what are these traces of? What is the foundation that has been destroyed, that was or still is under attack, but that we need in order to live? If the question is complex and controversial, it is first of all because the question itself contains two questions that are too often thought to be identical. The first concerns anthropology: what is man, and what are the limits beyond which we begin to destroy him as such? The second concerns cultural anthropology: what are the cultural referents that Western man cannot forgo except by losing what he himself defines as his own identity?

The twentieth century went so far in its questioning of foundational values and human limitations that it attempted to strip European man entirely of both. And in fact this is still going on. It is as if, in the process of dismantling our cultural edifice, the twentieth century could not be content with merely attacking its foundations, but had to attack the very ground on which this culture, like all others, rests.

The vertigo of self re-creation even goes so far as to deny, for example, that humans are inevitably sexed beings, and, consequently, that there is a complementarity between the two genders, man and woman: the open subversion of this norm prevents any properly anthropological discussion of the issue.[10] This ultimately represents a radical rejection of human finiteness, if it is true that sexuality expresses our fundamental insufficiency as a need for the other, which is described in all our myths of origin: the eternal God of the Bible does not create a laborer and a poet, but a man and a woman; the pride of the hermaphrodites, who believed themselves to be self-sufficient, writes Plato, led Zeus to cut them in half.[11] In various forms, this pretension to self-sufficiency oozes from every pore of late modernity.

Nonetheless, our relentless self-questioning focuses on, above all else, the essential reference points of European culture; it is no longer a matter of anthropology, but of cultural anthropology, even if the boundary remains difficult to establish. In this questioning, the sometimes clear and sometimes implicit intention is to challenge not only the human condition in general, but certain essential foundations of our culture. Within that framework, the scruple of which the dissidents speak arises in opposition not to human beings as they might be, but in opposition to Western human beings as they wish to be. We can indeed cast aside entire categories of our cultural referents, but at what cost? In this abandonment, will we remain conscious, thinking beings—the persons-as-subjects whose contours are outlined by our culture? Do we really want to reject this figure, the subjective self? This is the real question. As humans, we are structured by our awareness of finiteness. As Europeans, we live in a cultural world structured by the figure of the person-subject. Insofar as they are being contested, these two interlocking worlds call for justification.

36

Totalitarianism:
Between Religion and Science
(2001)

Tzvetan Todorov

Totalitarianism extends a promise of plenitude, of a harmonious life and of happiness. While it is true that the promise is not kept, it remains nevertheless, and we can always tell ourselves that next time it will be fulfilled and we will be saved. Liberal democracy does not extend the same sort of promise; it is only committed to allowing everyone to seek their own measure of happiness, harmony, and plenitude. In the best of circumstances, it insures the contentment of its citizens, their participation in the direction of public life, and justice in their relations with one another and with the State; it in no way promises salvation. Autonomy corresponds to the right to search for oneself, not to the certainty of finding. Kant seemed to believe that man should treasure this condition which gives him the means to emerge "from his self-imposed immaturity," [1] but in the end it remains uncertain whether everyone would, in fact, prefer maturity over immaturity, adulthood over childhood.

This promise of happiness for everyone gives us a way of identifying the category of thought to which the doctrine of totalitarianism belongs. As a theory, totalitarianism is a utopianism. When seen in the perspective of European history, utopianism is in turn revealed as an atheistic millennialism.

What is millennialism? It is a religious movement within Christianism (a "heresy") that promises believers salvation in this world, not in the kingdom of God. The original Christic message proclaimed the separation of two worlds; this is why, for instance, Saint Paul could proclaim that "there is neither Jew nor Greek, there is neither slave nor free, there is neither male nor female; for you are all one in Christ Jesus" (Gal. 3:28), without so much as questioning the status of master and slave, to say nothing of the other distinctions. From this perspective, equality and unity among men can be had only in the City of God; religion proposes to change nothing at the level of the world down here. Although it is true that Catholicism violated this principle when it became a state religion and involved itself in worldly affairs, it did not go so far as to promise salvation in this life.

This is exactly what the Christian millennialist movements that erupted since the thirteenth century preached. We have known since Norman Cohn's* pioneering work how diverse these movements could be. The new prophets announce the approach of the Last Judgment and, prior to this, the advent of the millennium, the thousand year reign inaugurated by the return of the Messiah. Their disciples decide that it is time to strip the rich of their wealth and institute perfect equality on earth. The Taborites of Bohemia, a radical sect of the fifteenth century, believed for their part that Christ's return was imminent and that his arrival would mark the dawning of a millennial kingdom characterized by equality and abundance—thus it was time to get ready. In the century following, Thomas Münzer took the lead of a millenarian revolt in Germany that condemned the wealth of princes as well as that of the Church, and incited peasants to seize it in order to accelerate the advent of a celestial kingdom on earth.

In contrast to these medieval or Protestant millennial movements, utopianism consists of the desire to build a perfect society through the efforts of man alone, without any reference to God. It is thus a second-degree deviation from the original Christian doctrine. Utopianism takes its name from utopia which is nothing more than an intellectual construct, an image of the ideal society. Utopia can have many functions. It can be a means of stimulating reflection or of critiquing the world as it is, but only utopianism proper attempts to introduce utopia into the real world. Utopianism is of necessity tied to coercion and violence (both equally present in those Christian millennialisms not content to wait for divine intervention), in that it seeks to introduce perfection into the here

---

* Norman Cohn, British historian and author of the influential work *The Pursuit of the Millennium* (1957).

and now while acknowledging that people are imperfect. This is why, as the Russian religious philosopher Semion Frank noted in 1941, "Utopianism, which presupposes the possibility of fully realizing the good by means of the social order, possesses an inherent tendency for despotism."[2] Totalitarian doctrines are particular cases of utopianism—the only ones we have known in the modern era—and of millennialism, meaning that, like *every* other salvation doctrine, they fall under the category of religion. To be sure, it is no accident that this religion without God prospers in the context of Christianity's decline.

The basis of this utopianism is, however, quite paradoxical for a religion. What we are dealing with is a doctrine brought into being before the advent of the totalitarian state, before the twentieth century—a doctrine that, at first glance, has nothing to do with religion: scientism. As Eric Voegelin notes, "Scientism has remained to this day one of the strongest Gnostic movements in western society." But millennialism itself grows in Gnostic soil.[3] And so we have to turn our attention to this additional doctrine.

Scientism takes as its point of departure a hypothesis about the structure of the world—that it is entirely coherent. Thus, as though the world were transparent, it can be known by human reason without lacunae. This task of knowing is entrusted to an appropriate praxis called science. No part of the world—material, spiritual, animate, or inanimate—can escape the grasp of science.

Obviously, this initial postulate has its consequences. If man's science manages to penetrate all of nature's secrets, if it allows him to reconstitute the chain of events contributing to each fact and every living being, it should then be able to modify these processes and to orient them in the desired direction. Science, an exercise in understanding the world, gives rise to technique, an exercise in transforming it. The sequence is already familiar to us: when primitive man, after having discovered the warmth of fire, tamed it and used it to heat his dwelling, the "natural" climate was transformed. Or, having much later recognized that certain cows produce more milk than others, or certain seeds more wheat per acre, modern man systematically practiced "artificial selection," which enhanced the work of natural selection. There is no contradiction here between an integral determinism that excludes free will, and the voluntarism of the technoscientist, which supposes exactly the opposite. If the transparency of reality also applies to the world of man, nothing prevents him from thinking about the creation of a new man, a species freed from the defects and impurities of its predecessor: what is logical for cows is logical for people. As Alain Besançon has concluded, here "Knowledge brings salvation." [4]

But what direction should this transformation of the species take? Who will have the competence to identify and analyze the meaning of these imperfections and of the perfection to which we aspire? In the examples already mentioned, the answer was simple: man wanted to be warm and to feed his hunger; his interest in these instances goes without saying. Everything that is good for man is good in general. But what if this entails the modification of the human species as such? Scientism tells us that science, once again, will provide us with the answer. The objectives of mankind and of the world are simply a by-product, an automatic effect, of the work of knowledge—so automatic in fact that the follower of scientism often does not even take the trouble to include them in his calculations. Marx, in his famous eleventh thesis on Feuerbach, declared with satisfaction that "philosophers have *interpreted* the world in various ways; the point however is to *change* it." [5] Not only does the technique (or transformation) proceed directly from science (or interpretation), but, moreover, the nature of this transformation does not even merit mentioning since this is itself the product of knowledge. A few decades later, Hippolyte Taine* would spell this out in full: "Science achieves morality by seeking only the truth." [6]

The notion that science produces the ideals of society and the individual along with other types of knowledge carries important consequences. If ultimate ends were merely an effect of individual choice then each person would have to allow that their choice might not coincide with their neighbor's; as a consequence it would become necessary to accommodate other interests, to practice tolerance and to look for compromises. Several conceptions of the good would coexist. But the same does not apply to the findings of science. Here, the false version is mercilessly dismissed and nobody thinks to ask for a little more tolerance on behalf of the refuted hypotheses. Since there is no room for several conceptions of the truth, an appeal to pluralism is out of the question; only errors are many, truth is one. If the ideal is the outcome of a demonstration, and not an opinion, then it must be accepted without dispute.

---

* Hippolyte Taine (1828–1893), the influential French historian.

Scientism rests on the existence of science, but it is not in itself scientific. Its underlying assumption, the total transparence of reality, cannot be proved or disproved. The same goes for its intended outcome—the production of objectives as part of the process of knowledge. At both its foundations and its summit, scientism demands an act of faith ("faith in reason" Renan[*] would say[7]). In this respect, it belongs to the family of religion and not to that of science. To be convinced, one need only look at the attitude adopted by totalitarian societies, built on scientistic premises, toward their own projects: while the normal rule of science is to allow free rein to criticism, these societies demand that objections be silenced and that submission be blind, just as one would in the case of religion.

Scientism is not science, this point needs to be emphasized. It is, rather, a worldview which appears more like an excrescence on the body of science. This is why totalitarian regimes can adopt scientism without necessarily encouraging scientific research. They have good reason not to since this would require submission solely to the quest for truth rather than to dogma. The Communists, like the Nazis, prohibited this course of action: the former by renouncing "bourgeois biology" (and thus Mendel[†]), the latter by condemning "Jewish physics" (and thus Einstein). In the Soviet Union, to challenge the biology of Lysenko,[‡] the psychology of Pavlov,[§] or the linguistics of Marr[¶] could land you in a concentration camp. And so these countries condemned themselves to scientific provincialism. The totalitarian states no longer needed cutting edge scientific research to execute their crimes: there's nothing scientifically prodigious about firearms, poisonous gas or blows from a cudgel. And yet, there is a relationship to science to be discovered in all of this. A mutation has taken place: as it became "possible" to grasp the universe in its totality, the means to improve it became equally global. It was this mutation that transformed the eternal

---

[*] Renan. See note on page 107.

[†] Gregor Johann Mendel (1882–1884), the Austrian Augustinian monk, whose work helped lay the foundation for the modern science of genetics.

[‡] Trofim Lysenko (1898–1976) was a Soviet biologist, for a time favored by Stalin, whose ideas had disastrous effects on Soviet agriculture.

[§] Ivan Pavlov (1849–1936) was a prominent Russian physiologist famous for the idea of the conditioned reflex.

[¶] Nicholas Marr (1865–1934), the Georgian-born linguist.

evil of man into the unprecedented evil of the twentieth century. Thus radical innovation was introduced into human history.

The monism of these regimes develops out of the same project: since a single rational thought can master the entire universe, there is no longer any need to maintain false distinctions, between groups in society, between spheres in the life of the individual, or between different opinions. Truth is one—the world of man must be one as well.

How does one situate scientism in history? If we restrict ourselves to the French tradition, its premises are to be found in Descartes. Although he begins by excluding everything having to do with God from the domain of rational knowledge, in what remains, the part of the world "in which theology doesn't dabble,"[8] total knowledge is deemed possible provided that it is entrusted to only reason and will. Hence it is not beyond man to think of himself as the master of nature and, in some ways, "like God"[9] himself. With such knowledge, a single "architect" might then rethink the organization of the state and its citizens (a project that Descartes judges possible but undesirable). The direction of change will at last be guided exclusively by the work of knowledge. Common good will develop automatically from scientific work, "its truths will dispose minds to sweetness and harmony."[10]

These ideas would later by taken up, amplified, and systematized by the "materialists" of the seventeenth and eighteenth centuries. Let's follow the example of nature instead of burdening ourselves with moral laws! says Diderot* facetiously—implying first of all, that one can know this nature (and who better than a scientist to procure this knowledge for us?), and that one then obey the precepts that automatically proceed from this knowledge. But it was mostly after the French Revolution that scientism insinuated itself into politics, insofar as the new State was supposed to be founded on the dictates of reason and not on arbitrary tradition. This notion proliferated in the nineteenth century among a wide range of thinkers, among both friends and enemies of the Revolution. So great was the prestige of science at this moment that one could even imagine it taking the place of faltering religion. This was the common claim

---

* Denis Diderot (1713–1784), the French philosopher and prominent Enlightenment figure. He was the co-founder and principle editor of the *Encyclopédie*.

among French utopianists and positivists like Saint-Simon* and Auguste Comte,† conservative dilettantes like the Comte de Gobineau,‡ and among learned historians like Renan and Taine, intellectual masters of the liberal intelligentsia and critics of democracy. It was during this period that the two major varieties of scientism were sketched out: historical scientism, of which Karl Marx was the most influential thinker, and biological scientism, of which Gobineau remains emblematic.

Thus scientism is incontestably a part of modernity, that is if one intends the word modernity to designate doctrines advocating that society receive its laws not from God or tradition, but from men themselves. It also implies the existence of science, of a knowledge that is mastered through human reason alone rather than being mechanically handed down from one generation to another. But it is not, as so many brilliant minds have often repeated, the hidden truth, the inevitable outcome of the whole of modernity. Totalitarianism, a regime inspired by modernity's principles, is not the secret and fatal slope of democracy. There is more than one family of thought at the core of modernity and neither voluntarism, the egalitarian ideal, the demand for autonomy, nor rationalism lead automatically to totalitarianism. The doctrine of scientism is perpetually combated by other doctrines which also lay claim to modernity in its broadest sense. In a particularly revealing manner, this struggle pits the partisans of scientism against those who are looked to as the thinkers of democracy, the humanists.

Humanists challenge the assumption of a total transparency of reality, and thus the possibility of knowing it without omission. Montesquieu, their representative in the first half of the eighteenth century, raised a dual objection. First, concerning every part of the universe, it needed to be subjected to what one today calls the "principle of precaution." The universe possesses, to be sure, a coherence that is knowable in theory; but this is far from true in practice. The concrete causes of each phenomenon are so numerous, the interactions so complex, that we can never be certain of the outcome of our knowledge. As long as doubt remains, it is better to refrain from radical and irreversible actions (which does not mean, however, from all action).

---

* Saint-Simon. See note on page 168.

† Auguste Comte (1798–1857) was a French philosopher. He is widely known as the founder of sociology and the doctrine of positivism.

‡ Gobineau. See note on page 206.

More fundamental still, no knowledge can ever present itself as absolute and definitive without endangering its status as knowledge and becoming instead just another act of faith. The ambitions of utopianism are therefore doomed from the outset: the absence of a global transparence authorizes only local and provisory improvements. The universality that followers of scientism claim and the one claimed by humanists are consequently not the same. Scientism is founded on a universality of reason, the solutions found by science apply by definition to everyone, even if they provoke the suffering of, or indeed, the loss of some. Humanism, on the other hand, assumes the universality of humanity: all human beings have the same rights and merit equal respect, even if their modes of living remain different.

The distinction between the two doctrines does not end here. The world of man is not simply a part of the universe; it has its specific features. This consists of the fact that men possess a consciousness of themselves that in some way permits them to detach themselves from their own being and to act counter to the determinations that they are subject to. Montesquieu writes, "Man, as a physical being, is like other bodies governed by invariable laws. As an intelligent being, he incessantly transgresses the laws established by God, and changes those that he himself establishes."[11] In retort to his friend Gobineau who was explaining to him that individuals obey the laws of their race, Tocqueville professed, "In my eyes human societies like individuals are something only through the exercise of freedom."[12] To believe that one understands man in his entirety is to understand him poorly. Even knowledge of animals is imperfect: it may turn out that the milk cows of today will become barren tomorrow. But the knowledge of man is unachievable in principle, insofar as people are animals endowed with the capacity for freedom. This is why one can never predict with certainty what their conduct will be from day to day.

It is moreover an acrobatic leap of logic to presume to derive what should be from what is. The observer of the world of human action discovers the effects not of right, but of might: the strongest survive at the expense of the weakest. But might does not make right, and with this we reply along with Rousseau that "it would be possible to employ a more logical method, but none could be more favorable to tyrants."[13] In order to decide upon the direction of change, therefore, one cannot simply observe and analyze facts, a task for which science is particularly well suited; one must invoke objectives that offer a voluntary choice, ones that presume both arguments and counterarguments. Ideals cannot be true or false, only more or less lofty.

Knowledge does not produce morality. Educated beings are not necessarily good. This is the major criticism that Rousseau addresses to his contemporaries, the men and scientists of the Enlightenment (of course Rousseau also belongs to the Enlightenment, but in a sense much more profound than Voltaire or Helvétius*). "We can be men without being scholars," [14] he says in one of his more memorable phrases. And, as for political regimes, democracy is a regime of all citizens, not only the knowledgeable and educated. The politics of democracy imply not knowledge of the truth, but free will (autonomy). This is why democracy fosters pluralism, not monism: not only errors are multiple, so too are human desires.

The democratic project, founded on humanist thought, does not lead to the establishment of a paradise on earth. This is not to say that it ignores the evil that is in the world and in man or that it resigns itself to evil, but it does not imagine that this evil can be radically extirpated once and for all. "And so must we do with good and evil, which are consubstantial with our life," [15] Montaigne writes, while Rousseau states that "good and evil flow from the same source." [16] If good and evil are consubstantial with our lives, it is because they give rise to human freedom, the possibility we have at any moment of choosing between several options. The common source of good and evil is our sociability and our incompleteness. This means that we need others to insure the sense of our existence. This need can be satisfied in two complementary ways: one can cherish others and seek to make them happy, or one can subjugate and humiliate them in order to revel in one's power over them. Having understood the inseparable character of good and evil, humanists abandon the idea of a global and definitive solution to human difficulties. Human beings can only be free from the evil that is in them by being "freed" from their humanity itself. It is futile to hope that a political regime or a powerful technology can bring definitive relief to suffering.

Scientism and humanism contradict one another in their definition of the objectives of human society. Scientism entirely excludes "subjectivity from its vision and along with it the contingency that makes up the will

---

* Claude Adrien Helvétius (1715–1771), another Enlightenment figure of lesser prominence than Voltaire whose philosophical ideas are often associated with utilitarianism.

of the individual. The objectives of society must develop out of the observation of the impersonal processes characteristic of humanity as a whole, indeed of the universe in its totality. Nature, the world, and humanity command; individuals only submit. For humanism, on the other hand, the role of individuals need not necessarily be reduced purely and simply to that of means. This reduction, Kant tells us, is possible in a limited and circumscribed fashion, in order to attain intermediate objectives; but the ultimate objective is still individual human beings: the whole of humanity but taken one person after another.

Violence as a means of imposing the good is not intrinsically linked to scientism, it has existed since time immemorial. The French Revolution did not need a scientistic justification to legitimize the Terror. However, at a certain point in time, elements that had hitherto remained isolated began to operate in conjunction with one another: the revolutionary spirit which implied recourse to violence, the millennialist dream of building a terrestrial paradise in the here and now, and finally the doctrine of scientism which postulated that total knowledge of the human species was attainable. This moment corresponds to the birth of totalitarian ideology. Even if the seizure of power took place in a peaceful manner (as did Hitler's, as opposed to Lenin's or Mussolini's), the project of creating a new society inhabited by the new man and of resolving every problem once and for all—a project that demanded revolution—was maintained in all totalitarian countries. One can be a follower of scientism without the millennialist dream and without the call to violence (like many technician-experts today) just as one can be a revolutionary without the doctrine of scientism, like so many poets at the beginning of the twentieth century who proclaimed their desire for a freeing of the primordial elements. Only totalitarianism demands the conjunction of these three forces.

Neither revolutionary violence nor millennialist aspirations lead by themselves to totalitarianism. In order to establish its intellectual premises, one has to add the proposition of a total mastery of the universe carried forward by the spirit of science and, moreover, by the doctrines of scientism. Conditioned by Cartesian radicalism and Enlightenment materialism, this doctrine blossomed in the nineteenth century: only then could the totalitarian project unfold. I must insist that it is only a question here of the ideological roots of totalitarianism—because obviously there are other roots: economic, social, and political (in a narrower sense).

When does the first outline of the totalitarian society emerge? Marx's writings and Gobineau's were published in the middle of the century; they illustrate scientism, but do not present a detailed picture of a future society (Gobineau, it must be said, was hardly a utopianist, since he only foresaw decadence). The theoretical and literary texts of Nikolai Chernyshevsky,* a great inspiration for Lenin, emerged in the 1860s: his scientistic manifesto *The Anthropological Principle in Philosophy* in 1860 and his *roman à thèse What Is to Be Done?* three years later. Nechayev's† *Revolutionary Catechism*, which deals more with revolutionary practice than a project for a society to be created, was written in 1869 and made public in 1871.

One of the most revealing texts emerging out of this context, and, at the same time, one of the least known, is the third *Dialogue philosophique* by Ernest Renan, which dates to 1871.[17] In it, a character named Théoctiste exposes, for the first time it seems, the principles of the future totalitarian state. Here, the ultimate objectives of society are not derived from the demands of individual beings, but from the species as a whole, indeed of living nature in its entirety. The great law of life is nothing more than the "desire to exist," more powerful than all other laws and human conventions. The law of life is the reign of the strongest and the subjugation of the weakest. From this perspective, the destiny of the individual is unimportant—it is to be sacrificed in the service of a higher endeavor. "The sacrifice of a living being to an end willed by nature is legitimate" (p. 623). Because we must completely obey the laws of nature, we must first of all know the nature of these laws. This is to be the task of the scientists. Once masters of knowledge, they quite naturally are attributed power. "The elite among intelligent beings, who master the most important secrets of reality, would dominate the world *by* the powerful means of action at their disposal and would cause the greatest reason possible to reign on earth" (p. 611). The world would thus be directed, not by philosopher kings, but by "positivist tyrants" (p. 614). Once initiated into the secret of the natural order of the universe, the latter would not be obliged to maintain it, but rather, as good technicians, should extend the work of nature in the improvement of the species. "It is up to science to take up the work at the point where nature left off" (p. 617). The species must be perfected,

---

* Chernyshevsky. See note on page 564.

† Nechayev. See note on page 564.

provided with superior intellectual and physical capacities, and purged, if need be, of every instance of defective humanity.

The future state founded on these principles opposes democracy at *every* step. The objective, indeed, is not to give power to *everyone*, but to reserve it for the best; not to cultivate equality but to encourage the spread of the supermen. Individual freedom, tolerance, and dialogue have no role to play because one always has at one's disposal a single truth which requires submission not debate. "The great work will be accomplished by science, not by democracy" (p. 610). Thus the new state justifies its efficacy, far superior to that of democracy which is obliged always to consult, to understand, and to convince. This opposition, in some ways surprising, is also revealing. Science and democracy are sisters born out of the same movement, a movement that endorsed autonomy and emancipation from the tutelage of tradition. If, however, science stops being simply knowledge about the world and becomes a guide for society, a producer of ideals (that is, if science mutates into scientism), it enters into conflict with democracy: the search for the truth should not be confused with the search for the good.

To ensure the proper order of affairs within a country, the scientistic state must provide itself with the appropriate tool: terror. The problem of the old tyrannies tied to religion was that they wielded a threat that was, alas, too fragile: from the moment man stops believing in hell or in devils, he thinks that everything is permitted! This decay has to be remedied by creating "not a chimeric hell, the existence of which one cannot prove, but a real hell" (p. 613). The creation of this space, a death camp that strikes terror into every heart and brings into being the unconditional submission of all is justified because it serves the good of the species. "The being who possesses science puts limitless terror into the service of truth" (p. 615). To institute this policy of terror, the scientific government places at its disposal a special corps of well-trained individuals, "obedient machines, indifferent to moral repugnance and capable of every type of ferocity" (p. 614). This demand reappears fifty years later in the mind of Dzerżhiński, the founder of the Soviet political police, the Cheka, who described his subordinates as "determined comrades, hard, solid, without souls."[18]

In terms of external policy, Renan continues, the scientists in power would have to have the ultimate weapon, one that insures the immediate destruction of the majority of the enemy population so that universal domination will be assured. "The day when those who are privileged with reason possess the means to destroy the planet, their sovereignty will be established; these privileged men will reign with absolute terror because they will hold the existence of everyone in their hands" (p. 615). Thus, strength of mind leads to material strength.

These are, in broad strokes, Renan's ideals, and one must admit that the utopianisms appearing half a century later bear an uncanny resemblance to his dream. The likeness is particularly striking with Nazism, where the project of producing a new man is given the same biological interpretation. Beyond this, Renan goes so far as to envisage the realization of utopia not in France, where it would come into conflict with other traditions, but in Germany, a country "that shows little concern for the equality or even the dignity of individuals" (p. 619). The correspondence with Communist society is not, however, any less pronounced, only better concealed. Communist society professed the ideal of equality but, we should remember, it by no means conformed to this ideal. In practice, the avant-garde role attributed to the party, and the underlying insistence of unconditional submission to the leaders, again reveals the cult of the superman at work in all totalitarian societies. In spite of egalitarian slogans to the contrary, daily life itself continued according to a well-established ritual of hierarchy.

Utopian scientism is the core of the totalitarian project. Can we say therefore that it is entirely alien to democracy? No. In all truth, scientism is but one tendency among many that exist in democracy. Every time we think that we totally understand the world and think that we must change it in the direction indicated solely by knowledge—by physics, by biology or by economics—we act in the spirit of scientism regardless of the type of the political regime we live in. The overflowing of scientism in democratic countries is quite frequent: one sees it for example as soon as political decisions are presented as ineluctable effects of economic laws discovered by scientists, or of natural laws accessible only to doctors and biologists. Politicians love to hide behind the authority of experts. Nevertheless, a fundamental distinction is lost as soon as scientism becomes a utopianism, a plan for a perfect society that must be carried out immediately. The great task, one might say in opposition to Renan, is accomplished by democracy, not by science. Instead of being in control of society, science is here in the service of society. This is also why democracy does not preach revolution, does not rely on terror and, in general, favors pluralism over monism.

Totalitarianism: Between Religion and Science

Fortunately, modern democracies have no aspirations of establishing a reign of perfection on earth and do not propose to produce an improved species of mankind, for, in contrast to the totalitarianisms of the twentieth century, these modern sorcerer's apprentices would be capable of going very far in this direction. They possess incomparable means of surveillance and control, wield weapons capable of the destruction of the entire planet, and count among their ranks scientists with the ability to master the genetic code and thus to manufacture, in the proper sense, a new breed of man. Compared to genetic manipulation, both the Communists' crude attempts to bring a new man into the world through reeducation and terror, and the Nazis' efforts to control reproduction and to eliminate allegedly inferior individuals and "races" seem like something from a distant past.

Should democracy, in resolutely turning its back on utopianism, completely renounce the idea of utopia? Not at all. Democracy is not a form of conservatism, a resigned acceptance of the world as it is. There is *no reason* to trap oneself in the logic of the "either/or" that totalitarians tried to impose on the spirit: one does not have to choose between a total renunciation of ideals and the desire to impose them by any means. Democracy, for its part, wants to replace what is with what should be—but it does not argue that the latter should be derived from the former. Lenin practiced monism and so subordinated the economic to the political. In democracy, the two remain distinct, but this does not mean that they are condemned to isolation. Economic forces will try to subordinate political agents: for their part, the latter can and should impose limits on the former on behalf of the ideals of society. A democratic utopia has the right to exist provided that it does not attempt to incarnate itself by force in the here and now.

What then are men's needs? The people of democratic countries or at least their spokesmen, have often believed that man aspires only to the satisfaction of his most immediate wants and material needs: more comfort, more ease, more leisure. In this regard, the strategists of totalitarianism have proven themselves superior anthropologists and psychologists. In a way that is less obvious and yet more imperious, man also needs goods that the material world does not provide. Human beings want their lives to have meaning, their existence to find its place in the order of the universe, for a connection to be established with the absolute. Totalitarianism, in contrast to democracy, claims to satisfy those needs, which is why it was freely chosen by the populations under consideration. Lest we forget, Lenin, Stalin, and Hitler were loved and wanted by the masses.

Democracies can ignore the human need for transcendence only at the risk of putting their very existence into jeopardy. How do they avoid that this need ends up in catastrophes like those that totalitarianism provoked in the twentieth century? Not by disregarding this aspiration but rather by resolutely separating it from the social order. The absolute and the structures of the state make poor bed-fellows; which is not to say that the absolute should simply disappear. Christ's original message is clear: "My kingdom is not of this world" (John 18:36): this does not mean that the kingdom does not exist, only that it is to be sought in the spirit of each individual and not in public institutions. When Christianity became a religion of the state, this message was set aside for centuries. A relationship with transcendence is no less necessary today than it once was; however, in order to avoid the totalitarian derivation, it must remain foreign to political programs (we will never build a paradise on earth), and yet it must continue to illuminate the internal lives of each one of us. One can experience ecstasy in front of a work of art or a landscape, in prayer or meditation, in the practice of philosophy or from the laughter of a child. Democracy does not fulfill the need for salvation or for the absolute; it cannot, on the other hand, afford to disregard its existence.

Acknowledgments

This is a book that has had a long gestation period, so there are many people to thank. Dan Mahoney and Paul Seaton first awakened me to the depth and profundity of dissident writers. After suggesting I read *The Captive Mind* years ago, Dan has continued to serve as a mentor as I explored the dissidents and began teaching them. I am forever grateful to them both. Jim Pontuso and Marketa Goetz-Stankiewicz have also encouraged my inquiries, especially in Havel and all things Czech. Peter Lawler gave me some crucial advice that would lead to the creation of the "Lessons" section of the book. They all made good suggestions about what to include as the contents took shape. A number of people read and commented on my introduction: Dan Mahoney, Paul Seaton, Marketa Goetz-Stankiewicz, Kate Graney, and Tim Burns. Peter Baehr is to thank for the title of the book.

Many people at Skidmore College deserve thanks. Jim Chansky let me try my hand at teaching a course on the dissidents during a summer term. Several student assistants helped me immensely. Leila Sterman was there at the very beginning, and her dogged pursuit of hard-to-find essays was critical. Without Leila, this project would never have gotten off the ground. Laurie Graham and Julia Grigel continued Leila's work as the book took its final shape. Amy Syrell and her staff in the Interlibrary Loan office at Skidmore have been terrific. Matthew Hockenos and Kris Szymborksi assisted me with many of the editorial footnotes. I want to thank

Acknowledgments

all of my colleagues in the Government Department for making teaching at Skidmore such a pleasure.

The Earhart Foundation and the Office of the Dean of the Faculty at Skidmore provided crucial financial support to cover permissions costs and as well as for my own work. I am grateful to Mark Hofmann, Associate Dean of the Faculty at the time, in particular.

Everyone at ISI Books has been terrific. An initial conversation with Jeremy Beer led to the proposal, and his encouragement at the beginning stages is much appreciated. Jennifer Fox has been a pleasure to work with throughout the process. Meghan Duke and Erica Ford did tremendous work gathering the permissions. Jed Donahue came on board at ISI in the middle of the process and saw things through to conclusion.

Finally, many thanks to my wife Natalie for her love and support. Not a day goes by when I am not thankful that she said yes when I popped the question. And there is no end to the joy of living with my two children Flagg and Maggie. I look forward to the day when they can appreciate the writings contained in this book.

Notes

The notes provided here from the essays by Friedrich, Besançon (both of his essays), Hassner, Malia, Burleigh, Delsol, and Todorov come from the authors themselves. The notes here from the essays by Strauss, Patočka, Solzhenitsyn, and Aron were provided by the editors of the essays in the place of their original publication in English.

I. Concepts

The Unique Character of a Totalitarian Society
Carl J. Friedrich

1. Sigmund Neumann, in *Permanent Revolution* (1942), treats them as basically alike; indeed his is the first comprehensive treatment of the general problems of totalitarian dictatorship. Franz Neumann, in *Behemoth* (1942 and later), on the hand, deals with the Hitler dictatorship as something quite distinctive, essentially the creation if not the creature of big business, the bureaucracy, and the army. Among earlier works, Alfred Cobban's *Dictatorship, Its History and Theory* (1939) on the one hand definitely links modern dictatorship with enlightened despotism, Bonapartism, and other tyrannical systems of the past, while on the other definitely treating Fascist and Communist dictatorship as alike. His book also undertakes to suggest the derivation of totalitarian dictatorship from Hobbes, Rousseau, and the French Revolution's doctrine of popular sovereignty; this theme has lately been developed brilliantly, though unconvincingly, by J. L. Talmon in *Totalitarian Democracy* (1952). Two other volumes also stressed the connection between Fascist and Communist dictatorship: *Dictatorship in the Modern World* (edited by

Notes

Guy Stanton Ford, 1935 and 1939), and Hans Kohn's *Revolutions and Dictator-ships* (1939). Among the books emphasizing either explicitly or by implication the distinctness of Fascism, mention might be made of E. B. Ashton (pseudonym), *The Fascist—His State and His Mind* (1937); Herbert W. Schneider, *Making the Fascist State* (1928); G. A. Borgese, *Goliath, the March of Fascism* (1937); Max Ascoli and Arthur Feiler, *Fascism for Whom?* (1938); and several books on Nazi Germany, including Frederick L. Schumann, *The Nazi Dictatorship* (1935 and later); Fritz Morstein Marx, *Government in the Third Reich* (1936 and later); Karl Loewenstein, *Hitler's Germany* (1939 and later). Konrad Heiden's *Der Führer—Hitler's Rise to Power* (1944), like the recent work by Alan Bullock, *Hitler—A Study in Tyranny* (1952), brings out the personal side of totalitarian dictatorship; this approach, while important, tends to obscure the uniqueness of totalitarian-ism. Bertram Wolfe's *Three Who Made a Revolution* (1938), and other works on Stalin, serve the same good purpose. The most searching study on the level where the impact of ideas upon political practice occurs is Hannah Arendt's *The Origins of Totalitarianism* (1951); it bears a certain resemblance to Hermann Rauschning's *The Revolution of Nihilism* (1939), and to Borgese's book cited above, but it devel-ops the important thesis that totalitarianism is an outgrowth of the establishment of dictatorship under modern conditions.

2. See *Constitutional Government and Democracy* (ed. 1941), chapter 20. The understanding of these political relationships is the most important aspect of soci-eties with which the student must be concerned; in the words of Aristotle, a politi-cal science is the highest or most important science.

3. This distinction was elaborated by Heinrich Rickert, *Kulturwissenschaft and Naturwissenschaft* (1898, 1910, and later), building upon studies of Wilhelm Dil-they, especially his *Einleitung in die Geisteswissenschaften* (1883). The point was central to the famous argument between Eduard Meyer and Max Weber, of which Max Weber's part is found in *Gesammelte Aufsaetze zur Wissenschaftslehre* (1922), "Kritische Studien auf dem Gebiet der kulturwissenschaftlichen Logik," 215–90.

4. Borgese, *Goliath*, sarcastically comments upon this very symptomatic escap-ism of the Western liberal. A striking instance of it, as far as the Soviet Union is concerned, is found in Maurice Hindus's *Mother Russia* (1942), but there are many others.

5. See Neumann, *Permanent Revolution*; Maxine B. Sweezey, *The Structure of the Nazi Economy* (1941); and R. A. Brady, *The Spiritual Structure of German Fascism* (1937).

6. Karl Loewenstein, *Hitler's Germany* (1940), and W. Ebenstein, *The Nazi State* (1943).

7. R. Hilferding, "State Capitalism or Totalitarian Economy," in *Modern Review* 1, 266–71.

8. James Burnham, *The Managerial Revolution* (1941).

9. The role of ideology is penetratingly discussed by Arendt, *Origins*, and in the article cited below, footnote 26.

10. This was written at the time Stalin was still living; there are some indica-tions, such as the appointment of Khrushchev instead of Malenkov to be general secretary of the party, that this may be less true in the future. But the searching inquiries of Merle Fainsod definitely point in this direction. See his "Controls and

Tensions in the Soviet System," *American Political Science Review*, 44, 266–82, and "The Komsomols—A Study of Youth under Dictatorship," *ibid.*, 45, 18–40, as well as *How Russia Is Ruled*, which I have been privileged to catch glimpses of in seminar discussions and conversations.

11. There have been considerable controversies on the question of the degree of rigidity of Soviet ideology. During the war it was customary among all those who wished to soft-pedal the potential conflict between the Soviet Union and the West to claim that ideology had become unimportant, in spite of the fact that Stalin and others repeatedly stressed it. For an indication of the "line," see as representative Robert E. Sherwood, *Roosevelt and Hopkins* (1948), especially pages 301–8. However, not only those who wished to play it soft, but also the self-styled "realist" school, denying the real significance of ideas and talking in terms of geographical and other kinds of "real" interest, have tended to take the line that Stalin was pursuing the policy of the Tsars of Russia and that ideology was little more than camouflage. Very interesting in this connection is Walter Lippmann's *U.S. Foreign Policy: Shield of the Republic* (1943), in which the two tendencies are combined. Lippmann, after demonstrating that the United States has never been willing to permit a power in continental Europe to become predominant, and then clearly recognizing that Russia will be the dominant power after the war (149), fails to draw the inevitable conclusion, except by way of insisting that the alliance must be maintained. He has some shrewd things to say about what will happen, if it is not (note the remark on page 148 on the conflict over territorial settlements), but characteristically Lippmann discusses the matter in terms of Russia rather than the Soviet Union, just as he speaks of Germany and the "German war" rather than Hitler and the Nazi state, thereby displaying his desire to minimize the ideological factor in terms of which this first world revolutionary war was actually fought. Barrington Moore, Jr., in *Soviet Politics—The Dilemma of Power* (1950), gives a discriminating discussion of the role of the ideology, to which he assigns a central role in the analysis of Soviet politics, while Julian Towster, in *Political Power in the U.S.S.R.* (1948), rightly started his discussion of Soviet government with a sketch of the underlying ideology. He speaks of it as "avowed theory" and comments at the outset that "an understanding of its [the USSR's] operative constitutional order would lack coherence without due attention to avowed theory." That the USSR's government is no "constitutional order" in terms of our analysis is obvious.

12. Recent developments suggest that the Soviet Union is abandoning this line again. As for Hitler's anti-Semitism, the damage done to his foreign policy, as well as the weakening of his domestic support are obvious. The problem has been explored in its ramifications by Hannah Arendt, *Origins of Totalitarianism*, chapters 6–9. However, her tendency is to overrate this aspect of Fascist ideology. Even early in the regime, mass support for Hitler was primarily based upon other factors, and anti-Semitism tended to weaken rather than strengthen Hitler's appeal with many, as was shown very convincingly on the basis of numerous psychological interviews by Theodore Abel, *Why Hitler Came into Power* (1938).

13. See also Harold D. Lasswell, *Power and Society*, § 6.5.

14. See Alfred Cobban, *Dictatorship—Its History and Theory* (1939); Carl Schmitt, *Die Diktatur von den Anfaengen des modernen Souveraenitaetsgedankens bis zum proletarischen Klassenkampf* (and ed., 1928).

15. The role of technology in the development of modern politics has received inadequate attention. Charles A. Beard, following Thorstein Veblen, occasionally lays stress upon it. James Burnham's *The Managerial Revolution* (1941) is built upon it, but the conclusions go beyond the evidence.

16. This is not strictly true, since the mass conversion continually attempted by totalitarian propaganda through the effective use of its monopoly of communications (factor 4) could not be carried through without it. This in turn affects the party and its dynamics.

17. In this connection the rate of literacy in Japan as contrasted with China used to seem significant, but would not seem to be similarly striking now. However, in our view the question as to whether China actually is a totalitarian dictatorship cannot be answered satisfactorily at the present time. No doubt the Chinese Communists are a totalitarian movement; but whether they will succeed in organizing China along totalitarian lines remains to be seen. If they do, the effect will probably entail the rapid reduction of illiteracy, as has happened in the Soviet Union in conjunction with the forward march of totalitarianism.

18. The objection that China does not fit this pattern—should not only be considered in the light of what is said in the previous footnote, but also in relation to the fact that the totalitarian developments in China are closely associated with the reception of these Western ideas. Sun Yat Sen's *Three Principles of the People*, probably the most influential book of modern China, provides ample evidence for this aspect of the matter.

19. See especially Stalin's great speech in the election of February 1946.

20. Konrad Heiden, in *Der Führer*, has given the most elaborate account to date, to which Alan Bullock's *Hitler* adds little. Very revealing, even as a title, is the book by E. Czech-Jochberg, entitled *Hitler—Eine Deutsche Bewegung* (1930).

21. From this our modern word state is in part derived, as the Medici party was called *it stato*. In the north, the estate of the king provided another source.

22. See, regarding this aspect, footnote 11 above.

23. See J. L. Talmon, *Totalitarian Democracy*; W. M. McGovern, *From Luther to Hitler* (1941); and Aurel Kolnai, *The War Against the West* (1938).

24. It is not a distinguishing feature of these totalitarian societies because such moral obtuseness has been recurrent in the history of human government. As far as amorality is concerned, Nero and Cesare Borgia yield little to contemporary dictators; indeed, their amorality seems more thoroughgoing, since they do not camouflage it by relating it to a presumably moral end, such as the Communist world society.

25. It may be recalled in this connection that Bodin, even though he seeks to give the sovereign very broad authority, declares the laws of succession inviolable. While it is incorrect to call these "constitutional laws," as has at times been done, it is clear that Bodin assumed that such a succession would be regulated by law. In a totalitarian dictatorship, such regulation is inconceivable.

26. That is why the dispute over the origins of totalitarianism is at once so sharp and so inconclusive; e.g., between Eric Voegelin, "The Origins of Totalitarianism" and Hannah Arendt's reply, *The Review of Politics*, 15, 68ff. Miss Arendt wisely remarks that her book is not really a study of the origins, but when she says that it "gives an historical account of the elements which crystallized into totalitarianism," she overstates the case for her remarkable book; for it deals only with

some of the elements, and they did not "crystallize," but were molded and used by the creators off totalitarianism. In her recent contribution to *Offener Horiz-ont—Festschrift fur Karl Jaspers* (1953), entitled "Ideologie and Terror," she rightly stresses the novelty and the creative aspect. In this connection, Bergsonian and Romantic prejudice to view all creation as somehow "good," and hence to over-look the "procreation in sin" and the possibility of fashioning the ugly which is wholly new. Man finds himself in a situation and he brings to his response such creative resources as are in him, both for good and evil.

On the Difficulty of Defining the Soviet Regime
Alain Besançon

1. Alain Besançon, *Présent soviétique et passé russe* (Paris: Hachette, 1980; reprinted 1986); originally published in *Contrepoint*, no. 20, 1976.
2. *Politics*, 3.7.
3. Rosa Luxemburg, *Centralisme et démocratie*, 1904.
4. Trotsky, *Nos tâches politiques*, 1904.
5. By Merle Fainsod (1958).
6. Cited by Solzhenitsyn in *The Gulag Archipelago* (French edition, le Seuil, 1974) vol. 1, 255. [Thomas P. Whitney renders Lenin's letter this way: "The basic con-cept, I hope, is clear . . . openly to set forth a statute which is both principled and politically truthful (and not just juridically narrow) to supply the motivation for the essence and the justification of terror, its necessity, its limits . . . it is necessary to formulate it as broadly as possible, for only revolutionary righteousness and a revolutionary conscience will provide the conditions for applying it more or less broadly in practice." See *The Gulag Archipelago*, vol. 1, trans. Thomas P. Whitney (Boulder, CO: Westview Press, 1998), 353.]
7. Raymond Aron, *Les étapes de la pensée sociologique*, (Paris: Gallimard, 1967). [Available in English as *Main Currents in Sociological Thought*, vol. 1 (New Bruns-wick: Transaction, 1998).]
8. Montesquieu, *The Spirit of the Laws*, bk. 5, ch. 13.
9. Raymond Aron, *Démocratie et totalitarisme*, (Paris: Gallimard, 1965), 319. [Available in English as *Democracy and Totalitarianism* (Ann Arbor: University of Michigan Press, 1990).]
10. Ibid., 287–88.
11. Ibid., 291.
12. Kostas Papaioannou, *L'ideologie froide*, (Paris: J.-J. Pauvert, 1967), 165.
13. Op. cit., 275: The key passage from *The Gulag Archipelago* is: "The imagina-tion and interior strength of Shakespeare's wicked characters stopped at ten cadav-ers. Because they did not have *ideology*. Ideology! It is ideology which brought the sought-for justification of wickedness, the long-term firmness necessary for wickedness. . . . It is in this way that the inquisitors based themselves upon Chris-tianity, conquerors upon the nation's glory, colonizers upon civilization, Nazis on race, Jacobins (today and yesterday) upon equality, fraternity, and the happiness of future generations." [*The Gulag Archipelago*, vol. 1, trans. Thomas P. Whitney, 173–74.]
14. Aron, *Démocratie et totalitarisme*, 302.

15. Ibid., 301–2.
16. Ibid., 294–95.
17. Annie Kriegel analyzed these two notions in "Notes sur l'idéologie dans le parti communiste français," *Contrepoint*, no. 3, 95–104.
18. Aron, 283–84.

Communist Totalitarianism:
The Transatlantic Vagaries of a Concept
Pierre Hassner

1. C. Friedrich and Z. Brzezinski, *Totalitarian Dictatorship and Autocracy* (New York: Harper, 1956).
2. A. Besançon, *Court traité de soviétologie à 'usage des autorités civiles, militaires et religieuses* (Paris: Hachette, 1976).
3. E. Voegelin, *The New Science of Politics* (Chicago: University of Chicago Press, 1952).
4. G. Breslauer, *Five Images of the Soviet Future: A Critical Review and Synthesis* (Berkeley: University of California Press, 1978).
5. "Conservateur de quoi?" *Commentaire*, (Autumn 1978), 357–59; and *Anatomie d'un spectre: l'économie politique du socialisme réel* (Paris: Calmann-Levy, 1981), 28–38.
6. S. Bialer, *Stalin's Successors* (Cambridge: Cambridge University Press, 1980).
7. See A. Inkeles and R. Bauer, *The Soviet Citizen: Daily Life in a Totalitarian Society* (Cambridge, Mass.: Harvard University Press, 1959).
8. K. Deutsch, "Cracks in the Monolith: Possibilities and Patterns of Disintegration in Totalitarian Systems," in *Totalitarianism* (Cambridge, Mass.: Harvard University Press, 1959).
9. P. Wiles, "Comment on Tucker's movement-regimes," *American Political Science Review*, 55 (1961), 290–93; P. Hollander, "Observations on Bureaucracy, Totalitarianism and the Comparative Study of Communism," *Slavic Review*, 26:2 (June 1967), 302–7; W. Odom, "A Dissenting View on the Group Approach to Soviet Politics," *World Politics*, July 1976, 542–67.
10. In *L'Italie et le fascisme* (1926), 221.
11. E. Halevy, *L'éra des tyrannies* (Paris: Gallimard, 1938).
12. W. Gurian, *Der bolschewismus* (Freiburg, 1931); E. Voegelin, *Die politischen Religionen* (Vienna, 1938).
13. M. Curtis, "Retreat from Totalitarianism," in C. Friedrich, M. Curtis and B. Barber, *Totalitarianism in Perspective: Three Views* (New York: Praeger, 1969), 153–80.
14. Z. Brzezinski, "Totalitarianism and Rationality," *American Political Science Review*, 50 (1956), 751–63.
15. R. Löwenthal, "Totalitaire and demokratishe Revolution" [1960], reprinted in B. Seidel and S. Jenkner, *Wege der Totalitarismus-Forschung* (Darmstadt, 1968), 359–82.
16. R. Tucker, "The dictator and Totalitarianism," *World Politics* 17 (1965), 555–84.
17. R. Tucker, "Does Big Brother really exist?," in *1984 Revisited: Totalitarianism*

Notes

in Our Century, ed. Irving Howe, (New York: Harper, 1983), 89–112.

18. P. Wiles, "Comment," 290–3; J. Azrael, "Varieties of De-Stalinization," in *Change in Communist Systems*, ed. Chalmers Johnson (Stanford: Stanford University Press, 1970), 135–52.

19. A. Meyer, *The Soviet Political System* (New York: Random House, 1965).

20. G. Skilling, "Soviet and Communist Politics: A Comparative Approach," *Journal of Politics*, 22:2 (May 1960), 300–13.

21. J. Hough, "The Soviet system: petrification or pluralism?" in *Dilemmas of Change in Soviet Politics*, ed. Z. Brzezinski (New York: Columbia University Press, 1969).

22. F. Castles, "Interest articulation: a totalitarian paradox," *Survey*, (Autumn 1969), 116–33.

23. Odom, "A Dissenting View," 542–67.

24. Susan G. Solomon, ed., *Pluralism in the Soviet Union: Essays in Honour of Gordon Skilling* (London: Macmillan, 1983).

25. J. Hough, "Pluralism, corporatism and the Soviet Union," ibid., 58.

26. W. Taubman, "The Change to Change in Communist Systems: Modernization Post-Modernization, and Soviet Politics," in *Soviet Politics and Society in the 1970s*, ed. H. Morton and N. Tokes (New York: Free Press, 1974).

27. J. Kirkpatrick, *Dictatorship and Double Standards* (Washington, D.C.: American Enterprise Institute, 1982).

28. Michael Walzer, "Failed Totalitarianism," in *1984 Revisited*, ed. Howe, 103–21.

29. See the contributions of A. Smolar, J. L. Domenach and J. Rupnik to *Totalitarismes*, ed. G. Hermet, P. Hassner and J. Rupnik (Paris: Economica, 1984).

30. A. Zinoviev, *Homo sovieticus* (Paris: Jiilliard, 1983).

31. M. Djilas, "The Disintegration of Communist Totalitarianism," in *1984 Revisited*, ed. Howe, 136–48.

32. W. Odom, "Choice and Change in Soviet Politics," *Problems of Communism*, (May–June 1983), 3–22.

33. M. Friedberg, "Cultural and Intellectual Life," in Robert S. Byrnes (ed.), *After Brezhnev: Sources of Soviet Conduct in the 1980s* (Bloomington, Indiana University Press, 1983).

34. K. Papïaoannou, *L'idéologie froide* (Paris: Pauvert, 1967).

35. Kolakowski, "Totalitarianism and the Lie," in *1984 Revisited*, Howe, ed.

36. Claude Lefort, *L'invention démocratique: Les limites de la domination totalitaire* (Paris: Fayard, 1981).

From Under the Rubble, What?
Martin Malia

1. See my article, "The August Revolution," *The New York Review of Books*, Sept. 26, 1991, for a more complete account of the collapse.

2. This model can be found in their classic *Totalitarian Dictatorship and Autocracy*, (Cambridge, MA: Harvard University Press, 1956).

3. In Chalmers Johnson, ed., *Change in Communist Systems* (Stanford, CA, Stanford University Press, 1970, 33–116).

4. See his monumental series, *History of Soviet Russia*, published in the 1950s.

5. Deutscher's main work was, of course, his outstanding biographies of Trotsky—*The Prophet Armed: Trotsky, 1879–1921*, (New York: Oxford University Press, 1954); *The Prophet Unarmed: Trotsky, 1921–1929*, (London and New York: Oxford University Press, 1959); and *The Prophet Outcast, Trotsky, 1929–1940*, (London and New York: Oxford University Press, 1963); and of Stalin—*Stalin: A Political Biography* (New York and London: Oxford University Press, 1949).

6. Leopold Haimson, "The Problem of Social Stability in Urban Russia, 1905–1917," *Slavic Review* (Columbus, OH), part 1, December 1964, 619–42; part 2, March 1965, 1–22.

7. The list of books that make up this wave is too long to include here. A good "short course" can, however, be found in the collection of articles in Daniel Kaiser, ed., *The Worker's Revolution in Russia, 1917: The View from Below*, (Cambridge: Cambridge University Press, 1987).

8. The two classic examples of this trend are Stephen F. Cohen, *Bukharin and the Bolshevik Revolution*, (Oxford: Oxford University Press, 1973); and Moshe Lewin, *Lenin's Last Struggle*, (New York: Pantheon, 1968).

9. See, for example, Sheila Fitzpatrick, ed., *Cultural Revolution in Russia, 1928–1931*, (Bloomington, IN: Indiana University Press, 1978); Sheila Fitzpatrick, *Education and Social Mobility in the Soviet Union, 1921–1934*, (Cambridge: Cambridge University Press, 1979); and her *The Russian Revolution*, (Oxford and New York: Oxford University Press, 1982); see also Jerry Hough, *The Soviet Prefects: The Local Party Organs in Industrial Decisionmaking*, (Cambridge, MA: Harvard University Press, 1979).

10. I am referring to Lynne Viola's *The Best Sons of the Fatherland*, (Oxford: Oxford University Press), 1987; and J. Arch Getty's *The Origins of the Great Purges: The Soviet Communist Party Reconsidered*, (Cambridge: Cambridge University Press, 1985).

11. See his *The Soviet Syndrome*, trans. Patricia Ranum, (New York: Harcourt, Brace, Jovanovich, 1978), for a good concise summary of his thought.

12. This position is forcefully and concisely argued by Leszek Kolakowski, "Marxist Roots of Stalinism," in Robert C. Tucker, ed., *Stalinism: Essays in Historical Interpretation*, (New York: Norton, 1977).

II. Nature

National Socialism as a Political Religion
Michael Burleigh

1. *The Autobiography of Bertrand Russell 1914–1944* (Boston: Little, Brown, & Co., 1968), 142.

2. Ray Monk, *Bertrand Russell: The Spirit of Solitude 1872–1921* (New York: Free Press, 1996), 579–80.

3. Bertrand Russell, *The Practice and Theory of Bolshevism* (London: Allen & Unwin, 1920), 15–16.

4. Emilio Gentile, *The Sacralization of Politics in Fascist Italy* (Cambridge, MA: Harvard University Press, 1996), 32.

5. Franz von Papen addressing representatives of the Bavarian economy, cited in Uriel Tal "'Political Faith' of Nazism prior to the Holocaust" (Tel Aviv 1978), 7.

6. Victor Klemperer, *I Will Bear Witness. A Diary of the Nazi Years 1933–1941* (New York: Modern Library, 1998), 1, entry dated 14 July 1934, 74.

7. Victor Klemperer, *The Language of the Third Reich*. LTI-Lingua Tertii Imperii. A Philologist's Notebook (London, 2000), 34.

8. Peter Schoettler, "Das Konzept der politischen Religionen bei Luci Varga und Franz Borkenau'" in Michael Ley, Julius H. Schoeps (eds.), *Der Nationalsozialismus als politische Religion* (Bodenheim, 1997), 190.

9. See William Johnes, "The Path from Weimar Communism to the Cold War; Franz Borkenau and "The Totalitarian Enemy" in Alfons Soellner, Ralf Walkenhaus, Karin Wieland (eds.), *Totalitarismus. Eine Ideengeschichte des 20. Jahrhunderts*, (Berlin: Akademie Verlag, 1997), 34–52.

10. Franz Borkenau, *The Totalitarian Enemy* (London: Faber & Faber, 1940) quotations from 121–22 and 140–41. This theme was subsequently explored with great insight and scholarship by Norman Cohn, *The Pursuit of the Millennium Revolutionary Millenarians and Mystical Anarchists of the Middle Ages* (London: Oxford University Press, 1970), especially 287–88; "As in the Nazi apocalypse the 'Aryan race' was to purify the earth by annihilating the 'Jewish race,' so in the Communist apocalypse the 'bourgeoisie' is to be exterminated by the 'proletariat'. And here we are faced with a secularized version of a fantasy that is many centuries old. . . . However modern their terminology, however realistic their tactics, in their basic attitudes Communism and Nazism follow an ancient tradition—and are baffling to the rest of us because of those very features that would have seemed so familiar to a chiliastic propheta of the Middle Ages."

11. Eric Voegelin, *The History of the Race Idea: From Ray to Carus* (Baton Rouge: Louisiana State University Press, 1998).

12. Eric Voegelin, *Die politischen Religionen* (Munich 1996), and available in English as *Political Religions Toronto Studies in Theology*, 2nd edition, vol. 23 (Toronto: Edwin M. Ellen Press, 1986). The best guides to Voegelin's thought are his *Autobiographical Reflections*, ed. Ellis Sandoz (Baton Rouge: Louisiana State University Press, 1989), but see also Ellis Sandoz, *Eric Voegelin's Thought: A Critical Appraisal* (Durham, NC: Duke University Press, 1982); (ed.) *Eric Voegelin's Significance for the Modern Mind* (Baton Rouge: Louisiana State University Press, 1991); Barry Cooper, *Eric Voegelin and the Foundations of Modern Political Science* (Columbia, MO: University of Missouri Press, 1999); Glenn Hughes, ed., *Politics of the Soul: Eric Voegelin on Religious Experience* (Oxford 1999). Hans Maier, "Ein Schwieriger swischen den Fronten", *Frankfurter Allgemeine Zeitun* (8 April 2000), ii, is an outstanding discussion of Voegelin's period at Munich University after the Second World War. I am most grateful to Bernd Weisbrod for this reference.

13. Raymond Aron, "Les Religions Séculières" idem *Une histoire du XXe siècle. Antholoie* (Paris 1996), 139–222, contains most of Aron's essays on this theme, commencing with his 1944 piece "L'avenir des religions séculières."

14. The most recent analysis of the Soviet regime as a political religion is Arthur Jay Klinghoffer, *Red Apocalypse: The Religious Experience of Soviet Communism* (Lanham: University Press of America, 1996). See also Alain Besançon, *The Rise of the Gulag* (New York: Continuum, 1981); James Billington, *Fire in the Minds*

of Men: Origins of the Revolutionary Faith (New York: Basic Books, 1980); Eric Hoffer, *The True Believer* (New York: Time, Inc., 1963).

15. For a fascinating discussion of the literature see Philippe Burrin "Political Religion: The Relevance of a Concept," *History and Memory* (1997), 9, 321–49.

16. See especially Robert N. Bellah, "Civil Religion in America," idem., *Beyond Belief: Essays on Religion in a Post-Traditionalist World* (Berkeley: University of California, 1991), 180–81.

17. Adam Zamoyski, *Holy Madness. Romantics, Patriots and Revolutionaries 1776–1871* (London: Penguin Books, 2000), 309.

18. Zamoyski, *Holy Madness*, 408–9.

19. George L. Mosse, *The Nationalization of the Masses. Political Symbolism and Mass Movements in Germany from the Napoleonic Wars through the Third Reich* (Ithaca: Cornell University Press, 1975); and his important book *The Fascist Revolution Toward a General Theory of Fascism*, (New York: H. Fertig, 1999), 1–44.

20. John H. Johnston, *English Poetry of the First World War* (Princeton: Princeton University Press, 1964), 30.

21. George L. Mosse, *Fallen Soldiers* (New York: Oxford University Press, 1990).

22. George L. Mosse "The Poet and the Exercise of Political Power," *Masses and Man: Nationalist and Fascist Perceptions of Reality,* (Detroit: Wayne State University Press, 1987), 87–103; see also the remarkable passages on Hitler in Modris Eksteins, *Rites of Spring: The Great War and the Birth of the Modern Age* (New York: Dover, 1989), 331ff.

23. Jonathan Glover, *Humanity: A Moral History of the Twentieth Century* (New Haven: Yale University Press 1999), 16.

24. Hermann Ullstein, *The Rise and Fall of the House of Ullstein* (London: Nicholson and Watson, 1940), 142–3.

25. Gentile (note 4), 54.

26. Tal (note 5), 31.

27. Ian Kershaw, *The Hitler Myth* (Oxford: Oxford University Press, 1987).

28. Sabine Behrenbeck, *Der Kult um die töten Helden* (Vierow 1997).

29. Feldman, "New Thinking about the 'New Man'", 147–48.

30. Klaus Vondung, *Magie und Manipulation* (Goettingen 1971); Hans-Joachim Gamm, *Der bräune Kult* (Hamburg 1962), Peter Reichel, *Der schöne Schein des Dritten Reiches* (Berlin 1996); Jennifer McDowell "Soviet Civil Ceremonies", *Journal for the Scientific Study of Religion* (1974), 13, 265–79; Victoria E. Bonnell, *Iconography of Power Soviet Political Posters under Lenin and Stalin* (Berkeley: University of California, 1997).

31. George Orwell "Mein Kampf", *New English Weekly* (21 March 1940) reprinted in Peter Davidson (ed.), *The Complete Works of George Orwell,* vol. 12, *A Patriot After All: 1940–1941,* 116–18.

32. Fritz Stern, "National Socialism as Temptation" in his *Dreams and Delusions: The Drama of German History* (New Haven: Yale University Press, 1987), 147ff.

33. Max Domarus (ed.), *Hitler: Speeches and Proclamations* (London 1990), 2, speech dated 6 September 1938, 1146.

34. Christopher Dawson, "Religion and the Totalitarian State," *The Criterion* (1934), vol. 14, 8.

35. Saul Friedländer, *Nazi Germany and the Jews* (New York: Harper, 1997), vol. 1, 89–92.

Notes

36. Mary McCarthy "General Macbeth," *Harper's Magazine* (June 1962).

37. Mikhail Heller, *Cogs in the Wheel: The Formation of Soviet Man* (New York: Knopf, 1988), 193.

38. Reinhold Niebuhr "The Religion of Communism," *The Atlantic Monthly* 147, (1931), 469.

39. The seminal study here is Saul Friedländer's *Kitsch und Tod* (Munich 1986). Interestingly, while this essay penetrates to the essence of the Nazi phenomenon, its approach has not led to more detailed researches along these lines.

40. Philippe Burrin, *Hitler and the Jew: The Genesis of the Holocaust* (London: Arnold, 1989); Christian Gerlach, "The Wannsee Conference, the Fate of German Jews, and Hitler's Decision in Principle to Exterminate all European Jews," Omer Bartov (ed.) in *The Holocaust: Origins, Implementation, Aftermath* (London: Routledge, 2000), 106ff.

41. Deutschland-Berichte der SOPADE (1937), 4 report dated 4 April 1937, 497–99.

42. Hannah Arendt, *The Origins of Totalitarianism* (San Diego: Harcourt Brace, 1973), especially page 189ff.

43. For the above see mainly Omer Bartov "Progress and Catastrophe." *Tikkun* 14 (2000), 41–8.

44. Richard Bessel, *Germany after the First World War* (New York: Oxford University Press, 1993); Gerald Feldman "Kriegswirtschaft und Zwangswirtschaft", Wolfgang Michalka (ed.), *Der Erste Weltkrieg: Wirkung, Wahrnehmung, Analyse* (Munich: Piper, 1994), 472–73.

45. Feldman (note 29), 147–63.

46. Klemperer (note 6), 18.

47. Simonetta Falasca-Zamponi, *Fascist Spectacle: The Aesthetics of Power in Mussolini's Italy* (Berkeley: University of California, 1997), 100–18.

48. Friedrich Reck-Malleczewen, *Diary of a Man in Despair* (London: Duck Editions, 2000, 1955) entry dated April 1939, 74.

49. William Sheridan Allen, "Die deutsche Öffentlichkeit und die 'Reichskristallnacht'—Konflikte swischen Werthierarchie und Propaganda im Dritten Reich," D. Peukert, J. Reulecke (eds.), *Die Reihen fast geschlossen: Beiträge zur Geschichte des Alltags unterm Nationalsozialismus* (Wuppertal 1981), 396–411.

50. The most recent study is Radu Ioanid, *The Holocaust in Romania: The Destruction of Jews and Gypsies under the Antonescu Regime, 1940–1944* (Chicago: Ivan R. Dee, 2000), 177ff.

51. Uriel Tal, "Violence and the Jew in Nazi Ideology," Salo W. Baron, George S. Wise (eds.), *Violence and Defense in the Jewish Experience* (Philadelphia: Jewish Publication Society of America, 1977), 213.

52. Omer Bartov, *Hitler's Army* (New York: Oxford University Press, 1991), and Rab Bennet, *Under the Shadow of the Swastika: The Moral Dilemmas of Resistance and Collaboration in Hitler's Europe*, (London: Cassell, 1999), 130–74.

53. Max Domarus (ed.), *Hitler: Speeches and Proclamations* vol. 2, (London: I. B. Taurus, 1990), speech dated 8 October 1935, 955.

54. See especially Richard Breitman, "Himmler and the Terrible Secret," *Journal of Contemporary History* vol. 26, (1991), 431–51.

55. *International Military Tribunal*, vol. 29, Doc-1919-PS, 110–73.

III. Origins

German Nihilism
Leo Strauss

1. For the distinction between the closed society and the open society, see Henri Bergson, *The Two Sources of Morality and Religion* (Notre Dame, IN: University of Notre Dame Press, 1977), chs. 1 and 4.
2. For Glaukon's protest, see *Republic*, 372c-d; see also Leo Strauss, *The City and Man* (Chicago: Rand McNally and Co., 1964), 93–96.
3. "We, however, stand in the middle of the experiment; we are attempting things that have no foundation in experience. Sons, grandsons and great-grandsons of godless men, to whom even doubt has become suspect, we march through landscapes that threaten life with higher and lower temperatures." See Ernst Jünger, Der Arbeiter; *Herrschaft und Gestalt* (Hamburg: Hanseatische Verlaganstalt, 1932), 193–94.
4. Carl Mayer, "On the Intellectual Origin of National Socialism," *Social Research* 9 (May 1942), 225–47.
5. "Their Finest Hour" (a speech delivered first in the House of Commons and then broadcast, June 18, 1940).
6. Strauss is referring to Oswald Spengler. See *The Decline of the West* (New York: Knopf, 1939), 36. At Cannae the Romans suffered a crushing defeat in the Second Punic War against Hannibal (216 BC).
7. Goethe, *Faust* I, 1851–55.
8. See Caesar, *The Gallic Wars*, vol. I, 30–54.
9. Livy, *The History of Rome*, 25.31, 5–11.
10. Aristotle, *Politics*, 2.7, 1269a.
11. "Permanent peace is a dream, and not even a beautiful one, and war is a law of God's order in the world, by which the noblest virtues of man, courage and self-denial, loyalty and self-sacrifice, even to the point of death, are developed. Without war the world would deteriorate into materialism." Letter to Dr. J. K. Bluntschli, 11 December 1880, in *Field-Marshal Count Helmuth von Moltke as a Correspondent*, trans. Mary Herms (New York: Harper and Brothers, 1893), 272.
12. "Über den Schmerz," in *Blätter und Steine* (Hamburg: Hanseatische Verlaganstalt, 1934), 154–213, in particular, 213.
13. Nietzsche, *Beyond Good and Evil*, 252–53.
14. See Virgil, *Aeneid*, 5.851.

Is Technological Civilization Decadent, and Why?
Jan Patočka

1. See two reports by the Club of Rome: Dennis Meadows, Donella Meadows, Jorgen Randers, W. Behrens, *The Limits of Growth* (New York: Universe Books, 1972); and Meadows, et al., *Beyond the Limits* (Post Mills: Chelsea Green, 1992).
2. "hekatombs . . . myriatombs"—i.e., instead of "hundreds" of sacrifices, countless sacrifices. Sacrifice is an important theme in Patočka's thought: see "The Dangers

of Technicization in Science according to E. Husserl and the Essence of Technology as Danger According to M. Heidegger" in *Jan Patočka: Philosophy and Selected Writings*, trans. and ed. Erazim Kohák (Chicago: University of Chicago Press, 1989), especially pages 335–39. Patočka is also referring, mockingly, to the public housing developments that were erected by the Communists around Prague.

3. See Auguste Comte, *The System of Positive Polity*, trans. J. H. Bridges et al. (London, 1875–77).

4. The turn of the last century saw a number of studies of suicide, including Émil Durkheim's famous *Suicide, a Study in Sociology*, trans. J. A. Spaulding and G. Simpson (Glencoe: Free Press, 1951). See also Tomáš Masaryk's *Suicide and the Meaning of Civilization*, trans. W. B. Weist and R. G. Batson (Chicago: University of Chicago Press, 1970).

5. Émil Durkheim, *Les formes élémentaires de la vie religieuse* (Paris: Presses Universitaires de France, 1968), 312–13.

6. Heraclitus, DK 22 B45; "You would not find out the boundaries of the soul, even by travelling along every path: so deep a measure does it have [*houto bathun logon echei*]" (trans. KRS, 203).

7. Eugen Fink, *Metaphysik der Erziehung im Weltverständnis von Plato und Aristoteles* (Frankfurt am Main: Klostermann, 1970).

8. Ibid.

9. Gilles Quispel, "Faust: Symbol of Western Man," in *Eranos Jahrbuch 1966* (Zürich: Rhein-Verlag, 1967).

10. Ibid. Julian the Apostate ("the one who denounces the religion"), briefly emperor from 361–63 AD, sought to reverse the Christianization of Rome. Contemporary Neoplatonists were aggressive critics of Christianity.

11. See Friedrich Nietzsche, *The Will to Power*, trans. Walter Kaufmann and R. J. Hollingdale (New York: Vintage, 1968), sec. 572, bk. 2, sec. 1: "History of Christianity."

12. See Paul's First Epistle to the Corinthians, chap. 20: "Where is the wise man? Where is the debater of this age? Has not God made ludicrous the wisdom of the world [*sophia tou kosmou*]?"

13. Philippus Aureolus Paracelsus (1493–1541) was a Swiss alchemist and physician who wrote on medicine.

14. "Man's condition. Inconstancy, boredom, anxiety."—Blaise Pascal, *Pensées*, trans. A. J. Krailsheimer (New York: Penguin, 1966) 36. The "aesthetic stage" is the first stage of Kierkegaard's "stages on life's way." See Søren Kierkegaard, *Either/Or*, trans. Walter Lowrie (New York: Doubleday, 1959), vol. 2, 159–338.

15. Durkheim, op. cit., 305–6.

16. (a) The "wars of liberation" refer to a series of conflicts between 1809 and Napoleon's eventual defeat in 1814 wherein, among other problems, Napoleon faced a brutal British-backed guerrilla insurgency in Spain, war with Austria, not to mention total disaster in Russia; (b) the year 1848 saw a series of revolutionary crises in France, Italy, Austria, and Prussia, most of which were brutally repressed.

17. This is a reference to a relatively outdated slang expression—as in "that was really *happening*."

18. See Ernst Jünger, *Die Totale Mobilmachung*, in *Sämtliche Werke*, Zweite Abteilung, vol. 7, essay 1: *Betrachtungen zur Zeit* (Stuttgart: Klett-Kotta, 1980).

19. See Jacob Burckhardt, *The Civilization of the Renaissance in Italy* (1860), trans. S. G. Middlemore (New York: Harper and Row, 1958).

20. This is a reference, of course, to Martin Heidegger.

IV. Seduction

The Smatterers
Aleksandr I. Solzhenitsyn

1. Lydia Chukovskaya, the daughter of a well-known children's writer Kornei Chukovsky (1882–1969), is one of the Soviet Union's leading dissident writers and the author of two short novels, *The Deserted House* and *Going Under*. She was expelled from the Writer's Union in January 1974.

2. A reference to the extensive industrial pollution of Lake Baikal and its surroundings and to recent protests on environmental grounds.

3. Magnitogorsk is a major city in the Urals that underwent most of its development in the twenties and thirties and became a showplace of Soviet industry.

4. Presumably a reference to Eisenstein's film *Alexander Nevsky*.

5. Andrei Amalrik (b. 1938), a nonconformist Soviet writer, imprisoned in 1965 and subsequently exiled to Siberia for having produced "anti-Soviet" and "pornographic" works. In 1966 Amalrik was permitted to return to Moscow; in May 1970 he was again arrested on trumped-up charges as a result of his writings, and in July 1973 was sentenced to three years forced labor. This sentence was commuted in November 1973 to three years exile in Siberia.

Aleksandr Solzhenitsyn and European "Leftism"
Raymond Aron

1. Aleksandr Solzhenitsyn, *The Oak and the Calf* (New York: Harper and Row, 1974), 119.

2. Aleksandr Solzhenitsyn, *The Gulag Archipelago*, vols. 1-2 (New York: Harper and Row, 1974), 173–74.

3. A left-wing worker.

VI. Lessons

Moral Destruction
Alain Besançon

1. Heinrich Himmler, *Discours secrets* (Paris: Gallimard, 1978).

2. Tragedy understood as the pervasive principle of reality.

3. Raymond Aron, *Démocratie et totalitarisme* (Paris: Gallimard, 1965), 302.

4. Ibid.

Notes

The Traces of a Wounded Animal
Chantal Delsol

1. Václav Bělohradský, "Sur le sujet dissident," *Le Messager européen*, no. 4 (1990): 23–46.
2. Milan Kundera, *Risibles Amours* (Paris: Gallimard, 1970). Published in English as "Edward and God" in *Laughable Loves* (Alfred A. Knopf, Inc., 1974).
3. Arthur Koestler, *Darkness at Noon*, trans. Daphne Hardy (New York: Bantam Books, 1968), 137.
4. Ibid.
5. Bělohradský, "Sur le sujet dissident."
6. Predrag Matveievitch, "De la dissidence dans l'autre Europe," in *Fondation Charles Veillon* (Bussigny, 1993), 17.
7. As I reread these lines, I came upon a very similar analysis of the same passage in the Declaration in Marie Balmary, *Abel, ou La traversée de l'Eden* (Paris: Grasset, 1999).
8. Mircea Eliade, *Commentaires sur la légende de Maître Manole* (Paris: L'Herne, 1994), 245.
9. See my work *Les Idées politiques au XXème siècle* (Paris: Presses Universitaires de France, 1991), 87.
10. See Didier Éribon, *Réflexions sur la question gay* (Paris: Fayard, 1999).
11. Plato, *The Symposium*, 190c ff.

Totalitarianism: Between Religion and Science
Tzvetan Todorov

1. "An Answer to the Question: What is Enlightenment? (1784)," in Immanuel Kant, *Perpetual Peace and Other Essays*, trans. Ted Humphrey (Indianapolis, IN: Hackett Publishing Co., 1983), 41.
2. Semion, Frank. "Eres' utopizma," *Po tu storonu levogo i pravogo* (Paris: YMCA Press, 1972), 92.
3. Eric Voegelin, *The New Science of Politics* (Chicago: University of Chicago Press, 1952), 127.
4. Alain Besançon, *Les origines intellectuelles du léninisme* (Paris: Calmann-Lévy, 1977), 128.
5. Karl Marx, "Theses on Feuerbach," in Friedrich Engels, *Ludwig Feuerbach and the Outcome of Classical German Philosophy* (New York: International Publishers, 1941), 84.
6. Hippolyte Taine, *Derniers essais de critique et d'histoire* (Paris: Hachette, 1894), 110.
7. Ernest Renan, *L'Avenir de la science, Oeuvres complètes*, t. III (Paris: Calmann-Lévy, 1949), 1074.
8. René Descartes, *Principes de philosophie*, I, 76; Ouevres et lettres (Paris: Gallimard, 1953), 610.
9. Descartes, *Les passions de l'âme*, 152; ibid. (note 8), 768.

10. Descartes, *Principes de philosophie* (note 8), 568.

11. Charles Louis de Secondat Montesquieu, *L'espirit des lois*, I, 1 (Paris: Garnier, 1973), 9.

12. Alexis de Tocqueville, "Lettres à Gobineau," in *Oeuvres complètes*, t. IX (Paris: Gallimard, 1951), 280.

13. Jean-Jacques Rousseau, Le Contrat social, I, 2; *Oeuvres complètes*, t. III, (Paris: Gallimard, 1975), 353.

14. Rousseau, *Emile*, IV, op. cit., t. IV, 601.

15. Michel de Montaigne, *The Complete Works of Montaigne: Essays, Travel Journal, Letters*, trans. Donald M. Frame (Stanford: Stanford University Press [1958] 1967), 835.

16. Rousseau, "Lettre sur la vertu, l'individu et la société," *Annales de la Société Jean-Jacques Rousseau* XLI (1997), 325.

17. Ernest Renan, *Dialogues philosophiques, Oeuvres complètes*, t. I, 602–24. Further page references in text.

18. Feliks Dzerżhińsky, "Intervention of December 7, 1917," in *Lenin i VChk: Sbornik dokumentov* (Moscow: 1975); cited by N. Werth, "Un Etat contre son peuple," in *Le Livre noir du communisme* (Paris: Laffont, 1997), 69.

Sources and Permissions

635

Sources and Permissions

"The Smatterers," from *From Under the Ruins*, by Alexander Solzhenitsyn. Copyright 1974 by YMCA-Press. By permission of Little Brown & Co., publishers.

Heretical Essays in the Philosophy of History by Jan Patočka, reprinted by permission of Open Court Publishing Company, a division of Carus Publishing Company, Peru, IL, from *Heretical Essays in the Philosophy of History* by Jan Patočka copyright XXX.

"Ideology and Terror: A Novel Form of Government" by Hannah Arendt from *Review of Politics*, 15:3, 1953; "The Origins of Totalitarianism" by Eric Voegelin from *Review of Politics*, 15:1, 1953; and "Totalitarian Religions" by Waldemar Gurian from *Review of Politics*, 14:1, 1952. All reprinted by permission of Cambridge University Press.

"Our Muzzled Freedom" (pages 320–27) from *The Gulag Archipelago* 1918–1956 by Aleksandr I. Solzhenitsyn. Authorized Abridgement with a New Introduction by Edward E. Ericson, Jr. Copyright 1985 by The Russian Social Fund. Perennial Classics Introduction copyright 2002 by Edward E. Ericson, Jr. Reprinted by permission of HarperCollins Publishers. Parts I–IV translated by Thomas P. Whitney. Parts V–VII translated by Harry Willetts. Abridged by Edward E. Ericson, Jr. For additional territory: The Harvill Press/Random House/20 Vauxhall Bridge Road/London SW1V 2SA/ United Kingdom.

"The Image of the Body and Totalitarianism" by Lefort, Claude. edited by John B. Thompson., *The Political Forms of Modern Society: Bureaucracy, Democracy, Totalitarianism*, pages 292–306, copyright 1986 Massachusetts Institute of Technology, by permission of The MIT Press.

"National Socialism as a Political Religion" by Michael Burleigh from *Totalitarian Movements & Political Religions*, reprinted by permission of Taylor & Francis via Copyright Clearance Center.

"Totalitarianism: Between Religion and Science" by Tzvetan Todorov from *Totalitarian Movements & Political Religions*, reprinted by permission of Taylor & Francis via Copyright Clearance Center.

"The Marxist Roots of Stalinism" by Leszek Kolakowski from *My Correct Views on Everything* reprinted by permission of St. Augustine's Press via Copyright Clearance Center.

Sources and Permissions

"On the Difficulty of Defining the Soviet Regime" by Alain Besancon and translated by Daniel Mahoney and Paul Seaton from *The Present Soviet Union and Past Russia*, reprinted by permission of Alain Besancon.

"Three Riders of the Apocalypse" by Aurel Kolnai originally published in *Appraisal: The Journal of the Society for Post-Critical and Personalist Studies*, vol. 2, reprinted by permission of Richard Allen and Dr. Francis Dunlop.

"German Nihilism" by Leo Strauss from *Interpretation*, vol. 26/3 (Spring 1999), 353–78; reprinted by permission of Nathan Tarcov, Literary Executor, Estate of Leo Strauss, and *Interpretation*.

"A Treatise on Ticks" by Poitr Wierzbicki and "Ticks and Angels" by Adam Michnik reprinted from *Survey*, Vol. 25, No. 1 (Winter 1980), 160–85

Every effort was made to obtain permission for the material presented in this volume.

About the Contributors

HANNAH ARENDT (1906–1975), an influential philosopher and one of the premier public intellectuals of the postwar period, was a student of Martin Heidegger. Her many books include *The Origins of Totalitarianism* (1951), *The Human Condition* (1958), and *On Revolution* (1963). She taught in The Committee on Social Thought at the University of Chicago, at The New School in New York City, and was a fellow at Yale University and Wesleyan University.

RAYMOND ARON (1905–1983), the preeminent French political thinker in the years after 1945, taught at several French universities, most notably the Sorbonne and the Collège de France. Aron published many, many books across a range of disciplines including the 1955 masterpiece, *The Opium of the Intellectuals*. He edited the journal *La France Libre* during World War II, and wrote columns for *Le Figaro* (1947–1977) and *L'Express* (1978–1983).

ALAIN BESANÇON (b. 1932) is a prominent French historian whose books include *The Falsification of the Good: Soloviev and Orwell* (1994) and *A Century of Horrors: Communism, Nazism and the Uniqueness of the Shoah* (2007). He taught at L'École des Hautes Études en Sciences Sociales, where he became a director of studies in 1977.

VÁCLAV BENDA (1946–1999) was a Czech mathematician and philosopher. A founding member of the Committee for the Defense of the Unjustly Persecuted (VONS), Benda was also a spokesman for Charter 77. He wrote articles on mathematics and philosophy, as well as influential samizdat essays. In 1996, he was elected to the upper house of the Czech parliament.

About the Contributors

MICHAEL BURLEIGH (b. 1955) is an award-winning British historian. He founded the journal *Totalitarian Movements and Political Religions* and has taught at Oxford, the London School of Economics, Rutgers University and Washington and Lee University. His books include *The Third Reich: A New History* (2001), *Earthly Powers: Religions and Politics in Europe from the Enlightenment to the Great War* (2006), and *Sacred Causes: Religion and Politics from the European Dictators to Al Qaeda* (2006).

CHANTAL DELSOL (b. 1947) teaches philosophy at the Université de Marne-la-Vallée near Paris, where she helped found the Institut Hannah Arendt in 1993. Among her writings available in English are the books *Icarus Fallen: The Search for Meaning in an Uncertain World* (2003) and *The Unlearned Lessons of the Twentieth Century: an Essay on Late Modernity* (2006).

CARL FRIEDRICH (1901–1984), one of the earliest academic analysts of totalitarianism, taught at Harvard University, as well as at the University of Heidelberg. His works include *Totalitarian Dictatorship and Autocracy* (1956) and *The Philosophy of Law in Historical Perspective* (1958).

WALDEMAR GURIAN (1902–1954) was a Russian political scientist and journalist. Born in St. Petersburg, he emigrated to Germany, where he converted to Catholicism and studied with Max Scheler. He moved to the United States in 1937, where he became a professor of political science at the University of Notre Dame and, in 1939, founded the journal *Review of Politics*. Gurian is the author of *Bolshevism: Theory and Practice* (1932), *Hitler and the Christians* (1936), and *Bolshevism: An Introduction to Soviet Communism* (1952), among other works.

PIERRE HASSNER (b. 1933) is Senior Research Fellow Emeritus at the Centre d'Études et de Recherches Internationales (CERI) in Paris. He has also lectured in international relations at the Institut d'Études Politiques de Paris, the European Center of Johns Hopkins University in Bologna, the University of Chicago, and Harvard University. His books include *Violence and Peace: From the Atomic Bomb to Ethnic Cleansing* (1996). In 2003 Hassner was awarded the Prix Tocqueville.

VÁCLAV HAVEL (b. 1936) is a Czech politician and playwright. He wrote many influential samizdat essays during the 1970s and 1980s, served as a spokesman for Charter 77, and led the Civic Forum in 1989. He served as the last president of Czechoslovakia from 1989–1992 and the first president of the Czech Republic from 1993 to 2003. His books include *Open Letters: Selected Writings 1965–1990, The Garden Party and Other Plays* (1994), and *To the Castle and Back* (2008).

About the Contributors

EVA KANTŮRKOVÁ (b. 1930) is a Czech novelist, essayist, and playwright. She served as spokeswoman for Charter 77 and helped found the Civic Forum in 1989. Her books in English include *My Companions in the Bleak House* (1987). She was elected to the Czech parliament in 1990.

LESZEK KOLAKOWSKI (1927–2009) was a Polish philosopher who taught at the University of Warsaw, McGill University, Yale, Oxford, and the University of Chicago. He lost his teaching position at the University of Warsaw in 1968 due to his political beliefs and was exiled shortly thereafter. He is the author of more than thirty books, including the three-volume work *Main Currents of Marxism* (1978, 2005) and *My Correct Views on Everything* (2005). He was awarded the Order of the White Eagle, Poland's highest honor, and was the first recipient of the United States Library of Congress's John W. Kluge prize for Lifetime Achievement in the Humanities and Social Sciences.

AUREL KOLNAI (1900–1973) was born in Budapest to a Jewish family, but converted to Catholicism in 1926. He taught philosophy at Bedford College in London and Marquette University in Wisconsin. His publications include *The War against the West* (1938), *The Utopian Mind and Other Papers* (1995), and *Privilege and Liberty and Other Essays in Political Philosophy* (1999).

CLAUDE LEFORT (1924–2010) spent most of his academic career at the Sorbonne and at the École des Hautes Études en Sciences Sociales, where he was a research director between 1976 and 1990. His books include *The Political Forms of Modern Society: Bureaucracy, Democracy, Totalitarianism* (1986), and *Complications: Communism and the Dilemmas of Democracy* (1999).

MARTIN MALIA (1924–2004) was a distinguished Sovietologist and historian of Russia. He taught at Harvard University before taking a position at the University of California, Berkeley, where he spent most of his teaching career. Malia's works include *Alexander Herzen and the Birth of Russian Socialism 1812–1855* (1961), *The Soviet Tragedy: A History of Socialism in Russia, 1917–1991* (1995) and *Russia under Western Eyes* (2000).

PIERRE MANENT (b. 1949) is Research Director at the Centre d'Études Sociologiques et Politiques Raymond Aron, part of the École des Hautes Études en Sciences Sociales. His works include *Tocqueville and the Nature of Democracy* (1996), *The City of Man* (1998), *A World Beyond Politics? A Defense of the Nation-State* (2006), *Democracy Without Nations?* (2007), and *Le Regard politique* (2010).

About the Contributors

ADAM MICHNIK (b. 1946) is a Polish historian, writer, and editor. He was a founder of the Workers' Defense Committee (KOR) and a member of the Polish Sejm from 1989–1991. He is the editor in chief of the Polish newspaper *Gazeta Wyborcza*, and is the author of several books, including *Letters from Prison and Other Essays* (1985), *The Church and the Left* (1993), and *Letters from Freedom: Post-Cold War Realities and Perspectives* (1998).

CZESLAW MILOSZ (1911–2004) was a Polish poet and essayist. After serving briefly in the Polish diplomatic service during the postwar years, he requested political asylum in France. In 1960 he began teaching at the University of California, Berkeley. *The Captive Mind*, his brilliant study of intellectuals seduced by Communism, was published in 1953. His other books include *To Begin Where I Am* (2002), *New and Collected Poems: 1931–2001* (2003), and *Legends of Modernity: Essays and Letters from Occupied Poland, 1942–1943* (2006). He was awarded the Nobel Prize for literature in 1980.

JAN PATOČKA (1907–1977) was a distinguished Czech philosopher and student of Edmund Husserl. He was also a principal founder of and a spokesman for Charter 77. He taught at Charles University in Prague before being forced to retire because of his political beliefs. His books include *Heretical Essays in the Philosophy of History* (1996), *An Introduction to Husserl's Phenomenology* (1996), and *Plato and Europe* (2002), all published posthumously.

MARTIN PALOUŠ (b. 1950) was one of the early signatories of Charter 77 and a founding member of the Civic Forum. He studied chemistry at Charles University and was also a student of Jan Patočka's. He is currently the Permanent Representative to the United Nations for the Czech Republic. He has previously held the positions of Czech Ambassador to the United States and Deputy Minister of Foreign Affairs. Palouš has also taught at Charles University in Prague, Northwestern University, and Central European University in Budapest.

ALEKSANDR I. SOLZHENITSYN (1918–2008) was a Russian novelist and historian. His *Gulag Archipelago* (1973) has been called the most important book of the twentieth century. His novels include *One Day in the Life of Ivan Denisovich* (1962), *In the First Circle* (1968, 2009), *Cancer Ward* (1968), and the cycle of novels called *The Red Wheel*. He was awarded the Nobel Prize for Literature in 1970.

LEO STRAUSS (1899–1973) was one of the most influential political philosophers of the twentieth century. His works include *Natural Right and History* (1953), *On Tyranny* (1963), and *The City and Man* (1964). Strauss taught political philosophy for many years at the University of Chicago.

About the Contributors

TZVETAN TODOROV (b. 1939) is a Bulgarian-born French philosopher. He has taught at Harvard University, Columbia University, and the University of California, Berkeley. His books include *Voices from the Gulag: Life and Death in Communist Bulgaria* (1999), *Fragility of Goodness: Why Bulgaria's Jews Survived the Holocaust* (2001), and *Hope and Memory: Lessons from the Twentieth Century* (2003).

LEOPOLD TYRMAND (1920–1985) was a Polish writer and editor. In the 1950s he wrote for the Polish Catholic-liberal weekly *Tygodnik Powszechny*. He left Poland for the United States in the mid-1960s, and thereafter contributed to many publications including *The New Yorker, Commentary*, and *The Wall Street Journal*. He was co-founder and vice-president of the Rockford Institute. Tyrmand edited two anthologies of writings from the Paris-based Polish émigré journal *Kultura: Kultura Essays* and *Explorations in Freedom: Prose, Narrative and Poetry from Kultura*, both published in 1970.

ERIC VOEGELIN (1901–1985), the distinguished Austrian-born philosopher, taught at the University of Vienna, Louisiana State University, and the University of Munich. Among his books are *The New Science of Politics* (1952), *Hitler and the Germans* (1999), and the multi-volume work *Order and History* (the initial volumes published in 1956–1957). Volume 5 of his collected works, *Modernity Without Restraint* (1999), contains his important essay *The Political Religions*, first published in Vienna in 1938, one month after the Nazis annexed Austria.

PIOTR WIERZBICKI (b. 1935) is a Polish journalist, writer, editor, and music critic. He joined the democratic opposition movement in the 1970s and was interned under martial law from December 13, 1981 to July 10, 1982. From 1993 to 2005 he served as the editor in chief of *Gazeta Polska*.

Index

Afanasyev, Yury, 85
Akhenaton, Pharaoh, 195–96
"Aleksandr Solzhenitsyn and European 'Leftism,'" 366–76
Aleksandr Solzhenitsyn: The Ascent from Ideology, xxxv
Alexander II, Czar, 152
alienation
    concepts of, xx, 28
    existentialism and, 546
    human rights and, 598
    Leninism and, 179–80
    nature and, 98, 103, 166–67
    separation and, 533
    socialism and, 565
    totalitarianism and, 309–12, 317, 360
All Our Yesterdays, 376
Allen, William Sheridan, 211
"alternative culture," 469
Althusser, Louis, 375
Amalrik, Andrei, 166, 361
Amendola, Giovanni, xvii, 193
ancien régime, 187–88, 588
And Quiet Flows the Don, 366
Animal Farm, 580
Annals of Communism series, xxv
anthropocentric humanism, xxxiv–xxxv
Anthropological Principle in Philosophy, 612
anti-fascism, x–xi, 403
anti-political politics, 306, 308

anti-religious policies, 3–15
anti-Semitism, 261–63
Antonescu, Ion, 251
Apology of Socrates, 522
Applebaum, Anne, xii
Aquinas, Thomas, 24
Aragon, Louis, 555
Arendt, Hannah, viii, x, xiv–xv, xviii, xxii, xxvii–xxviii, xxxvii, 6, 8–9, 53–54, 57–58, 60, 64, 67, 77, 85, 124, 177, 207, 260–67, 286, 562, 581–83
Aristotle, xxviii, 25, 31–35, 37, 50, 75–76, 233, 277, 580, 582–83
Aron, Raymond, x, xvii, xix, xxv–xxvi, xxviii, xxx, xxxvii, 38–45, 50–53, 56, 58, 97, 177, 196, 366, 566–67, 575–76, 582–83
Ash, Timothy Garton, xviii
Ashes and Diamonds, 404
Assault on Ideology: Aleksandr Solzhenitsyn's Political Thought, xxxv
atheism, 3, 10, 110, 225–26, 348
Athenian polis, 17, 263
Attali, Jacques, 74
authentic/inauthentic, 272–73, 278, 287–88
authoritarian regimes, xviii, 4–10, 48, 59, 64–65, 375
authoritarianism, xvi, 7, 53–59, 65–67, 71, 75–79, 86

Index

Index

Index

Index

Index

Index

Index

Index

Index

Index

Index

Index

Index

Index